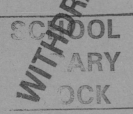

The Miles Kelly
Book of
Life

The Miles Kelly Book of Life

Miles Kelly
PUBLISHING

First published in 2006 by
Miles Kelly Publishing Ltd
Bardfield Centre, Great Bardfield, Essex, CM7 4SL

2 4 6 8 10 9 7 5 3 1

Publishing Director Anne Marshall
Editorial Director Belinda Gallagher
Art Director Jo Brewer
Proofreaders Judy Barratt, Stephen Setford
Design Concept Warris Kidwai
Designers Sally Lace, Peter Radcliffe
Indexer Hilary Bird
Picture Research Manager Liberty Newton
Picture Researcher Laura Faulder
Production Elizabeth Brunwin
Reprographics Anthony Cambray, Mike Coupe, Stephan Davis, Ian Paulyn

Planners, Authors and Consultants Camilla de la Bedoyere, Rupert Matthews,
Steve Parker, Stephen Setford, Barbara Taylor

ISBN 1-84236-715-3
ISBN 978-1-84236-715-5

Printed in China

British Library Cataloguing-in-Publication Data
A catalogue record for this book is available
from the British Library

www.mileskelly.net
info@mileskelly.net

The publisher would like to thank the following artists
whose work appears in this book:
Richard Draper, Ian Jackson, Mike Saunders

All other artworks are from Miles Kelly Archives

The publishers would like to thank the following picture
sources whose photographs appear in this book:
Page 175(t) Fred Bavendam/Minden Pictures/FLPA, (b) R.Dirscherl/FLPA;
184(t) Norbert Wu/Minden Pictures/FLPA; 185(b) Norbert Wu/Minden Pictures/FLPA

All other photographs from:
Castrol, CMCD, Corbis, Corel, digitalSTOCK, digitalvision, Flat Earth, Hemera, ILN
John Foxx, PhotoAlto, PhotoDisc, PhotoEssentials, PhotoPro, Stockbyte

CONTENTS

PREHISTORIC LIFE 10–69

PLANTS 70–129

WATER LIFE 130–189

INSECTS & OTHER INVERTEBRATES 190–249

REPTILES & AMPHIBIANS 250–309

BIRDS 310–369

MAMMALS 370–429

HUMAN BODY 430–489

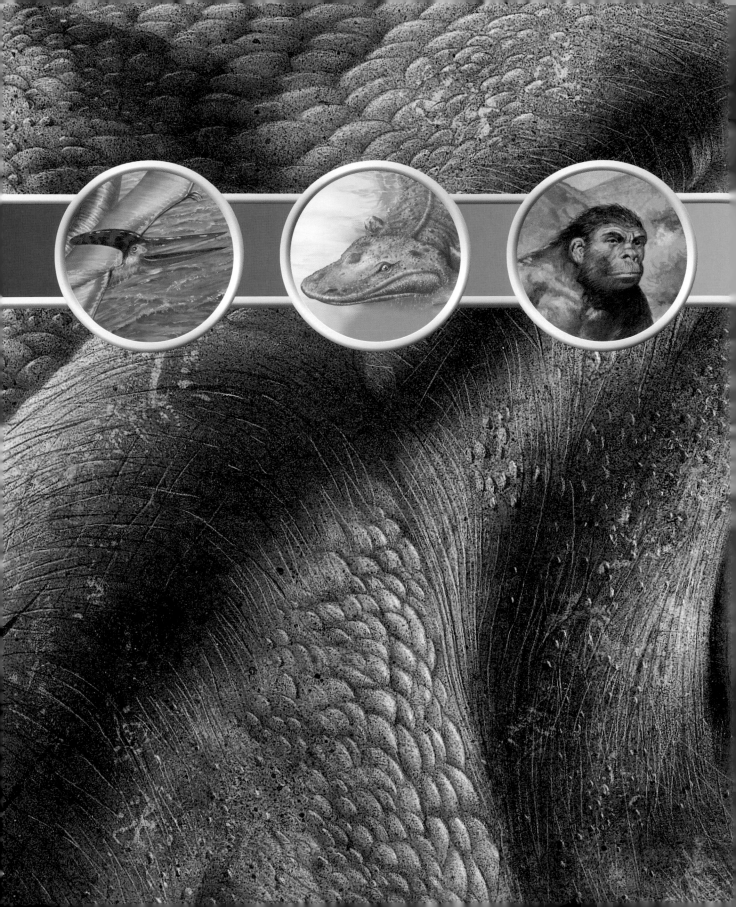

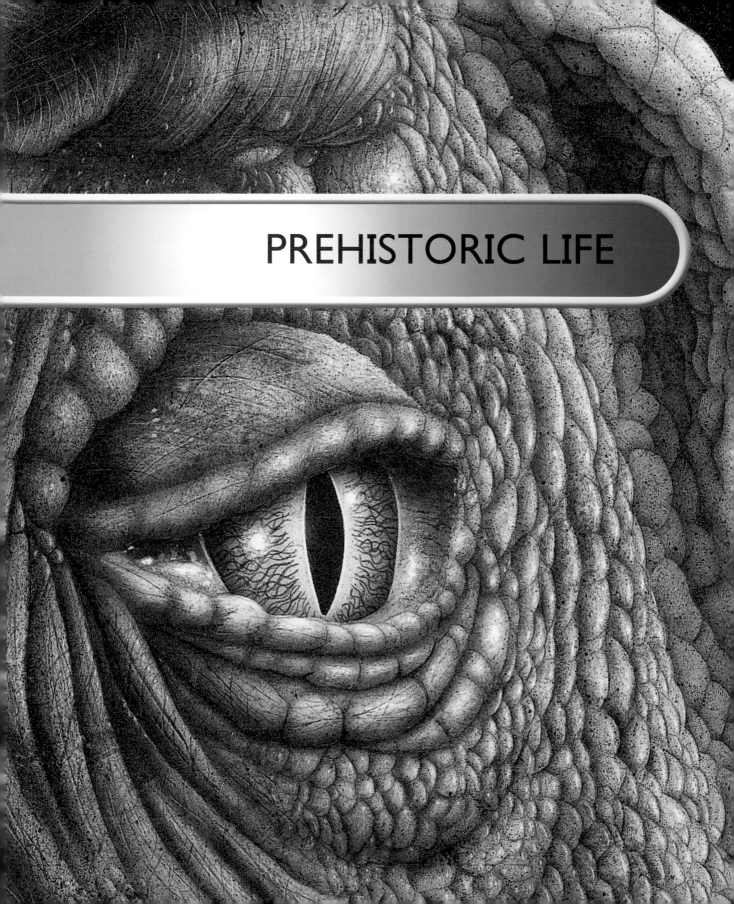

PREHISTORIC LIFE

Studying the Past

The prehistoric animals in this section lived many thousands or even millions of years ago. Nobody has ever seen one of them alive. We know about these animals because bones, teeth and other remains have been preserved in rocks as fossils. By studying the fossils, scientists called palaeontologists can discover what the animals looked like and how they lived.

○ Information about prehistoric animals comes not only from fossils, but also from 'trace' fossils. These were not actual parts of the animals' bodies, but other items or signs of their presence.

○ Trace fossils include footprints, egg shells, marks made by claws and teeth, and coprolites – fossilized droppings.

○ The majority of prehistoric animals are known from only a few fossil parts, such as several fragments of bones.

○ The dinosaurs were a group of prehistoric reptiles. When producing reconstructions, fossil parts of other similar dinosaurs are often used by scientists to 'fill in' missing bones, teeth and even missing heads, limbs or tails.

Amazing

Several museums have complete *Brachiosaurus* skeletons on display, but only the one in the USA is real. All the rest are copies.

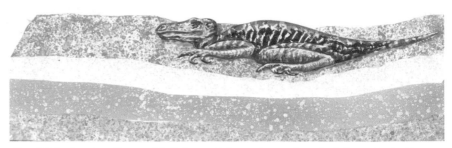

A *Velociraptor* dies and falls into a lake or river, where it sinks to the bottom. The flesh and other soft body parts rot away, or are eaten by water creatures.

The bones and teeth are buried under layers of mud and sand. Silica and other minerals from the rock seep into the bones, filling any available gaps.

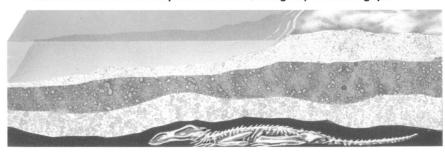

Over a period of millions of years, minerals replace the original dinosaur bones entirely, but preserve their shape and form. The bones have become fossils.

If the rock containing the fossils is lifted up and eroded, the fossils become exposed. They may then be seen by a scientist so that they can be excavated.

Find out more

Mollusc marker fossils p. 17

An excavation by palaeontologists in the field. Each fossil must be carefully recorded, together with the precise place where it was found.

○ Soft body parts from modern reptiles, such as lizards, are used as a guide for the reconstruction of a dinosaur's muscles and guts, which are added to the fossils.

Fossilized body parts

The hard parts of an animal's body were the most likely parts to form fossils, especially teeth, bones, claws and horns.

○ On rare occasions, palaeontologists discover remains of an animal's body that dried out rapidly so that quite a few parts were preserved as mummified fossils.

○ Most fossils are of bones or teeth, because these hard objects are preserved more easily than soft body parts. Over millions of years, the original objects rot away and are replaced by minerals from the surrounding rocks. The fossils can be very heavy, and they are often fragile as well. Sometimes rare fossils of skin or muscles are found.

○ Palaeontologists study fossils by comparing them to the bones of other animals. They search for animals that have teeth of a similar shape to those of the fossil. If two animals have similar teeth, then it is likely that they both ate similar foods.

○ The marks left on bones by muscles show how strong the dinosaur was and in which direction it could move its legs, neck and other parts of its body.

○ The palaeontologist must remove the fossil from the surrounding rocks, called the matrix. Some types of rock can be dissolved away with chemicals, but most need to be scraped away with metal hooks and chisels.

○ The most delicate fossils are coprolites, which are preserved animal droppings. Coprolites include the world's largest known droppings, made by a sauropod dinosaur, which would have weighed about 10 kg when fresh.

Dietary clues

If coprolites (fossilized droppings) are broken open, their contents can reveal to palaeontologists what the animal had been eating and how much food it consumed.

Palaeontologists who study fossil footprints can tell how fast the animal was moving when it made the prints. These Tyrannosaurus prints are close together and the heels have made shallow impressions, so the dinosaur must have been walking slowly at the time.

Famous fossil finds

1822 Dr Gideon Mantell discovers the first dinosaur fossils in Sussex, England. They belong to *Iguanodon*.

1858 Joseph Leidy discovers the first dinosaur skeleton in New Jersey, USA. It is a *Hadrosaurus*.

1878 Coal miners at Bernissart in Belgium discover 40 complete *Iguanodon* skeletons.

1909 Earl Douglass unearths the largest collection of fossils ever found, in Utah, USA.

1925 Dinosaur nests and eggs are discovered for the first time by Roy Andrews digging in the Gobi Desert, central Asia.

1969 Fossils of *Deinonychus* are found by John Ostrom.

1974 Hundreds of fossils are found in a remote area of Xigong Province, China.

1993 Largest dinosaur, *Argentinosaurus*, and largest land animal ever, is discovered.

1995 Discovery of fossils of the 14.3-m-long *Giganotosaurus*, the largest meat-eating animal ever to walk the Earth.

1998 Discovery of *Caudipteryx* in Liaoning, China, shows that some smaller dinosaurs were covered with feathers.

Earliest Life

For many millions of years after it formed, the Earth was a dead world. There was no life anywhere on the planet. About 3300 million years ago (mya), the first plants evolved in the sea, followed around 1200 mya by the first single-celled animals. About 700 mya, the first multi-celled animals appeared in the oceans. Similar to worms and jellyfish, these animals fed both on plants and on other animals.

❍ Invertebrates (animals that do not have a spinal column) were the first multi-celled animals to live on Earth, in the prehistoric seas.

◀ **Stromatolites such as these exist off the coasts of western Australia, southern Africa, eastern Greenland and parts of Antarctica. They are made up of the fossils of algae and bacteria.**

❍ One of the earliest-known fossils of a multi-celled animal is around 600 mya. This is a creature called *Mawsonites*, which may have been a primitive jellyfish or worm.

▼ **Charnia was a prehistoric animal that grew in feather-like colonies attached to the seabed, like the sea pens of today. Charnia fossils date to around 700 mya.**

▲ **The Cooksonia plant had forked stems ending in spore-filled caps. The earliest examples of Cooksonia, found in Ireland, date from 430 mya.**

❍ The earliest plant fossils are found in stromatolites. These are limestone deposits formed by bacteria and simple plants called algae. Some stromatolites are over 3000 million years old.

❍ The very first animal-like organisms that fed on other organisms or organic matter were single-celled and sometimes called protozoans.

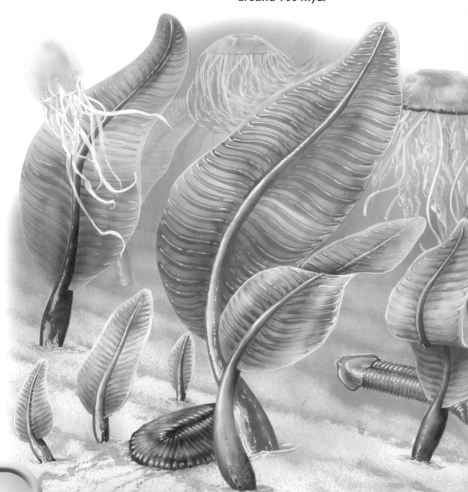

Find out more

Trilobite seas pp. 16–17

Vertebrate ancestor

Pikaia was a small, worm-like creature that is thought to be the ancestor of all vertebrates (animals with backbones). *Pikaia* looked a little like an eel with tail-fins. Its fossil remains were found in the 530 million years old mudstone deposits of the Burgess Shale in Canada. *Pikaia* was the first-known chordate – an animal with a stiff supporting rod, called a notochord, along its back. In later animals, this rod developed into a backbone. The chordate group includes all vertebrates, as well as marine animals called tunicates and acraniates.

❍ The soft bodies of worms means that they do not make good fossils.

❍ Marine worms called seruplids make hard tubes around their bodies. The tubes fossilize better than the worms' bodies.

❍ Small, shelled invertebrates emerged in the Cambrian Period (505–590 mya). They included the archaeocyathids, which had bodies that were like two cups, one inside the other. The groups of shellfish that live today evolved millions of years later.

Ⓐ Anomalocaris *was a 60-cm-long predator. Its fossil remains have been found in the rocks at Burgess Shale, Canada.* Anomalocaris *had a circular mouth and fin-like body parts.*

Early lichens

Lichens, such as those shown here, are a partnership between an alga and fungus. Early lichens – like modern-day ones – grew on rocks and, over time, eroded part of the rock and helped form soil.

❍ One early invertebrate is *Spriggina*, named after Reg Sprigg, a geologist. He discovered its fossilized remains near Ediacara, in southern Australia, in 1946.

❍ Another famous invertebrate discovery was made by Roger Mason, an English schoolboy, in 1957. This was the fossil of *Charnia*, an animal that was similar to a living sea pen.

❍ Worms are invertebrates that usually have long, soft, slender bodies. They were among the earliest multi-celled animals to live in the prehistoric seas.

❍ Fossilized remains of serpulid tubes are quite common in rocks of the Mesozoic and Cenozoic Eras (248 mya to the present).

❍ The 530-million-year-old mudstone deposits of the Burgess Shale, Canada, contain the fossil impressions of the annelid worm *Canadia*. In annelid worms, the body is divided into segments. Palaeontologists think that millipedes and other arthropods evolved from annelids.

Ⓥ Ottoia *was a sea worm whose fossil remains palaeontologists discovered in large numbers in the Burgess Shale rock strata of North America.* Ottoia *lived in burrows on the seabed and fed by filtering minute food particles from the water.*

Key dates

4600 mya	Earth forms from a mass of space dust and gas.
3300 mya	First simple plants, algae, begin to appear in the world's oceans.
700 mya	First water animals appear – worms, jellyfish and sponges.
450 mya	First fish evolve in the oceans.
410 mya	Plants appear on land.
400 mya	Insect-like animals called arthropods move on to land.
350 mya	First amphibians evolve from fish and begin to live partly on land.
330 mya	One group of amphibians evolves into reptiles.
230 mya	First dinosaurs evolve.
220 mya	Small group of the therapsid reptiles evolve into mammals.

Trilobite Seas

About 600 mya, animals with hard body parts appeared for the first time. These animals included molluscs and echinoderms, both of which survive to this day, and trilobites, which are now extinct. For millions of years, creatures such as these dominated life in the ocean. A few molluscs even began to live on land, although only in damp areas.

○ Trilobites belonged to the invertebrate group called arthropods – animals with segmented bodies and hard outer skeletons.

○ Trilobite means 'three lobes'. Trilobites' hard outer shells were divided into three parts. The first trilobites appeared about 530 mya. By 500 mya, they had developed into many different types.

Starfish

Starfish are echinoderms that have five arms radiating out from the central mouth and stomach region. They hunt smaller animals, especially shellfish and molluscs.

○ Trilobites had compound eyes, like insects' eyes, which could see in many different directions at once.

○ Trilobites had long, thin, jointed legs. They moved quickly over the seabed or sediment covering it.

▼ *Most ammonites had spiral shells, but in some the shells grew straight like a cone, or were bent and twisted into bizarre shapes.*

○ Trilobites became extinct around 250 mya – along with huge numbers of other marine animals.

○ Ammonites belong to the cephalopod group of molluscs.

○ Ammonites were once widespread in the oceans, but, like the dinosaurs, died out at the end of the Cretaceous Period (about 65 mya).

○ The number of ammonite fossils that have been found proves how plentiful these animals once were.

○ Ammonites were predators and scavengers. They had very good vision, long seizing tentacles and powerful mouths.

Find out more

Prehistoric arthropods pp. 18–19

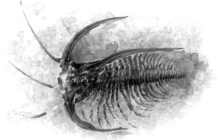

Mollusc marker fossils

This snail is a mollusc. Molluscs are crucial in palaeontology, because their shells fossilize easily and occur in great numbers. Some molluscs evolved quickly, and their rapid-changing shapes are used as 'marker fossils' to date rocks.

◐ *Trilobites were most numerous during the Cambrian, Ordovician and Silurian Periods, between 542 and 410 mya, although they survived to the Late Triassic Period, 250 mya. Many trilobite fossils are actually the remains of shed outer shells, or exoskeletons.*

⬆ *Like starfish, sea cucumbers are echinoderms. They live on the seabed and feed on tiny animals that they filter from mud and sand.*

❍ Ammonites had multi-chambered shells that contained gas and worked like flotation tanks, keeping the creatures afloat.

❍ Modern molluscs include gastropods (slugs, snails and limpets), bivalves (clams, oysters, mussels and cockles) and cephalopods (octopuses, squids and cuttlefish).

❍ The first molluscs were probably tiny – about the size of a pinhead. They appeared during the Mid-Cambrian Period, about 550 mya.

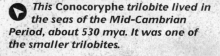

◐ *This Conocoryphe trilobite lived in the seas of the Mid-Cambrian Period, about 530 mya. It was one of the smaller trilobites.*

Prehistoric Arthropods

*T*he most successful animals of all have been the arthropods: animals that have jointed skeletons around the outside of their bodies. The arthropods include spiders, crabs, insects and centipedes, as well as hundreds of other types of animal. Today, there are about 1.2 million species of arthropod, but many more than this existed during prehistoric times.

○ Arthropods form the largest single group of animals. They include insects, crustaceans (crabs or lobsters), arachnids (spiders) and myriapods (millipedes) – any creature with a segmented body and jointed limbs.

○ The earliest known remains of arthropods come from the 530-million-year-old mudstone deposits of the Burgess Shale in Canada.

○ Arthropods were one of the first – if not the first – groups of animals to emerge from the sea and colonize the land, around 400 mya.

△ *The flying arthropod* **Meganeura** *would have resembled this modern-day dragonfly. It had large bulging eyes that allowed it to spot the movements of prey. However,* **Meganeura** *was up to 15 times the size of a living dragonfly, and had much stronger legs.*

○ Arthropods were well suited for living on land. Many of them had exoskeletons (outer skeletons) that prevented them from drying out. Their jointed limbs meant they could move over the ground.

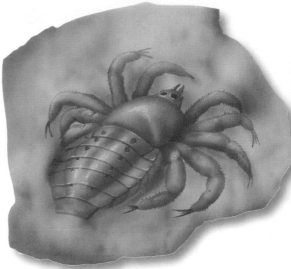

△ *Early spiders were among the first creatures to live on land. One of the earliest-known spiders is* **Palaeocharinus,** *which was discovered in 400-million-year-old rocks in Rhynie, Scotland.* **Palaeocharinus,** *seen here preserved in amber (fossilized resin from ancient trees), was 0.5 mm long. It would have hunted tiny mites that fed on rotting plant matter.*

Amazing

Arthropods have paired limbs, which can be specialized as legs, pincers, paddles or almost any other form.

△ **Arthropleura** *, the largest land arthropod, was as long as a human is tall. Despite its size, it was a plant eater rather than a predator.*

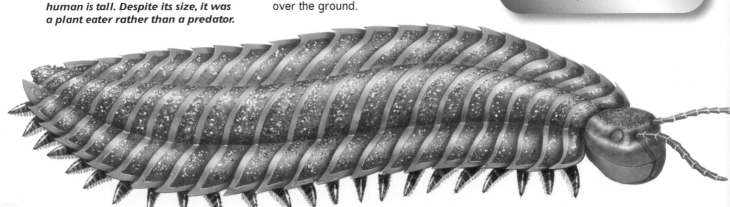

Giant plants

When the first arthropods moved from the water to the land, they found much of it covered by dense vegetation. The largest plants were the giant clubmosses, which stood 30 m tall.

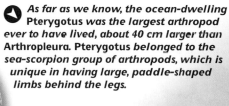

As far as we know, the ocean-dwelling Pterygotus *was the largest arthropod ever to have lived, about 40 cm larger than* Arthropleura. Pterygotus *belonged to the sea-scorpion group of arthropods, which is unique in having large, paddle-shaped limbs behind the legs.*

○ The largest-ever land arthropod was a millipede-like creature called *Arthropleura*, which measured 1.8 m long.

○ Like woodlice, *Arthropleura* ate rotting plants. It lived on the floor of forests in the Carboniferous Period (360–286 mya).

○ The first land-living insects appeared during the Devonian Period (408–360 mya).

○ The Cretaceous Period (144–65 mya) saw a big rise in the number of flying insects, because of the emergence of flowering plants.

○ Many flowering plants rely on flying insects to spread their pollen, while flying insects, such as bees, rely on flowers for food (nectar and pollen).

○ Bee-like insects date back to the Late Cretaceous Period, while modern bees first appeared around 30 mya.

Insects and pollination

The evolution of winged, pollinating insects, such as these honeybees, is closely linked to the evolution of flowering plants. Bees, as well as other flying insects, help these plants to spread by carrying pollen from the male part of one flower to the female part of another as they feed on nectar.

Ancient Fish

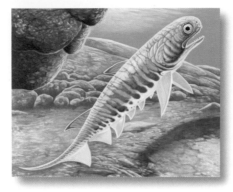

Fish first appeared in the ocean about 450 mya. These early fish did not have jaws, and they fed by sucking up small, soft-bodied animals. Fish with jaws appeared about 430 mya, but at first their skeletons were made of gristle rather than bone. Only about 350 mya did fish with bone skeletons become numerous.

❍ Early fish were called agnathans, which means 'jawless'. Agnathans ate by sieving plankton through their simple mouth opening, as well as scooping up algae from the seabed.

❍ Later jawless fish had more streamlined, deeper bodies and eyes at the front of their heads. This suggests they were not restricted to the seabed.

❍ Lampreys and hagfish are living relatives of agnathans. They have soft bodies, look like eels, and are jawless.

❍ Most of the jawless fish became extinct about 350 mya.

❍ Acanthodians are jawed fish with bony skeletons. Jaws and teeth gave these fish a huge advantage over agnathans. The acanthodians were able to eat a greater variety of food and become predators, and also defend themselves more effectively. As the jawless agnathans declined, the acanthodians flourished.

◀ *Climatius, an acanthodian (jawed fish) lived around 400 mya. Another name for acanthodians is 'spiny sharks'. Although they were not sharks, many of these fish had spines on the edges of their fins.*

❍ As acanthodians developed jaws, so they developed teeth, too. The earliest fish teeth were cone-like projections along the jaw, made out of bone and coated with hard enamel.

▼ *Bothriolepis had eyes on the top of its head. Its mouth was lined by a set of cutting plates and was situated under the head. These features lead palaeontologists to believe that Bothriolepis was a bottom-dwelling sediment feeder.*

▲ *Hemicyclaspis and other early jawless fish could swim much farther and quicker than most invertebrates. This meant they could more easily search for and move to new feeding areas.*

◀ *Hybodus was a blunt-headed prehistoric shark that lived between 250 and 125 mya, in the time of the dinosaurs. It looked quite similar to modern sharks, but had very different jaws.*

Find out more

Sea reptiles pp. 38–39

Lobe-finned fish use their muscular fins to provide swimming power, enabling them to move with agility but restricting their speed.

Amazing

Early fish were the first animals to have brains in their heads. Other creatures had nerve connections and sensory organs spread around their body, or concentrated in more than one place.

○ Bony fish have internal skeletons and external scales made of bone. They first appeared in the Late Devonian Period (about 360 mya), and evolved into the most abundant and diverse fish group.

○ There are two types of bony fish – ray-finned fish and lobe-finned fish. There were plenty of prehistoric lobe-finned fish, but only a few species survive today. They belong to one of two groups – lungfish or coelacanths.

Pleuracanthus

The first fish to have jaws with teeth were the sharks. *Pleuracanthus* was a shark that lived about 350 mya in lakes and rivers.

○ The teeth of early acanthodians varied greatly. Some species had sharp, spiky teeth, while in others the teeth were like blades or even flat plates. Each tooth shape was an adaptation to eating a particular type of food.

○ Placoderms were jawed fish that had bony plates covering the front part of the body. They appeared in the Late Silurian Period (about 415 mya) and were abundant in the seas of the Devonian Period (408–360 mya).

Eusthenopteron using its fins to move out of the water. Eusthenopteron, which means 'good strong fin', was once thought to be the closest ancestor to tetrapods (four-legged animals). However, palaeontologists have since found another fish, Panderichthys, which was an even closer relative.

Ancient shark tooth

A fossilized tooth from a prehistoric *Megalodon* shark (left), compared to a tooth from a modern great white shark (right). The most common fossil remains of fish, like those of many other vertebrates, are teeth, because teeth are made of a long-lasting substance called enamel.

From Fish to Amphibians

About 350 mya, one group of fish evolved primitive lungs that allowed them to breathe air. They also had four legs, which had evolved from stout fins. These were the first amphibians – animals that are able to live in water or on land. As millions of years passed, the amphibians became increasingly adapted to life on land, but they still needed to return to water to lay their soft eggs.

○ A fossil of an animal from which amphibians may have evolved has been found in Lode, Latvia. This is *Panderichthys*, a fish with paired muscular fins, from which limbs probably developed. The skull of *Panderichthys* is nearly identical to that of later amphibians.

Early amphibian fossils

A fossil of *Acanthostega* from Greenland. The early amphibian fossils have been found only in Greenland and nearby areas of North America and western Europe.

▶ *Scientists think that **Ichthyostega's** shape and behaviour were similar to that of a seal. Like a seal, it could probably tuck its limbs alongside its body when swimming. On land, it might have used its forelimbs to drag the rest of its body over the ground.*

○ Tetrapod means 'four-legged'. All early tetrapods were amphibians, as they were animals that could survive both in water and on land. The size of tetrapods increased during the Carboniferous Period (360–286 mya). This may have been because there was more oxygen in the atmosphere – produced by the huge forests that existed at the time.

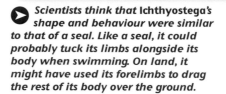

○ Tetrapods adapting to the land had to face a range of challenges, such as greater temperature variations and more ultraviolet radiation from the Sun.

○ *Acanthostega* was one of the earliest tetrapods. It had a fish-like body, which suggests that it spent most of its life in water. Its fossil remains were found in rock strata dating from the Late Devonian Period (around 370 mya).

Amazing

Scientists know that over 100 groups of amphibians existed 250 mya. By 150 mya, however, all but two of these groups had become extinct.

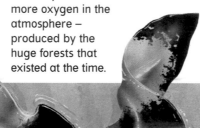

◀ **Acanthostega** *may have evolved from lobe-finned fish such as* **Eusthenopteron** *and* **Panderichthys***. It shared a number of features with these fish, including a similar set of gills and lungs, and a tail-fin and braincase.*

Find out more

Lobe-finned fish p. 21

Bulky amphibian

Mastodonsaurus was a big, bulky amphibian. Like some other early amphibians, it could live out of water for long periods of time, but had to return to water to lay its eggs.

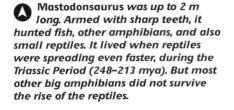

A **Mastodonsaurus** *was up to 2 m long. Armed with sharp teeth, it hunted fish, other amphibians, and also small reptiles. It lived when reptiles were spreading even faster, during the Triassic Period (248–213 mya). But most other big amphibians did not survive the rise of the reptiles.*

❍ *Acanthostega*'s legs were well-developed, with eight toes on the front feet and seven on the rear ones. The number of toes on its feet surprised palaeontologists – they had previously thought all tetrapods possessed five toes.

❍ *Ichthyostega* was another early tetrapod. Like *Acanthostega*, it was discovered in Greenland in rock that was 370 million years old. Its body was around 1 m long. Palaeontologists think that its body was probably covered in scales.

❍ Temnospondyls were a group of amphibians that emerged in the Carboniferous Period (360–286 mya). They were the biggest early tetrapods.

❍ Leposondyls were an early tetrapod group that appeared between 350 and 300 mya. They were mostly about the size of modern newts (10–15 cm long).

❍ Modern amphibians, such as frogs, salamanders and caecilians, belong to the lissamphibian group, which evolved between the Late Carboniferous and Early Triassic Periods (300–240 mya).

Early amphibians

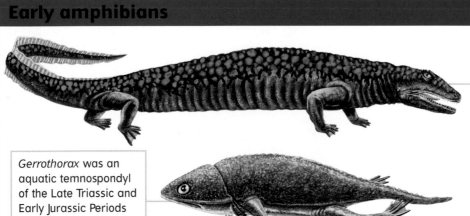

Eogyrinus was an amphibious tetrapod that lived around 310 mya. It grew up to 4.5 m long and had a skull similar to a crocodile's and a body similar to an eel's.

Gerrothorax was an aquatic temnospondyl of the Late Triassic and Early Jurassic Periods (215–208 mya). Like most temnospondyls, it was a predator.

One theory about *Diplocaulus*' skull shape is that it was used for defence, and difficult for predators to swallow. Another idea is that it helped the animal to move through the water.

Triadobatrachus, from Triassic Madagascar, is the earliest-known frog. Salamanders and caecilians first appeared in the Jurassic Period (213–144 mya).

The First Reptiles

Some time around 330 mya, one group of amphibians evolved a waterproof skin, which meant that they could live in arid places without drying out too quickly. They also evolved a new type of egg that could be laid on dry land, unlike amphibian eggs, which need to be laid in water. These and other evolutionary changes made them into the first reptiles.

Pangaea

At the time that the first reptiles lived, all the continents on Earth were joined together in one vast landmass called Pangaea. Later, the continents began to separate. Even today, they are still moving slowly across the face of the globe.

Amazing

The first reptiles appeared in the same place as the first amphibians had appeared some 80 million years earlier – in Greenland and nearby areas.

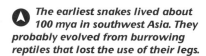

⌃ The earliest snakes lived about 100 mya in southwest Asia. They probably evolved from burrowing reptiles that lost the use of their legs.

◯ Compared to amphibian limbs, reptile legs were better adapted to moving around on land. In addition, reptiles had a more effective circulatory system for moving blood around their bodies, and bigger brains.

◯ Reptiles also had more powerful jaw muscles than amphibians, and thus would have been better predators. Early reptiles ate millipedes, spiders and insects.

⌖ Varanosaurus was a synapsid (mammal-like) reptile that lived in North America in the Early Permian Period, about 286 mya. There are important similarities between the skulls of synapsid reptiles and mammals.

Find out more

Egg fossils p. 29

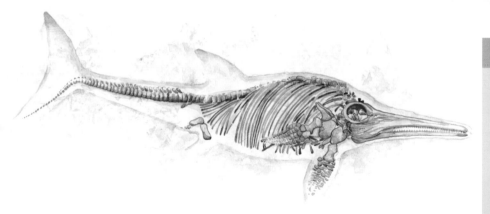

Reptile eggs

Reptiles broke the link between reproduction and water by laying hard-shelled eggs on land. This snake shell contains the developing young (embryo), a food store (yolk) and a protective liquid (amniotic fluid).

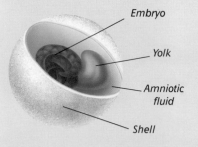

Embryo
Yolk
Amniotic fluid
Shell

○ Reptiles evolved eggs that were covered by a protective shell. The shell enabled reptiles to lay their eggs safely on land without risk of them drying out.

○ One advantage of shelled eggs was that reptiles did not have to return to water to breed, so they could colonize new areas. Another advantage was that reptiles could hide their eggs better on land – eggs laid in water are easy pickings for hungry animals.

○ A reptile embryo completes all its growth phases inside its egg – when it hatches it looks like a miniature adult.

○ By the Late Carboniferous Period (about 300 mya), reptiles developed openings in their skulls, behind the eye socket. These openings allowed room for more jaw muscles.

○ Over time, four types of reptile skull developed. Each belonged to a different reptile group.

○ Anapsids had no openings in their skull other than the eye sockets. Turtles and tortoises are anapsids.

○ Euryapsids had one opening high up on either side of the skull. Sea reptiles, such as ichthyosaurs, were euryapsids, but this group has no surviving relatives.

The fossilized remains of an Ichthyosaurus, showing the impression of its body in the rock. Many examples of Ichthyosaurus fossils have been discovered in rocks from the Jurassic Period (213–144 mya) in England and Germany.

○ Synapsid reptiles had one opening low down on either side of the skull. Mammals are descended from the synapsid group.

○ Diapsid reptiles had two openings on either side of the skull. Dinosaurs and pterosaurs were diapsids; so too are birds and crocodiles.

Hylonomus, meaning 'forest mouse', was one of the earliest reptiles. Fossil hunters discovered its remains in fossilized tree stumps at Joggins in Nova Scotia, Canada. It is thought that this little reptile hunted insects and other invertebrates, which it caught with its cone-shaped teeth. Hylonomus lived about 320 mya during the Mid-Carboniferous Period.

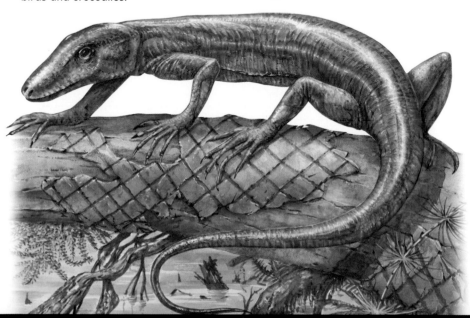

A Reptilian World

By about 270 mya, the reptiles dominated the land. The amphibians were not so well adapted to life on dry land, so they survived only in damp areas or near bodies of water. At first the synapsids were the most numerous reptiles, but later the anapsids, then the diapsids took over.

Proganochelys, an ancestor of modern turtles and tortoises, had a 60-cm-long shell, but it was unable to pull its head or legs inside.

Cynognathus means 'dog jaw'. Like other synapsid reptiles, it had strong muscles for opening and closing its jaws, which made it a powerful killer.

Some fossil discoveries revealed to scientists how the continents have moved about over the Earth's surface. The reptile *Lystrosaurus* lived about 200 mya. Its fossils have been found in Europe, Asia, Africa and Antarctica. *Lystrosaurus* could not swim, so all the continents must have been joined together at the time. Over millions of years, they drifted apart, eventually reaching their current positions.

Some reptiles had very sharp teeth – and not just the predators. The plant-eating *Moschops* was as big as a rhino and lived in southern Africa about 270 mya. Its teeth were long and straight, and ended with a sharp edge like a chisel. It could easily bite tough leaves and twigs off bushes.

Find out more

Pangaea p. 24

As well as acting as a heat-regulator and allowing its body to quickly warm up or cool down, *Dimetrodon*'s large fin might have helped it to attract mates or ward off rivals.

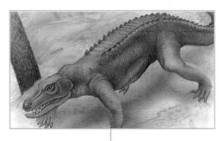

Fossils of *Protosuchus*, meaning 'first crocodile', have been discovered in Arizona, dating back to around 200 mya. Although *Protosuchus* was similar to living crocodiles in many ways, its legs were much longer.

Diictodon was a mammal-like reptile that lived about 260 mya. A plant-eater and a burrower, *Diictodon* was an advanced form of a synapsid known as a dicynodont.

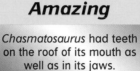

Amazing

Chasmatosaurus had teeth on the roof of its mouth as well as in its jaws.

Chasmatosaurus was an early archosaur and a forerunner of the dinosaurs. It lived about 250 mya and grew up to 2 m long.

Thrinaxodon had three different types of teeth. These were small front teeth for nipping and biting, larger canine teeth for stabbing, and rough-edged cheek teeth for shearing. It used its teeth to good effect when preying on smaller creatures.

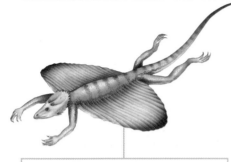

Coelurosauravus, which was around 60 cm long, lived in forests in Europe and Madagascar. Palaeontologists initially mistook its gliding rods for fin spines, and thought it was a fish.

The Dinosaurs Appear

The dinosaurs were a group of prehistoric reptiles that held their legs underneath their bodies, like modern mammals. The skull bones of dinosaurs were unlike those of other reptiles. Dinosaurs were closely related to crocodiles. It is thought that birds probably evolved from one type of dinosaur.

How to identify a dinosaur

1 Legs are held directly under the body, not sprawling sideways as in other reptiles.

2 Ankle has a simple joint that allows only limited movements, unlike most other reptiles, which have ankles capable of twisting in all directions.

3 Hips are joined solidly to the backbone, not loosely as is more usual in reptiles.

4 Long hind legs. Nearly all dinosaurs had hind legs that were significantly longer than their front legs.

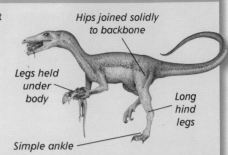

Hips joined solidly to backbone

Legs held under body

Long hind legs

Simple ankle

The Age of the Dinosaurs

Dinosaurs existed on Earth between about 230 and 65 mya. This huge stretch of time is divided into three periods: the Triassic, the Jurassic and the Cretaceous. Together, these periods make up the Mesozoic Era, also known as the 'Age of the Dinosaurs'.

Triassic Period 248–213 mya

Archosaurs became important, and the first real dinosaurs emerged. There were small two-legged carnivores (meat eaters) and larger herbivores (plant eaters).

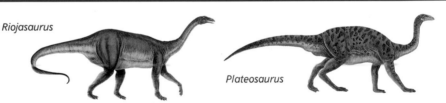

Riojasaurus

Plateosaurus

Jurassic Period 213–144 mya

The dinosaurs diversified greatly in the Jurassic. Giant dinosaurs took over as the dominant animals, such as the giant plant eater *Barosaurus*.

Barosaurus

Heterodontosaurus

Apatosaurus

Cretaceous Period 144–65 mya

There were more types of dinosaur in the Cretaceous than in the other periods, including huge carnivores and armoured herbivores.

Tyrannosaurus rex

Spinosaurus

Deinonychus

Egg fossils

The remains of embryonic dinosaurs have been found within a few fossilized eggs. Fossils show that dinosaur eggs varied greatly in size and in shape, with some being smaller than a modern hen's egg.

▲ *Ornithosuchus was an early archosaur that may have been related to ancestors of the dinosaurs. It was about 4 m long and was a hunter with powerful muscles.*

❍ The name 'dinosaur' means 'terrible lizard'. It was given to these ancient reptiles in 1842 by English scientist Richard Owen.

❍ Dinosaurs belong to a group of reptiles known as the archosaurs, which means 'ruling reptiles'. This group includes crocodiles and several types of reptiles that are now extinct.

❍ Dinosaurs are classified according to the shape of their hip bones. Saurischian dinosaurs had hip bones shaped like those of modern reptiles – the name 'saurischian' means 'reptile-hip'. The ornithischian dinosaurs had hip bones that resemble those of modern birds – 'ornithischian' means 'bird-hip'.

❍ Hundreds of different types of dinosaur have been named by scientists, but nobody is certain how many there were in total. Thousands of dinosaur fossils remain buried and have not yet been discovered.

▲ *One of the oldest known dinosaurs was Herrerasaurus, which lived in South America about 230 mya. It was about 4 m long and hunted other animals. Herrerasaurus had jaws filled with sharp teeth, curved backwards. These would have been able to grip struggling prey and stop them from wriggling free.*

❍ *Compsognathus*, a hunting dinosaur, was the smallest of all dinosaurs. It was about the same size as a chicken, and weighed around 2.5 kg. *Compsognathus* had a long tail and neck, so it may have reached over 1 m in length, but would have stood only about 40 cm tall. *Compsognathus* probably hunted insects and small lizards for food.

❍ The biggest dinosaurs laid the largest eggs that have ever existed. The eggs were about 40 cm across, or as large as a football, and were probably laid by sauropod dinosaurs.

▲ *Unlike most reptiles, dinosaurs cared for their young for the first few months of life. This helps to explain why the dinosaurs were so successful.*

Family lifespans

Millions of years ago	Family
220–160	Prosauropods
190–65	Sauropods
180–65	Nodosaurids
170–80	Stegosaurids
150–80	Spinosaurs
140–65	Iguanodontids
125–65	Dromaeosaurs
110–65	Ankylosaurids
110–65	Ornithomimids
105–65	Pachycephalosaurids
100–65	Ceratopsids
95–65	Hadrosaurids
85–65	Oviraptosaurs
80–65	Theropods

All dates are approximate

Early Dinosaurs and Relatives

*I**t is thought that the first dinosaurs emerged during the Mid-Triassic Period, around 230 mya, in South America. They quickly spread across the entire world, and evolved into a large number of different species. By 190 mya, the dinosaurs had become the dominant animals on Earth, and they remained so for more than 120 million years.***

❍ *Coelophysis* is a dinosaur that has been found in vast numbers. Hundreds of fossilized *Coelophysis* have been excavated in North America. The most dramatic find came in 1947 at the Ghost Ranch in New Mexico, USA. Scientists found the fossils of an entire pack of these animals, almost 100 strong. It is thought that the *Coelophysis* were killed by a sandstorm.

❍ *Herrerasaurus*, a powerful predator, was up to 4 m long and weighed more than 100 kg. It is one of several very early dinosaurs that lived from about 228 mya in what is now South America.

Plateosaurus

Plateosaurus ('flat reptile') was one of the first big plant-eating dinosaurs. It grew up to 8 m long and lived 220 mya in what is now Europe. It could rear up on its back legs and use its long neck to reach food high off the ground.

❍ In 1988, an almost complete skeleton of *Herrerasaurus* was unearthed in the foothills of the Andes Mountains near San Juan. The narrow jaws were full of sharp, back-curving teeth. The long, strong rear legs allowed rapid movement.

❍ Only very few remains of *Saltopus* have been discovered, near Elgin in Scotland. *Saltopus* was a tiny dinosaur, about the size of a small pet cat. The hands of *Saltopus* had five fingers each, which was a primitive or 'old-fashioned' feature for a meat-eating dinosaur. Over millions of years the number of fingers reduced to three or even two per hand.

Amazing

Dinosaurs and mammals first appeared at about the same time, but it was the dinosaurs that ruled the Earth. Mammals became important only after the dinosaurs had died out.

❍ When its fossils were first studied, some experts considered *Ornithosuchus* to be a very early, primitive type of dinosaur. However, it is now classed as a member of a related reptile group, the thecodonts. Some thecodonts may have given rise to the dinosaurs. *Ornithosuchus* was up to 3 m long and had sharp teeth suited to catching big victims and tearing their flesh. It probably ran on all fours or on just its rear legs.

❍ *Scaphonyx* was not a dinosaur, but a member of the reptile group called rhynchosaurs or 'beaked reptiles'. They were plant eaters and ranged from about 2 m in length down to less than 40 cm. *Scaphonyx* was one of the larger rhynchosaurs, and it used its hooked upper jaw to grab fern-fronds and other ground-level plant growth.

❶ *Riojasaurus **was a prosauropod that lived in South America right at the end of the Triassic Period (213 mya).***

❍ Rhynchosaurs were very common at the start of the Age of Dinosaurs, but these reptiles soon faded away, perhaps because the carnivorous dinosaurs found them easy prey.

❍ *Staurikosaurus* was some 2 m in length and weighed around 15 kg. The small, pointy teeth of *Staurikosaurus* were suited to snapping up little prey, from dragonflies to slugs.

❍ *Eoraptor* lived at the same time and place as *Herrerasaurus*, but it was much smaller, only one metre from nose to tail-tip, and would have stood knee-high to an adult. It had unusual leaf-like teeth at the front of its mouth, and the more typical meat eater's sharp, curving teeth towards the rear. Light and agile, *Eoraptor* probably grabbed any small creature as prey.

Find out more

Giant dinosaurs pp. 32–33

Coelophysis *was a slim, lightweight dinosaur. It could probably trot, jump, leap and dart about with great agility. Sometimes* Coelophysis *ran upright on its two back legs. At other times it might bound along on all fours like a dog, reaching speeds of more than 30 km/h.*

○ *Thecodontosaurus*, 'socket-toothed lizard', was named in 1843, making this herbivore one of the first few dinosaurs to receive an official scientific name. Its remains are scarce but reveal a long-necked and very long-tailed plant eater, as shown by its small, leaf-shaped teeth. These had serrated (wavy or saw-like) edges for slicing through vegetation. In general shape, *Thecodontosaurus* looked like the later dinosaur giants called sauropods – but it was only 2 m in length.

○ *Mussaurus* weighed twice as much as an adult human. It lived in Argentina, South America, and fed on low-growing plants such as ferns and horsetails. The first remains of *Mussaurus* to be studied were babies that had probably just hatched from their eggs. They were about the size of today's rats, and among the smallest of all dinosaur fossils. Only later were remains of adult *Mussaurus* found.

Specialized feet

One of the secrets of *Plateosaurus*'s success as a plant eater may have been its front feet, which could be hyper-extended. This flexibility meant that *Plateosaurus* may have been able to grasp branches while feeding.

When Mussaurus, 'mouse reptile', *hatched from its egg, it was only about 25 mm long. It probably stayed near the nest until it had grown to more than 20 cm in length. An adult* Mussaurus *was more than 3 m long.*

The first remains of the dinosaur Thecodontosaurus *were found in Bristol, England, in 1843. They lay in rocks from the Carboniferous Period, more than 100 million years before the first dinosaurs existed. Scientists later realized that* Thecodontosaurus *had been fossilized inside a cave formed within the older rocks. In fact,* Thecodontosaurus *lived about 180 mya.*

Giant Dinosaurs

During the Jurassic Period (213–144 mya), dinosaurs spread to all the world's major continents. The group diversified into many new types of animal. The largest dinosaurs of all were the sauropods – plant eaters with heavy bodies, long necks and even longer tails. The prosauropods, their predecessors, included the first dinosaurs to grow as heavy as an elephant.

❍ *Cetiosaurus*, 'whale reptile', got its name because the fossil backbones (vertebrae) from this dinosaur were originally identified as from a whale. This Mid-Jurassic sauropod showed a mix of features from earlier prosauropods and later, larger sauropod plant eaters. At 25 tonnes in weight, and about 15 m in length, *Cetiosaurus* remains have been associated with water plants and animals. *Cetiosaurus* may have lived in swamps and fed on soft-leaved aquatic plants.

❍ *Barosaurus* from the Late Middle Jurassic had an enormously long, strong neck and tail, but a relatively small body. Its total length was about 25 m, and it weighed in the region of 30 tonnes. The neck had 16–17 cervical vertebrae, or neck bones, some almost one metre in length.

🔺 *The heaviest land animal ever was probably* **Argentinosaurus**. *Not much is known about this giant, but it is thought that it weighed over 100 tonnes and measured 35 m from head to tail.* **Argentinosaurus** *had a huge body but a small head and brain.*

Big bones

The sauropods had huge bones. The thigh bone, or femur, of *Barapasaurus* was as tall as an adult person, at about 170 cm.

🔻 **Brachiosaurus** *was one of the biggest dinosaurs that ever lived. It weighed over 50 tonnes – more than a huge juggernaut truck. It was also one of the tallest dinosaurs. Its head could reach to 13 m above the ground. During the warm, damp Jurassic Period, plants thrived in most areas, covering land that previously had been barren.*

Find out more

Riojasaurus p. 30

Amazing

Scientists think that the heart of *Argentinosaurus*, the largest of the sauropod dinosaurs, may have weighed around 1 tonne.

Gastroliths

Piles of rounded, smoothly polished stones, up to the size of soccer balls, are often found with the remains of huge plant eaters, such as *Brachiosaurus* and *Diplodocus*. The likely explanation is that these are gastroliths, or 'stomach stones'. The dinosaurs swallowed them deliberately to help grind up their mountainous meals of plant food. In the process, the stones became smooth and shiny, as if in a grinding mill.

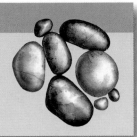

○ *Shunosaurus* was a smaller sauropod from the Middle Jurassic. It had the typical long neck, bulky body and long tail of its group. *Shunosaurus* was about 11 m long and probably weighed more than 10 tonnes. Its most noticeable feature was a tail club made of enlarged end-of-tail bones, possibly armed with several spikes. This would be an effective defensive weapon when swung at marauding carnivores.

▶ *Massive plant-eaters, such as Barosaurus, thrived on the high-level fronds, needles and leaves of towering tree-ferns, gingkoes and conifers.*

○ *Rhoetosaurus* was one of the first Australian dinosaurs to be named. It had many similarities to its sauropod cousin *Shunosaurus*. Its fossils come from Roma, Queensland, and show a robust-bodied plant eater about 15 m in length and 15 tonnes in weight.

○ *Seismosaurus* was a huge sauropod, sometimes hailed as the longest of all dinosaurs. However, estimates of 55 m from nose to tail-tip are based on only partial fossils, and 40–49 m is perhaps more likely. Fossils of *Seismosaurus* were found in New Mexico, USA. It was named 'earthquake reptile', from the idea that the ground shook as it lumbered along, although *Argentinosaurus* was probably twice as heavy as *Seismosaurus*.

○ Sauropods probably lived in groups or herds. We know this from their fossilized footprints. Each foot left a print as large as a chair seat. Hundreds of footprints together showed that many sauropods walked along with each other. They most likely spent most of the time eating, perhaps as much as 20 hours out of every 24. They had huge bodies that would have needed vast amounts of food, but only small mouths with which to gather it.

Awesome dinosaurs

	Length	Weight
Argentinosaurus	35 m	100 tonnes
Seismosaurus	40–49 m	50-80 tonnes
Brachiosaurus	30 m	50 tonnes
Brontosaurus	20 m	20–30 tonnes
Diplodocus	23–27 m	12 tonnes

All measurements are approximate

Stegosaurs

For millions of years the ornithischian (bird-hipped) dinosaurs remained small and relatively rare. Then, about 160 mya, a new family of large ornithischians appeared. These were the heavily armoured, plant-eating stegosaurids. They spread across the world in large numbers. After around 50 million years of success, the stegosaurids died out and were replaced by other types of dinosaur.

○ Stegosaurs are often called 'plated dinosaurs', from the large, flat plates or slabs of bone on their backs. Stegosaurs probably first appeared in eastern Asia in Early Jurassic times, and then spread to other continents.

○ Stegosaurus, 'roof reptile', measured about 9 m from nose to tail and weighed 3 tonnes. Its fossils date from Late Jurassic and Early Cretaceous times.

○ Found in China and named after the Tuo River, Tuojiangosaurus was a stegosaur 7 m in length and 1 tonne in weight. With the discoveries of Stegosaurus in North America and Lexovisaurus in Africa, it showed how the stegosaurs had spread to most continents by the Late Jurassic Period.

▶ The stegosaur Tuojiangosaurus had up to 15 pairs of bony plates projecting from its neck, back and tail. Like other stegosaurs, Tuojiangosaurus wielded its muscular tail as a defensive weapon. With cone-shaped plates underneath and long spikes at the end, the tail could deliver a powerful, wounding blow to any aggressors.

Tuojiangosaurus

Most scientists display pictures of the larger dinosaurs having dull colours, but the Chinese scientists who discovered Tuojiangosaurus suggested that it may have been brightly coloured.

○ One of the enduring puzzles about the stegosaur group of dinosaurs is the reason for the tall, triangular or diamond-shaped plates on their backs. These plates were made of lightweight bone, probably covered by skin in life, and little use for protection.

○ The plates may have worked as heat-absorbers, soaking up the Sun's warmth so that this herbivore could get moving more quickly in the morning than other cold-blooded dinosaurs.

Amazing

The last stegosaurs may have lived in India about 80 mya. At that time, India was an island continent, so the stegosaurs would not have faced competition from types of dinosaur that evolved elsewhere.

Find out more

Armoured dinosaurs pp. 44–45

○ Most stegosaurs had no teeth at the front of the mouth, but instead had a horny beak, like that of a bird, for snipping off leaves. They chewed their food with small, ridged cheek teeth.

➤ *To protect against the teeth and claws of predators, Stegosaurus had tough, studded hide and bony teeth set into the skin of its throat. The skull of Stegosaurus was tiny compared to its massive, bulky body, so its brain was small as well. Situated in the hip area was a large gathering of nerves and nerve tissue. It is thought that this helped to co-ordinate the movements of the legs and tail, reducing the amount of nerve signals that the brain needed to cope with.*

○ Like other group members, *Tuojiangosaurus* had tall triangles or leaf-shaped plates of bone along its back. These were probably arranged sticking upright in two rows. The bird-like beak cropped low vegetation, and the four large spikes at the end of the tail were arranged as two V-shapes in a formidable defensive weapon.

○ The plant-nipping 'beak', low-slung head, arched back with projecting bony plates, and spiky tail show that *Kentrosaurus* was a member of the stegosaur group. Indeed, its name means 'spiked reptile'. Its fossils, along with those of *Brachiosaurus* and many others, were unearthed at a famous site called Tendaguru in what is now Tanzania, east Africa.

What colour were dinosaurs?

Fossils are not original living material, but rock and stone, made of minerals. So a fossil's colour is that of its minerals. This means we cannot tell the colours of dinosaurs or other long-extinct animals from their fossils. Some dinosaurs may have been camouflaged in dull browns and greens, like living alligators and turtles. But others may have been bright and colourful, like some types of lizard and snake are today. To produce life-like models and pictures, such as those in this book, colours are chosen by intelligent guesswork and comparisons with living reptiles.

Stegosaurus may have had brightly coloured skin

➤ **Kentrosaurus** *had an unusual defensive display – a combination of plates and spikes running the length of the body and tail. Kentrosaurus was more than 1 tonne in weight and around 5 m in length.*

Hunter Dinosaurs

During the Jurassic Period (213–144 mya), the hunting dinosaurs diversified to take on many different forms. Some evolved to become larger and more powerful creatures able to hunt other large dinosaurs. Others become smaller, faster and more nimble, so that they could catch lizards or insects.

◀ Compsognathus was a carnivorous dinosaur and is relatively rare in terms of fossil finds. At 1 m long and 3 kg in weight, it was one of the smallest dinosaurs, and probably fed on insects and small reptiles. Compsognathus was fast and agile, but it is likely that it moved in packs for self-defence.

First name

Megalosaurus was the first dinosaur to receive an official scientific name, in 1824. That was 18 years before the name 'dinosaur' itself was coined for this group of reptiles.

Amazing

The teeth of hunting dinosaurs were attached only weakly to the jaws and were easily broken. The dinosaurs had to grow new teeth continually.

Find out more

Giant dinosaurs pp. 32–33

▶ **Eustreptospondylus** *ran speedily on its strong back legs and four-toed feet, although only three toes touched the ground. The large head had long jaws filled with sharp teeth. Its name, 'well-curved vertebrae', refers to the shape of the joint surfaces on its backbones.*

○ *Dilophosaurus* was 6 m in length and half a tonne in weight, It was one of the earliest sizeable theropods (meat-eating dinosaurs). Its fossils are known from Arizona, USA, and Yunnan, China. It was a lithe and agile hunter with sharp, curved fangs, easily able to run down prey such as the newly hatched young of herbivorous sauropods.

○ *Eustreptospondylus*, from the Middle Jurassic Period, was a fierce predator that roamed near what is now Oxford, England. Much larger than its equivalent carnivores today, the big cats, *Eustreptospondylus* was 7 m long and weighed a quarter of a tonne.

○ The vast sauropods were the biggest-ever meals on four legs. Great predators took advantage of these meat-mountains. The largest predator in the Late Jurassic was *Allosaurus*, 'different/strange reptile'.

○ A smallish predator about 2 m long, *Coelurus* was named 'hollow form' after its tube-like limb and tail bones. The spaces in the bones helped save weight so that this slim, agile meat eater was just 15 kg. Its fossils come from Wyoming, USA, and it has given its name to a general group of small, speedy carnivores – the coelurosaurs. These probably fed on small prey such as lizards, worms, grubs and insects.

○ *Ceratosaurus* was named 'horn reptile' after the rhino-like projection on its snout. It also had a jutting bony ridge above each eye. This theropod was about 6 m long and weighed almost 1 tonne. It lived around the same time and in the same region of North America as the even larger *Allosaurus*, and their fossils have been found together in some places.

○ The big, powerful, meat-eating *Carnotaurus* is a member of the carnosaur group of dinosaurs.

▲ **Dilophosaurus** *was named 'two-ridge reptile' after its head crest, which consisted of two narrow, curved plates of bone. Like the horns of Carnatosaurus, the crest may have been a sign of maturity and readiness to breed, or a feature that distinguished between males and females.*

○ *Carnotaurus* fossils come mainly from the Chubut region of Argentina, South America. *Carnotaurus* lived about 100 mya. A medium-sized dinosaur, *Carnotaurus* was about 7.5 m in total length and weighed up to 1 tonne.

○ The name *Carnotaurus* means 'meat-eating bull'. *Carnotaurus* had two cone-shaped bony crests or 'horns', one above each eye, where the horns of a modern bull would be. Rows of extra-large scales, like small lumps, ran along *Carnotaurus* from its head to its tail.

▲ **The eyebrow 'horns' of Carnotaurus** *are a puzzling feature. They do not seem large or strong enough to be weapons, and in any case, this dinosaur was already a very large and powerful creature. The horns may have grown with maturity, indicating that the owner was an adult and able to breed.*

Allosaurus

Allosaurus fossils were discovered at the Cleveland–Lloyd Dinosaur Quarry, Utah, USA. *Allosaurus* fossils have also been found in Africa, which was joined to America during the Jurassic Period, when this dinosaur was alive. At 12 m long and 2-plus tonnes in weight, *Allosaurus* almost rivalled the great *Tyrannosaurus*, although it lived 70 million years earlier. Dinosaur Quarry was once a death trap for these huge hunters. Other dinosaurs became stuck in what looked like a pool, but was in fact thick mud. Passing *Allosaurus* tried to eat them, but were sucked under the mud and died. This happened year after year – so far, remains of more than 65 *Allosaurus* have been found.

Sea Reptiles

During the Mesozoic Era, the Age of Dinosaurs (248–65 mya), several groups of reptiles left the land and evolved to live in the seas. They still breathed air and most laid their eggs on dry land. These reptiles remained the largest animals in the seas until the end of the Mesozoic, when they became extinct.

Ichthyosaurus

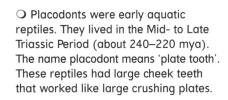

Fossils of prehistoric marine reptiles such as *Ichthyosaurus* created a sensation in the early 19th century because fossil hunters discovered them before they had found any dinosaur remains.

❍ *Archelon* was a giant sea turtle and the largest turtle ever to have lived. *Archelon* lived in the seas off North America during the Late Cretaceous Period (70 mya). It weighed about 2.3 tonnes and fed on the different types of squid that swam in the Cretaceous seas. *Archelon* had very powerful front flippers that propelled it through the water.

❍ Placodonts were early aquatic reptiles. They lived in the Mid- to Late Triassic Period (about 240–220 mya). The name placodont means 'plate tooth'. These reptiles had large cheek teeth that worked like large crushing plates.

❍ *Placodus* was a placodont. It had a stocky body, stumpy limbs, and webbed toes. It may have had a fin on its tail.

Amazing

Scientists are not certain whether the different groups of sea reptiles are closely related to each other or not.

❍ *Placodus* means 'flat tooth'. It probably used its flat teeth, which pointed outwards from its mouth, to prise shellfish off rocks.

❍ Nothosaurs were another group of reptiles that returned to live in the seas. *Nothosaurus* was, as its name implies, a nothosaur. Its neck, tail and body were all long and flexible. Its total length was about 3 m and its approximate weight was 200 kg.

▼ **In the Late Cretaceous, a shallow sea covered what is now Texas. Elasmosaurus** *lived in the sea and* **Pteranodon** *swooped down to catch fish.*

Pteranodon

Elasmosaurus

Find out more
Mistaken identity p. 63

Leatherback look-alike

Archelon fossils show that it was similar to, but much bigger than, modern leatherback turtles. Its front limbs were thinner and longer than its hind ones, and were of more use to it in the water. Females used their back limbs to dig nests for their eggs, which they laid on land.

○ Plesiosaurs were marine reptiles that were plentiful from the Late Triassic through to the Late Cretaceous Periods (215–80 mya). They were better adapted to a marine lifestyle than the nothosaurs or placodonts. Their limbs were fully-developed paddles, which propelled their short bodies quickly through the water.

○ Many plesiosaurs had a long, bendy neck, which ended in a small head with strong jaws and sharp teeth. The diet included fish, squid and probably pterosaurs (flying reptiles), which flew above the water in search of food.

○ The first *Plesiosaurus* fossil was discovered at Lyme Regis, on the south coast of England, by Mary Anning in the early 19th century. The fossil, which is in the Natural History Museum, London, is 2.3 m long.

○ *Plesiosaurus* was not a fast swimmer. It used its flipper-like limbs to move through the water, but it had a weak tail that could not propel it forward very powerfully.

○ Ichthyosaurs looked similar to sharks, which are fish, and also to the later dolphins, which are mammals. When one type of animal evolves to look like another, scientists call it convergence.

○ Some fossilized skeletons of *Ichthyosaurus* and other ichthyosaurs have embryos (unborn infants) inside. This shows that ichthyosaurs gave birth to live young, as opposed to laying eggs like most other reptiles

○ Ichthyosaurs were plentiful in the Triassic and Early to Mid-Jurassic Periods (248–155 mya), but became rarer during the Late Jurassic and Cretaceous Periods (155–65 mya). Fossil-hunters have found ichthyosaur remains all over the world – in North and South America, Europe, Russia, India and Australia.

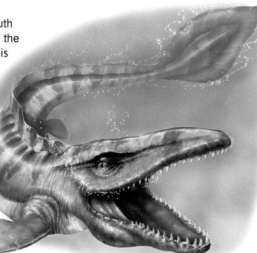

A *Mosasaurus was a fast, powerful swimmer. It had an enormous tail and paddle-shaped limbs, which it probably used as rudders.*

Swimmers

The 2-m-long *Placodus* used its plate-like side teeth to crunch up molluscs that it scraped off the seabed.

Nothosaurus was an aquatic reptile that could use its webbed feet to move over land.

The early ichthyosaur *Mixosaurus* used its paddle-like limbs for movement.

Peloneustes's streamlined body enabled it to swim quickly to catch squid, cuttlefish and ammonites.

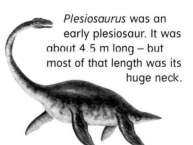

Plesiosaurus was an early plesiosaur. It was about 4.5 m long – but most of that length was its huge neck.

Browsing Dinosaurs

At the start of the Cretaceous Period (144 mya), a change came over the dinosaurs. The sauropods became much rarer, and were replaced by a group of smaller browsing dinosaurs that had been around in small numbers since the Triassic Period. These were the ornithischians – the bird-hipped dinosaurs.

Saurolophus lived in both Asia and North America in the Late Cretaceous (about 70 mya). It was 9 m long.

Lambeosaurus grew to be 9 m long. It rested on all fours when feeding.

Plateosaurus lived in Europe in the Late Triassic (225 mya). It was a prosauropod dinosaur.

Triceratops weighed over 10 tonnes and lived in large herds across North America.

Iguanodon was able to walk on its hind feet when moving quickly or over long distances.

Muttaburasaurus lived in Australia during the Early Cretaceous Period (130 mya).

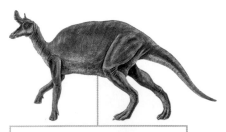

Lambeosaurus may have reached 16 m long, according to one partial fossil.

Euoplocephalus lived 75 mya in Late Cretaceous North America, and grew to be 5 m long.

Parasaurolophus had a hollow crest on its head that was up to 2 m in length.

Edmontonia is named after the place Edmonton, in Canada, where its fossils were found.

Stegosaurus must have eaten short bushes and plants, as it could not raise its head much.

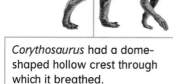

Scelidosaurus may have been the ancestor of later stegosaurs and ankylosaurs.

Edmontosaurus grew to be at least 13 m long and ate tough, coarse plants.

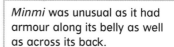

Minmi was unusual as it had armour along its belly as well as across its back.

Corythosaurus had a dome-shaped hollow crest through which it breathed.

Kentrosaurus had spikes where other stegosaurs had plates. These may have been used to defend the dinosaur from attack.

Leaellynasaura had particularly large eyes, which suggests that it may have fed at night.

Stegoceras had a dome of solid bone on its skull that was used in head-butting contests.

Polacanthus fossils are very rare and no complete skeleton has ever been found.

Horned Dinosaurs

About 85 mya a new type of dinosaur evolved: the ceratopsians, or horned dinosaurs. At first they were quite small, around 1.8 m long, but they rapidly spread across Asia and North America, becoming larger and more numerous. The largest ceratopsian was Triceratops, which grew to over 9 m in length. By 65 mya, ceratopsians were among the most numerous of all dinosaurs.

○ Scientists have identified about 30 types of horned dinosaur, but there were probably many others.

○ The earliest horned dinosaurs were quite small and had no horns. One of these was *Protoceratops*, which lived in Asia about 85 mya.

▲ Centrosaurus *was one of the most numerous of the horned dinosaurs. It grew to be about 6 m long.*

○ The later horned dinosaurs were larger and had several horns, such as *Styracosaurus* from North America, which lived 80 mya. Dinosaurs that had armour, such as *Euoplocephalus*, lived at the same time.

○ The horned dinosaurs became numerous and widespread because of their teeth and jaws. The large frills at the back of the skull allowed for powerful muscles to work the jaws, which were filled with dozens of sharp, slicing teeth. Ceratopsians were able to slice up and swallow large quantities of tough plant food that other dinosaurs were unable to eat.

○ Some horned dinosaurs, such as *Centrosaurus,* lived in herds and probably migrated in search of food. So far, there is little direct evidence that dinosaurs behaved in this way, although fossils of the forest dinosaur *Plateosaurus* have been found in what was then a desert. The *Plateosaurus* may very well have been migrating between forests when it died.

○ *Triceratops* had three extremely sharp horns, which may have been used to fight off attacks from hunting dinosaurs, such as *Tyrannosaurus*. The horns may also have been used to settle disputes between rival horned dinosaurs fighting over feeding grounds or to see who would lead the herd.

Styracosaurus

Chasmosaurus

Triceratops

▲ *Ceratopsians were a group of dinosaurs with distinctive neck frills, horned faces and parrot-like beaks. They had very powerful jaws, allowing them to feed on tough plants. It is likely that they moved in herds. A mass grave of ceratopsians unearthed in Canada contained at least 300 skeletons.*

Psittacosaurus

Psittacosaurus was an early ceratopsian, about 2 m long, whose fossils come from east Asia. It had the characteristic bird-like beak, but had not yet evolved the face horns or neck shield. *Psittacosaurus* was about the size of a farmyard pig. Later members of the group would be enormous, like *Triceratops*. Fossil evidence shows that when newly hatched from their eggs, baby *Psittacosaurus* were hardly longer than a human hand.

Find out more

Tyrannosaurus p. 50

Amazing

Most horned dinosaurs had very similar bodies, so scientists can tell the different types apart only if the heads are found.

Dinosaur horns

A dinosaur horn had a two-part structure: an inner bone core and an outer protective covering of a substance called keratin. This is similar to the composition of horns in modern mammals, such as antelope.

❍ An amazing discovery in China showed the remains of an adult *Psittacosaurus*, a small ceratopsian, surrounded by about 34 young or juveniles. This suggests that the adult was caring for the youngsters in a crèche or nursery, when they all perished in a sudden disaster.

▲ *It is thought that the success of the horned dinosaurs was due to the plants they ate.*

◑ *Protoceratops was the first in the ceratopsian group of dinosaurs. It had a small frill that protected its neck area and a tough beak for cropping vegetation.*

▼ Triceratops *had a short sturdy neck guarded by a bony frill larger than a dining table. In some ceratopsians, the frill was mostly tough, bony skin, which meant that it was a lot lighter.* Triceratops *moved in herds, giving it some protection from predators.*

❍ At 9 m long and weighing 5 tonnes, *Triceratops* would have charged with twice the bulk and power of a rhino. But most of the time it probably snipped off vegetation with its sharp, parrot-like beak, and munched this food with its many sharp-ridged cheek teeth.

Ceratopsian facts

Torosaurus had one of the largest skulls of any land animal – it was in excess of 2.6 m long.

Some horned dinosaurs did not have horns, such as the early *Psittacosaurus*, which lived in Asia about 95 mya.

Horned dinosaurs became more numerous as flowering plants spread, so some scientists think they were good at eating these new plants.

The different types of horned dinosaur are distinguished by their horn shapes.

The large neck frills may have been brightly coloured and used to threaten other dinosaurs.

The horned dinosaur *Monoclonius* is known only from very few fossils.

Styracosaurus had horns pointing backward from the head instead of forward, as in most horned dinosaurs.

Armoured Dinosaurs

Among the rarest dinosaur fossils are those of the armoured dinosaurs. Very few of these fossils have been found, and usually only part of the dinosaur is preserved as a fossil. The armoured dinosaurs existed from 180 mya until 65 mya. Their fossils are found on most continents, so they were a highly successful group.

○ The most heavily armoured dinosaur was *Ankylosaurus*, which lived in North America about 70 million years ago. Its back was covered by plates of solid bone, while spikes and knobs stuck out at odd angles. The head was covered by thick sheets of bone, and even the eyelid had a covering of bony armour.

○ The plant-eating *Ankylosaurus* grew to be over 11 m long and stood almost 3 m tall. Its teeth were adapted to eating plants, but the jaw muscles were weak, so it must have fed on soft plant food.

Pachycephalosaurus **means 'thick-headed reptile', due to the domed and hugely thickened bone that characterized this kind of dinosaur. Rivals would head-butt each other during fights. The butting could be very fierce, but after several clashes the weaker dinosaur would retreat.**

Nodosaurids

Hylaeosaurus was part of the nodosaurid group of dinosaurs. The bodies of these dinosaurs were protected by spikes and plates, but they did not have a tail club. Like all armoured dinosaurs, nodosaurids had a soft, vulnerable belly, so they held their body quite close to the ground when they moved.

It was not only members of the armoured dinosaur group that had body armour. Triceratops, a ceratopsian, had a bony neck frill and incredibly tough skin to protect it from predators such as Tyrannosaurus.

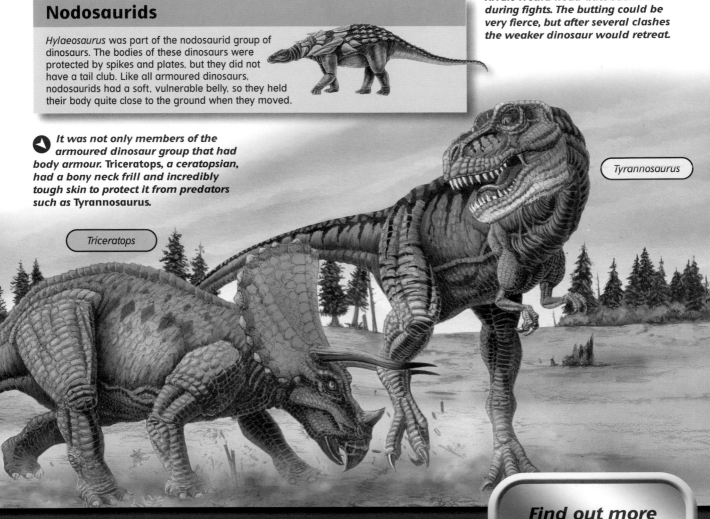

Tyrannosaurus

Triceratops

Find out more
Triceratops p. 43

○ At the end of its tail *Ankylosaurus* had a huge mass of solid bone. It may have used its powerful tail muscles to swing this heavy weight at an attacker. Used like this, the tail club could have seriously injured even the largest of the hunting dinosaurs.

○ 'Bone-head' dinosaurs are properly called pachycephalosaurs. These dinosaurs had skulls that were topped by massively thick layers of solid bone. *Stegoceras* was a bone-head that lived in North America about 70 mya and grew to 2 m in length. Like other types of pachycephalosaur, it ate plants and walked on its two hind legs.

○ *Wannanosaurus* is the smallest pachycephalosaur discovered to date, measuring just 60 cm long. It lived in China about 70 million years ago.

○ The largest pachycephalosaur was *Pachycephalosaurus*, which grew to be over 8 m long. The size of most other forms of bone-head is unclear, as the bodies are rarely fossilized intact. Only the thick bone of the skull is found.

○ The pachycephalosaurs used their heads to fight with in head-butting contests. When two *Stegoceras* fought, they would lower their heads and charge straight at each other.

Thick head

Pachycephalosaurus had the thickest skull bone of any creature – more than 25 cm thick.

○ Fossils of *Scelidosaurus* have been found in North America, Europe and possibly Asia. *Scelidosaurus* was a plant eater of the Early Jurassic Period, about 200 mya. From nose to tail, *Scelidosaurus* was about 4 m long. It probably walked on four legs, but may have reared up to gather food.

Body armour

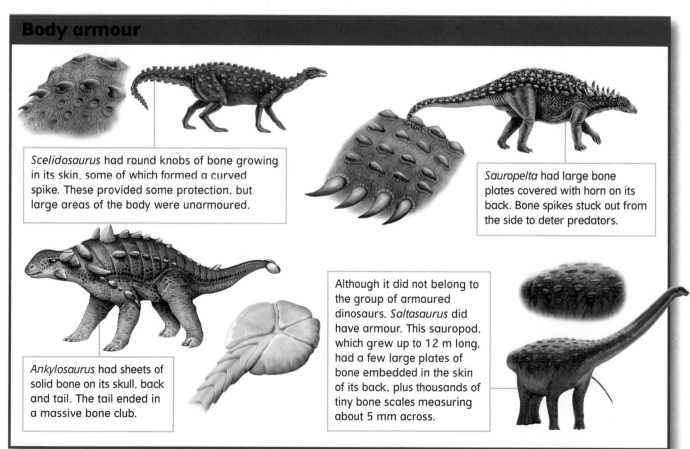

Scelidosaurus had round knobs of bone growing in its skin, some of which formed a curved spike. These provided some protection, but large areas of the body were unarmoured.

Sauropelta had large bone plates covered with horn on its back. Bone spikes stuck out from the side to deter predators.

Ankylosaurus had sheets of solid bone on its skull, back and tail. The tail ended in a massive bone club.

Although it did not belong to the group of armoured dinosaurs, *Saltasaurus* did have armour. This sauropod, which grew up to 12 m long, had a few large plates of bone embedded in the skin of its back, plus thousands of tiny bone scales measuring about 5 mm across.

Flying Reptiles

The skies above the dinosaurs were filled with flying animals, but they were very different from modern birds. First to take to the air were the pterosaurs, or winged reptiles. These creatures diversified into hundreds of different types. Later, the birds appeared, probably having evolved from a small type of dinosaur about 170 mya.

Pterodactyl

▶ Some excellently preserved fossils of flying reptiles, such as this pterodactyl, show that some had fur on their bodies. This suggests that they may have been warm-blooded, like modern birds and mammals.

○ Most scientists think that birds are descended from a small hunting dinosaur of some kind. This little creature probably looked like *Protoarchaeopteryx*, which was about the size of a modern turkey and was covered in feathers. The front legs of *Protoarchaeopteryx* were not strong enough to be used as wings, but were longer than those of most small hunting dinosaurs.

Quetzalcoatlus

○ Several different types of small dinosaur were covered in feathers. The first dinosaur to be found with fossilized feathers was *Sinosauropteryx*, which lived about 125 mya in China. This predator was 1.3 m long and was covered in small feathers. It probably used the feathers to help it keep warm.

◀ *Quetzalcoatlus belonged to a family of pterosaurs called the azhdarchids. These flying reptiles had giant wingspans, long necks and toothless beaks. The name 'azhdarchid' comes from the Uzbek word for a dragon.*

○ Several different sorts of reptile were able to glide from tree to tree, but the first vertebrate able to fly properly was a pterosaur, or winged reptile. One of the earliest pterosaurs was *Rhamphorhynchus*, which had a wingspan of about 1.5 m and lived 180 mya in Europe.

○ *Quetzalcoatlus* of North America was the largest pterosaur and also the largest flying animal ever known. *Quetzalcoatlus* had a wingspan of about 12 m and weighed an amazing 100 kg. As far as is known, it probably flew slowly, soaring on air currents while looking for food.

○ Over the millions of years that pterosaurs existed, they evolved dramatically. The earliest pterosaurs lived about 220 mya. They were small, agile flyers with long, bony tails. The latest pterosaurs lived 65 mya and were huge, soaring creatures. However, the wings of all the pterosaurs were composed of leathery flaps of skin supported by fourth fingers, which had evolved to be extremely long.

○ *Archaeopteryx* was the earliest known bird – its name meant 'ancient wing'. It lived in Europe about 150 mya, and had feathers that were laid out exactly as in modern birds. It lacked strong muscles attached to its wings, so it was probably a weak flyer.

◀ *Sinosauropteryx was a hunting dinosaur that was covered in feathers. The name means 'Chinese lizard wing'.*

Sinosauropteryx

Find out more

After the dinosaurs pp. 54–55

Dual discovery

Fossil-hunters have found *Rhamphorhynchus* fossils alongside those of the early bird *Archaeopteryx*, in Solnhofen, Germany.

Amazing

Flying reptiles had hollow bones, so that their bodies were as light as possible. This means that their bones became fossilized only rarely – usually when they fell into a lake or sea.

▼ **Dimorphodon** *had a wingspan of between 1.2 and 2.5 m. Palaeontologists think that it lived and hunted along seashores and rivers.*

▶ **Archaeopteryx** *is the first known flying bird, but it would not have been a very efficient flyer because of its primitive skeleton and long tail.*

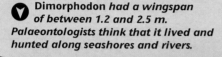

Archaeopteryx

Dimorphodon

○ Pterodactyls were another group of pterosaurs. They lived in the Late Jurassic through to the Late Cretaceous Periods (160–65 mya). They lacked the rhamphorhynchoids' long, stabilizing tail, but they were more effective and agile fliers. They were also lighter than rhamphorhynchoids, because they had more hollow bones.

○ It has been a long-standing debate among experts whether some prehistoric reptiles, such as pterosaurs, were cold- or warm-blooded. In 1971, a fossil of the pterosaur *Sordes pilosus* provided strong evidence that it was warm-blooded.

The birds take over

By about 100 mya, the birds were evolving into a variety of forms that gradually took over the lifestyles of the smaller pterosaurs. Faced with this competition, only the larger pterosaurs were able to survive. *Pteranodon* had a wingspan of 7 m, but others were even larger.

◀ **Ichthyornis** *looked like a modern seagull and lived in the Cretaceous Period.*

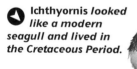

Ichthyornis

Five largest flying animals ever

	Place	Time	Wingspan
Quetzalcoatlus	North America	Late Cretaceous	12 m
Pteranodon	North America	Mid-Cretaceous	9 m
Tropeognathus	South America	Mid-Cretaceous	6.5 m
Cearadactylus	South America	Mid-Cretaceous	5.5 m
Ornithodesmus	Europe	Early Cretaceous	5 m

Raptors

The word raptor (which means 'thief' or 'hunter') is used to describe the small, fast-moving hunting dinosaurs of the Cretaceous Period (144–65). Scientists do not agree on the exact relationships between the different raptor groups, but they probably are related somehow. All these dinosaurs walked on their hind legs, and used their claws for hunting.

❍ Long, lean and lithe, the carnivore *Baryonyx* was named 'heavy claw' from the massive curved claw on the first digit or thumb of each front limb. Fossils associated with *Baryonyx* include many fish scales, so this hunter may have lurked in swamps and hooked up fish to eat with its long, low, crocodile-like jaws and teeth. *Baryonyx* was about 10 m in length and about 2 tonnes in weight.

Giant claw

The claw of *Baryonyx* was over 30 cm long, making this the largest dinosaur claw ever found.

▲ **When Avimimus *was discovered in 1981, it was suggested that it may have been feathered as the bones showed features similar to those of modern birds. At the time the idea was not taken seriously, but we now know that many smaller dinosaurs had feathers. The limbs of* Avimimus *were too small and weak to work as wings for flight.* Avimimus *lived in what is now the Gobi Desert of Mongolia.**

❍ One of the therizinosaurs, or 'scythe reptiles', *Therizinosaurus* was a massive dinosaur that resembled its earlier cousin *Beipiaosaurus*. The reason for its huge hand claws remains a puzzle – pulling down vegetation, ripping up nests of ants and termites, self-defence and many other reasons have been suggested.

❍ *Therizinosaurus* had a long, giraffe-like neck and a toothless, beak-like front to its mouth. It was 12 m in length and weighed 2 tonnes or more. It probably walked semi-upright on its rear limbs. Scientists are unclear as to what it ate.

❍ *Avimimus* was a small theropod (carnivorous dinosaur) about 1.5 m long, and very light, at only 10 kg. It used its strong, sharp beak to peck for food such as small animals and perhaps plants.

Amazing

It was by studying raptors that scientists first realized that dinosaurs must have been fast-moving, relatively intelligent reptiles. Until then, dinosaurs had been thought to be slow and stupid.

▶ **The raptors were among the most intelligent of the dinosaurs. Troodon had the largest brain in comparison to its body of all the dinosaurs, so it was probably the brightest – though it would still have been less intelligent than any mammal.**

Find out more

Sinosauropteryx p. 46

Good vision

Troodon was 2 m long and lived in North America 70 mya. Its skull had big sockets for large eyes, indicating that it was a night hunter.

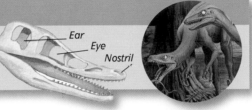

Ear
Eye
Nostril

❯ Struthiomimus *is something of a mystery to scientists. It was able to run quickly and had strong claws, which are adaptations to hunting – but it had no teeth! Some think that it ate eggs, others that it ate insects. A few scientists believe it was a true hunter that swallowed lizards and mammals.*

❍ Struthiomimus was similar in size and shape to a modern ostrich. Its long bony tail gave a total length of 4 m. Its powerful, sharp-clawed hands would be able to scratch, grasp and dig well.

❍ *Caudipteryx* was a turkey-sized dinosaur with various bird-like features. It had a beak, feathers on its body and front limbs, and a long, feathered tail. Its fossils come from China, and were the first to be found with feather impressions.

❍ *Beipiaosaurus* is a strange recent find from China. It was about as tall as a person and had very long claws on its front limbs, placing it in the dinosaur group called therizinosaurs. Fossil impressions show filament-like 'feathers' covering its limbs, and perhaps its body too. *Beipiaosaurus* probably ate plant foods, but little is known of its way of life.

❍ Deinonychus, 'terrible claw', grew to 3 m long and weighed about as much as an adult human.

❯ *Deinonychus was a type of dromaeosaur (meaning 'swift reptile'). A combination of sharp teeth and claws and long, strong legs for jumping onto prey made Deinonychus a powerful hunting machine. The main weapon was the sharp, curving claw on the second toe of each hind foot. This claw was kept folded back when walking, but was flicked forward to attack prey. Deinonychus hunted in packs, which enabled these dinosaurs to attack prey much larger than themselves.*

Raptors and relatives

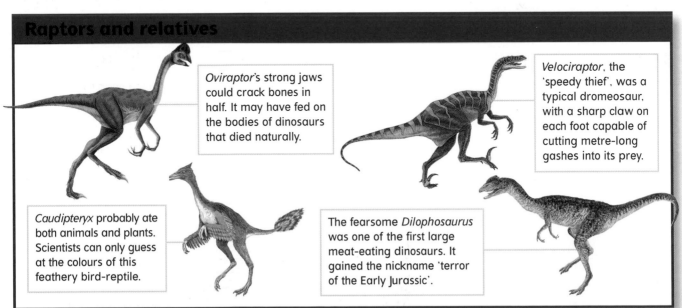

Oviraptor's strong jaws could crack bones in half. It may have fed on the bodies of dinosaurs that died naturally.

Caudipteryx probably ate both animals and plants. Scientists can only guess at the colours of this feathery bird-reptile.

The fearsome Dilophosaurus was one of the first large meat-eating dinosaurs. It gained the nickname 'terror of the Early Jurassic'.

Velociraptor, the 'speedy thief', was a typical dromeosaur, with a sharp claw on each foot capable of cutting metre-long gashes into its prey.

Large Hunters

The most massive hunting dinosaurs of all – the carnosaurs – lived in the Cretaceous Period (144–65 mya) and survived right to the end of the Age of Dinosaurs. They were enormously powerful, but may not have been able to move quickly. Some scientists think that these meat eaters may have fed by scavenging from dinosaurs that had died of disease, rather than by hunting live prey.

▶ **Tyrannosaurus** *may have taken 20–50 years to reach adult size. This would have depended largely on how much food was available, as in reptiles such as crocodiles today.*

○ Fossils of *Tyrannosaurus* ('tyrant lizard') were found in North America in 1902. *Tyrannosaurus*, one of the last dinosaurs, was up to 13 m long, 6 m high, and 6 tonnes in weight. For over 90 years, it was believed to be the largest meat eater to walk the Earth.

◤ **Albertosaurus,** *like the other carnosaurs, was a massive, powerful hunter of the Cretaceous Period. It had clawed feet and hands, strong muscular legs, razor-sharp teeth and a strong skull to protect it when attacking prey at speed.*

○ *Tyrannosaurus*'s 50 or so teeth grew to 30 cm in length, and its mouth opened so wide that it could easily have swallowed a 10-year-old child. This great predator lived in North America and was one of the last dinosaurs.

○ In 1994, *Tyrannosaurus* lost its claim to be the biggest-ever meat eater when fossils of an even larger carnivore named *Giganotosaurus*, 'giant southern reptile', were found in Patagonia, Argentina.

○ *Giganotosaurus* was over 14 m in length and weighed up to 8 tonnes. Its puny arms had three-fingered hands. Its teeth, shaped like arrowheads, were over 20 cm long. *Giganotosaurus* preyed on huge sauropod dinosaurs.

○ *Spinosaurus* was a huge meat eater, almost as large as *Tyrannosaurus*. It lived in North Africa and had a long, low, crocodile-like head similar to that of *Baryonyx*.

On the move

Tyrannosaurus's powerful rear legs contrasted greatly with its puny front limbs, or 'arms'. As it pounded along, its thick-based tail would have balanced its horizontal body and head, which was held low. The rear feet were enormous, with each set of three toes supporting some 3–4 tonnes in weight.

Find out more
Hunter dinosaurs pp. 36-37

Scent detector

Tyrannosaurus had very large nasal cavities which indicates to scientists that it had a very good sense of smell.

The predator Spinosaurus *had a distinctive 'sail' on its back. The sail would have been almost 2 m tall.*

○ *Albertosaurus* was about 9 m long and weighed perhaps 3 tonnes. Like its huge relative *Tyrannosaurus*, it had tiny, seemingly useless arms, each with a two-fingered hand.

○ The carnosaurs were well equipped for hunting large prey – including other dinosaurs. They all had massive mouths armed with long, sharp teeth in powerful jaws. They had long, strong back legs for fast running, and enormous toe claws for kicking and holding down victims.

The eyes of the carnosaurs, such as Tyrannosaurus, *were positioned so that both faced forwards. This enabled the hunter to judge the distance, speed and direction of prey with great accuracy.*

Amazing

The teeth of large hunting dinosaurs were serrated, like a steak knife, so that they could cut up meat more easily.

○ *Spinosaurus* gave its name to a group of similar theropods (meat-eating dinosaurs) – the spinosaurs.

○ *Spinosaurus* had a 'sail' on its back, formed of skin held up by long bony rods – neural spines that projected from its vertebrae (backbones). The sail may have been a temperature regulator that worked in a similar way to the back plates of *Stegosaurus*.

○ *Albertosaurus*, the smaller and slightly earlier cousin of *Tyrannosaurus*, may have hunted young plant-eating dinosaurs such as hadrosaurs, or perhaps scavenged on the dead bodies of the adults.

Dinosaur Periods

The Mesozoic Era

The vast stretches of time over which the Earth has existed have been divided up by scientists into named divisions. Each division has certain features in common. For instance the time from the start of life up to around 248 mya is called the Palaeozoic Era, which means 'the time of ancient life'. The time from 65 mya to today is called the Cainozoic Era, or 'the time of modern life'. The time between 248 and 65 mya is known as the Mesozoic Era, meaning 'the time of middle life'. Dinosaurs lived during the Mesozoic Era. Every era is divided into Periods, each of which has a distinguishing feature. The Cretaceous Period (144–65 mya), for example, saw deep beds of chalk laid down in many parts of the world. These illustrations are 'snapshots' showing some of the dinosaurs that were alive at different times in the Mesozoic Era.

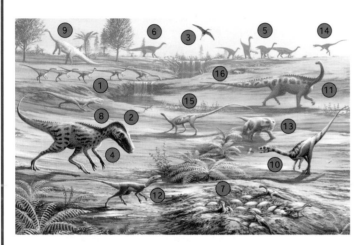

230–220 mya · Mid- to Late Triassic

1	Coelophysis	9	Plateosaurus
2	Eoraptor	10	Procompsognathus
3	Eudimorphodon	11	Riojasaurus
4	Herrerasaurus	12	Saltopus
5	Massospondylus	13	Scaphonyx
6	Melanorosaurus	14	Staurikosaurus
7	Mussaurus	15	Thecodontosaurus
8	Ornithosuchus	16	Thrinaxodon

200–160 mya · Early to Mid-Jurassic

1	Anchisaurus	10	Megalosaurus
2	Barapasaurus	11	Megazostrodon
3	Barosaurus	12	Rhoetosaurus
4	Cetiosaurus	13	Scelidosaurus
5	Dilophosaurus	14	Scutellosaurus
6	Dimorphodon	15	Seismosaurus
7	Eustreptospondylus	16	Shunosaurus
8	Heterodontosaurus	17	Yunnanosaurus
9	Lesothosaurus		

Find out more

The age of the dinosaurs p. 28

150–135 mya · Late Jurassic to Early Cretaceous

1 *Allosaurus*
2 *Apatosaurus*
3 *Archaeopteryx*
4 *Brachiosaurus*
5 *Camarasaurus*
6 *Ceratosaurus*
7 *Coelurus*
8 *Compsognathus*
9 *Diplodocus*
10 *Kentrosaurus*
11 *Mamenchisaurus*
12 *Ornitholestes*
13 *Rhamphorhynchus*
14 *Sauroposeidon*
15 *Tuojiangosaurus*

120–80 mya · Mid-Cretaceous

1 *Argentinosaurus*
2 *Baryonyx*
3 *Beipiaosaurus*
4 *Caudipteryx*
5 *Deinonychus*
6 *Giganotosaurus*
7 *Iberomesornis*
8 *Iguanodon*
9 *Leaellynasaura*
10 *Maiasaura*
11 *Minmi*
12 *Ornithodesmus*
13 *Polacanthus*
14 *Psittacosaurus*
15 *Repenomamus robustus*
16 *Spinosaurus*
17 *Stegosaurus*

75–65 mya · Late Cretaceous

1 *Albertosaurus*
2 *Avimimus*
3 *Corythosaurus*
4 *Edmontonia*
5 *Edmontosaurus*
6 *Euoplocephalus*
7 *Lambeosaurus*
8 *Parasaurolophus*
9 *Pteranodon*
10 *Saltasaurus*
11 *Stegoceras*
12 *Struthiomimus*
13 *Therizinosaurus*
14 *Triceratops*
15 *Troodon*
16 *Tyrannosaurus*
17 *Zalambdalestes*

After the Dinosaurs

All dinosaurs on Earth had died out by about 65 mya, along with many other types of reptile and other animals. Scientists are not sure what caused this mass extinction. Perhaps a large meteorite hit the Earth, causing widespread devastation and a dust cloud that blocked the Sun; or huge volcanic eruptions may have caused drastic climate change.
New types of life emerged to replace the dinosaurs.

The creodonts

Several of the mammal groups that appeared soon after the dinosaurs died out were very successful, but then died out themselves. The creodont mammals, such as this *Sinopa*, had become the most numerous hunters by 50 mya, but 13 million years later they were extinct, perhaps because more intelligent carnivores had evolved.

❍ After the dinosaurs became extinct, huge flightless birds – known as 'terror birds' – seized the opportunity to become the dominant predators of their day. *Titanis* was one such terror bird. It had an enormous head and powerful legs, like those of its dinosaur ancestors, so it could outrun its prey. Some experts believe that *Titanis* is the ancestor of ducks, geese and other related birds.

The colossal Argentavis, whose fossils were discovered in 1979, is an ancestor of modern North American turkey vultures.

❍ *Archaeopsittacus* was an early parrot of the Late Oligocene Epoch (28–24 mya). *Ogygoptynx* was the first-known owl. It lived in the Palaeocene Epoch (65–58 mya). *Aegialornis* was an early swift-like bird, which lived in the Eocene and Oligocene Epochs (58–24 mya). It may be the ancestor of today's swifts and hummingbirds.

❍ *Argentavis* was an enormous, vulture-like bird of prey – the largest one ever discovered. Its wingspan was more than 7 m, which is double the size of the largest modern living bird, the wandering albatross. Individual *Argentavis* feathers could measure up to 1.5 m long. *Argentavis* lived between 8 and 6 mya.

Some scientists believe that dinosaurs may have been killed by a giant meteorite – a lump of space rock – that smashed into the Earth. The impact would have thrown up vast clouds of water, rocks, ash and dust, blotting out the Sun for many years. Plants would not have been able to grow in the gloom, so plant-eating dinosaurs – and the meat-eating dinosaurs that preyed on them – would have died out.

Find out more
The birds take over p. 47

○ *Gallinuloides* was an early member of the chicken family. *Gallinuloides* fossils have been found in Wyoming, USA, in rock strata of the Eocene Epoch (58–37 mya). The earliest-known vultures lived in the Palaeocene Epoch (65–58 mya). The earliest-known hawks, cranes, bustards, cuckoos and songbirds lived in the Eocene Epoch.

○ The earliest mammals were small, shrew-like creatures that appeared in the Late Triassic Period (220–213 mya). It was only after dinosaurs became extinct around 65 mya, that mammals started to evolve into larger and more varied forms.

Amazing

Scientists are not able to date rocks very precisely. This means that the 'sudden' disappearance of the dinosaurs may have happened in a single day, or taken up to 500,000 years.

○ Mammals (and birds) have bigger brains than reptiles, and are also warm-blooded. These abilities meant that mammals could be adaptable – something that ensured their success in the changing climates of the Tertiary and Quaternary Periods (65 mya to the present). During the Eocene Epoch, (58–37 mya), mammals became the most dominant animals on land.

Early rodents

The first rodents, such as this *Platypittamys*, lived in North America about 60 mya.

➊ *Leptictidium was a small mammal that had the combined features of a weasel, a shrew and a kangaroo. Like other small carnivores, it probably hunted at night.*

○ *Leptictidium*, 'delicate weasel', was a small carnivorous mammal up to 90 cm long that lived 50–40 mya. It hopped on long hind legs, a bit like a kangaroo. It fed mainly on insects, but also ate small lizards, mammals and invertebrates.

○ Most mammals produce live young, unlike reptiles and birds, which lay eggs.

➊ *Titanis was the largest of the 'terror birds', which roamed the Americas about a million years ago. It stood some 3 m tall and preyed on many types of mammal. The terror birds may have been driven to extinction when humans arrived in the Americas about 30,000 years ago.*

○ In placental mammals, the offspring stays inside its mother's body, in the womb, until it is a fully developed baby – at which point it is born. Marsupial mammals give birth to their offspring at a much earlier stage. The young then develop fully in their mothers' pouch, or marsupium. After the young of mammals are born, their mothers feed them milk, produced in their mammary glands.

Major mass extinctions

Vendian Extinction	About 560 mya, around 75 per cent of all types of plant and animal on Earth vanished.
Permian Extinction	About 225 mya, around 70 per cent of all animal species living in the seas suddenly became extinct.
Cretaceous Extinction	About 65 mya, most of the land animals and several groups of sea animals became extinct. The dinosaurs died out at this time.
Modern Extinction	Over the past 10,000 years, many larger land animals, such as mammoths, moas and deer, became extinct as humans hunted them and turned their habitats into farmland.

Mammals Take Over

By about 55 mya, the mammals had emerged as the most successful animals on land. They had increased in size and had diversified to lead new types of lifestyle that no mammal had led before. Birds and reptiles had lost the contest to take over from the dinosaurs.

❍ The first specialist mammal plant eaters (herbivores) appeared in the Late Palaeocene Epoch, around 60 mya. They ranged in size from the equivalent of modern badgers to pigs. These early herbivores were rooters or browsers – they foraged for food on the floors of their forest homes. It was not until the very end of the Palaeocene Epoch, about 58 mya, that the first large herbivores evolved.

🔺 *Merycoidodon was a herbivore that lived around 30 mya. It was about the size of a sheep, with a large head and a long body.*

🔺 *Some prehistoric camels had horns. Synthetoceras had a pair of horns at the back of its head, and also an extraordinary Y-shaped horn growing from its nose. It probably used its horns to fight enemies and also to show off to others of its kind at breeding time.*

❍ Condylarths were the first hoofed mammals. They lived in the Early Tertiary Period (65–40 mya). All later hoofed mammals are descended from condylarths. The earliest condylarths had claws as opposed to hooves. Later ones evolved longer limbs, tipped with nails or hooves, for running away quickly from carnivores.

Amazing

By 55 mya, nearly every group of mammal alive today had appeared somewhere on Earth – along with several other mammal groups that later became extinct.

❍ Perissodactyls are plant-eating, hoofed mammals with an odd number of toes on their feet. The three living groups of perissodactyls are horses, tapirs and rhinoceroses. The two extinct groups of perissodactyls are brontotheres and chalicotheres. During much of the Tertiary Period (65–2 mya), perissodactyls were the most abundant form of hoofed mammals. They then declined and artiodactyls (even-toed mammals) became dominant.

Oxyaena

Oxyaena, shown here, was a typical creodont predator, with a strong body and sharp teeth. The foot structure of *Oxyaena* suggests that it could climb trees. It probably fed on birds, small mammals, eggs and insects.

Find out more

Bigger and bigger p. 59

Prehistoric sonar

Like this living bat, prehistoric bats such as *Icaronycteris* probably used sonar to sense their surroundings and hunt for prey. Bats use sonar by making high-pitched sounds and then listening to the echoes that bounce back off objects.

Pakicetus *could run fast and swim well. It probably lived alongside rivers and streams, and hunted animals both in and out of the water.*

○ Artiodactyls are hoofed mammals with an even number of toes on their feet. Pigs, camels, giraffe, sheep, goats, cattle, hippopotamuses, deer, antelopes and their ancestors are all artiodactyls. Like the perissodactyls, the artiodactyls first appeared about 50 mya. During the Miocene Epoch (24–5 mya), the artiodactyls became the most successful hoofed mammals.

The colossal **Andrewsarchus** *lived a bit like a modern bear. It hunted hoofed mammals, but also scavenged other predators' leftovers and ate leaves, berries and insects. No entire* Andrewsarchus *skeleton has been found, only its 83-cm-long skull.*

○ *Andrewsarchus* is one of the largest meat-eating land mammals that has ever existed. It lived in East Asia in the Late Eocene Epoch (around 40 mya).

Condylarths, *such as the rat-sized, forest-dwelling* **Hyopsodus,** *were the ancestors of hoofed mammals.* Hyopsodus *had claws, not hooves.*

○ The success of the artiodactyls lay more in their stomachs than in their feet. They evolved more advanced digestive systems, which allowed them to process the tough grasses that had replaced the earlier, softer, forest plants.

○ The ancestors of primates were small insectivorous (insect-eating), shrew-like mammals. The first known primate was *Plesiadapis*, which lived about 60 mya in Europe and North America. It was a squirrel-like tree climber.

○ The primates are a group of mammals that include lemurs, monkeys, apes and humans. Primates have a much greater range of movement in their arms, legs, fingers and toes than other mammals. They also have a more acute sense of touch because their fingers and toes end in flat nails, not curved claws – so the skin on the other side evolved into a sensitive pad.

○ *Icaronycteris* is the earliest-known bat. Its fossils dating back 55–45 million years. *Icaronycteris* looked like a modern bat, but the tail was not joined to the legs by skin flaps, as it is in bats today.

The early primate **Plesiadapis** *had a long tail and claws on its fingers and toes, unlike later monkeys and apes, which had toe- and fingernails.*

Browsers and Grazers

The larger animals that feed on plants tend to be either browsers, meaning that they eat leaves or fruits from bushes and trees, or grazers, meaning that they eat grass. These animals need to be able to chew and digest plant food, and they form the main prey of the hunter mammals.

○ Ruminants are a very successful group of plant-eating mammals that first appeared about 40 mya. Modern ruminants include cattle, sheep, deer, giraffes, antelopes and camels. All these animals can eat quickly, store plant material in the stomach and then bring it back to their mouths again, to chew it and break it down. This process is called 'chewing the cud'.

Hippo-like rhino

In the course of evolution, some animal families produced creatures quite unlike their modern forms. The rhinoceros *Teleoceras*, which lived 25 mya, was more like a hippo than a rhino. Its short legs suggest that it spent most of its time in water, perhaps resting in lakes or rivers by day, and grazing on grass or reeds at night.

○ *Archaeomeryx* was an early, rabbit-sized ruminant that lived in Asia. It is the ancestor of the chevrotain – a small, hoofed mammal also known as the mouse deer. Camels were the next ruminants to evolve. They were followed by cattle, sheep and deer, which were more advanced ruminants because they had four-chambered stomachs.

▼ Around 40 mya, the largest animal walking the Earth was Uintatherium. *This plant eater was over 3 m long and nearly 2 m tall at the shoulder, about the same size as a cow. Its fossils were found near the Uinta River in Colorado, USA.*

○ *Brontotherium*, whose name means 'thunder beast', was a large herbivore somewhere between a rhinoceros and an elephant in size. Herds of *Brontotherium* roamed across grassy plains and through forests in North America and Asia about 40 mya.

Amazing

Plant leaves, including grass, are a widely available source of food, but they are difficult to digest. Most animals that feed on them have large guts to cope with the task.

○ *Brontotherium* had thick legs and short, broad feet, with four toes on its front feet and three toes on its hind feet. *Brontotherium* used its big, square molar teeth to crush the soft leaves it ate. It had a thick, Y-shaped horn on its snout. Palaeontologists think that *Brontotherium* used its horn to ward off predators. The horn was larger in males than females, suggesting that the males also used their horns for display and to fight rivals.

○ *Paraceratherium* is the largest land mammal ever to have lived. It could be as tall as 6 m at the shoulder. It was also an early rhinoceros, but unlike its living relatives, had no horns on its snout. Remains of *Paraceratherium* have been discovered in Europe and Central Asia, where it lived between 30 and 16 mya.

Find out more
Woolly mammoth p. 67

Bigger and bigger

Most types of animal will evolve into larger forms over time, unless there is a good reason not to do so, such as a lack of food. Larger animals can defend themselves better against hunters, and may also dominate other members of their own species.

Brontotherium stood 2.5 m tall and was the largest of the brontotheres.

Moeritherium was 60 cm tall, but its descendants evolved into the much larger elephants.

Platybelodon stood 3 m tall, and was the largest and last of the shovel-tusk elephants.

Arsinoitherium

Arsinoitherium lived about 30 mya in Africa. It was up to 2 m tall and had 44 teeth, of which most had rough surfaces for grinding tough plant food. Scientists do not know how Arsinoitherium was related to other animals.

○ Paraceratherium had long front legs and a long neck, which it used like a giraffe to reach leaves on the high branches of trees. Males were larger than females, and had heavier heads with more dome-shaped skulls. In comparison with the rest of its body, Paraceratherium's skull was quite small.

○ Elephants and their ancestors belong to an order of animals called Proboscidea, meaning 'long-snouted'. (Another word for elephants is proboscideans.) The ancestors of elephants appeared around 40 mya. They were trunkless, and looked a bit like large pigs.

○ Moeritherium is the earliest-known of these elephant ancestors. Its name comes from Lake Moeris in Egypt, where fossil-hunters first discovered its remains. It was 2 m long and weighed 200 kg, and probably spent much of its life wallowing in rivers or shallow lakes, like a hippopotamus. The upper incisor teeth of Moeritherium were longer than the other teeth, forming short tusks.

The largest-ever mammal on land was a type of rhino, but without a nose horn. Paraceratherium measured 8 m long and weighed over 15 tonnes – heavier than three elephants. Despite its size, it was a peaceful plant eater.

○ Platybelodon was an early – but not the first – member of a group of prehistoric elephants called mastodonts. It lived about 25 mya in the cold regions of northern Europe, Asia and North America. Its lower jaw ended in two wide, flat, spade-like tusks.

○ Platybelodon was 6 m long and weighed 4–5 tonnes. It ate tough plant material such as tree branches.

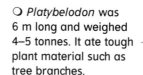

Hunter Mammals

The carnivores, a group of meat-eating mammals, evolved about 55 mya in Europe. By about 30 mya, they had diversified to produce the bears, dogs, cats, raccoons, seals and others. Nearly all meat-eating mammals alive today belong to this group, although there were several other groups of predatory mammals in the past.

○ Cats are the most highly developed of the carnivores. They are the fastest and most intelligent land hunters, with the sharpest claws and teeth. Cats evolved along two lines.

○ One group was the sabre-tooths, which included *Smilodon*. This group is extinct today. Sabre-tooths specialized in killing large, heavily-built animals with thick hides, which explains the sabre-tooths' long canine teeth.

The terrifying Smilodon *was not the ancestor of modern tigers, lions or domestic cats. It belonged to the sabre-tooths, a different branch of the cat family. Smilodon stabbed its prey with its long canine teeth. It then tracked the wounded animal, and when the victim had bled to death, it moved in to feed.*

○ Entelodonts were large pig-like mammals that lived in Asia and North America in the Miocene Epoch (24–5 mya). They are the ancestors of modern pigs. One entelodont was *Dinohyus*, which probably fed off plant roots or scavenged for prey. *Dinohyus* was one of the largest entelodonts, standing at least 2 m tall at the shoulder with a skull that was around 1 m long.

○ The felines, the other cat group, were faster and more agile than the sabre-tooths, which became extinct because their prey became faster and able to outrun them. The felines, however, continued to be successful hunters.

Cat-like marsupial

While *Thylacosmilus* had much in common with sabre-tooth cats, it had some differences too. Unlike true cats, it was a marsupial, its sabre-teeth never stopped growing, and it could not retract its claws.

○ *Thylacosmilus* was a carnivorous marsupial that lived on the grassy plains of South America in the Pliocene Epoch (5–2 mya). *Thylacosmilus* was about the size of a modern jaguar, growing up to 1.2 m long and weighing about 115 kg.

The fierce-looking Dinohyus, *also known as Daeodon, may well have scavenged for its food like modern hyenas. Its powerful neck muscles and large canine teeth suggest it could have broken bones and eaten flesh.*

Find out more

The creodonts p. 54

○ Smilodon preyed on large and slow-moving creatures, such as prehistoric bison, mammoths, giant camels and ground sloths. Smilodon was truly a top predator, with no real enemies and no direct competitors – until the emergence of modern humans.

○ Dogs developed long snouts, which gave them a keen sense of smell, and forward-pointing eyes, which gave them good vision. Dogs also developed a mixture of teeth – sharp canines for stabbing, narrow cheek teeth for slicing and, farther along the jaw, flatter teeth for crushing.

○ Hesperocyon was one of the earliest dogs, living between 37 and 29 mya. Hesperocyon was the size of a small fox. It had long legs and jaws, forward-pointing eyes and a supple, slender body.

A *Part of a pack of* **Hesperocyon** *dogs, tracking the scent of their prey. Organized hunting in packs is an example of dogs' intelligence.*

○ The sabre-tooth cat Smilodon was a fierce predator that lived between 1 mya and 11,000 years ago in North and South America. One of Smilodon's most distinctive features was its huge, curved canine teeth, which could be up to 25 cm long. Smilodon was only a little larger than a big lion, but was around twice its weight, at 200 kg.

V *Dinictis was a member of the cat family that lived in North America about 30 mya. It hunted fast-running mammals.*

A *Some predators have changed little over millions of years. A very early kind of otter,* **Potamotherium,** *lived in Europe about 23 mya. It looked much like the otters of today. The body shape was so well suited to hunting fish in woodland streams that otters have remained almost unchanged ever since this time.*

○ Like Smilodon, Thylacosmilus had very long, upper canine teeth, which it used to stab its prey. Also like Smilodon, Thylacosmilus had very powerful shoulder and neck muscles, which meant it could press its huge canines down with great force.

○ Thylacosmilus became extinct after the land bridge between North and South America was re-established. It could not compete with the more powerful carnivores that arrived from North America.

Father of the cats

Scientists often give names to prehistoric animals that describe their place in evolutionary history. The *Patriofelis* lived about 40 mya and was one of the very first cats. The name means 'father of the cats'.

Mammals Spread Out

By 40 mya, the continents of Earth were separated much as they are now, though with a few differences. The mammals had already spread to all continents and dominated life on land everywhere. One group of mammals, the whales, had taken to life in the sea.

○ The growth of grasslands and the decline of forests in the Miocene Epoch (24–5 mya) speeded up changes to herbivores' bodies. They developed faster legs to outrun carnivores in open spaces. They also developed better digestive systems to cope with the new, tough grasses.

○ South America was separated from the rest of the world for much of the Tertiary Period (65–2 mya).

The first horse was hardly larger than a pet cat. Hyracotherium *lived in Europe, Asia and North America about 50 mya. It stood only 20 cm tall and lived in woods and forests.*

○ Like Australia, South America's isolation meant that certain mammals evolved there and nowhere else. The main difference between them was that South America had placental mammals as well as marsupials.

Procoptodon *was a giant kangaroo that stood around 3 m tall. In Australia, plant-eating marsupials such as kangaroos and wallabies occupied the position taken by hoofed mammals in other parts of the world.*

○ South America's placental mammals included the giant ground sloths and huge rodents the size of bears.

○ Glyptodonts were giant armadillos that lived in South America from 5 mya to 11,000 years ago. They had dome-like shells and armoured tails that ended in a spiked club. The tail served as a support when they reared up on their hind legs to defend themselves or to mate.

Rabbit-like rodent

Protypotherium from South America was a rabbit-like rodent that was about 50 cm long. It was related to hoofed mammals, but had claws instead of hooves.

○ The glyptodonts also had powerful jaws and huge cheek teeth that could constantly be replaced, unlike most other mammals. These constantly growing teeth meant they could chew through the toughest plants without wearing down their teeth.

○ The formation of the Panama isthmus (a strip of land) relinked South America to North America about 3 mya. Many South American mammals journeyed north. Some, such as guinea pigs, armadillos, and porcupines, were very successful in their new homes. Others, including the glyptodonts, eventually died out. This might be because of climate change – or because humans hunted them to extinction.

Amazing

The only places where mammals do not occur naturally are volcanic islands that erupted from the sea in isolation from other landmasses. But even these are now inhabited by mammals that have been carried there by humans.

○ *Megatherium* was a giant ground sloth – an extinct type of sloth that lived about 5 mya. *Megatherium* stood about 7 m tall. It had huge, powerful arms and massive claws, which it used to pull down branches and even uproot trees. It had short hind legs and a strong tail that it used for extra support when it stood on its rear legs to reach the tallest branches.

○ *Megatherium* lived in parts of South America, such as present-day Bolivia and Peru. *Megatherium* walked on its knuckles on its forelimbs and on the side of its feet on its hind legs.

❍ *Megatherium*'s size would have put off most predators, but it also had very tough skin – an extra defence. The remains of ground sloth skin found in caves in South America show that it was strengthened by tiny lumps of bone.

❍ Australia has a unique natural history because it became isolated from the rest of the world around 40 mya. Australia's native mammals, living and extinct, are mostly marsupials – mammals that give birth to tiny young, which then develop in their mother's outside pouch.

❍ Early Australian marsupials date from the Oligocene Epoch (28–24 mya), but most fossils come from the Miocene Epoch (24–5 mya) or later.

🔽 *For almost 50 million years, South America was like a giant island, separated from North America by an ocean. Many strange animals evolved in South America at this time that were found nowhere else in the world.*

Mistaken identity

The prehistoric whale *Basilosaurus*, which means 'king of the lizards', was so named because the first person to examine its remains thought it was a gigantic plesiosaur – a prehistoric marine reptile.

🔺 *At 3.4 m long, the giant wombat* Diprotodon *was the largest marsupial ever to have lived. It had tusks for its front teeth, but its cheek teeth were like a kangaroo's.*

❍ Fossils show that a giant kangaroo, *Procoptodon*, and a giant wombat, *Diprotodon*, lived in Australia in the Miocene Epoch. Two marsupial carnivores preyed on these giant herbivores. One was the lion-like *Thylacoleo*, the other was the smaller, wolf-like *Thylacinus*.

❍ *Basilosaurus*, which appeared about 40 mya, was an ancestor of modern whales. It measured 20–25 m long – the same as three elephants standing in a row – and ate sea animals such as large fish and squid.

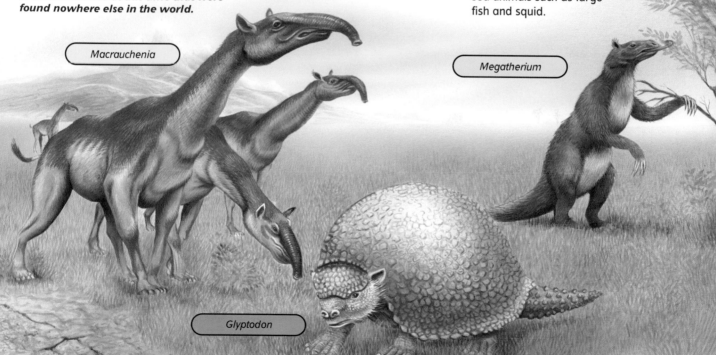

Macrauchenia

Megatherium

Glyptodon

Early Humans

Scientists believe that some time around 5 mya, a type of ape that lived on open grassland in Africa evolved to walk upright on its hind legs. This was the start of the evolutionary line that was to lead to modern humans. There have been many different types of creature in this group, not all of them directly related to the main human line.

○ The fossil record of hominids (early humans) is patchy. Most early hominid fossils have been found in the Great Rift Valley region of East Africa, which stretches through Ethiopia, Kenya and Tanzania. Probably the most important site for evidence of human ancestors is Olduvai Gorge in northern Tanzania.

○ One of the earliest-known hominids is *Ardipithecus ramidus*, which lived about 4.5 mya. It was similar to a chimpanzee, except that it walked on two legs. It lived in woods and forests, sleeping in trees at night, but foraging on the ground for roots by day. A full-grown *Ardipithecus ramidus* male was about 1.3 m tall and weighed about 27 kg.

○ The hominid *Australopithecus afarensis* probably lived 3.5 mya. Its brain was the size of a chimpanzee's, and it had the short legs and long arms of modern apes.

Fragile fossils

Early human fossils are rare and, because they are fragile, are usually broken. This fossil skull of a *Homo habilis* has been reconstructed from broken pieces and misses the lower jaw.

○ *Australopithecus afarensis* was small, only measuring between 90 and 120 cm. *Australopithecus afarensis* ate seeds, fruits, nuts and occasionally meat.

○ *Australopithecus africanus*, 'the southern ape of Africa', was the first australopithecine hominid to be found. It probably lived 2.8–2.3 mya.

○ *Paranthropus boisei* lived 2.3–1.4 mya. It had bigger jaws and teeth than modern humans, but a much smaller body. It fed on plant foods such as roots and tubers. Males were about 1.37 m tall. This was one of several hominids that developed in East Africa in response to climate change.

○ *Homo habilis* is one of the earliest-known members of the genus *Homo*, to which we belong. It lived 2.4–1.6 mya. *Homo habilis* means 'handy man' – it could use its hands to gather fruit and crack nuts. It also used sticks and stones as simple tools. The males were around 1.5 m tall and about 50 kg in weight.

○ *Homo ergaster* was the first 'human-looking' hominid. It appeared about 1.9 mya. It was up to 1.8 m tall, with long, thin limbs and a straight spine.

Amazing

All modern human populations originating outside Africa are descended from a small group of about 150 individuals that left Africa about 90,000 years ago.

○ *Homo erectus* was a hominid that probably lived from 1.8–0.3 mya. It spread beyond Africa and settled in Europe and Asia. There is evidence that *Homo erectus* used fire.

○ *Homo neanderthalensis* – or Neanderthals – lived between 230,000 and 28,000 years ago across Europe, Russia and parts of the Middle East. They were 30 per cent heavier than modern humans, with sturdier bodies and shorter legs. They buried their dead, cooked meat and made tools and weapons.

○ *Homo sapiens*, 'wise man', may have appeared in Africa about 150,000 years ago. This is the species to which human beings belong. The first *Homo sapiens* outside Africa appeared in Israel, 90,000 years ago. By 40,000 years ago, *Homo sapiens* had spread to many parts of the world, including Europe and Borneo.

○ *Homo sapiens* probably arrived in North America about 30,000 years ago. They would have crossed the Bering land bridge – which formed when sea levels fell during the ice age that was occurring at the time – from present-day Siberia to present-day Alaska.

Early tools

Homo erectus made the first carefully designed tools between 600,000 and 300,000 years ago. They were either held in the hand for cutting or thrown at animal prey. The later invention of attaching a stone tool to a wooden handle allowed humans to make more useful spears and axes.

Find out more

Fossilized body parts p. 13

Human evolution

The story of human evolution is complex. While the key points have been established quite firmly, the links between them and the way in which the different hominid groups are related are subjects of great debate and disagreement. All dates here are approximate.

4.5 mya

Ardipithecus ramidus. Scientists gave it its name from the Afar language of Ethiopia – 'ardi' means 'ground', while 'ramid' means 'root' – words that express its position at the base of human history.

3.5 mya ago

Like other australopithecine hominids, *Australopithecus afarensis* walked on two legs. This was the most efficient way for it to move over land in search of food. It fed by day and slept at night.

2.8–2.3 mya

Australopithecus africanus was about 1.3 m tall and lived across Africa. It probably used bits of wood and bone as tools for finding and preparing food. It is likely to have foraged for fruits, seeds, and roots.

2.3–1.4 mya

Paranthropus boisei was another species of australopithecine ('southern ape'). Males had large jaws and robust skulls with bone crests on top, to which powerful chewing muscles were fixed. Females lacked these muscles.

1.9–0.6 mya

Homo ergaster was different from earlier hominids. It was taller, with a more lightly built face, and had smaller cheek teeth. *Homo ergaster* was the first hominid with a protruding nose, rather than just nostrils.

1.8–0.3 mya

Stone hearths in caves that were used by *Homo erectus* prove that it had mastered fire, which provided protection, warmth, light and the means to cook food. *Homo erectus* is known to have practised cannibalism.

150,000 years ago–present

Cave painting, cooking and complicated tool-making are all features of early *Homo sapiens*. *Homo sapiens* looked different from previous *Homo* species, having a higher forehead and a more prominent chin.

95,000–13,000 years ago

In 2004, Australian scientists discovered the remains of an entirely new species of human, *Homo floresiensis*, which lived on the remote Indonesian island of Flores. It was just 1 m tall, with a grapefruit-sized skull.

The Ice Age World

About 2 mya, the climate of the Earth underwent a profound change. Long periods of intense cold lasting thousands of years began, interrupted by equally long periods of warm weather. During the cold periods, which we now call ice ages, Arctic-style weather spread across much of the globe.

○ Woolly mammoths (scientific name *Mammuthus primigenius*) lived between 120,000 and 6000 years ago. They lived on the steppes of Russia and Asia and the plains of North America during the ice ages of the Quaternary Period (1.6 mya to the present).

○ To survive these cold places, woolly mammoths were designed for warmth and insulation. Their woolly coats were made up of two layers of hair – an outer layer of long, coarse hairs, and an inner layer of densely packed bristles. They also had very tough skins – up to 2.5 cm thick – beneath which was a deep layer of body fat.

○ Male woolly mammoths could grow up to 3.5 m long and 2.9 m high at the shoulder, and weigh up to 2.75 tonnes. They had long tusks that curved forward, up and then back.

○ They used their tusks to defend themselves against attackers, and probably also to clear snow and ice to reach low-lying plants. Many well preserved woolly mammoth remains have been found in the permanently frozen ground of Siberia.

○ The woolly rhinoceros (scientific name *Coelodonta*) lived from 1.8 mya to 10,000 years ago. To help it survive the ice-age climate, it had long, thick fur, short legs and small ears. Woolly rhinoceroses lived on the plains of northern Europe, Russia and China.

Horns or claws?

When woolly rhinoceros horns were discovered in Russia in the 19th century, many people thought they were the claws of a giant bird.

Woolly rhinoceros

Cave lion

Amazing

The next ice age may arrive within the next 100 years or so, or it may not begin for another 150,000 years. Nobody really knows.

Find out more

Dinosaur horns p. 43

The Irish elk

Scientists used to believe that, because *Megaloceros*'s antlers were so big, they could only have been used for display purposes – to scare off rivals. In the 1980s, however, research proved that these antlers were used for fighting. The antlers of *Megaloceros* reached 3.7 m across and weighed around 220 kg, meaning that they made up an amazing 15 per cent of the entire animal.

○ Woolly rhinoceroses were herbivores, feeding on low-growing plants such as mosses, herbs and dwarf shrubs.

○ Woolly rhinoceroses had a pair of horns on their snout, which were made of matted hair. The front horn would have been up to 1 m long on adult males. Woolly rhinoceroses could reach a length of 3.5 m, and weigh up to 4 tonnes.

○ The closest living relative of the woolly rhinoceros is the Sumatran rhino of Indonesia.

○ *Megaloceros* is one of the largest species of deer ever to have lived. Adult males were 2.2 m long, 2 m tall at the shoulders and weighed 700 kg. This deer lived between 400,000 and 9000 years ago.

○ *Megaloceros* is known as the Irish elk because a large number of fossils of the species have been discovered in Ireland, particularly in peat bogs. But *Megaloceros* lived all over Europe, the Middle East, China and North America, too. *Megaloceros* had a much broader, flatter snout than modern deer, which suggests it was a less fussy eater and probably just hoovered up plant food in enormous quantities.

○ Like modern deer, *Megaloceros* males shed their antlers and grew a new pair every year. For antlers as big as *Megaloceros*'s, this required a huge intake of nutrients and minerals. About 10,000 years ago, falling temperatures led the dwarf willow bush – a major source of the nutrients *Megaloceros* needed to grow its antlers – to decline. This may be why *Megaloceros* died out. Another theory is that early humans, who greatly prized *Megaloceros*'s antlers, hunted it to extinction.

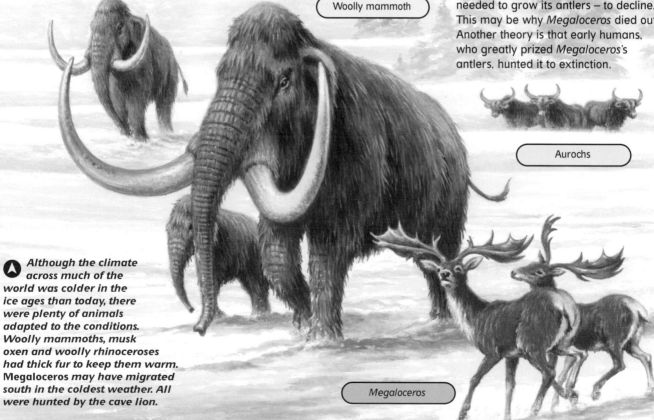

Woolly mammoth

Aurochs

Although the climate across much of the world was colder in the ice ages than today, there were plenty of animals adapted to the conditions. Woolly mammoths, musk oxen and woolly rhinoceroses had thick fur to keep them warm. Megaloceros may have migrated south in the coldest weather. All were hunted by the cave lion.

Megaloceros

Glossary

Acanthodian A group of fish characterized by having jaws.

Agnathan A group of fish characterized by not having jaws.

Amber Fossilized tree sap.

Ammonite A type of cephalopod with a long, often spiral shell.

Amphibian A group of animals characterized by living in the water when young, but mostly on land when adult.

Anapsid A group of reptiles characterized by having no holes on the sides of their skulls.

Archosaur A group of diapsid reptiles that includes dinosaurs, pterosaurs and crocodiles.

Arthropod A group of animals characterized by having an exoskeleton.

Artiodactyls A group of hoofed mammals with an even number of toes on each foot.

Bats A group of mammals characterized by having wings and being able to fly.

Birds A group of animals characterized by having feathers, laying eggs and other features.

Bivalve A shellfish with two shells of roughly equal size.

Carnivore Any animal that eats only or mostly meat.

Carnosaur A general term for large theropods.

Cephalopod A type of mollusc with a single, long shell.

Ceratopsian A family of ornithischian dinosaurs characterized by having horns on their heads.

Condylarth A group of plant-eating mammals that were the first to have hooves on their feet.

Coprolites Fossilized droppings.

Creodont A family of meat-eating mammals.

Diapsid A group of reptiles characterized by having two holes set on the sides of their skulls.

Dinosaur A group of reptiles characterized by having legs that were tucked underneath the body.

Echinoderm A group of animals characterized by having five or more arms and a central body.

Entelodonts A group of hoofed mammals that were the ancestors of modern pigs.

Euryapsid A group of reptiles characterized by having a hole set high up on the sides of their skulls.

Fossil A part of an animal or plant that has been preserved in rock.

Gastrolith A stone swallowed by some animals to aid the digestion of tough plant foods.

Gastropod A mollusc with one shell.

Glyptodont A group of mammals similar to giant armadillos.

Herbivore Any animal that eats only or mostly plants.

Hominids A group of primates that includes humans and their ancestors.

Ichthyosaur A group of marine reptiles that looked like modern dolphins.

Invertebrate An animal without a backbone.

Keratin A material produced by many animals. Keratin is a major component of fingernails.

Lepospondyls A group of small amphibians adapted to spend their adult lives in damp or wet places.

Lobe-finned fish Fish that have a strong, muscular limb at the base of their fins.

Mammal A group of animals characterized by giving birth to live young and producing milk.

Marsupial A group of mammals that gives birth to immature young that then live in a pouch until fully developed.

Matrix The rock inside which a fossil is found.

Mollusc A creature with a shell or shells and a soft body.

Nodosaur A family of ornithischian dinosaurs that had bone armour and spikes, but no tail club.

Nothosaur A group of reptiles that hunted fish in coastal waters, coming ashore frequently.

Ornithischian One of two main types of dinosaur. Ornithischians had hips shaped like those of modern birds. All ornithischian dinosaurs were plant eaters.

Pachycephalosaurs A family of ornithischian dinosaurs that had very thick skull bones.

Palaeontologist A scientist who studies prehistoric animals and plants.

Pangaea The name given to the landmass that formed when all the continents of the world joined together.

Perissodactyls A group of hoofed mammals with an odd number of toes on each foot.

Placental A group of mammals that gives birth to young that are fully developed and so do not live in a pouch.

Placoderm A group of jawed fish with bone armour on their heads and the front parts of their bodies.

Placodont A group of marine reptiles that had strong crushing teeth and may have fed on shellfish.

Plesiosaur A group of marine reptiles with long necks and four legs adapted to be flippers.

Predator A meat-eating animal that actively hunts and kills other creatures for food.

Primate A group of mammals that are characterized by having five-fingered hands able to grip small objects.

Proboscidea The family of mammals that includes elephants and their ancestors.

Prosauropod A family of saurischian dinosaurs that could walk on two or four legs and ate plants.

Protozoa Animals consisting of just one single cell.

Pterodactyls A group of pterosaurs characterized by having a short tail.

Pterosaurs A group of archosaur reptiles that had wings and could fly.

Raptor A group of small, fast moving theropods that had one claw on its hind foot larger than the others.

Ray-finned fish Fish that have fins composed almost entirely of thin bones and skin.

Reptile A group of animals characterized by having scaly skins and laying eggs.

Rhynchosaurs A group of plant-eating diapsid reptiles.

Rodents A group of plant-eating mammals characterized by having two pairs of long, sharp teeth at the front of the mouth.

Ruminant A group of hoofed mammals with specialized stomachs able to digest plant food very efficiently.

Saurischian One of two main types of dinosaur. Saurischians had hips shaped like those of modern lizards.

Sauropods A family of plant-eating saurischian dinosaurs that walked on four legs and reached enormous sizes.

Scavenge To feed on meat taken from the body of an animal that has died from disease or other natural causes.

Silica A type of mineral that is a major component of many different types of rock.

Sonar A method of detecting objects in the dark by bouncing sound waves off them.

Stegosaurs A family of plant-eating ornithischian dinosaurs that had plates or spikes growing along the back.

Synapsid A group of reptiles characterized by by having a hole set low down on the sides of their skulls.

Temnospondyl A group of amphibians adapted to spend their entire adult lives on dry land.

Tetrapod An animal with four limbs.

Thecodonts A group of archosaur reptiles that may have been the ancestors of the dinosaurs.

Therizinosaurs A group of theropods characterized by having long, curved claws on the arms.

Theropod A general term for two-legged meat-eating dinosaurs.

Trilobite A group of arthropods characterized by having a body divided into three sections.

Vertebrae The bones that are joined together to form the backbone.

Vertebrate An animal with a backbone.

Warm-blooded Any animal that is able to generate its own body heat rather than simply absorbing heat from the environment.

PLANTS

World of Plants

Plants contribute to the well-being of our world in all kinds of ways, including giving off oxygen, and anchoring the soil in place with their roots. We also rely heavily on plants for food, drinks, medicines, clothes, timber and paper, as well as fuels such as coal and oil.

▼ *The oldest living trees are bristlecone pines, some of which are more than 4000 years old. They have a long lifespan, because they grow very slowly and live in cool, dry areas, such as Nevada, Utah and California in the USA.*

▶ *The small, hardy rowan, also known as mountain ash, grows up to 15 m tall. It is most common throughout western and northern parts of the UK.*

❍ The first plants to appear on land were simple plants, such as liverworts, ferns and horsetails. These plants grow from tiny, simple structures called spores.

❍ Fossil leaves identical to those of today's gingko trees have been found in rocks formed during the Jurassic Period, 213–144 million years ago.

❍ The gingko is the world's oldest living seed-plant.

▶ *Chocolate is made by grinding the kernels of cocoa beans to a paste called chocolate liquor. The liquor is hardened in moulds to make chocolate.*

❍ Algae vary from microscopic single-celled organisms to huge seaweeds called giant kelp. 'Forests' of giant kelp grow off the coast of California, USA.

❍ Because algae often live very differently from plants, many scientists classify them not in the plant kingdom (Plantae), but in a separate kingdom (Protista), along with slime moulds. Other scientists class only single-celled algae as protists.

❍ Resin comes from several pine tree species. It is used in the preparation of paints, varnishes and glues.

❍ Cotton cloth is made from the fluffy white fibres around the seeds of *Gossypium* plants.

Cacao tree

Pod

Plant power

What all plants share is the ability to capture the energy in sunlight. Plants, such as this sunflower, use this energy to fuel their own life processes, such as growth and reproduction. Animals, in turn, derive energy from plants by eating them. In this way, plants power all life on Earth.

Plant groups

There are about 375,000 species of plant. The biggest plant family is the flowering plants, or angiosperms, with over 250,000 species. Other important plant groups are mosses and liverworts (seen here), ferns and horsetails, and conifers and cycads. Fungi used to be classed as plants, but as they cannot make their own food, they are now put in a class of their own, which includes about 100,000 species.

▼ *Like all conifers, Corsican pines produce cones. The cones look very different from flowers, but they serve the same purpose – making the seeds from which new trees grow.*

▲ *One orchid flower may produce more than 2 million tiny seeds. An orchid seed needs the help of a fungus to sprout and obtain food.*

▲ *A fern reproduces by spores, not by seeds. Ferns are among the oldest plants living on land.*

○ Unlike animals, most plants cannot move from one place to another. Their movement mainly involves growing towards the Sun to get light. Plants also have no real senses, such as sight and hearing, with which to detect their surroundings in the way that animals do.

○ The features of a plant determine which group it belongs to. Features include its height, whether it grows on its own or near many more of its kind, and what kind of soil it prefers. Other important clues as to which group a plant belongs to are its leaves and flowers.

○ Coal is a soft rock made from dead plants that lived in swamps hundreds of millions of years ago. The decaying plants were buried under mud. Over time, heat and pressure turned them into coal.

○ Palms are a very ancient group of plants, and fossil palms have been found dating back 100 million years to the time of the dinosaurs.

Cycad

▲ *The cycads and gingkos of today are the direct descendants of the first seed plants to appear on land.*

▶ *Many animals, including giant pandas, depend on plants for food, so plants are the first link in food chains.*

Amazing

Cycads were widespread by about 250 million years ago. They were probably eaten by some dinosaurs.

Find out more

People and plants pp. 126–127

Large and Small

Plants range from tiny mosses that absorb water from damp air to giant trees that draw water and other foods from the ground and pump it up more than 100 m to their topmost leaves. Trees are the biggest plants, and the biggest single living thing on Earth is a tree.

Bonsai trees and shrubs have been pruned and starved of food and water to stunt their growth.

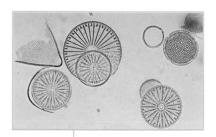

Microscopic diatoms are at the start of ocean food chains. Most phytoplankton (drifting plants) are very tiny, so they are called nanoplankton or microplankton.

Some flowering plants are enormous – a Chinese wisteria in California has branches 150 m long and produces 1.5 million flowers every year. The biggest flower belongs to the smelly rafflesia of Southeast Asia. Its metre-wide flower (below) smells like rotting meat, to attract insects.

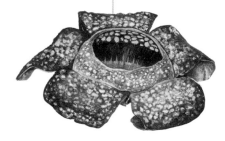

'General Sherman', in California, USA, is the most massive living tree. It is a giant sequoia over 83 m tall and 11 m across.

Bamboo looks like a tree but is actually a giant grass. It is the tallest grass (growing up to 25 m) and the fastest-growing plant, shooting up almost 1 m per day.

Measuring up to 2 m across, the leaves of the giant water-lily of tropical South America are so big and strong that this heron can stand on them and walk across a pond.

Amazing

The world's smallest flower is the *Wolffia angusta* duckweed of Australia. This is a floating water plant 0.6 mm long and 0.33 mm wide. It can only be seen clearly when viewed under a magnifying glass.

Tallest, biggest, longest

Tallest grass	Bamboo	25 m
Tallest cactus	Saguaro	18 m
Biggest fern	Norfolk Island tree fern	20 m
Biggest seed	Coco-de-mer palm	20 kg
Biggest carnivorous plant	Nepenthes vines	10 m
Longest leaf	Raffia palm	20 m
	Amazonian bamboo palm	20 m
Longest seaweed	Giant kelp	60 m

The banyan or Indian fig tree puts out wide-spreading branches that send down hundreds of hanging roots. These take hold of the soil and act as supports for the branches. The biggest-known banyan is in the Botanical Gardens in Calcutta, India. It has an estimated 1,775 hanging roots, and its huge canopy covers an area the size of a small forest.

The world's tallest flower is the 2.5 m titan arum, which grows in the tropical jungles of Sumatra.

The orchid family is one of the largest and most diverse of all plant families, containing between 20,000 and 25,000 different species.

Coast redwoods are about 112 m high – the length of a soccer pitch.

The African baobab has a barrel-shaped trunk that stores water. Some of the largest trees can measure up to 54 m around the outside of the trunk.

Super-giant trees

Some trees are so high they seem to touch the sky. Here are five record-breaking trees of different species.

1

Eucalyptus
Australia
132.6 m

2

Douglas fir
USA
126.5 m

3

Douglas fir
USA
116 m

4

Mountain ash
Australia
114 m

5

Coast redwood
USA
112 m (still growing)

Find out more

Trees pp. 96–97

Parts of Plants

There are four major parts to a flowering plant: the roots, the stem, the leaves, and the flowers. The root, stem and leaves keep the plant alive and fixed into the soil, while the flowers make seeds from which new plants grow.

❍ The leaves are the plant's green surfaces for catching sunlight. They use the Sun's energy for converting carbon dioxide and water into the sugar glucose, which the plant needs to grow. This process is known as photosynthesis.

❍ Some flowering plants, like tulips, produce just a single flower. Others, including the dog rose, have many flowers that develop separately.

❍ In some plants, such as the corn marigold, flowers are grouped together in clusters known as flowerheads.

❍ Flowers contain a plant's reproductive organs. For seeds to develop, the flower has to be pollinated.

❍ Some plants produce underground food-storage organs known as bulbs, corms and tubers.

Amazing

One wild fig tree near Ohrigstad, Mpumalanga, South Africa is believed to have roots that reach down to a depth of 120 m.

The vanilla orchid produces the flavouring vanilla, which is extracted from the plant's fruit, or 'pod'.

❍ There are two kinds of root: fibrous roots and taproots. Grass plants have many long, thin fibrous roots that spread out in the soil in every direction. The carrot is a taproot – this root has a swollen part below the stem that is used to store food for the plant. Side roots grow out from a taproot.

❍ The stem of a plant must hold up the leaves, so that they can absorb sunlight and make food. It must also hold up the flowers, so that they can collect pollen and make seeds. Many plant stems have tough fibres inside to strengthen them and help keep them upright.

Many plants that grow from seeds have flowers, although not all are as bright and colourful as these buttercups

Petals

Stamen

Sepals

Carpel

Flowers usually open only for a short time. Before they open, they are hidden in tight green buds

Tea leaves

Tea is the dried leaves of the evergreen tea plant, which grows in the tropics, mostly at an altitude of between 1000 and 2000 m. Tea plants can grow 9 m tall, but they are pruned to 3 m on tea plantations. Workers called 'tea pluckers' pick leaves from mature tea plants by hand. The leaves are then taken to a nearby factory to be dried, crushed and treated.

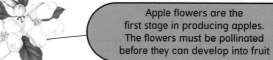

Apple flowers are the first stage in producing apples. The flowers must be pollinated before they can develop into fruit

Apples, like other fruits, contain seeds that are released when the fruit dries up, rots or is opened by animals

Leaves allow plants to 'breathe'. They also absorb sunlight, which provides the energy needed to create the plant's food

Tiny hairs grow along the outside of a plant's root. The hairs help the plant to absorb water and minerals from the soil

Tube-like channels called xylem carry water to all parts of a plant. Other tubes, called phloem, carry energy-rich sap

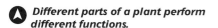

△ **Different parts of a plant perform different functions.**

❍ Fruits are protective structures that form around seeds after pollination.

❍ When a seed begins to grow, its first root is called a primary root. This branches into secondary roots.

❍ The roots, bulbs, flowering heads and leaves of some plants are edible. Carrots and parsnips are roots. Onions are bulbs. Cauliflower and broccoli are the flowering heads of plants belonging to the cabbage family. We eat the leaves of lettuces, and the fruits of many plants, such as apples.

Seaweed ice cream

This farmer is harvesting seaweed. Many seaweeds are edible, and in some places are considered delicacies. In addition, seaweed is used as an ingredient in many food products, including ice cream. Most of the water in ice cream freezes into very small ice crystals. Adding chemicals from seaweed slows down the growth of ice crystals in the ice cream, and helps to keep the ice cream smooth. Seaweed is also used in cosmetics and as a fertilizer for farm crops.

❍ The root's tip is covered with a cap of slimy cells. This cap protects the root tips from being worn away as they grow through the ground. Contractile roots shorten when the soil dries out, pulling a plant down into the ground.

◀ *Roots grow down into soil or water. They hold the plant in place, preventing it from being blown away. They also hold the soil in place. When trees are cut down, the soil is easily blown away by the wind or washed away by water.*

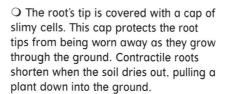

△ *Sugar cane is a tropical grass with woody stems 2–5 m tall. It grows in places such as India and Brazil. Sugar juice is made from cane by shredding and crushing the stems and soaking them in hot water to dissolve the sugar.*

Find out more

Plant food pp. 82–83

Plants and Water

Water is essential for plant life. Plant cells cannot do their jobs without water, nor can photosynthesis take place to feed the plant. Water also helps keep plant cells rigid. Without enough water, the cells go limp and the plant wilts.

○ If you break open a celery stalk, you will see fibres sticking out of the end. These fibres are made from groups of xylem tubes that carry water through the plant. Groups of tubes like these are called vessels. Inside the vessels are coils of cellulose. These help to keep the tubes open so that water can always pass along them.

▼ *The tubes that carry water and food through a leaf are called veins, because they are similar to the veins that carry blood through an animal's body.*

▶ *Plants do not use any energy in sucking up water or pumping it to their leaves. Water passes into the roots of a plant from the soil. Inside the root, the water is pulled through the plant to the leaves in tiny tubes, or xylem. Water that evaporates through holes in the leaves is replaced with more water, which travels up the stem to the leaves.*

Water escapes from leaves as water vapour

Water flows up inside stem through tube-like channels called xylem

Roots spread out in soil to collect water

Water enters plant through its roots

○ Near the tip of each root are tiny, delicate hairs. They grow out a short way into the soil and collect water. The water moves along the hair and into the root, where it enters a water tube. As the tip of the root grows through the soil, the hairs further back die and new hairs grow at the root tip.

Find out more
Waterplants pp. 110–111

○ Plants lose water by transpiration. This is evaporation through the leaf pores, or stomata.

○ As water evaporates through the stomata, more water is drawn up to replace it through the xylem.

○ If there is too little water coming up from the roots through the xylem, then the cells collapse and the plant wilts.

▲ *The leaves of waterplants have a waxy coating that prevents too much water from being lost or gained.*

○ In plants, water fills up the tiny cells from which they are made and keeps them rigid, in the same way that air keeps a balloon inflated.

○ For a plant, water also serves the same function as blood in the human body. It carries dissolved gases, minerals and nutrients to where they are needed.

○ Some water oozes from cell to cell through the cell walls, in a process called osmosis.

○ Water in a plant's xylem tubes contains many dissolved substances besides water.

Rainforest orchids

Orchids living high on rainforest trees have special roots that absorb water from the air. Their thick, waxy leaves help to stop water escaping from the plant.

▶ *If a plant does not get enough water, its leaves will soon start wilting and losing colour. Eventually, the leaves will drop off completely and the plant will die.*

Amazing

Some algae are made up of 98 per cent water. All algae need water for reproduction.

How water escapes

Inside a leaf are tiny spaces. When water reaches these spaces, most of it changes into a gas called water vapour. The water vapour is then lost to the surrounding air through pores (holes) on the underside of the leaf called stomata. More water is drawn up the plant to take its place. If the air outside the leaf is hot and dry, water vapour escapes quickly, so the plant needs plenty of water to keep up the supply to the leaves.

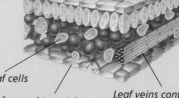

Waterproof wax coat

Green leaf cells

Leaf pores (stomata)

Leaf veins containing tiny tubes

Leaves

Leaves are a plant's powerhouse, using sunlight to make sugar, the plant's fuel. Many leaves are broad and flat to catch the maximum amount of sunlight. Other shapes and styles may help to conserve water or help plants to cling to surfaces.

▼ *A cactus has spines instead of wide, flat leaves. This reduces water loss in dry habitats. The spines also collect dew and trap a layer of moisture around the plant.*

○ Leaves come in many different shapes and sizes, but there are two main types: needle-shaped leaves and broad leaves.

○ Conifers, such as pine trees, have needle-shaped leaves.

◄ *Many shrubs, such as magnolias and buddleias, and trees, such as willows, cherries, sweet chestnuts and cork oaks, have long narrow leaves.*

Long, narrow willow leaves

▲ *Maple trees, which grow in places where it is not always sunny, have broad leaves that are adapted to taking in as much light as possible. Such leaves would shrivel and die in very hot, dry places.*

○ Broad leaves are made by some trees and other woody plants in the flowering plant group. A broad leaf may be just a single leaf, such as an oak tree leaf, or be made from a group of leaflets, such as an ash tree leaf.

○ Leaves are joined to the stem by a stalk called a petiole.

○ The flat part of the leaf is called the blade.

○ The leaf blade is like a sandwich, with two layers of cells holding a thick filling of green cells.

► *The modern gingko tree is like a 'living fossil' – its leaves are identical to those of trees that grew 160 million years ago.*

◄ *The leaves of some trees become more colourful just before they fall, turning to shades of yellow, gold, orange and red. The colours change as the leaves lose their chlorophyll (green colouring), which allows other colours in the leaves to become visible.*

○ The green in the leaf comes from the chemical pigment chlorophyll. This traps the Sun's energy, so that the plant can make sugar by photosynthesis.

○ Chlorophyll is held in tiny bags in each cell called chloroplasts.

○ To cut down water loss in dry places, leaves may be rolled-up, long and needle-like, or covered in hairs or wax.

○ Climbing plants, such as peas, have leaf tips that coil into stalks called tendrils. The tendrils help the plant cling to vertical surfaces.

Amazing

The world's largest leaves belong to the raffia palm. They grow up to 20 m long.

Find out more

Plant food pp. 82–83

○ Magnolia trees have the largest leaves and flowers of any tree outside the tropical forests.

○ Bougainvillea (a tropical plant) does not produce colourful flowers, but has colourful leaves instead.

○ The leaves of the water hyacinth swell up with air to help the plant float.

⋀ *You can identify trees by their leaves. Features to look for are not only the overall shape, but also: the number of leaflets on the same stalk; whether leaflets are paired or offset; and whether there are 'teeth' around the edges of the leaves.*

⋀ *Some plant leaves have parallel veins, while others possess a branching network of veins, in which the veins are of different sizes.*

How many leaves?

The average oak tree grows and sheds at least 250,000 leaves every year.

⋁ *Palms have a few very large leaves called fronds. The fronds grow from the main bud at the top of a tall thin trunk. If the main bud at the top of the trunk is damaged, the tree will stop growing and die.*

Palm tree

Raffia palm

Feathery fronds

Tree ferns, which grow in tropical regions, can reach heights of up to 25 m. Their branchless trunks are topped with clusters of feathery leaves called fronds.

frond

Leaf shapes

Plants have developed many different shapes of leaf in order to survive in different conditions.

Tri-part leaf

Heart-shaped

Multiple

Simple

Spiky

Plant Food

Imagine being able to feed yourself just by standing in a field in all types of weather. Most plants are able to do this, using a process called photosynthesis. 'Photo' means 'light' and 'synthesis' means 'making', which is exactly what plants are able to do – they make food using light.

Stealing food

Mistletoes are semi-parasitic plants that wind around trees. They draw some of their food from the tree and make some from sunlight with their own leaves.

○ Photosynthesis occurs in special parts of a plant's leaves called chloroplasts. They contain chlorophyll, a green pigment that absorbs energy from sunlight.

○ The energy fuels a chemical reaction between water and carbon dioxide.

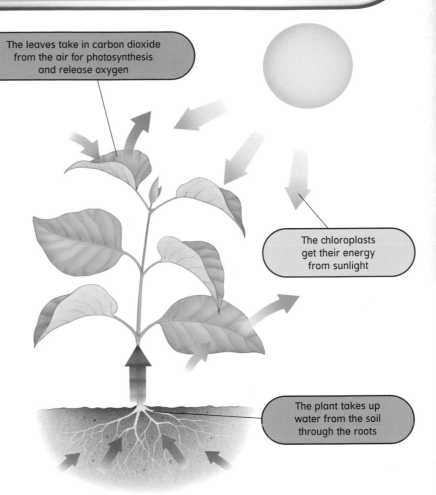

The leaves take in carbon dioxide from the air for photosynthesis and release oxygen

The chloroplasts get their energy from sunlight

The plant takes up water from the soil through the roots

Like other fungi, mushrooms cannot make their own food by photosynthesis, so they feed off 'hosts', such as trees.

Every green plant is a remarkable chemical factory, taking in energy from the sun and using it to split water into hydrogen and oxygen. The plant then combines the hydrogen with carbon dioxide from the air to make sugar – the fuel the plant needs for growth.

○ The carbon dioxide comes from air drawn into the leaf through pores on the underside called stomata. The water is drawn up from the soil by the roots.

○ The chemical reaction produces the sugar glucose, which is then transported around the plant to where it is needed. Oxygen is produced as a waste product, and escapes into the air.

○ Sunlight contains light of different colours. Chlorophyll absorbs mostly red and blue light. Green light reflects off the leaf, which is why plants appear green.

○ Some of the glucose produced by photosynthesis is burned up at once, releasing energy and leaving behind carbon dioxide and water. This process is called respiration.

Find out more
Fungi and lichens pp. 86–87

- Plants also use glucose to make cellulose, which builds cell walls.

- Some glucose is combined into larger molecules called starches, which are easy for the plant to store. The plant breaks these starches down into sugars again whenever it needs extra energy.

- Starch from plants is the main nutrient we get from food such as bread, rice and potatoes.

- In cacti and some other plants, food is made in the stems, rather than the leaves.

- Some bacteria, such as cyanobacteria, can also make food by photosynthesis.

▲ *Seaweeds don't have roots, stems, leaves or flowers, but they are plants and make their food from sunlight.*

Oxygen for life

One of the waste products in photosynthesis, oxygen gas, is released back into the air through a plant's leaves. Animals, including humans, and also plants, all need oxygen to live. This release of oxygen from photosynthesis helps all living things on Earth.

Canadian pondweed gives off bubbles of oxygen gas in water.

◄ *Green leaves contain the chemical chlorophyll. During photosynthesis, plants spread out their leaves to expose a large area of chlorophyll and trap as much sunlight as possible. The leaves are usually arranged so that they do not overshadow each other.*

Amazing

Together, the world's plants produce a combined total of about 150 billion tonnes of sugar each year by photosynthesis.

▼ *Potatoes are tubers – the swollen tips of underground stems. They store energy in the form of starch, which is made from glucose produced by the leaves during photosynthesis.*

Carnivorous Plants

Plants that trap insects for food are known as carnivorous plants. They live in places where they cannot get enough nitrogen from the soil, so they obtain the nitrogen they need from the bodies of their insect victims.

▶ Insects are lured into the jaw-like leaf trap of the Venus fly-trap by nectar. Once the insect lands, the 'jaws' clamp shut on the victim in a fraction of a second. The plant immediately secretes digestive juices that first drown, then dissolve, the insect.

○ There are 550 species of carnivorous plant, living in places from the high peaks of New Zealand to the swamps of Carolina, USA.

○ The butterwort gets its name because its leaves produce droplets of liquid that make them glisten like butter. These droplets contain the plant's digestive juices.

○ The sundew can tell the difference between flesh and other substances, and only reacts to flesh.

○ The sundew's leaves are covered in tentacles that ooze a sticky substance called mucilage.

○ The sundew wraps up its victims in its tentacles and suffocates them with slime in under ten seconds.

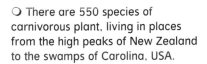

The fly touches trigger hairs that send an electrical signal to cells on the side of the trap

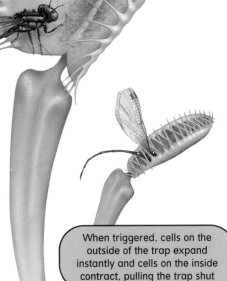

When triggered, cells on the outside of the trap expand instantly and cells on the inside contract, pulling the trap shut

▲ Monkey cup (Nepenthes) pitchers have a lid that acts as a landing platform for insects. It also helps to prevent rainwater from diluting the digestive juices inside the pitcher. Many Nepenthes plants have two types of pitcher, one on the ground and one higher up the stem. The pitchers grow from 5 cm to 35 cm in length.

Types of trap

Some carnivorous plants, including pitcher plants and monkey cups, use passive traps, which do not move. Others, such as sundews and Venus fly-traps, use active traps, in which the plant moves to capture an insect.

Albany pitcher plant *Cephalotus*	Pitfall (passive)
Cobra lily *Darlingtonia*	Pitfall (passive)
North American pitcher plant *Sarracenia*	Pitfall (passive)
Monkey cup *Nepenthes*	Pitfall (passive)
Venus fly-trap *Dionaea*	Steel-trap (active)
Sundew *Drosera*	Fly-paper (active)
Butterwort *Pinguicula*	Fly-paper (active)
Bladderwort *Utricularia*	Mousetrap (active)

Pitcher plants

The strange leaves of pitcher plants develop from the tips of leaves, which extend into tendrils and then swell like balloons. At first they are full of air, but soon they begin to fill with digestive juices. The shape and size of the pitchers varies with the species, but they are all named after their pitcher, or jug, shape. The smallest ones hang from trees, while the largest ones, such as the rajah pitcher, sit on the ground and hold several pints of fluid. Insects attracted to the pitcher by its scent or colour slide down the walls and drown in a soup of digestive juices at the bottom. Unlike some carnivorous plants, the traps of pitcher plants are passive, which means that they do not move to catch their victims.

In the wild, animals such as spiders, mosquitoes and tree frogs make their homes inside pitcher plants. Some insect larvae are also immune to the digestive juices and are able to live in the pitchers, feeding on the pieces of plants and animals that build up at the bottom of the pitcher.

Insect lands on sticky tentacles

❍ A Venus fly-trap's trap will only shut if touched at least twice in 20 seconds.

❍ Insects are lured to many carnivorous plants by sweet-tasting nectar – or the smell of rotting meat.

❍ The juice of a pitcher plant will dissolve a chunk of steak to nothing in a few days.

❍ The bladders of bladderworts were once thought to be air sacs to keep the plant afloat. In fact, they are tiny traps for water insects.

Tentacles covered in drops of sticky mucilage

When an insect lands on the sticky tentacles of a sundew, it struggles to free itself, but this struggling stimulates the tentacles to tighten their grip. The tentacles then produce a digestive juice that dissolves the victim.

Amazing

Venus fly-traps sometimes catch small frogs, and the rajah pitcher is said to eat mice.

One-way slide

Insects that slide into a North American *Sarracenia* pitcher plant cannot get back out. The pitcher's sides have a dusting of fine wax particles to make them slippery, while downward-pointing hairs nearer the bottom of the tube make escape impossible.

Find out more

Plant food pp. 82–83

Fungi and Lichens

*F*ungi are not plants, because they have no chlorophyll to make their food. So scientists put them in a group or kingdom of their own. Lichens are a remarkable partnership between algae and fungi.

Amazing

One toadstool may produce as many as 1 million spores a minute, for several days.

○ Fungi were once thought to be simple plants with no leaves. We now know that there are many differences between fungi and true plants. Some of these differences are linked to the types of chemicals that make up fungi, which are different from those of even the simplest true plants.

○ Lichens are able to survive in some of the most difficult conditions on Earth – in poor soils, on rocks and in some of the coldest regions, including the Arctic and Antarctic, and high mountains. They can survive in such harsh conditions because they are made up of both fungi and algae – neither of which would survive on their own.

○ Fungi are a huge group of 50,000 species. They include mushrooms, toadstools, moulds, mildews and yeasts.

○ Because fungi cannot make their own food, they must live off other plants and animals (their 'hosts') – sometimes as partners, sometimes as parasites.

○ Fungi feed by releasing chemicals called enzymes to break down chemicals in their host. The fungi then use the chemicals as food.

○ *Penicillium* moulds are common fungi that grow on rotten fruit. One species, *Penicillium notatum*, produces a chemical that kills bacteria. It is used in the antibiotic drug penicillin, which is a treatment for bacterial infections.

Spore star

At the centre of an earth star fungus is a ball-shaped object with a hole in the top. When the fungus is fully grown, spores escape from the hole into the air.

○ Cheeses such as Camembert, Roquefort, Stilton and Danish Blue get their distinctive flavours from chemicals made by moulds added to them to help them ripen. The blue streaks in some cheeses are actually moulds.

◀ *The algae in lichens are tiny green balls that make food from sunlight to feed the fungi. The fungi make a protective layer around the algae and hold water.*

New mushrooms

Mushrooms reproduce by releasing millions of tiny spores. The first stage of a new mushroom is a network of thread-like hyphae called a mycelium. This develops a fruiting body, which is able to produce more spores.

Fruiting body sheds spores

Spores germinate and grow into mycelium

Fruiting body forms

○ Parasitic fungi feed off living organisms; fungi that live off dead plants and animals are called saprophytic fungi.

○ Truffles are fungi that grow near oak and hazel roots. They are prized for their flavour and sniffed out by dogs or pigs.

○ There are 20,000 species of lichen. Some grow on soil, but most grow on rocks or tree bark.

○ There are around 400 species of lichen in the Antarctic. Some Arctic lichens are over 4000 years old.

○ Lichens are tolerant of salty conditions, and are often found on seashore rocks.

○ Some lichens are used to make antibiotics and fabric dyes. Lichens are very sensitive to harmful chemicals in the air, especially sulphur dioxide, so they are also used to monitor air pollution.

Find out more

Woodland fungi p. 118

Types of fungus

Glistening ink cap
Coprinus micaceus

The deceiver
Laccaria laccata

Delicious milk-cap
Lactarius deliciosus

Soft slipper toadstool
Crepidotus mollis

Morel
Morchella deliciosa

Garlic mushroom
Marasmius scorodonius

Club foot
Clitocybe clavipes

Yellow brain fungus
Tremella mesenterica

Honeytuft fungus
Armillaria mellea

Shaggy parasol
Pholiota squarrosa

Shelving tooth
Steccherinum septentrionale

Golden spindles
Clavulinopsis fusiformis

Shaggy ink Cap
Coprinus comatus

Honey scaly mushroom
Pholiota squarrosoides

Turkey tails
Trametes versicolor

Puffball
Lycoperdon perlatum

Russet shank
Collybia dryophila

Upright coral
Ramaria stricta

Tawny grisette
Amanita fulva

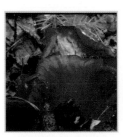

Lobster mushroom
Hypomyces lactifluorum

Plant Defences

Plants have defences to discourage animals from eating them. These defences include very tough leaves, stinging leaves, spines, thorns and prickles. Nasty-tasting or poisonous chemicals make sure that the animal does not eat the same plant again.

Camouflaged plants

Pebble plants grow in deserts in southern Africa. They develop thick, round leaves, coloured like stones and pebbles, to provide camouflage and protection against animals that might eat them.

○ *A thicket of thorny stems like this keeps animals at a distance. Few animals would risk eating such a prickly mouthful.*

○ *There are about ten species of water hemlock. These poisonous plants have clusters of white flowers. Water hemlock is also called cowbane or beaver poison in North America.*

○ The rosary pea has pretty red-and-black seeds that are often used to make bracelets. But eating just one of these seeds can kill a man.

○ Hemlock belongs to the parsley family, but it is highly poisonous. It was said to be the plant used to kill the Ancient Greek philosopher Socrates.

○ *Needle-like stinging hairs grow out from the surface of a nettle plant's stem and leaves. When an animal brushes against a stinging hair, the tip breaks off and a poisonous sap is pushed into the animal's skin. Each hair can only sting once.*

Amazing

The deadly nightshade plant is poisonous to humans, but birds and rabbits can eat it without harm.

○ Birthwort is a poisonous vine, but its name comes from its use in the past to help women through childbirth.

○ Crowfoots, such as aconite and hellebore, and spurges, such as castor-oil and croton, are all poisonous plants.

○ Many heathland shrubs, such as gorse, are thorny to stop animals eating them.

Find out more
Saguaro cactus p. 112

Poisonous plants

There are thousands of plants around the world that are at least partly poisonous. Some parts of edible plants are poisonous, such as potato leaves and apricot and cherry stones. Some plants are toxic to eat; some toxic to touch; some create allergic reactions through the air with their pollen. Poison ivy contains an oil that irritates and inflames the skin. People can be poisoned simply by walking barefoot through the leaves.

Poison ivy

○ Death cap fungi contain deadly phalline toxins, which kill most people who eat the fungi.

○ Yews are grown in many European churchyards – perhaps because the trees were planted on the sites by pagans in the days before Christianity. But the bark of the yew tree and its seeds are poisonous.

○ A cactus spine is really just a leaf stalk. Spines grow out of side branches called areoles. Extra spines protect the delicate growing tip of the cactus.

▲ *Fly agaric contains a poison called muscarine. It rarely kills, but makes you feel sick and agitated. Fly agaric was once used as a poison to kill flies.*

○ In drier regions, trees such as acacias are armed with spines to protect them against plant-eating animals. The thorns can be up to 50 cm long.

○ About 75 kinds of mushroom and so-called toadstools are toxic to humans. Most belong to the Amanita family, including destroying angels, death caps and fly agarics.

○ False morel is a poisonous sac fungus with a cap 3–9 cm across. True morels are harmless.

▶ *The sharp spines of cacti, such as this prickly pear, prevent animals from reaching the water stored in their swollen stems, which is vital to the plants' survival.*

Plants without Flowers

It is difficult to imagine just what tiny mosses and ferns could have in common with giant conifer trees, such as the redwoods of North America. But there is one key similarity – neither the mosses and ferns nor the redwoods reproduce from flowers.

Spores and seeds

One of the main differences between primitive plants – including ferns, mosses, liverworts and horsetails – and more advanced plants is the way they reproduce. Primitive plants produce spores instead of seeds. A fern, for example, produces thousands of tiny spores that are blown to a new place by the wind.

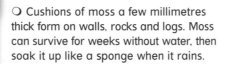

○ Huge numbers of algae in the seas make most of the oxygen we breathe, even for those people who live far from the coast.

○ Mosses and their relatives, the liverworts, are low-growing plants found mostly in moist areas. They have no waterproof outer layer to protect them from drying out. They also lack a system of vessels to transport water and other materials to different parts of the plant.

▶ *Most algae, such as these seaweeds, live in the sea, or in lakes and ponds. They have no roots, leaves or flowers, although some seaweeds have leaf-like fronds and root-like holdfasts for clinging to rocks.*

▶ *Most ferns need damp conditions to grow. Many species live around the bases of trees deep within forests.*

○ Mosses are slightly more complex than liverworts, but both lack true roots. To anchor themselves to surfaces, they have small shoots called rhizoids.

○ Like mosses and liverworts, ferns grow mainly in damp areas and need to have a ready supply of water or moisture. But ferns also have some of the features of more advanced plants, including proper roots, stems and leaves, and systems of tubes (xylem and phloem) called vascular bundles that carry water and sap. These adaptations mean that ferns are able to grow much larger than mosses or liverworts.

○ Cushions of moss a few millimetres thick form on walls, rocks and logs. Moss can survive for weeks without water, then soak it up like a sponge when it rains.

○ Sphagnum, or peat moss, can soak up 25 times its own weight in water.

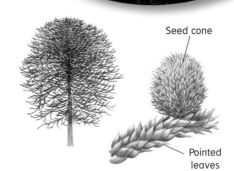

Seed cone

Pointed leaves

▲ *The monkey puzzle tree is native to Chile and Argentina. It is so called because European settlers puzzled at how monkeys could reach the seed cones on the prickly maze of branches. They failed to realize that there were no monkeys there at all.*

○ Male moss cells can only swim to fertilize female cells when the moss is partly under water. So mosses often grow near streams, where they are more likely to get splashed with water.

○ Fern spores are made in sacs called sporangia. These are the brown spots on the underside of the fronds. From these the spores spread out, and some settle in suitable places to grow.

Amazing

The spore cases of the stag's horn clubmoss produce a bright yellow powder that was once used to make fireworks.

Mosses reproduce from minute spores in two stages. First tadpole-like male sex cells are made on bag-like stems called antheridae and swim to join the female eggs on cup-like stems called archegonia. Then a stalk called a sporophyte grows from the ova. On top is a capsule holding thousands of spores. When the time is right, the sporophyte capsule bursts, ejecting the spores. If spores land in a suitable place, male and female stems grow and the process begins again.

Archegonia

Antheridae

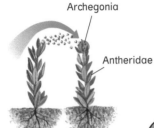

5. The process begins again

4. The sporophyte capsule bursts

3. The fertilized egg grows into a sporophyte

2. One sperm cell unites with the female egg cell

1. Male sperm cells swim to join the female egg

○ Once a fern spore has settled, it develops into a tiny heart-shaped plant known as a prothallus, which makes both male and female sex cells. When bathed in rain, the male cells swim to the female cells, fertilizing them. A new root and stem then begin to grow, forming a proper fern frond, and the tiny prothallus dies.

○ Conifers are trees with needle-like, typically evergreen leaves that make their seeds not in flowers but in cones.

○ With gingkos and cycads, conifers make up the group of plants called gymnosperms, all of which make their seeds in cones.

○ The monkey puzzle tree is thought to be the most primitive living conifer. Males and female plants of this species are separate trees.

Conifer cones

Cones are the tough little clusters of scales on coniferous trees. Male cones produce a yellow dust called pollen. Female cones make seeds when they receive pollen. All cones are green and quite soft when they first form, then turn brown and hard as they ripen. The cone scales open to release the seeds when they are ripe.

Horsetails are a group of tall, fern-shaped plants that have existed on Earth for millions of years. They have leaf-like parts that resemble the spokes of a wheel, and cone-shaped reproductive parts that produce spores. Horsetails often grow as weeds on disturbed ground.

There are about 10,000 different species of fern. A typical fern has small roots, an underground stem called a rhizome and a spreading crown of fronds (leaves) that grows from the soil's surface. The stem creeps horizontally through the soil.

Find out more

Coniferous forests pp. 116–117

Flowering Plants

There are more than 250,000 species of flowering plant, including flowers, vegetables, grasses, trees and herbs, which are all divided into two main groups: the monocotyledons, such as grasses and bulb-plants, and the much larger group, the dicotyledons.

Seed leaves

Dicotyledons are plants that sprout two leaves from their seeds. Monocotyledons are plants that sprout a single leaf from their seeds. A cotyledon is a seed leaf.

○ Before a flower opens, the bud is enclosed in a tight green ball called the calyx. This is made up of tiny green flaps called sepals.

○ The colourful part of the flower consists of groups of petals. The petals make up what is called the corolla. Together, the calyx and the corolla form the perianth. If petals and sepals are the same colour, they are said to be tepals.

○ The *Puya raimondii* plant takes up to 150 years to grow its first flower – and then it dies!

▶ *Monocots, such as wheat, tend to grow quickly and their stems are usually stay soft and pliable. The veins in monocot leaves run parallel to each other. Monocots also develop a thick tangle of thin roots, rather than a single long 'tap' root, as in dicots.*

○ There are about 50,000 species of monocot plants – about a quarter of all flowering plants.

○ The flower parts of monocots, such as petals, tend to be set in threes, or multiples of three.

○ Monocot stems grow from the inside. However, dicots have a cambium, which is a layer of growing cells near the outside of the stem. Monocots rarely have a cambium.

○ Monocots are thought to have first appeared about 90 million years ago. They most probably developed from dicot plants that lived in swamps and rivers, and which resembled water lilies.

○ There are about 175,000 dicot species – over three-quarters of all flowering plants.

○ Dicots grow slowly. At least 50 per cent have woody stems.

○ Dicot flowers have sets of four or five petals.

▶ *Desert plants may look dead until the rain comes, when they suddenly burst into life, growing and flowering quickly so that the desert briefly blooms.*

Monocots and dicots

Monocots	Dicots
Grasses	Roses
Rushes	Magnolias
Sedges	Geraniums
Cereals	Hollyhocks
Bamboos	Daisies
Palm trees	Apple tree
Orchids	Buttercups
Tulips	Dandelions
Daffodils	Poppy
Lilies	Hibiscus

Find out more

Pollination pp. 100–101

1. The fully formed flower is packed away inside a bud. Green flaps or sepals wrap tightly round it

2. Once the weather is warm enough, the bud begins to open. The sepals curl back to reveal the colourful petals

3. The sepals open wider and the petals grow outwards and backwards to create the flower's beautiful corolla

At the right time of year, buds begin to open to reveal flowers' blooms so that the reproductive process can begin. Some flowers last just a day or so. Others bloom for months on end before the eggs are fertilized and grow into seeds.

4. The flower opens fully to reveal its bright array of pollen sacs or anthers

Amazing

The biggest flowerhead is the *Puya raimondii* plant from Bolivia, which can be up to 2.5 m across and have 8000 individual blooms.

Growers control the amount of light, water and warmth in greenhouses, so that plants such as these cyclamens all flower together.

○ Most dicots have branching stems and a single main root called a taproot.

○ The leaves of dicot plants usually have a network of veins, rather than the parallel veins seen in monocots.

There are now few meadows with rich displays of wildflowers like this. Most wildflowers are smaller and more delicate than their garden cousins.

Flower parts

All flowers are arranged according to a similar plan. There are four circles of parts. The outer circle is made of sepals, with a circle of petals inside it. Within the petal circle is a circle of male parts, and the innermost circle is made up of female parts. In irregular flowers, the different parts are not always equally spaced, and may vary in number or size. Some parts may even be missing.

Flowers

More than 80 per cent of all green plants have flowers. Flowers make seeds that develop into new plants. A plant that lives for only one year flowers at the end of its life. Most plants that live for many years flower every year.

These flowers come from the flax plant. Flax was the most important vegetable fibre in Europe before cotton. It is still used to make linen.

The pink or white flowers of the dog rose are scented and have five petals.

Thrift flowers grow at the tips of grass-like tufts on cliffs, rocks and salt marshes from April to October.

All cacti produce flowers that bloom only for a few days before they lose water and die.

Bird of paradise flowers have a flat 'landing platform' for the birds that visit to feed on nectar.

In augumn the woodland forest floor is covered with dead leaves. The leafless trees allow plants to flower in spring.

Poppies die as soon as they have flowered. Each flower produces hundreds of seeds.

The yellow stigmas of the purple saffron crocus make saffron, a valuable spice.

Apple blossoms are usually pink. They get their colour from anthocyanin pigments, which also turn leaves red in autumn.

Iris flowers have brightly coloured lines on the petals that point the way to the sweet nectar at the base of the three largest petals. These lines are sometimes called honeyguides.

Passion flowers have, in the middle of their flowers, an unusual ring of filaments.

Horse chestnut trees grow upright white flower spikes that look like candles.

Primrose flowers provide a vital source of nectar for early spring butterflies, such as the brimstone. Flowers grow from the base of the plant on long stalks.

The orange flowers of Colville's glory tree from Madagascar hang in grape-like clusters.

Snowdrops flower early in the year, using energy stored in underground bulbs.

Daisies look like a single bloom, but they actually consist of many small flowers. Those around the edge each have a single petal.

The bolls picked for cotton develop from the seed pod that is left after the petals of the cotton flower have dropped off in summer.

Grasses have inconspicuous, tiny, green flowers clustered at the top of tall stems.

Find out more

Flower advertisement p. 101

Trees

Trees have one tall, thick, woody stem called a trunk. The trunk is at least 10 cm thick, and it allows the tree to stand up by itself. Trees act as the Earth's 'lungs', enriching the air with oxygen. The trunks provide timber, and rubber is made from tree sap.

▶ *This is a typical broadleaved tree, with branches growing out from the trunk. The trunk and branches have five layers. These are (from the centre out): heartwood, sapwood, cambium, phloem and bark. Heartwood is the dark, dead wood in the centre of the trunk. Sapwood is pale, living wood, where tiny pipes called xylem carry sap from the roots to the leaves. The cambium is the thin layer where the sapwood is actually growing; the phloem is the thin, food-conducting layer.*

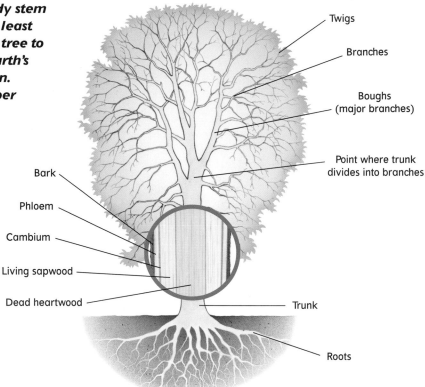

Twigs

Branches

Boughs (major branches)

Point where trunk divides into branches

Bark

Phloem

Cambium

Living sapwood

Dead heartwood

Trunk

Roots

Amazing

The world's fastest-growing tree is the tropical pea tree *Albizia falcate*, which can grow by up to 10 m in a single year.

○ In cool temperate regions and the Arctic, most evergreen trees are conifers such as pines and firs. They have needle-like leaves.

○ The trunks of conifers typically grow right to the top of the tree. The lowest branches are the longest, because they have been growing for the longest amount of time. The upper branches are short, because they are the youngest. So the tree has a conical shape.

◀ *Bark protects the inside of a tree from drying out, and helps to prevent damage by insects and fungi. It also insulates the tree against very hot or very cold weather. As the wood inside the bark grows, the bark splits, peels or cracks in a way that is different for each type of tree. For example, pine bark (seen here) splits into plates.*

○ The needles of some pines grow up to 30 cm long. The biggest needles ever belonged to the extinct Cordaites, at more than 1 m long and 15 cm wide.

○ Trees with wide, flat leaves are called broadleaved trees. They usually have crowns with a rounded shape.

○ A leaf falls because a layer of cork grows across the leaf stalk, gradually cutting off its water supply.

Tree types

Deciduous	Evergreen
Oak	Pines
Beech	Firs
Birch	Spruce
Chestnut	Yew
Aspen	Holly
Elm	Redwoods
Maple	Hemlock
Rowan	Cedars
Larch	Monkey puzzle

Find out more

Broadleaved woodlands pp. 118–119

○ The leaves of broadleaved trees are all wide and flat to catch the sun, but they vary greatly in shape.

○ Trees such as birches and poplars have small triangular, or 'deltoid', leaves. Trees such as aspens and alders have round leaves.

Growth rings

If a tree is sawn across, you can see the annual growth rings, which show how much the tree has grown each year. The edge of each ring marks where growth ceased in winter. Counting the rings gives the tree's age.

All trees have flowers, but the flowers of conifers are usually tiny compared with those of broad-leaved trees, such as this cherry blossom tree.

The bark of cork trees, which grow in Portugal, Spain, and other countries, is made into corks for bottles.

○ Limes and Indian bean trees have heart-shaped, or 'cordate', leaves.

○ Maples and sycamores have leaves shaped a bit like hands, which is why this leaf-shape is described as 'palmate'.

○ Ash and walnut trees both have lots of leaflets on the same stalk, which gives them a feathery, or 'pinnate', look.

○ Shrubs are small, tree-like plants. Bushes have more branches than shrubs, and are usually smaller. Shrubs have woody stems and several branches, spreading out near to the ground.

○ Shrubs provide useful cover for wildlife, especially birds and small mammals. Gardeners often grow bush roses, fruit bushes such as gooseberries, and ornamental shrubs such as fuchsias, azaleas and rhododendrons.

The world's most massive tree is a giant sequoia named 'General Sherman' growing in Sequoia National Park, California, USA. It is almost 84 m high and measures 26 m round its trunk. It weighs about 2500 tonnes – equivalent to the combined weight of 350 elephants – and contains enough wood to make five billion matches.

Seasonal leaves

There are two kinds of trees: evergreen, which hold on to their leaves all year round, and deciduous, which lose their leaves in autumn in temperate regions and grow new ones the following spring (tropical deciduous trees lose their leaves at the start of the dry season). An evergreen tree does lose some leaves during the year, but not all at once; it always has some leaves on its twigs to make it look green.

Around the World

Trees and plants naturally grow close together in rainforests, coniferous forests and broadleaved forests. They also occur in grasslands, deserts and swamps, and on mountainsides. In addition, people plant trees in towns and gardens, and also in plantations, where trees are grown for timber and other products.

Young palms have short, wide trunks at first, and then grow up from a single point at the plant top.

Baobab trees have thick trunks that store water to help them survive the dry season in Africa.

Plantation trees are usually planted close together in straight lines, making them easier to look after and cut down.

Poplars are fast-growing members of the willow family. There are 35 different species.

Bluebells are a common sight on woodland floors in the UK during spring. Bluebells grow from bulbs underground.

Bamboos have woody stems resembling thin tree trunks. A bamboo is a type of grass, not a tree.

Acacia trees provide welcome shelter for animals on Africa's savanna grasslands.

Maple leaves turn yellow or orange in autumn before falling off, leaving the branches bare in winter.

The beautiful pink flowers of cherry trees attract insects, which carry pollen from tree to tree.

Amazing

On a warm day, a large oak tree takes up about 1140 l of water from the soil. As much as 98 per cent of this water is lost through the tree's leaves by evaporation.

Find out more

Swamp cypress p. 110

Forest trees, such as these in an American rainforest, compete with each other for sunlight by growing as tall as possible.

Trees can even survive in deserts, by sending down long roots to reach water hidden deep underground.

Perched high up on tree branches, plants such as this stag's horn fern are nearer to the light than plants growing on the forest floor.

In Japan, flowering cherry trees are grown for their striking blossom; most of them do not produce fruit.

Swamp cypresses have a wide, fluted base to the trunk, which helps them to stay upright in waterlogged ground.

Jacaranda trees are often grown in warm parts of the world for their attractive blue or purple flowers.

Fungi kill many trees, such as this sugar maple. The fungus feeds on food made by the tree, causing the middle to rot and weakening the tree.

A giant sequoia tree produces about 2000 cones per year. Each cone contains about 200 seeds.

Palms, such as this coconut palm, are not true trees, even though they have woody trunks.

Rainforests are home to half the world's animal and plant species. This is Puerto Rico's El Yunque forest.

The trees of New England, USA, are famous around the world for the brilliant golden, red and orange colours of their autumn leaves.

Pollination

Before a flower can make seeds, male pollen has to be transferred to the flower's female stigma. This is called pollination. Pollen can be carried from flower to flower by insects and other animals, and also by wind and water.

▶ *Within a flower is a ring of male parts called stamens. Each has a long, thin stalk – the filament – topped by a brush- or bag-like anther, which contains the male reproductive cells inside their pollen grains. At the centre of the flower are the female parts, known as the carpel. This has a sticky pad, called the stigma, on top of a long stalk, called the style, which widens at its base into an ovary. Inside the ovary are the female reproductive cells in their ovules (eggs).*

❍ Some flowers are self-pollinating, meaning that pollen moves from an anther to a stigma on the same plant.

❍ In cross-pollinating flowers, the pollen from the anthers must be carried to a stigma on a different plant of the same species.

❍ Bees and butterflies are drawn to blue, yellow and pink flowers, while white flowers attract night-flying moths.

◀ *To attract male bees, the bee orchid has a lip that looks and smells just like a female bee. But if no bees come along, the orchid can bend over to pollinate itself.*

❍ Many flowers have honey guides – markings to guide the bees in. These are often invisible to us and can only be seen in ultraviolet light, which bees and some other insects can see.

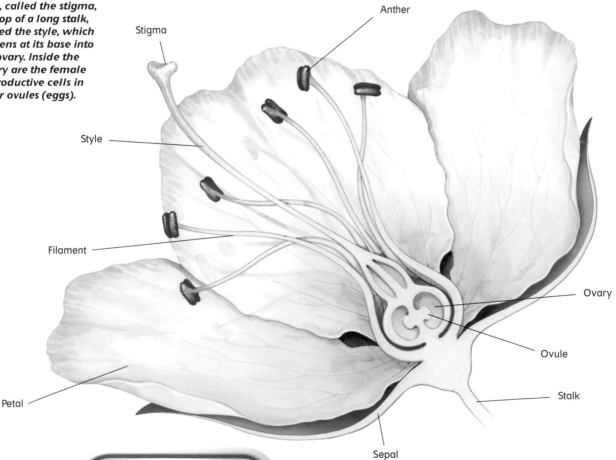

Stigma

Anther

Style

Filament

Petal

Ovary

Ovule

Stalk

Sepal

Find out more
Flowers pp. 94–95

Male catkins releasing pollen

Female catkins

Male catkins

A *Some trees grow groups of flowers called catkins that hang down from a twig. Stamens hang outside the flowers in a catkin. They make pollen that is blown away by the wind. The slender, green, female catkins of the silver birch look very different from the long, drooping male catkins.*

○ Bees collect pollen on their back legs to feed to their young.

○ A flower can only use pollen that has come from the same species of plant.

Flower advertisement

To attract insects, some flowers have brightly coloured petals and a powerful scent. Near the base of the petals the flower makes a sugary juice called nectar for insects to drink. As insects search for the nectar, they pick up sticky pollen with their bodies from the anthers. When they visit another flower, the insects transfer the pollen from their bodies to the other plant's sticky stigma.

○ Flowers that are pollinated by animals, make a small amount of spiky pollen. The spikes help the pollen to stick to hairs on the bodies of passing insects or other animals. The spikes hold the pollen in place as the animal flies between flowers.

▼ *The cuckoo pint, or lords and ladies, smells like cow-dung to attract the flies that carry its pollen.*

Amazing

Flower pollen causes an allergic reaction in some people. This is known as hay fever.

○ Wind-pollinated flowers, such as grass flowers, have no need of bright colours or scents, so they are dull and have no smell. The stamens hang out of the flowers so that the wind can blow the pollen away.

○ Many flowers contain both the male reproductive organs (stamens) and the female reproductive organs (carpel), but some plants have only one or the other.

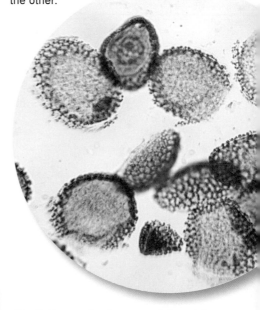

◄ *Pollen grains have an elaborately patterned cell wall, which prevents the pollen from drying out. The pattern of the cell wall differs in pollen of different plant species.*

Animal pollinators

Most pollen is carried on the bodies of insects. Many tropical flowers use bats to transport their pollen. Some flowers rely on bird pollinators, such as this hummingbird. Hummingbirds need the high-energy nectar from the flowers to power their rapid flight.

Seeds

Seeds are the tiny, hard capsules from which most new plants grow. Seeds develop from the plant's egg after it has been fertilized by pollen. Each seed contains a baby plant, plus a store of food to keep it alive until it grows leaves to make its own food.

▶ *Lotus plants are water plants that produce their seeds in a flat seed head. When the seeds are ripe, they fall into the water and float away.*

❍ All 250,000 flowering plants produce 'enclosed' seeds. These are seeds that grow inside sacs called ovaries, which turn into a fruit around the seed.

❍ The 800 or so conifers, cycads and gingkos produce 'naked' seeds, which means there is no fruit around them.

❍ After maturing, seeds go into a period called dormancy. During this time, the seeds are scattered and dispersed.

❍ Some scattered seeds fall on barren ground and do not grow into plants. Only those seeds that fall in suitable places will begin to grow.

◀ *Sycamore seeds have 'wings' to help them spin away on the wind.*

❍ Fruits are often eaten by animals. The seeds get dispersed when they are passed out in the animal's body waste. Some seeds stick to animal fur. They have burrs (tiny barbs) that hook on to the fur, or even a sticky coating. Fruits such as geraniums and lupins explode, showering seeds in all directions.

❍ Drupes are fleshy fruits whose seeds are contained inside hard, woody 'stones'. Drupes include plums, cherries, apricots, and peaches.

❍ Nuts, such as acorns, are hard, dry fruits that contain a single seed.

What are fruits?

Scientists define a fruit as the ovary of a plant after the eggs have been pollinated and grown into seeds. Fleshy fruits, such as oranges, have soft, juicy flesh. In other fruits, such as hazelnuts and almonds, the flesh turns to a hard, dry shell. Fleshy fruits can be either berries, such as oranges, which are all flesh; aggregate fruits, such as blackberries, which are lots of berries from a single flower; or multiple fruits, such as pineapples, which are single fruits from an entire multiple flowerhead.

Almonds

Blackberries

Pineapple

❍ Many seeds are light enough to be blown by the wind. The feathery seed cases of some grasses are so light that they can be blown several kilometres.

❍ Some seeds can be dispersed by water. Their fruit wall contains air spaces or oil droplets to give them buoyancy.

▶ *Tumbleweed plants uproot themselves and roll along in the wind to scatter their seeds.*

How a seed forms

When a pollen grain lands on the stigma of a flower, it grows a tube down the style and into the ovary. The tip of the pollen tube then breaks open, releasing a male nucleus, which joins with the female nucleus of the ovule, or egg. This joining together is called fertilization, and the new cell that forms is the start of a seed.

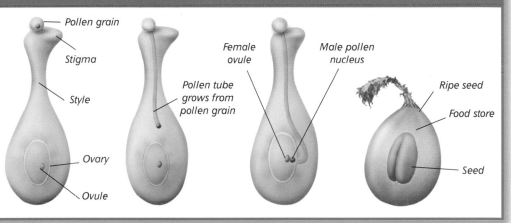

Pollen grain

Stigma

Style

Ovary

Ovule

Pollen tube grows from pollen grain

Female ovule

Male pollen nucleus

Ripe seed

Food store

Seed

▶ *When dandelions mature, they form feathery seeds that are blown away by the wind and float through the air like tiny parachutes.*

Animal helpers

Seeds are carried away from the parent plant to make sure that they do not compete for the same space, light and water. Some fruits make themselves attractive to animals so that they will be eaten. When an animal eats the the sweet, juicy fruit, the seeds are not digested. Instead, they leave the animal's body in its droppings, and so get a supply of manure to help the new plants grow. As well as eating many fruits and seeds, squirrels also bury them so that they have food for the winter. Sometimes these buried food stores are forgotten, and the seeds sprout into new plants.

▶ *Milkweeds have large seed pods that burst open when they are ready to release their seeds.*

○ Nuts and shelled peanuts are not true nuts, but simply large seeds.

○ Nuts are a concentrated, nutritious food, consisting of about 50 per cent fat and 10–20 per cent protein. Peanuts contain more food energy than sugar and more protein, minerals and vitamins than liver.

Special seeds

The fruits of the elm, ash, lime and hornbeam are fitted with 'aerofoils' or 'wings', which enable them to glide very long distances.

The largest seed in the world comes from the giant fan palm, or coco-de-mer, which grows on the Seychelles Islands of the Indian Ocean. One seed can weigh 20 kg.

Giant redwoods grow from tiny seeds less than 2 mm long. It would take 271,000 redwood seeds to make 1 kg.

The world's smallest seeds are those of epiphyhtic orchids. Over 990 million seeds are needed to make 1 g.

Amazing

Some lotus seeds have sprouted after being in a dormant (resting) state for 400 years.

Find out more

Fruit and vegetables pp. 124–125

Spreading without Seeds

Some plants only grow once, from a seed. Many plants die back each year but grow again and again from parts of the root or stem. This is called vegetative reproduction.

Potato tubers

A potato plant grows underground stems, which swell up with stored food at the tips to form tubers, called potatoes. The 'eyes' of the potato can grow into new plants using the food stored in the potato. They are the buds on the swollen stem.

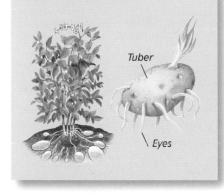

Tuber

Eyes

▲ *Daffodils are typical monocots, with long lance-like leaves and petals in threes. Daffodil bulbs store food during winter, and in spring they provide the plant with the energy it needs to grow new leaves and flowers.*

○ Plants such as lupins grow on the base of an old stem. With age, the stem widens and the centre dies, leaving a ring of separate plants around the outside.

○ Cuckoo pint, or lords and ladies, grows from a swollen underground stem called a corm. A corm is a round shape and is covered with a few thin scales or leaves.

○ Tubers store starch from one growing season to fuel early growth in the next.

○ Plants can also reproduce by sending out long stems, called runners, which crawl over the ground, or suckers, which grow under the ground.

○ The prickly, woody stems of bramble plants grow up to 3 m in length, often arching over and rooting on the ground.

○ Many plants spread by creeping underground stems called rhizomes. These form buds that push their way up through the soil as they grow stems.

○ Tulips grow from bulbs, which are shortened underground stems that store food in their fleshy scales.

▶ *One of the first woodland flowers of the year, lesser celandine is able to bloom early by using the energy stored in its underground tubers.*

New plants from old

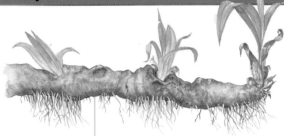

Garlic bulbs are separated into four or five segments called cloves. Bulbs and corms produce bulbets and cormlets attached to the parent bulb. These can be detached and grown into new plants.

Plants such as irises sprout from thick stems called rhizomes. These rhizomes grow sideways beneath the ground.

Bulbs, such as those of tulips, daffodils and onions, look like corms, but they are actually made of swollen leaves wrapped around a short underground stem. This is why bulbs have layers.

Some flowers, such as crocuses and gladioli have a bulbous base to their stem. This is called a corm.

○ Tulips are monocots that produce one large, bell-shaped bloom at the end of each stem. There are about 100 species of wild tulip, growing right across Asia.

○ Carolus Clusius set up a flower garden in Leiden, Holland, in the late 1500s. Here the first tulips from China were grown, and the Dutch bulb industry began.

○ Potatoes were grown in South America 1800 years ago. They were brought to Europe by the Spanish in the 16th century.

Amazing

New strawberry plants sprout from long, spindly stems called runners, which grow above ground.

A *Lilies, such as these tiger lilies, also grow from bulbs. Lilies are one of the largest and most important flower families, containing about 4000 species.*

Shoots from roots

The blackthorn is a deciduous, thorny shrub that often forms dense thickets by sending up shoots (suckers) from the roots, Blackthorn belongs to the rose family, and is an ancestor of garden plums.

Find out more

Life-cycles pp. 108–109

Plant Growth

Inside a seed is a tiny plant, or embryo, waiting to grow. When the seed settles in the soil, it takes in water, swells up and breaks open so that the new plant can grow out. This process of sprouting is known as germination.

○ Some seeds, such as those of the ironbark tree, need to be scorched by fire before they will germinate.

○ Coconut palm trees grow on tropical beaches and the coconuts fall and germinate on the beach. They can also fall into the sea, sometimes travelling for 2000 km in different ocean currents before washing up on another warm beach, where they may sprout and grow into a new coconut palm.

Amazing

Some bonsai trees are hundreds of years old, even though they are still very tiny trees.

▼ *Palm trunks do not get thicker like tree trunks; they simply grow taller. Some palms have trunks no bigger than a pencil; others are 60 m high and 1 m across.*

○ When a new plant has used up the food store in its seed, it must find another source of food. The root obtains water and minerals, growing strong enough to hold the plant in place. The shoot grows towards the light, so that the first leaves can make food.

Old tree, new life

Trees are dying in forests all the time. In the past, foresters used to clear away dead trees or chop down those that were dying. But it has now become clear that these trees play a vital part in the woodland ecosystem. As the rotting tree is broken down, it not only provides food for plants, fungi, insects and bacteria, but it also enriches the soil.

○ Only certain parts of a plant, called meristems, can grow. These are usually the tips of shoots and roots. Because a plant grows at the tips, shoots and roots mainly get longer rather than fatter. This is known as primary growth. Later in life, a plant may grow thicker or branch out.

▼ *Hundreds, or even thousands, of poppy seeds sometimes sprout together, filling meadows and crop fields with carpets of colourful flowers.*

Find out more

Seeds pp. 102-103

1. The seed sends a root down and a shoot up

2. The shoot bursts into the air

3. The stem and roots grow longer, and the plant soon begins to grow new leaves

▶ *When a seed germinates, a root (or radicle) grows down from it and a green shoot (or plumule) grows up. The first leaves to come up are the seed leaves, or cotyledons, of which there can be one or two. The cotyledons are food stores.*

◀ *Lichens may be hundreds of years old, even though they measure only a few millimetres across.*

○ Poppy seeds can lie buried in soil for years until brought to the surface by ploughing, allowing them to germinate.

○ Most lichens are extremely slow-growing. In fact, the colourful rock lichen *Acarospora chlorophana* may only grow a few millimetres each century.

○ In plants such as the broad bean, the cotyledons (seed leaves) stay underground.

○ Cycads have fern-like leaves growing in a circle round the end of the stem. New leaves sprout each year and last for several years.

○ The fastest growing plant in the sea is the giant kelp, which can grow 45 cm in a single day. Giant kelp can reach a total length of up to 60 m.

○ Oak trees can live for a thousand years or more, and grow up to 40 m tall. In Europe, oaks are the oldest of all trees.

○ The welwitschia plant, from the deserts of southern Africa, can live for up to 2000 years.

◀ *Pollarding is cutting the topmost branches of a tree so that new shoots grow from the trunk to the same length. The signs of pollarding are easy to see in trees during winter, when the leaves are gone.*

Gum tree growth

Eucalyptus trees, or gum trees, grow best in warm places that have alternate wet and dry seasons, such as Australia and the southern United States. In winter, eucalyptus trees simply stop growing and produce no new buds. Eucalyptus leaves provide the koala with its staple food, but can be harmful to other animals.

Life-cycles

*E*ach species adopts a life-cycle that will maximize its chances of survival. Some plants, called annuals, grow from seeds, produce their own flowers and seeds, and die within a single year. Others, known as biennials, complete their life cycle in two-years. Plants called perennials live for many years.

Annual seeds

As soon as a seed forms, it has a tiny living plant inside it. The seed of an annual plant may fall from its parent plant in the autumn and lie all winter in the ground. The following spring, the tiny plant bursts out of the seed and grows steadily for a few months. Finally it makes flowers and, after its seeds have formed and spread, the plant dies. Most crops are annuals, including peas and beans, squashes, and cereals such as maize and wheat. Many weeds are annuals, too.

Amazing

Most perennials spread by sending out shoots from their roots, which develop into new stems.

○ With an annual, forming flowers, fruits and seeds exhausts the plant's food reserves, so the green parts die.

○ Annuals have shallow roots so that they can quickly colonize bare ground.

○ Lobelia, an annual plant, was once used by the Native Americans as the medicine 'Indian bacco'.

○ A biennial flowers in its second year. In the first year, it builds up an underground food store, such as a bulb or taproot, to see the plant through the winter. Biennial beetroots develop leaves and a fleshy, red root in the first year; they are harvested before the next growing season.

▶ Perennials, such as tulips, have a thick underground food store, called a bulb, corm or rhizome that stays alive during winter, when the rest of the plant has died away.

○ Perennials may not bloom in the first year, but after that they will bloom every year.

○ Since they bloom for many years, perennials do not need to produce as many seeds to survive.

○ Some perennials are herbaceous – that is, they have soft stems. The stems wither at the end of each summer, and new stems grow next spring.

○ Herbaceous perennials spend winter as dormant underground bulbs, corms, tubers, roots and rhizomes.

○ Other perennials have woody stems, such as trees, shrubs and vines. Their stems stay alive and grow longer with each growing season.

○ Woody perennials spend winter above ground, but stop growing during this time.

○ A woody perennial will only flower when it has grown into a mature plant, which can take many years.

Ephemerals

The seed of the shepherd's purse plant sprouts soon after it lands in the soil. Such plants that grow quickly, flower, set seeds and die in a few weeks are called ephemeral plants. There are many life-cycles of the shepherd's purse, one after the other throughout the year. This means that shepherd's purse seeds are being spread around at regular intervals, so there is a better chance that some may find a place to grow.

◀ Perennials from temperate (cool) regions – such as asters, irises, wallflowers, lupins, peonies and primroses – need a cold winter to encourage new buds to grow in spring.

Annuals	Biennials	Perennials
Poppy	Wallflowers	Aster
Lobelia	Carnations	Iris
Petunia	Sweet William	Lupin
Buttercup	Evening primrose	Daffodil
Sunflower	Beetroot	Begonia
Peas and beans	Carrot	African violet
Squash	Foxglove	Gloxinia
Maize	Honesty	Columbine
Wheat	Forget-me-not	Oak tree

Short life-cycles

Annuals, such as poppies, complete their life-cycle in a single growing season; biennials, such as wild callet, complete theirs in two. Annuals and biennials are popular with gardeners, since they are easy to grow and come in a wide range of colours and sizes.

Annual

An annual plant invests its energy in reproducing as rapidly as possible. The parent plant dies soon after its seeds are dispersed. The entire cycle – from seed to growing, flowering plant and back to seed again – takes no more than a year.

Seed capsule

The seedling germinates

Buds form

Plant flowers and poppy seeds form

Biennial

Biennials form a root, perhaps a short stem and a rosette of leaves in the first year. Their food store ensures that they can continue their development the following year, when they flower, form seeds and then die, completing their life-cycle.

The wild callet plant grows for one year

Buds form

Flowers begin to open

Flower blooms

Flowers pollinate and are fertilized

Seeds form and are dispersed

Seeds grow in the ground

The seedling germinates

Young plant

○ Tropical perennials, like begonias, will die if left outdoors in temperate winters.

○ Polyanthus are a cross between two perennials – the primrose and cowslip.

○ Ephemerals (short-lived plants), such as chickweed or groundsel, can take over bare soil quickly and become weeds (plants growing in the wrong place).

◀ *The stems of woody perennials do not wither, but most shed their leaves in autumn.*

Find out more

Plant growth pp. 106–107

Waterplants

A plant is over 90 per cent water, so it is not surprising that plants manage to live in water perfectly well, provided that they are able to obtain enough sunlight. Some plants float on the surface, while others root in the bottom of ponds or streams.

○ Giant water lilies have huge leaves with the edges upturned, like a shallow frying pan, to keep them afloat.

○ Many grass-like plants grow in water, including reeds, mace, irises and rushes, such as bulrushes and cattails.

○ Sedges are like grasses, but they have solid, triangular stems. They grow in damp places near the water's edge.

○ Rushes have long, cylindrical leaves and grow in tussocks in damp places along the bank.

○ Reeds are tall grasses with round stems, flat leaves and purplish flowers. They grow in dense beds in open water.

○ Free-floating plants, such as duckweed and frogbit, are common in marshes. In rivers, they would be washed away.

Water hyacinths are purple American water flowers. They grow quickly, and can clog up slow streams.

○ Water horsetails are modern relatives of plants that dominated the vast swamps of the Carboniferous Period, 360–286 million years ago.

Papyrus

Papyrus is a tall, grass-like water plant that grows in Africa's River Nile. Stems were rolled flat by the Ancient Egyptians to write on. The word 'paper' comes from papyrus.

Swamp, or bald, cypress trees grow in swampy areas of North America. Their trunks are wide at the base, which helps to support them in the shifting mud. Their roots grow cone-shaped 'knees' above the water to take in air, since waterlogged mud does not contain much oxygen.

Find out more
Seaweed ice cream p. 77

Amazing

Water hyacinths grow so quickly that they may double in number every ten days.

○ Seaweeds are red, green or brown algae. Red seaweeds are small and fern-like, and grow 30–60 m down in tropical seas. Brown seaweeds, such as giant kelp, are big and grow down to depths of about 20 m, mostly in cold water. The small- to medium-sized green seaweeds are found in rockpools and coastal rocks in temperate and tropical regions.

○ Some seaweeds, such as the bladderwrack, have gas pockets to help their fronds (leaves) float.

▼ *Huge numbers of wildfowl, including great crested grebes, spend the winter in reedbeds. In many parts of the world, reeds are cut and used as roofing materials.*

▲ *Mangrove trees help to protect tropical shorelines by trapping mud with their roots and preventing the land from being washed away by tides or storms.*

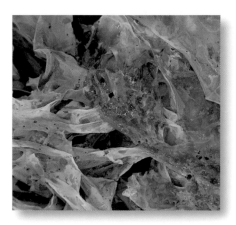

▲ *Rushes produce clusters of tiny green or brown flowers, which are pollinated by the wind. The flower parts are arranged in sixes.*

▲ *Seaweeds grow mainly on rocky shores, or underwater close to the coast. They hold on to the rocks to prevent being washed away. The part that attaches the seaweed to a rock is called a holdfast, and it resembles a root. It grips the rock tightly like a sucker. Seaweeds have tough, leathery fronds (leaves) to stand up to the pounding of the waves. Their bodies are flexible, so that they can move in the water currents without breaking.*

Water lilies

The flat leaves of water lilies float on the surface of the water. Inside the plant, there are plenty of air spaces to help the plant to float. Water runs easily off the waxy surface of the leaves, which stops them from becoming waterlogged. The breathing pores (stomata) are on the top surface of the leaf, rather than underneath, as in land plants. This allows the gases needed for breathing and making food (photosynthesis) to pass easily from the air into the leaf. Water lily leaf stalks are soft and bendy, so they are less likely to snap as the water moves.

Desert and Grassland

Grassland forms where there is not enough rain for trees to grow. in grassland habitats, there is usually a long dry season and a short rainy season. A desert is a place where little rain falls. Plants cannot thrive in deserts without mineral-rich soil and sufficient water.

Zebra

Wildebeest

Gazelle

○ Grasslands cover nearly a quarter of the Earth's land surface.

○ Temperate grasslands include the prairies of North America, the pampas of South America and the steppes of Eurasia. The tropical grassland of Africa is known as savanna.

○ Meadow grass is the most common of all grasses, found on grasslands all over the world – and in garden lawns.

Saguaro cactus

Huge saguaro cacti from Arizona and California in the USA and also Mexico may live for over 200 years. They do not usually grow 'arms' until they are 75 years old. The pleats in the stem expand like a concertina as the cactus soaks up water. Up to 90 per cent of the weight of a cactus comes from the water stored in its fleshy stem.

◀ *On Africa's savanna grasslands, different grazing animals avoid competing for food by eating grass of different heights. Zebras, for example, eat tall grass, while wildebeest eat the middle shoots and gazelles browse on the lowest shoots.*

○ The many prairie flowers include blazing stars, coneflowers, sunflowers, asters and goldenrods.

○ Eurasian grasslands bloom with vetches, trefoils and orchids, as well as many kinds of herb.

○ When grasslands are destroyed by farming, the soil can be blown away by the wind. This is what turned the Great Plains region of North America into a 'dust bowl' in the 1930s.

○ Many grassland trees are said to be sclerophyllous. This means they have tough leaves and stems to save water.

○ The mesquite has roots that can reach depths of up to 50 m.

○ Window plants grow almost entirely underground. These are cigar-shaped plants that poke down into the ground, leaving just a small green 'window' on the surface to catch sunlight.

▼ *Cacti have to pollinate, like all other flowering plants. Every few years, many cacti produce big, colourful blooms to attract insects quickly.*

Mutual benefits

Africa's grasslands are home to vast herds of grazing animals. They arrive as soon as the rains have turned the grasslands green with new growth. The animals eat the grass, but the grass also benefits, since the animals produce huge amounts of droppings that enrich the soil with nutrients.

○ The quiver tree drops its branches to save water in times of drought.

○ During the brief rainy season, grasses and herbs grow quickly. The land becomes green with new growth, and brightly coloured flowers blanket the ground. The flowers create seeds rapidly, but dry out and die once the rains stop.

Find out more

Prickly pear cactus p. 89

❍ Some flowering desert plants are visible for only a few days. Their seeds lie dormant (inactive) in the soil, perhaps for years, until a the rains come. Then the plants germinate and bloom quickly. These quick-growing flowers are called ephemerals. Their whole life-cycle – from one generation of seeds to the next – can last just two or three weeks.

❍ Desert plants have special adaptations to stop water evaporating from their leaves. Most have small, hard, tough-coated leaves. The reduced surface area means there is less leaf exposed to hot sunlight, which makes the plant's water evaporate. Other desert plants, such as cacti, have no leaves at all.

❍ In most deserts, there are usually plants with special adaptations to cope with daytime heat and lack of water. Adaptations include deep roots, the ability to reach water far underground, or spreading roots that cover a wide aras close to the surface. Shallow roots are able to take up surface moisture quickly from heavy dews and occasional rains. Swollen stems are also used store precious water.

Amazing

On Africa's savanna grasslands, elephant grasses can grow up to 4 m in height.

▼ *The largest plants in most deserts are called succulents. Their thick, fleshy stems or leaves store water to help the plant survive dry periods.*

Joshua cactus

Saguaro cactus

Prickly pear cactus

Grasses of the world

Many grasses reproduce by sending out underground stems or long shoots, from which a new plant grows. If the top of the grass is cut, eaten or burnt, new grass then grows from underground shoots.

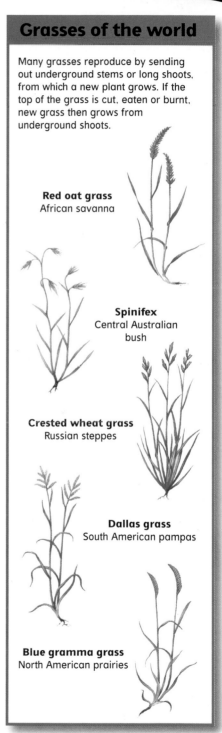

Red oat grass
African savanna

Spinifex
Central Australian bush

Crested wheat grass
Russian steppes

Dallas grass
South American pampas

Blue gramma grass
North American prairies

Rainforest

Tropical rainforests are warm and wet, with over 2000 mm of rain per year and average temperatures in excess of 20°C. These conditions make them the world's richest plant habitats. Flowering plants originated in tropical rainforests.

○ Most rainforest trees are broadleaved and evergreen.

○ Trees of the Amazon rainforest include rosewood, Brazil nut, rubber, myrtle, and laurel, as well as palms. Trees in the African rainforest include mahogany, ebony, limba, wenge, agba, iroko and sapele.

Amazing

Half the world's remaining rainforest will be gone by 2020 if it continues to be cut down at the current rate.

Amazon rainforest

Covering much of northern South America, the Amazon rainforest is home to more species of plants and animals than any other place on Earth. For this reason, conservationists are very concerned to protect areas of rainforest that are being cut down by people wanting to grow crops or build settlements.

▲ Rainforest trees are covered with epiphytes – plants with roots that do not reach the soil, but which take water and minerals from rainwater and plant debris that falls on them.

○ Many rainforest plants have big, bright flowers to attract birds and insects in the gloom. Flowers pollinated by birds are often red, those by night-flying moths white or pink, and those by day-flying insects yellow or orange.

▶ Most rainforests receive between 150 and 400 cm of rain each year. Plants grow quickly in the warm, wet conditions. In order to expose their leaves to sunlight (to make food by photosynthesis), some rainforest trees grow up to 50 m tall.

Find out more
Animal helpers p. 103

▶ *The roots of the strangler fig plant grow down to the ground around the roots of rainforest trees, strangling them by taking their water supply. The tree then dies away, leaving the fig roots as a hollow 'trunk'.*

○ The gloom means that many plants need large seeds to store enough food while they grow. They produce fragrant fruits that attract animals. The animals eat the fruits and spread the seeds via their droppings. Fruit bats, for example, are drawn to mangoes.

○ Many trees grow flowers on their trunks to make them easy for animals to reach. This is called cauliflory.

○ Many plants are parasitic. This means that they feed on other plants. Parasitic plants include mistletoes and rafflesia.

○ Epiphytes are often known as 'air plants', because they seem to live on air, being attached neither to the ground nor to any obvious source of nutrients.

○ Epiphytes in tropical forests include various orchids, ferns and bromeliads.

○ Some tropical forests blanket the sides of mountains. The trees here are shorter, and more plants grow on or near the ground. The highest mountain rainforests are called 'cloud' forests, because much of the forest is covered in low clouds, providing moisture for all kinds of mosses, ferns and herbs.

○ Many rainforest trees have a symbiotic relationship with fungi that live on their roots. The fungi get energy from the trees, and in return they supply the trees with phosphorus and other nutrients.

○ Some ants that live in rainforests, such as leaf-cutter and harvester ants, line their nests with leaves. The ants cut up the leaves to provide food for fungi. The fungi, in turn, provide food for the ants.

▲ *Durian fruits attract mammals, such as orang-utan, with their strange smell. The mammals eat the durian fruit and help to disperse its seeds in their body waste.*

Brazil nuts

Brazil nuts are harvested from rainforest trees when they fall to the forest floor. The nuts develop inside a round, woody capsule that looks like a large coconut. Inside each capsule there are 8–24 nuts, arranged like the sections of an orange. The nuts are taken out of the capsules and dried in the sunshine.

▶ *The leaves of the tallest trees form a scattered top level of the rainforest, called the emergent layer. Sunlight passing between these trees allows a second, lower, more even layer to grow. This is the main canopy, and it is the densest part of the rainforest. The canopy is tangled with vines and epiphytes. This layer blocks out most of the remaining sunlight, so the forest's lower layers – on or near the ground – have few plants. Some seedlings grow there, as well as fungi and other organisms that do not need much light.*

Emergent layer

Canopy

Understorey

Forest floor

Coniferous Forests

The evergreen conifer forests of the cool regions that border the Arctic Circle – such as the north of Asia, northern Europe and North America – are called boreal forests. The word boreal means 'northern'. Winters in boreal regions are long and very cold.

Softwood timber

Softwood is timber that comes from coniferous trees such as pine, larch, fir and spruce. Between 75 and 80 per cent of the natural forests of northern Asia, Europe and the USA is made up of softwood trees. Pines grow fast and straight, reaching their full height in less than 20 years – which is why they provide 75 per cent of the world's timber.

○ For nine months of the year boreal forests are cold and dark, but they spring to life in the brief warmth of the three-month summer.

○ In Russia and Siberia, boreal forest is called taiga, which is a Russian word meaning 'little sticks'.

○ Many conifers are cone-shaped, which helps them to shed snow from their branches in winter.

○ The needle-like shape and waxy coating of conifer leaves helps the tree to save water.

○ Soft, or white pines, such as sugar pines and piñons, grow their needles in bundles of five, and produce little resin.

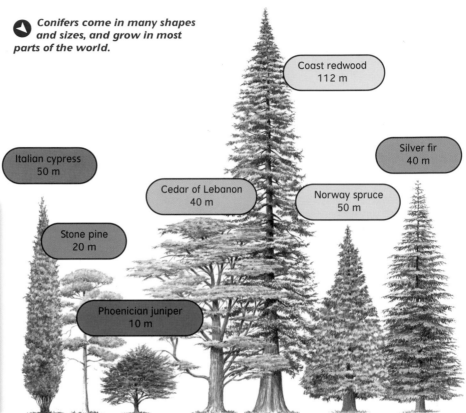

Conifers come in many shapes and sizes, and grow in most parts of the world.

Coast redwood
112 m

Silver fir
40 m

Italian cypress
50 m

Cedar of Lebanon
40 m

Norway spruce
50 m

Stone pine
20 m

Phoenician juniper
10 m

Christmas trees are usually spruce or fir trees. The modern Christmas tree tradition began in Germany, but the use of evergreen trees as a symbol of eternal life was an ancient custom of the Egyptians, Chinese and Hebrews.

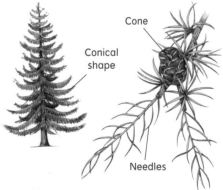

Cone

Conical shape

Needles

Boreal forests are mostly evergreen conifers such as pine (especially Scots pine), spruce, larch and fir. Most conifers are instantly recognizable from their conical shapes, their evergreen, needle-like leaves and their dark brown cones.

❍ Hard or yellow pines, such as Scots and Corsican pines, grow their needles in bundles of two or three, and make lots of resin.

❍ Eurasian pines include the Scots pine, Corsican pine, black pine, pinaster pine and stone pine.

❍ North American pines include eastern white pines, sugar pines, stone pines, piñons, Ponderosa pines, Monterey pines, jack pines and lodgepole pines.

❍ The sugar pine is the biggest of all pines, often growing up to 70 m tall and 3.5 m thick. The eastern white pine has valuable, fine white wood.

❍ Other North American forest trees include balsam firs and black spruces.

❍ Boreal forest trees are good at recovering after fire. Indeed, jack pine and black spruce cones only open to release their seeds after a fire.

▶ *The leaves of conifers may be scale-like, as they are here, or needle-like. The scale-like leaves cling to the stem.*

▶ *Conifer cones are green at first, but turn to brown as they ripen. In warm, dry weather, the cone scales open to release the conifer seeds, which are blown away by the wind on papery wings.*

Forest floor

As trees in coniferous forests grow very close together and keep their leaves all year round, little light reaches the forest floor, so only mosses, lichens, and other small plants can grow there. The soil in coniferous forests usually freezes once a year, making it difficult for plants to obtain water.

▼ *In the coldest boreal forests, water – which all plants need for survival – is locked away as ice all winter long. To adapt to these conditions, conifers have developed thin, needle-like leaves. The narrow shape of the leaves allows little water to evaporate, so the tree is able to conserve its water supplies to see it through the icy winter. Conifers are evergreen, meaning that they do not drop their leaves each year.*

Amazing

Boreal forests cover about 1.5 billion hectares – about 11 per cent of the Earth's land area.

Find out more

Trees pp. 96–97

Broadleaved Woodlands

Forests of broadleaved, deciduous trees grow in temperate regions such as North America, western Europe and eastern Asia, where there are warm, wet summers and cold winters. Very few woodlands in Europe are entirely natural; most are 'secondary' woods, growing on land once cleared for farms.

Massive branches spread out from the sides of the tree

Acorns sit in cups at the end of long stalks

Oak leaves have 3–6 rounded lobes on each side, and almost no leaf stalk

The pedunculate, or English oak, is probably the most common British tree and grows up to 35 m in height. The acorns have long stalks, called peduncules.

Amazing

About 300 insect species can be found in a mature oak tree, and up to 40,000 caterpillars.

Plenty of light can filter down through deciduous trees, so that all kinds of bushes and flowers grow in the woods, often blooming in spring before the trees develop their leaves. Bluebells may grow so closely together that they carpet spring woodland with a stunning and unique display of brilliant violet-blue flowers.

○ In moist western Europe, beech trees dominate woods on well-drained, shallow soils, especially chalk soils; oak trees prefer deep clay soils. Alders grow in waterlogged places.

○ In drier eastern Europe, beeches are replaced by durmast oak and hornbeam, and in Russia by lindens.

○ In North American woods, beech and linden are rarer than in Europe, but oaks, hickories and maples are more common.

○ Buckeye and tulip trees dominate in the Appalachian Mountains of North America.

○ A wide range of shrubs grow under the trees in broadleaved woods including dogwood, holly and magnolia, as well as woodland flowers.

Bluebell

Woodland fungi

Many different species of fungi grow in the dark, damp environment of the forest floor. They feed on rotting wood and other plant material. Fly agaric has a special relationship with birch tree roots. The fungus takes sugars from the tree, but in return the fungus provides the tree with nutrients that it cannot easily obtain from the soil.

Wood blewit

Death cap   Dryad's saddle

Fly agaric

Mealy tubaria   Many-zoned bracket fungus

Devil's boletus

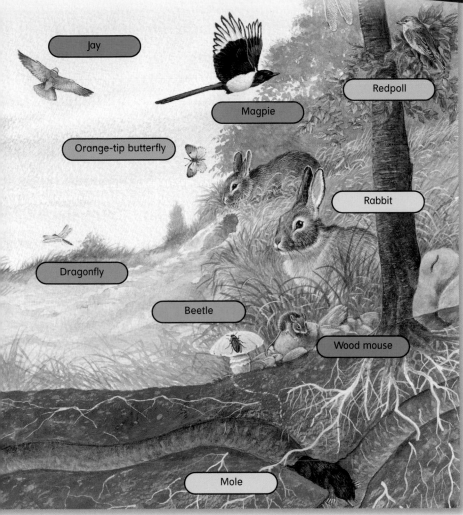

Jay

Magpie

Redpoll

Orange-tip butterfly

Rabbit

Dragonfly

Beetle

Wood mouse

Mole

Hazel tree has a broad crown

Smooth, round hazel nuts sit in ragged green or brown, leafy husks

Round, slightly hairy leaves have pointed tips

Female catkins look more like leaf buds with tiny red tassels

Male hazel catkins

🔺 *Hazel is common in the understorey of oak woodlands. It is often coppiced – cut back to the base to produce a mass of tall, straight sticks.*

🔺 *Broadleaved woodland with a mixture of trees and shrubs provides home for many animal species.*

❍ Ferns and mosses grow on the woodland floor. Creeping plants, such as ivy, climb up tree trunks to reach the light.

❍ Tannin from oak bark has been used for curing leather since the days of ancient Greece.

❍ Oak wood is very strong and durable, and so was the main building wood for centuries. It was used for making timber frames for houses and for building ships.

❍ Maple syrup comes from several North American maple trees, including the sugar maple and the black maple. The syrup is 'sweet-water' sap. It is different from ordinary sap, and flows from wounds during thaws, when there is no growth.

❍ Few flowers can grow in beech woods during summer, because of the deep shade cast by the trees and the thick carpet of fallen leaves. Beech nuts are very nutritious, and are eaten by birds and small mammals.

Leaf fall

Losing their leaves in autumn helps trees to save water as they 'shut down' their food-gathering system for winter. Food pipes inside the tree branches are sealed, and as the leaves are cut off from their food supply they die. The chlorophyll that keeps the leaves green breaks down, and the leaves turn red, yellow and brown before falling to the ground. Enough food is stored within the tree to ensure that buds can grow in spring.

Find out more

How many leaves? p. 81

Cold Places

*O*n mountaintops and in polar regions, plants have to survive long, freezing winters, strong winds and thin, frozen soils. Small plants, such as mosses and lichens, are common. Flowers appear only in the brief summer months.

Mountain survival

Conditions get colder, windier and wetter higher up mountains, so plants get smaller and hardier. In Australia, eucalyptus trees grow near the tree-line. In New Zealand, Chile and Argentina southern beeches grow. Alpine flowers like purple and starry saxifrage have tough roots that grow into crevices and split the rocks. There are few insects high up, so flowers like saxifrage and snow gentian have big blooms to attract them. Alpine flowers such as edelweiss have woolly hairs to keep out the cold. Tasmanian daisies grow in dense cushion-shapes to keep warm.

○ Around the shores of the Arctic, within the Arctic Circle, are vast regions of boggy, marshy land called tundra. The Arctic tundra supports more than 400 species of flowering plants, including heathers or lings, crowberry, bilberry, anemones, stonecrops and saxifrages.

○ Willow trees grow in the Arctic, but because of the cold and fierce wind, they are less than 10 cm tall, spreading out along the ground rather than growing upwards.

▲ *The coffee plant is a mountain plant that grows best at altitudes of 1000 to 2500 m. Coffee beans are not actually beans at all; they are the seeds from inside the red coffee berries. Coffee berries appear green at first, then turn yellow and eventually bright red as they ripen.*

Amazing

The Arctic poppy is the flower that blooms the nearest to the North Pole.

▼ *Colourful flowers blossom on the tundra during the brief summer, when the Sun never sets. Short, stunted, twisted willow and birch trees cling to the ground in more protected hollows, spreading their roots wide in the shallow areas of thawed soil. Caribou, or reindeer, scrape away the snow to feed on reindeer moss – a type of lichen.*

Find out more

Boreal forest in winter p. 117

▶ *Crocuses and other spring flowers grow and even blossom while there is still a covering of snow on the Arctic soil.*

○ Some flowers that grow in the Arctic turn and face the Sun all day to absorb as much light as possible and to keep warm.

○ Many Arctic plants are evergreen, so they are ready to make the most of the brief summer.

○ Butterflies and bees are rare in the Arctic, so many plants, including mustard, rely on the wind for pollination.

○ The soil is so poor in the Arctic that seeds make the most of the nutrients in animal corpses, such as those of musk oxen. Arctic flowers often spring up inside skulls and near bones.

○ Some plants have dark-coloured leaves and stems, which soak up the Sun's warmth quickly and help to melt the snow.

○ Numerous types of conifer, including pines, firs, spruces and larches, grow on lower mountain slopes.

○ Above a certain height, known as the tree-line, conditions become too cold for trees to grow.

○ Above the tree-line, stunted shrubs, grasses and tiny flowers grow. This is known as alpine vegetation.

○ To make the most of the short summers, the alpine snowbell grows its flower buds the previous summer, then lets the buds lie dormant through the winter under the snow. When the snow melts, the flower buds emerge.

○ Mountain plants have various adaptations to cope with the extreme conditions at high altitude. Their leaves are hairy, to withstand cold and frost, and the plants keep close to the ground as they grow, which shelters them from the wind. They often form small mounds, or cushions, in which leaves and shoots in the centre are protected from the cold by the leaves around the outside.

○ The only part of Antarctica with a real variety of plants is the Antarctic Peninsula, which juts northwards and extends just beyond the Antarctic Circle. About 350 plant species – mostly lichens, mosses and algae – grow there, as well as three species of flowering plant.

◀ *The dwarf willowherb rarely grows more than 30 cm high – any higher and it will quickly be killed by the ice-cold Arctic wind.*

Frozen soil

Most plants in polar regions must grow in the top 30 cm or so of soil. Below that depth, the soil remains constantly frozen – even during the summer. This is called the permafrost region.

Cereals

Cereals such as wheat, maize, rice, barley, sorghum, oats, rye and millet are the world's major sources of food. Cereals are grasses, and we eat their seeds, or grain. We also process the grains into food such as flour, oils and syrups.

Amazing

The world grows enough wheat in a year to fill a line of trucks stretching a quarter of the way to the Moon.

○ In the developed world – that is, regions such as North America and Europe – wheat is the most important food crop. But for half the world's population, including most people in Southeast Asia and China, rice is the staple food.

Popcorn

Popcorn is a popular snack food. When heated in a saucepan, the kernels make a loud 'popping' noise and literally jump out of the pan. The 'popped' popcorn can then be eaten straight away, with salt or sugar for extra taste.

◀ *The ear, or head, of a corn plant is called a cob. It is covered with tightly packed yellow or white kernels of seeds. The kernels are the part of the plant that is eaten.*

○ Many grains are used to make alcoholic drinks such as whisky. A process called fermentation turns the starch in the grains into alcohol. Special processing of barley creates a food called malt, which is used by brewers to make beer and lager.

◀ *Wheat grows over more farmland than any other crop. It is the basic food for 35 per cent of the world's population.*

○ Maize, or corn, is the USA's main crop, and the second most important crop around the world after wheat. Rice is the third key crop.

○ Popcorn has no starch, unlike most other corn. When heated, moisture in the kernels turns to steam and expands, causing the kernel to explode.

○ Wheat was one of the first crops ever grown. It was planted by the earliest farmers at least 10,000 years ago.

○ Pasta is made from durum (hard-grain) wheat. Italians have been using it in their cooking since the 13th century, but now pasta dishes are popular worldwide.

○ When grain is ripe it is cut from its stalks. This is called reaping.

○ After reaping, the grain must be separated from the stalks and chaff (waste). This is called threshing.

○ After threshing, the grain must be cleaned and separated from the husks. This is called winnowing.

◀ *A combine harvester is an agricultural machine that reaps the grain, threshes it, cleans it and then pours it into bags, or reservoirs.*

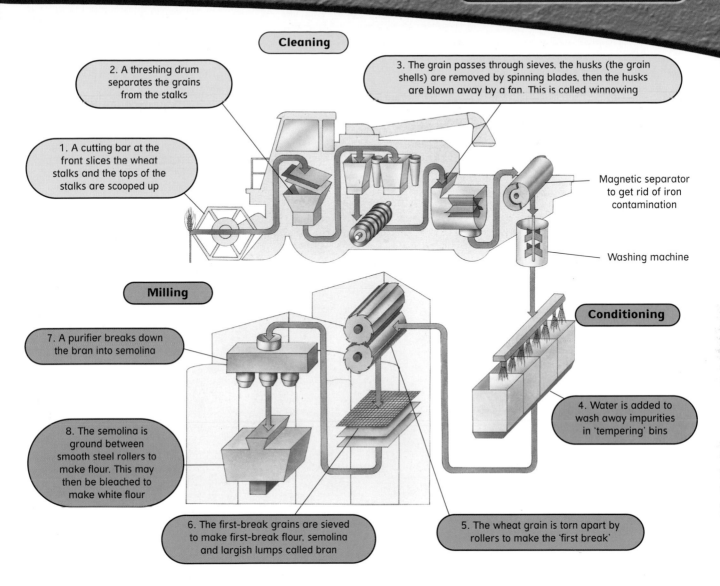

Cleaning

2. A threshing drum separates the grains from the stalks

3. The grain passes through sieves, the husks (the grain shells) are removed by spinning blades, then the husks are blown away by a fan. This is called winnowing

1. A cutting bar at the front slices the wheat stalks and the tops of the stalks are scooped up

Magnetic separator to get rid of iron contamination

Washing machine

Milling

7. A purifier breaks down the bran into semolina

Conditioning

4. Water is added to wash away impurities in 'tempering' bins

8. The semolina is ground between smooth steel rollers to make flour. This may then be bleached to make white flour

6. The first-break grains are sieved to make first-break flour, semolina and largish lumps called bran

5. The wheat grain is torn apart by rollers to make the 'first break'

○ A lot of wheat is fed to livestock, but 95 per cent of all rice is eaten by people.

○ Brown rice is rice grain with the husk ground away. White rice is rice grain with the inner bran layer ground away as well, and is far less nutritious.

○ Rice provides more than 20 per cent of the calories consumed by humans.

A *Harvesting wheat and using it to make flour is a surprisingly complex process. The process is still carried out with simple tools in some parts of the world. But in the developed world, the entire process is largely mechanized.*

Rice growing

Rice has been cultivated since about 3000 BC. Rice seeds are first sown in drier soil, but when the young plants (seedlings) are about two months old, they are planted in paddy fields that are flooded with up to 10 cm of water. The water prevents weeds from overtaking the rice crop. The water is later drained, ready for the harvest. Rice can even be grown in hilly regions, with terraces of paddy fields being cut into the hillsides.

Find out more

Oldest crop plants p. 127

Fruit and Vegetables

Vegetables are basically any part of a plant eaten cooked or raw, except for the fruit. People also eat a wide variety of fruits, and a healthy diet includes at least five different fruits and vegetables every day.

Asparagus

Asparagus belongs to the lily family. Garden asparagus has been prized since Roman times. The edible young stems of the asparagus are called spears. If the spears are not harvested, they grow into tall, feathery plants. In Argenteuil, France, asparagus is grown underground to keep it white. White asparagus is especially tender and has the best flavour. Asparagus plants are perennials – they produce spears each year, and can do so for up to 25 years.

○ Green vegetables are the edible green parts of plants, including the leaves of plants such as cabbages and lettuces.

○ The leaves of green vegetables are rich in many essential vitamins, including vitamin A, vitamin E and folic acid (one of the B vitamins).

○ Pulses (beans and peas) are a good source of protein.

○ Citrus fruits are a group of juicy, soft fruits covered with a very thick, waxy, evenly coloured skin in yellow, orange or green. Citrus fruits include lemons, limes, oranges, grapefruits and shaddocks.

○ Fruits of temperate regions, must have a cool winter to grow properly.

○ The main temperate fruits are apples, pears, plums, apricots, peaches, grapes and cherries.

○ The best-known tropical fruits are bananas and pineapples. Others include guavas, breadfruit, lychees, melons, mangoes and papayas.

○ Berries are fleshy fruits that contain lots of seeds. Many plants produce berries, including tomatoes, grape vines and bananas.

○ Strawberries, raspberries and blackberries are not true berries. They are called 'aggregate' fruits, because they are made up of groups of tiny fruits, each containing one seed.

○ Grapes are found all round the world, in places where there are warm summers and mild winters.

○ Grapes are grown on woody grape vines. They can be black, blue, golden, green, purple or white, depending on the vine species. Grapes are eaten raw, pressed to make grape juice and wine, and dried as raisins.

Bananas

Banana plants are gigantic herbs with trunks that grow 3–6 m high. Bananas are picked green and unripe, shipped in refrigerated ships, then artificially ripened with 'ethylene' gas to turn them yellow. There are hundreds of varieties of banana.

A *Tropical fruits grow mainly in the tropics, where it is warm, because they cannot survive even a light frost.*

Amazing

Citrus fruits contain more vitamin C than any other type of fruit or vegetable.

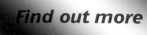

Find out more

What are fruits? p. 102

Fruit and vegetables

Spinach is rich in vitamins A and C, and also in iron.

Root vegetables are parts of plants that grow underground. Carrots are root vegetables that are a rich source of vitamin A.

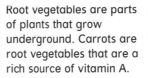

Vitamin C (ascorbic acid) is found in many fresh fruits and vegetables, especially citrus fruits. Vitamin C is important for the growth of bones, teeth, and blood vessels, and it aids the healing of wounds.

Grapes are juicy, smooth-skinned berries that grow in tight clusters on woody plants called vines.

The grapefruit is a typical citrus fruit. The juice of citrus fruits contains high levels of citric acid, which gives them their sharp flavour.

Lettuces are among the most popular green salad vegetables.

The peach is 87 per cent water, and has far fewer calories than fruit such as apples and pears.

Pears are the second most important temperate fruit after apples. The leading producer is China.

The pineapple plant grows on the ground and takes its food from the air or from decaying plant matter near its roots.

The tomato is not a vegetable, but a fruit called a berry.

A pea pod forms from the ovary of a pea plant. Only fertilized pea ovules can grow as seeds. When the pod is opened, it may contain some seeds that have failed to grow.

Plums came originally from Turkey's Caucasus Mountains, and Turkey is still the world's major grower of plums.

People and Plants

We would not be able to survive without plants. They form the basis of the food chain, and produce the oxygen that all living things need to breathe and stay alive. Plants also provide us with many useful materials, including wood, cotton, paints, rubber and medicines.

▶ Herbs are small plants used as medicines or to flavour food. Most herbs are perennial, and have soft stems that die back in winter. With some herbs, such as rosemary, only the leaves are used. With others, such as garlic, the bulb is used instead. Fennel is used for its seeds, as well as its bulb and leaves. Coriander is used for both its leaves and seeds. The flavour comes from what are called 'essential oils' in the leaves.

Labels on illustration: Rosemary, Thyme, Mint, Dill, Parsley, Fennel, Bay, Basil, Chives

○ The ancient Chinese and Greeks grew fruit trees, vegetables and herbs in gardens for food and for medicines.

○ In the 1500s, there were five famous botanical gardens in Europe designed to study and grow herbs for medicine.

○ The first botanical gardens were at Pisa (1543) and Padua (1545) in Italy.

○ Nutmeg, a sweet-flavoured spice, comes from the inner part of the seeds produced by the nutmeg tree, a kind of magnolia.

○ The Chinese have used the hollow stems of bamboo to make flutes since before the Stone Age. The Australian aboriginals use bamboo stems to make droning pipes called didgeridoos.

○ The date palm has been cultivated in the hottest parts of North Africa and the Middle East for at least 5000 years. Muslims regard it as the tree of life.

◀ Henbane is a pungent, poisonous herb. The drug hyoscyamine is made from this herb, which dilates the pupils of the eyes.

Maple syrup

Several North American maple trees produce maple syrup. Maple syrup was used by the Native Americans of the Great Lakes and St Lawrence River regions long before Europeans arrived in North America. Every spring, pipes inserted into the maple trees tap the sap into buckets. The liquid sap is heated until the water boils away, leaving maple syrup. About 30 l of sap are needed to produce 1 l of maple syrup. The leaf of the sugar maple tree is Canada's national symbol.

Amazing

A drug made from the Madagascar periwinkle, a perennial plant, helps children to fight the cancer leukemia.

Uses of wood

In the developing world, many people burn wood for fuel. About 90 per cent of the timber cut in India, for example, is burned for cooking on wood-stoves. Timber is also used for construction, furniture and (as pulp) for making paper for newsprint. In well-managed forests, new young trees are planted to replace the mature trees that are cut down. But many tropical forests are being felled thoughtlessly, for quick profits.

○ Eucalyptus wood is used to make a wide range of items, from boats to telegraph poles.

○ Most tropical trees are slow-growing hardwoods, such as teak and mahogany. Once cut down, they take many years to replace.

○ Teak is a deciduous tree that comes from India. It is one of the toughest of all woods and has been used to construct ships and buildings for more than 2000 years.

○ Chicle is a gum drained from the Central American sapota tree in the rainy season. It is the main ingredient in chewing-gum. The best quality chicle comes from Guatemala.

▶ *As humans take over larger and larger areas of the world, and as farmers use more and more weedkillers on the land, many wildflowers, such as this Lady's slipper orchid, are becoming very rare. Some are now so rare that they are protected by law.*

Oldest crop plants

		Year (BC)
Wheat		10,000
Pea		9000
Rye		6500
Bean		5000
Barley		4500
Lettuce		4500
Radish		3000
Rice		3000

○ Forests provide fuel, timber, paper, resins, varnishes, dyes, rubber, kapok and much more besides.

○ The Scottish physician James Lind (1716–1794) helped to eradicate the disease of scurvy – caused by a vitamin C deficiency – from the British Navy by recommending that sailors eat oranges and lemons on long sea voyages.

Find out more

Plant power p. 72

Plant products

Three of the most widely used plant products are cotton, wood and rubber. They are shown here with the plants from which they are derived.

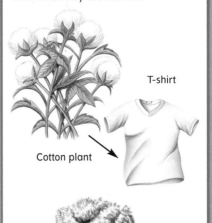

Cotton plant

T-shirt

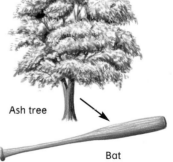

Ash tree

Bat

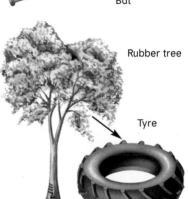

Rubber tree

Tyre

Glossary

Alga (plural: algae) A simple, plant-like organism that makes its own food by photosynthesis. Algae consist of one cell or many cells, ranging from microscopic diatoms to large seaweeds. They do not have roots, stems or leaves.

Angiosperm A flowering plant, such as a rose or an orchid. The seeds of an angiosperm are protected inside an ovary as they grow – the word 'angiosperm' means 'vessel seed'.

Annual A flowering plant that completes its whole life cycle in one year.

Antarctica A vast frozen continent, which surrounds the South Pole.

Anther The male part of a flower, which produces pollen.

Arctic The huge frozen ocean and cold lands around the North Pole.

Biennial A flowering plant that takes two years to complete its life cycle.

Bonsai A potted plant or small tree that is made to grow much smaller than it would do naturally.

Broadleaved tree A tree with wide, flat leaves. It may be an evergreen or a deciduous tree.

Bulb A short underground stem wrapped in swollen leaf bases, such as a daffodil or a tulip bulb.

Calyx A circle of sepals on the outside of a flower.

Camouflage Colours, markings or patterns that help plants to blend in with their surroundings and avoid being eaten.

Carnivorous plant A plant that eats animals, such as insects, as well as making its own food.

Carpel A female part of a flower in which seeds are made. A carpel usually consists of an ovary with a stalk (the style), which has a sticky tip (the stigma).

Cell Basic building block of all living creatures. Cell types have different jobs to do to keep the plant alive.

Chlorophyll A green pigment found in plants, which captures the light energy needed for photosynthesis.

Chloroplast A microscopic sac in green plant cells in which photosynthesis takes place.

Cone The reproductive structure of a typical gymnosperm. Male cones produce pollen, female cones seeds.

Conifer A tree, such as a pine, spruce or larch, which produces cones to make pollen and seeds.

Corm A swollen underground stem that contains stored food. New plants grow from its buds by vegetative propagation. Unlike bulbs, corms do not contain fleshy scales.

Corolla A circle of petals in a flower, inside the calyx.

Cotyledon The first leaf or leaves of a seed plant, found in the seed. Cotyledons store food for the new seedling and may be quite different from the plant's other leaves.

Cycad A gymnosperm, which has long, divided leaves (like a palm) and a massive stem. Male and female cones grow on separate plants.

Deciduous plant A plant that regularly sheds all its leaves, for instance before a very cold or a very dry season.

Dicotyledon A flowering plant with two cotyledons (seed leaves) in its seed. Dicots usually have broad leaves with a network of veins inside them. Their flowers have petals and other parts in fours or fives.

Ephemeral A short-lived plant, which completes its life cycle in a few weeks.

Epiphyte A plant that grows on the surface of other plants for support, but does not take water or food from them. The word 'epiphyte' means 'on top of a plant'.

Evaporation A process by which a liquid changes into a gas, such as liquid water turning into water vapour.

Evergreen A plant that keeps its leaves all year round, such as a fir tree.

Filament The stalk of a flowering plant stamen, which produces pollen.

Food chain A sequence of feeding links showing how plants are eaten by animals, which are, in turn, eaten by other animals.

Fossils The remains of living things, preserved in the rocks.

Frond The leaf of a fern.

Fruiting body A plant structure that makes spores, such as a mushroom.

Fungus (plural: fungi) A living thing that cannot make its own food but absorbs simple food substances from living or dead material.

Germination Process in which a new plant starts to grow from a seed or spore.

Gymnosperm One of the cone-bearing plants (conifers) or their close relatives that make seeds but do not have flowers.

Habitat The natural home of a plant or animal.

Meristem A growing point in a plant, usually at the tip of the roots and shoots.

Monocotyledon A flowering plant with only one cotyledon in its seed. Monocots have long, narrow leaves, with parallel veins. Their flowers have petals and other parts in threes.

Mycelium The network of hyphae that make up the body of a fungus.

Nectar A sugary liquid produced by flowers to attract birds, insects and other animals for pollination.

Ovary The part of the flower that contains ovules.

Ovule The part of the ovary in seed plants that contains the egg cell and develops into the seed after fertilization.

Parasite A plant that obtains its food from another species, usually causing harm to that species.

Perennial A plant that lives for many years.

Phloem The living food pipes inside plants through which sugary sap is carried up and down to all plant parts.

Photosynthesis The process by which green plants use the Sun's energy to turn carbon dioxide and water into sugary plant food.

Pollarding Cutting the top branches of a tree to encourage the growth of many thin stems from this point.

Pollen A fine yellow dust produced by the anthers and male cones of seed plants. Each pollen grain contains a male sex cell.

Pollination The transfer of pollen from the male part of a flower to the female part.

Rainforest A forest near the Equator where the weather is hot and wet all year round.

Respiration A process that takes place inside living cells in which food is 'burnt' in the presence of oxygen to release energy.

Runner A long stem that grows over the ground and then forms a new plant.

Seed A structure that forms from the ovule after fertilization and consists of a tiny plant with a food store, surrounded by a protective casing.

Sepal A leaf-like structure that protects the bud of a flower.

Species A group of similar living things that can breed together to produce fertile young.

Spore A small reproductive structure of a fern, moss, alga or fungus, which is capable of growing into a new plant. Spores are usually made up of one cell and are not the result of fertilization.

Stamen A structure that makes pollen in a flowering plant. A stamen is made up of a stalk, or filament, with sacs of pollen, called anthers, on the end.

Stigma A structure that receives pollen and is usually connected to the ovary by a stalk called a style.

Stomata Tiny holes in the surface of a leaf, which can open and close to control the movement of air and water vapour in and out of the leaf.

Style The stalk that links the stigma (receiving surface for pollen) with the ovary in a flower.

Symbiosis The close association of two different species in which both species benefit. The algae and fungi in a lichen live in a symbiotic partnership.

Taiga The vast coniferous forests that grow across northern Russia and Siberia.

Taproot The long, straight main root in gymnosperms and dicotyledons. In some plants, such as carrots and turnips, the taproot is used to store food.

Transpiration The evaporation of water from the leaves of plants. Transpiration pulls water up from the roots, through the stem and out through the leaves.

Tuber A rounded swelling at the end of an underground root or shoot, such as a potato.

Tundra Cold, treeless areas of the world, around the polar regions.

Vegetative propagation A process in which some plants can produce new plants from a small part of themselves without the need for flowers or seeds.

Xylem A system of water pipes inside plants, made up of columns of dead cells joined together. Water travels up from the roots to the leaves in xylem pipes.

WATER LIFE

Living in Water

Life began in the sea. Most of it remains there. From jellyfish to shellfish to swordfish, the oceans swarm with a vast array of creatures. And not just fish – there are also reptiles, such as sea snakes and turtles, and mammals, such as dolphins and seals.

Amazing

Of all the world's water, less than one-thirtieth is fresh – that is, not salty. Only a hundredth of this one-thirtieth is surface water (on land) – streams, ponds, rivers and lakes.

○ *Starfish are quite unlike any land animals. They have radials, or 'circular', body plans, no proper eyes or brains, and mouths on the undersides of their bodies.*

○ Altogether, oceans cover more than two-thirds of the Earth's surface. Their total area is about 362 million sq km. This means there is more than twice as much ocean as land, and that the oceans are by far the largest habitat for wildlife.

○ There are streams in the oceans. All the water in the oceans is constantly moving, but in some places it flows as currents, which take particular paths. One of these is the warm Gulf Stream that travels around the northern edge of the Atlantic Ocean.

○ Seawater is a 'soup' of tiny floating plants and animals called plankton. Plankton provides food for smaller fish, such as herrings and sardines. In turn, the smaller fish are eaten by larger ones, such as fearsome barracudas and ferocious sharks, building up the ocean food chains.

○ Fish are cold-blooded, with a body temperature the same as the water around them – except for tuna, whose muscles are so large and so active that they produce lots of heat, keeping the tuna 'warm' in the cold sea. Warm muscles work even better, which is why tuna swim so fast.

○ *A hard shell covers and protects the sea turtle's body. Compared to the freshwater turtle, the sea turtle has a flatter, less-domed shell, which helps it to swim faster.*

Find out more
Bluefin tuna p. 146

○ Some air-breathing animals are water-dwellers. They include the biggest creatures on our planet, great whales. Others are peaceful plant-munching manatees, secretive and almost-blind river dolphins, and long-tusked walruses and narwhals.

○ Leatherback turtles are true ocean wanderers. They dive down to depths of 1200 m for dinner. The biggest turtles in the sea (reaching up to 2 m long) they also make the deepest dives. Leatherbacks feed mostly on jellyfish.

How many fish?

There are about as many kinds, or species, of fish – almost 25,000 – as there are all other vertebrate animals (amphibians, reptiles, birds and mammals).

○ Some fish defend themselves with poisons, which they can jab into enemies using their stiff, sharp fin spines. The lionfish, or dragonfish, of Southeast Asia has large, lacy-looking fins and bright colours to warn predators of its venom. In contrast, the stonefish is camouflaged as a piece of rock for protection.

○ Mythical mermaids were believed to lure sailors to their deaths. Folklore tells how mermaids – who were depicted as half woman, half fish – confused sailors with their beautiful singing, with the result that the sailors' ships were wrecked on the rocks.

▲ *Water animals often defend themselves in the same ways as land animals. The porcupine-fish is the 'hedgehog of the sea'. Usually its spines lie flat, but as it gulps in water and swells up, they stick out for protection.*

▼ *Living things in water often look very different from those on land. This branching orange 'tree' is not a plant, but a soft coral – a group or colony of small animals called coral polyps, joined to each other.*

▲ *Porpoises are smaller, blunter-nosed cousins of whales and dolphins. The finless porpoise is one of the smallest, at only 1.5 m long.*

▶ *Aquatic (water-dwelling) animals, such as the octopus, are buoyed up by the water around them. This means their bodies do not need the strong, rigid support required by land animals. An octopus out of water becomes floppy and has trouble moving.*

Coelacanths rediscovered

Fish called coelacanths lived during the age of the dinosaurs, about 250 million years ago, and were thought to be extinct. However, from the 1930s coelacanth have been discovered in the Indian Ocean and also in Southeast Asia.

Range of Water Life

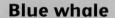

The underwater realm is home to an astonishing diversity of life. Plants range from microscopic one-celled algae to giant oarweeds as big as oak trees on land. Animal life is even more diverse, from weird alien-looking worms thicker than your arm to the largest of all animals, the great whales.

❍ Seaweeds range from tiny to gigantic and are the basis of ocean life. Even some farmers grow seaweed. It is delicious to eat, and is also a useful ingredient in products, such as ice cream and plant fertilizer.

❍ Sponges are the simplest of all creatures. They have no eyes or ears, nerves or brain, bones or muscles, but they are still animals.

▼ *The slate-pencil sea urchin is a member of the huge echinoderm group, which is found not on land nor in freshwater, but only in the salty water of seas and oceans.*

◀ *The leech is one of many thousands of worms that live in water. It grabs onto and sucks the blood of larger animals that wade into the water to drink.*

❍ Sponges have bodies that are made of many microscopic cells, and they take food into their bodies by 'eating'. A sponge sucks water into its bag- or flask-shaped body through many small holes in its wall, absorbs tiny bits of food through the wall's inner lining, and squirts the water out through a larger hole at the top.

❍ There are about 4500 different types of sponge in the sea and a few species in freshwater. The natural sponge that you might use in the bath is a long-dead, dried-out sponge.

▶ *Sometimes the sea-living versions of common land animals can be very dangerous. This coneshell, found in tropical shores, resembles a harmless snail, but it hides a vicious sting that can cause intense pain for many hours.*

Blue whale

The biggest animal on the planet lives in our oceans. It is the amazing blue whale, which can measure up to 30 m in length and can weigh up to a massive 200 tonnes.

▼ *In a large group called a school, fish like these yellow snappers have less chance of being eaten by a predator.*

❍ The most familiar worms are called annelids. They have a long body made of many sections or segments.

❍ Many annelids live in water, including, on the seashore, ragworms, fanworms and tubeworms, in the sea, leaf-shaped, blood-sucking leeches, and, in the stagnant water of swamps and ditches, bloodworms.

Find out more
Feathery feeder p. 169

▲ **Life on a coral reef is based on seaweeds, which vary from large, green plants swaying in the current to tiny growths of algae on the reef rocks.**

◯ A typical fish lives in water, has a long, slim body, large eyes, a finned tail that swishes from side-to-side for swimming, body fins to control its movements, a covering of scales, and feather-like gills on either side of its head that take oxygen from the water.

◯ Many fish lack one or more of these features. Eels are long and thin like snakes and usually scaleless, lungfish can breathe out of water, and many catfish have leathery skin or bony plates rather than scales.

◯ Whales, dolphins, seals, sea lions and walruses are warm-blooded mammals that have adapted to ocean life.

◯ Seals and sea lions are known as pinnipeds, meaning 'fin feet'. They have flippers instead of legs – far more useful for swimming. They also have streamlined, bullet-shaped bodies, and a layer of fatty blubber under the skin, to keep warm in chilly waters.

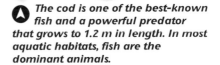

▲ **The cod is one of the best-known fish and a powerful predator that grows to 1.2 m in length. In most aquatic habitats, fish are the dominant animals.**

Amazing

In 2006 scientists discovered the world's smallest fish in a swamp in Sumatra, Southeast Asia. Called paedocypris, this tiny fish is just 8 mm long, the size of this line ——— .

◀ **Gorgonian coral grows in an elaborate system of branches, like a lacy fan. It is made by a colony of tiny, simple, anemone-like animals called coral polyps.**

Sea otters

Sea otters are the smallest sea mammals. These playful creatures live off the Pacific coast among huge forests of giant seaweed, called kelp. They use the kelp to anchor themselves as they sleep. When they take a snooze, they wrap a strand of kelp around their body to stop them being washed out to sea.

Breathing in Water

Gills are like 'inside-out' lungs. They have the same branching, frilly structure, but they are outside the body, in contact with the water. Dissolved oxygen seeps from the water to blood flowing through the gills. Most water-dwellers, including fish and crabs, and molluscs such as octopuses and sea-slugs, have some type of gills.

Amazing

Some fish not only breathe with their gills but feed with them too – the gills have comb-like rakers that gather small bits of food.

Most seals and sea lions can hold their breath for a few minutes under water as they chase prey, such as fish. After hunting they 'haul out' of the ocean and rest on a bank or rock.

Shellfish, like clams, mussels and oysters, have frilly gills inside their shells. The shell must gape open to allow in a flow of water, which brings dissolved oxygen.

❍ In fish gills water flows in through the fish's mouth and over the feathery, thin-walled, blood-filled gills. Oxygen passes from the water to the blood that flows through the gills enabling the fish to 'breathe'. Stripped of oxygen, the water then flows out through the gill slits on either side at the rear of the fish's head.

❍ Lungfish are well-adapted to life in slow, muddy rivers, weedy lakes and shallow swamps. Like other fish they have gills. However, if the water lacks oxygen, for example when it is very shallow and warm, lungfish can also swallow air into their tube-like lungs.

❍ South American and African lungfish can survive drought, when their water dries up, by burrowing into the damp mud beneath the riverbed. As the dry season arrives and the rivers and pools shrink, the lungfish noses and presses the mud aside to form a vase- or tube-shaped chamber. It curls up in here and then its skin makes a layer of mucus (slime). This goes hard to form a waterproof lining or cocoon for the chamber.

Bed in the mud

In their cocoon in the mud, lungfish can survive for several years. They get their nutrients and energy by breaking down their own muscles.

Find out more
African lungfish p. 150

▶ *The gill slit on the 'neck' is clearly visible in this barracuda. The gill flap (operculum) covering the gills themselves is tilted so water can flow out through the slit.*

○ Most sharks must swim continuously, so that water flows over their gills and they can breathe. Some sharks can lie still and make the water flow over their gills by 'pumping' the muscles of their mouth and neck.

○ Whales, dolphins and porpoises have to come to the surface for air. This is because they are mammals, like we are. Sperm whales hold their breath the longest. They have been known to stay underwater for nearly two hours.

○ Amphibians breathe air into lungs, but they can also absorb oxygen and 'breathe' through their skin. However, their skin must stay damp or the oxygen cannot pass through.

○ The axolotl, a type of salamander, keeps its tadpole gills even when adult.

▶ *Moray eels, such as the spotted moray, lurk in cracks and caves. To breathe they open their mouths and turn to face the current, which brings water to flow over the gills.*

▼ *Sea slugs have tufts of gills on their backs, which often contain poisons to deter other animals from nibbling them. The sea-slugs' scientific name – nudibranch – literally means 'naked gill'.*

▼ *When a fish opens its jaws wide to feed or 'yawn', the red, blood-filled gills can be seen on either side at the rear of the mouth chamber.*

○ Some creatures, such as worms and flatworms, have no special parts for respiration. Oxygen can pass straight through their skin. Their flattened shape means that no part inside their body is more than a few millimetres away from the skin, and oxygen can easily seep this distance.

○ There are venomous (poisonous) snakes in the sea. Just like other reptiles they must come to the surface to breathe air into their lungs. Banded sea snakes cruise around coral reefs in search of their favourite food – eels.

How gills work

Like other fish, sharks breathe underwater using their gills. Most sharks have five gill slits on either side. However, the slits are not covered by a hard flap or gill cover as in bony fish.

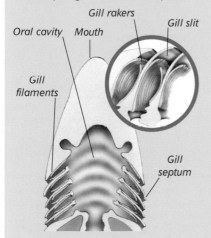

Gill rakers
Gill slit
Oral cavity   Mouth
Gill filaments
Gill septum

Moving in Water

Water is very dense, so streamlining (a smooth body-shape) enables fish, dolphins, seals and other sea creatures to move through it easily. Speedy fish, such as marlin, tuna and wahoo, have long, slim bodies that narrow to a point. Thrust (the force to move forwards) comes from the tail, which is pulled from side to side by huge blocks of muscles along either side of the body.

The scallop's two-part shell is not only for protection. The scallop flaps the two halves, or valves, together and swims jerkily over the seabed propelled by jets of water.

❍ Fish swim using a side-to-side movement of their bodies. Muscles make up approximately 70 per cent of a fish's weight. A fish uses its fins for steering – the tail fin, for example, acts as a rudder.

Fastest fish

Measuring the top speed of big, fast ocean fish is very difficult. But the sailfish can probably reach speeds of about 100 km/h.

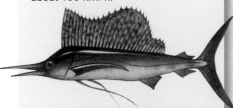

❍ Not all fish are the same shape, and their shape often determines how they move. Flatfish have flat bodies, shaped for lying on the seabed rather than swimming. Eels are long and thin and swim mainly by wriggling – just like a snake – rather than using fins, and by reversing the wriggle they can swim backwards.

❍ Most fish have several fins that help them to swim and cut through the water. On the back are the dorsal fins. Pectoral fins are on the lower sides near the front, and pelvic fins on the lower sides near the tail. The anal fin is on the underside just in front of the tail. The tail itself is called the caudal fin. A shark's dorsal (back) fin stops its whole body swinging from side to side while swimming.

❍ A dolphin's tail, called its flukes, looks similar to a fish's tail. A dolphin swims by arching its body up and down, not bending from side-to-side like a fish. Its flukes are not its 'legs' – they have no bones within them. However, its flippers, like a seal's flippers, are its 'arms', with hand and finger bones inside.

Amazing

The slowest fish are certain kinds of seahorses. They swim with just the dorsal fin on the back and have a top speed of 0.015 km/h, which is about 4 mm per second.

Swift and fierce, makos are strong, muscular hunting sharks that can swim at great speed. They have long, streamlined bodies with very pointed snouts, and grow up to 4 m in length.

Rays, like the stingray, swim by rippling their side 'wings', which are really their fleshy pectoral fins.

Sea turtles move by 'flying' with their flippers. The flippers flap up and down in a figure-of-eight motion and work like the wings of a bird, rather than pushing water backwards like oars or paddles.

Find out more
Fastest penguin p. 153

◔ A fish's shape gives clues to how fast it swims. The yellowtail surgeonfish has a tall, bulky body and small triangular tail, which means it is a relatively slow mover.

❍ Penguins have strong wings but they cannot fly – at least, not in the air. However, they make flapping movements very similar to flying when they are swimming underwater.

❍ The limbs of seals are modified into powerful flippers that help in swimming. A seal's strong, torpedo-shaped body makes it a great swimmer.

❍ Eared seals have long rear flippers that are more mobile than those of true seals. Their front flippers are also large and more powerful. Eared seals mainly use their front flippers to paddle.

◔ The conger eel grows to 3 m long. Eels have no separate tail fin but one, long 'wraparound' fin along the back, rear-end and underside. They are not strong swimmers and spend much time hiding in cracks and caves.

▲ The penguin holds its beak, head and neck out straight in front and folds its feet back, to make itself more streamlined, for greater swimming speed.

Kicking and swimming

Many animals live both on land and in water, so they use their legs and feet to run and swim. Otters, crocodiles and frogs have toes that are joined with flaps of skin, called webbing, to make a broad surface area for kicking and swimming. The webbed rear feet kick to swim and the front legs steer through water. Frogs also move by leaping, which enables them to escape from predators quickly.

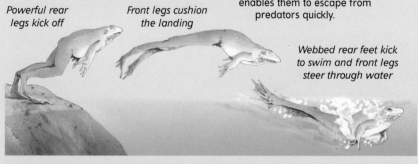

Powerful rear legs kick off

Front legs cushion the landing

Webbed rear feet kick to swim and front legs steer through water

Freshwater Food Chains

A *food chain occurs when a plant is eaten by a herbivorous animal,* which is then eaten by a carnivorous animal, and so on. Food chains link together into food webs. In freshwater many food chains begin with water plants, such as water-lilies or pondweeds, as well as plants around the banks, such as rushes, reeds and sedges.

Sensitive fish

A catfish is a 'living tongue' with taste buds over most of its body. It can also detect tiny electrical pulses from the living bodies of other creatures nearby, allowing the catfish to find prey hidden in the mud.

The blood-sucking river lamprey is only one of many parasites that infest larger water animals.

Amazing

The food chain between a seaweed and a swordfish can have as many as a dozen links.

The Nile crocodile cannot chew. It often holds its prey and then spins around like a spinning top to tear off chunks that are small enough to swallow.

○ Food chains in water tend to be longer than those on land. In a river the chain might have six or seven links: for example, from plant to river snail, small fish, crayfish, larger fish, otter and finally crocodile.

○ The water flea, or pond flea, daphnia, is a crustacean named after its similarity to an insect. It has two antennae (feelers), which have many branches like tiny trees.

○ Water fleas are very common inhabitants of ponds and streams. They eat microscopic bits of plant and tiny creatures, and in turn are important food for fish, grubs, worms and similar creatures.

○ Many small or young fish are 'minnows', but the minnow is also a distinct kind, or species. It is only 10 cm long and a common victim of bigger fish. Minnows are common links in food chains between tiny plants and animals and larger predators.

Eating the dead

Snapping turtles feed on carrion, such as drowned deer and pigs, finding them by smell. They have been used to locate the bodies of people murdered and thrown into deep lakes.

● *The painted terrapin eats mainly water plants, but it also eats some worms and grubs. Animals like this that eat both plants and creatures are known as omnivores.*

● *The water opossum, or yapok, of South America links food chains in water and on land. It hunts in pools and rivers for fish, frogs, crayfish and insects. Then it returns to land to rest, sleep and breed – and perhaps be caught by a land predator, such as a jaguar.*

❍ The stone loach, like the minnow, is a common link in freshwater food chains. It feeds on small worms and other little creatures in the stones and mud, and is then eaten by larger fish.

❍ A fish of fast and gravel-bottomed rivers, the nase lives in Europe and western Asia. It is a herbivore and scrapes small plants off the stones with its hard, horny lips.

❍ The pike is a powerful hunter up to 100 cm long with a mouthful of sharp teeth. It dashes out of water plants to ambush its prey. In many rivers and lakes, it is the top carnivore at the end of various food chains.

❍ The lamprey usually lives as a parasite. It sticks onto a larger fish, its host, and rasps its way through the skin to suck the fish's blood and body fluids. Lampreys are very strange fish, with an almost prehistoric body design. They lack jaws: the mouth is a round sucker edged with tiny teeth.

● *The pike seizes its prey with its long, wide mouth armed with small but very sharp teeth. Pike live in weedy lakes and rivers all around the northern parts of the world.*

❍ The Nile crocodile is the top predator in many watery areas of Africa. It grabs large animals or birds that come to drink, drags them under the surface to drown them, then tears off chunks of flesh and bone to swallow. One meal can last a Nile crocodile six months.

● *The great crested newt, an amphibian, may be hand-sized but it could be the top carnivore in a small pond. It is a fierce hunter of smaller water animals, like worms, aquatic insects and baby fish.*

Find out more

Marshes and swamps pp. 150–151

Marine Food Chains

Plants are the basis of all food chains, but plants seem to be missing in the open ocean. However, they are there, in the form of tiny floating algae called phytoplankton. They are eaten by tiny animals, called zooplankton, and so the oceanic food chains build up.

○ Copepods are crustaceans that are amongst the most numerous of all animals. Each one has a shield-like body-case and fringed limbs that it waves to swim. It also uses these to gather food. In the sea, copepods feed and reproduce in the brightly lit water close to the surface. Vast clusters or swarms of copepods feed on microscopic plants and animals. Along with krill, copepods are the main food for fish and other sea animals.

Fast food in the sea

Herring are a family of small, silvery marine fish that swim in large schools. They are often found in the temperate, shallow waters of the North Atlantic and the North Pacific. Herring feed on small fish and plankton. They are, in turn, an important part of the diet of larger creatures, such as sharks, seals, whales and seabirds. There are more than 360 species (kinds) in the herring family, which includes fish such as sardines, anchovies, shad, menhaden and sprats.

○ Krill look like small shrimps and are usually 2 to 3 cm long. Millions of them, along with other small creatures, make up plankton. Krill are eaten by many creatures including seabirds, penguins, fish like the huge whale shark, and great whales.

○ Marine iguanas are plant eaters, or herbivores. Most lizards prefer life on land, where it is easier to warm up their cold-blooded bodies, but marine iguanas depend on the sea for their food. They dive underwater to graze on the algae and seaweed growing on the rocks and corals.

Rays, like the spotted stingray, crunch up shellfish that they find buried in the sand by detecting tiny weak pulses of natural electricity from the shellfish's muscles.

○ Killer whales are types of dolphin and live in all seas, even in cold Arctic and Antarctic regions. They feed on many kinds of fish, squid and similar prey. They are also the only type of whale or dolphin that regularly hunts warm-blooded victims, including porpoises, great whales, seals, sea lions and seabirds (such as penguins) – and even other dolphins.

Sharks, like this sand tiger shark, are meat-eating fish, and nearly all of them live in the sea. Some chase prey, others lie in wait to grab victims. Others are scavengers, feasting on the dying and dead bodies of other animals, such as whales and seals.

The lionfish is at the end of a food chain. Almost no hunter attempts to eat it, because of the poison in its sharp fin spines. However, when it dies it becomes food for detritivores – small worms, crabs and similar creatures that consume the rotting flesh of carcasses.

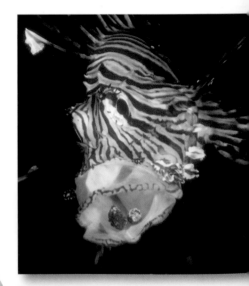

Find out more

Greenland sharks p. 153

Large fish like the lunar-tail grouper gulp down one meal and then rest or swim slowly for several days, until hungry again. Grumpers usually hide under rocky overhangs or in cages.

○ Many seabirds eat fish or squid. The gannet's feeding technique is to plummet headfirst into the ocean and catch a fish in its beak. It dives at speed and hits the water hard. The gannet's head is protected with sacs of air that absorb most of the shock.

○ Fish, such as herring, have no obvious protection except for their darting speed – and being in a huge group. The colony moves together, twisting and turning almost as one. The effect is to make the shoal resemble a single massive animal, a 'super-organism' to confuse, or frighten off, predators.

Amazing

Basking sharks are the second-biggest of all fish, reaching 10 m in length and 6 tonnes in weight. Like whale sharks, basking sharks filter small animals, such as krill, and other bits of food from the sea.

Krill-eater seal

The crabeater seal is a poorly named water animal. It lives and feeds in the Southern Ocean where there are, in fact, no crabs – its main food is krill.

Shark diets

The porbeagle shark uses its keen eyesight to chase after its favourite food of small shoaling fish, such as mackerel. With a sudden swish of its tail, it dashes into the shoal and picks out a victim.

The thresher's tail is as long as its body. It swipes the tail at speed through the water to slap and stun smaller fish, which the thresher then returns to bite into pieces or swallow whole.

The tiger shark is famous for trying to eat nearly everything, in the hope that it might be tasty. However, some of the items it swallows are not even food – such as tin cans and beach shoes.

The wobbegong is well camouflaged to blend into rocks and seaweed. It lies in wait for smaller fish, or similar prey, to swim just above it, then it rears up to grab them.

The silvertip shark is a sleek, fast swimmer that pursues other midwater creatures, mainly smaller fish, by making a surprise lunge.

Breeding in Water

Compared with land animals, water animals and plants have one benefit when breeding: they can use water currents in a river or sea to carry away their eggs or seeds and spread them far and wide. This means some water creatures are found in almost every sea and ocean around the world.

Scented courtship

Sharks have a complicated way of getting together, known as courtship. They give off scents, or 'perfumes', into the water to attract a partner. Then the two rub one another, wind their bodies around each other, and maybe even bite the other.

○ Cuttlefish normally live alone but they come together in small shoals to breed. Each cuttlefish uses colour and pattern to signal its readiness to mate as waves of black, yellow and brown stripes pass rapidly along its body.

○ On land a female and male animal usually mate when the sperm pass into the female's body to fertilize the eggs – internal fertilization. However, in water, many kinds of frogs, fish, shellfish, worms and other animals simply release their eggs and sperm into the water, and leave fertilization to chance – this is external fertilization.

▲ After baby turtles hatch from their eggs, they must dig their way up to the surface and then race down the beach to the sea. Many predators, such as lizards, foxes, otters, jackals, and gulls and other seabirds, gather along the shore to feast on the susceptible babies.

○ Water creatures attract a mate at breeding time, just like animals on land. Sounds and scents travel much farther in the water than in air, and sounds go faster too, so many water-dwellers make use of these to draw the attention of a breeding partner.

○ Whales, dolphins and porpoises, in particular, make a whole range of squeaks, clicks and grunts as they court. As they come closer to each other they also use touch – they will stroke and caress their partners, too.

▼ Female turtles return to the beach where they hatched to dig their nests. After they have laid their eggs, they go straight back to the water. Hawksbill turtles may lay up to 140 eggs in a clutch (a single nest), while some green turtle females clock up 800 eggs in a year.

Find out more

Travelling salmon p. 146

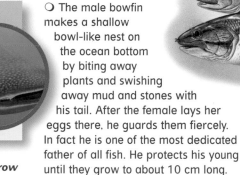

Baby sharks

Some sharks have hundreds of babies at once. The whale shark may give birth to as many as 300 pups, each about 60 cm long.

○ Some fish change sex as they grow up. Groupers may start as males, then turn into females as they get bigger. This depends partly on how many other male and female groupers there are in the area.

○ A baby catshark develops slowly in its protective case, called a mermaid's purse. As it gets larger its store of food, the yolk, shrinks. Finally it hatches after about eight months.

○ The male bowfin makes a shallow bowl-like nest on the ocean bottom by biting away plants and swishing away mud and stones with his tail. After the female lays her eggs there, he guards them fiercely. In fact he is one of the most dedicated father of all fish. He protects his young until they grow to about 10 cm long.

○ Some sharks gather in large groups, or shoals, to breed. Hammerheads come together in hundreds or even thousands, so the females and males can choose partners for mating. Bonnet-head, nurse and dogfish sharks also form breeding shoals.

Amazing

Male seahorses have the babies. They don't exactly give birth, but they store the eggs in a pouch on their belly. When the eggs are ready to hatch, a stream of miniature seahorses billows out from the male's pouch.

○ The male bowfin of North America is larger than the female, has a spot at the top of his tail, and provides more parental care for his young than almost any other fish in the ocean.

○ Some mother sharks, such as mother catsharks, lay eggs. Each egg has a strong case in which there is a developing baby shark, called an embryo. The case has long threads, which stick to seaweed or rocks. Look out for empty egg cases on beaches. They are known as mermaids' purses.

○ In some areas all the coral animals breed at once, usually to fit in with the tides and currents of the ocean. The corals release so many eggs and sperm into the water that it turns cloudy and if you are underwater you can see only a few metres ahead. Gradually the cloudiness is swept away and spread out by the currents.

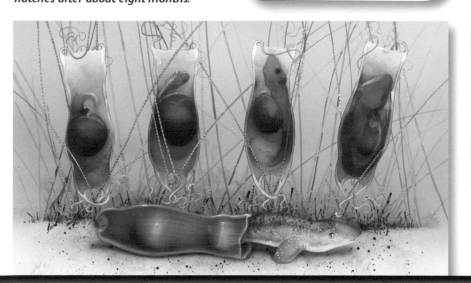

○ The sailfin goby erects its dorsal fin, holding it up like a sail when it wants to warn away another goby in its territory – or when it wants to attract a partner at mating time.

Long-distance Swimmers

Animals such as whales and birds combine methods of navigating – using the position of the Sun, Moon and stars, large landmarks such as mountains or cliffs, and even the Earth's magnetic field. Turtles, lobsters and fish navigate using the 'smell' and 'taste' of natural chemicals that change in different rivers or parts of the ocean.

❍ Most billfish, like the white marlin, make seasonal migrations. They move north or south in summer and return to the tropics in winter. The white is the smallest of the four kinds of marlin, weighing about 70 to 80 kg. It lives in the warmer regions of the Atlantic Ocean. (Largest is the black marlin at 700 kg or more.)

❍ The alewife, a type of shad and cousin to the herring, migrates like the salmon. It grows up along the Atlantic coasts of North America, then swims up rivers to spawn (lay eggs). It reaches about 40 cm in length. However, some alewives stay all their lives in freshwater, mainly in the Great Lakes of the USA and Canada, and are smaller.

❍ Many types of shark travel long distances in the course of their lives. As all the world's seas and oceans are connected, it's easy for sharks to cover huge distances.

◉ *Flyingfish have enlarged side fins that work as wings. They do not flap but glide across the water's surface. For their size these fish make great journeys, travelling hundreds of kilometres in a few days to new feeding grounds.*

◉ *Bluefin tuna are powerful, muscular fish that can reach speeds of 90 km/h. Their muscles make so much heat that these fish become warm-blooded. They feed in large shoals on different types of fish, then swim more than 2000 km in a few days to coastal areas to breed.*

◉ *Spiny lobsters spend the summer feeding off the coast of Florida, but head south in autumn to deeper waters. They travel about 50 km along the seabed, in columns that may be more than 50 lobsters strong. They keep together by touch, using their long, spiky antennae (feelers).*

❍ Blue sharks make the longest migrations of all sea animals. They follow the Gulf Stream current across the Atlantic from the Caribbean Sea to Europe, and swim south along the African coast, then cross the Atlantic again to return to the Caribbean. A blue shark can cover a distance of more than 6000 km in less than one year.

❍ Sharks may have a built-in compass. People use magnetic compasses to find their way across the seas or remote lands. The compass detects the natural magnetism of the Earth and points north–south. Sharks may be able to detect the Earth's magnetism too, using tiny parts of their bodies, and this could help them find their way across oceans. Other animals, such as certain birds and turtles, can also do this.

Travelling salmon

Salmon spend from two to six years in their home river, then head out to sea where they grow up to 1.5 m long, and become powerful and fast as they feed on smaller fish. After between one and four years at sea, they head back upriver to breed in the stream where they hatched. Most then die, but some make the journey twice.

Find out more
Indus River dolphin p. 149

▶ Some killer whales, or orcas, are always on the move. They cover thousands of kilometres yearly and are known as 'transients'. Yet other groups, or pods, of killers are 'residents' who stay within a small area for most of their lives.

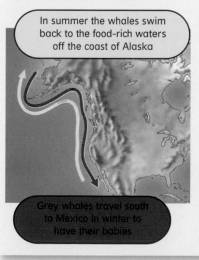

▲ River dolphins make seasonal journeys, following their food, such as fish. They may cover several hundred kilometres through one year.

Grey whales

Grey whales migrate, or travel, farther than any other mammal. The whales may swim nearly 20,000 km in a year, journeying there and back between Mexico and Alaska.

In summer the whales swim back to the food-rich waters off the coast of Alaska

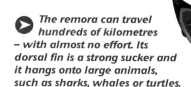

Grey whales travel south to Mexico in winter to have their babies

▶ The remora can travel hundreds of kilometres – with almost no effort. Its dorsal fin is a strong sucker and it hangs onto large animals, such as sharks, whales or turtles.

○ Baby loggerhead turtles make a two-year journey. They are born on beaches in Japan. The hatchlings hurry to the sea and set off across the Pacific to Mexico – a journey of 10,000 km. They spend about five years in Mexico, then return to Japan to breed.

○ The secretive and little-known river dolphins live in some of the largest rivers in the world. There are five kinds, or species – two in the Indian region, two in South America and one in China. Their regular journeys along the river to follow prey during their seasonal migrations are greatly disrupted by dams, hydroelectrics schemes and irrigation channels.

○ Common eels hatch in the Sargasso Sea in the West Atlantic and drift to Europe with the ocean currents, developing as larvae. They grow up in freshwater rivers and lakes, and swim back to the Sargasso Sea to mate.

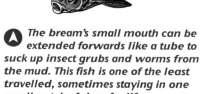

▲ The bream's small mouth can be extended forwards like a tube to suck up insect grubs and worms from the mud. This fish is one of the least travelled, sometimes staying in one small patch of river for life.

Amazing

Many kinds of microscopic sea plants (algae) migrate vertically – up and down. They rise to the surface by day to use the Sun's light for growth, then sink by night away from the small surface animals who eat them.

Rivers and Lakes

A river provides many habitats for different animals. It starts as a stream of cold, clear water rushing over a stony bed, slows into a small river with a sandy bed and tree-fringed banks, and finally becomes wide, sluggish and muddy-bottomed. Lakes also vary greatly – for example, from shallow to very deep.

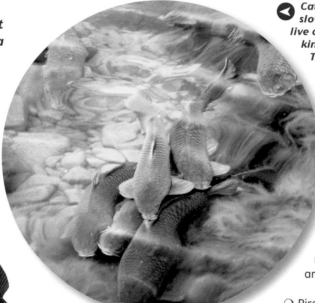

❍ Catfish tend to favour deep lakes, slow rivers, and canals. They usually live on or near the bottom, eating all kinds of worms and similar food. They use their long 'whiskers', called barbels, to detect prey.

❍ In a pond the dragonfly's eggs hatch into young forms called nymphs. Like the tadpole, the nymph does not look much like its parent, lacking wings. But, like its parent, it is a fierce hunter of small prey.

◀ *The piranha's teeth are very sharp but also thin, like triangular blades. They easily snap if the prey struggles to get free.*

❍ The smooth newt preys on many small water creatures – including small fish, worms and even its own tadpoles.

❍ Rainbow trout are fish of fast-flowing streams, where the water contains plenty of dissolved oxygen. Some kinds stay in freshwater all their lives. Steelhead rainbows migrate out to sea, like salmon, and then return to breed.

❍ Piranhas have razor-sharp teeth and gather around a large animal in the water to tear off chunks of flesh. They live in South American rivers and swamps. They feed on other fish and insects and fruit, but as a ferocious predatory group they can attack and kill small mammals and even humans.

◀ *Most pelicans live near freshwater. They are strong swimmers and the largest diving birds of all. They use the stretchy throat pouch as a scoop for catching fish.*

Freshwater shark

Only one kind of shark regularly travels up rivers, especially in South America. The bull shark has attacked people fishing, washing or bathing in lakes, 2000 km from the sea.

○ The sturgeon is a huge fish, up to 3 m long, that lives for part of each year around the sea coast. In spring it swims up rivers to breed. The female lays more than two million small, sticky, black eggs, which people collect and eat as a delicacy called caviar.

○ River otters swim at great speed, twisting around in a split second as they chase prey. The main forward force comes from the otter pushing with the rear webbed feet. The front feet are held against the body except when moving slowly, when the otter paddles with all four feet.

○ The river otter's bushy whiskers can feel the way in muddy water, to detect prey such as worms and shellfish by touch. When swimming fast, the otter stretches its head and neck out forwards to make its front end more pointed and streamlined.

○ On their migration upriver, salmon swish their long, flexible bodies to swim against the current, leaping up rapids and waterfalls more than 3 m high.

○ River dolphins have tiny eyes and are almost blind, because sight is little use in muddy water. However, they can swim fast and hunt food using the squeaks and clicks of echolocation or sonar, like other dolphins (and also bats). They find their prey of fish and similar animals by sound too, grabbing the victims in their long beaks equipped with more than 100 small, sharp teeth.

○ The Indus River dolphin has tiny eyes and is almost blind. It travels through muddy water by using echolocation, or by feeling its way – it drags its flipper through the riverbed.

Amazing

The huge mouth of the wels, or European catfish, is big enough to swallow a two-year-old child.

○ As the boto river dolphin comes to the surface and breathes out, the noise it produces sounds like a human sigh. Its back has a low hump rather than a dorsal fin.

Fighting-fish

These small fish, only 5 to 7 cm long, live naturally in ponds and sluggish rivers in the Thailand region. The males have been bred for thousands of years to produce many different varieties of fighting-fish, in an array of colours and sizes. Some have very long fins, which they spread out as a threat to rivals.

○ Each type of fish has its own preference for water speed, temperature and clarity. The grayling prefers clear, cool streams and brooks.

Greatest aquatic freshwater habitats

River Amazon	South America	Most water, 200,000 cu m/sec
River Nile	Africa	Longest, 6695 km
Lake Superior	North America	Greatest area, 82,400 sq km
Lake Baikal	Central Asia	Deepest, 1620 km

Marshes and Swamps

During a long, hot summer, some marshes may start to dry out. The pools shrink, and water creatures are crowded into smaller areas. The heat also drives oxygen from the water, so aquatic animals that breathe underwater by gills begin to suffocate.

African lungfish

African lungfish fish grow to 2 m long and are fearsome hunters of smaller water creatures, such as fish, frogs, crayfish, lizards and water birds. At breeding time the male wriggles and digs a hole in the sand or mud for the female to lay her eggs. He guards these while they develop and hatch.

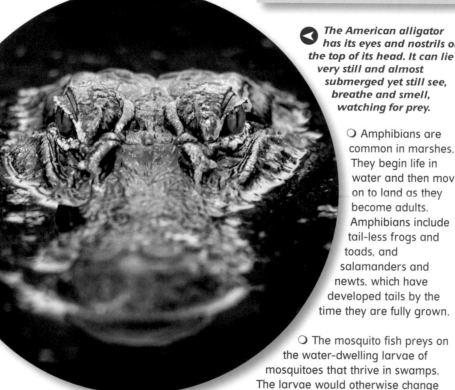

The American alligator has its eyes and nostrils on the top of its head. It can lie very still and almost submerged yet still see, breathe and smell, watching for prey.

❍ Amphibians are common in marshes. They begin life in water and then move on to land as they become adults. Amphibians include tail-less frogs and toads, and salamanders and newts, which have developed tails by the time they are fully grown.

❍ The mosquito fish preys on the water-dwelling larvae of mosquitoes that thrive in swamps. The larvae would otherwise change into adults and become pests.

The arapaima, or pirarucu, can breathe by gills and also by gulping air into its throat and down to its swim bladder. This huge fish of the Amazon region grows to lengths of more than 4 m and can weigh more than 200 kg.

❍ Some marsh animals cope with a drought by 'sleeping'. They enter a period of inactivity called aestivation, similar to hibernation. They burrow deep into the damp mud for protection and stay there until the autumn rains fill the pools again.

❍ Like other lungfish, the South American type does not breathe air through its nostrils as in land animals. It gulps air down its throat and gullet (oesophagus) and through a slit into its lungs. This lungfish reaches about 1.2 m in length and, like its African relative, its lower fins are long feelers.

❍ Reptiles are common in many swamps in warmer regions. Crocodiles and alligators lurk in the shallow muddy water. Various kinds of snakes swim well and some dive after fish and frogs. Freshwater turtles grab small animals or graze on the waterweeds.

❍ Several kinds of wading birds are found in marshy areas. Herons stand very still, waiting for a fish or frog to swim past, so they can jab it with their spear-like beak.

❍ Many kinds of snail live in the water of swamps and marshes. Most feed on water plants, rasping at them with a tiny, file-like 'tongue', called a radula, covered with hundreds of tiny teeth.

▲ Crested newts hide among pond weeds and water plants during breeding season. But as summer passes, they leave the water to hunt for their food on land.

Reddish egret

The reddish egret, a small heron, stalks prey in shallow water much more than its fellow herons or egrets. It often runs fast using the shadows from its wings to drive prey before it.

Amazing

In some tropical swamps the water can be more than 40°C – far too hot for us to bathe in. Decaying plants make the water acidic – it would rot our clothes in a couple of days. Yet fish and other creatures live here.

▶ As the climbing perch's marshy pool dries out, the fish can wriggle across land to another pool. It uses its strong pectoral (lower front) fins and the spikes on its gill covers to grip the ground, assisted by its tail, to move.

Find out more

Amazing p. 135

▶ The black caiman is the largest predator in South America. It can grow to 4.5 m long and lives in the swamps and pools of the Amazon region.

○ Swamps are home to various parasites – animals that live on others. Among such parasites are leeches. There are different types of leech for each type of host animal, such as the fish leech and the pond-snail leech.

○ To feed, the leech rasps a hole in the host's skin using its rounded mouth, edged with sharp, toothlike spines. It sucks up the blood and can swallow up to five times its own weight during a single meal.

○ The European pond turtle spends the cold winter in hibernation. Inactive in the mud at the bottom of the swamp, it wakes up in spring to feed and breed. But if the pools dry out, it enters aestivation (a drought-induced 'sleep') and once again stays inactive on the bottom.

○ Marshy pools are the 'nursery' for young forms of various insects, such as dragonflies, damselflies, caddisflies, mayflies and stoneflies. These are young forms of larvae, are wingless and also important food for frogs, fish and waterbirds.

Aquatic Extremes

On land, extreme conditions include scorching deserts and icy mountain-tops. Water habitats have many extremes too, including low and high temperatures, fast currents, and coastal salt lagoons, where the water is ten times saltier than seawater.

○ Brine shrimps can hatch from eggs that have been wetted after being dried out and preserved for more than 1000 years. These shrimps, like crustaceans, can also survive in water full of salt that is so hot it would almost scald us. These conditions are found in salty lagoons and salt pans in hot regions.

○ Few creatures can survive in the dark, icy-cold ocean depths. Food is so hard to come by, the deep-sea anglerfish does not waste energy chasing prey – it has developed a clever fishing trick. A stringy 'fishing rod' with a glowing tip extends from its dorsal fin or hangs above its jaw. This attracts smaller fish towards the anglerfish's big mouth.

○ Male emperor penguins balance an egg on their feet. They do this to keep their egg off the Antarctic ice, where it would freeze. The female leaves her mate with the egg to survive temperatures of −40°C for the whole two months that it takes for the egg to hatch. The male has to go without food during this time.

▼ *Animals of polar regions include polar bears and walruses, which are found in the Arctic (left), and penguins, which are found only in the Antarctic (right).*

○ Beluga whales live for part of the year among the icebergs and floes of the Arctic. Related to dolphins, the adult beluga whale is milky white in colour. Its name is derived from the Russian word *belukha*, meaning white. Belugas do not have a dorsal fin, which makes swimming under ice much easier.

▲ *This mother polar bear and her cubs are swimming in water that is below the freezing point of 0°C. The salt in seawater, and its continual movement with waves and currents, mean it does not freeze until several degrees below zero.*

Seal pup

Polar bear

Ribbon seal

Adelie penguin

Leopard seal

Emperor penguin

Squid

Chinstrap penguin

Ice fish

Walrus

Gentoo penguin

Harp seal

Common seal

Crabeater seal

○ **Bowhead whales venture farther north into icier water than any other large whale. They also have the biggest mouth of any whale, and the longest baleen (whalebone) at more than 4 m.**

○ Northern fur seals are found in the icy-cold waters of the North Pacific, particularly in the Bering Sea and the Okhotsk Sea. They have small external ears, and a thick layer of fat, or blubber, protects the northern fur seal from the extremely cold temperatures.

○ Fur seals also have dense fur, arranged in two layers. The coat has a thick undercoat of soft fur, covered by longer, coarser hair. These seals keep themselves warm by trapping air in their fur, providing a layer of insulation.

○ Some water animals never see daylight. They live their whole lives in underground lakes and streams in dark caves, feeding on bits and pieces washed into the cave from outside. They include blind fish, salamanders, shrimps and snails.

○ The walrus lies on the Arctic ice and 'sunbathes' in temperatures lower than −20°C. The male walrus is much larger than the female. He grows to 3.3 m long and more than 1200 kg in weight.

○ Anglerfish live in the deep black sea. They have a huge head and mouth. They also have numerous sharp teeth to trap their prey. Some anglerfish are only half a metre in length, while others grow up to 2 m.

○ **Arctic water is very cold, so Greenland sharks can swim only very slowly. Sometimes they lie on the seabed for days on end. The Greenland shark eats the meat from all kinds of dead bodies. These include whales, seals, dolphins, other sharks, squid and even drowned land animals, such as reindeer.**

○ **Fur seals, like the Northern fur seal, spend hours grooming themselves. They use their teeth and claws to spread waterproofing skin oils over their fur and to make sure the fur is free from mud and tangles, so it works well to keep in body heat.**

Fastest penguin

The fastest swimming bird is the gentoo penguin, which races under the water. It has been known to swim at speeds of 27 km/h.

Fencing whales

The 5-m-long narwhal is the most northerly of all mammals, surviving in the freezing Arctic seas. It has only two teeth. In the male of the species, the upper left incisor keeps growing and becomes a long, sharp tusk that can reach nearly 3 m in length. The other tooth stays about 20 cm long.

Amazing

Some hot springs have 'superheated' water. The water is under such great pressure as it spurts from cracks in the rocks, that it is hotter than boiling, yet some tiny life-forms called bacteria can live in it.

○ **Belugas are very noisy whales, making many different sounds from clicks to squeaks and squeals. These sounds echo between and under icebergs, making it difficult to locate the beluga's exact position.**

Rocky Seashores

The rocky shore is a very tough habitat with crashing waves, rolling boulders, hot sun, driving rain, chilly winds and the rise and fall of the tides. Almost any rock pool has inhabitants, such as anemones, crabs, shrimp, starfish, shellfish and small fish – and mainly gobies with their slippery leathery skin, big blunt heads, strong spiny fins and tapering tails.

Amazing

Some rocky islands are home to more than 50,000 gannets, which breed there every summer. The combined noise of their loud, harsh 'arrh' and 'urrah' calls can almost deafen a person.

○ Large seaweeds called kelp have long stems that anchor to the rocks below. They form a 'floating underwater forest' where many kinds of animals live, feed and hide.

○ Rock pools are teeming with all kinds of creatures. Limpets are a kind of shellfish. They live on rocks and in pools at shorelines. Here, they eat slimy, green algae. They have to withstand the crashing tide and to do so they cling to the rock with their muscular foot, only moving when the tide is out.

▶ *The male common dragonet is 30 cm long and a very colourful fish, with two tall back fins like brightly patterned yacht sails. Common dragonets live along the rocky shores of the East Atlantic Ocean and the Mediterranean Sea.*

▼ *Almost every crack, crevice and cave on a rocky shore is occupied – here by a scarlet shore crab. Crabs in particular battle with each other for the best hidey-holes.*

○ Starfish glide slowly over rocks. They can grow new arms. They may have as many as 40 arms, or rays. If a predator grabs hold of one, the starfish abandons the ray, and uses the others to make its getaway.

○ Some sea urchins wear a disguise. Green sea urchins sometimes drape themselves with bits of shell, pebble and seaweed. This makes the urchin more difficult for predators, or hunters, to spot in a rock pool.

○ The pale, mottled, silvery-brown of the rock goby is ideal camouflage on a seabed scattered with rocks and stones. Its fin spines are stiff and sharp, especially along the back (dorsal) fins. This puts off gulls, otters, bass, octopuses and other predators.

▲ *The seahorse usually hides among the seaweeds, rocks and coral of a rocky shore, holding on against the current and waves with its curly tail.*

Noisy gulls

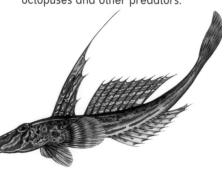

Kittiwakes belong to the gull family. It is believed that they were named because of their call, which sounds like 'kitti-wake'. They nest in large colonies on narrow cliff ledges. In fact they are the only species in the gull family that makes its nests on cliffs.

Find out more

Crabs pp. 170–171

Borrowed shells

The hermit crab borrows the leftover shell of a dead whelk or other mollusc – whatever it can squeeze into to protect its soft body.

When the tide comes in, anemones spread their stinging tentacles to catch small prey. As the retreating tide leaves the rocks dry, the anemones pull in their tentacles and look like blobs of pink jelly.

○ Like other gobies, the tiger goby feeds on a variety of small or young rock-pool creatures, such as sand shrimp, prawns, crabs and sea snails. Its stripes conceal it among the fronds of seaweeds and sea grasses, such as eel-grass. Its thick-skinned, tough-scaled, slimy body allows it to wriggle between pebbles.

○ Epaulette sharks can leave the water and move over dry land. They can drag themselves along the seashore from one rock pool to the next by using their strong pectoral fins like arms.

○ The oystercatcher feeds not only on oysters, but on mussels, clams, limpets and many other kinds of shellfish, and also on crabs, shrimps and worms. It has a chisel-like bill and strong neck muscles to stab and strike its food, carefully picking its spot to crack or lever open the shell.

Steller's sea lion is the largest type of sea lion, the male growing to almost 3 m in length. It lives along the rocky shores of the North Pacific Ocean, diving down nearly 200 m in search of squid, octopus and fish.

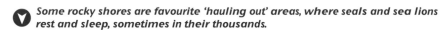

Some rocky shores are favourite 'hauling out' areas, where seals and sea lions rest and sleep, sometimes in their thousands.

Rock Pools

A rock pool is like a miniature underwater jungle. Most anemones are fixed to the rock, but shellfish, such as limpets, whelks and winkles, can glide slowly from under seaweed fronds. Then the high tide returns and brings with it cooler water and perhaps a dead fish or other source of food for scavengers such as the hermit crab and the shore crab.

Limpet

Blenny fish

Shrimp

Anemone

Crab

Starfish

Find out more

Borrowed shells p. 155

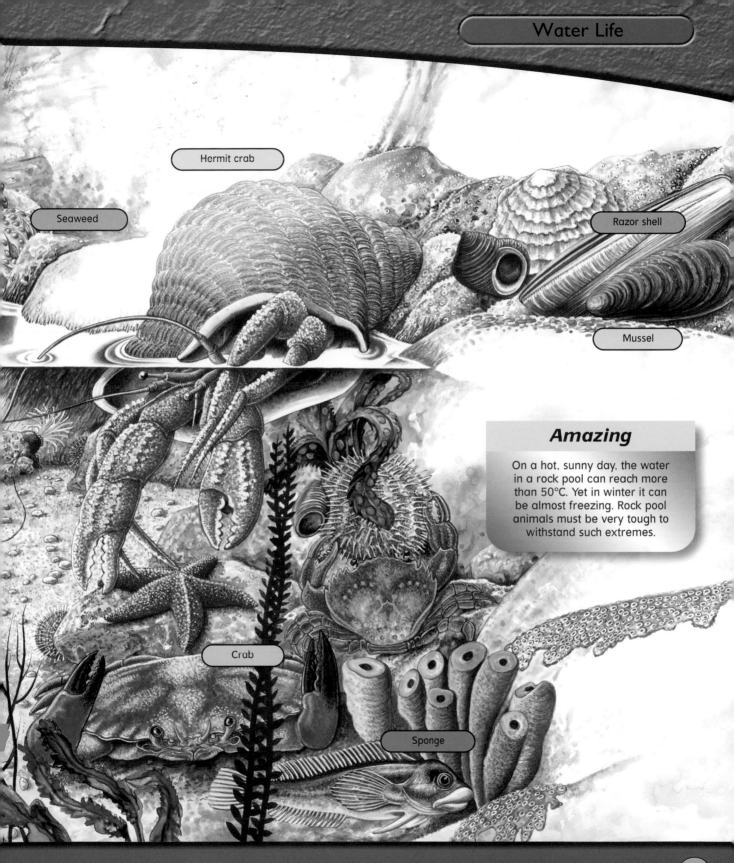

Hermit crab

Seaweed

Razor shell

Mussel

Amazing

On a hot, sunny day, the water in a rock pool can reach more than 50°C. Yet in winter it can be almost freezing. Rock pool animals must be very tough to withstand such extremes.

Crab

Sponge

Sandy Shores

When the tide is out, a sandy shore seems completely empty of living animals. However, just below the sandy surface are worms, shellfish, crabs, urchins and a host of other shore creatures all waiting for the sea to return.

○ Sand-eels are not proper eels but long, slim, eel-shaped members of the perch family, and close cousins of gobies. They grow to about 20 cm long and can quickly wriggle like worms into the sandy seabed, almost out of sight.

○ Carpet sharks are bottom-dwelling sharks. They have beautiful patterns on their skin that help them to blend in with their surroundings. Most of these sharks are found along sandy shores and near coral reefs. Wobbegong sharks, nurse sharks, zebra sharks, bamboo sharks and collared carpet sharks belong to this group.

Amazing

A puffin feeding can peck up more than a dozen sand-eels, which it holds in its beak as it flies back with them to its nest burrow, to feed its chicks.

Croc at sea

The largest-living reptile is the saltwater crocodile, also called the Indo-Pacific, Australian or estuarine crocodile. It can grow to more than 7 m in length.

○ The colourful 'feathers' of the peacock worm are actually frilly, antennae-like tentacles around its head. They are coated with sticky mucus that traps tiny floating pieces of food. The peacock worm makes its tube house from sand and mud glued with hardened mucus. The tentacles withdraw if danger threatens.

○ A young zebra shark's stripes may camouflage it as it lies on ridges of sand formed by water currents. The stripes also blend in with the shadows on the seabed formed by ripples on the surface above. As the shark grows, its stripes split into spots.

◄ *Some fish, like the yellowhead jawfish, make burrows in the sand. They rush back to these burrows and hide if danger appears.*

▼ *Sand-eels live in their thousands in and just below the tide zone. They are common food for larger fish, and for birds such as puffins and gulls.*

○ Gulls have a sharp, hooked bill, which helps them kill small birds and similar prey. They also have webbed feet to paddle on water surfaces. Gulls cannot dive underwater. They feed in shallow waters on worms, crabs and other animals that they find in the sand.

○ Some shores are swampy. This makes the border between land and sea hard to pinpoint. Muddy coastlines include tropical mangrove swamps that are flooded by salty water from the sea.

▼ *The red lizardfish lives along the warm sandy and muddy shores of the west Pacific Ocean. It has wide jaws with sharp teeth, and its shiny, heavy scales give its body a lizard-like appearance.*

▲ The common gull is a frequent visitor to beaches and muddy coasts. It pecks for crabs, worms and other food, and also feasts on dead fish and creatures left stranded by the tide.

▶ Flatfish, such as the peacock flounder, move slowly over the seabed, nosing for buried food such as worms and shellfish.

○ Mullets can swim from the salty sea into the brackish (part-salty) water of estuaries, where freshwater from a river flows into the ocean. The striped mullet reaches 90 cm in length and lives in warmer coastal regions around the world as well as out in the open sea. It feeds by sucking mud and sand into its mouth and filtering out tiny edible bits using its specialized gills.

○ The American manatee is found in warm waters from Florida, USA, around the Caribbean to northern South America. It lives along sandy shores in the sea and also swims into rivers and lakes. It can grow to 4.5 m long and 1500 kg in weight. Manatees eat huge amounts of water plants.

○ Birds, such as gulls and waders, feed along shores of sand and mud, probing for worms and shellfish. They often gather as the tide comes in, to catch animals coming up from out of the sand.

▶ A sawshark may lose and regrow as many as 30,000 teeth during its lifetime. Sawsharks swipe their long snouts through sand and mud to reveal small animals, such as shellfish and worms.

Shark camouflage

Angel sharks have wide, flat bodies the same colour as sand. They blend perfectly into the sandy seabed as they lie in wait for prey. They are called 'angel' sharks because their fins spread wide like an angel's wings.

▲ The leopard grouper is a day visitor to the sandy seabed, on the lookout for prey, such as a small fish, shrimps or worms. At night the grouper moves to a rocky area to sleep in a crevice or beneath an overhang.

Find out more

Shark diets p. 143

Seas and Oceans

The oceans are home to more than 250 species of mammals and reptiles, numerous small creatures, and more than 20,000 species of fish. Oceans are divided into two regions – the benthic zone, or the ocean floor, and the pelagic zone, which is the vast expanse of water.

❍ The pelagic zone is further divided into three other zones. The topmost of these, called the epipelagic zone, supports around nine-tenths of marine life. Apart from plants, many species of fish, reptiles and mammals dwell in the epipelagic zone.

❍ The twilight zone is just below the epipelagic zone. Very little sunlight reaches this zone, making it impossible for plants to survive here. However, animals, such as octopus, squid, hatchet fish, viperfish and other deep-sea fish, are found in this zone.

Amazing

The wandering albatross has the longest wings of any bird, measuring more than 3.5 m from tip to tip.

Sunbathing fish

Sunfish are named after their habit of sunbathing on the surface of the open ocean. The heaviest bony fish, the sunfish, lays an astonishing number of eggs – about 300 million. Most get eaten by other fish and sea animals.

◢ *Of all seabirds, albatrosses spend the most time over the ocean. They even sleep on the wing. When growing up, before they breed, they may not touch land for three or four years.*

❍ The midnight zone is the lowest subzone and is always completely dark and extremely cold. Very few creatures live in this zone and most of them do not have eyes.

❍ Marlin are large sea fish, closely related to swordfish, sailfish and spearfish. Marlin and sailfish are also called billfish. The upper jaw of a marlin extends to form a long, rounded spear-like snout. Marlin use this snout to capture food. The diet of marlin consists of squid, fish such as herring and mackerel, and crabs.

◀ *Mantas are the largest rays, measuring up to 7 m across the 'wings'. As water flows through the manta's scoop-like mouth, small creatures like krill are filtered out by comb-like parts on the gills.*

Fearsome nose

The swordfish may weigh 650 kg and be almost 5 m long. One swordfish drove its nose 55 cm into the timbers of a wooden ship, and the nose tip snapped off.

❍ The albatross is the largest seabird, weighing about 12 kg. It is commonly found in oceans of the Southern Hemisphere, but some species also dwell in the North Pacific. Albatrosses have a sharp bill with a hooked upper jaw. They also have tubular nostrils and webbed feet.

❍ Albatrosses are so heavy that they have to leap from cliffs to launch into flight. They prey on squid, cuttlefish and small marine creatures. Unlike gulls, these large birds can drink seawater.

❍ Beaked whales are medium-sized whales with long, narrow, beak-shaped mouths, like the mouths of dolphins. There are about 20 kinds of beaked whale, but some are very rare and seldom seen. The shepherd's beaked whale, which is some 7 m long, has been seen alive fewer than 20 times.

❍ Unlike most rays, which spend hours lying camouflaged on the bottom of the ocean, mantas spend much of their time swimming near the surface. The Pacific manta is the largest ray with a length of about 5 m. The Atlantic manta is slightly smaller.

⬆ *The nautilus is like a squid in a snail's shell. It hunts squid, fish and other prey using its huge eyes and sense of touch. It detects ripples made by moving animals and grabs victims with its numerous tentacles, passing meals to its mouth, which lies in the centre of the tentacle ring.*

Dolphins

The dusky dolphin is one of several types that does not have a narrow 'beak' for a snout. It lives in large groups, not only of its own kind, but also with other dolphins, whales, certain types of fish and even seabirds.

The pantropical spotted dolphin reaches about 2.2 m in length and weighs up to 110 kg. It swims fast and makes a series of low leaps or one very high one, hanging in the air before falling back to the sea.

The bottlenose dolphin lives in all warmer oceans and grows to about 3.5 m long. It sometimes chases fish up the beach and grabs them before wriggling back.

For centuries, artists have painted and sculpted common dolphins, which have very variable markings and colours. They live worldwide.

Risso's dolphin grows to 4 m long and weighs 370 kg. Its skin scars probably come from fights with its own kind at breeding time.

The spinner dolphin is one of the most acrobatic of all dolphins. It jumps high out of the water and spins around like a top. It lives in the open ocean and eats mainly fish.

Coral Reefs

Tiny animals build huge underwater rocks, cliffs and coves called reefs. These reefs are built up from coral, the leftover skeletons of sea creatures called polyps. Over millions of years, enough skeletons pile up to form huge, wall-like structures. Coral reefs are full of hidey-holes and make excellent homes for all sorts of amazing, colourful life. They are the sea's richest habitats.

○ Coral reefs are formed by colonies of coral polyps. A coral polyp is a tiny animal that uses minerals in the sea to produce a protective outer skeleton. These skeletons form hard and branching structures called coral reefs. Coral polyps use their tentacles to capture tiny creatures called zooplankton.

○ Coral reefs are found in warm and shallow waters, usually within 30° north and south of the Equator. They are home to numerous sea animals. Starfish, reef sharks, sponges, jellyfish, crabs, lobsters, anemones, eels and a huge variety of fish add to the colour and array of lifeforms in coral reefs.

Amazing

The fine, silvery sand of coral reefs is actually from fish droppings. It comes from the crunched-up food of fish such as parrotfish, who scrape off and swallow the rocky coral skeletons.

Living together

Clownfish are also called anemonefish. These fish live a sheltered life among the tentacles of sea anemones. The anemone protects the fish from predators, while the fish returns the favour by keeping its host's tentacles clean. Clownfish have a protective covering of mucus that helps keep them safe from the stings in the tentacles of the sea anemones.

▼ *Sea-squirts, or tunicates, are leathery, bag-like animals fixed to the coral rocks. Each draws in water through its upper opening, filters tiny bits of food from it, and squirts out the water through the side opening.*

○ There are three kinds of coral reef. These are fringing and barrier reefs, and coral atolls. Fringing reefs extend from the land into the sea. Barrier reefs are found further from the shore, separated from the mainland by a lagoon. Atolls are ring-shaped formations of coral islands, around a lagoon.

○ The Great Barrier Reef in the Coral Sea, off the northeastern coast of Australia, is the biggest of all coral reefs, although coral reefs are also found in the Indian Ocean and the Red Sea. Some of them also stretch along the Atlantic Ocean from Florida in the USA to the Caribbean Sea and Brazil.

▶ *A parrotfish snaps off pieces of coral with its beak-like front teeth and then crunches the coral with its back teeth.*

○ Coral reefs, especially the Great Barrier Reef, are major tourist attractions because of their fascinating structures, vibrant colours and rich marine life. A single coral reef may be home to as many as 3000 species of living things.

○ Gobies of tropical waters tend to have brighter colours than those in colder seas so that they can be noticed among the corals. The neon goby often rests on its pectoral (front side) fins, as though leaning on its 'elbows'. Like most gobies it swims only in short bursts. Otherwise it remains still, watching for food or danger.

○ Some coral-reef fish look like stones. Stonefish rest on the seabed, looking just like the rocks that surround them. If they are spotted, the poisonous spines on their backs can stun an attacker in a matter of seconds.

Find out more

Coral hot spots p. 165

Reef sharks, as their name suggests, live close to coral reefs. They are most common in the shallow tropical waters of the Indian and Pacific oceans. There are three main species of reef shark. These are the black-tip, the white-tip and the grey reef sharks. These sharks feed on squid, octopuses and reef fish, such as sturgeon and mullet.

Banded sea snakes use venom (poison) to stun their prey, but the yellow-bellied sea snake has a sneakier trick. Once its colourful underside has attracted some fish, it darts back – so the fish are next to its open mouth. The venom of sea snakes is more powerful than that of any land snake.

Cleaner wrasse are little fish that are 'paid' for cleaning. Larger fish, such as groupers and moray eels, visit the wrasse, which nibble all the parasites and other bits of dirt off the bigger fishes' bodies and from around the gills and eyes.

The orange ball anemone unfurls its tentacles only at night, as do many types of coral polyps. This means that by day the reef looks dull and drab. Only after dusk do its colours come 'alive', when they can be seen by divers with the help of a torch.

Parrotfish are usually found near coral reefs. They have long bodies and rather large heads, some about 1 m long. Others, such as the Indo-Pacific surf parrotfish, are much smaller, at around 45 cm. The jaw teeth of parrotfish are joined together to form a beak-like mouth. This beak is used to scrape algae and other food from coral reefs and rocks.

Coral reefs are home to some of the brightest colours in the living world, from vibrant anemones to rainbow-coloured fish.

Swimming snakes

About 30 kinds of snake are specialized to live in the sea, especially in and around coral reefs. They include the banded sea snake and the yellow-bellied sea snake. The biggest kinds grow to almost 3 m long.

Tropical Fish

The world's tropical seas teem with a seemingly endless range of beautifully coloured fish. The hues of some of these fish blend in with the corals and weeds. Others stand out from their surroundings, to make it clear that they occupy their own patch or territory of reef, or to attract a mate for breeding.

Leopard blennies live among branches of hard coral, well camouflaged among the patches of brightness and shadow by their leopard-like spots.

At breeding time the male and female banded butterfly fish pair up to mate and produce young.

Like most parrotfish, the yellowtail parrotfish has a hard, beak-like mouth for scraping small algae (plants) and coral animals from the rocks.

The clown triggerfish is found along rocks, shores and reefs of the Indian and West Pacific oceans.

The honeycombed cowfish has strong plates of bone in its skin, like a protective box. It grows to 50 cm long.

The coral grouper, also called the coral trout or coral bass, grows to 70 cm in length. It swims at depths from 5 to 50 m.

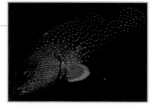

The barred hamlet fish is a curious but shy fish. It has electric blue lines that encircle the eye.

The well camouflaged long-lure anglerfish uses a lure to attract prey. It sits and waits for prey on the seabed.

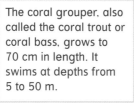

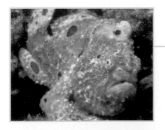

The squirrel fish is found in the Red Sea. It has large eyes and is a nocturnal fish, hiding during the day under ledges and in caves.

Trunkfish like the smooth trunkfish have a long snout and lips that can be extended forward or protruded.

This golden damselfish is being visited by a cleaner wrasse, which will pick small pests, bits of old skin and dirt from its body, fins, eyes and gills.

The longnose filefish is one of about 80 kinds of filefish. They are named from the small spines on their scales which give them a prickly feel, like a rasp.

Latticed butterflyfish are named from the criss-cross pattern on the side of the body. The belong to the group called chaetodontids, which includes more than 200 types of butterflyfish and angelfish.

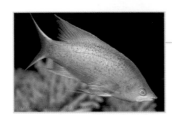

The purple queen is a member of the large basslet group, which includes dozens of colourful tropical marine fish.

The long, slim trumpetfish grows up to 1 m in length.

Tropical reefs are home for many kinds of angelfish, like the rock beauty with its brilliant yellow head and tail, but almost black body.

Blackbar soldierfish swim in a close-knit shoal or school, darting across the reef as they twist and turn together.

Coral hot spots

The world's top 10 are places where a huge variety of marine life is concentrated into a small area, and which are also under great threat:

1. Philippines
2. Gulf of Guinea
3. Sunda Islands
4. Southern Mascarene Islands
5. Eastern South Africa
6. Northern Indian Ocean
7. Southern Japan, Taiwan and southern China
8. Cape Verde Islands
9. Western Caribbean
10. Red Sea and Gulf of Aden

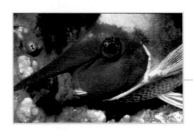

The unicorn fish is named from the long 'horn' above its mouth, which resembles the horn of the mythical horse called the unicorn. The horn is very short when young but gets longer with age.

Find out more

Amazing p. 162

Shallow Seas

Shallow coastal seas are the most productive parts of the ocean – that is, they have the most life. The waters receive plenty of sunlight even near the bottom, so plants can grow as food for a wide variety of animal life.

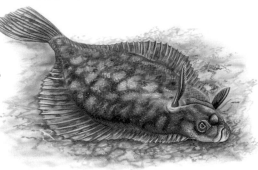

○ The great barracuda is well known as a fish with huge curiosity. It swims near divers and follows them, watching their movements and actions. This quiet menace is one reason for the barracuda's fearsome reputation.

○ Some barracuda attacks may be the result of these fish being provoked or surprised by divers or swimmers. But there are also tales of sudden bites for no apparent reason.

Soft bodies

Sea anemones are colourful creatures that are sometimes confused with coral polyps. Unlike corals, sea anemones do not have a skeleton to protect them. They attach themselves to solid surfaces, such as the seabed, corals or rocks.

▲ The flounder's flattened shape and dull colouring help to camouflage (hide) it on the seabed.

○ The green moray of coastal shallows grows to about 2 m in length and hides amongst seaweed and eel-grass. Divers' tales about moray eels say that their bites are poisonous, and once they have closed their teeth on something they never let go. But a moray soon lets go if it is hauled above the water.

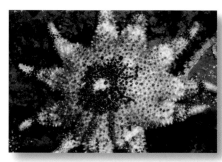

▲ Starfish with many arms and a wide central body, or disc, are known as sunstars. This pink sunstar makes its home along the west coast of the Americas.

Tigers of the sea

Barracuda are fearsome predators, which seize, maim and tear up other fish with their fang-like teeth. Great barracuda probably grow to about 2 m long, although some people claim they reach much larger sizes.

◄ Dugongs are members of the mammal group called sirenians, or sea-cows. They live in warm, sheltered waters around Africa, India, Southeast Asia, and Australia, munching plants such as sea grass.

▼ The rosy-lipped batfish 'walks' on its fleshy fins. It lives among seaweeds and rocks in the shallows around Pacific islands, such as the Galapagos Islands.

▲ This pencil urchin is a primitive, or cidarid, sea urchin. It can tilt its thick spines to 'walk' along the seabed.

❍ The Common porpoise is the most often-seen porpoise – partly because it has a very wide distribution, including the waters of the North Pacific and North Atlantic oceans, and the Mediterranean and Black seas. It is also because the common porpoise swims nearer shores and is not as shy of ships and busy waterways as the other species. It lives in groups of about ten and feeds mainly on fish and cuttlefish.

❍ Sea urchins are small creatures with spherical shells. Like starfish, sea urchins also have spines on their bodies. A sea urchin's spines are moveable and are used for defence and movement. Spines can be tiny or, in some cases, more than 20 cm long.

▼ The bites of moray eels, such as the green moray, are said to be poisonous. This is not so, but the bite may get infected by germs from the moray's mouth and teeth or the surrounding water.

❍ Sea urchins eat small plants and animals. Some eat sponges. Some fish, like triggerfish and pufferfish, can knock off the sea urchin's spines with their hard heads and eat the soft flesh in the shell.

❍ Flounder have a unique shape – they are flat and almost round. They belong to the group of fish known as flatfish. Both eyes of the flounder are located on the same side of the body – on the upper surface.

▶ Tiny porcelain crabs live among the stinging tentacles of anemones. The crab is protected against the stings and eats the anemone's leftover food to keep the anemone's tentacles clean.

❍ Not all flounders' eyes are on the same side. Some have both eyes on the left side, so they lie on the right side. Others have both eyes on the right side, so they lie on their left. Flounders prefer to live and swim close to the seabed.

❍ Others in the flatfish family include halibut, plaice, sole, dab, turbot, brill and windowpane. The liver oil of the halibut, one of the largest flatfish, contains more vitamins than even the famous cod liver oil.

❍ The dugong grows to about 4 m long and more than 800 kg in weight. It prefers shallow, sheltered coastal waters in the tropics to the open sea. Its favourite food is sea grass, which grows down to depths of about 4 m.

Amazing

The shallow waters of the continental shelf, around the edges of the great continents, form less than one-tenth of the ocean's area, yet contain more than nine-tenths of all ocean life.

Find out more
Living together p. 162

Simple Sea Animals

S ome water creatures seem to be little more than blobs of jelly or bundles of spines, without a brain or limbs, and with no complicated behaviour. Yet these creatures live in the seas in their millions – simple is not the same as unsuccessful!

○ Jellyfish, sea anemones and coral polyps are all members of the cnidarian group, containing almost 10,000 different species. Most live in the sea and have a jelly-like body or stalk, and a ring of tentacles that sting their prey.

○ Jellyfish are among the most feared sea animals. Found in oceans across the world, they are shaped like a bell and have poisonous tentacles. The body of a jellyfish is soft and does not have a fixed form. Its skin is almost transparent as nearly 98 per cent of its body is made up of water.

○ Jellyfish have a central cavity in their bell that acts as a stomach and intestine. They eat plankton, other jellyfish and small fish. Jellyfish do not have gills or lungs. Oxygen is absorbed and carbon dioxide is released through their membrane-like skin.

◄ *The see-through bodies of jellyfish, like this pencillate jellyfish, show their insides. You can see their breeding parts (as here) and also their last meal.*

▼ *The moon jellyfish, known as aurelia, grows to about 30 cm in diameter. It often gets washed into bays, estuaries and harbours in large swarms that can number many hundreds of creatures.*

○ Most sea anemones are very small, but some varieties may grow to more than 1 m in diameter. They have a cylindrical body and an opening at the top that serves as the mouth. The mouth of a sea anemone is surrounded by tentacles. These tentacles are used to grab food and for defence. The tentacles have stinging cells that paralyze the sea anemone's prey.

○ The tentacles also carry the prey into the sea anemone's mouth. Sticky mucus on the tentacles means they can grab even small fish.

○ Sea anemones that live in shallow waters secrete mucus or dig into the wet sand to prevent their bodies from drying out. Some can live for 70 to 100 years. Because of their vibrant colours they are much sought-after for display in aquariums.

► *Starfish, like these thin-armed orange stars, glide slowly over the rocks on their tube feet. They are looking for small plants and animals to scrape up and eat.*

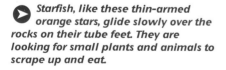

Amazing

The poison stings of the box-jelly from around Southeast Asia and Australia can kill a person within ten minutes.

Shadowy danger

The box-jelly is named after its squarish body, or bell. It's also called the sea-wasp from the burning pain of its stings. Its tentacles can trail for several metres and its body is very nearly see-through, so it is an unseen, dangerous menace for swimmers, who often wear 'stinger suits' as protection.

Feathery feeder

Feather-duster worms belong to the worm group called sabellids. They extend their feathery feeding tentacles outward to catch their food, but at the slightest hint of danger they withdraw into a protective tube, which lies part-buried in the sand or mud.

○ Most starfish have five arms, but some species have seven and others have up to 40 arms. Starfish have developed a unique way of moving. They have hundreds of tiny, tube-like feet underneath their arms, which help them to crawl.

○ Starfish do not have eyes. Instead, they have a small eye-spot at the tip of each arm. The eyes-spots are linked to a network of nerves. Starfish also have good senses of touch and smell. Some starfish can regenerate lost arms, and an entirely new starfish may be regenerated from a single arm attached to a portion of the central disc.

Sponges are the simplest animals with no proper muscles, eyes, nerves or brain. This vase sponge has growing on it an echinoderm, called a sea lily or crinoid, which is a stalked, upside-down version of its close cousin the starfish.

○ All echinoderms live in the sea. Their name means 'spiny-skinned' and they include starfish and urchins, most of which have sharp spines, sometimes poisonous. Other types of echinoderm include sea cucumbers, which are usually sausage-shaped and sort through seabed mud for food particles. Sea lilies are also echinoderms.

Not all corals build stony cups or containers around themselves. Soft corals lack hard outer cases and grow in tightly joined colonies.

Starfish are found in most of the oceans across the world. They live on the seabed and are usually active at night. Some types eat corals and shellfish.

Find out more

Porcelain crabs p. 167

Crabs and Crustaceans

Crustaceans, meaning 'crusty-case', are animals such as crabs, lobsters, prawns, shrimps, krill and barnacles, with a hard outer-body casing and several pairs of jointed legs. There are more than 40,000 species of crustacean, and most live in the sea. They are the equivalent of insects on land – they swarm in the oceans in their billions, and are important food for larger sea creatures, such as seals, dolphins and whales.

◯ Most crabs live in the sea, but a few species can be found in freshwater. The common shore crab can live in both salty and fresh water. It can even stay out of water for a few hours.

◯ Crabs have five pairs of limbs. One pair of large, claw-like limbs, called pincers, is used for grabbing prey. The rest of the limbs are used to move around. The rear part of the crab, called the abdomen, is very small and can be tucked under its shell. A crab also uses its pincers to defend itself. It digs a hole with the pincers and buries itself under the sand to hide from predators.

The ghost crab is so-called because it is white or light grey in colour. It hides in a burrow in the mud when the tide goes out.

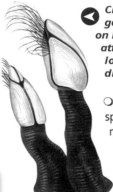

Crustaceans called goose barnacles grow on long, tough stalks attached to floating logs and other driftwood.

◯ Crabs have highly specialized gills that do not clog even when they stay in muddy waters. Unlike other crustaceans, crabs can move sideways. Owing to their peculiar body shape, it is easier for crabs to escape into their burrows this way. The Japanese giant spider crab is the largest of all crabs. With limbs outstretched it can measure more than 3.5 m across. It is found in the northern Pacific Ocean.

Cleaner and bait

The spotted cleaner shrimp not only cleans the tentacles of the sea anemone, but also attracts other marine creatures close enough for the anemone to prey on them.

Barnacles

Barnacles are small crustaceans found in oceans, seas and lakes across the world. The body of a barnacle is covered with a hard shell made up of plate-like structures. Some baleen whales have their heads covered with barnacles, which stick firmly and cannot be removed.

The banded coral shrimp sifts through the silvery coral sand, looking for any small bits of food. Shrimp and prawns help to keep the reef clean and recycle old, rotting bits of plants and animals.

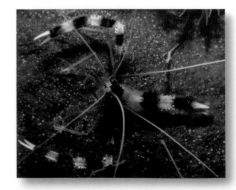

▷ *Robber crabs dig into the sand and hide during the day. They are excellent tree-climbers. They are also known as coconut crabs, because they can break open coconuts with their powerful pincers.*

○ Robber crabs get their name from the fact that they are easily attracted to shiny materials. They have been known to steal pots, pans and even mobile phones from houses and tents.

○ Lobsters belong to the same group as crabs, called the decapods. Unlike crabs, these crustaceans have elongated bodies. They are often confused with crayfish, which are smaller and mainly freshwater. Lobsters have big heads and their bodies are covered by a shell. They have five pairs of legs, one or more of which are modified into pincers.

○ Most lobsters live on the ocean floor, where they can hide by slipping into the spaces between rocks. They mostly feed on the remains of dead creatures. Lobsters also eat clams, snails, worms and sea urchins.

○ Shrimps and prawns are very similar in appearance. Both look like miniature lobsters. A hardened shell also covers their bodies, but this shell is not as thick or hard as that of lobsters.

○ Shrimps have bodies that are flattened from top to bottom, while the body of a prawn is flattened from either side. Shrimps crawl around the seabed, while prawns swim using five pairs of paddle-like limbs, which are located on their abdomen.

Amazing

One of the largest barnacles is the diadem barnacle, which grows almost as big as a fist – and lives firmly attached to the skin of a great whale.

▽ *Lobsters often have pincers of different sizes. The right pincer tends to be larger and blunt, for powerful crushing and crunching. The left pincer is normally smaller and narrower, for picking and cutting.*

▲ *The mantis shrimp uses its claws to smash crab shells and crack them open. Its movement is one of the fastest in the animal world – far too quick for us to see.*

Sea Snails and Shellfish

Sea snails and shellfish, along with octopus and squid, belong to the huge animal group called the molluscs. Most smaller molluscs have a hard, outer shell to protect the soft, fleshy body inside.

❍ There are more than 50,000 kinds of snail, including whelks, spire shells, limpets, top shells, winkles, cowries and cone shells.

❍ Snails belong to the class gastropoda, which means 'belly-footed animals'. Some sea snails live along the coast, in rock pools and shallow water, while others live on the deep ocean floor. Unlike land snails, some sea snails are very colourful.

▼ *A pearl is formed when a foreign object lodges itself inside the shell of an oyster, clam or mussel. These creatures coat the object with a substance called nacre, which usually lines the inside of the shell. Pearls are largely white or pale yellow in colour. However, some can be black, grey, red, green or blue.*

❍ Some sea snails swim or float along with the ocean currents. Others use their muscular feet, or lower parts of the body, for crawling over the seabed.

▼ *The Port Jackson shark is specialized to eat shellfish. It has broad, flat teeth at the back of its mouth for crushing them.*

Warning colours

Like sea snails, sea slugs are molluscs and have a soft and slimy body. However, their body is not enclosed in a hard shell. Some feed on poisonous sponges and take in the poisons, which go into their own tentacles. The sea slug's bright colours warn of its nasty poisonous taste.

❍ Most sea snails have four tentacles on their heads. One pair helps them to feel their way around, while the other often has eyes at the tip. Some species do not have eyes at all. These creatures have a tongue-like organ called the radula that consists of numerous tiny teeth. Some sea snails use the radula to pierce the shells of small animals.

Find out more
Sea slugs p. 137

Biggest shellfish

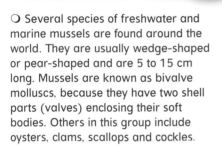

Giant clams are common in the tropical Pacific Ocean, especially among coral reefs. They can grow to 1.2 m across.

▶ *Concentric rings can be seen on the shells of mussels. These are formed during different seasons as the shell grows faster or slower and so they can show the mussel's age. These creatures have strong muscles to help them open and close their protective shells.*

❍ Several species of freshwater and marine mussels are found around the world. They are usually wedge-shaped or pear-shaped and are 5 to 15 cm long. Mussels are known as bivalve molluscs, because they have two shell parts (valves) enclosing their soft bodies. Others in this group include oysters, clams, scallops and cockles.

❍ Mussels breathe with the help of their gills. The gills have hair-like filaments, called cilia, over which water passes. The cilia are also used to capture food. Mussels are filter-feeders that feed on planktonic plants and animals. In some areas mussels are so plentiful that this filtering action actually clears the normally cloudy water.

❍ Most mussels have a strong and muscular tongue-shaped foot that extends from their body and sometimes remains outside their shells. They use this foot to dig. Towards the end of the foot lies the byssus gland, or pit, which produces a tough thread. The mussel uses this thread to attach itself to various surfaces, such as rocks.

❍ Clams belong to the same group as mussels, the bivalves, and are found across the world. Like other bivalves, clams have a two-part shell covering their body. Some clams can close their shells tightly when in danger. Clams also have a single muscular foot that helps them with digging. They use this foot to burrow into the sand.

▲ *Some sea slugs are hermaphrodites. This means the sea slug has both female and male breeding parts. After two individual hermaphrodites mate, both lay eggs.*

Amazing

The biggest pearl was found in a giant clam and was 12 cm across. One oyster had eight small pearls inside.

◀ *The conch is a tropical sea snail with a shell that is shaped like a rolled-up length of card. It peers out from inside the shell using its two eyes, each on a long, flexible tentacle.*

Octopus and Squid

S quid, octopus and cuttlefish are soft-bodied animals. They belong to a group of molluscs called cephalopods. All of them are fierce predators.

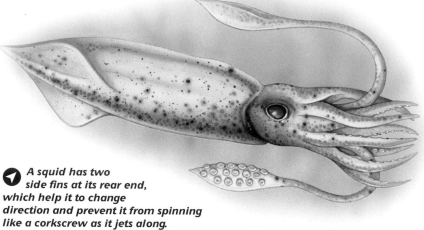

Amazing

The giant squid has the largest eyes of any animal. They are up to 40 cm across – about the size of a soccer ball.

A squid has two side fins at its rear end, which help it to change direction and prevent it from spinning like a corkscrew as it jets along.

○ When in danger, the squid shoots out a cloud of dark, ink-like liquid. This hinders the attacker's vision, allowing the squid to escape. The diet of a squid includes fish, crabs and shrimps, and smaller squid. Squid predators include whales, sharks and big fish. Squid is also a popular food for humans.

○ The cuttlefish looks like a small, flattened squid. It has a fin that runs around the entire length of its body. Like squid, a cuttlefish also has ten tentacles, eight of which are small. Cuttlefish move in the same way as squid, releasing jets of water for short bursts of speed.

Biggest octopus

The giant octopus grows over 7 m in length. The female may have as many as 280 suckers on each arm, while the male has only 100.

○ The skin of the cuttlefish has tiny spots of various colours. Using special muscles, the cuttlefish can control the size of these spots. Cuttlefish are also known as 'chamaeleons of the sea', owing to their ability to change colour according to their surroundings.

The octopus can squirt water from an opening called the siphon, seen here on the right. Just like squid and cuttlefish, the force of the water jet makes the octopus shoot backwards.

○ All squid have ten tentacles, or arms, two of which are long and slender. All the tentacles have suckers at the ends. They are used to grab prey. These creatures can swim very fast. They move by releasing jets of water through a fleshy tube called a siphon, located near the head.

○ Octopuses have soft, sack-like bodies and large eyes that can distinguish between different colours. The most striking feature of the octopus is its eight arms, or tentacles. Each tentacle has two rows of suckers, which help the octopus not only to hold its prey, but also to climb rocks.

Cuttlefish keep their two long tentacles hidden as they beat their fins to float above the seabed, looking for food such as crabs, shrimps and small fish.

Giant predator

The giant squid lives in the deep ocean and is rarely seen alive. In fact there may be more than one kind of this huge animal. Another even larger type may exist, called the titanic squid.

The giant octopus can spread out its body like a huge umbrella to catch ocean currents and float along over the sea. Alternatively, it can roll into a ball and sink quickly down to the seabed.

○ Octopuses use their arms to seize prey and pull it towards their mouth. They secrete poisonous saliva to paralyze the prey and they chew it using their beak-like mouths.

○ The main diet of the octopus consists of crabs and lobsters. Some species feed on small shellfish and plankton. In turn, octopuses are eaten by sharks and moray eels, among others.

○ Octopus are largely bottom-dwellers and live in small coves. They create a pile of debris in front of their hiding nook or lair to protect themselves.

Female reef squid lay their eggs in well-protected areas scattered around the reef. The females then die. The eggs are laid in clusters that are then fertilized by the male. The young squid congregate near islands several centimetres below the surface to avoid bird predators.

Find out more
Octopus p. 133

Sharks

S harks belong to the cartilaginous group of fish. There are more than 350 species in oceans across the world. Some sharks, like the bull shark, can also survive in freshwater.

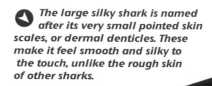

The large silky shark is named after its very small pointed skin scales, or dermal denticles. These make it feel smooth and silky to the touch, unlike the rough skin of other sharks.

Fearsome hunter

The world's biggest predatory, or hunting, fish is the great white shark. It is certainly large – at 6 m in length and weighing more than 1 tonne. Great whites live around the world, mainly in warmer seas. They have a fearsome reputation and have been known to attack humans.

○ Sharks are the primary predators, or hunters, of the ocean. They have special abilities to locate prey. The great white shark, the most feared predator of all, can smell a single drop of blood in 100 l of water.

○ The most powerful weapon that a shark has is its teeth. A shark can have as many as 3000 teeth set in three rows. The fish relies on the first row of teeth to strike the first blow. This first charge often injures or kills the prey.

○ Most sharks have a very good sense of smell. It is believed that almost a third of the shark's brain is devoted to detecting smell.

○ Sharks do not have external ear flaps. Instead, their ears are on the insides of their heads, on either side of the brain case. Each ear leads to a small sensory pore on the skin of the shark's head. It is believed that sharks can hear over a distance of 250 m.

○ A pair of fluid-filled canals runs down either side of the shark's body, from its head to its tail. This is the lateral line and helps the fish sense minute vibrations in the water. The lateral line canals are lined with tiny hair-like projections. These projections are triggered by even the slightest movement, which in turn alert the shark's brain.

○ Most sharks have torpedo-shaped bodies, which make them streamlined and so very good swimmers. They also have large tail fins that give them most of the power for swimming.

○ A shark's skin is not covered with smooth scales like bony fish. Instead, a shark's skin is covered with tiny, tooth-like structures called dermal denticles that mostly give the skin a sandpaper-like quality.

▶ *The white-tipped reef shark is so-called because of its white-tipped dorsal (back) fin. It grows to about 1.5 m in length.*

Find out more

Massive mouth p. 181

Amazing

The smallest shark is the dwarf lanternshark, at just 20 cm long. It is so small that it could lie curled up in your hand.

Types of shark

The mako shark swims at 55 km/h, much faster than a human sprinter. It races after prey such as mackerel, tuna and squid.

The nurse shark swims slowly and often rests on the seabed. It has dark spots when young but these fade with age.

The great hammerhead is a big and powerful shark, up to 6 m long. It has been known to attack people.

The sand tiger shark reaches about 3 m in length. It has thin, sharp teeth with gaps between them, leading to the nickname of 'snaggletooth shark'.

The tasselled wobbegong shark has frills of flesh around its mouth. These frills look like seaweed and act as the shark's camouflage.

Biggest fish

Whale sharks are the largest fish in the world. The average length is about 14 m. However, some are said to have grown to over 18 m in length.

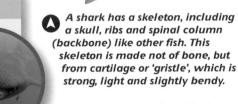

A shark has a skeleton, including a skull, ribs and spinal column (backbone) like other fish. This skeleton is made not of bone, but from cartilage or 'gristle', which is strong, light and slightly bendy.

○ Lemon sharks are found in the Atlantic and Pacific oceans and prefer to live in sub-tropical waters. They are found in abundance in the Caribbean Sea. They get their name from their colour. The upper part of the body is deep yellow or yellowish-brown. The belly is either off-white or cream.

○ The hammer-shaped head may improve the hammerhead shark's senses. The nostrils are at each end of the 'hammer'. Smells drifting from the side reach one nostril well before the other. By swinging its head from side to side, the hammerhead can pinpoint the direction of a smell more quickly. Hammerheads often swim close to the seabed, searching for buried fish and shellfish.

A strange looking shark, the frilled shark, has big frilly gill slits – the first pair reach right around its head like a collar. It has only one dorsal fin, instead of two as in most sharks. This fin is positioned far back towards the shark's tail.

Great Whales

The whale group, known as the cetaceans, contains about 83 kinds of whale, dolphin and porpoise. About 12 of these are baleen whales, whose long strips of baleen (whalebone) in the mouth filter seawater for small creatures such as krill. The rest are toothed whales, who catch prey such as fish and squid.

The humpback grows to 15 m in length and weighs 30 tonnes. It has the longest flippers of any whale, at 4 m.

Cuvier's beaked whale is one of the most numerous and widespread of the beaked whale group. It can grow to lengths of up to 7 m and is often covered in barnacles.

The baby beluga, or white whale, is dark grey or grey-pink when born. It gradually becomes paler over about five years.

The blue whale is the longest and heaviest whale, and lives in oceans all around the world.

Pilot whales are also called 'blackfish', although they are not fish. They are among the whales that regularly become stranded along beaches and coasts.

A baby whale like this grey whale calf is born tail-first. Its mother helps it to the surface to breathe. The baby will grow to 15 m long and weigh 35 tonnes.

Find out more

Grey whales p. 147

Pygmy sperm whales or lesser cachalots tend to lie at the surface when resting. They suddenly disappear with a splash when approached by a boat. They are about 3 m long.

The killer whale or orca is not a true whale, but the largest kind of dolphin. It reaches 9 m in length and 10 tonnes in weight. It can kill and eat almost any creature in the sea, and also feeds by 'surfing' onto a beach and grabbing a young seal or sea lion.

Amazing

The smallest of the great whales is the minke. Even so it is far larger than any land animal – growing to lengths of up to 10 m and weighing up to a massive 10 tonnes.

The northern bottlenose whale can reach up to 9 m in length and 7 tonnes in weight. It can dive underwater for long periods, holding its breath for up to two hours. It ranges widely across the North Atlantic Ocean.

Sowerby's beaked whale lives in the North Atlantic, roaming as far as Iceland and the southern tip of Greenland.

Right whales have a large head and bow-shaped lower jaw. They are easily recognized because of the presence of light-coloured wart-like growths called callosites. These are usually located on the head, near the blowhole and around the eyes and jaws.

Baleen

Numbers of plates or 'straps' of baleen (whalebone) in the whale's mouth:

Sei whale	700
Blue whale	660
Minke whale	600
Bowhead whale	580
Right whale	480
Grey whale	320

The sperm whale is the biggest-toothed whale. It ventures into waters around the Arctic and Antarctic, which are cold even in summer.

Twilight Zone

The gloomy midwater zone covers depths of about 100 m to 1000 m, depending on the clarity of the seawater – below this it's nearly or completely pitch black. In the tropical and subtropical oceans many little-known, large-eyed, colourful fish swim in the dimness, often sporting long or spiky fins.

The bramble shark is one of the deeper-swimming sharks, often found at depths of 500 to 1000 m. Some of its skin scales, or dermal denticles, are especially large, giving it a thorny defence. It eats fish and crustaceans, such as shrimps and crabs.

Amazing

The central part of the Pacific is the deepest area of ocean on average, at 4300 m – and more than 99 per cent of this vast habitat is completely dark.

❍ Some sharks glow in the dark – especially lanternsharks. They live in deep, dark water and have glowing spots on their bodies, particularly around their mouths and along their sides. The spots may attract curious small creatures, such as fish and squid, so the shark can snap them up.

Take away the water, and vast areas of the sea are immense sandy or muddy plains with several thousand metres of water above them. This is the world's biggest habitat.

❍ Most fish with light-producing organs live in deep water. But the lantern-eye, which is 30 cm long, favours midwater depths around Southeast Asia. The fish is named from the curved patch below each eye. This appears white by day. However, at night it glows lantern-bright and even flashes on and off when the fish is agitated.

The cookie-cutter shark is only 50 cm long. It takes neat bites of flesh out of larger fish with its very sharp teeth, then dives to deeper water, down to 500 m, to rest and to digest its tasty meal.

Find out more

oceans pp. 160–161

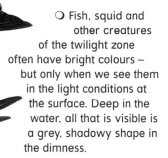

> The opah is usually found at depths from about 150 to 500 m. However, it is a rare fish, and seldom seen.

○ Fish, squid and other creatures of the twilight zone often have bright colours – but only when we see them in the light conditions at the surface. Deep in the water, all that is visible is a grey, shadowy shape in the dimness.

Lengthy fish

Oarfish are considered to be the longest bony fish in the world. They usually grow to around 6 m in length, but some have been reported to reach over 16 m.

○ The bright, bulky opah, or moonfish, is found in midwaters around the world. Strong and heavy, up to 1.5 m long and 75 kg in weight, it lacks teeth and looks far from speedy or agile. Yet the opah still manages to catch fast-swimming prey, such as squid and whiting, in its protruding, thick-lipped mouth.

○ The dealfish has an unusual fan-like tail, which points upwards as though joined to the body at right angles compared to other fish. There is also a distinctive red fin along almost the entire back of the fish. Dealfish grow to 2.5 m in length and dwell in the eastern North Atlantic. They feed on small squid and fish.

○ The John Dory has a tall but thin body when seen head-on. It is equipped with a protrusible mouth, which opens forward like a wide tube to engulf victims. The John Dory is 65 cm long and found in the Mediterranean Sea and eastern Atlantic Ocean.

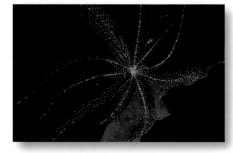

▲ Feather-stars are thin, feathery cousins of starfish and urchins. They are some of the deepest-living of all animals, with some kinds found well below 5000 m. They glide across the seabed, filtering tiny bits of food from the muddy ooze.

Massive mouth

The megamouth shark has a massive mouth, more than 1.3 m wide. Its soft, flabby body is about 5 m long. Megamouths open their great mouths as they swim through shoals of small sea creatures, such as krill and young fish. The little prey get trapped inside the mouth and swallowed.

> Jellyfish sometimes sink down into the twilight zone by day, to avoid being seen by predators such as turtles. They rise at night to catch their prey, which include small fish and squid.

The Abyss

The world's most constant habitat is also its most mysterious. The ocean depths are endlessly black and cold. Fish and other animals live on the 'rain' of rotting debris floating down from above – or eat each other.

○ On the bottom of the deep sea, there is almost no light at all. Some creatures here have huge eyes to peer in the gloom. Others find food mainly by smell and touch, and also by sensing weak pulses of electricity given off in the water by the active muscles of their swimming prey.

○ The dwarf sperm whale is similar in shape to a porpoise, without the usual sperm whale's bulging forehead. It reaches about 2.5 m in length. It is found most often in warmer seas, especially in deep areas off the coasts of South Africa, India and Australia. It is rarely in the open ocean like the pygmy sperm whale.

○ Prey is scarce in the vast blackness of the deep ocean, so fish like the gulper have large mouths to grab whatever they can. This eel is a relative giant of the depths at 60 cm long.

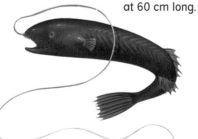

A The long-rod anglerfish has a body about 15 cm long, but its bendy, whip-like 'fishing rod' may be 20 cm or more.

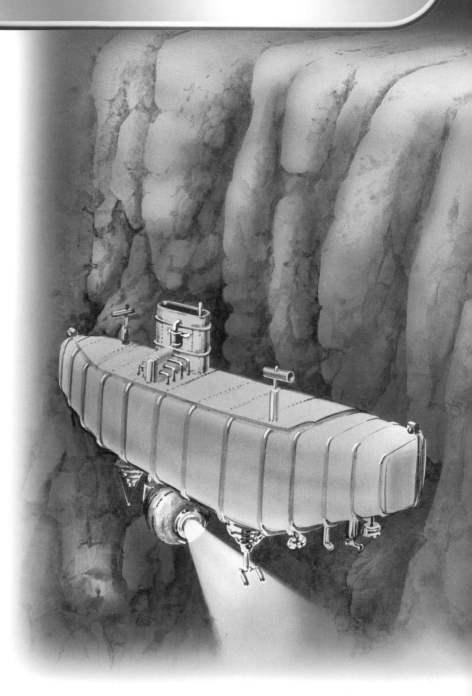

A On 23 January 1960, US Navy Lieutenant Don Walsh, and Swiss scientist Jacques Piccard set a record by descending to the bottom of the Challenger Deep, in the US Navy submersible Trieste. They reached a depth of 10,900 m. They saw various new types of sea creature. Their work continues today as present-day deep-sea explorers go on to make discoveries of life in the depths of the ocean.

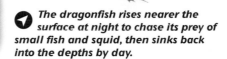
The dragonfish rises nearer the surface at night to chase its prey of small fish and squid, then sinks back into the depths by day.

○ About 1500 different deep-sea fish give off light. As well as tempting prey, light also confuses predators.

○ The lantern fish's whole body glows, while the dragonfish has light organs dotted along its sides and belly. The belly alone of the cookiecutter shark gives off a ghostly glow.

○ The snaggletooth, like several other deep-sea fish, has rows of glowing or bioluminescent spots along its sides. These may signal to others of its kind at mating time.

Walking fish

The tripod fish is one of the deepest-dwelling of all fish, found more than 6000 m below the surface. It 'walks' along the soft mud of the seabed on the long spines of its two lower side fins (pelvics) and lower tail. It probably eats small shrimp and similar shellfish.

○ The tassel-chinned anglerfish is hardly larger than your thumb. This anglerfish has extraordinary fleshy tassels on its chin that resemble seaweed, as well as the usual glowing lure on a fine spine projecting from its forehead, which it uses to attract prey.

○ The viperfish looks fearsome and is one of the larger predators of the ocean depths, yet it is only 30 cm long. The general lack of food in the deep sea means animals are mostly small.

○ The first spine or ray on the back (dorsal) fin of the viperfish is very long and flexible. It has a blob-like tip that glows in the darkness. Small creatures come to investigate and the viperfish grabs them in its wide, gaping jaws lined with long, needle-shaped teeth.

○ As well as tempting prey, light also attracts mates at breeding time. Many deep-sea fish are rare and live in a vast habitat, so any feature that can help them to find a mate and reproduce is extremely helpful.

The light organs or photophores along the body of the viperfish may be used to attract other viperfish when mating.

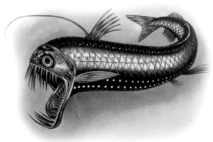

Sponges grow in every part of the ocean, including the great depths. Their chambers and canals become home to other creatures, such as crabs and shrimps.

Biggest hunter of all

The mighty sperm whale is more than 20 m long and 40 tonnes in weight, making it the largest toothed whale – and by far the largest predator, or meat eater, on Earth. Sperm whales regularly dive more than 1000 m below the surface and stay under for an hour as they hunt near the ocean floor for fish, squid, crabs and similar food.

Find out more
Sponges p. 169

Deep-sea Hot Springs

All life on Earth, including sea life, depends on light energy from the Sun – or so it was thought. In the blackness of the deep sea are animals that get energy from another source. This is the minerals gushing up in super-hot water from deep below the seabed.

○ Hot springs are found on the sea floor along the mid-ocean ridge. They are formed when water seeps under the Earth's hard outer surface (crust). This water is heated by the red-hot magma rock far below and shoots up through cracks in the ocean floor.

○ The temperature of water in and around a vent (hot spring) can reach 400°C. This water is rich in minerals and the gas hydrogen sulphide.

Amazing

At each visit in a submerisible to a new area of deep-sea vents, scientists discover dozens of unknown kinds of fish, crabs, worms and other creatures.

Deep-sea ratfish

Chimaeras are also called ratfish after their long, tapering tails. Most are about 1 m long. They are cousins of sharks and rays with a skeleton of cartilage, not bone. Several kinds live in the very deep ocean.

▷ The teeth of deep-sea predatory fish, such as this fearsome-looking swallower, are thin, sharp, pointed and needle-like, to firmly impale scarce and precious prey so that it cannot wriggle free.

○ As the minerals solidify around the vent, they build up strong chimneys that get taller and taller. One such chimney was measured to be the height of a 15-storey building – about 50 m.

○ On the seabed there are worms as long as cars. Giant tubeworms cluster around hot spots on the ocean floor. They feed on tiny particles that they filter out from the water. Some are more than 3 m long with bodies as thick as a human arm.

▽ The gulper eel is almost all mouth, and its stretchy jaws can extend to swallow a victim bigger than itself. It is sometimes caught by the crabs at deep-sea hot springs.

▽ Deep-sea vent tubeworms have bright red, frilly gills to gather oxygen and also collect tiny food particles. They have microbes in their bodies – types of bacteria that help them to feed on the minerals spurting from below.

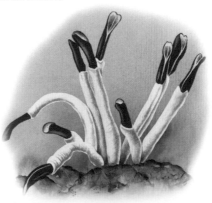

Known species at hydrothermal vents

1980	about 20
1990	more than 100
2000	more than 250

Most recent big vent discovery
Lau Basin, South Pacific

Depth	approx 2500 m
Length of crack	400 km
Scientists involved	about 100

Find out more

Long-rod anglerfish p. 182

○ Living amongst the giant tube worms are blind white crabs, various kinds of bivalve molluscs, such as mussels and clams, pink eyeless fish and many other species found nowhere else, and in no other habitat, in the world.

○ The scalding water mixes with the surrounding cold water to create chimney-like jets of warm water. These jets are often black because of the mineral content in the water. As a result these hydrothermal vents are also called black smokers.

○ Most deep-sea hot springs are in the middle of the Atlantic Ocean and around the edges of the Pacific Ocean. Such areas are where the Earth's surface rocks are on the move, with frequent earthquakes. Earthquakes happen on land and also underwater, when they cause huge waves that are known as tsunamis.

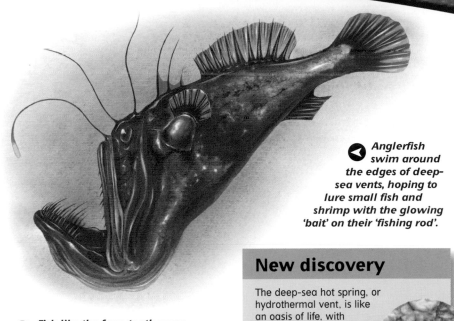

▶ *Anglerfish swim around the edges of deep-sea vents, hoping to lure small fish and shrimp with the glowing 'bait' on their 'fishing rod'.*

▼ *Fish like the fang-tooth seem flabby and floppy, but they live deep in the ocean under incredible water pressure, which would squash a land animal in an instant.*

New discovery

The deep-sea hot spring, or hydrothermal vent, is like an oasis of life, with many kinds of creatures thriving there. All around is the cold blackness of the deep sea, with very little life. Hydrothermal vents were first discovered in 1977 near the Galapagos Islands along the eastern Pacific Ocean basin. Scientists travelling in the submersible *Alvin* observed these vents about 2500 m below the ocean's surface.

Marine Biology

Marine biology is the study of life in the oceans and other related environments, such as estuaries and lagoons. Biological oceanography and marine biology are often confused with each other. Both study sea creatures. However, biological oceanography studies the effects of changing oceans on marine life.

Amazing

Every year more than a million young people at colleges and universities around the world choose to study aquatic biology – lakes, rivers, seas, oceans and the things that live in them.

Crabs are 'cleaners of the sea', feeding on the remains of plants and animals. Biologists are interested in how crabs are affected by pollution. Fewer crabs would mean that debris could pile up on the seabed.

Fish experts

Ichthyologists deal with various aspects of fish, such as their classification, behaviour, evolution and habitats.

○ Marine biology includes several sub-fields, such as the study of aquaculture, environmental marine biology, deep-sea ecology, ichthyology, marine mammology and marine ethology.

○ Environmental marine biology is the study of the health of oceans and the effect of coastal development on the marine environment. It also looks at the impact of pollutants, such as oil spills and other chemical hazards, on the surrounding marine life.

Marine biology has exciting, even heart-stopping moments, such as filming a great white shark through the open roof of a protective shark cage.

○ Deep-sea ecology takes a closer look at how water creatures in the deep adapt to the dark and cold environment.

○ Ichthyology is the study of fish – both marine and freshwater. Marine mammology is a relatively new subject that deals exclusively with the study of marine mammals, such as whales, dolphins and seals.

○ Marine ethology helps us understand the behaviour of marine animals in their natural environment. It also focuses on ways to save endangered species whose habitats are threatened by human activity or changes in the environment.

> *Herring, such as this Atlantic herring, used to be found in shoals many kilometres long, with hundreds of thousands of fish. But trawlers have caught most of them and now their numbers have depleted. Marine biologists study the herring's life-cycle, and the size of catches, to see if the fish can recover its numbers.*

◯ Marine biologists use various advanced methods to collect data for their research. Several new tools, such as plankton nets, remotely operated vehicles and fibre optics have made studying the oceans much easier.

◯ Artificial underwater habitats are built about 20 m below the water's surface to accommodate scientists who work underwater for longer periods.

◯ The study of sharks is sometimes called elasmobranchology. Knowing more about sharks – things such as how they breed and what they need to survive – will help us to conserve them and stop shark species from dying out. To find out how sharks live, scientists have to study them in the wild. This is called 'fieldwork'.

◯ Scientists also catch sharks and other sea animals so that they can study them in captivity. This lets them look closely at how sharks swim, eat, breed and behave. In aquariums, scientists test sharks' reactions to see how their brains and senses work.

◯ In laboratories, scientists study things such as sharks' blood, skin and cartilage to find out how their bodies work.

> *Many anglers understand aquatic biology. Much of our knowledge of water life comes from people who catch fish, crabs and other creatures, whether for sport as here, or out at sea in huge trawler ships for food.*

> *Although flat, the skate is not a flatfish but a type of ray, up to 3 m in length. It has long been caught for food yet little is known about its life and habits – for example, why it moves quite long distances during the summer months.*

Exploring underwater

The invention of the aqualung by French divers Jacques Cousteau and Emile Gagnan in 1942 popularized diving. A high-pressure cylinder, worn on the diver's back, is connected to the mouth with a hose that has a valve. This was the first 'self-contained underwater breathing apparatus', abbreviated to SCUBA.

Find out more

Sharks pp. 176–177

Glossary

Aestivation When an animal becomes inactive to survive a long period of dryness or drought.

Algae Simple plants including seaweeds that do not have proper flowers, fruits or roots.

Amphibians Main animal group that includes frogs, toads, salamanders and newts, where the larvae (young or tadpoles) mostly live in water while the adults live mainly on land.

Anal To do with the lower or rear end of an animal, such as the anal (lower rear) fin of a fish, or the end of an animal's digestive passageway.

Annelids Major group of worms with many body sections or segments, including earthworms and water-dwelling worms such as lugworms, ragworms, fanworms and leeches.

Aquatic Living in water, either in fresh water (streams, ponds, rivers, lakes), brackish (part-salty) water, or saltwater (seas, oceans).

Baleen The long strap-like parts hanging from the upper jaw inside the mouth of a great whale, which have brush- or comb-like edges to filter small food items from the water.

Benthic Living on the bottom of a sea, ocean, lake or river (compare Pelagic).

Bill Another word for a bird's beak.

Blubber Thick layer of fat just under the skin in cold-water animals such as seals, sea lions, walruses and whales.

Brackish Water which is part-salty and part-fresh, as found in the mouths of rivers and some coastal lagoons.

Camouflage When a living thing blends in or merges with its surroundings, using features such as body shape, colours, patterns and even movements.

Carnivore An animal that eats mainly other creatures rather than plants.

Cetacean A member of the whale, dolphin and porpoise group.

Cilia Tiny hair-like structures used in various ways by animals, such as to create a current of water.

Cnidarians Main group of soft-bodied, simple animals including jellyfish, sea anemones and coral polyps.

Cold-blooded An animal that cannot generate its own body heat, and so has a body temperature which is similar to the temperature of its surroundings.

Courtship When animals get together and give off scents, make sounds and perform displays, to attract a partner for breeding.

Crustaceans Main group of animals usually with a hard body casing and jointed limbs, which includes water fleas (daphnia), barnacles, krill, shrimps, prawns, crabs and lobsters.

Decapods Group of crustaceans which includes crabs, lobsters, shrimps and prawns (the name means 'ten limbs').

Detritivore A scavenging-type animal that eats mainly dead, dying and decaying material as food.

Dorsal On the upper surface or back, such as the dorsal fin of a fish.

Echinoderm Main group of 'spiny-skin' animals that all live in the sea, including starfish, sea urchins, sea lilies, feather stars and sea cucumbers.

Echolocation Sending out sounds such as squeaks or clicks, and listening for the returning echoes, to work out the position of nearby objects.

Embryo A very early, small stage in the development of a living thing from an egg.

Epipelagic zone The brightly lit surface waters of a sea or ocean, above the twilight zone.

Estuary The mouth or end of a river, where it widens and flows into the sea.

Flatfish Group of fishes where the body is flattened from side to side and the fish spends much time lying on one side (left or right) on the seabed.

Flukes (a) The tail parts of a whale, dolphin, porpoise or sirenian (dugong or manatee). (b) Thin, leaf-shaped animals that often live as parasites inside other creatures.

Food chain A series of events when a plant is eaten by an animal, which is eaten by another animal, and so on.

Food web Many food chains that have plants and animals in common and so join or link together.

Fresh water Water that is not salty, that is, it has only tiny amounts of salt (mainly sodium chloride) dissolved in it.

Gills Body parts specialized to take in dissolved oxygen from the water around.

Gill rakers Comb- or brush-like parts on the gills of some animals that filter small items of food from the water.

Habitat A certain kind of environment or surroundings, such as a pond, slow river, deep lake or open ocean.

Herbivore An animal that eats mainly plant foods rather than other creatures.

Hibernation When an animal becomes inactive to survive a long period of cold, usually the winter.

Kelp Large seaweeds with flattened fronds ('leaves') shaped like straps, blades or fans.

Larva The young stage of an animal as it is growing up, when it usually looks different from the adult – for example, the tadpole of a frog.

Marine To do with seas, oceans and water with dissolved salts (mainly sodium chloride).

Midnight zone The unlit, black waters of the deep sea or ocean, below the twilight zone.

Migration Long-distance journey, usually carried out at the same time or season each year.

Molluscs Huge main group of animals with soft bodies often encased in a hard shell, including shellfish like mussels and oysters, and snails, slugs and octopus.

Mucus Sticky, slimy substance made by many animals for various reasons, such as for capturing food, protection or sticking to a surface.

Nudibranchs Sea-slugs, which are saltwater cousins of slugs on land.

Omnivore An animal that eats a mixture of foods including plant material and animal flesh.

Operculum The bony flap covering the gills of animals such as fish, with a gap or slit along its rear edge.

Parasite A living thing which obtains a need such as food or shelter from another living thing, called its host, and causes harm to the host.

Pectoral To do with the front limbs or the shoulder region, for example, the pectoral fins are the front side fins of a fish.

Pelagic Living in open water, above the bottom (compare Benthic).

Pelvic To do with the rear limbs or the hip region, for example the pelvic fins are the rear side fins of a fish.

Phytoplankton The tiny plants of the plankton.

Pinniped 'Flipper or fin feet', the group name for seals, sea lions and walruses.

Plankton The floating 'soup' of tiny plants and animals, many too small to see without a microscope, found in seas and oceans (marine plankton), and also in large lakes (freshwater plankton).

Polyp An animal with a simple shape, usually a stalk-like body with a ring of tentacles on top, as in coral polyps (coral animals) that build coral reefs.

Predator a hunting animal that pursues and catches other creatures for food.

Prey A creature that is caught and eaten by another animal, the predator.

Respiration The activity of breathing, or getting oxygen from the surroundings into an animal's body.

School A large group of water animals, especially fish, that swim close together and twist, turn and move in the same direction together.

Sirenians Small group of sea mammals, sometimes called sea cows, that includes dugongs and manatees.

Tusk A very large or long tooth, as in the narwhal.

Twilight zone The dimly lit waters of a sea or ocean, below the epipelagic zone.

Valve In shellfish or bivalves such as mussels, one part of the two-part shell.

Venom A poisonous or harmful substance, especially as used by animals such as poisonous snakes and venomous fish like the stonefish.

Vertebrate An animal with a spinal column or backbone made of individual bones called vertebrae.

Warm-blooded Any animal that is able to generate its own body heat rather than simply absorbing heat from the environment.

Webbing In water animals, flaps of skin between the fingers or toes that give a greater thrust or pushing force when swimming.

Yolk A food store for the developing young in the eggs laid by some female animals, such as sharks.

Zooplankton The tiny animals of the plankton.

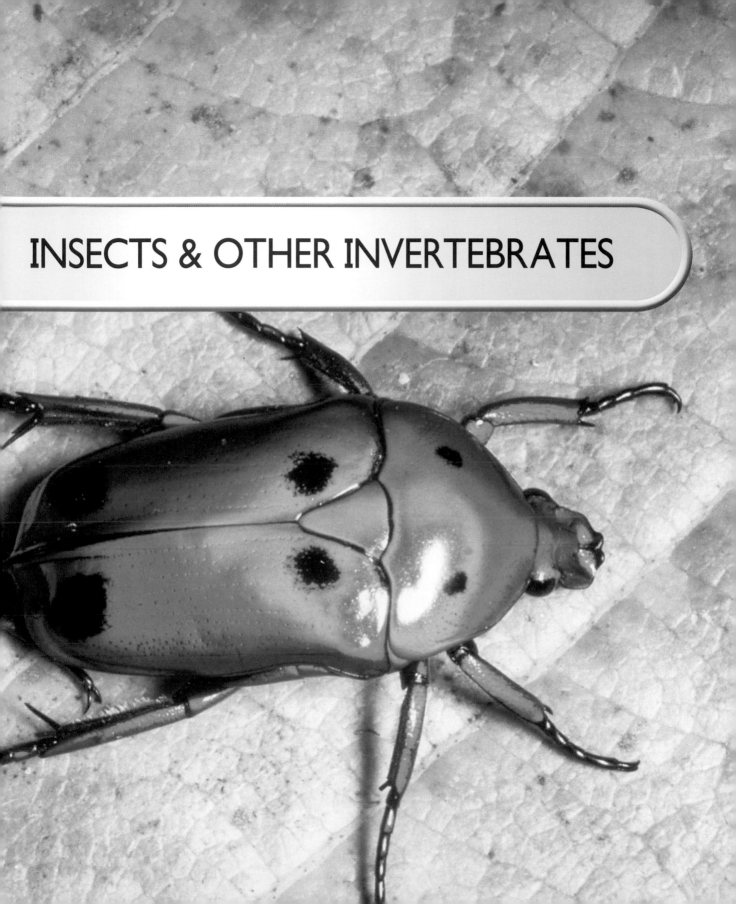

INSECTS & OTHER INVERTEBRATES

Land Invertebrates

Invertebrates are animals that do not possess a backbone. Invertebrates are an incredibly diverse and widespread group of animals with relatively few features in common. They are found in virtually every type of habitat, but are most numerous in the oceans. However, certain types of invertebrate, such as insects and spiders, are well adapted to life on land.

Amazing

A species of earthworm found in Asia is known to climb trees to save itself from drowning after a heavy downpour.

○ Invertebrates were the first animals to evolve, perhaps as long ago as one billion years (although the fossil record goes back only about 600 million years, so we cannot be sure).

○ Invertebrates make up about 97 per cent of all known animal species. They include arthropods, molluscs, worms and echinoderms.

○ **Woodlice are crustaceans that have adapted to life on land. They live in damp environments and can often be found in rotting wood and under stones, and also in people's homes.**

○ Invertebrates are cold-blooded animals. This means that they depend on their surroundings to maintain their body temperature.

○ Arthropods are invertebrates with a flexible external skeleton of hard, jointed plates made of a substance called chitin. This is called an exoskeleton. Arthropods include insects, arachnids (spiders and scorpions), crustaceans and myriapods.

○ Myriapods are land-dwelling arthropods with long, tube-like bodies and many legs. They live in soil and leaf litter. Myriapods include centipedes and millipedes.

○ **Insects, such as this buckeye butterfly, form the largest invertebrate group. Butterflies evolved when flowering plants were beginning to spread over the land, and they were among the first pollinating insects.**

Leeches

Leeches are segmented worms that live on land and also in water. They can feed on both dead and decaying plant matter. Some feed on insects and other worms, such as earthworms, while other species suck the blood of mammals, including humans.

Invertebrate facts

World's largest earthworm	South African giant earthworm	1.36 m long
Shortest earthworm	*Chaetogaster annandalei*	0.5 mm long
Largest land snail	African giant snail	20 cm average shell length
Largest arachnid	*Heterometrus swannerdami* scorpion	18 cm long
Smallest arachnid	Gall mites	0.25 mm
Longest myriapod	*Scolopendra moristans* centipede	33 cm long
Most legs	*Illacme plenipes* millipede	750

About 3000 species of centipede have been discovered so far. Most are relatively small, being 0.5–5 cm long, but the giant centipede can reach up to 30 cm in length.

○ Land-dwelling arthropods have a waxy waterproof coating on their exoskeleton to protect them from drying out. However, crustaceans lack this coating, so the majority live in water. Woodlice are among the few crustaceans that live on land.

○ Worms are slender, soft-bodied creatures. The three most important groups are roundworms, flatworms and segmented worms. Garden earthworms are a type of segmented worm.

○ Some invertebrates are parasitic, meaning that they live on or in the bodies of other animals, which are referred to as hosts. Ticks and leeches are external parasites. Some flatworms and roundworms, including tapeworms and flukes, are internal parasites

○ Slugs and snails are molluscs with a muscular 'foot' for moving around, and a tongue covered in tiny teeth for rasping at food.

○ Most invertebrates change shape as they grow, and this change is called metamorphosis. It allows the adults and young to have different lifestyles.

○ Some invertebrates feed on the remains of dead plants and animals. Known as 'decomposers', these animals perform a valuable role in breaking down and recycling the natural world's waste material.

This colourful Flavescens slug is using its muscular foot to wind its way along a grass stem. Flavescens slugs are pests of banana plantations in southern Africa.

Roundworms

Round, or nematode, worms are among the most common animals. They inhabit virtually every type of environment. Parasitic roundworms are a major cause of human and animal disease.

Most snails spend the day inside their hard, protective shells, emerging at night to search for food. Like slugs, they move by sliding over mucus secreted by their large, muscular foot.

The earthworm is a very useful invertebrate, since it makes the soil fertile by burrowing and adding its excretions (body waste). Its feeding and tunnelling activities allow air to permeate the soil and decompose organic matter, which aids plant growth.

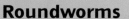

Find out more
Growth and change pp. 200–201

Insects

Insects are by far the most common type of animal. More than nine out of ten living species are insects. They flourish in nearly every part of the world, except under the sea and in the very coldest places. Insects are so successful because of their powerful exoskeletons, their ability to fly and their small size.

◀ *Trapped in sticky tree resin millions of years ago, this insect was preserved as the soft resin turned into hard amber. It is difficult to find insect fossils, because the soft bodies of insects usually decay before they have a chance to become fossilized.*

Amazing

In the past, doctors would insert maggots in wounds to eat dead flesh and disinfect the wounds by killing bacteria.

○ Insects have an open circulatory system without lots of tubes for carrying blood. The heart of an insect is a simple tube that pumps greenish-yellow blood all over the body.

▼ *This diagram of a honeybee shows the main parts of an insect's body. A honeybee has two pairs of wings.*

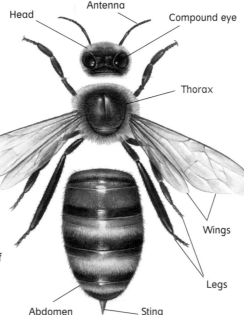

Head
Antenna
Compound eye
Thorax
Wings
Legs
Abdomen
Sting

○ The segmented body of an insect is divided into three parts: head, thorax (middle section) and abdomen (rear section).

○ All insects have six legs that are joined to the thorax. They usually have either one or two pairs of wings, which are also joined to the thorax.

○ Insects have an exoskeleton, which is a strong outer skeleton that protects the insect's body.

○ The muscles and delicate organs of insects are enclosed and protected within this exoskeleton.

○ The head contains the antennae, eyes, brain and mouthparts.

○ The digestive and reproductive systems of insects are contained within the abdomen.

Social insects

Social insects – termites, ants, bees and wasps, for example – live together with their own kind in large, complex groups called colonies. Within a colony, the insects work together as a team to find food and shelter. Usually only one female in the colony, the queen, lays eggs.

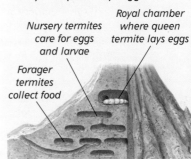

Nursery termites care for eggs and larvae
Royal chamber where queen termite lays eggs
Forager termites collect food

○ Insects breathe through special openings on the sides of the body known as spiracles.

○ Insects have a tiny brain, which is just a collection of nerve cells fused together. The brain sends signals to control all the other organs in the body.

○ Like all other invertebrates, insects are cold-blooded. Their body temperature changes with that of their surroundings, so their growth and development depends upon how hot or cold the weather is.

Insect records

Longest	Giant stick insect	33 cm
Shortest	*Dicopomorpha echmepterygis* wasp	0.21 mm long
Fastest flying	*Austrophlebia costalis* dragonfly	58 km/h
Fastest runner	*Periplaneta americana* cockroach	5.4 km/h
Largest egg	Malaysian stick insect	1.3 cm long
Most offspring	Cabbage aphid	Potentially billions!
Strongest	Rhinoceros beetle	Can carry 850 times its own weight

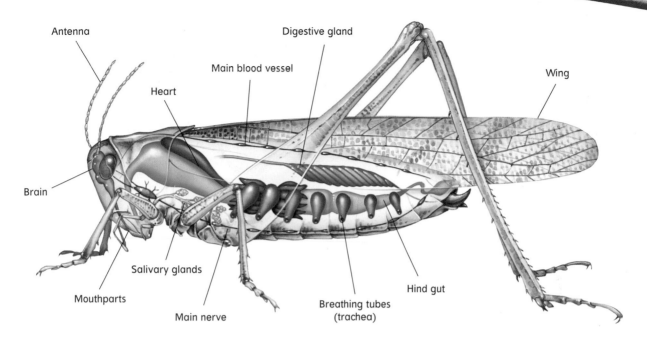

Antenna

Digestive gland

Main blood vessel

Wing

Heart

Brain

Salivary glands

Mouthparts

Main nerve

Breathing tubes
(trachea)

Hind gut

Flowering plants and pollinating
animals, such as this honeybee,
have evolved together, each totally
dependent upon the other. This process
is known as co-evolution.

Insect senses

Insect eyes are of two different types.
Compound eyes, which are made up of
many tiny lenses, are good at detecting
movement. Simple eyes only register
light and dark. An insect's antennae, or
'feelers', function as organs of touch,
smell, and taste.

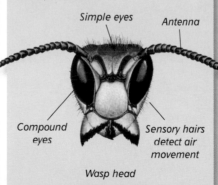

Simple eyes

Antenna

Compound
eyes

Sensory hairs
detect air
movement

Wasp head

Some insects damage crops
and are considered pests.
Mealybugs (scale insects)
are pests of citrus trees and
greenhouse plants.

A grasshopper has the body parts
of a typical insect. Insects breathe
through a network of tubes (trachea)
that lead from small holes (spiracles)
along the body.

❍ Insects have always been of great
importance to human civilizations, and
some insects are reared for the materials
that can be obtained from them. For
example, silkworms are bred for the silk
they produce, and honeybees are kept
for the honey and wax they provide.

❍ Insects play a major role in the
pollination of flowers. In fact, there are
many plants that depend entirely on
insects for pollination.

Find out more

Termites pp. 232–233

Arachnids

There are about 75,500 species of arachnid. Arachnids include a variety of creatures, including spiders, scorpions, ticks, mites, harvestmen and pseudoscorpions. Fossils of arachnids suggest that they were among the first land-dwelling animals. These creatures can be found almost anywhere on Earth, but they are most common in dry and tropical regions.

➤ Spiders are predatory arachnids that use fangs to inject venom into their prey. Some spiders spin silken webs to catch their prey.

➤ Sun spiders are not true spiders. These nocturnal hunters usually bite off the legs of their prey before eating the victims head-first. Most species feed on spiders, scorpions, ticks and mites.

➤ The sensory hairs on the legs of this spider are clearly visible. Lacking ears, a mouth and a tongue, such hairs enable spiders to touch, taste and hear things in the world around them.

❍ Arachnids have eight legs. They also have two pairs of appendages (the chelicerae and the pedipalps) at the front of the body, which are used to grasp and hold prey.

❍ Diverse in size, arachnids range from just a few millimetres to more than 20 cm in length. Their hard, segmented body casing, or exoskeleton, protects them from enemies. The exoskeleton is made of carbohydrates and calcium.

❍ An arachnid's body is divided into two parts: the cephalothorax (joint head and thorax) and the abdomen. The cephalothorax has sensory organs, mouthparts, stomach and limbs, while the abdomen contains the heart, lungs, gut, reproductive organs and anus.

❍ Arachnids do not have teeth and jaws to chew their food, and most cannot digest solid food. This is why they suck fluids from their prey's body.

Pseudoscorpion

Pseudoscorpions are not scorpions. Although they look like scorpions, they do not have the long tail with the sting at the tip. They produce venom in their pincer-like pedipalps. Pseudoscorpions have silk glands, which have openings on the jaws, or chelicerae. They use the silk to spin cocoons, in which they moult and live during winter.

○ Arachnids use sensory hairs, simple eyes and slit sensory organs to detect and interpret their surroundings.

○ Arachnids are ecologically important to humans, since they help to control the populations of pest insects.

○ The lifespan of arachnids is fairly short. In temperate regions, they usually live for about a year, but in warmer places their lifespan can be longer.

○ When caught by predators, some arachnids drop their captured limbs in order to escape.

○ Arachnids are classified as invertebrates – animals that do not have backbones.

○ Arachnids are cold-blooded creatures that get warmth from their environment.

▲ *At first glance, spiders and harvestmen appear similar. But whereas spiders have two distinct body parts, separated by a waist or stalk, harvestmen have a 'one-piece', rounded or oval body. Furthermore, harvestmen do not have organs capable of secreting silk thread for spinning nests and webs.*

▶ *Scorpions are feared by humans because of their powerful sting. Their grasping, pincer-like appendages can also be a scary sight.*

○ Instead of having lungs, arachnids have two types of breathing mechanism – book lungs and tracheae.

○ Sometimes the legs of an arachnid are used for catching and holding enemies.

▶ *Many mites are so small that they may be invisible to the naked eye (shown here x 75), but they are an important group of arachnids. Some mites are free-living, others are parasites.*

Ticks

Ticks are parasites that feed on the blood of mammals, such as humans, deer, sheep, dogs and cows. A tick is about the size of a rice grain (shown here x 75). It climbs on to a host animal, grips tightly with its legs and sinks its mouthparts into the host's skin. When it has gorged itself on blood, its bag-like body swells up like a balloon and the tick drops off the host.

▼ *All spiders can make silk. They pull it out of organs called spinnerets, usually with their legs, and use it to make webs and wrap up prey and eggs.*

Amazing

Pseudoscorpions often attach themselves to the legs of insects, such as house-flies, crane flies and beetles, to hitch rides. They can also walk backwards.

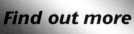

Find out more

Spider silk and webs pp. 242–243

Courtship and Reproduction

Males and females must come together and mate to produce the next generation. Many species use scents to find mates, but others use sounds, dances, light displays, and even gifts. After the females have laid their eggs, most insects show little interest in their offspring. However, some species at least make sure there is a ready food source for the young (larvae) that hatch.

▲ Many spiders attach their silken egg-sac to a plant or other surface, while others conceal it in a nest chamber. Some spiders even carry their eggs around with them.

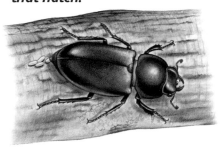

▲ Female stag beetles lay their eggs in rotting tree trunks. The larvae feed on the decaying wood.

○ Male cicadas, crickets and grasshoppers 'sing' to attract mates, while the male buzzing spider drums his abdomen on a leaf to signal to females.

○ Butterflies and moths perform elaborate courtship flights, or 'dances', and they also may produce chemical scents called pheromones to attract the opposite sex.

○ Bolas spiders can make pheromones that are identical to those produced by some female moths, and the spiders use them to attract and trap male moths.

○ Some male insects and spiders present courtship 'gifts' to the females. Male dance flies give food items wrapped up in silk to impress potential mates.

○ The female earwig guards her eggs until they hatch, cleaning them regularly. Unusually for an insect, she also looks after and feeds her young until they can fend for themselves.

Fireflies

The firefly is not a fly but a type of beetle. Male fireflies 'dance' in the air at dusk, flashing lights from their abdomens as they fly. Female fireflies stay on twigs and leaves and flash in reply as part of their courtship. The lights are made by chemicals in the beetles' bodies.

○ Scorpions give birth to live young. The females of some species bend their legs to make a 'birth basket' that catches the young as they are born.

○ Spiders wrap their eggs in silk to form a protective egg-sac. Some baby spiders (or spiderlings) have an egg-tooth that they use to cut their way out of their egg.

Wrestling beetles

Stag beetles have huge, antler-like jaws. Rival males use these to wrestle with each other for the right to mate with females. The contest ends when one beetle retreats or is tipped over onto its back.

After mating, the female Colorado beetle lays clusters of 20–45 eggs.

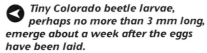

Tiny Colorado beetle larvae, perhaps no more than 3 mm long, emerge about a week after the eggs have been laid.

○ Baby spiders move from one place to another using a silken strand released from their body. The wind then carries this thread and the spiders hang on for a free ride. This method of dispersal is called ballooning.

○ Caterpillars – the larvae of butterflies and moths – are plant eaters. Most caterpillars eat only particular plants. The adult females make sure that they lay their eggs on leaves of the correct species, so that when their young hatch there is plenty of food at hand.

○ Parasitic wasps, such as ichneumon wasps, lay their eggs on or inside the bodies of other insects. When the larvae hatch, they eat the host insect and may even pupate inside its body.

After mating, the female black widow spider sometimes eats the male. She mates only once in her lifetime, which is why she's called a 'widow'. The female stores the male's sperm in her body.

○ The larvae of colony-forming social insects, such as ants, bees, wasps and termites, get perhaps the best care of any young insects. The adult worker insects in the colony tend and protect the eggs, and nurture the larvae once they have hatched.

A honeybee hive, showing some of the cells used for storing pollen, honey, eggs and developing larvae. Worker bees feed the larvae on 'royal jelly' (a nutritious form of saliva) at first, and later on honey and pollen.

Amazing

Some male moths can detect a female's pheromones from more than 11 km away.

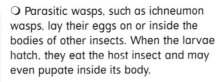

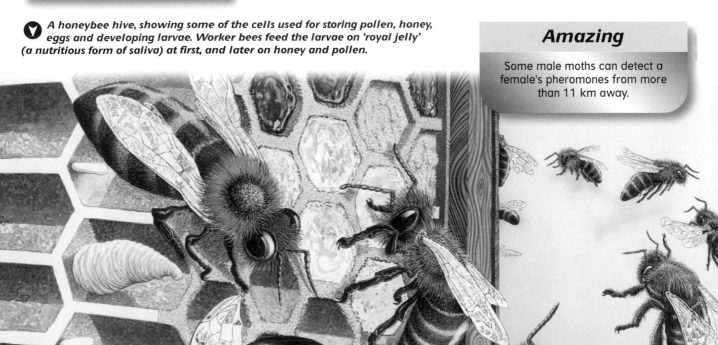

Growth and Change

All arthropods must shed their hard exoskeleton periodically in order to grow, since it will not stretch. This is known as moulting. However, the development from egg to adulthood varies between the different groups, and between species.

❍ To moult, insects expand their body by swallowing air or water, or by raising their blood pressure. The exoskeleton splits, and the insect wriggles free.

❍ A soft new exoskeleton is exposed when the insect gets rid of its old one. The new exoskeleton is bigger than the old one, allowing the insect to grow.

❍ The new exoskeleton hardens and becomes darker in colour.

❍ The larval stage between moults is known as an instar.

❍ Moulting takes a long time, and the insect is vulnerable to attack during this period, so most insects moult in secluded places. Moulting is controlled by chemicals called hormones in the insect's body.

A *A young adult dragonfly emerges during its final moult. After resting for a while, it will pump blood into its short crumpled wings to spread them out to their full adult size.*

Different lives

In the insect world, the young and adult animals often have not only different bodies but also very different lives, with contrasting surroundings and diets.

Damselfly nymphs (left) live underwater, feeding on fish, tadpoles and water beetles. The adults (right) are aerial hunters that catch insects such as flies and mosquitoes on the wing.

Polyphemus caterpillars (left) feast on the leaves of shrubs and trees such as oak and willow. Adult *Polyphemus* moths (right) lack functioning mouthparts and do not feed at all.

Cicada nymph

The larva of the cicada may live underground for more than ten years. Different types of cicadas stay in the soil for different periods of time. The American periodic cicada is probably the record-holder, taking 17 years to change into a pupa and then an adult.

Cicada larva

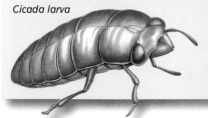

Amazing

A caterpillar grows about 2000 times bigger than its size at the time of its birth. If a 3 kg human baby grew at the same rate, the baby would weigh as much as a bus in a month.

1. Female butterfly lays tiny eggs, usually under leaves

2. Caterpillar hatches from egg and eats leaves

3. Caterpillar becomes pupa

4. Pupa's case splits open

5. Adult butterfly emerges

This diagram shows complete metamorphosis in a butterfly. The larvae of butterflies and moths are called caterpillars, the larvae of beetles are known as grubs, and the larvae of many flies are called maggots.

Non-stop moulting

In two primitive insect groups, silverfish and bristletails, moulting does not stop at maturity, and there is no change in form between young and adults. Many insects only go through 5–10 moults, but silverfish can moult up to 60 times in a lifetime. Silverfish are named after the tiny, shiny scales that cover their carrot-shaped body. Like bristletails, they have three bristle-like 'tails', as well as abdominal projections called styles that help them to move over steep or uneven surfaces.

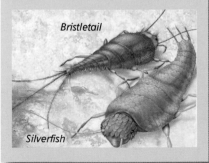

Bristletail

Silverfish

○ With some insects, such as grasshoppers and dragonflies, the young, which are known as nymphs, resemble their parents, although they are smaller and without wings.

○ Nymphs gradually develop into adults through a series of moults. As their bodies go through little change, this type of development is called incomplete metamorphosis

○ Other insects, such as butterflies, moths, beetles, bees, wasps and ants, have greater changes in body shape between the young (larval) stage and adulthood. They are said to experience a complete metamorphosis.

Crickets and grasshoppers go through incomplete metamorphosis. The wings develop gradually within 'wing buds' on the outside of the nymph's body. At the final moult, the nymph becomes a fully formed adult, capable of breeding.

○ In insects, moulting ceases at adulthood, but arachnids moult throughout their lives. Although they increase in size, there is no real change in appearance, since immature arachnids merely look like smaller versions of the adults.

Cricket nymph   Old skin   Mature adult

Find out more

Caterpillars p. 221

Wings and Flight

Insects fly to escape from danger, to find suitable mates, to hunt for food, or to find a new place to lay their eggs. Some insects can fly very long distances in search of food, while others can cross entire continents when they migrate. Wings help to distinguish between different insect groups.

Amazing

A large butterfly flaps its wings once or twice each second. Some tiny flies flap almost 1000 times each second.

○ Insects were the first animals to evolve the power of flight.

○ Most insects have evolved two pairs of wings, which help them to fly. The earliest insects had wings that helped them to glide through the air. These wings evolved into sturdier wings that could be flapped up and down.

Some flies are fierce predators, using their aerial prowess to snatch other insects in flight.

ⓐ *Dobsonflies look like dragonflies. Adults have veins on their wings, which are grey in colour.*

○ Not all insects can fly. Some insects have lost their wings during the course of evolution, while others have become skilled fliers.

○ In many groups of flying insects, the larval stage is wingless.

○ Insect wings are membrane-like structures. They have veins and nerves running across them, through which blood and oxygen are circulated. The wing edge is usually thicker and sturdier than the main part of the wing. This helps the wing to slice through the air more easily during flight.

○ The veins provide support to the wings and allow them to twist in flight.

○ The wings are attached to the insect's thorax (middle section) by strong muscles, which help the insect to flap its wings.

Migrating monarchs

Every autumn, huge numbers of monarch butterflies fly from cold northern areas of North America to the warmth of Florida, California and Mexico. In spring, new generations of monarchs make the long return journey north again.

⭕ If the air is cool, insects need to bask in the sun to warm up their flight muscles before take-off is possible. Bumblebees can also 'shiver' their flight muscles in order to generate heat.

⭕ In insects, such as beetles, the front pair of wings is hard and protects the hind wings, which are more delicate. In flies, the hind wings are reduced to knob-like structures called halteres, which help the insect to balance itself in the air.

◀ *In beetles, the front wings have evolved into hard wing cases that prevent damage to the fragile hind wings. This Colorado beetle is opening its wing cases in preparation for take-off. You can see the hind wings unfolding underneath.*

◀ *The thin tissues of a butterfly's wings are nourished and supported by tubular veins. The wings are covered in thousands of tiny scales and hairs.*

⭕ In some insects, such as wasps and butterflies, the front and hind pairs of wings are linked to produce two (rather than four) flying surfaces.

⭕ Some insects, such as dragonflies, butterflies and locusts, may save energy by gliding between wingbeats.

◀ *Dragonflies and damselflies flap their wings in a figure-of-eight pattern. This movement helps to create air currents near the wings that balance the insect while flying.*

▲ *One of the strongest insect fliers is the Apollo butterfly of Europe and Asia. It flaps high over hills and mountains, then rests on a rock or flower in the sunshine.*

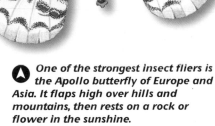

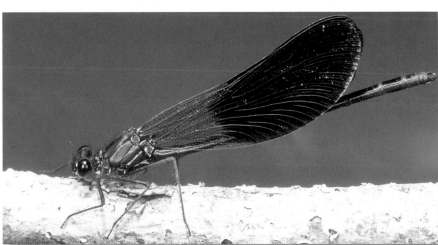

Hawkmoths

Hawk moths, or sphinx moths, are among the fastest flying insects, capable of flying at up to 50 km/h. Many, such as Darwin's hawk moth shown here, can hover in mid-air as they use their long tongues to suck nectar from deep within flowers.

Find out more

Dragonflies pp. 230–231

Legs and Movement

One feature that sets arthropods, such as insects and arachnids, apart from most other invertebrates is their jointed limbs. By being able to walk, run, jump, or swim, they are better equipped to find food and find mates, and to colonize new habitats.

○ The number of legs varies from six in insects to eight in arachnids (such as spiders and scorpions) and several hundred in millipedes.

○ Each leg usually ends in a claw that helps the animal to grip surfaces.

○ Some arthropods, including flies and spiders, have tiny bristles or adhesive pads on their feet that enable them to walk on smooth, vertical surfaces, hang upside down, or even walk on water.

○ Most insects walk by moving three of their six legs at a time. The front and back legs on one side and the middle leg on the other side stay put, forming a stable tripod shape. The other three legs move forwards.

True legs

Prolegs

Anal claspers

▷ *When a jumping spider spots prey, it rapidly increases its blood pressure, forcing its rear legs to extend and hurl the spider through the air towards its victim.*

○ Muscles in the thorax (the middle section of an insect's body, to which the legs are attached) move the legs to and fro, while muscles inside the legs themselves bend them at the joints.

○ When a spider walks, it moves four of its eight legs at a time. The first and third leg on one side of its body move with the second and fourth leg on the other side.

○ A spider uses muscles in its legs to bend the legs at the joints. However, spiders have no muscles to extend their legs, so this is done by raising the blood pressure in the legs.

○ Legs are used for many other purposes apart from movement, including holding onto the opposite sex during mating, catching prey and manipulating food, and feeling the surroundings.

▽ *Some aquatic insects, such as this water boatman bug, have flattened, hairy legs. The insects use their legs like oars to 'row' themselves through the water.*

Flea

A flea can leap 30 cm high, which is more than 100 times its body length. It has rubbery pads at the base of its hind legs. These are kept compressed, like coiled springs, until they are released by a trigger mechanism, catapulting the flea into the air.

◁ *Like other insects, caterpillars have six legs. These are at the front of the body. Behind them are five pairs of gripping 'false legs' – four pairs of muscular projections called prolegs, and a pair of sucker-like anal claspers at the rear.*

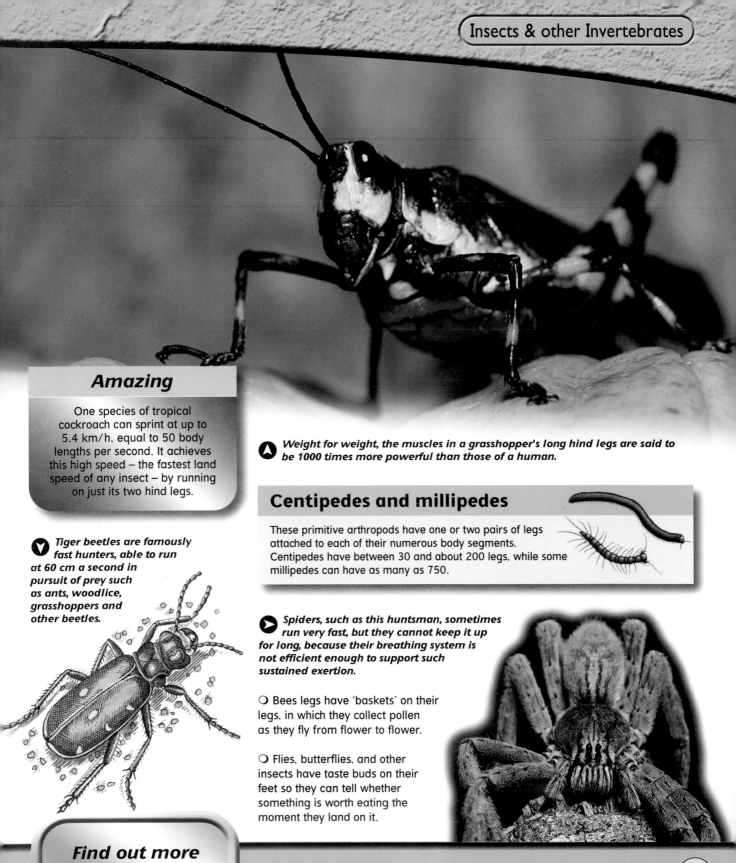

Amazing

One species of tropical cockroach can sprint at up to 5.4 km/h, equal to 50 body lengths per second. It achieves this high speed – the fastest land speed of any insect – by running on just its two hind legs.

Tiger beetles are famously fast hunters, able to run at 60 cm a second in pursuit of prey such as ants, woodlice, grasshoppers and other beetles.

Weight for weight, the muscles in a grasshopper's long hind legs are said to be 1000 times more powerful than those of a human.

Centipedes and millipedes

These primitive arthropods have one or two pairs of legs attached to each of their numerous body segments. Centipedes have between 30 and about 200 legs, while some millipedes can have as many as 750.

Spiders, such as this huntsman, sometimes run very fast, but they cannot keep it up for long, because their breathing system is not efficient enough to support such sustained exertion.

○ Bees legs have 'baskets' on their legs, in which they collect pollen as they fly from flower to flower.

○ Flies, butterflies, and other insects have taste buds on their feet so they can tell whether something is worth eating the moment they land on it.

Find out more

Water bugs p. 213

Food and Feeding

The diets of insects and arachnids are almost as varied as their appearance. Some species are specialist feeders, eating only one particular kind of plant or preying on just a few kinds of animal. Others are generalists, feeding on a broad range of foods. There are also scavengers that take whatever they can find, including decaying plant and animal tissues.

◀ Spiders, such as this tarantula, use their jaws, pedipalps and digestive fluids to liquidize their prey.

Antlion trap

Antlions are insects like lacewings. Some antlion larvae make a pit in the sand by moving around in a spiral path and throwing out sand. The larva then waits inside the pit and feeds on insects that fall into it. When the prey struggles to escape, the larva throws sand at it to make it fall back down into the pit. The larva then sucks the body juices from its victim.

◀ The devil's coach-horse beetle has powerful mouthparts and tears apart dead and dying small caterpillars, grubs and worms.

○ Insects that chew their food, such as grasshoppers and beetles, have two sets of 'jaws'. At the front are serrated mandibles, which chop up and grind food. Behind these are the less powerful maxillae, which move the food down into the stomach.

○ Many insects that feed on liquid foods have tube-like mouthparts. Butterflies and moths have a long tongue, called a proboscis, that they use to probe flowers and suck up nectar. When not in use, the proboscis coils up under the head.

○ Many bugs, including aphids and cicadas, feed on plants. They have syringe-like mouthparts that they use to pierce plant stems and drink the nutrient-rich sap.

○ Some ants drink the liquid called honeydew that aphids and other bugs excrete as they feed on plant sap. The ants will defend the aphids from predators to protect their food source.

○ Piercing sucking mouthparts are also used by predatory insects, such as assassin bugs and robberflies, to inject saliva into their prey and digest the victim's internal tissues and organs. The predator drinks the dissolved innards.

○ Wasps and bees have both jaws and a proboscis. They use their proboscis to sip nectar from flowers, and their jaws for building nests.

▼ When ants find food, they form a chemical trail of pheromones so that other ants can find their way from the nest to the food source.

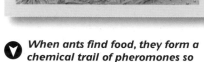

Crab, or flower, spiders prey on nectar-feeding insects, such as bees, hoverflies and butterflies. They seize prey with their front legs and inject it with a paralyzing venom.

Tiger beetles have huge eyes to locate their prey. These fierce predators use their massive biting jaws to catch and cut up their prey, such as insects and other invertebrates.

○ Termites and wood-boring beetles have a diet of wood. Their stomachs contain microbes (bacteria and protozoa) that break down cellulose – one of the main ingredients of wood.

○ When larvae become adults, they may change their diet as well as their appearance. Adult parasitic wasps, for example, are often vegetarian, but their larvae are carnivorous. In some insect species, such as mayflies, the adults do not eat at all.

○ The jaws of arachnids (spiders and scorpions) are known as chelicerae. They also have leg-like mouthparts called pedipalps, which they use to manipulate food items.

A preying mantis has powerful front legs armed with sharp spines. The mantis uses these to impale its victims, before shredding them with its sharp cutting mouthparts.

○ Arachnid mouths are too small to eat solid food, so arachnids release digestive fluids to turn the prey into a soupy mass that can be sucked up.

Amazing

One species of cockroach can go for about 3 months without eating, surviving off its body fat. It can even live for 40 days with neither food nor water.

Caterpillars have strong jaws with overlapping 'teeth' or plates to chew or grind up leaves. When the caterpillar pupates, it loses these mouthparts and develops the sucking proboscis of an adult butterfly or moth.

House-flies

House-flies often vomit some portion of their last feed on top of their next meal. This makes the new food material easier to digest. Most of the time, house-flies do not eat all the food and leave some particles behind. These remaining food particles can spread a variety of diseases.

Colour and Camouflage

Insects have some of the best types of camouflage in the entire animal world. Camouflage is when a living thing is coloured and patterned so that it blends in with its surroundings, making it difficult to spot. Camouflage can help a predator to creep up unnoticed on its victims. Many insects that are preyed on use camouflage to avoid predators.

❍ Insects that live in grass or on leaves – such as katydids, mantids and many stinkbugs –– are often coloured green to conceal them amongst the lush vegetation.

▼ *The tiger swallowtail caterpillar has large eyespots on its body to scare off predators. These circular markings look like the eyes of a larger, more dangerous animal, such as a snake, and persuade attackers to back off.*

❍ Leaf insects have flattened bodies and fringes on their legs that give them a leaf-like outline. Their markings look like the ribs and veins of leaves, and the body may even have brown edges to make them resemble a dying leaf.

❍ Many moths have a mottled colouration to help them blend in with the lichen covered tree trunks on which they rest during the daytime.

▶ *In its caterpillar (larval) stage, the monarch butterfly eats milkweed plants, which are poisonous to predatory birds. The monarch retains the toxins in its body as an adult, and its striking orange–and–black colouring warns birds not to eat it.*

❍ Stick insects and praying mantises look like twigs and leaves. Predators often miss out on a meal because these insects blend into their environment very well.

▼ *The peppered moth has both a light, speckled form and an all-black form. The latter survives better in urban areas, where it is well-camouflaged on the darker surfaces of smoke–polluted trees. The lighter, speckled form is more common in the countryside.*

Hornet mimic

The hornet moth has transparent wings and a yellow-and-black striped body, making it look like a large wasp called a hornet. It even behaves like a hornet when it flies. Predators, such as birds, avoid hornet moths because they look as though they might sting.

Hornet

Hornet moth

With their long, thin bodies, stick insect look remarkably like leafless twigs, especially when they remain perfectly still or sway with the wind.

With its green colouration and the wavy edge to its body, this stinkbug resembles a tiny leaf.

○ Monarch butterflies are bitter-tasting and poisonous, so most birds do not eat them. Viceroy butterflies are harmless, but they have orange-and-black wings similar to those of monarch butterflies. Birds avoid viceroy butterflies because they think that they are also poisonous.

○ Adults and caterpillars of some moths and butterflies have large, eye-like spots to scare away predatory birds.

○ The velvet ant is actually a wasp. It resembles an ant, and can easily attack ant nests with this disguise.

○ Some harmless insects mimic (imitate) harmful insects in appearance and behaviour. This often fools predators into leaving them alone.

○ Hoverflies are stingless, but their bodies are marked with yellow-and-black stripes that make them resemble wasps or hornets. Because of their coloration, predators avoid the harmless hoverflies, assuming them to be stinging insects.

○ Some spiders also use warning and camouflage colours. Crab spiders, for example, are able to change colour to match the flower on which they choose to hide. They blend in with their surroundings, and pounce on any insects that come to sip nectar from the flower.

○ Sometimes colour is used not to hide an insect, but to warn predators to steer clear of it.

○ Insects with stings or that are poisonous to eat usually have brightly coloured bodies. Black, yellow, orange and red are often used as warning colours. Poisonous chemicals are either made in the insect's body or obtained from a toxic plant on which it feeds.

This crab spider, camouflaged white against its host flower, has caught a hoverfly.

Amazing

If a crab spider is placed on a flower that is a different colour to the one on which it has been hiding, it can take up to two days for the spider to copy the new colour.

Thornbugs

The thornbug has a pointed extension to its thorax that resembles a thorn. By day, it sits still on a twig pretending to be a real thorn. It moves about and feeds at night. The unusual body shape not only camouflages the bug, but also acts as protective armour – any predator that tries to eat it risks injury.

Find out more

Self-defence pp. 210–211

Self-defence

*T*he threat of becoming a meal for another animal is always close at hand for insects and arachnids. Hiding from predators or fleeing when danger threatens are the first-choice survival tactics. But if camouflage proves ineffective and escape is not possible, these creatures either need to be able to fight back or have other means of defending themselves against predators.

▲ *This caterpillar is protected from attack by birds and other predators by its irritating hairs. Some other caterpillars have sharp spines for protection.*

Chemical spray

The bombardier beetle can twist the end of its abdomen to squirt a boiling, irritating liquid in almost any direction. The liquid evaporates immediately it is sprayed, forming a gas that briefly blinds the enemy and enables the bombardier beetle to run away.

▲ *When ants sting, they inject a venom called formic acid. The sting of the bulldog ant, shown here, is extremely painful to humans.*

❍ Some caterpillars and larvae have special glands that secrete poison when they are attacked. Predatory birds soon learn to avoid them.

❍ Stick insects and weevils are known to 'play dead' when attacked. They simply keep very still, and attackers will usually leave the insects alone, because most predators do not eat dead prey.

❍ Ants, bees, wasps and scorpions can sting their attackers and pump toxic venom into the wound. Spiders have a venomous bite.

❍ Honeybees sting only once and die soon after. The jagged sting remains stuck in their victim's skin, which tears out the honeybee's insides.

❍ Wasps can sting many times over, because their stings are smooth and can be pulled out of their victims' bodies and used again.

❍ Some beetles release unpleasant-tasting, sticky yellow blood (hemolymph) from their 'knee-joints', which gums up the attacker's mouth and antennae.

◗ *When an earwig is being threatened, it raises its tail in an effort to make itself appear bigger.*

Amazing

When they are threatened, tarantulas hurl tufts of barbed hairs at their attacker. This leads to skin irritation and pain.

○ Moths, grasshoppers and mantids suddenly show the bright colours on their hind wings to startle a predator. These are called flash colours.

○ Some insect larvae and adults have spiny projections on their body to make them difficult to swallow.

○ Harvestmen spray a smelly liquid at attackers, or smear it over themselves to achieve the same deterrent effect.

○ Some animals adopt an aggressive pose when threatened. Australia's highly venomous funnelweb spider raises its front legs and exposes its deadly fangs. This display persuades many predators to back off.

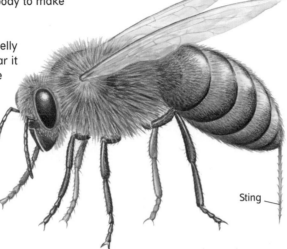

▶ *A honeybee's jagged sting is a modified ovipositor (egg-laying tube), so only female bees can sting. Male bees do not have the necessary equipment at the end of their abdomen.*

Sting

▲ *A lobster moth caterpillar confuses predators by suddenly changing shape. It raises its head and tail over its body (making it look like a tiny lobster) and waves a pair of filaments at the end of its abdomen. Lobster moth caterpillars can also squirt formic acid over their predators.*

Click beetle

The click beetle measures about 12 mm long. When in danger, it falls on its back and pretends to be dead. But it slowly arches its body and then straightens with a jerk, flicking itself up to 25 cm into the air with a loud 'click'. This frightens predators and gives the beetle a chance to escape.

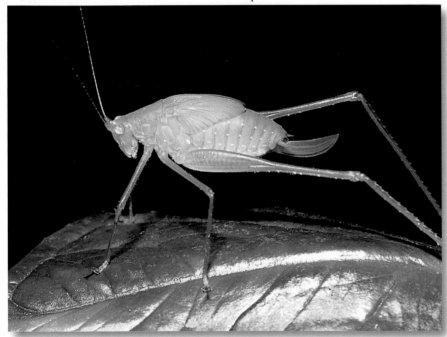

▲ *Insects, such as katydids, can shed a limb when an attacker grabs them by the leg. This phenomenon is known as autotomy.*

Bugs

The word 'bug' is sometimes used to mean any insect, but in science it refers to a specific group of insects with piercing and sucking mouthparts. There are around 82,000 species of bug, ranging from tiny bugs just a few millimetres long to giant water bugs, up to 6.5 cm in length, that prey on frogs, fish and occasionally even small birds.

Assassin bugs

Assassin bugs are predatory. They grab their prey with their powerful front legs and 'assassinate' it by injecting venom. The venom paralyzes the prey and partially dissolves and disintegrates it. The bug then sucks up the liquid food. An assassin bug may take several days to eat a large victim.

○ Bugs generally have compound eyes and two pairs of wings. The first pair is partially hard and protects the delicate, membrane-like second pair of wings.

○ Some bugs do not have wings, while the nymphs of all bugs are wingless.

○ All bugs undergo incomplete metamorphosis. There is no pupal stage, so the bugs grow into adults by moulting again and again. The nymphs resemble the adult bugs.

○ Bugs can survive on land, in air, on the surface of water and even under water. There are very few places where you would not find a bug.

○ Some bugs can give out a very bad odour. This is a defence strategy.

Stinkbugs have glands on their undersurface, from which they secrete a foul-smelling fluid. This fluid has a strong effect on many animals and helps to protect the bug from predators. In some stinkbugs, the thorax extends down the back to form a protective shield that covers most of the abdomen. These stinkbugs are also called shield bugs.

Spittlebugs

Spittlebug nymphs produce a sticky liquid and blow it into a frothy mass of white bubbles, which is sometimes known as 'cuckoospit'. As well as hiding the nymph from predators, these bubbles also protect the young bug from the drying effects of the sun.

○ Bugs feed on plant and animal juices. There are some bugs, such as bed bugs, that are parasites. They live by sucking blood from other animals.

○ Carnivorous bugs are predatory and help to control pests, while herbivorous bugs can be a threat to crops. Bugs are sometimes cannibalistic, eating weaker individuals of their own kind.

○ Some people cultivate certain species of bug to obtain dyes from them, while others enjoy bugs as food. Bugs are often harvested on a commercial scale for various purposes.

Amazing

Male cicadas are the loudest of all insects. The song of some species can be heard more than 400 m away. The sound of thousands of cicadas in a single tree can be louder than a pneumatic drill.

Find out more

Cicada nymph p. 200

Water bugs

Giant water bugs store air in a dip between the roof of the abdomen and the wings. To renew this air supply, they swim to the surface and take in more air through a snorkel-like tube.

Male cicadas sing loudly to attract females with the help of special drum-like membranes called timbals. Female cicadas do not produce any sound because their timbals are not developed.

The long, thin legs of a water strider help to spread out its weight. The surface of the water bends into small dips around the end of each leg, but does not break.

Backswimmers have claws on the end of each leg to help them hang upside down from the surface of the water or grip onto water plants.

The water scorpion is a predator. Its legs are suited to catching prey, such as tadpoles, and its mouthparts are adapted to sucking fluids from the prey's body.

The squash bug of North America feeds on the juices of cucumbers, squashes, melons and other gourds. While feeding, the squash bug injects a toxic substance into the plant. As a result, the plant wilts and dies.

213

Wasps

Wasps are related to bees and ants. They have four transparent wings, two large compound eyes and sharp cutting jaws with jagged edges. Wasps are solitary as well as social insects. Social wasps live in huge colonies, while solitary wasps live alone. There are about 17,000 species of wasp, but only about 1500 species are social.

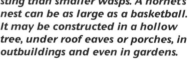

These social wasps will not store food in their nest, as the cells face downwards and are open at the bottom. The queen wasp glues her eggs inside the cells to prevent them from falling out. Workers feed the larvae with chewed up insects and caterpillars.

The tarantula hawk is a spider-hunting wasp. It stings tarantulas to paralyze them, and then stores the spiders in its nest as food for its larvae.

○ Wasp nests can be simple or complex. Some nests are just burrows in the ground, while others are built with mud and twigs and may contain many cells and tunnels.

○ Each nest has at least one queen wasp, as well as workers and males.

○ Not all wasps bother to build nests. Some wasps, such as cuckoo wasps, lay their eggs in the nests of bees and other wasps.

○ Other species of wasp lay their eggs in stems, leaves, fruits and flowers, instead of building nests.

Although hornets are protective of their nest, they are far less likely to sting than smaller wasps. A hornet's nest can be as large as a basketball. It may be constructed in a hollow tree, under roof eaves or porches, in outbuildings and even in gardens.

Fig pollinators

Fig wasps lay their eggs on wild figs. This causes the formation of seed galls inside the figs, and in the process pollinates them. The trees can only be pollinated by these wasps. Each fig wasp species pollinates a particular species of wild fig tree.

Find out more

Hornet mimic p. 208

▼ *Male velvet ants have wings and cannot sting. Velvet ants are actually wasps. The females, which do not have wings, move about on the ground like ants, and their sting can be painful.*

▶ *The giant wood wasp looks menacing, but it is actually harmless. It belongs to a group of wasps called horntails, after the spine at the end of their abdomen. Females inject a wood-rotting fungus as they lay their eggs in tree trunks. When the larvae hatch, they eat both the wood and the fungus.*

❍ Adult wasps feed on nectar, and fruit and plant sap, while wasp larvae feed on insects.

❍ Many species of wasp are parasitic in the larval stage, which means that they live on or inside another insect, known as a host, and feed off its body.

❍ Wasps are helpful for controlling pests, such as caterpillars.

❍ Gall wasps are named after their habit of causing the formation of tumour-like growths in plants, known as galls.

❍ A female gall wasp injects her eggs into a woody plant host. When the eggs hatch, the larvae release chemicals that cause the plant to cover them with soft tissues in the form of a gall. The larvae feed on the gall and pupate inside it.

❍ Sawflies are wasps that have a saw-like ovipositor (egg-laying tube) for inserting eggs into plant tissue.

▼ *Hornets are huge, robust, social wasps, up to 30 mm long. Apart from their larger size, hornets can be distinguished from other wasps by their deeper yellow coloration.*

▲ *Gall wasps are usually about 2–8 mm long. They have a humped thorax and their shiny abdomen is oval in shape. The wings have fewer veins than those of other types of wasp.*

Ichneumon wasps

These wasps parasitize the larvae and pupae of other insects, such as moths, beetles, flies and other wasps. The female uses her long ovipositor (egg-laying tube) to deposit eggs on or inside the body of the host insect, sometimes drilling through several centimetres of wood to reach it. When the ichneumon larvae hatch, they feed on the host larva.

Wasp records

Largest	Tarantula hawk wasps	6.7 cm long, 11.4 cm wingspan
Smallest	Dicopomorpha echmepterygis	0.21 mm long
Lightest	Caraphractus cintus	0.005 mg
Largest recorded nest	Vespula germanicus	3.7 m long, 1.75 m diameter

Bees

There are approximately 20,000 species of bee. Many bees live alone, but over 500 species are social and live in colonies. Bees belong to the same insect group as ants and wasps. Bees look like wasps, but they have more hair and thicker, more robust, bodies. Unlike wasps, bees also have specialized organs for carrying pollen.

▶ *Honeybee workers crowd around their queen. The workers lick and stroke her to pick up powerful scents called pheromones, which pass on information about the queen and tell the workers how to behave.*

❍ Bees feed on pollen and nectar collected from flowers. Pollen contains protein and nectar provides energy.

❍ Bees form the most important group of pollinating insects. They are mainly attracted to blue and yellow flowers, and visit these flowers more often.

❍ Bees have two kinds of mouthparts. The first kind, found in honeybees, is adapted for sucking. The other kind is adapted for biting. This is found in carpenter bees.

❍ The antennae are the organs of touch and smell. Bees use their antennae to detect flower fragrances and to find nectar.

❍ Bees have five eyes. They have two compound eyes and three simple eyes, or ocelli. Bees cannot see red, but they can see ultraviolet light, which is invisible to the human eye.

❍ Social bees, such as honeybees, bumblebees and stingless bees, secrete wax to build their nests. A honeybee colony may contain 3000 to 40,000 bees, depending on the species, the season and the locality. The colony consists of a single queen bee, female workers and male drones.

Amazing

Many flowers have patterns of lines on them that reflect ultraviolet light. Although the patterns are not visible to the human eye, these 'honey guides' direct bees and other insects to the nectar.

▲ *A carpenter bee is not as hairy as a bumblebee, with short hairs on its abdomen or sometimes no hair at all. Female carpenter bees lay their eggs in holes that they drill in wood.*

Honeycombs

Honeybees collect the nectar of flowers, and other plant secretions, and turn it into honey. It is then altered chemically into different types of sugars and stored in hexagonal wax honeycomb cells. The honeycomb is used in the winter to provide food for the larvae and other members of the bee colony.

Find out more

Honeybee hive p. 199

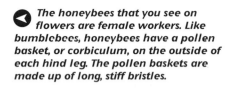

The honeybees that you see on flowers are female workers. Like bumblebees, honeybees have a pollen basket, or corbiculum, on the outside of each hind leg. The pollen baskets are made up of long, stiff bristles.

The solitary mason bee builds its nest in wood or in the soft mortar between bricks. While not dangerous to humans, these bees can damage walls and buildings.

Bumblebees collect pollen from flowers in structures called pollen baskets on their back legs. The bee combs the pollen dust from its body and packs it tightly into the pollen baskets until they are full.

○ The male drones do not have stings and their function is to mate with the queen bee. On average, the queen lays 600–700 eggs per day.

○ Worker bees perform various tasks, such as cleaning the nest, producing wax and collecting food for the colony. They also guard and feed the larvae and keep them warm.

○ The queen bee secretes pheromones, that tell worker bees that she is alive and well. The pheromones also inhibit the development of worker bees into queens. Once she lays eggs, the fertilized eggs become female worker bees and the unfertilized eggs become male bees.

○ When a colony becomes overcrowded, some of the bees fly off to a different location. This phenomenon is called swarming. It is a part of the annual life-cycle of the bee colony.

Halictus bees are relatively small bees, usually 5–10 mm long . A few species are attracted to perspiration, and are known as sweat bees.

Leaf-cutter bees are named after their habit of cutting pieces of leaf to make a protective casing for their eggs. These mainly solitary bees may nest in the soil, in hollow plant stems or in woody tunnels.

Honeybee facts

Honeybees can fly up to 14 km in search of food

Some queen bees can lay as many as 1500 eggs per day

The bees keep the temperature in their nest at a constant 33–34°C, whatever the weather outside

Queen bees can store sperm in their bodies for up to 5 years

On each trip, a bee could return with half a million grains of pollen

To make 0.5 kg of honey, workers may fly 88,000 km and visit 2 million flowers

In the course of its life, a single worker bee produces about 0.8 g of honey

Each worker larva is fed about 1300 meals a day

Bee communication

Worker honeybees communicate the location of food to the rest of the hive by 'dancing'. The dances may be circular or in a figure of eight, accompanied by waggles of the abdomen and high-pitched buzzing.

Ants

Ants are among the most successful insects on Earth. There are more than 9000 different species. Scientists believe that ants evolved from wasps millions of years ago. Ants are social insects that live in huge colonies. These colonies consist of the queen ant, female workers and male ants.

▼ *The army ants of tropical America march in columns up to one million strong and eat almost 50,000 insects a day. To cross gaps, some of the ants form bridges with their bodies, allowing the rest of the army to swarm over the living bridge. These nomadic ants do not build permanent nests, but they do make temporary nests called 'bivouacs'. No nesting material is involved – the workers simply link up to form chains that surround the queen and young.*

○ In ant colonies, the different ants divide themselves into groups that perform various tasks. Some ants are cleaners and some take care of the ant larvae, while others gather food or defend the nest.

○ The queen ant is the largest ant in the colony. When she matures, the queen ant flies off in search of a suitable place to build a new colony.

○ Queen ants nip off their wings once they find a place to breed. Smaller worker ants also have wings.

Amazing

Birds allow ants to crawl on their bodies and spray them with formic acid. Known as anting, this gets rid of parasites from the birds' feathers.

○ Worker ants take good care of the eggs. At night, they carry the eggs into deep nest tunnels to protect them from cold. In the morning, the workers carry the eggs back to the surface to warm up.

○ Male ants die shortly after mating with the queen ant.

Ant nests

Most ants live in anthills that are made of mounds of soil, sand and sticks, but some ant species nest in trees. Anthills consist of numerous different chambers and tunnels. Each chamber is used for a specific purpose, such as a food store, 'nursery' for the young, or resting area.

Find out more

Bulldog ant p. 210

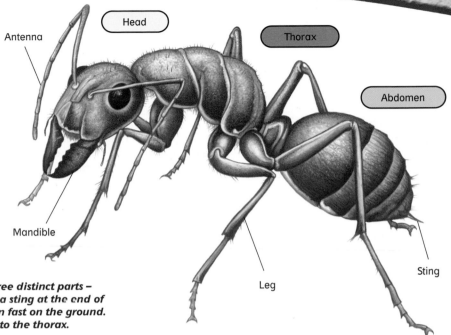

○ An ant has two stomachs. One stomach carries the ant's own food, while the other carries food that will be shared with other ants. This secondary stomach is called the crop.

○ Ants have compound eyes. However, their eyesight is normally poor and they depend on their antennae to sense their surroundings. Some species of ant are completely blind.

○ Ants use their powerful jaws, called mandibles, to dig holes, as well as to bite and carry food. The size of the mandibles varies between ant species.

Antenna

Head

Thorax

Abdomen

Mandible

Leg

Sting

▼ *The body of an ant is divided into three distinct parts – head, thorax and abdomen. There is a sting at the end of the abdomen. Ant legs are adapted to run fast on the ground. Two pairs of wings may also be attached to the thorax.*

▲ *Leafcutter ants feed on a fungus that they grow in their underground nests. They cut out bits of leaves from plants and carry them back to the nest to fertilize their 'fungus garden'.*

▼ *Weaver ants make their nests in tall trees, using sticky secretions produced by their larvae to 'sew' leaves together.*

Communication

Ants communicate with the help of their feelers (antennae), which are sensitive to touch and scent. They also leave scent trails behind them to let the other ants know exactly where to find the food source. Each ant colony has a unique smell that helps the members to identify each other. This also helps the ants to detect an intruder in the nest.

○ Ants are 'intelligent' insects. Experts have calculated that an ant brain can function as fast as a powerful computer.

○ Ants are capable of lifting loads between 20 and 50 times heavier than their own body weight.

○ Ants spray formic acid on predators to defend themselves. People once obtained formic acid by boiling ants.

Butterflies and Moths

There are more than 165,000 species of butterfly and moth. There is no scientific distinction between butterflies and moths, but butterflies tend to be brightly coloured and fly by day, while most moths are active after sunset and have a duller coloration. Butterflies and moths are important pollinators of plants, carrying pollen from plant to plant as they feed on flower nectar.

▼ *Although butterflies pollinate plants, not all species are welcomed by farmers and gardeners because their caterpillars are crop pests. The caterpillars of the small white butterfly, for example, are pests of brassica crops such as cabbage and Brussels sprout.*

Amazing

Some moth species drink the tears of hoofed animals such as cattle, deer, horses, tapirs, pigs and elephants.

Butterfly or moth?

Butterflies usually have more delicate and slender bodies than moths. Moths tend to have more plump and robust bodies. While resting, most butterflies fold their wings straight up above their backs (right). Most moths rest either with their wings spread flat (left) or folded like a tent over their bodies. The antennae of a butterfly are plain stalks ending in a club (or a hook, in the case of skipper butterflies). The antennae of moths come in many different shapes, ranging from single strands to feathery branches, but they never end in a club.

▲ *A butterfly drinking nectar from a flower using its proboscis.*

❍ The wings of butterflies and moths are covered with millions of microscopic scales, which overlap each other like roof tiles.

❍ In some species of moth, the females do not have wings.

❍ Both butterflies and moths undergo complete metamorphosis. This means that their bodies change completely as they become adults.

❍ Butterflies and moths pass through four different stages of development during their life-cycle. They begin life as an egg laid on a plant. The egg hatches into a larva called a caterpillar. The caterpillar then develops into a pupa or chrysalis. Finally, the pupa matures into a butterfly.

❍ Most moth caterpillars weave a structure around themselves for pupation. This is called a cocoon and is made of silk, leaves or soil. Most butterflies do not weave such cocoons and the pupae are naked.

❍ Most caterpillars moult four or five times before they enter the pupa or chrysalis stage.

Butterfly and moth records

Largest	Queen Alexandra's birdwing butterfly, Hercules moth and Bent-wing ghost moth	28 cm wingspan
Smallest	*Stigmella ridiculosa* moth	2 mm wingspan
Fastest flying	Death's-head hawk moth	54 km/h
Longest recorded migration	Monarch butterfly	3432 km
Longest tongue	Madagascan hawk moth	28 cm
Coldest living	Woolly bear caterpillar	Can survive to −50°C

○ In some species, the caterpillars are armed with stinging hairs containing poisons. These hairs cause irritation or pain when touched.

○ Caterpillars usually eat leaves. They have jaws with overlapping edges and grinding plates for slicing up and chewing their food.

○ Adult butterflies and moths only consume liquid food, such as flower nectar and liquids from rotten fruits or vines. Some butterflies and moths even feed on liquid animal waste.

○ Butterflies and moths have a long, straw-like structure called a proboscis under their head, which helps them to suck nectar and other juices.

○ Butterflies and moths protect themselves from predators, such as birds, lizards, bats and spiders, by mimicry and camouflage.

▲ *There may be 200 to 600 tiny scales on every square millimetre of the wings of a butterfly or moth, such as this white peacock butterfly.*

Eyespots

Some moths and butterflies have large spots on their wings. From a distance, these spots resemble the eyes of a larger, more fearsome animal and scare away potential predators.

Caterpillars

Caterpillars have a tube-like body made of flexible tissue, with three pairs of thoracic (true) legs and several pairs of fleshy, abdominal prolegs. The head is equipped with jaws, short antennae and often simple eyes. All caterpillars have silk-producing organs.

The small postman caterpillar is covered with sharp spines for protection.

When a gypsy moth caterpillar needs to find a new tree to feed on, it swings by a silk thread and allows the wind to carry it away.

Yellow-necked caterpillars are considered pests, because they eat the leaves of trees such as apple, oak, cherry and walnut.

World Butterflies and Moths

Butterflies and moths are ancient insects. Fossil records show that moths date back 140 million years and butterflies 40 million years. One feature that butterflies and moths have in common is that they cannot survive extreme cold weather. Not one single moth or butterfly is found in Antarctica.

Atlas moths are among the largest moths, with a wingspan of up to 25 cm. When they fly, these moths are often mistaken for birds.

Apollo butterflies are mostly found in mountains and hilly regions of Europe and Asia. They have a furry body to protect them from the cold.

As beautifully marked as many butterflies, the diurnal Zodiac moth flits through the tropical rainforest in Queensland, Australia.

The death's head hawk-moth has a skull-like pattern on its thorax. Long ago, the presence of this moth was considered to be a sign of death.

This young monarch butterfly has recently emerged from its pupa.

The small postman butterfly of Central and South America is found on the edges of tropical forests and in wetlands.

Bhutan glory butterflies of northeast Asia were collected in large numbers in the past. Now, their numbers have been greatly reduced and they are very rare.

For butterflies, tortoiseshells have a comparatively long life as adults, surviving for about ten months from one summer to the next. They hibernate during winter.

The hummingbird hawk-moth hovers in front of flowers, beating its wings so fast that they are almost invisible. The rapidly beating wings produce a high-pitched hum, like the wings of a hummingbird.

The painted lady butterfly occurs in temperate regions across Asia, Europe and North America, especially around flowery meadows and fields. Its caterpillar feeds mainly on thistle plants.

The beautiful Rajah Brooke's birdwing is found high in the rainforest canopy from Malaysia through to Sumatra and Borneo. It was named after the British Rajah Brooke of Sarawak.

Female red admiral butterflies lay their eggs on nettle leaves. The caterpillars feed inside a protective tent made of folded leaves held together by silk threads.

Peacock butterflies use the false eyes on their wings to scare predators away. They also open and close their wings rapidly to make a scraping sound as predators approach.

Amazing

Many moths do not feed in their adult stage and so lack mouthparts. This is not the case with adult butterflies.

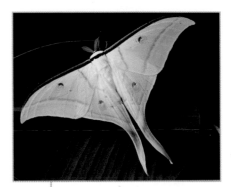

Moon moths occur throughout the world, but they are mostly seen in tropical countries. Moon moths are so-called because the marks on their wings resemble a new moon.

Find out more

Migrating monarchs p. 202

Beetles

Without a doubt, beetles are the most successful animal group on Earth. There are at least 360,000 beetle species, making up about one-third of all animal species. Beetles are found in almost every type of habitat, from mountaintops to deserts, and in all sizes, ranging from 0.25 mm up to 20 cm in length.

▷ *This cockchafer beetle has opened its elytra and spread its wings. Cockchafers are relatively weak fliers.*

○ Beetles eat a wide variety of plants and animals. Beetles, in turn, are eaten in vast numbers by other, larger animals, including reptiles, birds and mammals.

○ The shape of a beetle's mouthparts indicates the type of food it eats. Predatory tiger beetles, for example, have serrated, sickle-shaped jaws for slicing up prey, while weevils and seed beetles have long snouts for boring into wood and seeds.

○ In beetles, the front wings have become hardened. These 'wing cases', or elytra, meet in the middle to cover and protect the more delicate hind wings that the beetle uses for flying.

○ In flight, the elytra are held up out of the way of the hind wings. They provide little lift, but they help to keep the beetle stable in the air.

○ Although some beetles have a dull coloration, many species, including scarabs and wood-boring beetles, have bright, metallic-looking colours.

○ Some beetles produce special chemicals called pheromones to attract mates.

○ Other beetles have more unusual courtship techniques. Deathwatch beetles, for example, tap their heads on the walls of their wooden tunnels.

Gardener's friend

Ladybirds, or ladybugs, are almost circular in shape. They are usually bright pink, orange or red, with black, red or orange spots. The number of spots may vary from species to species. These beetles are one of the most beneficial insects because they feed on aphids and other insect pests that damage crops. Ladybirds are sometimes bred on a large scale and are then introduced into farms or greenhouses to get rid of pests.

▷ *Screech beetles are aquatic beetles that actively hunt their prey in the water, swimming with a 'dog paddle' motion that involves all six legs.*

◁ *Rhinoceros beetles are named after the horns on their heads. This beetle has two horns, but some rhinoceros beetles have three or even five horns. Rhinoceros beetles do not use their horns as a defence against predators. Instead, they use them to fight with other males for food and to attract female beetles for mating. The very tough exoskeleton protects the beetle's body like a suit of armour.*

Sacred scarab

The scarab, or the dung beetle, was sacred to ancient Egyptions. It was associated with the creator-god, Atum. This beetle was believed to have come into being by itself, from a ball of dung. Images of scarab beetles were often carved on ancient Egyptian precious stones and jewellery. The carvings were thought to bring good luck and ward off evil.

Find out more

Tiger beetle p. 207

▼ **Stag beetles live in damp wooded areas, especially near oak trees. Their mandibles (jaws) resemble the antlers of a stag – hence the name.**

○ Firefly beetles flash lights from their bodies when searching for mates at night. Each firefly species uses a different flashing sequence.

○ Beetles undergo complete metamorphosis. Their eggs hatch into worm-like grubs (larvae) before pupating into adults. In some species the larval stage lasts for several years.

○ Some beetles, such as Colorado beetles, are pests that attack crops and devour food stores.

○ Woodworm and deathwatch beetles destroy the timbers of houses. Other beetles are a threat to living trees – the elm bark beetle spreads the fungus that causes Dutch elm disease.

○ Beetles perform an important role as 'decomposers', eating dead plants and animals and returning them to the soil as nutrients.

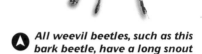

▲ **All weevil beetles, such as this bark beetle, have a long snout with biting jaws at the tip.**

▶ **The deathwatch beetle's habit of tapping on house timbers in the quiet of the night was once believed to be a warning of approaching death.**

▼ **The Goliath beetle is one of the largest and heaviest insects in the world. Males grow up to 12 cm and weigh about 115 g. Despite their size, Goliath beetles are good fliers. They produce a low, helicopter-like whir while flying.**

▼ **The great diving beetle has a flattened, streamlined body, which helps it to move rapidly through water. When swimming, it moves its back legs together, rather than alternately like most other water beetles. When the beetle stops swimming, it floats to the surface of the water.**

Beetle records

Longest Hercules beetles		19 cm
Heaviest Goliath beetle		Over 100 g
Smallest Featherwing beetles		0.2 mm
Longest living Jewel beetles		30 years or more
Coldest living Arctic beetle		Can survive below −60°C
Highest jump Click beetle		30 cm

Flies

Scientists define a fly as an insect with two wings. Although we call many other insects flies, such as butterflies and dragonflies, they are not true flies, because they have four wings. In place of hind wings, true flies have a pair of knob-like structures called halteres, which are used for balancing in flight.

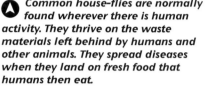

▲ Common house-flies are normally found wherever there is human activity. They thrive on the waste materials left behind by humans and other animals. They spread diseases when they land on fresh food that humans then eat.

▼ Despite its name, the mantisfly is not a true fly, since it has four wings. With grasping fore legs and delicate wings, this insect looks like a cross between a praying mantis and a lacewing.

○ Flies are found all over the world, from the icy polar regions to the equatorial rainforest. There are about 122,000 species of true fly.

○ Flies have large compound eyes made up of many individual lenses. Each of a house-fly's two compound eyes contains about 4000 lenses.

○ The claws and sticky pads on a fly's feet allow it to cling on to smooth surfaces and walk upside down with ease.

▲ Bee-flies have a long tongue for sucking nectar from flowers. Their maggots eat the larvae of solitary bees.

Robber fly

Huge compound eyes provide the robber fly with the excellent vision it needs to be an effective aerial predator. A robber fly's proboscis (mouthpart) is a piercing, stabbing organ.

Parasite carrier

A female mosquito uses her needle-like mouthparts to pierce a victim's skin and suck up blood. She injects a salivary fluid to keep the blood flowing and stop it from the clotting. Most female mosquitoes have to feed on the blood of other animals to reproduce. They need the protein extracted from blood for the development of their eggs. Mosquitoes are known to spread many infectious diseases between humans by feeding like this, including yellow fever and dengue fever. The female *Anopheles* mosquito spreads malaria.

▲ Crane flies have extremely narrow wings. They have a thin body and long legs, and resemble large mosquitoes. These insects cannot bite. Crane fly larvae are also known as leatherjackets, because of their tough, brown skin.

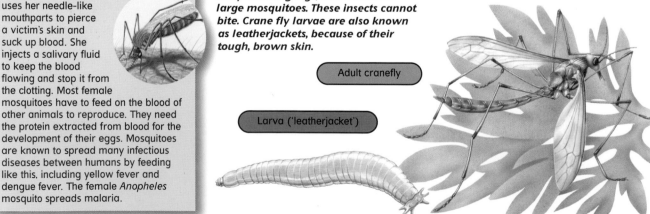

Adult cranefly

Larva ('leatherjacket')

 Swarms of tiny flies called midges gather on warm evenings near ponds, lakes, and streams. Some midges bite animals and feed on their blood.

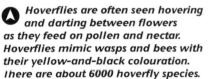 Hoverflies are often seen hovering and darting between flowers as they feed on pollen and nectar. Hoverflies mimic wasps and bees with their yellow-and-black colouration. There are about 6000 hoverfly species.

Adult vinegar flies live for just two weeks, during which time they feed on nectar and other sugary solutions.

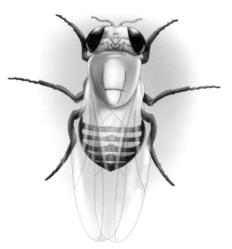

○ Flies can perform amazing aerial manoeuvres, including hovering, flying backwards, and landing on the ceiling.

○ In flies, metamorphosis is complete. The legless, simple-bodied fly larvae are called maggots.

○ Fly maggots live in soil or water, or in moist rotting plant and animal tissue.

○ A fly's mouthparts are adapted to sucking or sponging up liquid food such as blood, flower nectar, and even dung. A few fly species feed on living body tissues.

○ Some adult flies, including robber flies, are ferocious aerial predators that chase and catch other insects on the wing.

○ Flies pollinate flowers, but they also spread diseases such as malaria and sleeping sickness.

Amazing

House-flies are known to spread 40 serious diseases. A single fly can harbour as many as 33 million infectious organisms inside its intestines, and another 500 million on its body surface and legs.

Horse flies are among the fastest flying insects, reaching maximum speeds of 39 km/h. Female horse flies suck and feed on the blood of animals, including humans. The males feed mainly on flower nectar.

Find out more

House-flies p. 207

Crickets and Grasshoppers

Crickets and grasshoppers live throughout the world (except in the coldest regions), wherever there are fields, forests and grasslands. There are 28,000 species, most of which have wings. The front pair are leathery and flap-like, while the long rear pair are used for flying. Instead of flying away from danger, crickets and grasshoppers often leap away on their powerful back legs.

❍ Crickets are nocturnal and have keen hearing and eyesight. Compound eyes help crickets see far and in many directions at the same time. Round, flat hearing organs are found on the front legs.

❍ Grasshoppers tend to be active during the day. They have large eyes, and their ears are located on the abdomen rather than on the legs. Their antennae are generally shorter than those of crickets.

❍ Crickets are omnivorous and feed on crops, vegetables, flowers, green plants, small animals, clothes and each other.

❍ Grasshoppers are herbivorous (plant-eating) insects. They feed on a variety of plants, grasses and crops, using their mandibles to chew up the tough food.

❍ Some cricket and grasshopper species destroy crops, and so they are considered to be pests,

❍ All crickets and grasshoppers undergo incomplete metamorphosis.

Grasshoppers can leap more than 200 times their own length. Once in the air, they flap their wings to help them travel even further.

Field crickets are usually found in green fields and forested areas. They feed on plant seeds, smaller insects and fruits. Some species of field cricket become cannibalistic when there is a shortage of food.

Amazing

The largest locust swarms can contain up to 50 billion insects, and cover 1,000 sq km of land. Such swarms can devour enough crops in a single day to feed around half a million people for a whole year.

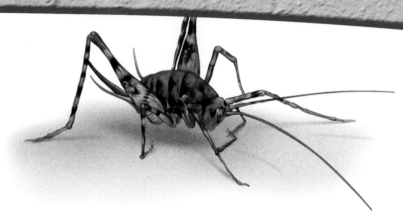

The long, sensitive antennae of the cave cricket help it to find its way around in the dark. The tail-like projections, called cerci, at the end of the cricket's abdomen also have a sensory function.

Mole crickets

The front legs of the mole cricket are broad and spade-like for tunnelling. The males dig special burrows to amplify their songs. Females lay their eggs in underground chambers.

○ Female crickets have long, needle-like ovipositors to lay eggs. They carry the eggs until they find a safe place where the eggs can hatch into nymphs.

○ After mating, the female grasshopper may lay her eggs in low bushes, or dig a hole in the soil with her abdomen to deposit eggs from her ovipositor. She protects her eggs with a hard shell covering called an egg-pod.

When a grasshopper is at rest, the wide, delicate, back wings are folded like a fan underneath the long, narrow front wings. The front wings are lifted up to allow the rear flying wings to spread out when the grasshopper flies.

○ Grasshoppers and crickets sing during the mating season to attract a mate or scare away rivals.

○ Crickets produce these sounds by rubbing the bases of their specially modified forewings. Grasshoppers rub ridges on their legs against a tough vein on their wings.

Locust swarms

Locusts are grasshoppers. When conditions are right, locusts can breed in vast numbers. Huge locust swarms many millions strong fly off to find new feeding areas. Since each locust can eat its own weight in plant food each day, these swarms can devastate farm crops.

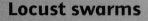

Find out more
Grasshopper anatomy p. 195

Dragonflies and Mantids

Dragonflies and mantids are among the insect world's top predators. Dragonflies are fast-flying, highly manoeuvrable predators that patrol over rivers, ponds and streams, plucking flying insects from the air. By contrast, mantids, such as the praying mantis, are ambush predators. These insects sit in wait for prey and then snatch it with their spine-studded folding front legs.

○ Dragonflies can measure up to 12 cm in length. They have long, colourful, slender bodies with two pairs of veined wings. Their large, compound eyes give them excellent eyesight.

○ Larger dragonflies are called hawkers while the smaller ones are called darters. Dragonflies have huge compound eyes, which cover the insect's entire head.

○ Metamorphosis is incomplete. Adult dragonflies survive on land but their nymphs live underwater.

A praying mantis moves its long front legs very rapidly to grab its prey. Sharp spines stop the prey from escaping. The mantis bites deeply into its victims with its powerful jaws.

Dragonflies and damselflies capture their prey with the help of their legs, folding them like a basket to form a trap beneath their body. Once the prey has been captured by the basket, it is transferred to the mouth.

Amazing

Dragonflies are among the fastest-flying insects. They can fly at 30 to 50 km/h.

Many damselflies rest with their wings folded over their back. Dragonflies hold their wings straight out when perching.

Mayfly nymphs

Mayflies are smaller cousins of dragonflies and damselflies. Mayfly nymphs live underwater for up to three years. The lifespan of an adult mayfly is short and ranges from a few hours to a few days. It lives just long enough to mate and reproduce, and does not feed.

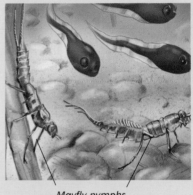

Mayfly nymphs

◯ The praying mantis gets its name from its posture. It holds its front legs together as if it were praying.

◯ The praying mantis can grow up to 6.5 cm in length. It has a triangular head that can turn in a full circle. It is generally green or brown in colour.

◯ Praying mantises are carnivorous and feed on a variety of other insects, including butterflies, grasshoppers and moths. They can even attack small lizards, frogs and birds. Small mantises can become cannibalistic, especially when there is no food.

◯ Males and females mate while they fly. Once they have mated, the female dragonfly deposits her eggs in water or inside water plants.

◯ The dragonfly nymphs that hatch from the eggs feed on fish, tadpoles and other small aquatic animals.

◯ Damselflies are beautiful, slender relatives of dragonflies. They sit and wait for suitable prey to fly within range, while dragonflies actively hunt in the air.

◯ Damselflies are usually found near water, and their nymphs live in the water until they mature into adults.

◯ Damselfly nymphs have external gills on the tip of their abdomen for breathing underwater. In dragonfly nymphs, these gills are internal.

Praying mantises have good camouflage to protect themselves from predators. Their body colour blends in with their surroundings.

Each one of a dragonfly's wings can move independently. This makes the dragonfly a very versatile flyer, able to hover, turn at 90 degree angles, dart backwards and forwards, and come to a sudden stop.

Mantisfly

Mantisflies are named after their folded pair of front legs, which look like those of praying mantises. Although these insects look similar, they are not related.

Termites

Termites are soft-bodied insects that are believed to have evolved from an ancient cockroach-like ancestor. Their fossils date back to the early Cretaceous Era, around 130 million years ago. Termites are distributed all over the world. However, they are better adapted to warm and humid weather than to cold climates. They are most common in the tropics and sub-tropics. There are about 2750 species.

○ There are two main types of termites – ground termites (also known as subterranean termites) and wood termites. Ground termites nest in soil and wood termites nest in wooden planks and other wooden structures.

○ The mouthparts of termites are modified for the purpose of chewing wood. They have antennae, which can be either bead-like or thread-like.

○ Termites have a soft cuticle (an outer covering) that dries up easily, which is why they live in dark, warm and damp nests.

○ Termites are social insects that live in well-organized groups or colonies. A termite colony is a highly integrated unit in which each and every function is divided among the various termites.

Wood is difficult to digest. Wood termites have bacteria and other single-celled organisms in their guts to help them digest tough plant material and wood.

Amazing

When a nest is invaded by ants, the soldiers of some termite species can 'explode' to cover the intruders with sticky fluid.

○ Small termite colonies may contain hundreds or thousands of termites, but a very large colony can be home to millions of termites.

○ There are different categories of termite in a colony – the king, the queen, workers and soldiers. All these categories are referred to as castes. The worker and soldier castes are unable to reproduce.

To help them feed on termites, southern Asia's sloth bears have lost their incisor teeth. The bears dig into termite mounds and insert their muzzle. They close their nostrils to keep out the termites, purse their lips and then suck up the insects through the gap in their teeth.

Termites nest underground or in hollow tree stumps, shrub roots, the timbers of buildings and even in books. Some nests rise above ground and are known as termite mounds. Made of soil and saliva, these mounds can be 8–9 m high. They are a common sight in tropical regions.

Queen and king

The king termite helps the queen to set up the colony and mates with her. The queen lays eggs and looks after the colony. Once there are enough worker termites, the queen no longer looks after the young ones. Initially, the queen lays a small number of eggs. As the colony matures, she can lay many more eggs – as many as 36,000 eggs a day. The queen may grow to such a size that she can no longer move.

▶ *Worker ground termites are normally smaller, softer and paler than soldiers. The soldiers, which defend the colony, are unable to feed themselves, so the workers have to keep them supplied with food.*

❍ In a colony, termites communicate with each other about the direction and presence of food through vibrations, physical contact and chemical scents called pheromones.

❍ At a certain time of year, large numbers of winged, sexually mature males and females ('reproductives') are produced. These fly off in all directions to form new colonies.

❍ Workers form the majority of the colony's population. They carry out most of the routine tasks needed to maintain the colony, from taking care of the eggs and repairing the nest, to foraging for food and feeding the young.

❍ Soldiers defend the colony against attack, using powerful jaws that protrude from an enlarged, hardened head.

Giant appetite

Like sloth bears, giant anteaters feed on termites. They break open termite mounds with their clawed forelimbs and catch the termites using their long, sticky tongue, which can be up to 60 cm long. They can devour up to 30,000 ants a day.

Termite or ant?

Termites are sometimes called white ants because termites and ants look quite similar. However, they can easily be distinguished. Ants have elbowed antennae, while termites have straight antennae. Termites also have two pairs of large wings, which overlap each other on their backs when at rest. These wings are equal in size, unlike those of ants. The thorax has a broad joint with the abdomen, whereas ants, bees and butterflies have a narrow, pointed 'waist'.

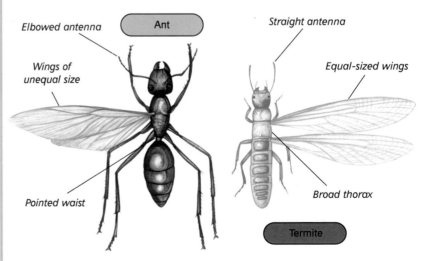

Elbowed antenna — Ant — Straight antenna

Wings of unequal size — Equal-sized wings

Pointed waist — Broad thorax — Termite

Find out more

Ants pp. 218–219

Cockroaches, Fleas and Lice

Cockroaches, fleas and lice are not related groups of insects, but they are all viewed with distaste because they are seen as pests. Cockroaches infest human homes, while fleas and lice are parasites that suck the blood of mammals and birds.

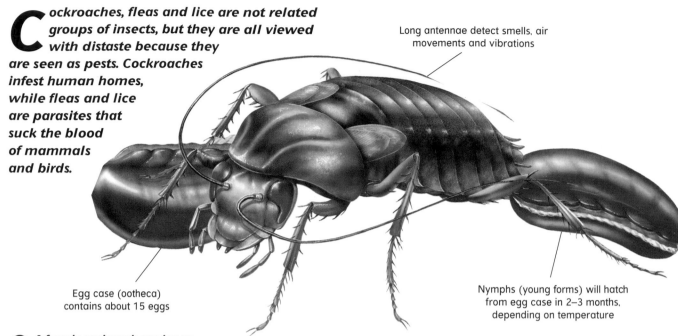

Long antennae detect smells, air movements and vibrations

Egg case (ootheca) contains about 15 eggs

Nymphs (young forms) will hatch from egg case in 2–3 months, depending on temperature

⊘ *A female cockroach can lay up to 30 to 40 eggs at a time, and reproduce four times in a year. She stores the eggs in a brownish egg case called an ootheca. The cockroach may either carry this egg case around with her or hide it somewhere. The young cockroaches are called nymphs.*

Clean cockroaches

Cockroaches are not dirty creatures. They work hard to keep themselves clean in order to preserve a coating of wax and oils that prevents them from drying out. It is the bacteria they carry that makes them dangerous.

○ There are about 4000 known species of cockroach. Well-known cockroach species include oriental black beetles and croton bugs.

○ Cockroaches are found everywhere, especially in bat caves, peoples' homes, under stones, in thick grass and on trees and plants. The cockroaches found in caves are usually blind.

○ Cockroaches can be winged or wingless. Adult cockroaches measure 1–9 cm long. They are nocturnal insects that prefer damp surroundings.

Amazing

Fleas carry various deadly diseases. They can transmit bubonic plague, which killed a quarter of the population of Europe in the mid-1300s.

○ Cockroaches are swift-moving creatures. Their legs are adapted for fast running. They also have flat, oval-shaped bodies that enable them to hide in narrow cracks in walls and floors.

○ Most cockroach species are omnivorous. Their main food is plant sap, dead animals and vegetable matter, but they will even eat shoe polish, glue, soap and ink.

○ Metamorphosis is incomplete in cockroaches. Adults can live for up to two years. Males and females are very similar in appearance.

○ Cockroaches are decomposers. They play an important role in balancing the natural environment by digesting forest debris and animal waste matter. But household cockroaches are considered pests, because they can contaminate food with bacteria and spread diseases among humans.

Unchanged by time

Cockroaches are so good at surviving that they have changed little since they first appeared around 300 million years ago. They survived the dinosaurs and the ice ages, and are still successful insects today.

○ There are about 2000 species of flea, ranging from 0.1 to 1 cm in length. Fleas undergo complete metamorphosis.

○ Fleas are ectoparasites – parasites that live on the outside of their host. They feed on the blood of birds and mammals.

○ Fleas are themselves subject to parasitism by external mites and internal nematode worms.

○ Lice are small insects measuring up to 11 mm long. Two types of lice that frequently affect humans are the head louse and the body louse.

○ Lice have three needle-like structures, called stylets, that can pierce the skin. These are held back by a specially adapted tongue. After piercing the skin, the lice suck the blood with a pumping action of their throat.

Pests

Madagascan hissing cockroaches push air out of breathing holes in the sides of their body to make a hissing sound, which they use to deter predators and also to attract mates.

A fast runner, the death's head cockroach lives on the ground, searching through leaf litter or bat droppings for scraps of food. This cockroach is named after the strange markings on its thorax, which look like skulls or vampires.

Unlike other pest cockroaches, oriental cockroaches do not have sticky pads on their feet and cannot climb slippery or smooth surfaces. They can survive for about a month without food, if water is available.

Domestic dogs and cats are prone to flea attack, but a flea will only feed on human blood if it is very hungry. The larvae eat decaying material in nests and carpets.

A louse's body is flattened, which helps it to lie close to its host's skin. The head louse attaches itself to the hair or scalp with the help of claws on its legs.

Other Insects

Insects are the most numerous and successful creatures on Earth. More than one million species of these six-legged creatures (hexapods) are known to science already, and new species are being discovered all the time. It is thought that the true number of species may be 5–10 million.

Stylops are small, parasitic insects. The male is shown here. The female is maggot-like and never leaves the body of her host.

A lacewing has two similar pairs of wings, which are covered with a delicate network of veins. When the lacewing rests, it holds its wings together like a roof over its body.

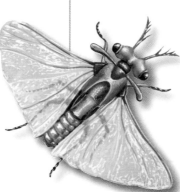

Book lice are transparent and so small that they are almost invisible to the naked eye. Book lice can, however, wreak havoc amongst valuable collections of books by eating the glue that binds the pages.

A stick insect has an extremely long, thin body, with thread-like antennae made up of as many as 100 segments.

Scorpionflies have an elongated head with a long 'beak' that ends in biting jaws. The rear body part of some males is curled upwards, similar to a scorpion's tail.

Adult antlions resemble dragonflies, having a long slender body and four delicate wings. Unlike dragonflies, antlions are nocturnal insects.

Find out more

Antlion trap p. 206

Non-insect hexapods

Some six-legged animals are not considered true insects, mainly because the mouthparts are located in a pouch on the underside of the head. The mouthparts are pushed out of the pouch when the animal feeds. These animals are all wingless, and many lack antennae and eyes.

Diplurans are small, blind, soft-bodied hexapods with pincer-like cerci. They are often found in small groups in the soil, or under rocks or tree bark.

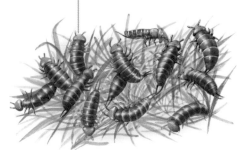

A proturan has neither eyes nor antennae. Instead, it has a sensory organ on its head and uses its front two legs as antennae. Most species are microscopic.

Springtails have a spring-like organ, known as a furcula, under their abdomen. It helps them to leap high into the air.

Leaf insects are related to stick insects. They have flat, irregularly shaped bodies that resemble leaves.

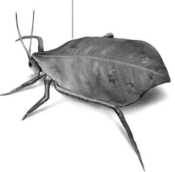

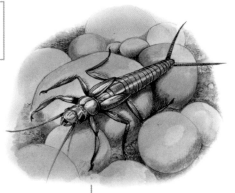

A common sight in houses, silverfish have a long, shiny body covered in scales. They feed on paper, glue, and food scraps.

Earwigs are nocturnal insects. They live in the soil and can dig tunnels as deep as 1.8 m under the ground in order to escape cold weather.

Stonefly nymphs (seen here) live in streams and lakes. The adult stoneflies are poor fliers, spending much of their time resting on stones.

Scorpions

Scorpions have been around for more than 400 million years. They are easily identified by the venomous sting at the end of their tail and their lobster-like pincers. These nocturnal creatures are found in tropical and warm temperate regions, in a range of habitats from deserts to rainforests.

▶ *A scorpion uses its sting for defence, to fight rivals at mating time and to subdue large or struggling prey. It arches over its tail and stabs downwards with the stinger. The scorpion snips up its victim with its jaws, liquidizes the edible parts with saliva and then sucks up the resulting mush. Any indigestible remains are discarded.*

Amazing

At night, scorpions are said to be able to use the stars to navigate and orient themselves.

❍ Scorpions grab their prey with their pincers, or pedipalps. Then they use their sting to inject venom, which paralyzes their victim.

❍ Scorpions can be tan, red, black or brown in colour. As in other arthropods, a hard exoskeleton protects the scorpion from external damage.

❍ The tiny sensory hairs covering the body and legs help scorpions to detect temperature changes and movement around them.

❍ Scorpions have book lungs, which are gill-like structures for breathing.

Scorpion reproduction

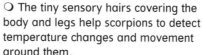

For scorpions, mating is an elaborate ritual. The male scorpion grabs the female and performs dance-like movements before mating. After mating, the female retains the eggs in her body and gives birth to live young. The female takes good care of her young and carries them on her back for about ten days or until their first moult, after which they have to fend for themselves.

▲ *Although they are a widespread group of invertebrates, most arachnids are terrestrial (land-dwelling). Scorpions are most commonly found in warm countries. The imperial, or emperor, scorpion lives in west Africa.*

Most dangerous

Few animals are more deadly than the fat-tailed scorpion of north Africa. Its lethal venom, which is as toxic as a cobra's, can kill an adult human in a few hours if the victim is not treated with anti-venom. As it is often found near human homes, this scorpion is greatly feared.

○ The size of a scorpion's pincers usually indicates how dangerous it is. Large pincers reduce the need for a powerful sting. However, scorpions with small pincers are less able to defend themselves, so they compensate for this by having a much stronger venom.

○ Once it is dark, scorpions come out of their daytime nesting places, such as crevices, burrows or under rocks, to hunt for food or to find a mate.

○ In some species, the male scorpion is eaten by the female when mating is over.

▼ *Whip scorpions are arachnids, but they are not true scorpions. They are usually larger than scorpions and their whip-like tails do not carry stings.*

> *Scorpions belong to the most ancient family of arachnids. When they sense danger, scorpions, such as this wood scorpion, brandish their pincers and arch their tail over their back, ready to strike at the attacker.*

○ The layer of fat under a scorpion's exoskeleton helps it to survive when food is scarce. In fact, scorpions can live without eating for up to a year.

○ Young scorpions moult from four to nine times before they become adults.

○ With each moult, the scorpion cracks open its old exoskeleton and wriggles out of it. Initially the new exoskeleton is very soft, but it hardens with time.

○ The average lifespan of a scorpion is around three to five years, but some species are known to live for as long as 25 years.

> *Like spiders, scorpions, such as this giant (desert) hairy scorpion, have bodies that are divided into two sections – a cephalothorax and an abdomen. They have four pairs of legs and a pair of pincer-like pedipalps. Their powerful biting and chewing jaws are called chelicerae.*

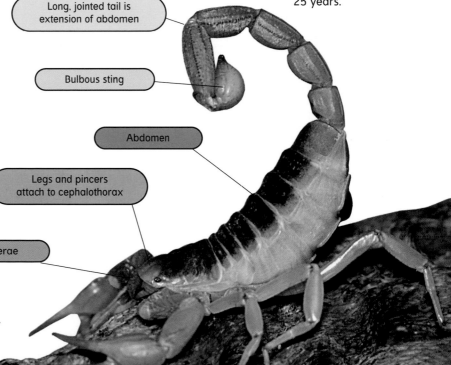

Long, jointed tail is extension of abdomen

Bulbous sting

Abdomen

Legs and pincers attach to cephalothorax

Chelicerae

Find out more

Arachnids pp. 196–197

Spiders

Famous for their web-spinning activities, spiders are predatory arachnids that use fangs to inject venom into their prey. There are about 40,000 spider species. Although widely disliked, only a few spider species are harmful to humans, and many help to keep our homes free of flies and other unwanted insects.

▶ *Some spiders can only see the difference between light and shadow, but others – including this jumping spider – are believed to have excellent eyesight. Jumping spiders can spot moving prey up to 25 cm away.*

❍ Most spiders have six or eight eyes. Spider eyes are 'simple', meaning that they do not have multiple lenses like the compound eyes of many insects.

❍ The hairs that cover a spider's body are connected to its nervous system (a bunch of nerves in the cephalothorax) and work as sensory organs. Some hairs can detect movements in the air to alert the spider to nearby prey. Other hairs are taste-sensitive.

Amazing

Spider webs were once used to dress wounds, in the belief that the silk would staunch the flow of blood and help it to clot.

❍ Blood flows freely inside a spider. This is a similar blood system to the type of open circulation seen in insect bodies. However, some spiders also have veins and arteries to ensure that blood reaches all parts of the body.

◀ *House spiders are the most common spiders and are often spotted in houses and gardens. They are also found in woodpiles and under logs. These spiders feed on small invertebrates, such as beetles, cockroaches, earwigs and even earthworms.*

Body structure

The body of a spider, such as this wolf spider, is divided into two distinct parts, known as the cephalothorax and the abdomen, connected by a slender stalk, called the pedicel. There are six pairs of appendages. The first is a pair of jaws (chelicerae). These are equipped with fangs and connected to venom-producing glands. Males carry sperm cells in the second pair of appendages (pedipalps). Females use their pedipalps to hold food. The remaining four pairs of appendages are walking legs.

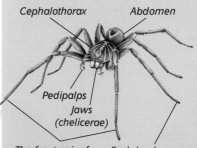

Cephalothorax   *Abdomen*

Pedipalps
Jaws (chelicerae)

The front pair of legs are often used as sensory feelers

Each leg has seven segments and at least one claw at the tip

Find out more

Silk production p. 242

Water spiders live in freshwater ponds, lakes and slow streams. They construct a bell-shaped web under the water and fill it with air, which they trap in their hair at the surface. They stay inside their 'diving bell' and only leave it to collect more air or catch prey such as small fish and aquatic insects.

Spiders in folk tales

Myths and traditional tales from many parts of the world feature spiders or spider webs. Some of the best-known spider stories come from West Africa and the Caribbean. They describe the adventures of Anansi, a cunning spider, and are an encouragement to children to be clever.

❍ Male spiders are generally smaller than females. They may also be a different colour.

❍ When the male finds the right partner, he usually mates with her immediately. However, some species secrete pheromones (chemical signals) to attract a mate. These spiders also have elaborate courtship rituals.

❍ Some females eat the male after mating. The male is often too weak to defend himself from this attack.

❍ The female lays her eggs inside special silk cocoons called egg-sacs. Each sac may have hundreds of spider eggs. The egg-sacs are either carried around by the mother spider or hidden in her web or nest.

❍ Spider eggs take a few weeks to hatch. Small spiders come out of the eggs. These are known as spiderlings. Young spiders may live in a group until they mature, but some spiderlings live alone.

The female tarantula will tend and protect her egg-sac. She may become aggressive if the eggs are threatened.

❍ Spiderlings moult a couple of times before they become fully grown adults.

❍ Most species are solitary insects and only come together to mate. Some spiders, however, live as a community in which a group of females share one web.

❍ Spiders are useful to humans, because they prey on many pest insects, including those that attack rice fields and cotton, apple and banana plantations.

Spider records

Largest	Goliath bird-eating spiders	28 cm legspan
Heaviest	Female bird-eating spiders	120 g
Smallest	Male midget spiders	0.4 mm legspan
Fastest	House spiders	1.9 km/h
Highest living	Jumping spiders	Up to 6700 m
Most venomous	Brazilian wandering spiders	0.006 mg of venom can kill a mouse
Longest living	Bird-eating spiders	20–25 years
Largest eyes	Ogre-faced spiders	1.5 mm across
Most eggs	Bird-eating spiders	Up to 3000
Least eggs	*Oonops domesticus*	2

Spider Silk and Webs

All spiders can make very thin, fine threads called silk. Spiders spin their silk for many reasons. About half of the 40,000 different kinds of spiders make webs or nets to catch prey. Some spiders wrap up their living victims in silk to stop them escaping, so the spider can have its meal later. Some female spiders make silk bags, called cocoons, where they lay their eggs, and others spin protective silk 'nursery tents' for their babies.

❍ Spider silk is made of protein particles. Inside the spider's body, this silk is liquid in form.

❍ The liquid silk hardens as the spider pulls it out to form a fine thread. Spider silk is very elastic and stretchy.

❍ Different types of silk are used for different purposes. Sticky silk is used to capture prey, while non-sticky silk is used to make webs strong.

❍ Spiders normally weave webs during the night and usually finish making them by early morning.

❍ Spiders depend on wind currents to lay the first thread of the web. They float the thread in the air and wait for it to stick to a plant stalk or some other support. Then the spider walks across the thread and continues weaving the rest of the web.

▼ *When an insect blunders into a web, the spider is alerted by the vibrations caused by the struggling prey. The spider rushes over and wraps it in silk, sometimes first giving the insect a paralyzing bite to subdue it.*

❍ Different groups of spiders spin different-shaped webs. For example, some webs are sheet-like, others like funnels, and some are irregular in shape. The most familiar webs are the wheel-shaped webs built by orb spiders.

❍ Orb webs are very light but they are made in such a way that the delicate web can support the spider as well as the struggling prey. In fact, the web can handle a weight that is thousands of times heavier than the silk of which it is made.

▲ *An orb-weaver may spin over 100 webs in its lifetime, each involving up to 100 m of silk and taking from 40 minutes to several hours to build.*

❍ Sheet webs are also common among spiders. The spider weaves a sheet of sticky silk and lays it flat. Right above the sheet, it weaves a number of non-sticky silk threads. Insects that fly past the web will trip on the non-sticky threads and fall into the sheet below.

❍ Not all spider webs are built against supporting structures. Some spiders use the web like a net. The net is thrown over the unsuspecting prey, which is then wrapped in silk.

❍ To avoid getting stuck inside their own webs, spiders smear a special substance over their bodies and have oil glands on their feet. They only tiptoe while moving over the web. A spider also knows where it has laid the sticky and non-sticky silk threads.

Silk production

Spiders have silk producing glands in their body that are linked to spinning organs, called spinnerets, at the tip of the abdomen. Spinnerets have openings called spigots and spools, through which silk emerges. Each spigot secretes silk of a different thickness. Several types of silk can be spun at the same time.

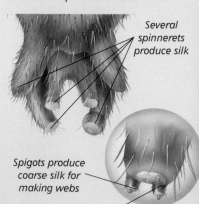

Several spinnerets produce silk

Spigots produce coarse silk for making webs

Spools produce fine silk for wrapping prey

Bolas spider

The bolas spider makes a sticky ball and attaches it to a length of silk. It then whirls this 'rope' around like a lasso to catch flying insects.

 A spider begins making its web by creating a strong framework of silk. It then fills the frame with sticky, circular threads that trap prey, such as flies.

1. Silk comes from inside the spider's body. The spider starts a web by building a bridge

3. It adds more threads to make a complete framework

2. Then it makes a triangle shape

4. Finally, the spider fills the frame with circular threads

5. A spider's web is strong enough to catch large insects, but it is easily damaged by larger animals and people

Amazing

A strand of spider silk is stronger than a steel wire of the same thickness.

Spiders that Hunt

Spiders are carnivores. They feed on all types of insect. Some bigger species can even attack small mammals and birds. The spider injects paralyzing venom into its prey. The prey is partly digested by this venom, and the spider then sucks out the liquidized innards. Not all spiders spin webs to catch prey – some are active hunters that stalk or chase prey. Other spiders ambush or even set traps for their victims.

○ Venom glands are located near the fangs on the spider's head.

○ For some animals, spider venom is lethal, while other animals are left paralyzed by it. Spider venom can affect animals in two ways – it can be either neurotoxic or necrotic.

○ Neurotoxic venom affects the entire nervous system of the animal. It can cause paralysis and pain in areas other than where the spider has bitten. Necrotic venom only affects the tissues where the spider bites. The skin in this area can form blisters or turn black.

○ Most spiders pose no threat to humans. However, the venom of brown recluse spiders, black widows and Brazilian wandering spiders is powerful enough to kill a person.

Amazing

The bite of the male Sydney funnelweb spider can be fatal for primates (humans, apes and monkeys), but it does not pose a threat to other mammals, such as cats and dogs.

▼ *When jumping spiders leap, they often produce a tough line of silk, called a dragline, which keeps them secure in case they fall or are blown off course.*

▼ *The giant crab spider often hides on flowers and attacks insects, such as bees and wasps, that come to feed there.*

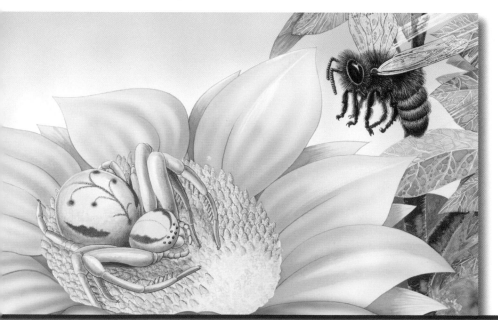

Raft spider

Raft spiders live near water. A raft spider touches the surface with its sensitive legs, feeling for vibrations caused by insects, fish or frogs. By spreading its legs out wide and taking quick steps, it can run over the water to catch prey. Raft spiders often crawl down water plants when danger threatens, and they can stay underwater for up to an hour.

A spitting spider has silk glands that are connected to its poison fangs. When it spots its prey, it spits a sticky, silken substance over the prey to immobilize it. The spider may swing its head from side to side while spitting to create a zig-zag stream that binds the prey to the ground.

Trapdoor spiders

Trapdoor spiders make burrows in the ground. They build a silk-hinged earthen door at the opening of their burrows. The spiders wait for prey to come near and then rush out of this door to grab a meal. Some species stretch a silk 'trip-wire' from the burrow. As soon as a prey trips on the silk line, the spider rushes out and bites the victim.

○ Bird-eating spiders come out to hunt at night. They do spin webs, but usually chase their prey. They silently and suddenly dash to catch small mammals or drag hummingbirds from their nests.

○ Raft spiders, also known as fishing spiders, dive underwater for 10–15 minutes at a time when hunting for prey such as tadpoles, aquatic insects, and small fish and frogs.

○ A jumping spider leaps by means of muscular contractions in its body, which force blood into the legs. This causes the legs to extend rapidly. Some species do not jump but scurry around in an ant-like manner.

○ Crab spiders hide themselves and lie in wait for their prey. As they can change their colour to match their environment, it is difficult for their prey to spot them. This helps the spiders to make surprise attacks. Some crab spiders resemble tree bark, leaves or fruits, while others look like bird droppings.

○ Wolf spiders are named after their wolf-like habit of chasing and pouncing on their prey. They are also known as ground spiders or hunting spiders.

The wolf spider lies in wait, still and silent, ready for an insect or spider to pass by. As its prey approaches, such as this cricket, the wolf spider pounces.

○ Jumping spiders are active predators that usually hunt by day. They stalk their prey until they are within jumping range, then leap on the unsuspecting victim.

Find out more

Mouse spider p. 247

Spiders of the World

Spiders are found almost everywhere, from deserts, forests and grasslands to caves, houses and even ponds. They range in size from those as large as dinner plates to tiny spiders smaller than a pin-head. Many spiders have a dull brown or grey colouration, but others are brightly coloured with eye-catching yellows, reds, and oranges.

The Australian redback spider is one of the most deadly of a group called widow spiders. These spiders get their name because once they have mated, the female eats the male.

Female spiders spin a silk cocoon around their eggs, forming an egg-sac. This protects the eggs and stops them from drying out.

The familiar wheel-shaped webs of orb-weavers have spirals of sticky silk that prevent jumping or flying insects from escaping.

Bird-eating spiders feed primarily on small birds, such as hummingbirds and warblers. Their main enemy are spider-hunting wasps.

Tarantulas usually dig underground burrows, but some live in burrows dug by rodents or other animals. Tarantulas eat a variety of animals, from insects and small reptiles to small birds and frogs.

Crab spiders, such as this gold-leaf crab spider, are named after their crab-like shape and their ability to walk sideways.

Argiope spiders are also called 'writing spiders', because of the zigzag pattern that they build into their webs.

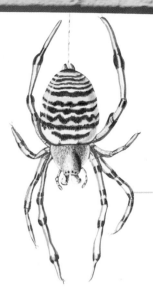

White-backed garden spiders have very distinctive striped markings of silver, yellow and black. They build large webs, and often hang upside down near the centre.

Golden-silk spiders weave very strong orb-webs that look like gold thread in the sunshine.

North America's shamrock spider gets its name from the pattern on its abdomen, which may resemble a shamrock (a type of clover).

Brown recluse spiders are native to the United States. Despite their shy nature, these highly venomous spiders are often found in homes and garages, lurking in dark corners or basements.

Amazing

In some countries, people eat spiders. Blue legged tarantulas, for example, are said to taste like chestnuts when eaten raw, and like the marrow of chicken bones when cooked.

Mouse spiders belong to the trapdoor family of spiders. They have grey stomachs covered with hair, which looks like mouse fur.

Funnelweb spiders are named after their habit of making sheet-like webs that funnel into a tubular retreat at one point.

Many spiders wrap their prey in silk to immobilize them, but fishing spiders simply grasp their victims with their fangs and eat them.

Find out more

Arachnids pp. 196–197

Glossary

Abdomen The third part of an insect's body, behind the head and thorax.

Anal claspers Gripping, sucker-like projections at the end of the body of caterpillars and male dragonflies.

Antennae (singular: antenna) A pair of structures on an insect's head that are sensitive to smell, taste and touch.

Anti-venin A medicine given to counteract the effects of venom.

Aquatic Living most or all of the time in water.

Arachnid An arthropod with eight legs.

Arthropod An invertebrate animal with an exoskeleton.

Autotomy The ability of an animal to shed a limb in order to escape predators.

Bask To lie in the sunshine for warmth.

Bug An insect with needle-like mouthparts for piercing and sucking.

Camouflage The way that an animal's colour, markings, patterning or shape helps it to blend in with its surroundings.

Cannibalistic Describes an animal that may eat members of its own species.

Carnivorous Eating mainly or only meat.

Caterpillar A moth or butterfly larva.

Cell The microscopic building blocks from which all living things are made. A cell is also a hexagonal space in a wasp or bee nest, used to store food or eggs.

Cephalothorax Part of an arachnid's body: the head and thorax fused together.

Cerci Sensory projections at the end of the abdomen of some insects.

Chelicerae An arachnid's muscular jaws. In spiders the chelicerae are tipped with fangs.

Chrysalis A hard case that protects the pupa of an insect, especially a butterfly or moth.

Cocoon A silken case around an insect pupa or the eggs of spiders.

Cold-blooded When an animal cannot maintain a constant body temperature. Its body temperature depends on the temperature of its surroundings.

Colony A group of insects that live together in a nest and are all offspring of the same female – the queen.

Complete metamorphosis When an insect undergoes distinct stages in its development, in which the young look very different to the adults.

Compound eyes Eyes that are made up of many different parts, each with a tiny lens at the surface.

Courtship Animal behaviour that leads to the selection of a mate and to mating.

Decomposers Organisms that break down the remains of other living things.

Drone A male bee who mates with the queen but does no work in the colony.

Egg-sac A silken bag spun by a female spider around her eggs to protect them.

Egg-tooth A temporary tooth that a baby spider uses to pierce its egg shell.

Elytra The wing cases of a beetle.

Exoskeleton The tough, waterproof casing of an arthropod's body.

Eye spots Markings on an insect's body or wings that resemble the eyes of a larger animal.

Fangs Pointed mouthparts, often hollow for injecting venom into prey.

Fossils The remains of living things, preserved in the rocks. Impressions in rock of footprints or skin are also fossils.

Gall A growth that forms on a plant around eggs laid by certain wasps.

Grubs Insect larvae, especially those of beetles, wasps and bees.

Habitat The natural home of a plant or animal.

Halteres A pair of small, knobbed structures, one on each side of a fly's body. They help a fly to control its flight.

Hexapod A non-insect six-legged arthropod, such as a springtail.

Hibernate To enter a sleep-like state in which the body functions at a low level and thus uses little energy. Hibernation helps some animals to survive the winter.

Honey guides Lines or patterns on a flower that guide insects to the nectar.

Honeydew A sweet liquid that oozes out of the rear of sap-feeding bugs.

Host An animal on or in which a parasite lives and feeds.

Incomplete metamorphosis When an insect develops from a larva into an adult without going through a pupal stage. The young resemble the adults.

Insect An arthropod with six legs and a head, thorax and abdomen.

Instar The stage in an insect's life-cycle between two moults.

Invertebrate An animal without a backbone. Insects, arachnids, worms, snails and slugs are all invertebrates.

Larvae (singular: larva) The first stage of an insect's life-cycle after hatching from its egg.

Maggot The larva of a fly.

Mandibles An insect's main pair of jaws, which chop up food.

Mating The coming together of male and female animals to produce young.

Maxillae The second pair of jaws in an insect, used to help guide food into the mouth.

Metamorphosis The change of a young insect through several growth stages into its adult form.

Migrate To travel in search of food, better weather or breeding sites.

Mimic The use of colours and patterns to copy another animal's appearance.

Moulting Shedding an old skin, to reveal a new skin underneath.

Nectar A sugary liquid produced by plants that attracts pollinating insects such as bees and wasps.

Nymph The larvae of insects such as dragonflies and grasshoppers.

Omnivorous Feeding on a wide variety of food, both plants and animals.

Ovipositor A female insect's egg-laying tube.

Paralyze To affect an animal's nervous system or muscles so that it cannot move.

Parasites Organisms, such as fleas, ticks and mites, that live and feed on or inside other living things.

Pedipalps The second pair of leg-like appendages at the front of an arachnid's body, usually covered in sensory hairs.

Pheromone A chemical that some animals produce to attract a mate.

Pollen Tiny grains made by the male parts of a flower. Pollen must reach the female parts of a flower so that seeds can form (pollination). Bees, wasps, flies and other insects help this process by carrying pollen between flowers as they feed.

Predator An animal that hunts and kills other animals for food.

Prey An animal that is hunted by other animals for food.

Proboscis The tube-like mouthparts of moths, butterflies and some flies.

Prolegs Muscular, leg-like projections on a caterpillar's body.

Pupa (plural: pupae) The resting stage of an insect's life-cycle, when it changes from a larva to an adult.

Queen An egg-laying female in a colony of ants, bees, wasps or termites.

Saliva A liquid produced by glands in the mouth that makes it easier to swallow and digest food.

Sap A nutrient-rich liquid found in plants.

Sensory hairs Tiny hairs attached to nerves that enable insects and arachnids to detect things by touch and even taste.

Silk Threads of protein made by spiders and some insects.

Simple eyes Eyes with only one lens. Spiders and some insects have simple eyes.

Social insects Insects that live together in colonies.

Species A group of similar living things that can breed together to produce fertile young.

Spinnerets Tubes at the end of a spider's abdomen, through which the spider squeezes silk to spin a web.

Spiracle Tiny breathing holes on an insect's abdomen.

Sting The sharp body part used to inject venom into attackers or prey.

Thorax The middle section of an insect's body.

Timbals Drum-like structures on the legs of some insects for producing mating calls.

Venom A poisonous liquid used by an animal to kill or paralyze prey.

Web A network of silken threads woven by a spider and used to trap prey.

Wing cases The hard coverings of a beetle's hind wings.

Workers The insects in a colony that build the nest, find food and care for the young. Workers cannot breed. There are worker bees, ants and termites.

REPTILES & AMPHIBIANS

Every Shape and Size

Reptiles and amphibians come in every shape and size. There are around 8000 species of reptile, and 5000 amphibian species. They range from tiny frogs to giant, dinosaur-like lizards. The joint study of reptiles and amphibians is called herpetology, from the Greek word **herpeton**, *meaning 'crawling things'.*

○ Reptiles and amphibians are vertebrates, which means that they have a backbone. This is a strong, flexible support column to which other body structures are attached. Mammals, birds and fish are also vertebrates.

Early reptiles

The first reptiles evolved from amphibians 330 million years ago, in the Carboniferous Period. They were more successful than their amphibian ancestors because their tough-shelled eggs did not need to be laid in water, enabling early reptiles to colonize dry land.

○ Both reptiles and amphibians are cold-blooded, which means that their body temperature is determined by the temperature of their surroundings.

○ Amphibians spend part of their life on land and part in water. Frogs, toads, newts and salamanders are all amphibians.

○ The life cycle of most amphibians involves a change from an aquatic larva that takes in oxygen through gills to a land-dwelling adult that breathes through lungs.

⊳ *The world's tiniest reptile is the Jaragua lizard of the Caribbean, which is just 16 mm long. A Brazilian frog is one of the smallest amphibians. Its body length is just 9.8 mm.*

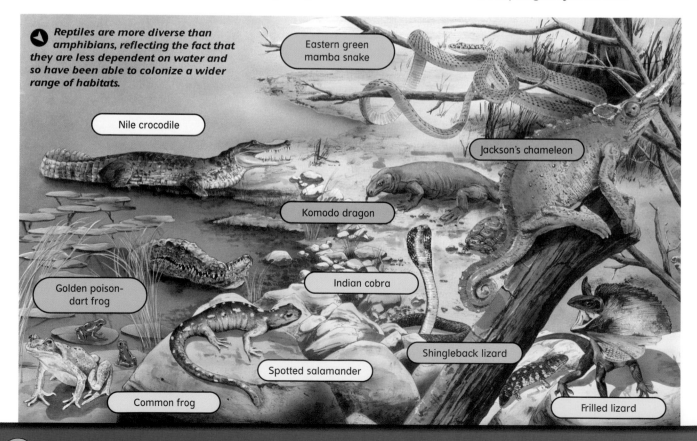

⊳ *Reptiles are more diverse than amphibians, reflecting the fact that they are less dependent on water and so have been able to colonize a wider range of habitats.*

Eastern green mamba snake

Nile crocodile

Jackson's chameleon

Komodo dragon

Golden poison-dart frog

Indian cobra

Shingleback lizard

Spotted salamander

Common frog

Frilled lizard

Ancient ancestors

The 'golden age' of reptiles was 230–65 million years ago, when the reptile group called the dinosaurs dominated life on Earth. Many dinosaurs were placid herbivores, but others, such as *Tyrannosaurus* (shown here), were fierce predators.

Amazing

To cool themselves, desert tortoises urinate on their legs. When the urine evaporates, it takes away body heat.

○ Most amphibians live close to water in temperate and tropical parts of the world. They lay their eggs in water.

○ Some amphibians have adapted to survive cold and dry conditions.

○ Reptiles are scaly skinned animals that live in many different habitats, mainly in warm regions.

○ Many reptiles spend their whole lives away from water.

○ Some reptiles do spend time in water, but most reptiles lay their eggs on land.

○ Reptiles do not have a larval stage, and emerge fully formed from their eggs.

Reptiles

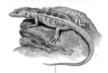

Crocodiles, alligators, caimans and gharials are large, leathery skinned reptiles that form the crocodilian group. (More than 20 species.)

The highly successful lizards usually have four legs and a tail. (About 4500 species.)

Snakes are legless, predatory reptiles with long, cylindrical bodies. (Nearly 3000 species.)

Turtles and tortoises are reptiles with hard shells. Together they are known as chelonians. (Just under 300 species.)

Amphisbaenians are burrowing, legless, worm-like reptiles that are related to lizards. (About 150 species.)

Tuataras are the last survivors of an ancient group of reptiles. (Only 2 species.)

Amphibians

Frogs and toads are tailless amphibians with muscular back legs. (Around 4400 species.)

Salamanders, newts and the eel-like sirens are amphibians with tails. (More than 450 species.)

Caecilians resemble worms or snakes and have only the tiniest of feet, or none at all. (Under 200 species.)

Temperature Control

Reptiles and amphibians are cold-blooded, which means that they cannot use the food they eat to make their own body heat. Instead, they must absorb heat from their surroundings in order to make their bodies work. They control their body temperature mainly by moving between hot and cold places during the course of the day.

Many reptiles are found in hot deserts and dry grassland. Their thick skin means that as little water as possible escapes from their bodies. Some amphibians also manage to survive in arid conditions, sheltering in burrows and storing water in their bladder to keep themselves alive.

Aestivation

During dry periods, some reptiles and amphibians aestivate – that is, they enter an inactive state that is similar to hibernation. The freshwater spotted turtle of North America aestivates in the muddy beds of lakes and rivers, or even in muskrat burrows.

❍ Reptiles mainly live in warmer parts of the world. They often bask in the sun in order to gain enough energy to hunt.

❍ Reptiles need a certain level of warmth to survive. This is why there are no reptiles in very cold places, such as at the North and South Poles or at the very tops of mountains.

❍ Amphibians, too, are absent from the poles, but some can be found in mountains as high up as 4500 m. Many amphibians hibernate through winter.

Amazing

The Australian water-holding frog survives long desert droughts by shedding the outer layers of its skin to form a cocoon that it fills with water.

❍ A few frogs and salamanders can survive temperatures as low as −6°C by releasing a substance called glycerol into their bloodstream. This acts like a kind of anti-freeze, and prevents the cells of their bodies from icing up.

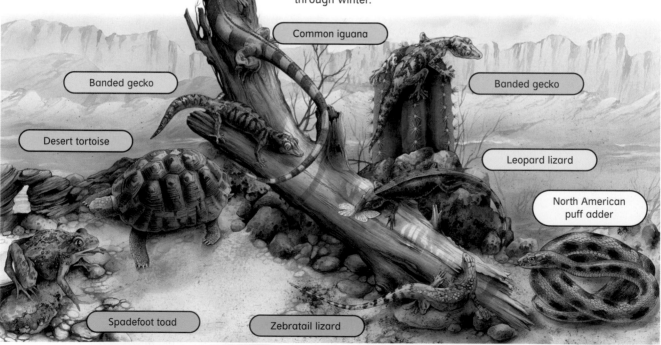

Common iguana

Banded gecko

Banded gecko

Desert tortoise

Leopard lizard

North American puff adder

Spadefoot toad

Zebratail lizard

Find out more

Marine iguana p. 264

Temperature control in crocodilians

To cool off, this Morelet's crocodile has opened its jaws to let moisture evaporate from its mouth.

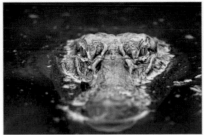

Crocodilians, such as this American alligator, submerge themselves in water when they get too hot.

Like all reptiles, Nile crocodiles rely on basking in the sun to gain sufficient energy for hunting.

▶ *Chameleons and many lizards can adjust the colour of their skin to absorb more heat from the sun.*

○ Like reptiles, many amphibians live in very hot places. But sometimes it can get too hot and dry for them. The spadefoot toad of Europe, Asia and North America buries itself in the sand to escape the heat and dryness.

○ A spadefoot toad can survive losing 60 per cent of its body water.

○ Many burrowing frogs that live in hot, dry places are able to store water in their bladder.

○ A basking frog loses water from its skin, so basking is restricted to species that live near permanent water.

○ Even reptiles can get too hot sometimes. When this happens, they hide in the shade of a rock or bury themselves in the sand. Some reptiles escape the heat by having a nocturnal lifestyle, meaning that they are mostly active at night.

○ Reptiles need very little water compared to many other animals. Because they don't use food to create body heat, many can survive in places with scarce food supplies, such as deserts.

▲ *The Great Plains toad burrows into soft mud and under rocks during daylight hours to avoid drying out.*

Hibernation

When the weather turns especially cold, many amphibians and some reptiles go into a sleep-like state called hibernation. Frogs may hide in the mud at the bottom of ponds or under stones and logs in autumn, and hibernate there right through until spring.

▲ *In common with other lizards, this agama from Africa gets itself warm by lying, or basking, in the sun.*

Introduction to Reptiles

Reptiles include lizards, crocodilians, chelonians, tuataras, snakes and amphisbaenians. A reptile's skin looks slimy, but it is in fact quite dry. It retains moisture so well that reptiles are a dominant animal group in deserts. The skin often turns darker to absorb the sun's heat.

Amazing

When it finds water, a thirsty desert tortoise may drink more than 40 per cent of its own body weight in water in just over an hour.

○ Flying reptiles dominated the skies during the Mesozoic Era, 248–65 million years ago.

○ Some reptiles can take to the air today – if only for a few seconds. They do not really fly but glide between branches or down to the ground. Gliding helps animals to travel further, escape predators or swoop down on passing prey before it gets away.

○ Fossils of shelled reptiles similar to today's chelonians (tortoises and turtles) date back about 220 million years to the Triassic Period.

Many reptiles that spend much of their time in trees are coloured green, such as this basilisk lizard. They blend in with their leafy surroundings, making it difficult to see them unless they move.

Amphisbaenians are burrowing reptiles of tropical and subtropical regions. They are generally only seen on the surface when heavy rain floods their tunnels. Using their thick heavy skulls, amphisbaenians batter their way through the soil in search of worms, insects and larvae to eat.

○ Snakes were the last of the existing reptile groups to appear on Earth. It is likely that they evolved from lizard ancestors 150–100 million years ago, during the late Jurassic or early Cretaceous Period.

○ Part of the reason for the great success of the lizards is their size – only a few exceed 30 cm in total length. Being relatively small, and thus not requiring large supplies of food, they are able to survive where their larger reptile relatives cannot.

○ Crocodilians, like many reptiles, are perfectly at home in water. Their streamlined body shape, heavily webbed feet and massive muscular tail make them impressive aquatic hunters.

Airborne reptiles

Some reptiles can take to the air. Flying snakes make their bodies into parachutes by raising their rib cage and flattening their body. Flying geckos have webbed feet and folds of skin along their legs, tail and sides, which turn the lizard into an expert glider. The flying dragon lizard has 'wings' made from skin stretched out over ribs that project beyond the body. The wings fold away when not in use.

Find out more

Flying frogs p. 303

Living fossil

The tuatara is the only survivor of a group of animals that became extinct 60 million years ago. No one knows why the tuatara survived and the others died out. The two tuatara species live on about 30 offshore islands in New Zealand. A solitary, nocturnal animal, the tuatara eats invertebrates, small lizards and amphibians, birds' eggs and chicks.

▼ *The wedge-shaped head, narrow neck and brown-green scale pattern of the Gaboon viper make this snake almost impossible to spot among the leaves of the forest floor.*

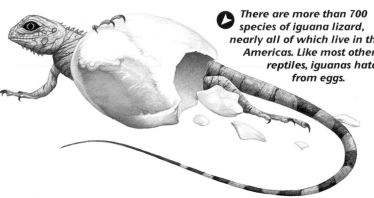

▶ *There are more than 700 species of iguana lizard, nearly all of which live in the Americas. Like most other reptiles, iguanas hatch from eggs.*

❍ When resting, the tuatara breathes just once each hour. Furthermore, this reptile may still be growing when it is 60 years old. This slow lifestyle and growth rate may partly explain why the tuatara is believed to be able to live for as long as 120 years.

❍ A tuatara may share the burrow of a seabird such as a petrel or shearwater. The bird's droppings attract a range of insects, including beetles and crickets, which are the tuatara's favourite food. The tuatara pays for its lodgings by keeping the burrow insect-free.

▼ *Crocodilians are more social animals than other reptiles, and there have been claims that they sometimes cooperate when hunting.*

Anatomy of Reptiles

A reptile's body relies on the same basic life-support systems as other vertebrates (animals with backbones), using many of the same organs, including a heart, lungs, kidneys and liver. But there are several key differences, most notably the tough skin in which these animals are clad.

❍ Reptiles have dry, scaly, waterproof skin. This prevents their bodies from drying out.

❍ The skin consists of scales made of keratin – the same sort of material that forms human fingernails and toenails.

❍ A reptile's scales may be rough or smooth, and they can form very thick, horny plates called scutes. In some species the skin contains bony plates called osteoderms.

Amazing

The green-blooded skink is the only vertebrate to have green pigment (colouring) in its blood. Scientists are uncertain as to the function of this pigment.

❍ All reptiles shed their outer skin to replace their scales. Snakes shed their skin in one piece. In lizards, crocodilians, chelonians and tuataras, the old skin comes away in flakes or chunks.

❍ Unlike the limbs of mammals and birds, a reptile's legs support its body from the side. This gives it a sprawling gait when it moves.

Crocodilian throat flap

Crocodilians have no lips, so they cannot make their mouths watertight when submerged. Instead, they have a special flap in their throats that seals off the windpipe, so that they do not drown when they dive below the surface.

❍ Snakes, amphisbaenians and some lizards have lost their legs.

❍ In many reptiles, bone growth does not stop when the animals reach sexual maturity.

❍ When reptiles get old, they do not permanently lose their teeth like mammals do, but continue to replace the teeth that they shed.

❍ Chelonians (tortoises and turtles) lack teeth, but they chop up their food with a horny beak. This is always growing, so it never gets worn down with use.

❍ Sea snakes have an enlarged lung, part of which forms a special chamber to aid the snake's buoyancy.

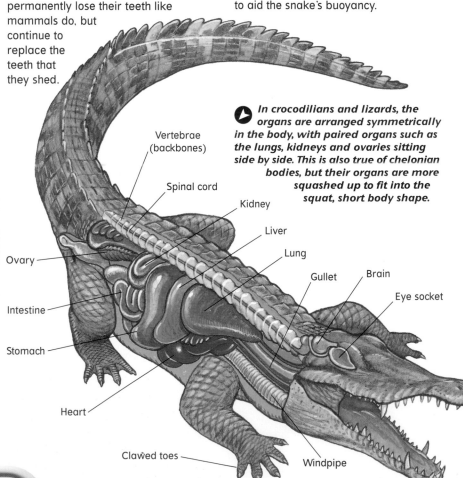

▶ *In crocodilians and lizards, the organs are arranged symmetrically in the body, with paired organs such as the lungs, kidneys and ovaries sitting side by side. This is also true of chelonian bodies, but their organs are more squashed up to fit into the squat, short body shape.*

Vertebrae (backbones)

Spinal cord

Kidney

Liver

Lung

Gullet

Brain

Eye socket

Ovary

Intestine

Stomach

Heart

Clawed toes

Windpipe

Find out more
Amphibian anatomy pp. 296–297

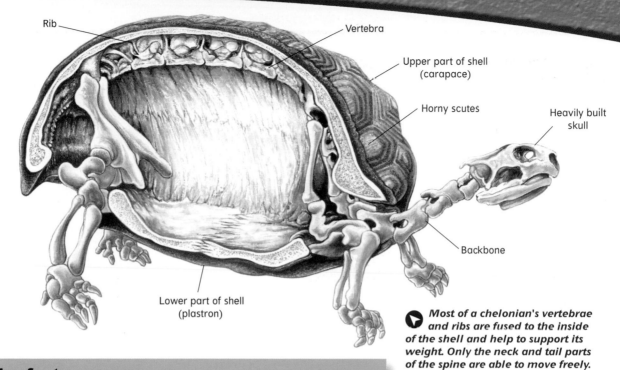

Rib

Vertebra

Upper part of shell
(carapace)

Horny scutes

Heavily built
skull

Backbone

Lower part of shell
(plastron)

Most of a chelonian's vertebrae and ribs are fused to the inside of the shell and help to support its weight. Only the neck and tail parts of the spine are able to move freely.

The majority of a snake's organs are elongated to fit into the reptile's long, thin body. The paired organs are staggered, rather than side by side. The enlarged right lung does all the breathing, the small left lung is redundant.

Gecko feet

Geckos have an unusual adaptation – hairy feet. Each foot has about 500,000 tiny hairs, and each hair tip has thousands of microscopic 'stickers', creating a powerful adhesive. This enables the gecko to walk on any surface, including vertical ones, and even hang by one toe.

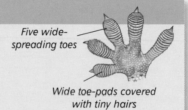

Five wide-spreading toes

Wide toe-pads covered with tiny hairs

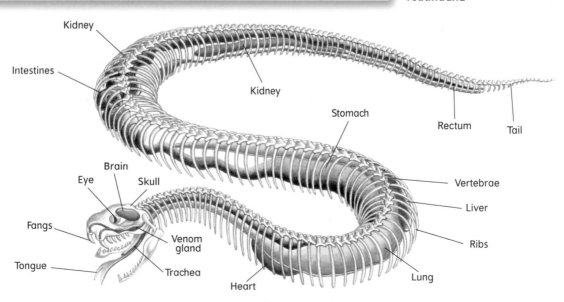

Kidney

Intestines

Kidney

Stomach

Rectum

Tail

Brain

Eye

Skull

Vertebrae

Fangs

Liver

Venom
gland

Tongue

Ribs

Trachea

Heart

Lung

Reptile Senses

*L*ike other vertebrates, reptiles find out about the world around them using their senses of sight, smell, hearing and touch. However, the development of these senses varies between the different reptile groups. And some reptiles have acquired additional senses to help them find and capture prey.

❍ Lizards, snakes and chelonians have a depression in the roof of the mouth called the Jacobson's organ, which allows them to 'taste' the air.

❍ Crocodilians, chelonians and most lizards have good eyesight, but many snakes do not. In fact, some snakes that live underground are blind. They only emerge when lack of food forces them to the surface.

❍ Geckos and iguanas cannot blink. Instead of having movable eyelids, they have a fixed transparent scale over each eye called a brille. Snakes also have brilles. The brilles are shed with the rest of the skin when the reptile moults (or 'sloughs').

▲ *Each of a chameleon's turret-like eyes can swivel independently, allowing it to search for prey (or predators) in all directions.*

❍ You can usually tell whether a reptile is active by day or night from its eyes. If the pupil is a slit that closes almost completely in sunlight, the animal is nocturnal. A wide, round pupil means a reptile is active by day.

▲ *Chelonians, such as this giant Galapagos tortoise, have poor hearing, but excellent senses of smell and sight. They also have a Jacobson's organ.*

❍ Snakes of the pit viper, python, and boa families can detect the body heat of nearby prey using special sensory areas on their faces. In pythons and boas, these are slits in the lip scales, but in pit vipers they form a pit (hole) on each side of the head.

▲ *The web-footed gecko of southwest Africa lives in the Namibian desert. To keep its eyes clear of dust and sand, it constantly licks them with its long tongue.*

Find out more

Amphisbaenian p. 256

In most crocodilians, the eyes, ears and nostrils are positioned on the top of the head. This enables them to breathe and monitor their surroundings while drifting along unnoticed just under the water's surface.

○ Marine turtles migrate vast distances each year as they swim to their nesting beaches. They possibly use the position of the Sun in the sky as their guide, but there is also evidence that they may be able to sense the Earth's magnetic field and use this to help them navigate.

○ Many lizards, including iguanas, can see in colour. This is important, because it enables them to distinguish between the sexes. Iguanas communicate using their colourful crests, head ornaments and throat fans.

○ Only crocodilians and lizards have external ear openings. One African gecko has such thin skin over its ear-openings that if you were to look at it with the openings lined up precisely, you would see light coming through from the other side.

○ Chelonians and snakes have poor hearing. Although snakes are not very good at detecting air-borne sounds, their skull bones can pick up vibrations travelling through the ground.

○ The burrowing amphisbaenians find food by detecting the scent and sound of prey animals in their tunnels.

Jacobson's organ

Snakes and some lizards, such as monitors and Gila monsters, constantly flick out their forked tongues. The tongue collects airborne scent particles and transfers them to the Jacobson's organ in the roof of the mouth. This is lined with special cells called chemoreceptors, which analyse the scent for evidence of nearby prey.

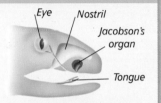

Eye   Nostril

Jacobson's organ

Tongue

Third eye

Tuataras and many lizards, including iguanas (seen here), have an eye-like structure under the skin on top of the skull. The function of this 'third eye' is uncertain. It is thought to register day length, and may influence behaviour such as basking, hibernation and even breeding.

Amazing

Tests with a blind rattlesnake showed that when its heat pits were covered up, its success rate in hitting a target fell from 98 per cent to 27 per cent.

Rattlesnakes are pit vipers. Their heat pits are lined with a layer of cells called thermoreceptors, which detect heat given off by warm-blooded animals. This allows them to track prey such as mammals or birds in the dark. The heat pits tell the snake not only the location of the prey, but also how far away it is.

Reptile Reproduction

Following courtship and mating, most reptiles lay eggs. The eggs allow young reptiles to develop in safety, even though they are outside their mother's body. The eggs are laid in a nest that is usually well hidden – such as in a pile of rotting vegetation, in the sand on a beach, or in a hole by a river bank. Few reptiles show any interest in their young once they have hatched.

○ Most reptile eggs are much tougher than those of amphibians. This is because the eggs must be able to survive life out of water. The shells prevent the eggs from drying out.

○ Lizards and snakes lay leathery-shelled eggs. Crocodile and tortoise eggs have a hard shell rather like birds' eggs.

When young American alligators are ready to hatch, they make high-pitched calls from inside the egg. Hearing these cries, the female opens the nest. She may use her jaws to help the baby reptiles emerge from their eggs. The mother will stay with and defend her young for up to two years.

Inside an egg

The egg yolk provides food for the young, called an embryo. The shell protects the embryo from the outside world, but also allows oxygen and water into the egg, which are vital for the embryo's growth. A bag of protective fluid cushions the embryo from knocks.

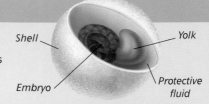

Shell — Yolk

Embryo — Protective fluid

○ On Fernandina Island in the Galapagos, marine iguanas incubate their eggs in the mouth of a volcano.

○ The majority of reptiles abandon their eggs immediately after laying them. Making sure that the eggs are hidden from predators is as much as most reptiles do for their offspring.

○ In certain lizards, such as skinks, and some snakes, including cobras and pythons, the female stays with the eggs and will try to drive away intruders.

○ Female pythons remain coiled round their eggs for several weeks. Indian and green tree pythons actually keep their eggs warm by 'shivering' – contracting their muscles to generate heat.

○ Crocodilians take more care of their offspring than most reptiles. They will aggressively defend the nest and also remain with their young for some time after hatching. This may be anything from just a few months to a couple of years, depending on the species.

Amazing

In crocodilians, chelonians and some lizard species, the sex of the young depends on the temperature at which the eggs are incubated. Higher temperatures tend to produce more males, and lower temperatures more females.

Reptile eggs

Alligators lay their eggs in a mound of plants and earth. A typical clutch contains between 35 and 40 eggs.

A ground python's egg is large compared to its body. A female is about 85 cm long, and her eggs 12 cm.

The Javan bloodsucker lizard lays strange eggs like this. No one knows why their eggs are so very long and thin.

Galapagos giant tortoises lay round eggs like this one. The eggs hatch up to 200 days after they were laid.

❍ Some whiptail and wall lizards can reproduce by parthenogenesis. This means that the female is able to produce eggs that can develop without having been fertilized by a male.

❍ Young reptiles hatch out of eggs as miniature adults. They do not undergo a change, or metamorphosis, like amphibians do.

❍ The young reptiles are able to feed themselves as soon as they hatch from their eggs.

Female sea turtles only come ashore to lay their eggs. They deposit the eggs in a hole on the beach, which they dig in the sand with their hind flippers.

❍ Some snakes and lizards do not lay eggs. Instead, they give birth to fully developed live young. Animals that do this are said to be viviparous.

The black ratsnake lays 12–20 eggs in a hidden area, such as under hollow logs or among leaves, or in an empty burrow. The eggs hatch 65–70 days later. The hatchlings have large appetites and quickly double their size.

Egg tooth

A baby reptile, such as this Burmese python, uses a sharp lump on the end of its snout to cut its way out of the egg. This 'egg tooth' falls off soon after the animal has hatched.

Egg tooth

Reptiles – Food and Feeding

Reptile diets vary greatly. Some species feed mainly on plant matter while others are out-and-out carnivores (meat eaters). Many reptiles are omnivorous, eating a wide range of foods. Some carnivorous reptiles actively hunt for food, but many are not fast-moving enough to catch prey in this way, so they lie in wait and ambush their victims.

Cannibalism

Few animals prey on mature crocodilians, but cannibalism within species sometimes occurs. In some places, saltwater crocodile hatchlings are known to have been eaten by older offspring. Cannibalism usually occurs between juveniles, probably as a survival instinct where there are too many crocodiles competing for a limited supply of food.

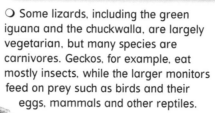

○ Some lizards, including the green iguana and the chuckwalla, are largely vegetarian, but many species are carnivores. Geckos, for example, eat mostly insects, while the larger monitors feed on prey such as birds and their eggs, mammals and other reptiles.

○ Some lizards have a very specialized diet. The marine iguana of the Galapagos, for example, eats only seaweed, while the thorny devil of Australia exists on a diet of ants, eating up to 2500 in one meal. There are also species whose diet comprises mainly water snails, or even scorpions.

○ Most carnivorous lizards simply grab their prey and swallow it. Some species, however, will first shake their victims vigorously or thrash them against rocks to subdue them.

○ Snakes usually swallow small animals while they are still alive, but bigger creatures may be either killed first or injected with venom to prevent them from struggling.

○ Amphisbaenians are thought to feed on burrowing invertebrates, such as earthworms and beetle larvae.

○ Chelonians (tortoises and turtles) use the sharp edges of their horny jaws to cut up food.

Amazing

On rare occasions, a snake may accidentally be eaten by another snake when both try to devour the same prey.

▼ *The chameleon lizard is a highly efficient hunting machine. Each eye can move independently, so the chameleon is able to look in two different directions at once. When a tasty fly buzzes past, the chameleon shoots out an incredibly long tongue in a fraction of a second and draws the fly back into its mouth.*

When the chameleon spots an insect, it then swivels its other eye to look at the prey. This is because it is easier to judge distances with two eyes

▲ *The marine iguanas that live in the Galapagos Islands graze on seaweed growing on submerged rocks. Before each dive into water to feed, the iguanas must warm themselves in the sun to gain enough energy.*

○ Crocodiles pull large prey animals into the water, stun them with a blow from their long, powerful tail and then drown them.

○ A crocodilian does not have teeth designed for slicing up prey or chewing, so larger food items need to be broken up into swallowable chunks. The crocodile grabs a piece of the victim's body and twists like a corkscrew until a lump of flesh tears off.

The chameleon's tongue is almost as long as its body

Two eyes give the brain two slightly different angles to look at the object, so it is easier to tell how far away it is

Find out more

Chameleons pp. 282–283

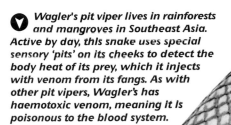

▼ *Wagler's pit viper lives in rainforests and mangroves in Southeast Asia. Active by day, this snake uses special sensory 'pits' on its cheeks to detect the body heat of its prey, which it injects with venom from its fangs. As with other pit vipers, Wagler's has haemotoxic venom, meaning it is poisonous to the blood system.*

Giant herbivore

Many tortoises are herbivores (plant eaters), often using their fore feet to hold plants down while they nibble the shoots. The jaws of the Galapagos giant tortoise are well adapted to feeding on whatever vegetation it comes across. It can even cope with prickly cacti.

○ Tortoises are mainly plant eaters, grazing or browsing on fruit and leaves. Freshwater turtles are more carnivorous than their land-dwelling cousins.

○ Some sea turtles feed on marine invertebrates, including jellyfish, while others eat seaweed and plants such as seagrass.

○ A reptile may change its diet as it grows older. Some freshwater turtles, for example, eat insects when they are young, but feed on aquatic vegetation as adults.

○ Nile crocodiles, too, eat insects after hatching, but as juveniles they move on to crabs, fish and birds. The adults will take mammals as large as buffaloes.

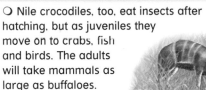

▲ *The common snapping turtle lives in rivers, lakes and swamps in North America. It will eat almost anything swallowable that comes within lunging range. This one has caught a sunfish.*

▶ *Crocodiles and alligators are especially adapted to lie almost submerged in the water. They wait in the shallows for animals to come to drink, or drift silently towards their prey, then leap up and grab their victim before dragging it under water.*

Reptile Defences

Reptiles are eaten by many other animals. Tough skin, horny plates and hard shells protect some reptiles from attack, and various species use camouflage to evade detection by predators. But reptiles have also developed a wide range of ingenious ways to help them avoid becoming a meal for another animal – and survive at least long enough to grow up and breed.

Snake mimic

The non-venomous milksnake mimics the colouration of the venomous coral snake. Predators that try to eat a coral snake get bitten, suffer pain, and learn to avoid the snake in future – and any other species that resemble it. The milksnake's patterning is slightly different from the coral snake's, but it is close enough to fool many predators.

The European grass snake pretends to be dead so that predators leave it alone. It rolls onto its back, wriggles as if dying, and then lies still with its mouth open and its tongue hanging out. It even releases a liquid from its anus that mimics the smell of a rotting corpse.

When a predator grabs a five-lined tree skink by the tail, the lizard can contract its tail muscles so that the tail snaps at a specially weakened joint called the fracture point. The skink scampers off, leaving the confused predator holding a twitching blue tail. The tail eventually grows back.

○ By increasing their blood pressure, horned lizards can burst blood vessels and squirt a jet of blood from their eyes at attackers nearly 1 m away.

○ The spitting cobras of Africa and Asia can spray venom into the eyes of an approaching enemy. The venom is forced at high pressure through tiny holes in the tips of the fangs. When hunting prey, the cobras inject their venom by biting.

○ Many lizards can shed their tail if it is grasped by a predator. The tail will eventually grow back, but it may not be so well formed as the original.

○ The blue-tongued skink flashes its bright blue tongue at predators. The startled predator halts its attack, allowing the lizard to slip away.

Stuck fast

Many reptiles can inflate their bodies with air to deter predators by making themselves look larger. The chuckwalla lizard puffs itself up for a different reason. When danger approaches, the chuckwalla wedges itself into a rock crevice, then inflates its body so that predators cannot pull it out.

A frilled lizard in full display is an amazing sight. This lizard has a large flap of neck skin that normally lies flat. When faced by a predator, it spreads this out to form a huge, stiff ruff that makes it look bigger and scarier.

○ The armadillo lizard of South Africa has spiny skin on its back, but a soft belly. When threatened, it curls up into a ball and stuffs its tail in its mouth, protecting its belly from the teeth and claws of its enemy.

○ The Australian shingleback lizard's tail is shaped like its head. This possibly confuses predators and gives it a chance to escape. If a predator does attack, it may strike at the tail and inflict a non-fatal wound.

When crocodiles are threatened, they can move so quickly that they almost appear to leap out of the water. This is known as tail-walking.

○ Some snakes can pretend to be dead. Most predators steer clear of dead animals, since they may have died of diseases that could infect the predator as well.

○ Turtles and tortoises pull their head and legs into their hard shells to avoid danger. Box turtles have a hinged lower shell (plastron) that enables them to close their shell almost completely, creating an almost impregnable, armour-plated 'box'.

When alarmed, the non-venomous hognose snake raises its head, hisses and flattens its neck into a cobra-like hood, giving the impression that it is about to deliver a deadly bite.

Amazing

The basilisk lizard of Central America has scaly fringes on its long toes that enable it to run over the surface of water to escape its enemies.

Marine Reptiles

Some reptiles venture into the ocean, and a few spend their entire lives at sea. Marine reptiles need to get rid of the excess salt that they absorb from seawater, which could be lethal. Turtles 'cry' extra-salty tears to reduce their salt levels. In crocodiles and marine snakes, special glands in the mouth excrete a concentrated saline solution, which is then washed away.

○ The marine iguana of the Galapagos is the only lizard that spends much of its life in the sea.

○ When in water, a marine iguana may dive for 15 minutes or more, pushing itself along with its tail.

○ Marine iguanas slow their heart rate down when they dive, so that they use less oxygen.

Young sea turtles

Female sea turtles lay their eggs in holes on beaches. They cover the eggs with sand before returning to sea. When the young turtles hatch, they have to dig their way up to the light and air. As they scuttle down the beach towards the water, many fall victim to seabirds and other predators.

○ Sea snakes can stay submerged for up to five hours and move rapidly through the depths.

○ The sea snake and the sea krait (another type of marine snake) have a paddle-like end to the tail, to help them move swiftly through the water.

○ Sea kraits lay their eggs on land, but sea snakes spend their whole lives in the ocean, even giving birth there.

○ Tens of thousands of sea kraits are taken from the oceans each year both for their meat and their skin, which is made into goods such as shoes and bags.

○ Floating sea snakes often find themselves surrounded by fish, which gather at their tail to avoid being eaten. When the snake fancies a snack it swims backwards, fooling the fish into thinking that its head is its tail.

○ Sea turtles have light, flat shells so that they can move easily underwater.

○ Female sea turtles come ashore briefly to lay their eggs, but the male turtles never touch dry land again after leaving the beaches on which they hatched.

◀ *The marine iguanas of the Galapagos islands expel excess salt from nasal glands. The coating of salt gives their faces a whitish appearance. The skin colour of iguanas from different Galapagos islands varies, possibly because they feed on different types of seaweed.*

Sea turtles

The Pacific, or olive, ridley is the smallest of all the sea turtles. It lives in warm waters and feeds on shrimps, jellyfish, crabs, sea-snails and fish.

The green turtle of subtropical and tropical waters grazes on seagrass, mangrove roots and leaves. The young also eat jellyfish, sponges and molluscs.

The hawksbill turtle was nearly hunted to extinction for its beautiful shell, and also for its eggs. It is now protected in many countries.

Saltwater crocodile

Several crocodile species inhabit coastal regions, but the saltwater crocodile is more at home in the ocean than most. It can travel great distances by sea. One male was believed to have swum at least 1360 km to reach the Caroline Islands in the Pacific Ocean.

Amazing

Leatherback turtles have been recorded diving down to 1200 m. They may even exceed depths of 1500 m as they search for large congregations of jellyfish.

Yellow-bellied sea snake

Banded sea snakes

Paddle-like end to the tail

Bands act like camouflage to help break up the outline of the snake's body

○ Sea turtles are the fastest of all chelonians. Their flipper-like front legs 'fly' through the water. Their back legs form mini rudders for steering. Pacific leatherback turtles have managed speeds of up to 35 km/h.

○ Leatherback turtles feed on jellyfish. The turtles often mistakenly swallow floating plastic debris, much of which is translucent like their prey. They have also been found with plastic fishing line in their stomach, presumably eaten because it resembles the trailing tentacles of a jellyfish.

◄ *In the oceans, it is difficult for snakes to control their temperature by basking, so marine snakes are found mainly in tropical waters, which are usually warm all-year round.*

Chelonians

Land-living chelonians are known as tortoises. All chelonians have four limbs, a shell, and a horny, toothless beak. There are two parts to the shell: the shield on the reptile's back is known as a carapace, while the flat belly section is called the plastron. Tortoises have a high, domed shell that is difficult for predators to bite or crush.

○ The shell is made up of two layers: an inner layer of bone covered by an outer layer of horny plates called scutes, which are made of keratin.

○ A chelonian's ribs are fused to its shell, so the ribs cannot move to draw air into the lungs. Instead, special muscles at the tops of the legs pump air into the lungs so that the reptile can breathe.

○ Tortoises shed their skin, but it comes off in small pieces rather than as lumps.

○ Most tortoises are primarily herbivorous, feeding on plant leaves and fruits, but they will also eat tiny animals such as caterpillars.

○ Tortoises live mostly in hot, dry regions and will hibernate in winter if brought to a cold country.

▶ *Tortoises are placid and very slow moving, with an average walking speed of 0.2–0.5 km/h.*

Amazing

A giant tortoise can support a one-tonne weight – about the weight of an average car.

▲ *The Texas tortoise is found in northeastern Mexico and Texas, USA. It eats prickly pear cacti and other succulent plants. A low reproduction rate and heavy collection from the wild by pet suppliers have severely reduced its numbers.*

High, rounded upper shell

Clawed feet

Sturdy club-shaped legs

Find out more

Chelonian skeleton p. 259

Galapagos giant tortoise

This huge tortoise has a massive shell, powerful legs and a long neck. It lives on the Galapagos islands in the Pacific Ocean. where it spends most of its time basking in pools or mud, or grazing on grasses or shrubs in small groups. Like many of the Galapagos species, it is at risk, and breeding programmes have been set up to increase numbers.

○ Turtles and tortoises live to a great age. The greatest authenticated age is for a male Marion's tortoise, which was taken from the Seychelles to Mauritius in 1766. It died 152 years later, but since it was mature when it was found, its true age could have been nearly 200.

○ The Galapagos giant tortoise, the world's largest tortoise, grows to 1.2 m in length. The size and shell shape of this tortoise vary according to which of the individual Galapagos islands the animal originates from.

○ Giant tortoises were once kept on ships to provide fresh meat during long sea voyages.

○ Some birds of prey carry tortoises high into the air and drop them onto rocks below, so that the shells crack and the birds can get to the meat inside.

▶ *The leopard tortoise lives in Africa. it was named after the yellow-and-black markings of its shell, which are reminiscent of a leopard's coat.*

○ The smallest tortoise in the world is the speckled Cape tortoise of Africa, measuring 6–8 cm long. Being so small makes the tortoise vulnerable to a range of predators, but it also enables the tortoise to squeeze under rocks to hide.

○ The desert tortoise lives in dry habitats in the southwestern United States and northern Mexico. It lays its eggs in a hole or under a rock or log. When the eggs hatch some weeks later, the babies must fend for themselves.

○ In many chelonian species, the scutes on the shell have 'growth rings' that show how much they have grown each year. Counting the growth rings can help to determine the chelonian's age.

◀ *To avoid the hottest part of the day, the desert tortoise burrows into the soil with its large front legs, which have wide feet and stout claws.*

Armour plating

When threatened, tortoises and turtles draw their head and legs inside their hard shell, leaving nothing for the predator to get its teeth or claws into. The chelonian simply sits tight until the danger has passed.

Egg laying records

Most eggs per clutch	242	Hawksbill turtle
Most eggs per season	1100 plus	Greenturtles
Least eggs per clutch	1 or 2	Pancake tortoise, big-headed turtle, and other species

Turtles

Turtles are chelonians that spend much, or even all, of their time in water. They have flatter, more streamlined shells than tortoises, and this shell shape helps them to move easily through the water. Like tortoises, turtles have no teeth, so they use their sharp jaws to slice up food.

The alligator snapping turtle lives in deep rivers and lakes in the USA. To hunt, it opens its jaws so that fish can see what looks like a wriggling worm, but is actually just a pink, fleshy lure on the bottom of its mouth. When fish come to investigate, the turtle snaps them up.

Turtle migration

Some sea turtles are among nature's greatest travellers. Every three years, green turtles gather together to swim 2300 km or more from their feeding grounds off the coast of Brazil to breeding sites such as Ascension Island, in the South Atlantic. Here they lay their eggs ashore by moonlight at the highest tide. They bury the eggs in the sand, to be incubated by the heat of the Sun.

○ Sometimes called terrapins, freshwater turtles have webbed, clawed feet that make them well-equipped for both moving on land and swimming in water.

○ Some freshwater turtles have soft, flexible shells that enable them to squeeze under rocks or into nooks and crannies to evade predators.

○ Freshwater turtles lay their eggs on land. The female digs out a hole for the eggs with her back legs.

○ Young freshwater turtles are usually insect-eaters, but most change to a diet of aquatic plants as they grow. Some freshwater turtles are carnivores. They lie motionless and then ambush their prey.

○ The carnivorous alligator snapping turtle is the largest freshwater turtle. Males weigh up to 100 kg.

○ Algae growing on the shell of the alligator snapping turtle make the turtle resemble a rock as it lies motionless on the bottom of rivers and lakes.

○ Some freshwater species, including the matamata and the Chinese soft-shelled turtle, have long noses that act as 'snorkels', enabling the turtles to breathe at the surface while the rest of their body remains submerged.

○ The common snake-necked turtle of Australia has such a long neck that it has to be folded sideways to fit under its shell.

○ In sea turtles, which rarely emerge on to land, the limbs are clawless flippers, rather than legs.

○ Sea turtles feed, mate, and even sleep at sea. Females come ashore only once each year to lay their eggs. They use their flippers to drag themselves up the beach so that they can deposit their eggs in the sand.

Sharp jaws

Fleshy lure

Freshwater turtles

The South American matamata turtle lies on the bottom of rivers and eats fish that swim past.

The Indian softshell turtle (also known as the narrow-headed turtle) is a very fast swimmer that feeds on fish.

The eastern box turtle of North America eats several plant and mushroom species that are poisonous to humans.

The painted turtle of North America can often be seen basking on a favourite log in the morning, sometimes in communal groups.

Sea turtles swim with regular beats of their wing-like front flippers. The rear flippers are used for steering.

Hawksbill

Loggerhead turtle

Green turtle

Leatherback turtle

○ Some species of sea turtle feed only on seaweed as adults. Others eat marine invertebrates, such as jellyfish, shrimps, sea urchins and molluscs, as well as fish.

○ The leatherback sea turtle is the world's heaviest chelonian. Adults typically weigh at least 450 kg. One leatherback washed up on a beach in Wales, UK, in 1988 weighed 961 kg.

Amazing

Young sea turtles make easy, appetizing meals for many predators, including crabs, seabirds and fish. Probably less than 1 per cent of all young green turtles that hatch survive to reach adulthood.

Stinkpot

When threatened, the stinkpot turtle of eastern North America releases a smelly yellow secretion from a pair of glands on its thighs. This secretion smells so foul that most predators back off. If they don't, the turtle can deliver a nasty bite.

Crocodilians

Crocodilians are large reptiles with powerful bodies, thick skin and snapping jaws. These semi-aquatic predators inhabit lakes, rivers and lagoons. Some species will journey out to sea. As well as crocodiles, this reptile group includes alligators, caimans and gharials. Crocodiles are mainly found in Africa, Asia and Australia, although a few species live in Central and South America.

○ Crocodiles have remained unchanged for millions of years. The ancestors of crocodilians lived alongside the dinosaurs 200 million years ago, and today's crocodilian species are the nearest we have to living dinosaurs.

○ Crocodilians can stay underwater for many minutes or even hours.

○ Crocodiles sometimes store prey underwater so that the victim's body starts to rot and is easier to dismember.

○ Most crocodiles have eyes and nostrils at the top of their heads, which enable them to drift along just under the surface of the water unnoticed.

○ Crocodiles are fast swimmers. They swish their powerful tail from side to side to propel themselves forward, and paddle and steer with their webbed rear feet.

○ Crocodiles lay their eggs near water, either in a mound of vegetation or in a hole in the ground.

◄ *The gharial of Asia is a slender crocodilian with a narrow snout. Its legs are weaker than those of other crocodilians, and it spends most of its time in the water.*

○ A Nile crocodile can shut its jaws with a devastating force of up to 2000 kg per sq cm. However, the muscles used to open the crocodile's mouth are weak. Incredibly, its jaws can apparently be held shut with a thick rubber band.

Strong jaws

▲ *With their tough skin, large teeth and powerful jaws, crocodilians are formidable predators.*

▲ *Africa's Nile crocodile eats a range of large vertebrate animals, including antelopes and young hippos. However, fish and smaller vertebrates often form the bulk of its diet.*

Amazing

Nile crocodiles allow small birds, such as spur-wing plovers, to walk into their open mouths to pick food from between their teeth.

The skin on the back has ridges formed by dozens of tiny bones called osteoderms

Short front legs for moving on land

Find out more

Crocodile anatomy p. 258

Crocodilian ancestor

Protosuchus was one of the ancestors of the crocodiles. It lived about 220 million years ago during the Triassic Period. It had quite a short skull, which shows that it had not yet adapted fully for eating fish. *Protosuchus* probably ate small lizards.

Short skull

Long legs will become shorter as Protosuchus *evolves*

○ The saltwater, or estuarine, crocodile ranges through the tropical regions of Asia and the Pacific. At up to 7 m long and with a maximum recorded weight of more than 1 tonne long, it is the largest reptile in the world.

○ Up to 2000 people each year are believed to be killed by saltwater crocodiles, making them the most dangerous of all crocodilians.

○ On muddy river banks, crocodiles usually slither along on their belly, with their legs splayed out to the side. On dry land, they can walk at 2–4 km/h on all fours, with their body raised off the ground. They can even make short gallops with their tail held up in the air, reaching speeds of up to 18 km/h.

Muscular tail for swimming

▶ *This female West African dwarf crocodile is laying her eggs in a hole, dug near to water.*

Parental care

Crocodilians show an unusually high level of parental care compared to most reptiles. A mother crocodile will carry her newly hatched babies to safety in her open mouth.

Webbed hind feet for paddling

The skin on the belly is smooth and was once prized as a material for shoes and handbags

▼ *A large prey animal, such as a zebra or wildebeest, can provide a crocodile with enough energy to last several months until its next meal.*

Biggest crocodiles and alligators

1	Estuarine crocodile	7 m
2	Indian gharial	6 m
3	Nile crocodile	5 m
3	American crocodile	5 m
4	American alligator	4 m

Alligators and Caimans

Alligators are found both in the southeastern United States and in the Yangtze River in China. There are now only a few hundred Chinese alligators left in the wild. Caimans are the alligators' South American relatives. Gharials are restricted to the north of the Indian subcontinent.

○ Alligators have broader snouts than crocodiles. When the mouth is shut, the fourth tooth on the lower jaw is visible in a crocodile, but not in an alligator.

○ Alligators are generally smaller than their crocodile cousins.

○ American alligators had been hunted almost to extinction by the 1950s. They were given legal protection, and their numbers in the wild have now recovered strongly.

○ As in all crocodilians, male and female American alligators look alike, although the males tend to grow larger than the females.

Alligator farms

Crocodiles and alligators have long been hunted by humans. To meet the demand for their skin and meat, crocodiles and alligators are now bred and reared in captivity on 'farms', such as this alligator farm in Florida, USA. Farming eliminates the need to kill wild crocodilians.

○ A male American alligator courts a female by stroking her with his front legs and rubbing her throat with his head. He even blows bubbles past her cheeks to encourage her to mate with him.

▽ *Over the last 100 years, the population of the South American black caiman is believed to have fallen by 99 per cent, largely due to it being hunted for its skin.*

△ *American alligators prey on a wide range of animals, including fish, snakes, turtles and mammals. They will sometimes rear up suddenly on their tail to snatch birds perched on overhanging branches.*

Amazing

Crocodilians often swallow stones to help them grind up their food. The stones also probably act as ballast, enabling the reptile to float without tipping over.

Find out more

Hatching alligators p. 262

The common caiman has the srongest body armour of almost any crocodile. It eats fish, water birds, river snails – and even piranhas.

❍ Chinese alligators move into elaborate underground burrows to avoid the worst of the winter weather.

❍ Crocodilians have few natural enemies, but jaguars and large anacondas have been observed killing caimans in South America. Similarly, hippos and elephants have been known to kill crocodiles, in this case probably to protect their young.

❍ Crocodilians communicate by slapping their heads on the water's surface or snapping their jaws together. Male American alligators roar loudly during the breeding season.

❍ The American alligator lives in lakes, swamps and marshes. In mid-summer, when the water levels fall, it digs holes to create deeper areas of water that will last until the rains return.

With only its eyes and snout projecting above the surface, the American alligator resembles a floating log as it lies low in the water.

The spectacled caiman gets its name from the ridge between its eyes. This looks like the bridge of a pair of spectacles.

❍ Caimans in Venezuela bury themselves in soft mud at the driest time of year. They wait encrusted in the mud for the water levels to rise again.

❍ In winter, alligators keep their snouts out of the water, so that breathing holes will form in the ice if the water's surface freezes over.

The female Chinese alligator buries her eggs under a mound of plant matter. As the vegetation rots, it gives off heat, which incubates the eggs. The alligator stays nearby to guard the nest until the eggs hatch.

Gharials

The gharial catches prey by sweeping its long, thin snout sideways through the water. Fish and frogs are impaled on the small, pointed teeth, and then flipped round by the gharial so that they can be swallowed head first.

Lizards

Lizards are a group of about 4500 scaly-skinned reptiles, varying from a few centimetres long to the 3-m long Komodo dragon. Most lizards live either on the ground, in rocky areas, or in trees. A number of lizards inhabit desert regions, and there are even some burrowing species that have lost their legs.

○ Lizards cannot control their own body heat, and so rely on sunshine for warmth. This is why they live in warm climates and bask in the sun for hours each day.

○ Lizards are able to tolerate unusually high levels of sodium and potassium in their bodies that would be lethal to birds and mammals.

○ Lizards move by walking, climbing or burrowing. Some can even glide.

○ Some burrowing lizards dig with their front limbs, but others have lost their legs and 'swim' through loose soil and sand. Climbing lizards often have long, sharp claws to give them a good grip.

Amazing

Some male agamid lizards appear to impress females by doing 'push-ups' and bobbing their heads up and down.

▶ *A Caribbean iguana surveys its surroundings. There are 700 plus species of iguana, nearly all of which live in the Americas.*

Venomous lizards

There are only two venomous lizards, the Mexican beaded lizard and the Gila monster (shown here) of the southwestern United States. The Gila monster's favourite food is birds' eggs. It bites humans only in self-defence. Its brittle teeth may break off and remain in the wound.

○ Most lizards lay eggs, although a few species give birth to live young. Unlike birds or mammals, a mother lizard does not nurture (look after) her young.

○ Lizards generally have sharp teeth along the edge of their jaws.

○ Like snakes, lizards shed their skin, but it tends to come off in large flakes rather than in one piece.

▶ *Geckos are small lizards that are mainly active at night. Their toes are covered in hairy pads, which help them to grip rough surfaces. Some geckos can even walk upside down.*

▲ *The desert-living thorny devil of Australia is covered in sharp spines to protect it from predators. The spines also condense dew and channel the water into the lizard's mouth, helping the lizard to survive in this inhospitable environment.*

❍ Most lizards are meat eaters, feeding on insects and other small creatures.

❍ Some types of lizard – geckos in particular – have adapted to living alongside humans. In some parts of the world, geckos are a common sight in buildings, where they feed on insects.

❍ Only one species, the marine iguana of the Galapagos islands, forages for food in the sea.

❍ A number of lizards – including the venomous Gila monster, which occurs in deserts of North America – can store fat in their tail. They live off this fat when their food is hard to find.

▶ *Slow worms are not worms at all. They are legless lizards that live in Europe, Africa and Asia. Slow worms are viviparous, which means that they give birth to live young.*

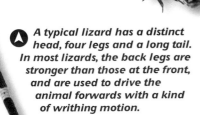

▲ *A typical lizard has a distinct head, four legs and a long tail. In most lizards, the back legs are stronger than those at the front, and are used to drive the animal forwards with a kind of writhing motion.*

Courtship and rivalry

In many reptile species, the males compete for the right to mate with females. The male anole lizard of Central and South America puffs out a bright red throat pouch to warn rivals to stay away. Two rival males may face each other with inflated throat pouches for hours at a time until one backs off.

Find out more

Frilled lizard p. 267

Large Lizards

Iguanas are large lizards that live around the Pacific and in the Americas. They have a crest of spines running from the head to the tail. The larger iguanas are the only vegetarian lizards, feeding on fruit, flowers and leaves. Monitor lizards are long-necked reptiles found in Australia, Asia and Africa.

Amazing

The longest lizard in the world is the Salvadori monitor of Papua New Guinea, which reaches lengths up to 4.75 m (although 70 per cent of this is taken up by the tail).

○ The green iguana lives high up in trees, usually beside water, but lays its eggs in a hole in the ground. It is an accomplished swimmer.

○ Like a chameleon, an iguana's eyes can swivel independently of each other, enabling the lizard to keep a look out for predators and prey in all directions.

○ The rhinoceros iguana of the West Indies gets its name from the pointed scales on its snout.

○ Water dragons are mostly large tropical lizards that swim well by lashing their tails from side to side.

○ Monitors have powerful limbs and a deeply forked tongue that is continually flicked out to 'taste' the air.

○ At least 20 of the 30 or so monitor species live in Australia. One of the largest is Gould's monitor, which uses its tail as a support when it stands on its back legs to survey the horizon. When threatened, Gould's monitor uses its tail like a club or a whip.

Early explorers told amazing tales of dragons living in faraway lands. It may be that these explorers had seen flying lizards or huge monitors such as the Komodo. Perhaps this how dragon myths started.

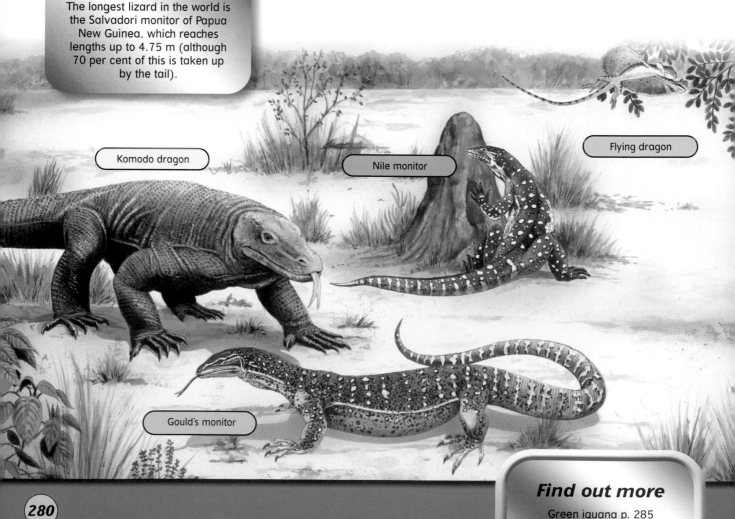

Komodo dragon

Nile monitor

Flying dragon

Gould's monitor

Find out more

Green iguana p. 285

▲ *Green iguanas will jump 6 m or more out of the trees to the ground or into water if they are disturbed.*

Wrestling monitors

At the beginning of the mating season, male monitors compete to win the right to mate with the females. Rival males rear up on their hind legs and wrestle until the weaker animal gives up.

❍ The rare Komodo dragon is a monitor lizard that lives on a group of islands in Indonesia and Southeast Asia. It is the largest lizard in the world, measuring up to 3 m long and weighing as much as 166 kg.

❍ The Komodo dragon eats mostly carrion (dead animals), but takes live prey whenever the opportunity arises.

❍ Komodos use their saw-like teeth to tear meat from prey such as water buffaloes, deer and wild pigs. Human victims have also been reported.

▼ *This rock iguana is found on Acklin's Island and surrounding cays (low islands of sand and coral) in the Bahamas.*

▲ *The Fijian banded iguana lives on the islands of Fiji and Tonga in the Pacific Ocean.*

❍ The female Nile monitor of southern Africa breaks open termite mounds and lays her eggs inside. The termites repair the hole, sealing in the eggs. When the young hatch, they must wait for the rains to soften the mud so that they can dig their way out.

❍ Nile monitors often raid the nests of crocodiles and turtles to steal their eggs.

▼ *The crested water dragon from Asia can stand up on its hind legs and sprint away to escape predators.*

Toxic saliva

The Komodo dragon is not built for long chases, so it prefers to ambush its prey, making a lunging bite with its wide jaws. If the victim escapes, the Komodo's saliva is so rich in toxic bacteria that the wound soon becomes infected, stopping the animal in its tracks. The Komodo follows the scent trail to the body of its prey.

Chameleons

Chameleons are a group of 85 lizard species, most of which live on the island of Madagascar and on the African mainland. Chameleons have adapted well to their life in the trees. They have long toes that can grip branches firmly, and a long tail that holds onto other branches like another hand. Tails like this are described as 'prehensile'.

○ Chameleons are famous for being able to change their skin colour to blend in with their surroundings. This is known as camouflage.

Changing colour

The chameleon can change its colour and pattern in minutes to blend in with its background. It uses tiny coloured particles, called pigments, in its skin that can clump together so they are not seen or spread out to show their hue. For example, when the chameleon moves from a leafy branch to dry twigs, it changes from green to brown.

▶ *The flap-necked chameleon is perhaps the most widespread chameleon species in southern Africa. The female descends from the trees to lay her eggs in a burrow that she excavates in the soil.*

○ Most lizards can change colour to a limited extent, but chameleons are expert colour-changers, transforming quickly to all sorts of colours.

▲ *Chameleons are unlike any other lizards. Their bodies are perfectly adapted to life in the trees. In fact, a motionless chameleon sitting on a branch, with its skin colour altered to match the background, is almost impossible to spot.*

Eyes housed in 'turrets' of skin

Flattened, leaf-shaped body

Long tail aids balance and can coil around branches

Clawed feet have two sets of fused toes for good grip

Find out more
Chameleon feeding p. 264

Male Jackson's chameleons have three 'horns' on the their head. They will aggressively defend their territory.

Amazing

Chameleons are so deaf that shouting next to a sleeping chameleon will not wake it up.

○ Chameleons also change colour when they are angry or frightened, and also when they are sick.

○ Male chameleons flush with bright colours to warn off rivals or predators, and to impress females.

○ Colour changing also help chameleons to control their body temperature. Their skin colour lightens to absorb more heat in the morning and evening. It becomes darker when the sun is at its strongest, so that the body absorbs less heat.

○ The smallest chameleon, the dwarf Brookesia, could balance on your little finger, while the biggest, Oustalet's chameleon, is the size of a small cat.

○ Chameleons have poor senses of smell and hearing, but their eyesight is probably the best in the lizard world.

○ Chameleons feed mainly on insects and spiders, hunting them in trees by day. They shoot out their tongue to trap prey on a sticky pad at the tip.

Fischer's chameleon lives in the mountain forests of Kenya and Tanzania. Its tail may be up to twice as long as the rest of its body.

○ The tongue is normally squashed up inside the chameleon's mouth.

Parson's chameleon is one of the largest chameleons, growing to well over 40 cm. It eats small vertebrates as well as insects. Being a large chameleon, it relies on camouflage to avoid detection, often remaining perfectly still for long periods.

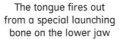

The tongue fires out from a special launching bone on the lower jaw

Once a chameleon has targeted its prey, spiral muscles inside its tongue contract widthways, propelling the tongue from the mouth like a sticky arrow. Different muscles reel the tongue back in, and the prey with it.

Chameleon eyes

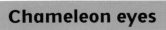

Chameleons rely almost entirely on sight to recognize predators, prey, mates and rivals. Each eye has a 180° field of view and can swivel independently of the other, giving the lizard the ability to see both to the sides and behind, as well as in front. Chameleons are also thought to have good colour vision.

Lizards of the World

Lizards occur in a wide variety of sizes, shapes and colours. They range from huge, dragon-like creatures to tiny, delicate reptiles that can sit on your finger. Some lizards have close associations with humans, and are welcome visitors to homes. The tokay gecko, for example, is thought to bring good luck to houses it enters.

The blue iguana of the Caribbean island of Grand Cayman grows to more than 1.5 m long, and can weigh in excess of 11 kg. Its numbers are now so low that the blue iguana is on the brink of extinction.

Marine iguanas congregate on rocky shores and cliffs. Females and young often lounge on top of each other, but males space themselves out more widely to define their territories.

Broad-headed skinks live in moist woodland. They often hunt insects high up in the trees, sometimes raiding the nests of paper wasps to eat the larvae.

The tokay gecko, the largest Asian gecko, hides during the day and emerges at night to hunt prey such as insects, mice and small birds.

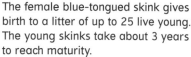

The female blue-tongued skink gives birth to a litter of up to 25 live young. The young skinks take about 3 years to reach maturity.

Galapagos land iguanas are large lizards that feed mainly on the fruit and leaves of prickly pear cacti.

Australia's shingleback lays down fat in its stumpy tail when when food is plentiful. The fat is broken down to provide energy when food is scarce.

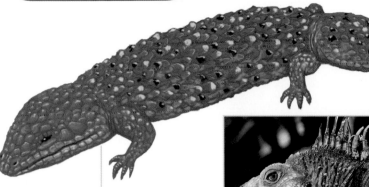

The green, or common, iguana of Central and northern South America has a crest of comb-like spines running down its body and tail. Green iguanas defend themselves with their sharp claws if attacked.

The frilled leaf-tailed gecko of Madagascar has a triangular head, long slender limbs, a broad, flat tail, and flaps of skin around the edges of its head and body.

The six-lined racerunner is the fastest reptile on land, having been recorded at reaching an amazing speed of 29 km/h.

The anole lizards of Central and South America and the Caribbean have a narrow head, a streamlined body and a long tail. They also have long legs and toes.

Chuckwallas are stout-bodied members of the iguana family, although they lack the crests seen on rainforest iguanas. They inhabit rocky desert regions of the southwestern USA and northwestern Mexico.

The orient knight anole lives in the forests of eastern Cuba, in the Caribbean, where it feeds on spiders, grubs, medium-sized and large adult insects, and also tree frogs.

The natural habitat of the Madagascan day gecko is forests and palm groves, but it often visits houses. Unlike most geckos, which are nocturnal, it is active by day. Its lifespan is about 10 years.

Snakes

Snakes are about 3000 species of legless reptile with long, slender, muscular bodies. Despite having no legs or claws, snakes are superb hunters that can move swiftly and tackle every type of terrain. They are also expert climbers, and many species can swim well. Snakes occur on all continents, except Antarctica. They are also found in the Indian and Pacific oceans.

❍ Snakes are thought to have evolved from burrowing lizards that gradually lost their legs as they adapted to an underground lifestyle.

Snake jaws

A snake has to swallow its prey whole, because it has no large back teeth for crushing its victims and cannot chew. The snake's jaw bones can separate to allow it to eat huge eggs or animals that are much larger than its head. A large snake can swallow an entire pig or deer.

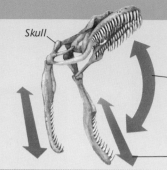

Skull

Lower jaws can detach from the skull to accommodate larger prey

Lower jaws work independently, with first one side pulling and then the other, to draw prey into the throat

❍ Most snakes reproduce by laying eggs, but some give birth to live young.

❍ A snake moves by gripping the ground or a branch with its scaly skin and pushing itself forward with muscles attached to its ribs.

❍ Snakes often weave their body along in a series of S-shaped curves, particularly over uneven surfaces. Burrowing snakes and some tree snakes use a concertina-like motion, bunching up their body and then straightening it out. Large, heavy snakes tend to move in a straight line.

❍ Sidewinding – a type of movement used by desert snakes – involves throwing the head and body forwards and sideways, and then following through with the rest of the body.

❍ Many swimming snakes have bands of colour along their bodies. This helps to break up their outline and blend them in with the ripples of the water.

Amazing

The Mozambique spitting cobra can accurately spit its venom into the eyes of an approaching person up to 3 m away.

The yellow ratsnake is a voracious predator of rodents, which it hunts at night. It will also eat lizards, frogs, birds and their eggs, and even young chickens, which makes it unpopular with farmers.

The female Massasauga rattlesnake of Canada and the United States gives birth to about 15 live young, which she leaves to fend for themselves. The baby snakes remain at the birth site for a few days until they have shed their skin for the first time.

The sidewinder is a viper that lives in the deserts of the United States. It lifts loops of its body clear of the ground as it moves sideways, leaving a series of marks in the sand shaped like sideways letter Js.

Sloughing

Before sloughing, a snake first rubs its snout on the ground to loosen its skin. The snake then wriggles out of the old, worn skin, revealing a new layer of scales beneath. The discarded skin often comes away in one piece.

○ A snake's skin does not grow with its body, so the snake must regularly shed its skin as it increases in size. This is called sloughing.

○ Snakes are generally solitary, usually coming together only to mate. However, some snake species congregate in large numbers to hibernate in communal dens. A den of common garter snakes, for example, may contain hundreds or even thousands of individuals.

○ The worm-like blind snakes and thread snakes spend almost their entire lives below ground. Their long cylindrical bodies, tough skulls and smooth, shiny scales are adaptations for a burrowing lifestyle. Their eyes are virtually useless.

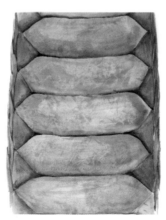

The belly scales of most snakes are particularly smooth, to enable the snake to move more easily over the ground. The scales also overlap, giving the snake more grip.

The emerald tree boa of northern South America is an agile climber. When hunting, it anchors itself to a branch with its tail and hangs down in a loose coil, ready to strike at prey.

Snake records

Largest recorded meal	One African rock python 4.9 m long consumed a 59-kg impala
Oldest recorded age	40 years 3 months 14 days – a male boa constrictor
Highest altitude	Himalayan pit viper, found up to 4900 m
Lowest altitude	Sea snakes often dive down at least 100 m
Longest dive	Dive by a yellow-bellied sea snake lasting 3 hours 33 minutes

Constricting Snakes

Constrictors include boas, pythons, anacondas, ratsnakes and kingsnakes. A constrictor kills its victims by squeezing them to death. It winds itself around the prey and gradually tightens its coils. Each time the animal breathes out, the snake applies a little more pressure, and the prey eventually suffocates.

Breathing while feeding

To avoid suffocating on a large meal, a snake, such as this boa constrictor, thrusts its windpipe forward as it swallows. The windpipe acts as a kind of snorkel, allowing the snake to breathe even though its throat is filled by the prey.

❍ Like all snakes, constrictors have to swallow their victims whole. A meal can often be seen as a lump moving down the body. Large prey make take several days to digest.

❍ Pythons are large tropical constricting snakes that live in moist forests in Asia, Indonesia and Africa.

❍ Pythons usually eat animals about the size of domestic cats, but occasionally they go for really big meals, such as wild pigs and deer.

❍ Boas and anacondas are the large constrictors of South America.

❍ Boas capture their prey by lying in wait, hiding motionless under trees and waiting for victims to pass by. In common with other snakes, boas can go for weeks without eating.

❍ Like many snakes, most constrictors begin life as eggs. Unusually for snakes, female pythons look after their eggs until they hatch by coiling around them.

Amazing

After eating a huge meal, such as a leopard, a python may not need to eat again for up to 12 months. One rock python was recorded as going for 2 years and 9 months between meals.

◀ *The stunning green tree python is found high up in the rainforest canopy in New Guinea and northern Queensland, Australia. It hunts at night for tree-dwelling mammals and roosting birds.*

Find out more

Malagasy tree boa p. 292

This ratsnake has caught its prey, a small meadow vole. It then loops its body around the vole, and stops it breathing by holding it very tight.

The tree boa from Trinidad hunts in the treetops for prey such as small mammals. When striking out to grab prey, it secures itself by gripping a branch with its prehensile tail.

○ Female boas do not lay eggs, but give birth to live young instead.

○ Boas have tiny remnants of back legs, called spurs, which the males use to stimulate females during mating.

○ Anacondas spend much of their lives in swampy ground or shallow water, lying in wait for victims to come and drink. One anaconda was seen to swallow a 2-m long caiman.

○ When frightened, the royal python of Africa coils itself into a tight ball, which is why it is sometimes called the ball python. Rubber boas do the same, but they hide their heads and stick their tails out aggressively to fool attackers.

The anaconda is the heaviest snake, weighing up to 220 kg. There have been many exaggerated claims about its size. In 1907, an anaconda measuring nearly 19 m was said to have been shot, but there was no proof to back up this incredible claim.

Reticulated python

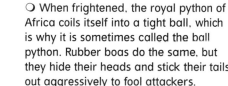
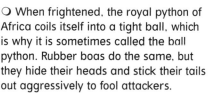

The reticulated python of Asia is the world's longest snake. In captivity, it can grow to 9 m long. In 1912, a specimen measuring 10 m was killed, but such giants have not been found in recent years.

Venomous Snakes

Venomous snakes use modified teeth called fangs to inject venom into their prey. Venom is a cocktail of harmful chemicals that either subdues or kills the victim. It reduces the risk of the snakes being injured in a long struggle, and also allows them to tackle prey much larger than themselves.

○ There are two main venom types. Neurotoxic venom attacks the victim's nervous system, stopping its heart or lungs from working or paralyzing its body. Haemotoxic venom affects the victim's blood and muscles.

○ Some venomous snakes have fangs at the front of the mouth, while in others the fangs are located at the rear.

○ Front-fanged snakes have long, hollow fangs. The fangs of taipans, sea snakes, cobras and mambas are fixed in place. Viper and pit viper fangs are hinged, so that they can be folded back out of the way when not in use.

○ Rear-fanged snakes, such as boomslangs, have shorter, fixed fangs. When the snake bites, venom flows down grooves along the edge of the fangs and into the wound.

Rattlesnake rattle

The 'rattle' at the tip of a rattlesnake's tail is a chain of modified scales. When threatened, the snake shakes the rattle by vibrating its tail, producing a warning sound that deters predators.

○ Of nearly 700 species of venomous snake, only about 50 have a bite that is potentially lethal to humans.

▶ *The mangrove snake of Southeast Asia is a rear-fanged species. It will bite readily to protect itself, although its venom is relatively mild. It lives in trees and shrubs near water, and feeds on reptiles, birds and small mammals.*

○ The king cobra of Southeast Asia is the world's longest venomous snake, being able to reach nearly 6 m in length.

○ In India, cobras kill more than 7000 people every year. The bite of a king cobra can kill an elephant in 4 hours.

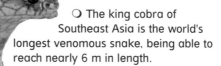

▲ *When on the defensive, a cobra rears up and spreads the skin of its neck in a hood to make itself look bigger. This often gives enemies a chance to strike it .*

○ Without treatment, victims of the taipan, black mamba, tiger snake, common krait, and king cobra have a 50 to 100 per cent risk of dying.

○ The sea snake *Hydrophis belcheri* has the most powerful venom of any snake – a mere 0.005 mg would be enough to kill an average-size man. Fortunately, the snake rarely bites people.

○ Sea snakes can stay submerged for five hours.

Amazing

Fer-de-lance (lancehead) snakes have 60 to 80 babies, each of which can give a dangerous bite.

Find out more

Rattlesnake p. 261

● Pope's pit viper is a tree-dwelling snake found on forested hills in Southeast Asia, where it preys on frogs, lizards, small mammals and possibly birds. It gives birth to live young.

○ Snake charmers use the spectacled cobra. It is not 'charmed' by the music (it has poor hearing) but by the movement of the charmer's pipe. The snake follows the pipe as if about to strike – its fangs have been removed to make it safe.

Folding fangs

Venom is made in glands on the side of the snake's head. As a viper or pit viper opens its jaws to strike at its prey, its hollow fangs flip down and lock into position ready for the bite. Muscles squeeze the venom glands as the fangs puncture the victim's flesh, pumping venom through the hollow fangs and into the wound.

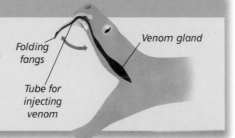

Folding fangs

Venom gland

Tube for injecting venom

● The king cobra is a good swimmer and spends much of its time around water.

○ A viper's venom kills its victims by making their blood clot. Venom from Russell's viper is used to treat haemophiliacs (people whose blood does not clot well).

○ The black mamba of Africa can race along at 25 km/h with its head raised and its tongue flickering.

● The Gaboon viper of western and southwest Africa has the largest fangs of any viper, measuring up to 5 cm in length. Here, the fangs are mostly covered by their fleshy sheaths.

Snakes of the World

Snakes occur on every continent except Antarctica, but they are more numerous in the tropics than elsewhere. Although they all share a similar body plan, the wide diversity of colour, markings, size and behaviour reflects the fact that snakes have adapted to different environments. New snake species are being discovered all the time.

Pine snakes are large, powerful constrictors that often burrow into the ground in search of prey. Their preferred habitat is pine woods.

Everglades ratsnakes are often found near water. They are very good swimmers, and will take to water readily to escape danger.

Wagler's pit viper is a medium-sized snake that changes its colour as it grows. The young (shown here) are mainly green; the adults have pale bars of spots on a black background. The females of this tree-dwelling species give birth to live young.

The green tree vipers of Asia are tree-dwelling venomous snakes with prehensile (gripping) tails.

The carpet python of Australia and New Guinea is often found around human settlements, where it preys on rats and other vermin.

The Malagasy tree boa lives on the island of Madagascar, off the eastern coast of Africa. It is closely related to the boa constrictor of Central and South America.

Eyelash vipers occur from southern Mexico to northern Peru. There are several colour forms, sometimes with a pattern that resembles lichen or moss on a tree trunk, as seen here.

The slender Natal green snake of Africa is active in the daytime, when it hunts prey such as frogs.

Copperheads are pit vipers that are related to rattlesnakes. They avoid confrontation and rarely bite humans.

The glossy-scaled mangrove snake is one of the largest tree-dwelling snakes in Asia. With its large mouth, the snake can swallow large birds' eggs and even squirrels.

Several pit vipers, including the cantil, or Mexican water moccasin, have a coloured tip to the tail. The snake wiggles the tip to lure potential prey, such as frogs and small lizards, within lunging range.

An inhabitant of Southeast Asia, the venomous monocled cobra gets its name from the eyespot on the back of its hood, which resembles a monocle.

The smooth green snake is a North American species that lives among thickets and shrubs close to water. Smooth green snakes feed mainly on insects – this one has caught a cricket.

Introduction to Amphibians

The word amphibian comes from the Greek amphibios, which means 'double life'. It refers to the fact that these animals can live both on land and in water. Amphibians are an important group of animals, being the first vertebrates to conquer land. Frogs, toads, newts, salamanders and caecilians are all amphibians.

❍ Amphibians are common in temperate (cooler) regions of the world, and in moist habitats, although many species can also be found in humid, tropical forests.

❍ When the weather turns especially cold, amphibians often hibernate. They burrow into mud at the bottom of ponds or under stones and logs.

Caecilians

Caecilians are mostly found in the tropics. They have a worm-like, limbless body, with a pointed head and a short tail. Some are burrowers, living in loose soil, while others are aquatic. Their primary sense is smell, and most cannot see because a thin layer of skin or bone covers the eyes.

❍ As spring arrives amphibians come out of hiding. The warmer weather sees many of them returning to the pond or stream in which they were born.

❍ Amphibians sometimes have long journeys back to their birthplace, and often they have to travel through towns and over busy roads.

Amazing

In many salamander species, if the animal loses an eye, a limb or its tail, the body part will regrow within a few months.

▶ *The African bullfrog has a massive body and a wide head with powerful jaws. It spends about ten months of the year underground to avoid the dry conditions, encased in a kind of water-filled cocoon. This species is very aggressive, and will defend its territory against intruders.*

Find out more
Temperature control pp. 254–255

Frog hazard

In some countries, signs warn drivers of the unusual hazard of large numbers of frogs or toads crossing the road to return to their breeding grounds.

○ White's tree frog is brown in the shade, but turns light green in sunshine.

○ Most amphibians are nocturnal, and active only when conditions are moist enough to prevent their bodies from losing too much water by evaporation.

○ Some amphibians, however, are active by day. Much of their behaviour revolves around controlling their temperature, such as basking in the sun to warm up and entering water to cool down.

○ Many amphibians live in places where food is only seasonally available, so they are active for just a few months or weeks of the year. They eat rapidly, storing fat to sustain them when food becomes scarce.

▶ *The strawberry poison-dart frog from Central America relies on poison to keep enemies at bay. Its bright red warning colouring says 'stay away' to predators.*

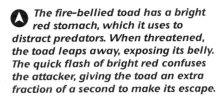

▲ *The fire-bellied toad has a bright red stomach, which it uses to distract predators. When threatened, the toad leaps away, exposing its belly. The quick flash of bright red confuses the attacker, giving the toad an extra fraction of a second to make its escape.*

○ Journeys to breeding grounds may be up to 5 km long, which is a long way to travel for an animal that measures just a few centimetres in length.

○ Amphibians have bare skin, with no hairs or scales. They possess poison glands in their skin. These produce secretions that are distasteful or even toxic to predators.

○ Some amphibians can alter the colour of their skin in response to changes in temperature or light levels.

▲ *The Goliath frog of western Africa is the largest frog in the world, measuring up to 40 cm long. It lives along jungle streams, and is an excellent swimmer and diver, with powerful hind legs and long, webbed toes. It rarely emerges from the water, and quickly jumps back in if disturbed. It eats small reptiles, other frogs and mammals.*

Amphibian records

Fattest toad	Cane toad	2.65 kg
Longest amphibian	Chinese giant salamander	1.8 m
Heaviest frog	African Goliath frog	3.66 kg
Biggest tadpole	Mexican axolotl	25 cm
Smallest frog	*Psyllophryne didactyla*	9.8 mm

Amphibian Anatomy

Although amphibian bodies are similar in many ways to those of other vertebrates (animals with backbones), there are some notable differences, especially in the way that they breathe. Amphibian skeletons have far fewer bones than those of other vertebrates, and their heart has three chambers, not four as in mammals.

Amazing

The African clawed toad has sense organs along its sides that detect vibrations in the water made by predators and prey.

❍ The flattened tails of newts make them expert swimmers.

❍ The burrowing, worm-like caecilians have a thick, bony skull to help them push their way through the soil.

❍ Caecilians have no limbs, but move by waves of muscular contraction that travel along their body.

❍ Oxygen can pass easily through the skin, which is important because most adult amphibians breathe through their skin as well as through their lungs.

❍ An amphibian's skin is kept moist by special glands just under the surface. These glands produce a sticky substance called mucus.

❍ Some salamanders have no lungs. They can absorb oxygen only through their skin and the lining of their mouth. If the skin dries out, oxygen is no longer able to pass through it, and the salamander dies.

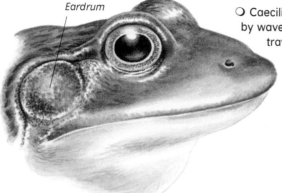

Eardrum

▲ *Frogs and toads, such as this American bullfrog, have large and well-developed eardrums and very good hearing.*

❍ Like humans, amphibians have five basic senses: sight, hearing, smell, touch and taste. However, they can also detect infrared and ultra-violet light, as well as the Earth's magnetic field.

❍ Frogs and toads have short backbones and greatly enlarged hind legs. The skull is flattened.

❍ Salamanders and newts have longer backbones than frogs or toads. They also have long tails, and their limbs are of roughly equal size.

❍ Caecilians have a tentacle on each side of the head between the eye and the nostril. They use these scent-detecting tentacles to locate prey.

❍ The average amphibian has skin that is moist, fairly smooth and soft.

◀ *Some frogs are adapted to living in trees. Their limbs are long and slim for gripping the branches, and their feet are specially adapted to enable them to climb vertically.*

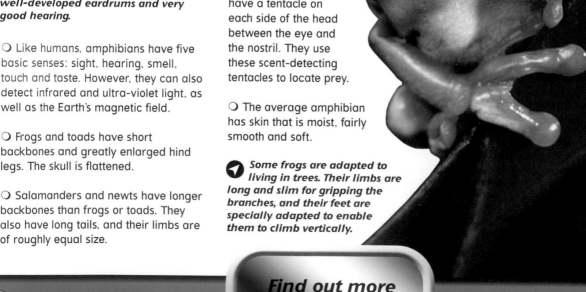

Find out more

Anatomy of reptiles pp. 258–259

Shedding skin

Like snakes and lizards, some frogs and toads shed their skin. The European toad sheds its skin several times during summer – and then eats it. This recycles the goodness of the toad's skin.

○ Amphibian larvae breathe through feathery external gills. Some species retain these gills into adulthood, but in most the gills are lost during metamorphosis.

○ Blood flows inside an amphibian's gills at the same time as water flows over the outside. As the water flows past the gills, oxygen passes out of the water, straight into the amphibian's blood.

○ Amphibian (and reptile hearts) have three chambers, whereas those of birds and mammals have four chambers.

This view of a frog's skeleton shows its highly developed rear legs and short backbone. The powerful rear legs enable frogs to make great leaps and to swim quickly in search of prey.

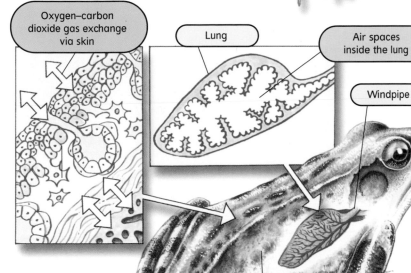

Oxygen–carbon dioxide gas exchange via skin

Lung

Air spaces inside the lung

Windpipe

Moist skin surface

Air tubes in an amphibian's lungs branch ever smaller, ending in millions of microscopic 'bubbles' called alveoli that form a huge surface area. Oxygen from inhaled air seeps into the blood passing through the alveoli. Waste carbon dioxide passes out of the blood and is exhaled from the lungs. This oxygen–carbon dioxide gas exchange also occurs between the air and blood vessels in the skin.

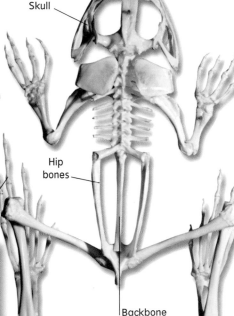

Skull

Hip bones

Long foot bones

Backbone

Freshwater creatures

Because their skin makes them vulnerable to moisture-loss, many amphibians ensure that they never stray far from water – freshwater, that is. There are no marine amphibians, because the high concentration of salt in the oceans would draw water from their bodies, causing them to dehydrate and die.

Life-cycle of Amphibians

Most amphibians are born and grow up in freshwater habitats such as ponds, pools, streams and rivers. They usually move onto dry land when they are adults and return to water to breed. As they grow, amphibians completely change their appearance. This change is known as metamorphosis.

○ Like fish and insects, amphibians lay many eggs – the more they lay, the greater the chance that some of their offspring will survive.

○ Frogs and toads generally lay between 1000 and 20,000 eggs. In salamanders and newts, the number of eggs laid varies from four or five to about 5000.

○ In frogs, toads and some newt and salamander species, the eggs are fertilized externally. The amphibians release their sperm and eggs into the water and leave fertilization to chance.

Ⓐ *When frogs mate, the chance of fertilization is increased by the male releasing his sperm straight onto the jelly-covered eggs that the female lays in the water.*

1. Frog spawn (eggs) float on top of fresh water

Adult toad

4. Froglets lose their tails and grow into adults

2. Tadpoles hatch from the eggs

Adult newt

3. Tadpoles grow legs and change into froglets

Ⓑ *Frogs pass through several stages as they develop. Fish-like tadpoles with gills hatch from eggs in the water and feed on tiny plants. As they develop into frogs, they begin to hunt for invertebrates such as insects and spiders.*

Find out more

Reptile reproduction pp. 262–263

Courtship ritual

The male great crested newt goes to great lengths to impress his mate. He swims in front of her, displaying the toothed crest on his spine. Then lashes his tail to waft secretions from his abdominal glands toward her. If she is receptive, she will take up the spermatophore (sperm packet) he has deposited.

Axolotl

In some species of salamander and newt, such as the axolotl of Mexico, the larvae never change into the adult form. The axolotl remains in the water and retains its gills throughout its life, becoming sexually mature in the larval state. This is known as neoteny, and it is also seen in the olm and the mudpuppy.

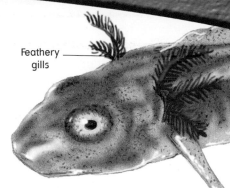

Feathery gills

◐ *Amphibian larvae are able to survive in water because they can breathe through large, feathery flaps called gills that extract oxygen from the water.*

○ The soft, jelly-like eggs, known as spawn, hatch into young, which must fend for themselves with no protection from their parents.

○ The young of amphibians, called larvae, have external feathery gills to breathe in water.

○ The fish-like larvae of frogs and toads are known as tadpoles. After about 7 to 10 weeks, the tadpoles grow legs and lungs and develop into frogs ready to leave the water.

○ In most salamanders and newts, the male leaves a 'packet' of sperm (called a spermatophore) on the ground or in a pond. The female then takes this into her body. Fertilization of the eggs is internal.

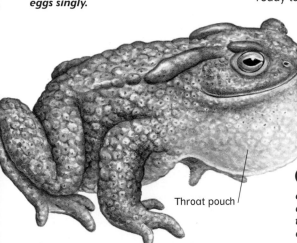

◐ *Most amphibians lay soft eggs. These may be in a jelly-like string, or a clump of tiny eggs called spawn, as with frogs and toads. Newts lay their eggs singly.*

Throat pouch

◐ *Frogs and toads, such as this common toad, can puff out their throat pouches. This amplifies the croaking love-calls they make to attract mates during the breeding season.*

Amazing

The male Darwin's frog swallows the eggs and keeps them in his throat until they hatch – and pop out of his mouth.

○ Some salamanders lay their eggs in damp places, such as under stones or logs, or in moss. Others attach them to rocks underwater.

○ In midwife toads, the male looks after the eggs, not the female. He winds strings of eggs around his back legs and carries them about until they hatch.

○ The female marsupial frog carries her fertilized eggs in a pouch on her back to keep them safe.

○ The male South American Surinam toad presses the eggs onto his mate's back, where they stay until the tadpoles hatch.

○ Many salamanders lack a free-living larval stage. A female fire salamander retains the fertilized eggs inside her body, where the young hatch out and develop. She then gives birth to live young that resemble miniature adults.

Amphibians – Feeding and Diet

Amphibians are carnivores that feed on living prey, rather than carrion (dead animals). Most amphibians have wide mouths for taking large prey. They tend to be generalist feeders, although invertebrates such as insects, spiders, snails and slugs form the bulk of the diet of adult amphibians. Unable to chew or break up food in their mouth, they have to swallow prey whole.

Cane toad

The cane toad is the greatest amphibian pest. It was introduced to Australia from tropical South America in the 1930s to eat beetles. Unfortunately, it also gobbles up native frogs and lizards, and even birds. Being poisonous to eat, it has also killed small crocodiles, snakes and monitor lizards.

○ The red-backed salamander of North America feeds on hundreds of different invertebrate species. Its choice of prey is limited only by the size of its mouth.

○ Some amphibians have highly specialized diets. The Mexican burrowing toad has a very small mouth, and feeds only on termites.

○ Newts are largely inactive creatures, and so do not feed frequently. If food is readily available, they tend to store fat, so that in colder months or in dry periods they can survive for longer without feeding.

○ Like their parents, the larvae of newts and salamanders are carnivorous, eating a wide range of aquatic invertebrates.

○ In some newts and salamanders, the fastest-growing larvae become cannibals and eat smaller larvae of their own species.

○ Frog and toad tadpoles tend to eat plant matter, although in a few species very large individuals may become cannibalistic.

Amazing

A wild African bullfrog that managed to get into a snake enclosure at South Africa's Pretoria Zoo devoured 16 venomous cobras.

○ Many frogs and toads can eat surprisingly large animals, including mice, birds, reptiles and snakes. They do not need to feed very often, since one meal can satisfy their energy needs for a long time.

▲ **Male Pacific tree frogs of North America are highly territorial. Their two-toned mating call can be heard several kilometres away.**

○ Amphibians usually find food by a combination of sight and smell. They tend to have large eyes because they are active at night.

○ Some species of salamander and newt are very sensitive to water currents made by prey animals.

Swallowing

As frogs and toads swallow their food, they tend to shut their eyes. This adds to the downward pressure and so assists in the swallowing motion.

Colorado River toad swallowing mouse

▲ **The eastern newt of North America consumes a variety of foods, including insects, small molluscs and crustaceans, as well as young amphibians and frogs' eggs.**

Find out more
Salamanders and newts pp. 306–307

A *Camouflaged by its colouring, the ornate horned frog of Argentina sits half-buried in leaf litter and moss on the forest floor, waiting for prey to pass by. It snaps up large insects, other frogs and small mammals with its huge mouth.*

○ Few frogs and toads actively hunt their prey. Most simply wait until food comes within range, and then either make an open-mouthed lunge or flick out their long sticky tongue to snare the prey.

○ Salamanders creep up slowly before striking. They move gradually towards prey and then suddenly seize it with their tongue or between their sharp teeth.

○ The worm-like caecilians feed mainly on earthworms, which they locate with the sensory tentacles under their eyes and grab with their curved teeth.

A *A fierce predator, the North American bullfrog – the continent's largest frog – feeds on reptiles, other frogs and small mammals.*

A *The cedros treefrog has adhesive discs on its toes. It waits for insects, which are plentiful in forests and woodland, and forms the bulk of its diet.*

Frogs and Toads

There are about 4400 species of frog and toad. The difference between frogs and toads is not clear cut. However, most frogs live in damp places and tend to have strongly webbed feet, long back legs and smooth skin. Toads generally spend their time on dry land. They don't have webbed feet and their skin is warty and quite dry.

○ Toads are normally shorter and squatter than frogs, with shorter legs.

○ Toads usually walk or waddle, whereas frogs tend to hop or leap. Most frogs can leap at least 20 times their own length.

Toad warts

Toads have drier, rougher, more lumpy skin than frogs. The bumps, or 'warts', on a toad's skin (shown here) release a fluid that can be poisonous, providing effective protection against predators such as otters and herons.

○ Toads tend to have thicker skin than frogs, which retains moisture better and enables them to spend longer on land.

○ The skin of some toads is so thick that it is used as a substitute for leather.

○ Some glass frogs that live in the forests of Central and South America have such thin, transparent skin that their bones, muscles and internal organs are visible through it.

○ Frogs and toads are meat eaters. They catch fast-moving insects by darting out their long, sticky tongues.

▲ *The giant treefrog is the largest frog in Australia, and one of the biggest tree frogs in the world. It is a tropical species that is found in the north-east of the country.*

○ Female frogs and toads are usually larger than males of the same species. The males often have thicker, more muscular front legs, with which they hold the females during mating.

○ In the breeding season, frogs and toads call to attract females.

○ Each species has its own unique call, enabling the females to locate the right male if several species are using the same pool for breeding.

◄ *The poison-dart frogs that live in the tropical rainforests of Central and South America get their name because local people tip their arrows and darts with deadly poison from glands in the frog's skin. Many of these species are very colourful, such as the blue poison-dart frog shown here.*

Find out more

Airborne reptiles p. 256

Flying frogs

A number of tree-dwelling frogs of Asia and
Central America are able to spread their huge
webbed feet and glide from tree to tree.
This helps them to escape from predators.
Some of these 'flying frogs' can glide up to 15 m.

Amazing

In 1935, 100 cane toads – a
species native to Central and
South America – were imported
to Australia. Within 50 years,
their numbers had increased to
plague proportions.

Swimming

Toads and frogs swim by kicking back with their powerful hind legs. Their large, webbed feet act like flippers,
helping to push them through the water.

| 1. Frog draws its legs up | 2. Pushes its feet to the side | 3. Begins to push legs back | 4. The main kick propels the frog fowards | 5. Frog begins to bring feet forwards | 6. Frog's legs are pulled up, ready to go again |

*Frogs are superb jumpers,
lifting their front legs off
the ground and propelling
themselves into the air with their
strong back legs. Many frogs also have
suckers on their fingers to help them
land securely on slippery surfaces.*

❍ The fish-like larvae (young) of frogs
and toads are called tadpoles. They live
in water and have a tail for swimming
and gills through which they breathe.

❍ As they grow, tadpoles lose their gills
and tail, grow legs and develop into
adults that breathe through lungs and
move around on land.

❍ The paradoxical frog of the Amazon
and the island of Trinidad is unusual.
The tadpole grows to about 17 cm long,
but during metamorphosis, it changes
into a tiny adult less than 7 cm in
length. No one knows why adults are
so small in relation to the tadpoles.

Frog and toad records

Least eggs	The tiny Cuban frog lays just a single egg
Most eggs	The female cane toad lays 30,000–50,000 per spawning
Most poisonous	An average golden poison-dart frog contains enough poison to kill about 1000 people
Highest altitude	The common toad has been found up to 8000 m in the Himalayas
Longest leap	5.35 m, made by a South African sharp-nosed frog – an amazing feat for a frog less than 7 cm long

Frogs and Toads of the World

Although the bodies of most frogs and toads are very similar in appearance, these amphibians can have dramatically different lifestyles. Some, for example, rarely move far from permanent bodies of water, while others spend almost their entire lives up in the trees.

The red-legged frogs of North America will eat any prey they can subsume that is not distasteful.

Male tinker reed frogs have a loud 'tack' mating call. The females lay their eggs in a firm mass suspended above the water among grass stems.

The poison in the golden poison-dart frog has been used to treat human heart-attack victims.

The attractive pine barrens frog is no more than 5 cm long. It inhabits brushy areas and forages at night for insects.

The toxins contained in the skin of poison-dart frogs not only deter predators, but they also help to prevent fungi and bacteria from forming on the frogs' moist skin.

When disturbed, the Rio Grande leopard frog of the USA and Mexico jumps in a zig-zag pattern to escape.

The eardrums of the male green frog of North America are about twice the size of its eyes.

Australia's orange-eyed tree frog has an 'arc-arc-arc' call. A mat of eggs is laid among aquatic vegetation.

Find out more
Ornate horned frog p. 301

The plump White's tree frog often lives in or near buildings in Australia. It hunts invertebrates at night.

The dyeing poison-dart frog reaches 6 cm in length. It is found in Suriname, French-Guiana, Guyana and Brazil.

The pig frog lives in swamps in the southeastern USA. Males make a low-pitched, pig-like grunt when calling.

The ornate horned frog of Argentina has such a large mouth that it can eat prey up to half its own size.

The female strawberry poison-dart frog lays unfertilized eggs beside the fertilized ones as food for her young.

The natterjack toad is easily recognized by a distinctive yellow line down its head. It gives off a smell of burning rubber when alarmed.

The guttural toad of southern Africa produces a distinctive loud, rattling call during the breeding season.

Fowler's toad of the eastern USA burrows into the ground in hot, dry periods, and also to escape the cold.

The red-eyed tree frog of the Central American rainforests rarely descends from the trees. It is a superb jumper.

Salamanders and Newts

There are more than 450 species of salamander and newt. These amphibians have a slender body, a long tail and, usually, four legs. They live in damp habitats, mostly in the northern hemisphere. Some salamanders spend their whole lives on land, while others are entirely aquatic. Newts are semi-aquatic salamanders that return to the water in the breeding season.

○ Newts and salamanders eat insects, snails and worms.

○ Newts and salamanders swim rather like fish. The make an 'S'-shape with their body as they move.

○ Like the tadpoles of frogs and toads, the larvae of salamanders and newts have feathery external gills.

○ In some species, such as the eastern newt of North America, there is a juvenile land phase, called an eft, between the larval and adult stages.

○ Several species are able to detach their tail. When they are attacked, the twitching tail distracts the predator, giving the newt or salamander a greater chance of escape.

Salamander at risk

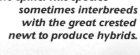

The axolotl is found only in Mexico's Lake Xochimilco. This salamander faces many threats to its survival. The introduction of carp and other predatory fish to its lake habitat reduced its numbers, as did the collection of wild axolotls for the pet trade and research. Pollution in the lake is now the greatest danger. The axolotl was once eaten as a local delicacy, but it is now protected by law.

○ Newts and salamanders tend to be well camouflaged, with skin patterns and colours that enable them to hide. However, some species are brightly coloured, often to indicate to predators that they are toxic (poisonous).

▶ *The marbled newt of France and Italy is more colourful than most of its European relatives. Only juveniles and females have the vivid orange stripe along the spine. This species sometimes interbreeds with the great crested newt to produce hybrids.*

Axolotl p. 299

North American salamanders

The Pacific giant salamander is unusual in that it can make a low-pitched call – most salamanders do not vocalize. It spends several years in the larval stage.

The California newt of the USA is about 15 cm long, just smaller than Europe's biggest newt, the warty newt.

The tiger salamander is the world's largest land-dwelling salamander, growing up to 40 cm long. It is found in a range of habitats from sea level to 3500 m.

The hellbender is entirely aquatic. Its baggy skin gives a large surface area for absorbing oxygen from the water.

Amazing

The fire salamander of Europe, Africa and Asia is so called because it often hibernates in logs, which may then be collected and used as firewood.

Shrinking gills

The mudpuppy salamander's gills change according to the oxygen content of its surroundings. The gills tend to be larger in warmer water, which contains lower levels of dissolved oxygen. The gills shrink in cold water – they do not need to be so large, because the water is richer in oxygen.

❍ Some species do not produce toxic substances, but are still brightly coloured. This is a highly effective defence, since predators assume that they are also toxic.

❍ The olm is a pale, thin, almost blind, cave-dwelling salamander from the lands bordering the Adriatic Sea.

◀ *The yellow-eyed salamander lives on the forest floor. It is nocturnal, and its large eyes help it to see in poor light. It lays its eggs underground, and the young that hatch resemble miniature adults.*

❍ If the Chinese spiny newt is seized by a predator, it pushes its sharp-tipped ribs through its skin. The ribs pass through its skin glands on the way and release an extremely unpleasant poison.

❍ In the eel-like aquatic salamanders called sirens, the front legs are small and the rear legs are absent.

❍ The four species of siren are found in the southern and central USA and in northeastern Mexico.

Glossary

Adapted Developed special features or behaviour in order to survive in a particular habitat.

Aestivation An inactive state, similar to hibernation, that helps some reptiles and amphibians to survive dry periods.

Amphibian A cold-blooded vertebrate with moist skin that either lives in water or has to return to water to breed.

Anatomy The body structure of an animal or plant.

Ancestor A plant or animal from which a later form of plant or animal evolved.

Aquatic Living most or all of the time in water.

Backbone A long 'bone' down the centre of a vertebrate's body, which is actually made up of many smaller bones called vertebrae (singular: vertebra). The backbone is also called the spine.

Ballast Something used to weigh down a floating object, and keep it stable in the water.

Bask To lie in the sunshine for warmth.

Brille A fixed transparent scale covering the eye of a snake or lizard.

Camouflage The way that an animal's colour, markings, patterning or shape helps it to blend in with its surroundings, so that it is difficult to see.

Cannibalism When an animal eats members of its own species.

Carapace The upper part of a chelonian's shell.

Carnivores Meat-eating animals.

Carrion The flesh of dead animals.

Cell The microscopic building blocks from which all living things are made. Different cells in an animal's body perform different tasks.

Chelonian A turtle or tortoise.

Chemoreceptor A sensory cell that detects air- or waterborne scent particles.

Cold-blooded When an animal cannot maintain a constant body temperature. Its body temperature depends on the temperature of its surroundings.

Communal Used by many animals.

Constrictor A snake that kills prey by coiling round it and suffocating it.

Courtship Animal behaviour that leads to the selection of a mate and to mating.

Crocodilian A crocodile, alligator, caiman or gharial.

Dinosaurs A group of reptiles that dominated the Earth 230-65 million years ago before dying out suddenly.

Eft The juvenile, land-dwelling stage in the life-cycle of some amphibians, between the larval and adult stages.

Egg-tooth A temporary tooth on the tip of a baby reptile's snout, which the reptile uses to pierce the shell of its egg.

Embryo A young, developing reptile before hatching or birth.

Evolved Changed gradually into a new species over millions of years.

Extinction When an animal species dies out completely.

Fang A sharp tooth, often hollow or grooved, for injecting venom into prey.

Fossils The remains of living things, preserved in the rocks. Impressions in rock of footprints or skin are also fossils.

Gills Feather-like growths that enable amphibian larvae to breathe underwater.

Gland Part of an animal's body that can produce hormones or liquids such as saliva and venom.

Habitat The natural home of a plant or animal.

Haemotoxic Damaging to blood cells. Haemotoxic venom causes death by excessive bleeding or blood clotting.

Heat pit A sensory organ on the head of some snakes that detects the body heat given off by warm-blooded prey.

Herbivore An animal that eats only or mostly plant material, such as leaves, stems, roots, seeds, nuts or fruit.

Herpetology The study of reptiles and amphibians.

Hibernate To enter a sleep-like state in which the body functions at a low level and thus uses little energy. Hibernation helps some animals to survive the winter.

Incubate To keep eggs warm enough until they are ready to hatch.

Invertebrate An animal without a spine. Insects, spiders, worms, snails and slugs are all invertebrates.

Jacobson's organ A pit in the roof of a reptile's mouth that detects airborne scent particles.

Juvenile An animal that is not yet an adult.

Keratin A hard substance from which horns, nails, claws and reptile scales are made.

Larvae (singular: larva) Young animals that look very different from their adult forms.

Mammal An animal that has hair (fur) and which feeds its young on milk.

Mangrove A coastal forest. Mangrove trees grow in seashore mud.

Mating The coming together of male and female animals to produce young.

Maturity The stage in an animal's development at which it is able to breed.

Metamorphosis The step-by-step change of a larva into an adult, which occurs in most amphibians.

Migrate To move from place to place in search of food, better weather or breeding sites.

Molluscs A group of animals (most with shells) that includes snails, slugs, octopuses, mussels and squid.

Mucus A fluid produced by the body of an animal.

Neurotoxic Harmful to the nervous system. Neurotoxic venom can cause paralysis and stop the heart and lungs from working.

Nocturnal Active at night.

Omnivorous Feeding on a wide variety of food, both plants and animals.

Organ Part of the body that performs a specific function. Lungs and gills, for example, are organs used for breathing.

Osteoderm A lump of bone in a reptile's skin that provides protection against predators. Crocodilians and some lizards have osteoderms.

Paralyze To affect an animal's nervous system or muscles so that it cannot move.

Parthenogenesis When a female can produce offspring without her eggs needing to be fertilized by a male.

Plastron The lower part of a chelonian's shell.

Predator An animal that hunts and kills other animals for food.

Prehensile Capable of grasping.

Prey An animal that is hunted by other animals for food.

Rainforest A forest near the Equator where the weather is hot and wet all year round.

Reptile A cold-blooded vertebrate with a tough, scaly skin.

Rival An animal competing for food, territory or mates.

Saliva A liquid produced by glands in the mouth to make it easier to swallow and digest food.

Scales Small, flat plates of keratin that cover the skin and protect it.

Scutes Scales that have developed into horny plates.

Sloughing Shedding old skin.

Spawn Floating clumps of amphibian eggs.

Species A group of similar living things that can breed together to produce fertile young.

Sperm Sex cells produced by a male animal.

Spermatophore A jelly-like 'packet' of sperm produced by some male amphibians.

Spurs Tiny remnants of back legs found on the body of male boas.

Tadpole The larval stage in the life-cycle of a frog or a toad.

Territory An area that an animal defends against intruders.

Thermoreceptor A sensory cell that detects heat.

Toxic Poisonous.

Venom A poisonous liquid used by an animal to kill or paralyze prey.

Vertebrate An animal with a backbone and an internal skeleton, such as a bird, reptile, mammal, amphibian or fish.

Viviparous Able to give birth to live young.

Vocalize To make sounds.

Yolk The yellow part of an egg. The yolk acts as a food store to nourish the embryo while it is growing in the egg.

Warm-blooded When an animal can generate its own body heat, rather than having to rely on absorbing heat from the environment.

BIRDS

What is a Bird?

Birds are warm-blooded vertebrates (animals with backbones). Their feathers keep them warm and help them to fly. They walk on two back legs, while their front limbs have become wings. All birds lay eggs.

Amazing

There are probably more than 100 billion wild birds in the world – compared to about 6.5 billion humans.

❍ The 9000 bird species are organized into about 180 families. Species in a family share certain characteristics, such as body shape.

❍ Bird families are organized into 28 or 29 larger groups called orders. Largest is the perching bird order, with more than 5000 bird species. The next largest is the swift and hummingbird order, with 429 species.

❍ Scientists believe that birds evolved from lightly built dinosaurs, such as *Compsognathus*, which ran on two legs.

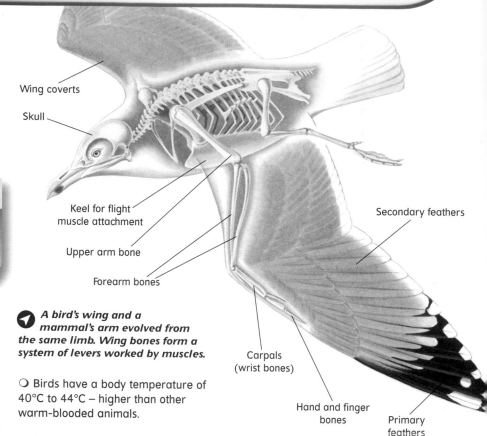

Wing coverts

Skull

Keel for flight muscle attachment

Upper arm bone

Forearm bones

Secondary feathers

Carpals (wrist bones)

Hand and finger bones

Primary feathers

◐ *A bird's wing and a mammal's arm evolved from the same limb. Wing bones form a system of levers worked by muscles.*

❍ Birds have a body temperature of 40°C to 44°C – higher than other warm-blooded animals.

❍ A bird's bones have a honeycomb structure. The bones are so light that they account for only about 5 per cent of the bird's total weight.

❍ A bird's muscles make up 30–60 per cent of their total weight. The biggest are the flight and leg muscles.

❍ The skeleton of a bird's wings has a similar structure to the human arm, but the wrist bones are joined. Also, a bird has only three fingers, not five fingers like a human.

◀ *The American jacana's extremely long, thin toes spread its body weight so well that it can run over the leaves of floating plants, such as lilies. The jacana feeds from the water's surface, and dives under water if threatened.*

First bird

Archaeopteryx ('ancient wing'), the earliest known bird, lived about 155 million years ago. It had feathers like a modern bird, but teeth like a reptile. It must have been a weak flyer, because its breast bone was too small to anchor powerful flight muscles. *Archaeopteryx* could not take off from the ground, and probably had to climb a tree before launching itself into the air. Its wingspan was about 50 cm.

Find out more

Feathers pp. 316–317

Night chorus

Known for their fast, loud, musical song, nightingales are named after their habit of singing at night, although they also sing during the day. Usually hidden in undergrowth, the nightingale's red-brown colours make it hard to spot. Nightingales are about 16 cm in length. The song of the nightingale often starts with a 'choc, choc' call, and consists of fluty, liquid trills and slow 'peeoo' notes.

○ No bird has more than four toes, but some have three, and the ostrich has only two. Four-toed birds have different arrangements of toes: in swifts, all four point forwards; in most perching birds, three point forwards and one backwards; and in parrots, two point forwards and two backwards.

○ A beak is made up of a bird's projecting jaw bones, covered in a hard horny material.

Hummingbirds can hover, move straight up or down, and even fly backwards. The heart rate of a tiny hummingbird reaches an astonishing 615 beats per minute when it flies.

○ Ravens and pigeons can work out simple counting sums. Parrots, budgerigars and mynahs can mimic human speech (though that is not the same as talking), and some parrots can name and count objects. The Galapagos woodpecker finch uses a twig as a tool to winkle out grubs from tree bark.

○ Most birds make sounds using a specialized voice box called a syrinx in the neck. Calls are usually short and harsh to warn of danger. Songs are longer and more tuneful. Each bird has an in-built ability to sing and mimic other birds.

A bird's egg, though seemingly simple, contains everything that the developing embryo inside needs to survive. The yellow yolk in an egg provides food for the embryo. The white provides food and moisture. The shell of an egg contains tiny pores, which allow oxygen to pass through the shell to the baby bird.

Feet and claws

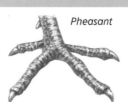

Osprey

Birds of prey use sharp, curved claws called talons to catch and carry prey.

Pheasant

In pheasants, two toes point forwards and two point backwards.

Duck

Ducks, geese and swans use their webbed feet like paddles in the water.

Robin

Perching birds have three forward-pointing toes and one backward-pointing toe.

Killdeer

Killdeers have only three toes on each foot, which helps them to run fast.

Woodpecker

Long, curved claws help woodpeckers to cling to vertical tree trunks.

Longest-lived

	Age (years)
Siberian white crane	82
Sulphur-crested cockatoo	80
Goose	80
Ostrich	68
Eagle owl	68
Macaw	64

Big and Small Birds

The world's largest bird is the ostrich. This long-legged bird weighs up to twice as much as an average adult human. In contrast, the bee hummingbird, the world's smallest bird, weighs only about as much as a small spoonful of rice.

○ The largest bird, the ostrich, weighs almost 80,000 times more than the smallest, the bee hummingbird.

○ *Aepyornis* (also known as the 'elephant bird') was a 3-m tall ostrich ancestor from Madagascar. It probably became extinct in the 17th century. The eggs of *Aepyornis* may have weighed as much as 10 kg – more than nine times the weight of an ostrich egg.

▶ *The wandering albatross has the longest wings of any bird. When outstretched, they measure as much as 3.3 m from tip to tip. The albatross spends most of its life in the air. It flies over the oceans, searching for fish and squid, which it snatches from the water's surface.*

○ Small birds have about 15 neck vertebrae, while the mute swan has 23. (Mammals have only 7.)

○ The 7182 feathers of a bald eagle weigh 677 g – more than twice as much as the bird's skeleton.

○ The bee hummingbird's nest is the smallest – only the size of a thimble.

○ Owls range in size from the least pygmy owl, at only 12–14 cm long, to the Eurasian eagle owl, at 71 cm. Female owls are usually larger than males.

▼ *The ostrich is the tallest (2.5 m), heaviest (150 kg) and fastest-running (55 km/h) of all birds. Ostriches favour the dry savanna (grassland) of Africa and survive well on a wide variety of foods, from seeds to lizards and frogs. The male shades the eggs and chicks from the scorching sun with his plume-like wing feathers.*

Amazing

The tallest bird ever, the giant moa of New Zealand, was 3.5 m tall. The moa is now extinct.

Find out more
Birds of prey pp. 346–347

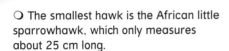

○ The smallest hawk is the African little sparrowhawk, which only measures about 25 cm long.

○ The storm petrel, no larger than a sparrow, stays at sea most of its life. It survives the stormiest weather despite its small size. Storm petrels have learned to follow ships, fluttering over the wake to pick up scraps. Their natural food is plankton (tiny animal and plant organisms), which they harvest from the surface of the ocean.

○ A prehistoric bird called *Diatrymia* was 2 m tall. It killed animals as large as a horse with its huge, hooked beak.

Small survivor

Europe's smallest bird, the goldcrest, still manages to migrate across the North Sea from Scandinavia to spend the winter in Britain. Like other tiny birds, it is very vulnerable to severe weather, but always seems to bounce back after cold seasons, which almost wipe it out.

▼ *The bee hummingbird is the world's smallest bird. Its body, including its tail, is only about 5 cm long and it weighs only 2 g. It lives on Caribbean islands and, like other hummingbirds, feeds on flower nectar. As it hovers in front of flowers, its tiny wings beat incredibly fast.*

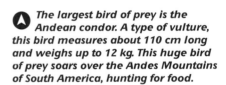

▲ *The largest bird of prey is the Andean condor. A type of vulture, this bird measures about 110 cm long and weighs up to 12 kg. This huge bird of prey soars over the Andes Mountains of South America, hunting for food.*

○ The American harpy eagle is so big that it can snatch large monkeys and sloths from rainforest trees.

○ Ravens are massive corvids (members of the crow family), which reach 65 cm in length. They are the biggest of all the songbirds. Ravens can kill prey, but they usually scavenge on dead animals. Long ago, they pecked at the bodies of criminals who had been hanged, so the raven became known as a bird of ill omen.

▲ *Eagle owls can hunt large prey and have been known to attack small deer and even foxes. Eagle owls are found mainly in high mountains and rocky, dry scrubland. Even real eagles keep away from these powerful predators. An eagle owl can weigh as much as an eagle, although it has a bigger head and shorter tail.*

Mini bird of prey

Falconets are the smallest birds of prey. The red-legged falconet is only 18 cm from beak-tip to tail end. Its legs are not red, but the feathers just above them are. This dainty bird is common in the open forests that cover the foothills of the Himalayan Mountains and stretch across to Southeast Asia.

Feathers

Birds are the only animals that have feathers. The feathers are made of keratin – the same material that makes up human hair and nails. Feathers keep a bird warm and protect it from the wind and rain. Wing and tail feathers allow most birds to fly.

❍ An antbird rubs a mouthful of ants over its feathers to clean them. The formic acid from the ants kills any lice and mites in the feathers.

Display feathers

To attract his mate, the blue bird of paradise hangs upside down from a twig, sprays out his wing and tail feathers, and arches his two long tail plumes into an M shape. Then he sways to and fro and makes a courtship call that sounds like the cough and splutter of an old motorcycle engine.

❍ The greater racquet-tailed drongo has two long, wire-like tail feathers with twisted tips that make a humming noise as the bird flies.

❍ The waxwing gets its name from the red markings at the tips of its wing feathers, which resemble drops of wax.

Amazing

A whistling swan can have more than 25,000 feathers, while the ruby-throated hummingbird has only 940 feathers.

❍ The male wattled starling loses his head feathers during the breeding season. Scientists investigating cures for human baldness are researching the bird's ability to regrow his head feathers each year.

Feather care

To clean its feathers, a bird, such as this cormorant, draws each feather through its bill. This is called preening. Many birds also take dust or water baths, or spread an oily liquid over their feathers to keep them waterproof.

▼ *Secretary birds are so-called because of the quill-like crests on the backs of their heads.*

▶ *Eighty per cent of a whistling swan's feathers are on its head and extremely long neck.*

❍ The soft, fluffy edges of an owl's feathers help to reduce flight noise, so that it can hunt almost silently.

❍ Bald eagles are not really bald. They have white feathers on their heads, which may make them appear bald from a distance.

> The colours of birds' feathers, such as this scarlet macaw, may help them to attract mates, or camouflage them so that they blend in with their surroundings.

○ A dense covering of three layers of feathers keeps penguins warm. An emperor penguin has about 12 feathers on each square centimetre of its body.

○ The long-tailed tit measures only about 14 cm long, and more than half of its length is made up by its tail feathers.

> The cormorant is often seen drying its feathers, perched with wings outstretched. Its feathers become sodden when it dives into the sea, which helps it to swim underwater in pursuit of fish.

Young penguins are covered with warm, thick down feathers, which makes them look very different from the adults. As the chicks grow up, the fluffy down is replaced by true feathers.

○ Special feathers on the heron's breast and rump crumble into a powdery substance. The bird rubs this into its plumage to remove dirt and fish slime.

○ The white feathers of the great egret were popular hat decorations in the late 1800s – more than 200,000 birds were killed for their feathers in a single year.

○ The female eider duck lines her nest with soft down feathers that she pulls from her own breast. Humans use eider down feathers to provide a warm lining for quilts and sleeping bags.

Types of feather

The four main feather types are down feathers that trap warm air next to the body, contour feathers that cover the body making it streamlined for flight, wing feathers that help give lift when flying and tail feathers that help a bird control its flight.

Down feather   *Contour feather*   *Flight feather (wing)*   *Tail feather*

Find out more

Penguins p. 363

Flight

Gliding, soaring, diving and hovering, birds are masters of the air. Apart from bats, they are the only vertebrate animals capable of flight. Among the largest of these flying aces are the storks, condors, swans and albatrosses.

○ Wings are a bird's front limbs. There are many different wing shapes. Small, fast-flying birds, such as swifts, have slim, pointed wings.

○ The heaviest flying bird is the great bustard. The male is up to 1 m long and weighs about 18 kg (the female is slightly smaller). The bustard is a strong flier, but it spends much of its life on the ground, walking or running on its strong legs.

○ A hummingbird's wings beat 50 or more times per second as it hovers in the air. The tiny bee hummingbird may beat its wings even faster, at an amazing 200 times per second.

○ *The swan is one of the world's heaviest flying birds, and it needs a long runway to take off. The swan gains speed by paddling or running over the water's surface. Once airborne, it is a powerful flyer, making a distinctive pulsing sound with its wings.*

How birds fly

In flight, a bird's flapping wings make circular and up-and-down movements – the wing tips pushing forward on the upstroke. Taking off for most birds involves flapping the wings to produce thrust and lift. Broad, rounded wings give the best lift and acceleration – useful for escaping a predator. Big birds, such as geese, run into the wind to generate enough lift to take off. Birds with long, narrow wings, such as swallows, can only take off from a high point – falling into the air and letting the air carry them.

○ Falcons are often seen flying in cities. The common kestrel hovers on fast-beating wings above rubbish bins as it searches for small mammal prey, such as mice and rats, while the peregrine dives down between New York skyscrapers to snatch pigeons flying far below.

○ The bateleur, a snake eagle, may fly as much as 300 km a day in search of food. The word *bateleur* means 'tumbler' or 'tightrope walker' in French, and refers to the rocking, acrobatic movements that the bird makes in flight.

○ *When diving, the peregrine falcon does not simply fold its wings and fall like many birds, but it actually pushes itself down towards the ground. This powered dive is called a stoop.*

○ An early member of the vulture family, *Argentavix* of South America, had an amazing 7.3 m wingspan.

○ There is an old saying that the weather will be good when swallows fly high, but bad when swallows fly low. This is based on fact: in wet weather, insects stay nearer the ground, so their predators – the swallows – do the same.

Find out more

Arctic tern p. 364

Longest wingspan

Wandering albatross	3.6 m
Marabou stork	3.2 m
Andean condor	3 m
Swan	3 m

Soaring birds

Birds that soar in the sky for hours, such as hawks and eagles, have long, broad wings. These allow them to float on rising air currents.

The common tern is often seen over rivers, hovering and swooping as it feeds. It nests in noisy colonies on beaches, sand dunes and islands. Colonies sometimes all take off at once, in silence, and fly over the sea before returning to the nesting site. The flight of a tern is light and graceful, with rapid changes of direction.

❍ In flight, a pelican flaps its wings 1.3 times a second. This is one of the slowest wingbeat speeds, when actively flying, of any bird.

❍ The red-breasted merganser is one of the fastest-flying birds. It can reach speeds of more than 65 km/h – and possibly even 100 km/h.

Wings and flight

Owls fly very quietly, so that they can hear sounds made by their prey. They swoop down on their victims in a surprise attack.

Eagles have huge, wide wings to help them soar in the sky as their keen eyes scan the ground below for prey animals.

Like other birds, pelicans use their wings and feet as 'air brakes' to slow them down as they land.

Hummingbirds are expert at hovering. These agile fliers can even fly upside down for brief periods.

With pointed wings and a long, forked tail, Arctic terns are fast, agile flyers. They make long migrations each year, and in their lifetime may travel over 1 million km.

Bigger birds, such as cranes, tend to fly in a straight line. Small birds usually fly with an undulating (up-and-down) motion.

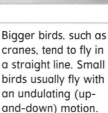

Flightless Birds

A small number of bird species have lost the ability to fly. Some run or creep about, whilst others have wings adapted for swimming. Flightless land birds live in Africa (ostrich), South America (rhea) and Australia and New Guinea (emu and cassowary).

Amazing

Ostriches are nearly seven times too heavy to fly, but they can run as fast as a racehorse.

○ The weka is a flightless rail that lives in New Zealand. Its diet includes seeds, fruit, mice, eggs and insects, and it also scavenges in rubbish bins.

○ The world's smallest flightless bird, the Inaccessible Island rail, weighs only 35 g – about the same as a small tomato. It lives on Inaccessible Island in the South Atlantic Ocean.

○ The kagu is a flightless bird that lives solely on the Pacific island of New Caledonia.

Dead as a dodo

The flightless dodo lived undisturbed on the island of Mauritius in the Indian Ocean until European sailors arrived in the 1500s. Sailors killed the birds for food and rats, and cats ate the eggs. By 1680, the dodo was extinct.

Ostrich eggs

Compared to other birds' eggs, ostrich eggs are the largest of all. However, compared to the size of the mother bird, they are the smallest eggs laid by any bird species.

○ The takahe is another flightless bird of New Zealand. Believed to have died out in the 19th century, the takahe was rediscovered in 1948.

○ Penguins have wings, but cannot fly. They spend as much as 85 per cent of their time in water, where they use their wings like flippers to help propel themselves along.

○ Penguins usually swim at 5–10 km/h, but can reach speeds of up to 24 km/h.

○ The largest bird in South America is the greater rhea, which stands 1.5 m tall and weighs up to 25 kg.

A *Emperor penguins have highly streamlined bodies, allowing them to dive to depths of 275 m when they hunt. They usually stay underwater for just a few minutes, although the record dive for these penguins is 18 minutes.*

○ Cassowaries are flightless birds that live in the rainforests of Australia and New Guinea. There are three species – all are large birds with long, strong legs and big, sharp-clawed feet. On the cassowary's head is a large horny crest, called a casque. Experts think that when the bird is moving through the dense forest, it holds its head down and uses the casque to help it break its way through the tangle of plants.

○ The emu is the largest bird in Australia. It measures 2 m tall and weighs as much as 45 kg. Although it cannot fly, it can run at speeds of more than 50 km/h on its long legs. Emus feed on fruit, berries, and insects.

10 flightless birds

Ostrich	Emu
Kiwi	Cassowary
Rhea	Penguin
Kakapo	Steamer duck
Weka	Calayan rail

Find out more

Ostrich p. 314

Rhea

Ostrich

Emu

Cassowary

Bennet's cassowary

Kiwi

Rhea
Smaller than the ostrich and emu, the rhea is still the largest bird in the Americas. It roams the pampas (grassland), often gathering in large flocks of a hundred or more birds.

Ostrich
Male ostriches have black feathers, while females, juveniles and chicks are well camouflaged by brownish feathers. In the breeding season, males defend their territories by patrolling and displaying, and by making loud, booming calls. They also inflate their bright pink necks.

Emu
The emu is almost as large as the ostrich, at nearly 2 m tall. These big, tough birds live in many parts of Australia, where they feed mainly on grasses, fruits, flowers and seeds.

Bennet's cassowary
This type of cassowary is about 100 cm tall. It has a fearsome reputation as a very dangerous bird. It may attack anything or anyone who comes too close to its nest, kicking out with its sharp claws.

Kiwi
The kiwi is well known, yet seldom seen. Its feathers are so thin and fine that the bird looks like a ball of fur. Kiwis creep about in the forest at night, pecking in the soil for worms and grubs.

Cassowary
Found in parts of northern Australia and New Guinea, the cassowary has colourful, turkey-like wattles (flaps of skin) hanging from its head and neck. To attract a female at breeding time, the male shows off these wattles.

Bird Beaks

A bird's beak, or bill, is used for feeding, preening the feathers (keeping them clean and combed), holding materials for building a nest and pecking at enemies. The shape of the beak reveals the type of food the bird eats.

○ A bird's beak is its feeding tool, so it is important to keep the beak clean and undamaged. A bird often jabs its beak into loose soil to remove sticky material and debris. Under the beak's covering of keratin are the bones of the upper and lower jaws – the maxilla and mandible. These flex, or move, with the head, to prevent damage to the beak.

Amazing

The Australian pelican has the largest beak of any bird, measuring up to 50 cm long.

▶ *Most black storks live in wet places, such as woodlands with streams and pools. They feed by wading slowly through shallow water, stabbing at prey with their spear-like beak. Black storks eat mainly fish, but also feed on frogs, invertebrates, birds, tortoises and small mammals.*

Beak shapes

The wrybill is the only bird with a beak that curves to the right. The wrybill is a type of plover that lives in New Zealand. It sweeps its beak over the ground in circles to pick up insects.

The upper and lower portions of the crossbill's beak cross over to help it prise open pine cones.

The hyacinth macaw has one of the most powerful beaks of any bird, strong enough to crack brazil nuts.

The sword-billed hummingbird has an extremely long beak and a long tongue for extracting nectar from flowers.

An owl's powerful hooked bill tears up mice, rats, rabbits, gophers, prairie dogs, and even squirrels and small monkeys.

○ A pelican catches fish in the large pouch of skin under its lower bill. The pouch can hold more food than the pelican's stomach. Most pelicans feed in groups, swimming along and herding fish together before scooping them up. The brown pelican uses a different hunting technique. It catches fish by diving head-first into the water, with its beak open, from a height of about 10 m.

○ Nightjars have the shortest beaks of all birds, at 8–10 mm long.

○ The huge beak of the whale-billed stork, or shoebill, is 23 cm long and 10 cm wide. The bird uses its beak to catch prey such as lungfish, young crocodiles and turtles.

Galapagos finches

The 13 species of finch that live on the Galapagos Islands off South America all have a different shape or size of beak, each one adapted to eating a particular type of food. This helps the finches to share out the limited food resources on the islands.

▶ *The puffin's beak can carry a neat row of up to 20 small fish, such as sand-eels. Out of the breeding season, the puffin's beak is not only duller in colour, but it is also smaller, because it loses its outer horny sheath.*

○ The western curlew plunges its long, curved beak into soft coastal mud to find worms, crabs, shrimps and shellfish.

○ The sword-billed hummingbird's 10.5 cm-long beak is longer than its body.

○ Seed-eating birds have strong, cone-shaped bills to crack open seeds.

○ The shovel-billed kingfisher is armed with its own spade for digging in mud – it uses its large, heavy bill to dig up worms, shellfish and small reptiles.

◀ *The spoonbill's long beak has a sensitive, spoon-shaped tip. The bird sweeps its beak through shallow water in search of fish and small creatures to eat.*

Toco toucan

The toco toucan of Brazil is the largest and best-known of the toucans. It sometimes perches on a branch near another bird's nest to steal the eggs or chicks. Intimidated by the toucan's great beak, the parent bird will not generally attack. When it sleeps, the toco toucan turns its head so that its long beak rests along its back. It also folds its tail over its head.

Find out more
Puffins p. 350

Feeding

A bird's beak is adapted to catch and eat all kinds of food. Birds of prey have hooked beaks, for tearing flesh. Fish-eaters, such as herons, have long, spear-shaped beaks. There are also specialized beak shapes for seed-eaters, nut-crackers, fruit-pickers and insect-snappers.

Filter-feeder

The flamingo uses its beak to filter food from shallow water. It stands in the water with its head down and its beak beneath the surface. Water flows into the beak and is pushed out again by the flamingo's large tongue. Bristles in the beak trap food items – such as worms, insects, shellfish and even algae – which the bird then eats.

❍ Swallows catch their insect food in the air as they fly.

❍ Locusts are the favourite food of the rose-coloured starling. Large flocks fly to wherever they are plentiful.

❍ The marsh harrier flies close to the ground searching for mice, rats, frogs, rabbits and fish. When it sights prey, the harrier seizes the victim with its sharp talons and tears it apart with its beak.

▶ *The woodpecker uses its special strong beak to bore into tree trunks and catch insects. The bird holds on tightly to a tree trunk with the help of its strong feet and sharp claws. Its stiff tail feathers also help to give it support. It starts to hammer into the trunk, disturbing wood-boring insects that live beneath the tree bark. The insects try to flee, but the woodpecker quickly snaps them up.*

Amazing

The bearded vulture drops bones from a great height to break them open so that it can reach the marrow inside.

◀ *Bee-eaters twist and dart at speed as they chase after flying insects, including bees and wasps. The bird rubs or bashes a bee or a wasp on a branch to remove the sting before eating it.*

Find out more
Gannet dive-bomber p. 350

○ If a Galapagos woodpecker finch cannot reach grubs in tree bark, it breaks off a cactus spine with its beak and uses the spine to extract the grubs.

○ The palm-nut vulture lives in Africa. Unlike most birds of prey, the palm-nut vulture is mostly vegetarian. Its main food is the husk of the oil palm fruit, although it also eats fish, frogs and other small creatures.

Honeyguide bird

The honeyguide bird uses the honey badger to help it obtain food. The bird feeds on bee grubs and beeswax. Although it can find the bees' nests, it is not strong enough to break into them. So it looks for the honey badger to help. It leads the badger, which also feeds on honey, toward the bees' nest. When the honey badger smashes into the nest, the honeyguide can also eat its fill.

The snail kite feeds only on water snails, and its long upper beak is specially shaped for this strange diet. When the kite catches a snail, it holds it with one foot while standing on a branch or other perch. It impales the snail's soft body on its sharp beak and shakes it free of the shell.

○ When hunting, a black heron holds its wings over its head like a sunshade. This may cut out the glare of reflected sunlight and help the bird to spot fish, or the patch of shade may attract fish to the area.

○ Prions feed on tiny plankton, which they filter from the water through comb-like structures on their beaks.

○ Secretary birds are famous for their ability to kill snakes on African grasslands. They have tough scales on their legs to help protect them from snake bites.

○ In contrast to other birds, the hoatzin, from northern South America, feeds almost entirely on leaves.

○ The green woodpecker probes rotting wood with its long tongue. Insects are trapped on the tongue's barbed, sticky, tip, and are extracted from the wood.

▶ *The gannet dives into the sea to catch prey such as herring and mackerel. It plunges through the air at up to 96 km/h. A specially strengthened skull helps to cushion the impact of the gannet's high-speed dive into water.*

Bird Senses

Almost all birds have excellent sight, and most depend on their eyes for finding food. Birds are also ten times more sensitive to changes of pitch and intensity in sounds than humans.

Sensitive bill

The avocet has a well developed sense of touch in its tongue and bill tip. It sweeps its slender, upturned bill from side to side to extract shrimps and other creatures from the mud in shallow water.

The golden eagle has keen eyesight and can see objects from a much greater distance than humans can. It can spot prey from a height of 1.6 km. Birds of prey tend to have eyes near the front of their heads, giving good forward vision.

○ A bird's outer ear consists of a short tube leading from the eardrum to the outside. In most birds, the ear openings are just behind the jaw.

○ A bird's eyes are often as big as its brain. The eye of a starling, for example, makes up as much as 15 per cent of the total weight of its head. (A human eye is only 1 per cent of the head weight.)

○ Birds have a poorly developed sense of taste. Most birds have less than 100 taste buds on their tongue, whereas humans have thousands.

Pittas are said to have the best sense of smell of any songbird. This may help them find worms and snails in the dim light of the forest floor. Rainbow pittas put wallaby droppings in and round their nests to disguise their own smell and keep tree snakes away from their eggs.

All-round vision

Birds that are preyed on by other animals have eyes on the sides of the head. This gives them a very wide field of view, enabling them to spot enemies or other dangers in most directions. They cannot, however, see very well directly in front of them or directly behind them.

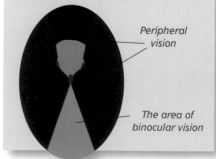

Peripheral vision

The area of binocular vision

Find out more

Lappet-faced vulture p. 357

Vultures can find dead animals when flying high in the sky. This could be because they can smell them, even from great heights.

Birds, such as this barking owl, have a clear third eyelid called the nictating membrane, or the blinking membrane. Birds can move this eyelid (far right) over the surface of the eye to keep it clean, and also to protect the eye from injury.

○ In experiments, albatrosses have been able to smell food from 30 km away.

○ The ostrich has the largest eyes of any land animal.

○ Kestrels can see ultra-violet light, which reflects off the urine a rodent uses to mark its tracks.

○ A great gray owl can hear a vole moving under 60 cm of snow 30 m away.

○ An owl's eyes cannot swivel in their sockets, so the owl has to turn its head to look in different directions. In fact, it can turn its head right round in a circle.

A barn owl's hearing is so good that it can detect and catch prey in complete darkness without using its eyes at all. The disc of feathers on a barn owl's face collects sound like a radar dish. A bird's ears are hidden under the feathers on the sides of their head. The ears of long eared owls are in fact just tufts of feathers.

Amazing

The eyes of birds of prey are five times more densely packed with light-sensitive cells than our own. This is why a peregrine can spot a pigeon flying up to 8 km away.

Defence

Birds may hide from predators or escape by running away or flying off. They also use their sharp beaks and claws to defend themselves. Some birds find safety in numbers.

○ Thousands of guillemots breed together in noisy colonies on rocky cliffs. They do not build nests but simply lay their eggs on the rock or bare soil. Most land hunters cannot reach the birds on the steep, narrow cliff edges. And any flying egg thieves are quickly driven away by the mass of screeching, pecking guillemots.

Ⓐ *North America's tiny elf owl (the smallest owl in the world) lives mainly in deserts. It often shelters and nests in the stems of cactus plants. The spiny stems help to protect the owl from predators and from the hot sun.*

○ If threatened, a rhea lies flat on the ground with its head stretched out in an attempt to hide.

○ Ostriches don't really bury their heads in the sand. But if a female is approached by an enemy while sitting on her nest on the ground, she will press her long neck flat on the ground, to appear less obvious.

○ The female dwarf cassowary, or moruk, is an extremely dangerous bird and will attack anything that comes near its nest with its 10-cm long claws.

○ If threatened by birds of prey, the hoopoe hides by flattening itself on the ground with its wings and tail spread out wide.

○ Antbirds have white spots on their back feathers, which they use to signal warnings to each other. They show the spots in particular patterns according to the message – like a sort of Morse code.

Ⓐ *The hoopoe lines its nest with animal excrement, perhaps so that the smell will keep enemies away!*

○ Kentish plover chicks have markings like the stones and pebbles of their nest site. If danger threatens, the chicks flatten themselves on the ground and are almost impossible to see.

○ Red-breasted geese often make their nests near those of peregrines and buzzards. This gives them protection, and they don't seem to be attacked by the birds of prey.

Bird or branch?

Birds have clever ways of hiding themselves from enemies. The tawny frogmouth is an Australian bird that hunts at night. During the day, it rests in a tree where its brownish, mottled feathers make it hard to see. When the bird senses danger, it stretches itself, with its beak pointing upwards, so that it looks almost exactly like an old broken branch or tree stump.

Changing colour

The ptarmigan has white feathers in the winter to help it hide from enemies among the winter snows in the Arctic. But in summer its white plumage would make it very obvious to predators, so the ptarmigan moults and grows brown and grey feathers instead.

▲ *Gannets are among many seabirds that breed in huge groups or colonies. The colony, or gannetry, is a noisy and crowded place. The birds swoop down in their hundreds, attacking and pecking any other animal that comes near. A gannetry may contain as many as 50,000 nests.*

○ When emperor penguin chicks are seven weeks old, they huddle together in large groups for warmth and protection. This keeps them safe while their parents are collecting food out at sea.

○ The pygmy seed-snipe of southern South America blends in with the plains landscape so well that it is almost invisible when it crouches on the ground.

◀ *The sunbittern's colourful display feathers could be a give-away to predators, but when it closes its wings, these are hidden, and it is well camouflaged in its rainforest home.*

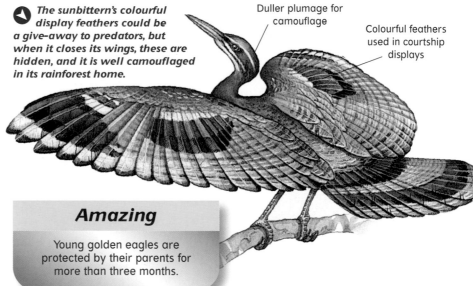

Duller plumage for camouflage

Colourful feathers used in courtship displays

Amazing

Young golden eagles are protected by their parents for more than three months.

Find out more
Owls p. 331

Night Birds

As night falls, some birds, including owls and nightjars, come out to feed. There is less competition for food at night, but finding it is more difficult in the dark. These birds need special adaptations for nocturnal living.

❍ The 150 or so species of owl are found in most parts of the world, with the exception of the far north, New Zealand and Antarctica. About 80 species of owl hunt mostly at night.

❍ Owls swallow their prey, such as mice and insects, whole.

❍ An owl's eyes are large and forward-facing to enable it to judge distances accurately when flying and hunting prey.

❍ The bristle-fringed beak of a nightjar opens very wide to help it snap up moths and beetles at night.

❍ There are about 70 species of nightjar. They are found in most warmer parts of the world, except New Zealand and southern South America.

Invisible owls

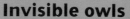

Owls roost (sleep) during the day. But their feathers blend so well into the background of tree trunks, branches and twigs, it is almost impossible to spot them. Even at night many owls, including the scops owl, are heard more often than they are seen. Scops owls screech loudly at night. They call 'chiup' every few seconds, on and on, time after time. They are so loud that they keep people awake at night. This is why they are also known as screech-owls.

❍ Nightjars are big-eyed, fluffy-looking, graceful flyers with some of the best camouflage in the bird world. Their mottled grey-brown plumage makes them almost impossible to spot as they sit perfectly still by day, among leaves and twigs on the ground or in a tree.

❍ Frogmouths are close cousins of nightjars, and, as their name suggests, they too have wide, gaping mouths. They also fly at night but are less agile than nightjars, diving down from a perch to catch prey on the ground. Many of these birds have strange calls that sound like engines or machines.

❍ The whip-poor-will, a North American nightjar, is named after its call. This can be repeated so often for so long that it becomes very irritating to human listeners. The whip-poor-will is fairly common in mixed broadleaved and conifer woods. It hunts close to the ground, snapping up large insects.

❍ The medium-sized African wood owl is common in south and east Africa. Many owls hunt at dusk, but the African wood owl only comes out in pitch darkness, and so it is heard but rarely seen.

Amazing

The desert-dwelling whip-poor-will is the only bird known to hibernate. It spends winter in a rock cleft or under a shrub.

❍ The oilbird lives in caves in South America. Like bats, the oilbird uses sounds to help it find its way in the dark. As it flies, it makes clicking noises and listens for the echoes that bounce back off nearby objects. At night, the oilbird leaves its cave to feed on the fruits of palm trees.

◀ *Unlike most birds, the kiwi has a good sense of smell, which helps it to find food at night. Using the nostrils at the tip of its long beak, the kiwi sniffs out worms and other creatures hiding in the soil. It plunges its beak into the ground to reach its prey.*

Find out more
Flightless birds pp. 320–321

○ The ghostly, black-rimmed white face and long 'ear tufts' of the white-faced scops owl make it one of the most distinctive members of the owl family. Its favourite hunting method is to sit and wait on a tree branch, then drop silently onto a passing victim below, such as a mouse or an insect, or even a scorpion.

Night parrot

The kakapo is the only parrot that is active at night. It is also a ground-living bird. All other parrots are daytime birds that live in and around trees. During the day, the kakapo sleeps in a burrow or under a rock, and at night it comes out to find fruit, berries and leaves to eat. It cannot fly, and is found only in New Zealand.

Owls – night hunters

Owls are the specialist night hunters of the bird world. They catch mainly small animals, such as mice, voles and lizards. The largest owls prey on rabbits and birds (including other owls), while smallest types hunt moths, beetles and other invertebrates. The fishing owls of Africa and Asia snatch fish, frogs and crayfish from shallow water using their long, unfeathered legs and sharp 'fish-hook' claws. The owl's velvety wing feathers have soft edges with fringes, which means that they are almost totally silent in flight. This enables the owl to swoop down undetected on its prey. Huge eyes give the owl good night vision, but its hearing is even better – four times more sensitive than the ears of a cat.

Wood owl

White-faced scops owl

Eagle owl

Horned owl

African wood owl

Pel's fishing owl

Spotted eagle owl

Cape eagle owl

Courtship

Male birds usually court the females before mating. They may show off their colourful or elaborate feathers or give singing or dancing displays. Some male birds demonstrate their skill at hunting or building nests to impress females.

Songs and calls

Birds make two sorts of sounds – simple calls, giving a warning or a threat, and more complex songs sung by some males at breeding time. One large group of birds is known as the songbirds, because of their singing abilities.

Canary

○ When courting, the male common iora fluffs up its feathers, leaps into the air and tumbles back to its perch again.

○ Bald eagles perform an amazing courtship display. The male and female lock their claws together and tumble through the air to the ground.

○ To attract females, the male lapwing performs a spectacular rolling, tumbling display flight.

▶ *The peacock's wonderful train contains about 200 shimmering feathers, each one decorated with eye-like markings. When courting, he spreads the train and makes it 'shiver' to attract a female.*

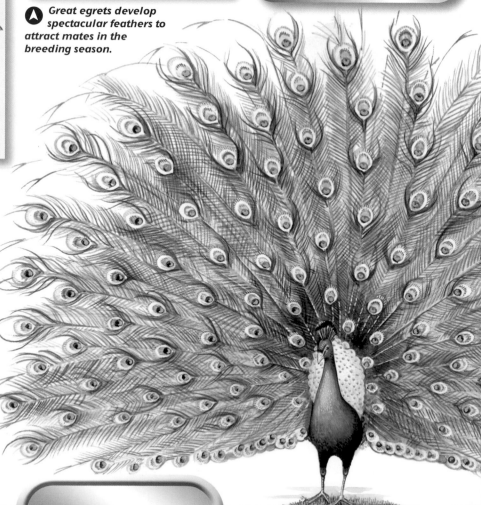

▲ *Great egrets develop spectacular feathers to attract mates in the breeding season.*

○ The loud booming call made by the male bittern in the breeding season can be heard up to 5 km away.

○ In the breeding season, male ruffs grow amazing feathers around the head and neck, and dance in groups to attract females.

Amazing

The crowned crane leaps up to 2 m into the air during its courtship display.

Find out more
Heron courtship p. 353

○ The noddy, a species of tern, gets its name from its habit of nodding its head during its courtship display.

○ When courting, a male bohemian waxwing gives the female a gift – a berry or an ant larva.

○ During courtship flights, the male woodpigeon makes a loud clapping sound with his wings.

When courting a mate, the male frigatebird clatters his beak and flaps his wings. He also inflates his red throat pouch into an eye-catching balloon.

The male blue-footed booby attracts a mate by dancing and holding up his brightly coloured feet as he struts about. Other species of booby have different coloured feet. The birds' strange name comes from the Spanish word bobo, *meaning 'clown'.*

When the male cape weaver has finished making a nest, he calls to the female.

○ Water birds called great crested grebes perform a courtship dance together. During the dance, they offer each other gifts – beakfuls of waterweed!

○ Courtship is the main reason why birds sing, although some species also sing outside of the breeding season. A female nightingale chooses a male for his song, rather than for his looks.

Building bowers

Bowerbirds are medium-sized, eat mainly fruit, and live in the forests of New Guinea and Australia. The male attracts or courts the female in an extraordinary way by building a bower. The bower's construction and appearance vary according to the species of bowerbird. It may be a simple mat of leaves and moss, a pile of twigs, or a large and elaborate structure shaped like a tower, tent, maypole or walk-along 'avenue'. The male may even decorate his bower with bright colours. He then dances, shows off his feathers and calls from his bower to bring a female near. But the bower is not a nest. After mating, the female leaves to build her nest in a bush and raise the chicks on her own.

Spotted bowerbird   Fawn breasted bowerbird   Black faced golden bowerbird

Nests and Eggs

Some birds, such as guillemots, are not nest-makers. But most birds dig or construct a nest to protect their eggs. Nesting materials include twigs, grass and mud. The cave swiftlet even makes a nest from its own saliva (spit).

 The 25 bee-eater species live mainly in rainforests in Africa, southern Asia and Australia. Carmine bee-eaters (shown below) nest in colonies in cliffs, usually near river banks, where they dig horizontal tunnels, often 2 m or more long, with their bills. Both parents incubate the eggs and rear the chicks.

 The paradise flycatcher makes a neat nest of plant roots held together with spiders' webs on a slender branch or twig.

❍ The tailorbird makes a cradle-like nest from two leaves, which it sews together with plant fibres or spiders' webs.

❍ Female manakins do all the nesting work alone. They build the nest, incubate the eggs and care for the young, with no help from the males.

❍ The crested oropendola weaves a hanging nest that may be up to 1 m long. The birds nest in colonies, and there may be as many as 100 large hanging nests in one tree.

❍ The penduline tit makes an amazing nest woven from plant fibres and suspended from the end of a twig. The walls of the nest may be 2.5 cm thick.

 Sociable weaverbirds make a huge shared nest in an acacia tree. Each male and female pair has its own chamber, but the whole nest may contain over 300 birds. They keep each other safe as they squawk, flap and peck at enemies that come too near. They also feed together, always watching each other. If one bird finds food, the others gather to share it.

❍ The grey partridge lays the largest egg clutch of any bird – on average 15 to 19 eggs, but some birds lay as many as 25 eggs at a time.

❍ The Eurasian cuckoo is a 'brood parasite' – it lays its eggs in the nests of other birds (the 'hosts'). Most birds take several minutes to lay an egg, but the cuckoo lays one in just nine seconds, so it can quickly take advantage of any brief absence of the host bird.

Hatching out

1. Bird chicks use an 'egg tooth' on their beaks to break a hole in the shell from inside the egg.

2. The chick pecks at the shell until a crack appears all the way round.

3. The chick then hooks its feet into the crack and pushes the two halves of the shell apart. It usually takes about a minute for the chick to emerge completely from the broken shell.

Find out more

Pear-shaped egg pp. 351

○ The male ostrich makes a shallow nest on the ground and mates with several females, all of whom lay their eggs in the nest. The chief female incubates the eggs during the day, and the male takes over at night.

○ Unusually for birds, female phalaropes are more brightly coloured than males. The female lays several clutches of eggs, leaving the male parent of each clutch to do all the caring for the young.

○ One pair of bald eagles in Florida, USA, built a nest that was 2.9 m wide and 6 m deep, and it weighed about 3 tonnes.

○ The tiny bee hummingbird lays the smallest egg, at 0.4 g in weight. The largest egg, laid by the ostrich, weighs 1–1.8 kg.

◀ **Blacknecked grebes make floating nests in marshes or freshwater lakes.**

Egg burrow

Bee-eaters lay their eggs in a chamber at the end of a burrow dug in an earth bank. Both parents incubate the eggs and feed the chicks.

Record-breakers

Largest communal nest
Sociable weaver: up to 300 nest chambers

Largest roofed nest
Hammerkop: up to 2 m wide and 2 m deep

Longest nest burrow
Rhinoceros auklet: up to 8 m

Smallest nest
Bee hummingbird: size of a thimble

No nest
Fairy tern: one egg laid on bare branch, leaf or cliff

Biggest egg
Ostrich egg: up to 17.8 cm by 14 cm, and strong enough to support weight of a person

Smallest egg
Bee hummingbird: 6.35 mm long

Largest clutch
Grey partridge: lays 15–19 eggs at one time

Longest incubation
Wandering albatross: 75–82 days

▼ **The bald eagle makes one of the biggest nests of any bird. The nest, or 'eyrie', is made of sticks and branches and is built in a tall tree or on rocks. Bald eagles use the same nests year after year, adding new nesting material each time.**

Amazing

An ostrich egg – the largest laid by any bird – has the same volume as 24 farmyard chicken eggs.

Eggs

Auk

Scarlet tanager

Catbird

House wren

Quail

Blue jay

Common snipe

Jacana

Hedge sparrow

Cetti's warbler

Caring for the Young

Many baby birds are blind, naked and helpless when they hatch, and have to be cared for by their parents. The young of ducks and geese hatch with a covering of feathers, and can find food hours after hatching.

Amazing

In just three weeks, a newly hatched cuckoo grows 50 times heavier. By laying eggs in other birds' nests, cuckoos avoid the hard work of feeding their hungry chicks.

○ Hawks and falcons care for their young and bring them food for many weeks. Their chicks are born blind and helpless. They are totally dependent on their parents for food and protection until they grow large enough to hunt for themselves.

▶ *Black-shouldered kite chicks are helpless when they hatch, but by the time they are five weeks old they have grown feathers and are ready to fly.*

▼ *All birds begin life as chicks that hatch from eggs. Like this gull, many parent birds feed and protect their chicks. The chick's downy coat is replaced by brown feathers. A year later, it grows the white and grey feathers of an adult gull.*

○ Swans carry their young on their back as they swim. This allows the parent bird to move fast without having to wait for the young, called cygnets, to keep up. The cygnets are also safe from enemies while they are riding on the parent bird's back.

Foster parents

These African flycatchers are busy feeding a cuckoo chick in their nest. The cuckoo has pushed the flycatcher's eggs out of the nest. The 'foster parents' rear the cuckoo chick as if it were their own.

○ A young golden eagle has grown feathers after 50 days and learned to fly after 70, but it stays with its parents for another month while learning to hunt.

○ A young bird is known as a fledgling from the time it hatches until it is fully feathered and can fly.

○ A young pelican feeds by putting its head deep into its parent's large beak and gobbling up any fish it finds.

○ To obtain food from its parent, a young herring gull has to peck at a red spot on the parent's beak. The adult gull then regurgitates (coughs up) food for the chick to eat.

Find out more
Nests and eggs pp. 334–335

▶ *Pigeons feed their young on 'pigeon milk'. This special liquid is made in the lining of part of the bird's throat, called the crop. The young birds are fed on this for the first few days of their life, after which they start to eat seeds and other solid food.*

❍ Young birds must learn their songs from adults. A young bird such as a chaffinch is born being able to make sounds. But, like a human baby learning to speak, it has to learn the chaffinch song by listening to its parents and practising the sounds.

❍ Shearwaters feed their young for 60 days, then stop. A week later, the chicks are so hungry that they take to the air to find food for themselves.

◀ *The female barn owl lays 4–7 eggs in a tree hole, barn or other building. These young barn owls are nesting in a barn.*

❍ Until their beaks have developed fully, young flamingos feed on a milky substance from their parents' throats.

❍ The sungrebe has an unusual way of caring for its young. The male bird carries his chicks in two skin pouches beneath his wings while they complete their development, even flying with them.

❍ Tiny quail chicks are born with their eyes open and their bodies covered in warm, downy feathers. They are able to follow their mother within one hour of hatching out.

◀ *Young little owls are fed by the male at first, but later the female little owl helps to bring them food as well. This little owl chick is eating a worm. The chicks leave the nest when they are about 26 days old.*

❍ The great spotted cuckoo lays its eggs in other birds' nests, but the chick is not quite as violent as in other cuckoo species. It does not tip out the unhatched eggs and chicks of the parent birds. But it does eat most of the food that the adults bring, so the other chicks starve. And being so big and strong, it may lean on the other chicks and squash them to death.

Follow the leader

Birds such as ducks and geese are able to run around and find food as soon as they hatch. Baby ducks follow the first moving thing they see when they hatch, which is usually their mother. This reaction is called imprinting. It is a form of very rapid learning that can happen only in the first few hours of an animal's life. Imprinting ensures that the young birds stay close to their mother and do not wander away.

Songbirds

Nearly half of all living bird species are songbirds, including sparrows, thrushes, warblers, tits, swallows and crows. Male songbirds usually sing complex songs when courting or defending their territory. Songbirds have grasping feet with four toes; the big toe points backwards.

Amazing

Some songbirds (such as the hawfinch and blackcap) lay eggs that hatch in only ten days.

The blackbird is an enthusiastic visitor to the bird-table. It is one of the earliest members of the dawn chorus, and likes to sit high on a tree or roof-top to sing its melodious, fluting song.

A bird usually sings to tell other birds to stay away from the territory where it lives and often feeds. The robin's bright red chest feathers also act as a 'keep out!' warning to other robins. In the breeding season, the birds sing to attract partners.

The red-billed scythebill has a long, curved beak to search for insects inside plants.

At 19 cm long, the great reed warbler is larger than most European warblers.

Manakins are small birds that live in Central and South America. There are about 57 species.

The chaffinch is the commonest of Europe's finches. It has a cheerful, attractive song.

Antbirds follow columns of army ants, and seize other insects as they flee from the ants' path.

Find out more

Songs and calls p. 332

The mistle thrush is the largest British thrush. It sings from the treetops in stormy weather.

There may now be as many as 150 million house sparrows in the USA.

The red-whiskered bulbul is a common sight in gardens and cultivated land in India, south China and Southeast Asia.

Shrikes are keen predators. Some species store prey by impaling them on thorns, creating a kind of gory 'larder'.

Skylarks make special, fluttering flights accompanied by a distinctive song.

The male northern oriole, also known as the Baltimore oriole, has vibrant orange and black plumage.

The northern mockingbird is the best mimic in its family, usually copying the sounds made by other bird species.

The 43 species of vireo live in North, Central and South America. They range in size from 10–16 cm.

Sunbirds use their long, slender beaks and tubular tongues to extract sweet liquid nectar from flowers.

The 26 species of fairy-wrens live in Australia and New Guinea, where they forage for insects on the ground.

Gamebirds

Gamebirds are mostly large, plump-bodied and spend much time on the ground. They are known as 'game' birds because they were hunted for their tasty meat – and still are in some regions.

○ The female red-legged partridge lays one clutch of eggs for her mate to incubate, and another clutch that she incubates herself.

○ The partridge family includes more than 90 species of partridge and francolin. These birds feed mainly on seeds.

○ In parts of Europe and North America, partridges are reared in captivity and then released and shot for sport.

▼ *Gambel's quails are gamebirds that live in deserts in the USA and Mexico. Sometimes Gambel's quails gather in groups of up to 200 birds.*

▼ *The wild turkey of North America lives in forest and scrub. It feeds on seeds, nuts, berries, leaves, insects and other small creatures that it finds on the ground. Farmyard turkeys have been bred from this wild relative.*

○ The helmeted guinea fowl, originally from Africa, was domesticated in Europe more than 2500 years ago.

○ A group of partridges is called a 'covey'. A covey usually consists of a male and female breeding pair and their young, plus a few other birds.

▲ *Wild guinea fowl are African birds named after a section of the west coast of Africa. They are noisy birds that live in flocks on the ground. At night, the guinea fowl sleep in trees.*

Colourful pheasant

The male common pheasant is a beautiful bird, with iridescent plumage on its head, bright red wattles (fleshy patches) around its eyes and sometimes a white neck ring. Originally from Asia, it has been introduced in Europe and North America, where it is widespread.

Find out more

Courtship pp. 332–333

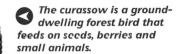

❍ The mallee fowl lays its eggs in a mound of plant matter. The heat given off by the rotting vegetation incubates the eggs. The chicks dig their way out of the mound after they hatch.

❍ Domestic chickens are descended from the red jungle fowl, which was first domesticated 5000 years ago. The jungle fowl still lives wild in Southeast Asia.

❍ All 49 species of wild pheasant are from Asia, except the Congo peafowl, which was first discovered in a Central African rainforest in 1936.

◄ *The curassow is a ground-dwelling forest bird that feeds on seeds, berries and small animals.*

❍ The 17 species of grouse live in North America, Europe and northern Asia.

❍ At 87 cm long, the western capercaillie is the biggest member of the grouse family. The female is only 60 cm long.

❍ During summer, western capercaillies eat buds, berries and leaves, but in winter they survive almost entirely on pine needles.

❍ To attract females and challenge rival males in the breeding season, the ruffed grouse makes a drumming sound with his wings.

❍ The 45 species of curassow and guan live from the southern USA to northern Argentina. The great curassow is 95 cm long and weighs 4.8 kg.

◄ *The crested wood partridge lives in woodland and forest in Southeast Asia. It feeds on insects, snails, fruit and seeds.*

Amazing

The crested argus pheasant has the largest and longest tail feathers of any bird, at up to 170 cm long and 12 cm wide.

▼ *A solitary bird, Temminck's Tragopan lives at altitudes up to 4600 m. In courtship, the male inflates his colourful throat wattle, which expands to cover his breast.*

Dancing display

The male argus pheasant of Southeast Asia has very long, ornamental wing feathers to impress his possible breeding partners. He prepares a special arena in a forest clearing by moving leaves and plants. Then he calls to the females before beginning his leaping, dancing courtship display.

▲ *The plumage of female gamebirds like this spruce grouse is usually drab brown for camouflage. This helps to protect the birds from enemies while they sit on their eggs and look after their chicks.*

Kingfishers and Relatives

Kingfishers are related to birds such as bee-eaters, rollers, hoopoes, todies and hornbills. Most of the birds in these groups have big bills and brightly coloured feathers. Kingfishers usually have a large head, a short neck and a pointed beak.

◀ Wood-hoopoes are busy birds that cackle constantly as they flap through the trees. They poke their long bills into bark to search for insects.

◯ A European bee-eater eats about 200 bees a day. Its summer diet is mainly bumblebees, and in winter it eats honeybees and dragonflies.

◀ Rollers use a diving method of hunting that is typical of this group of birds. They catch their prey in mid-air or by swooping to the ground.

◯ Motmots range in size from the 19-cm long tody motmot to the 53-cm long upland motmot. The ten motmot species live in forests from Mexico to northern Argentina. They all have downward-curving beaks, with jagged edges.

◯ Wood-hoopoes live in Africa, where they nest in tree holes. Groups of wood-hoopoes make loud calls and rocking movements, and pass bark to each other, in a display of territorial ownership.

Amazing

The kookaburra is the largest kingfisher. It is named after the sound of its call, which resembles noisy laughter.

◯ The 16 or so species of roller and ground roller live in southern Europe, Asia, Africa and Australia.

◯ Rollers get their name from their spectacular courtship flight, which involves rolling and somersaulting as they dive towards land.

◯ The cuckoo-roller lives only in Madagascar and the Comoros Islands in the Indian Ocean, where it catches chameleons and insects.

Find out more

Bee-eaters p. 324

Hornbill prison

The female hornbill lays her eggs in prison! The male hornbill walls up his mate and her eggs in a tree hole. He blocks the entrance to the hole with mud, leaving only a small opening. The female looks after the eggs and the male brings food, passing it through the opening. Even after the eggs have hatched, the female stays in the hole with her young for a few weeks while the male supplies her with food.

○ The broad-billed roller catches winged termites in the air. A roller will devour as many as 800 termites in a single evening.

○ Most kingfishers feed on fish. They catch their prey by plunging like an arrow into the water and grabbing the victim in their spear-shaped beak. They return to their perch with their prey.

○ A kingfisher may stun a slippery, struggling fish by beating it against a branch or rock before swallowing it.

○ The five species of tody are all insect-eating birds that live on the tropical Caribbean islands. Todies make their nests in 30-cm long tunnels, which they dig with their beaks.

○ Todies are tiny birds with mainly bright green plumage. Their hunting method is to sit and wait on a branch, then quickly fly into the open to grab a butterfly, beetle or other insect flying past. Todies can hover in mid-air almost as well as hummingbirds. This allows them to pick insects off leaves.

▶ *The long, pointed beak of most kingfishers, such as this malachite kingfisher, is ideally suited to catching fish.*

Grass diver

The tiny African pygmy kingfisher dives not into water, like the common kingfisher, but into grass, where it snatches grasshoppers and beetles.

◀ *The 50-cm long yellow-billed hornbill lives in southern Africa. All hornbills have large beaks. In many species, the beak is topped with a casque made of keratin and bone. A male hornbill may carry more than 60 small fruits at a time to his nest to regurgitate (cough up) for his young.*

343

Parrots and Relatives

Parrots are among the most lively, inquisitive and intelligent of all birds. A typical parrot has colourful feathers, a large head, big beady eyes and a strong, hooked beak to crush even the hardest seeds.

Different plumage

Male and female eclectus parrots have very different plumage. The male (shown here on the right) is bright green with a yellow bill; the female (left) is red with a blue belly and a black bill.

○ Parrots make many calls, and some mimic other sounds, including the human voice. The combination of colour, inquisitive behaviour, copying our speech, the ability to learn tricks, and being long-lived have all helped to make parrots popular pets.

○ The only flightless parrot is the New Zealand kakapo, or owl parrot, which is now extremely rare.

○ The palm cockatoo has an amazing courtship display. The male bird holds a stick in its foot and makes a loud drumming noise by beating the stick against the side of a tree.

Amazing

The hanging parrot hangs upside down from tree branches like a bat.

○ There are about 350 species in the parrot group, including birds such as macaws, budgerigars, lories and cockatoos. They live in Central and South America, Africa, southern Asia and Australasia

○ Macaws nest in tree holes high in rainforest trees. The female lays two eggs, which her mate helps to incubate. The young macaws stay with their parents for up to 2 years.

○ Macaws swallow beakfuls of clay from riverbanks. The clay may help to protect the birds from the effects of some plants and seeds that they eat, many of which are poisonous to other animals.

○ The pattern of feathers on each side of the red-and-green macaw's face is unique – no two birds look identical.

○ At 85 cm long, the scarlet macaw of South and Central America is one of the largest members of the parrot family.

The pet trade

People buying and selling caged birds has led to some species becoming endangered. Some pet birds, such as budgerigars, are bred in captivity, but others, including parrots, are taken from the wild, even though this is now illegal. The beautiful hyacinth macaw (shown here) used to be common in South American rainforests, but it is now rare as a result of people collecting the birds from the wild to supply the pet trade.

A *Rainbow lorikeets are active, noisy birds. They make shrill calls to each other as they fly about in the trees, and chatter constantly while feeding on seeds, fruit, nectar, pollen, berries, leaves and insects.*

○ With its bright red feathers, the scarlet macaw is also one of the most beautiful of all the parrots. It can fly at up to 56 km/h as it searches the rainforest for fruit, nuts and seeds to eat.

○ Cockatoos have a distinctive crest of feathers on the head, which they raise when they are alarmed or excited.

Find out more

Rainforest birds pp. 358–359

Sulphur-crested cockatoo
This large, yellow-crested bird forms flocks to feed on seeds and fruit. It is seen in parks and gardens in north and east Australia, and soon becomes tame at the bird table.

Gang-gang cockatoo
The male of this small cockatoo species makes a call like a rusty, creaking gate hinge. In the breeding season, he develops a bright red head.

Pink cockatoo
The white plumage of this tropical bird is flushed with soft pink. The pink cockatoo's head crest displays bands of scarlet and yellow when spread.

Palm cockatoo
Unusually dark for a cockatoo, this large species has a tall head crest. It uses its huge bill to crack open even extremely hard palm nuts and similar seeds. It inhabits tropical forests.

Hyacinth macaw
The world's largest parrot, from tropical South America, the hyacinth macaw feeds mainly in the trees, but it will also eat fallen nuts and fruit off the ground.

Red-tailed black cockatoo
These noisy birds gather in flocks of 200 or more. The scarlet patches on the tail shine brightly as the cockatoo flaps along slowly.

Pesquet's parrot
This parrot is a fruit-eating species that lives in Papua new Guinea. Pesquet's parrot digs a nest hole inside a dead tree and lays one or two eggs inside.

Long-billed corella
This cockatoo is unusual because it spends much time on the ground, digging for roots with its strong beak.

Sulphur-crested cockatoo

Gang-gang cockatoo

Pink cockatoo

Palm cockatoo

Hyacinth macaw

Red-tailed black cockatoo

Pesquet's parrot

Long-billed corella

Kea

Yellow-tailed black cockatoo

Kea
The kea is named after its piercing call. It lives in New Zealand and uses its long upper beak to tear flesh from fruits – and to rip flesh off dead animals.

Yellow-tailed black cockatoo
Dark except for its long, yellow-edged tail and yellow cheeks, this parrot from Tasmania and southeast Australia has a weird wailing call.

Birds of Prey

Some of the largest and fiercest birds are raptors, or birds of prey. They have powerful toes with sharp claws called talons to seize prey, and a pointed, hooked beak to tear off lumps of flesh. Most birds of prey have large eyes and hunt by sight.

The distinctive, adaptable bateleur eagle is widespread across Africa in grassland, mountain and desert regions.

The bearded vulture, unlike other vultures, has face and neck feathers.

The black eagle is large and black in colour, with a distinct V mark on its back.

The osprey's body measures 55–58 cm long, and it has an impressive 1.6-m wingspan. The females are slightly larger than the males.

The lappet-faced vulture has very broad wings. These are ideal for soaring high above the plains of its African home, searching for food.

Spikes under toes grip slippery fish

Talon

The laughing falcon's loud, repeated two-part call sounds slightly like the 'ha-ha!' of human laughter.

Bald eagles eat carrion (dead animals) and prey such as small birds and fish. They steal meals from other birds of prey and fight among themselves over food.

Biggest eagles

American harpy	91–110 cm
Philippine	86–102 cm
Golden	76–99 cm
Martial	81–96 cm
Verreaux's	81–96 cm
Bald	79–94 cm
Crowned	81–91 cm
New Guinea harpy	75–90 cm
White-tailed sea	70–90 cm
Imperial	79–84 cm
African fish	74–84 cm

Find out more

Owls – night hunters p. 331

Amazing

The Andean condor is the largest bird of prey. It weighs up to 12 kg and has a wingspan of over 3m.

One of the most powerful of all birds, Steller's sea eagle has a wingspan of 2.4 m and a massive beak to rip the flesh from fish, dead seals and beached whales.

The crested serpent eagle has a head crest of feathers. It hunts snakes and lizards as well as the usual prey.

The Egyptian vulture steals birds' eggs. It cracks the eggs by dropping them on the ground or by throwing stones at them.

Goshawks launch themselves off a high perch to catch birds and mammals.

Eleonora's falcon specializes in hunting small birds. It breeds unusually late in the summer, in colonies on rocky islands in the Mediterranean Sea.

The Jackal buzzard hunts mainly in mountainous country. It can be seen hovering on air currents searching for small mammals, birds and snakes to eat.

The sparrowhawk preys mostly on other birds, ranging in size from tits to pheasants.

Fish eagles use their lethally sharp talons to snatch fish from the water. Spikes on their toes help them to hold slippery prey.

Swans, Ducks and Geese

Most of these familiar waterbirds have broad bodies, webbed feet and flattened bills. In many species, the males are brightly coloured, while the females have drab, mottled brown feathers. The young birds are able to feed themselves soon after hatching.

○ Torrent ducks live by fast-flowing streams in South America's Andes Mountains. When young ducklings hatch from their eggs, they leap straight into the swirling waters.

○ There are more than 100 duck species, living all over the world, except in Antarctica.

○ Steamer ducks get their name from their habit of paddling over water with their wings as well as their feet, at speeds of up to 28 km/h.

○ Ducks have been domesticated for more than 2000 years for their meat and eggs.

◄ *The North American Trumpeter swan certainly lives up to its name, its loud, bugle–like cries carry over great distances. Trumpeters breed mainly in the far north of North America, especially Alaska. They move south for the winter, but only as far as the open water along the Canadian coast and on large lakes in national parks.*

○ Ducks feed on fish, shellfish, leaves and seeds.

○ Like cuckoos, the black-headed duck lays its eggs in the nests of other birds, particularly herons.

▼ *Black-necked swans are the smallest species of swan. The young swans, or cygnets, are light grey in colour, with black bills and feet. They sometimes ride on their parents' backs.*

Amazing

Barnacle geese make barking and yapping calls that sound like small dogs fighting.

◄ *Ducks, such as these white–faced ducks, are highly sociable birds that can adapt to a variety of aquatic environments.*

Find out more

Canada goose p. 364

○ The cinnamon teal is named from the glowing, rusty-red shades of the feathers on the head and body of the male, or drake. He also has bright, striped-looking wings folded along his back. But the female, as in most duck species, is a dull mottled brown.

▲ *The black swan makes a nest of sticks and other plant material in shallow water and lays up to six eggs. Both parents help to incubate the eggs.*

○ Whooper, trumpeter and mute swans are among the heaviest flying birds, weighing up to 16 kg.

○ Geese feed mostly on leaves, and can eat as many as 100 blades of grass in one minute.

○ Although quieter than other swans, the mute swan is not really mute, but makes many snorting and hissing calls.

○ Male swans are known as 'cobs' and females as 'pens', while baby swans are called 'cygnets'.

Fishing underwater

The red-breasted merganser is a saw-billed duck, so named because it has a serrated edge to its beak, which helps it keep a grip on fish caught under water. It flies low and fast over the water's surface, and is often seen swimming along with its head submerged as it scans for fish. After diving and catching a fish, the red-breasted merganser brings it to the surface to swallow it. The duck then performs a wing-flapping display, followed by a drink of sea water.

▲ *The male eider duck (above) has more striking colours than the brown and grey female. The female eider sometimes goes without food for two or three weeks while sitting on the eggs. After hatching, the ducklings are often looked after by one or more 'aunts', who oversee several broods.*

○ Most swans are white, but Australian black swans are not. Because of their unusual colour, they have been taken to lakes and ponds around the world as a dark, contrasting addition to the local white swans. In their original home of Australia, black swans breed in large colonies and often form huge flocks.

◄ *The male mandarin duck shows off his elaborate, colourful plumage in special courtship displays.*

Breeding pairs

The female and male Canada geese stay together to raise their family. They may keep together as a pair for several years. The pair nest in a natural hollow on dry ground close to water, lining the hollow with down feathers and grass.

Ocean and Shore

Many birds hunt for food in the oceans but rest and breed along the shore. Seabirds have waterproofed feathers, webbed feet and sharp bills to catch fish. Nesting in colonies on cliffs keeps the young birds safe from predators.

▶ *Puffins nest in burrows. While many other birds jostle for space on high cliff ledges, puffins dig a burrow on the clifftop. Here, they lay a single egg. Both parents feed the chick for the first six weeks.*

○ At up to 79 cm long, the great black-backed gull is the giant of the gull group. The little gull is one of the smallest gulls, at 28 cm long.

○ The kittiwake spends much more time at sea than other gulls. It usually only comes to land in the breeding season. This bird has very short legs, and it very rarely walks.

○ Fish and squid are the main food of shearwaters, but giant petrels also feed on carrion, and can rip apart whales and seals with their powerful beaks.

○ The Manx shearwater lays a single egg in a burrow. The male and female take turns at incubating the egg, and feeding one another.

○ Young shearwaters are fed on a rich mixture of regurgitated fish and squid, and may put on weight so quickly that they are soon heavier than their parents.

○ The guillemot can dive in water to a depth of 180 m as it hunts.

○ The auk family includes 22 species of diving birds, including auks, guillemots, puffins and razorbills. They live in and around the North Pacific, Atlantic and Arctic Oceans.

○ The common guillemot is the largest of the auks, at about 45 cm long and 1 kg in weight. The least auklet is the smallest auk, measuring 16 cm long and with a weight of just 90 g.

Amazing

Albatrosses can soar high over the waves for hours on end without flapping their wings, covering great distances with little effort.

Gannet dive-bomber

The gannet makes an amazing dive from a height of up to 30 m above the sea to catch fish. This seabird spots its prey as it soars above the ocean. Then with wings swept back and neck and beak held straight out in front, the gannet plunges like a dive-bomber. It enters the water, seizes its prey and surfaces a few seconds later.

▲ *There are about 48 species of gull found on shores and islands all over the world.*

Find out more

Wandering albatross p. 314

Pear-shaped egg

Guillemots their lay eggs on cliffs. A guillemot egg is pear-shaped, which means that the egg rolls round in a circle if it is pushed or knocked, and does not fall off the edge of the cliff.

▶ *The lower half of the skimmer's beak is longer than the upper half. This allows it to catch fish in a special way. The skimmer flies just above the water, with the lower part of its beak just below the surface. When it touches a fish, the skimmer snaps the upper part of its beak down to trap the prey.*

▶ *The Manx shearwater wanders widely over the ocean for weeks on each feeding trip, covering up to 500 km each day. Then it returns to its breeding colony, where thousands of these shearwaters nest in burrows.*

Curlew

▶ *The seashore provides birds with a rich source of food, including crabs, burrowing worms and shellfish. Curlews use their long, downward-curving bill to extract animals buried deep in mud or sand. Oystercatchers feed mainly limpets, mussels and other shellfish. The oystercatchers break open the shells by smashing them against rocks, or by severing the muscle that holds the two parts of the shell together.*

Oystercatcher

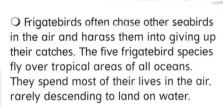

○ Frigatebirds often chase other seabirds in the air and harass them into giving up their catches. The five frigatebird species fly over tropical areas of all oceans. They spend most of their lives in the air, rarely descending to land on water.

○ The white-tailed tropicbird is noted for its amazing tail streamers, which measure up to 40 cm long.

○ The three species of tropicbird are all expert in the air. They can dive into the sea to find prey, but cannot walk on land. With their legs set far back on their bodies, they are only able to drag themselves along.

▲ *The white ibis lives on coastal islands, as well as freshwater ponds and marshes. It feeds on crayfish, insects, snakes, fish and crabs. It nests in grassy clumps and also in trees, up to a height of 15 m.*

○ Oystercatchers use their strong, blade-like beak to prise mussels off rocks and open their shells.

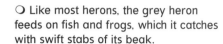

Rivers, Lakes and Swamps

A wide variety of birds live in wetland habitats, from herons, storks and pelicans to grebes, kingfishers and coots. There is plenty of food in the water, and the reedbeds and riverbanks provide safe nesting places.

◆ *The pelican collects fish in the big pouch that hangs beneath its long beak. When the pelican pushes its beak underwater, the pouch stretches and fills with water – and fish. When the pelican then lifts its head up, the water drains out of the pouch, leaving any food behind.*

❍ Young flamingos have grey feathers at first. Adult birds get their pink colour from pigments in the algae that they eat.

❍ The greater flamingo lives in huge flocks around lakes and deltas in Europe, Asia, parts of Africa, the Caribbean and Central America. It may live to be at least 50 years old.

▶ *A small bird called the dipper is well-adapted to river life. It usually lives around fast-flowing streams and can swim and dive well. It can even walk along the bottom of a stream, snapping up prey such as insects and other small creatures. The five different species of dipper live in North and South America, Asia and Europe.*

❍ Like most herons, the grey heron feeds on fish and frogs, which it catches with swift stabs of its beak.

❍ Cattle egrets nest in colonies – there may be more than 100 nests close together in one tree.

❍ Coots are the most aquatic of all the rails. They dive in search of plants and water insects to eat.

❍ The female moorhen makes a nest of dead leaves at the water's edge. The male helps to incubate the 5–11 eggs.

❍ Finfoots are aquatic birds that feed in the water on fish, frogs and shellfish. There is one species each in Africa, Southeast Asia and Central and South America.

Amazing

The green-backed heron of Japan tempts fish with 'bait', such as pieces of bread or feathers.

▲ *The painted stork lives in southern Asia, where it nests in trees on platforms made of sticks. It wades through freshwater lakes and marshes on its long legs, searching for food. The stork opens its downward-curving bill underwater and swishes it from side to side. The beak snaps shut as soon as it makes contact with a fish.*

Find out more

Filter-feeder p. 324

○ Kingfishers make their nests in tunnels along riverbanks. Using their strong beaks, a male and female pair excavate a tunnel up to 60 cm long, and then make a nesting chamber at the end. The female lays up to eight eggs, which both parents take turns to look after.

○ The male swan stays near the nest to defend his family against predators. When danger approaches, he spreads his wings, bends his neck, opens his beak, and hisses loudly to deter enemies. He will even peck at the intruder it if comes too close.

Heron courtship

The heron's beak and legs become brighter in colour during the breeding season when it is time to mate. It also moults its old feathers and grows new, brighter-coloured ones as part of its breeding appearance. Herons carry out a ritual 'dance' for their partners. This helps each bird to check that the other is fit and healthy, and thus a suitable mate for breeding.

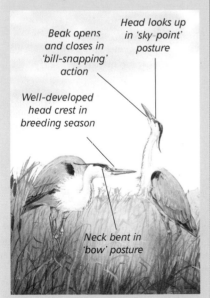

Head looks up in 'sky-point' posture

Beak opens and closes in 'bill-snapping' action

Well-developed head crest in breeding season

Neck bent in 'bow' posture

The yellow-billed stork is a common waterbird in Africa, especially in the eastern part of the continent. It lives on lakes, marshes and sometimes on coasts. Like certain other storks and also the bald ibis, it has bare skin around its face. This allows it to dip its head in and out of muddy water without getting its feathers dirty.

○ Horned grebes build a large nest of floating water weeds. The female and male take turns to sit on, or incubate, the eggs. Both the parents also feed the chicks and take turns to give them piggyback rides.

○ The male bittern's mating call is an extremely loud 'BOOM!' – almost like a cannon going off. However, at other times the bittern is a very secretive bird, well camouflaged among wetland reeds and rushes by its stripes and motionless, skygazing posture.

Lily-trotting jacana

The jacana is sometimes called the 'lily trotter', because of its unique way of moving over the leaves of water plants. Young jacanas often hide underneath floating leaves if danger threatens.

The long legs of a flamingo enable it to wade into extremely salty water without damaging its plumage. Flamingos use their feet to stir up mud in the shallows so that they can feed on bottom-dwelling animals.

In the Desert

Birds that live in deserts either get most of the moisture they need from their food, or they fly long distances to find water sources. During the hottest part of the day, these birds rest in the shade. Some desert species are active at night, when it is cooler.

Elf owls

The elf owl is one of the smallest owls in the world, measuring 14 cm long. It lives in the deserts of southwestern USA. It hunts at night, mainly catching insects and scorpions, but also mice and small birds, and on rare occasions snakes, and lizards. Elf owls may be attracted to bright lights such as campfires in their quest for flying insects.

❍ The little cinnamon quail-thrush of Australia hides in a burrow during the day to escape the hot sun. It emerges in the evening to find seeds and insects to eat.

❍ The verdin lives in the deserts of Mexico and the southwest of the USA, where it makes its nest on a cactus plant. The cactus spines protect the verdin and its eggs from predators.

❍ With few trees and bushes to perch in, desert birds spend most of their lives on the ground.

❍ The mourning dove is a desert bird of the southwestern USA. A fast flyer, it often travels great distances to find food and water.

❍ Turkey vultures soar over the American deserts searching for carrion (dead bodies) to eat.

❍ Insects are a favourite food of many desert birds, but some catch small mammals and others eat seeds.

▲ *The eagle-sized turkey vulture is the most widespread of the American vultures. In flight, it rolls and tilts its body from side to side.*

❍ Most desert birds are active at dawn and towards sunset, resting in shade for much of the day.

❍ Owls, poorwills and nightjars cool down in the desert heat by opening their mouths wide and fluttering their throats.

❍ Water is so precious in the desert that the roadrunner reabsorbs water from its droppings before excreting them.

❍ To keep out of the hot sun, burrowing owls rest and nest inside underground burrows dug by small mammals, such as rabbits and prairie dogs.

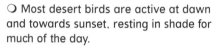

Elf owl

◀ *The fast-moving greater roadrunner lives in the western USA, where it preys on small snakes, as well as insects and mice. The greater roadrunner, a type of cuckoo, can move at a speed of 20 km/h or more on land.*

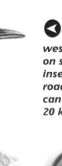

Find out more

Elf owl p. 328

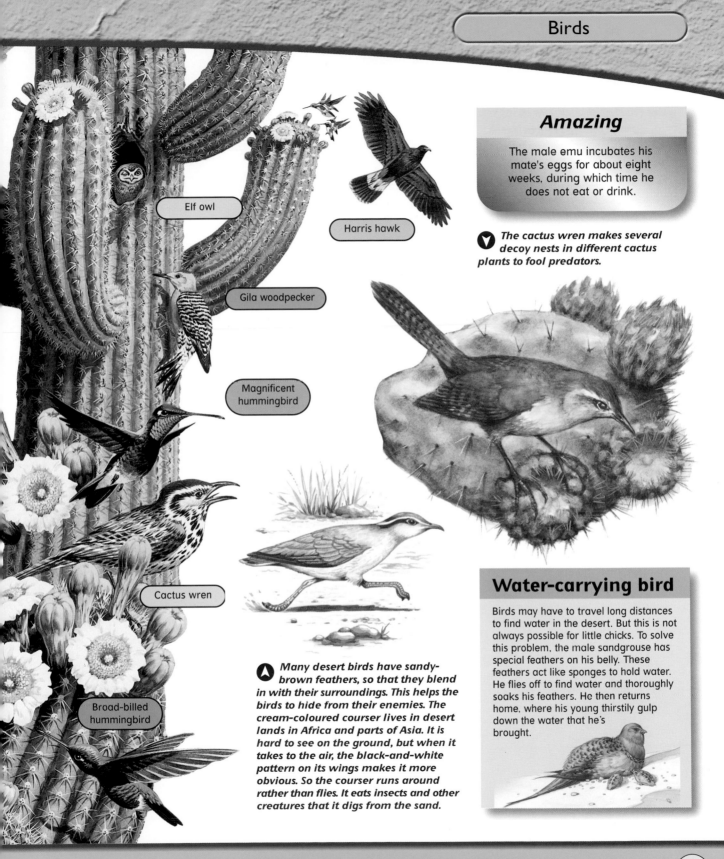

Amazing

The male emu incubates his mate's eggs for about eight weeks, during which time he does not eat or drink.

▼ The cactus wren makes several decoy nests in different cactus plants to fool predators.

Elf owl

Harris hawk

Gila woodpecker

Magnificent hummingbird

Cactus wren

Broad-billed hummingbird

▲ Many desert birds have sandy-brown feathers, so that they blend in with their surroundings. This helps the birds to hide from their enemies. The cream-coloured courser lives in desert lands in Africa and parts of Asia. It is hard to see on the ground, but when it takes to the air, the black-and-white pattern on its wings makes it more obvious. So the courser runs around rather than flies. It eats insects and other creatures that it digs from the sand.

Water-carrying bird

Birds may have to travel long distances to find water in the desert. But this is not always possible for little chicks. To solve this problem, the male sandgrouse has special feathers on his belly. These feathers act like sponges to hold water. He flies off to find water and thoroughly soaks his feathers. He then returns home, where his young thirstily gulp down the water that he's brought.

Grassland Birds

Grasslands are home to a variety of seed-eating and insect-eating birds, as well as carrion-feeding birds such as vultures. Long-legged birds, such as ostriches and rheas, can see over the tall grasses to watch for danger.

○ The yellow-billed oxpecker of the African grasslands sits on buffaloes' backs, pulling ticks from their skin.

○ Cattle egrets accompany large grassland mammals, feeding on the insects that live on or around them.

○ The crested oropendola is a grassland bird of South America. It hunts insects and other small creatures.

○ North America's largest owl, the great horned owl, includes quail and other grassland birds in its diet.

○ One of the biggest creatures on the South American pampas is the rhea, which feeds mainly on grass.

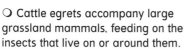
▽ *Rheas cannot fly, but they can sprint at speeds of up to 50 km/h. They use their wings for balance when running.*

○ The western meadowlark makes a ground nest of grass and pine needles in prairie grasslands.

○ A fast walker, the long-legged secretary bird of the African grasslands may travel 30 km a day in search of snakes, insects and birds.

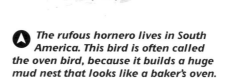

▲ *The rufous hornero lives in South America. This bird is often called the oven bird, because it builds a huge mud nest that looks like a baker's oven.*

○ Different species of vulture eat different parts of a body – lammergeiers (bearded vultures) even eat the bones of their prey.

○ In hot weather, some vultures cool down by squirting urine onto their legs. As the urine evaporates, it takes body heat away with it.

○ The female white-backed vulture lays one egg in a large stick nest made high in a tree. She incubates it for 56 days, during which time she is fed by the male. Both parents care for the chick.

○ The lappet-faced vulture is the largest vulture in Africa – it measures about 1 m long and has a huge 2.8 m wingspan. It also has a bigger beak than any other bird of prey.

▲ *Oxpeckers pluck lice, ticks and fleas from the skin of grassland mammals, such as buffalo or oxen. They also peck at wounds to keep them open, so they they can feed on the animal's blood.*

Woven nest

The male weaver bird makes a nest from grass, leaves and stems. He knots and weaves the pieces together to make a long nest, which hangs from the branch of a tree. The nest provides a warm, cosy home for the eggs and young. Its long entrance makes it very hard for any predator to reach inside.

The male weaver bird twists strips of leaves around a branch or twig

He first builds a round nesting chamber

Then he weaves a long entrance tunnel to help protect the eggs

Find out more

Ostrich p. 314

Long, bare neck

A vulture gets right inside a carcass with its long, flexible neck to peck at pieces of flesh with its sharp beak. The neck is mainly bare skin and has no large feathers, which would become soaked with blood.

▼ *Small and long-legged, the burrowing owl lives in grasslands throughout the Americas. They usually hunt in the evening, catching small birds, frogs and reptiles.*

❍ One of the largest and most powerful falcons, the saker is a bird of open country, especially dry scrub and steppe (grassland). It is found from eastern Europe across Central Asia to China. This majestic hunter seizes ground-living mammals, such as hares, marmots and pikas, and also preys on other birds.

▼ *The lappet-faced vulture scavenges for its food. It glides over the deserts of Africa and the Middle East, searching for dead animals or the scraps left behind by hunters such as lions. When it spots a meal, the vulture swoops down and attacks the carcass with its strong hooked bill. It usually dominates other species of vulture at carcasses, and often robs them of food.*

▼ *The lammergeier is also known as the bearded vulture, after the stiff black feathers that hang down from its face like a beard.*

Amazing

Flocks of one million or more red-billed quelea move like clouds over the African grasslands.

Rainforest Birds

Rainforests contain a greater variety of birds than any other habitat. The weather is warm all year round, and the trees and other plants provide plenty of food and safe nesting places. The birds live at different levels in the trees, to avoid competing for the same resources.

○ The king vulture of South America is the only vulture to live in rainforest. As well as feeding on carrion, it also preys on mammals and reptiles.

○ The sunbittern lives along river banks in the rainforests of South America, feeding on frogs, insects and other creatures.

○ The muscovy duck is now familiar in farmyards and parks in many parts of the world. However, it originally came from the rainforests of Central and South America.

○ The hoatzin builds its nest over rainforest rivers, so that if its chicks are threatened, they can quickly drop into the water to escape.

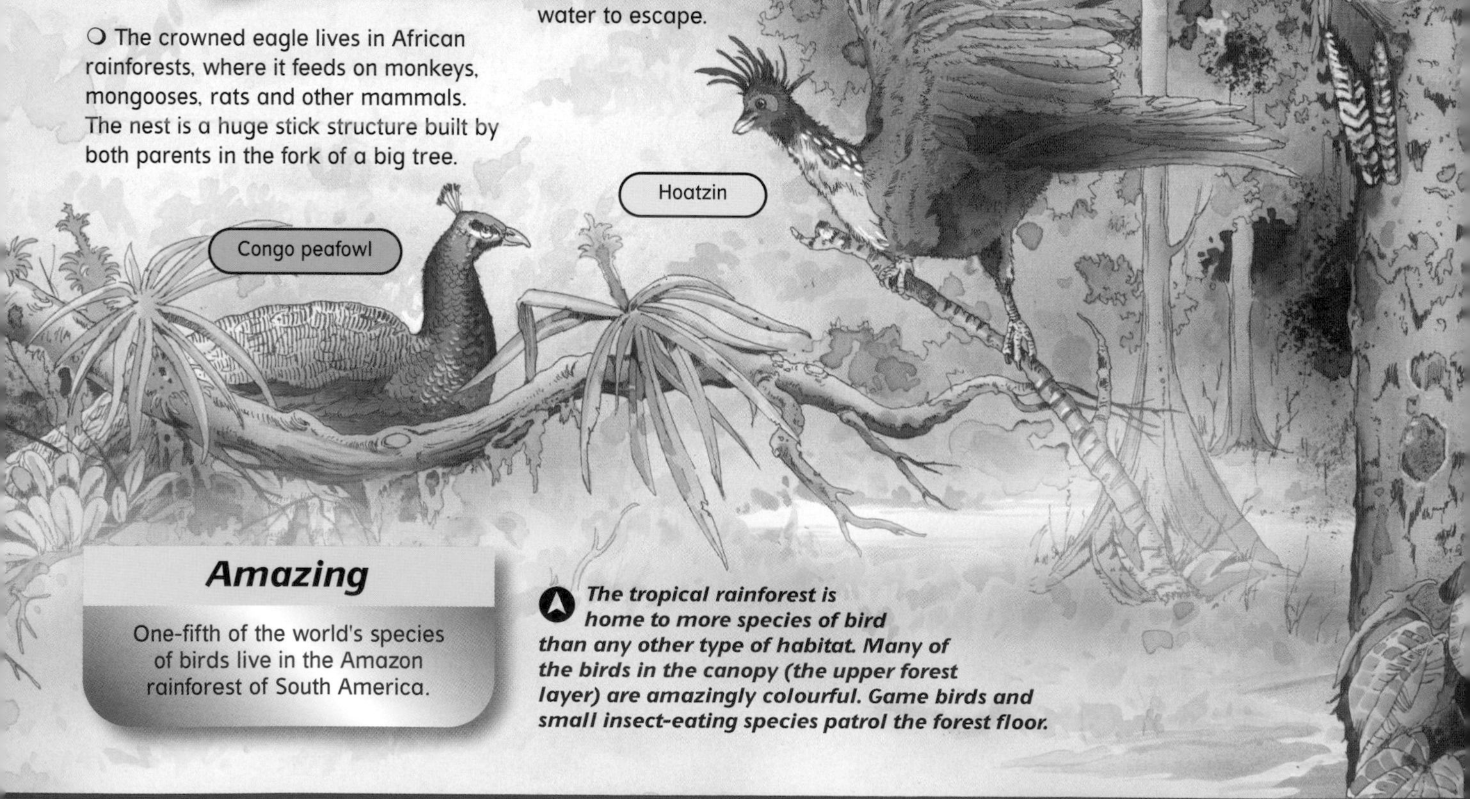

Hyacinth macaw

South America's Hyacinth macaw grows up to 1 m long. It nests in tree holes, laying a clutch of 2–3 eggs. Usually only one chick survives.

○ The crowned eagle lives in African rainforests, where it feeds on monkeys, mongooses, rats and other mammals. The nest is a huge stick structure built by both parents in the fork of a big tree.

Harpy eagle

Hoatzin

Congo peafowl

Amazing

One-fifth of the world's species of birds live in the Amazon rainforest of South America.

The tropical rainforest is home to more species of bird than any other type of habitat. Many of the birds in the canopy (the upper forest layer) are amazingly colourful. Game birds and small insect-eating species patrol the forest floor.

○ The 12 species of frogmouth live in the rainforests of Southeast Asia and Australia. Frogmouths feed on the wing, trapping insects in their wide, gaping mouth.

○ The colourful, long-tailed quetzal lives in Central America. It was sacred to the ancient Maya and Aztec civilizations, and it is the national bird of Guatemala.

○ To get airborne, the male quetzal jumps out of a tree backwards, to avoid tangling his extremely long tail feathers with the branches.

○ Toucans feed mostly on fruit, which they pluck from branches with their long beaks. They also eat some insects and small animals such as lizards.

○ Toucans usually nest in tree holes. The female lays 2–4 eggs, and the male helps with the incubation, which takes about 15 days.

○ The bearded greenbul lives in African rainforests and has a beautiful whistling call that it uses to keep in touch with others of its species in the dense jungle.

○ The quetzal has magnificent tail feathers, which are up to 90 cm long.

○ The scarlet macaw is one of the largest parrots in the world. It moves in flocks of 20 or so that screech loudly as they fly from tree to tree feeding on fruit and leaves.

○ The male red jungle fowl uses his 'cock-a-doodle-doo' call to attract females and warn off rival males.

○ Like the other 41 species in the bird of paradise group, the king bird of paradise lives mainly in rainforest. It feeds chiefly on fruits, along with some insects, frogs and other small animals. During his mating display the male holds out his wings and vibrates them like a fast-shaking fan.

Quetzal

Scarlet macaw

Jungle fowl

Crimson topaz

In the Amazon rainforest, a crimson topaz hummingbird darts across a sunlit clearing, its two long, black tail feathers trailing behind. This is a male impressing his mate. The female lacks the tail streamers, but she too has glittering plumage. She differs from most female hummingbirds, which have a duller colouring than the males to camouflage them while they are nesting.

Find out more

The pet trade p. 344

359

Forest and Woodland Birds

Coniferous forests and deciduous woodlands are rich habitats for birds because of the food and nesting places they provide. The cold winter weather does cause problems for the birds though. Many birds migrate to warmer places in winter.

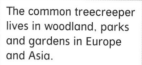

The common treecreeper lives in woodland, parks and gardens in Europe and Asia.

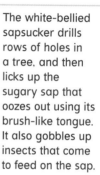

The song thrush makes its nest from dried stems lined with mud and rotting wood, bound with saliva to make a dry hard cup. The female lays 4–5 pale-blue, speckled eggs inside the nest.

The red-breasted nuthatch paints the entrance of its tree hole nest with sticky pine resin. This may stop insects and other creatures from getting into the nest, but the birds also have to take care not to get their own feathers stuck.

The white-bellied sapsucker drills rows of holes in a tree, and then licks up the sugary sap that oozes out using its brush-like tongue. It also gobbles up insects that come to feed on the sap.

The rifleman is a common sight on the North and South islands of New Zealand.

Great tits hatch blind and helpless, and are fed by their parents for about three weeks. They may make 1000 trips each day to find food for the young.

The jay is a shy bird and makes its nest low in a tree from twigs and earth, lined with roots and hair. It eats crops and animal prey, such as mice and small birds.

The bohemian waxwing makes a nest of twigs, moss and grass, usually in a conifer tree. The female incubates the 4–6 eggs, while the male keeps her fed.

Find out more
Honeyguide bird p. 325

The black-throated honeyguide eats beeswax, bee grubs, termites, ants, and the eggs of other bird species. Like the cuckoo, it is a brood parasite, meaning that it lays its eggs in the nests of other birds.

The tawny owl nests in tree holes, but it also uses old crow and heron nests, and squirrel dreys, as well as holes in farm buildings. The young owls are helpless at first and take 32–37 days to grow their feathers.

Amazing

Up to 50 per cent of all woodland bird species make their nests in tree holes.

The red-eyed vireo breeds in North America in the summer.

The pileated woodpecker has white neck stripes and a scarlet crest, making it easily recognizable. It lives in parts of the USA and Canada, in parkland and forests.

The willow warbler is full of nervous energy, and is forever on the move, flicking its wings as it busily forages for insects. A fine singer, the warbler sings its song from trees and bushes while moving through foliage in search of food. It also sings while flying.

When alarmed, the common pheasant runs away, crouching low to the ground. If danger is close by, the bird erupts into the air with a startling clatter of wings, before flying and gliding to safety.

Wrynecks resemble woodpeckers, but they lack the stiff tail feathers. They twist their heads oddly to look around when alarmed, hence their name.

Wild rock pigeons live in rocky areas in southern Europe, Asia and northern Africa. The pigeons that you might see in towns and cities are descended from this species.

Birds from Cold Places

The world's coldest places – near the poles or high on mountains – are extremely challenging habitats for birds. Species adapted to the cold may have thick feathers or layers of fat under the skin to keep them warm. Many birds migrate to escape the coldest weather.

High-living bird

Mountain-dwelling snow finches nest on rocky ledges at altitudes up to 5000 m. They can sometimes be seen eating food scraps left at open-air tables in ski resorts.

○ Some birds nest so high in the mountains that their chicks are safe from almost any predator. The alpine chough breeds at altitudes of more than 4000 m.

○ Most birds leave Antarctica in winter, but the southern black-backed gull stays all year round. It feeds on fish and birds' eggs, as well as some carrion.

○ The emperor penguin breeds in colder temperatures than any other bird. It can survive temperatures of –40°C as it incubates its egg.

○ The great skua is the biggest flying bird in Antarctica, at up to 5 kg and 66 cm long.

Scavenging shearwater

The sheathbill lives and breeds solely in Antarctica and its immediate surroundings, such as the Falkland Islands and the southern tip of South America. This aggressive scavenger feeds on young and injured seals and penguins, and also on food scraps from Antarctic research stations.

○ The laysan albatross breeds on central Pacific islands, but spends most of the year flying over the Arctic hunting for schools of fish to eat.

○ Tufted puffins nest only on cliffs and islands in the Arctic North Pacific. One colony of these birds contained as many as one million nests.

○ The Himalayan snowcock lives on the lower slopes of the Himalayan Mountains, where its grey and white feathers hide it among rocks and snow.

○ The Himalayan monal pheasant spends some of the year above the tree line, where it has to dig in the snow with its beak to find insects and other food.

○ Clark's nutcracker is a mountain bird, but weather conditions and availability of food mean that it lives at a variety of altitudes.

○ Most owls hunt at night, under cover of darkness. But nights in the flat, treeless tundra lands of the far north are too long, dark and cold for animals to be out and about, and an owl would have nothing to catch at night. So the snowy owl hunts by day over the tundra. It glides silently and swoops down to grab victims with its talons (claws). It carries the prey to one of its favourite perches and tears it up to eat with its strong, hooked beak.

○ The wallcreeper is an expert climber that can clamber up steep cliffs and walls in its search for insect prey. It lives high in mountains, such as the Alps and the Himalayas.

○ The tundra swan lays its eggs and rears its young in the tundra of the Arctic. The female bird makes a nest on the ground and lays up to five eggs. Both male and female care for the young. In autumn, the whole family migrates, travelling south to spend the winter in warmer lands.

Amazing

Penguins spend up to three-quarters of their life in the water, only coming to land or sea ice in order to breed.

Penguin species

Adélie penguin
African (black-footed or jackass) penguin
Chinstrap penguin
Emperor penguin
Erect-crested penguin
Fjordland crested penguin
Galapagos penguin
Gentoo penguin
Humboldt (Peruvian) penguin
King penguin
Little (blue) penguin
Macaroni penguin
Magellanic penguin
Rockhopper penguin
Royal penguin
Snares Island penguin
Yellow-eyed penguin

Emperor penguin
The largest penguin, at 1.2 m tall, is also the heaviest seabird. Each male holds his partner's single egg on his feet for some 60 days until the chick hatches.

Gentoo penguin
Gentoos feed largely on krill. In years when the krill are scarce, as part of their natural population cycle, gentoos may not try to breed at all.

Royal penguin
Royals live mainly on Macquarie Island, south of New Zealand. They number more than one million birds. Half of these live in a single huge colony.

Adélie penguin
These are the most southerly penguins. They breed on the cold coasts of Antarctica itself, during the brief summer when the water is ice-free.

Yellow-eyed penguin
Found as far north as New Zealand, this is one of the rarest penguins. Yellow-eyed penguins nest in isolated pairs, rather than in large groups or colonies.

Magellanic penguin
These penguins live as far north as Chile and Brazil. By day, their breeding sites resound with noisy, shrieking calls. But silence falls at night, when the penguins retreat into their burrows.

Chinstrap penguin
Named after the dark line on its chin, this is the most numerous penguin. Its large colonies total several million birds.

Rockhopper penguin
The rockhopper jumps with great skill around its stony breeding sites, on the bare and remote islands near Antarctica.

Little penguin
This is the smallest penguin, only 40 cm tall. Most penguins feed by day, but the little penguin does so at dusk, bringing food back to its burrow in the dark.

Emperor

Gentoo

Royal

Adélie

Yellow-eyed

Magellanic

Chinstrap

Rockhopper

Little

Find out more
Emperor penguins p. 320

Migration

Many birds migrate – that is, they make regular journeys each year to find food, water or nesting places, or to avoid bad weather. Not all birds survive, since the journeys are often long and dangerous, and require a lot of energy.

○ Many migrating birds have to build up fat stores to allow them to fly non-stop for many days without food.

○ A migrating bird can fly across the Sahara Desert in 50–60 hours without stopping to 'refuel'.

○ Most birds that migrate long distances fly at night.

○ The snow goose migrates nearly 5000 km, flying south from Arctic Canada at an altitude of 9000 m.

Cuckoo chicks fly south for the winter, about a month after the adult cuckoos have left.

○ Even flightless birds migrate. Emus make journeys on foot of 500 km or more, and penguins migrate in water.

○ Every year at least 5 billion birds migrate from North America to Central and South America.

○ The bobolink breeds in southern Canada and the USA, but migrates to spend the winter in South America.

Amazing

The Arctic tern travels farther each year and sees more hours of daylight than any other creature.

Huge flocks of geese and other birds make long journeys, called migrations, twice a year. They move away from cold regions in autumn, in search of food, and return to them again in spring. The term 'migration' comes from the Latin word migrare, which means 'to go from one place to another'.

Arctic tern   Golden plover   Canada goose

Arctic tern
The Arctic tern breeds in the Arctic during the northern summer. Then, as the northern winter approaches, the tern makes the long journey south to the Antarctic – a trip of some 15,000 km – where it catches the southern summer.

Canada goose
The Canada goose spends the summer in the Arctic and flies south in winter. In summer, the Arctic bursts into bloom and there are plenty of plants for the geese to eat while they lay their eggs and rear their young.

Golden plover
Every autumn, the American golden plover flies up to 12,800 km from North to South America. It breeds on the North American tundra, where it feasts on the insects that fill the air during the brief Arctic summer.

> Once a young swift has left its nest, it may not come to land again until it is about two years old and ready to breed. During this time, it may fly up to 500,000 km.

> Most hummingbirds do not migrate far, but tiny ruby-throated hummingbirds migrate from their summer breeding areas in eastern North America and fly almost 3000 km to winter in Mexico, the Caribbean and Central America. Although only 9 cm long, with wings just 12 cm across, they can reach speeds of about 44 km/h. Some birds fly non-stop for about 850 km across the Gulf of Mexico.

○ The common quail breeds in Europe and Asia, but migrates south to Africa and India in the winter.

○ The European bee-eater flies some 16,000 km between Europe, where it breeds, and Africa, where it overwinters.

> Common in open country, swallows often nest on ledges and beams in outbuildings and sheds, returning to the same nest each year. In autumn, flocks gather on telephone wires and reedbeds before leaving on their migration journey to Africa for autumn and winter.

○ Sand martins breed in the northern hemisphere, migrating south in winter in flocks containing thousands of birds.

○ Snow geese nest in the Arctic in the far north of North America, laying eggs even before the snow melts. They migrate to the coasts farther south for the winter.

○ Birds such as greylag geese and cranes tend to fly in a V-formation during migration. This may help to save energy, with different birds taking over the lead position.

Navigation

Migrating birds use various methods to find their way. Many navigate by the Sun, Moon, stars, landmarks, coastlines and prevailing winds. Some have a built-in compass, probably inside the brain, so that they can sense the direction of the Earth's natural magnetic field.

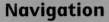

> In autumn, the common tern is seen moving in flocks. Most terns mate for life. Even if they don't stay together all year round, pairs meet up when they return to breeding sites.

Swallows and martins

There are about 80 species of swallow and martin found all over the world. Most migrate between breeding grounds and wintering areas. The house martin often lives near people, making its nest under the eaves of buildings or under bridges or other structures.

House martin

Find out more

Flight pp. 318–319

Endangered Birds

Over 10 per cent of the world's birds are in danger of dying out. They are especially threatened by habitat destruction, but other factors – including pollution, hunting, introduced species and the bird trade – are also putting their survival at risk.

Goose come-back

The Hawaiian goose is the world's rarest goose. Fifty years ago, there were only about 30 left. Now it is protected, and numbers are increasing.

❍ The mamo, a member of of the Hawaiian honeycreeper family, became extinct in 1899, partly because more than 80,000 birds were killed to make a cloak for King Kamehameha I of Hawaii.

❍ There are only about 600 black-faced spoonbills left.

❍ The endangered hyacinth macaw – at risk due to habitat destruction and illegal collecting for the bird trade – is now bred in captivity to help ensure its survival.

▶ *White-breasted mesites are a vulnerable species – they are exclusive to the island of Madagascar, where their natural habitat is under threat.*

Amazing

More than 80 of the world's 350 or so parrot species are in danger of extinction.

❍ The Fiji petrel was first discovered on the island of Gau Fiji in 1855, and was not seen again until 1984. Numbers are thought to be low.

❍ Probably less than 1000 red siskins remain in the wild – it has been a popular cage-bird since the mid 1800s.

❍ The Floreana mockingbird disappeared from one of the Galapagos Islands because rats were introduced.

❍ The short-tailed albatross has long been exploited for its feathers. This bird has been extremely rare since 1930.

❍ In New Zealand, Hutton's shearwater is preyed on by introduced stoats, while deer trample the burrows where it lives.

▶ *This rare Papuan hawk-owl lives in New Guinea forests, where logging is a major threat. It has a long, hawk-like tail and rounded wings.*

Most endangered birds

		Location	Reason
1	**Black-faced honeycreeper** *Melamprosops phaeosoma*	Hawaii	Habitat loss, restricted location
2	**Philippine cockatoo** *Cacatua haematuropygia*	Philippines	Habitat loss, cage-bird trade
3	**Djibouti francolin** *Francolinus ochropectus*	Djibouti	Hunting, habitat quality
4	**Montserrat oriole** *Icterus oberi*	Montserrat	Volcanic eruption, restricted location
5	**Asian white-backed vulture** *Gyps bengalensis*	Asia	Pollution
6	**Gurney's pitta** *Pitta gurneyi*	Myanmar, Thailand	Habitat loss, cage-bird trade
7	**Siberian crane** *Grus leucogeranus*	Asia	Habitat loss, degradation of wetlands
8	**Balaeric shearwater** *Puffinus mauretanicus*	Europe, Middle East	Introduced predators, entanglement in fishing lines
9	**Bali myna** *Leucopstar rothschildi*	Indonesia	Cage-bird trade
10	**Great Philippine eagle** *Pithecophaga jefferyi*	Philippines	Habitat loss, pollution, hunting

▶ The great bustard, with its 2.5 m wingspan, lives on the plains, steppes and farmland of Europe and Asia, feeding mainly on insects and plants. It is considered vulnerable.

○ Named after the small island in Cook Strait where it lived, the Stephen Island wren was killed off by the lighthouse keeper's cat. It may have been the only flightless songbird.

○ The huia, a species of wattlebird, has not been seen since 1907 and is now probably extinct. It was noted for having a different-shaped beak in males and females – the male's was straight and strong, the female's slender and curved.

○ The whooping crane is one of the world's most endangered birds, with only about 350 surviving in the wild in 2005.

○ The wood duck was hunted nearly to extinction in the 19th century for the male's colourful feathers, which were used as ornate fishing flies and hat decorations.

○ Many bird of paradise species are threatened by the felling of their rainforest homes for timber (the felling is sometimes done illegally).

▶ This mikado pheasant is very rare. It is now protected by law on its home island of Taiwan, in East Asia. A special reserve has been created to protect both it and Swinhoe's pheasant. In many areas, pheasant eggs and chicks are eaten by introduced animals, such as cats and rats.

▶ The mallee fowl is vulnerable and could become critically endangered. The male mallee fowl keeps a constant watch on his nest.

▲ The king vulture lives mainly in the rainforests of Central and South America. Although little is known about the life of king vultures in the wild, we do know that they are threatened by habitat loss and human settlement.

Rare eagle

Truly huge at 90 cm from beak to tail, the Philippine eagle equals the harpy as the world's biggest eagle. Despite its size and power, it is agile enough to pluck monkeys from tropical forest treetops. A threatened species, only a few hundred of these eagles survive in the mountains of certain Philippine islands. These eagles are now strictly protected and there is a captive breeding programme to increase numbers.

Find out more
The pet trade p. 344

Glossary

Adapted Well suited to a particular way of life or environment.

Antarctica A vast frozen continent, that surrounds the South Pole.

Aquatic Living in or near water.

Arctic The huge frozen ocean and cold lands around the North Pole.

Barbs The thin strands that make up most of a bird's feather. The barbs are held together by tiny, hook-like structures called barbules.

Bill The two hard mouthparts that birds use to catch and hold their food, care for their feathers and build nests. A bill is also called a beak.

Bird of prey A bird that hunts and kills other animals for food. Birds of prey have hooked bills, talons and keen senses.

Breeding season The time of year when pairs of birds come together to mate and raise a family.

Brood parasite A bird, such as a cuckoo, which has its eggs hatched and reared by another species of bird.

Camouflage Colours, markings or patterns that help animals to blend in with their surroundings and hide from predators or prey.

Carcass The dead body of an animal.

Carrion Dead or rotting animal flesh that is eaten by scavenging animals, such as vultures.

Casque A bony extension of the top part of a bird's bill, such as a cassowary.

Clutch A set of eggs laid by one female and incubated together.

Colony A large number of birds that gather together to breed or roost.

Coniferous forest A forest dominated by conifer trees, such as pine and spruce, which produce their seeds in cones.

Conservation Protecting and preserving species so they stand a better chance of surviving in the future.

Courtship Ritual behaviour and displays that form a bond between a male and a female before mating.

Cygnet A young swan.

Deciduous woodland Woodland dominated by trees such as oak and beech, which shed their leaves in the cold winter season.

Desert A place where more water is lost through evaporation than falls as rain. There is usually less than 25 cm of rain in a desert every year.

Domesticated Animals and plants kept by people for food or other uses.

Down Very soft, fluffy feathers, which help to trap air and keep a bird warm.

Drake A male duck.

Egg tooth A small, sharp point on the tip of a baby bird's bill, which helps it to break free of its eggshell and hatch out.

Embryo The early stage of a bird's development, before it hatches out of its egg.

Endangered Likely to die out in the near future.

Evolution The slow process by which living things change and adapt to their surroundings over many generations.

Extinction The permanent disappearance of a species.

Fledgling A young bird that has recently grown its feathers.

Flightless A bird that is unable to fly.

Flight feathers Large feathers that make up a bird's wings, providing power and lift during flight.

Flock A number of birds feeding or travelling together.

Formic acid A colourless, irritating acid squirted out by ants as a form of defence.

Gosling A young goose.

Habitat The natural home of an animal.

Hemisphere One of the two halves of the Earth. The Earth is divided along the Equator into the Northern Hemisphere and the Southern Hemisphere.

Hibernation A resting state, like a very deep sleep, which helps some animals to save energy and survive the winter.

Imprinting A process that usually occurs just after an animal is born in which a stimulus from the parent becomes permanently associated with a particular response. An example of this is young birds following their parents.

Incubation Sitting on the eggs to keep them warm so that baby birds will develop inside.

Keratin The tough protein from which feathers, human hair and human fingernails are formed.

Mammals A warm-blooded animal with hair, which feeds its young on mother's milk.

Migration The regular movement of animals from one area to another that takes place at certain times of the year. Many birds migrate each year between their summer and winter homes.

Monogamous Taking only one mate at a time.

Moulting The process of shedding old feathers and growing new ones. In birds, this usually happens once a year.

Navigate Finding a particular route or course from place to place.

Nectar A sugary liquid produced by flowers to attract birds, insects and other animals for pollination.

Nocturnal Active at night.

Owl A bird of prey that usually hunts at night. Many owls roost in trees during the day and have brown feathers for camouflage.

Parrot A colourful bird with a large, hooked beak and strong toes that help to grip branches and food.

Pigment A substance that gives colour, for instance to eggs and feathers.

Plankton Tiny creatures that drift with the movement of the water in the sea or in lakes.

Plumage The covering of feathers on a bird's body.

Pollinator An animal that carries pollen from flower to flower as it feeds on nectar.

Predator An animal that hunts and kills other animals.

Preening The process by which birds look after their feathers, using their bill and oil from their preen gland.

Prey An animal that is hunted and eaten by other animals.

Rainforest A forest near the equator where the weather is hot and wet all year round.

Raptor A bird of prey.

Regurgitate To cough up food that has already been swallowed in order to feed the chicks.

Roosting Sleeping or resting.

Sap Sugary food made by plants, especially trees.

Savanna An open grassland with scattered trees and bushes, usually in warm areas such as central Africa.

Skeleton A framework of bones that supports and protects an the body of an animal.

Species A group of similar living things that can breed together to produce fertile young.

Steppe An open grassland in central Asia with few trees or bushes. Summers are warm but winters are usually cold.

Streamlined A smooth, slim shape that cuts through air or water easily.

Syrinx A sound-producing organ ('voice-box') in birds, located where the windpipe meets the pipes leading to the lungs.

Talons The sharp, curved claws of birds of prey.

Territory An area that a particular bird occupies and defends against other birds of the same species. Birds usually nest in their own territory.

Tundra Cold, treeless areas of the world, found around the polar regions.

Vertebra One of the bones that makes up the vertebral column, or backbone, in vertebrate animals, such as birds, mammals, reptiles, amphibians and fishes.

Vulture A bird of prey that feeds mainly on carrion. The head and neck of a vulture are bare of feathers.

Warm-blooded Animals, such as birds and mammals, which can control their body temperature, keeping it at the same warm temperature all the time.

Waterfowl A bird such as a duck, a goose or a swan, which has webbed feet and a wide, flat beak. Waterfowl are well suited to living in or near water.

Wingspan The distance from the tip of one bird's wing to the tip of the other wing.

MAMMALS

What is a Mammal?

Mammals have bony skeletons, are usually covered in fur or hair, and feed their young with milk. Amazingly adaptable, mammals can be found in a large variety of habitats, from arid deserts to the icy Arctic. They are warm-blooded and are able to keep their bodies at a constant temperature.

Human 1.7 m tall

Blue whale 33.5 m long

Giraffe 5.5 m tall

○ There are about 4500 types, or species, of mammal, ranging in size from the giant blue whale to tiny shrews and bats. In fact, the blue whale is 100 million times bigger than what is possibly the world's smallest mammal – kitti's hog-nosed bat.

○ All mammals – except the duckbilled platypus and spiny anteater – give birth to live young. The two main mammal groups are placentals (such as cats) and marsupials (such as kangaroos), whose young develop in pouches.

○ Most mammals have good senses of sight, smell and hearing. Their senses help them to find food, and to protect themselves from predators. Many mammals live a nocturnal way of life; this means that they are most active at night, and have therefore developed excellent night vision.

▲ *The blue whale is the biggest mammal and the largest animal ever known to have lived. It can measure more than 33.5 m long – that's the length of seven family cars parked end to end – and weigh up to 210 tonnes. Its heart alone can weigh up to 700 kg. It spends all its life at sea.*

▲ *Mammals are adapted to a range of lifestyles. The African caracal, for example, has strong jaws and razor-sharp teeth to catch and hold its prey.*

▲ *This leopard seal's body is smooth and bullet-shaped. With its small, round head, flippers, and muscular body, it is able to propel itself through water at speed. On land, however, it is a clumsy mover.*

Amazing

The speediest mammal in the water is the killer whale, moving at around 55 km/h, sometimes in groups of 30 or more.

Find out more

Whales and dolphins pp. 420–421

Bear 2.4 m tall

African elephant 3.5 m tall

Human beings

Human beings are the mammal with the largest numbers in the world – more than six billion. We have hairy bodies, large brains and special mammary glands for feeding our young (babies) with milk.

❍ Fur and fat protect mammals from the cold. When they do get cold, mammals curl up, seek shelter or shiver. Some save energy in the winter by resting, or hibernating. Mammals are also able to cool their bodies down – by sweating, panting or resting.

Breathing

Mammals breathe air into their lungs. The air contains oxygen, a gas that is needed to release energy from food. Even mammals that live underwater, such as whales, need to come to the surface to breathe air. The bodies of small mammals, such as shrews, work so fast to stay warm that they need 20 times more oxygen, compared to their body weight, than a large mammal, such as a zebra.

❍ Most mammals move on four legs, but not all: sea-living mammals, such as whales and seals, have streamlined bodies that are well-suited to moving through water. Bats are the only group of flying mammals.

❍ Mammals have bigger brains, in relation to their body size, than other animals. Humans, chimpanzees, gorillas, orang-utans, baboons and dolphins are the world's cleverest creatures. Thanks to their large brains, mammals are able to learn and adapt, or change, their behaviour.

❍ Larger mammals, such as elephants, usually produce just one offspring (baby) and care for it over several years. Smaller mammals, such as rats, may have ten or more babies that grow quickly and are independent in just a few weeks.

❍ Most mammals are specialized feeders. This means that their bodies are suited to finding and eating particular foods. Carnivorous animals, which hunt or prey on others, for example, are often equipped with sharp and stabbing teeth. Herbivorous animals, which eat plant matter, digest their tough, fibrous food in specially adapted stomachs and long intestines.

❍ All mammals have three small bones in their ears. These bones, collectively known as the ossicles, transfer sound from the ear drum to the inner ear, from where nerves can carry the signals to the brain.

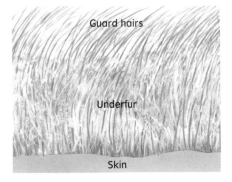

Guard hairs

Underfur

Skin

▲ *Most mammals have two layers of hair in their fur: a layer of soft, downy hair next to their skin traps warmth, while the guard hairs are normally coloured or patterned to provide camouflage.*

Mammal champions

Biggest rodent	Capybara (as big as a goat)
Biggest ungulate	Hippopotamus
Longest hair	Yak (hair up to 90 cm)
Largest bear	Polar bear (500 kg)
Smelliest mammal	Skunk
Sleepiest mammal	Dormouse
Slowest-moving mammal	Sloth
Heaviest tree-dwelling mammal	Orang-utan (up to 90 kg)
Mammal most at home in mountains	Pika (up to 6000 m altitude)
Most armoured mammal	Armadillos and pangolins

Mammals – Past and Present

Mammals appeared on our planet around 200 million years ago, when dinosaurs still roamed the land. When the dinosaurs died out, mammals, with their large brains, warm bodies and an ability to learn, went on to become a large and successful group of animals.

○ Before true mammals emerged, some reptiles, such as the dog-like cynodonts, had developed mammalian characteristics, such as hair and specialized teeth.

○ It is now believed that the first mammals evolved from small, carnivorous reptiles called therapsids. The limbs of therapsids were positioned below the body, rather than to the side of it, and this helped mammals move faster than reptiles.

Leopard camouflage

A close-up of a leopard's coat. The rosettes on a leopard's coat help this tree-climbing big cat to 'disappear' amongst the dappled shadows of a forest. The background colour varies from straw to deep chestnut and, occasionally, black.

> *The Uintatherium was about the size of a modern-day rhinoceros and was one of the first large mammals, living about 50 million years ago.*

○ We can imagine how mammals have evolved and changed by looking at fossils. These are remains, such as bones and teeth, that have been turned into stone over millions of years. Unfortunately, soft body parts, like brains and fur – which would tell us much about mammal ancestors – are rarely preserved as fossils.

○ Sabre-toothed cats became extinct around 10,000 years ago. *Smilodon* was the most famous sabre-toothed cat. It was the size of a large lion and its canine teeth, which it used to stab its prey, were a massive 25 cm long.

○ Thousands of animals have become extinct (died out) naturally during the course of evolution. Most extinctions happen when animals cannot adapt to changes in the environment.

○ Around 38 million years ago the world began to cool down, and ice formed in Antarctica. Mammals were able to control their body temperature, and this may have helped them survive such a dramatic change in climate.

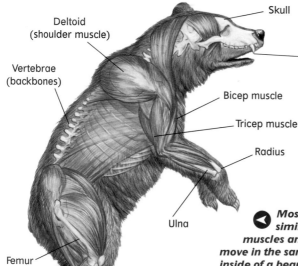

Deltoid (shoulder muscle)

Vertebrae (backbones)

Skull

Canine tooth

Bicep muscle

Tricep muscle

Radius

Ulna

Femur

Tibia

Tarsals

< *Most mammals have a similar body structure, with muscles and limbs that work and move in the same way. This view of the inside of a bear shows how muscles and bones work together to produce an animal's movement.*

Amazing

Mammals may have lived on our planet for approximately 200 million years – but microscopic bacteria have been around for 3.5 billion years.

Find out more

Monkeys pp. 424–425

North American mammoths had huge curling tusks. They were about 4 m high, making them taller than any elephant living today, and had an outer layer of hair up to 50 cm long. Mammoths became extinct around 12,500 years ago.

❍ The mammary glands, with which mammals suckle (feed) their young, evolved from sweat glands – some mammal-like reptiles may have leaked a sort of milk from sweat glands for their young.

❍ The bodies of most mammals are covered in a layer of hair, or fur. Some mammals have spines, horns and prickles, which are all made of strands of hair that have become thickened and strengthened to make them stiff.

❍ Not only is fur useful for keeping in body heat, it also gives protection – and it can act as camouflage or provide bright display colours and patterns for attracting mates. Sea mammals, such as whales, have only a tiny amount of bristles.

Many baby mammals are born helpless and depend on their mother's milk for all their nourishment. These kittens suck on their mother's teats to make her milk flow.

Longest hair

Musk oxen, along with yaks of Central Asia, have the longest fur of any animal. Some of the hairs in the outer coat are almost 100 cm long. These bulky animals can stay in the Arctic all year, surviving temperatures of −70°C.

❍ Many mammals show a more complicated range of behaviour than other creatures. In particular, they have a greater ability to learn from their own experiences. Some, including monkeys and dolphins, can even learn from one another, particularly their elders.

What Mammals Eat

All mammals begin their lives drinking their mothers' milk, but as they grow and develop they learn how to find their own food. While some mammals are hunters and predators, others graze on plants, forage for insects or scavenge for the remains of dead animals.

❍ To keep its body and brain warm and working well, a mammal needs to take in a lot of energy-giving food. Mammals may spend most of their waking hours looking for food. Wild horses, for example, can spend 16 to 20 hours feeding every day, taking about 30,000 bites during that time.

❍ Mammalian predators often hunt at dawn and dusk, when cold-blooded animals, such as lizards or insects, are less active – and easier to catch. Mammals that graze are more likely to be feeding during the day, when it is easiest for them to spot a predator.

❍ The teeth of a mammal are specialized to suit the kind of food that it eats. Meat eaters, for example, have sharp, piercing and slicing teeth. Plant eaters have teeth that can shear tough plants and grind them up.

▼ *The pika carefully chooses food to store in its burrow, avoiding plants that will rot too quickly. Storing food in this way is called caching.*

❍ Mammals have jaws that can move from side to side, as well as up and down. This means that mammals, unlike other animals, can chew their food.

❍ An animal needs to catch its food before it can eat it – and predatory mammals, such as cats, have paws that are equipped with razor-sharp claws for bringing down prey.

❍ Some plant eaters change their foods with the seasons. Pikas, which are small-eared relatives of rabbits, nibble buds and shoots in the spring, and grasses and herbs in the summer. In the autumn they store away leaves and grass to eat during winter.

◆ *The Australian numbat has a sticky 10 cm long tongue. It uses the tongue to scoop up small invertebrates.*

Amazing

Giraffes have long, black tongues, almost 0.5 m long, which they use to grab leaves and shoots.

Hedgehogs

Hedgehogs are most active at night, and they rely on their sense of smell to locate prey. They have small, sharp teeth and eat insects, grubs, slugs, worms and similar juicy creatures.

Lion

Incisors scrape meat from the bone

Carnassials slide against each other to slice flesh

Canines stab and pierce flesh

Horse

Incisors tear plants from the trees and ground

Row of large, broad-topped crushing molars grind plants and vegetation

Gap (diastema) where canines used to be before herbivores adapted to plant-eating lifestyle

🔺 *The lion is a carnivore. This means it eats meat and its teeth are suited to catching prey, tearing and chewing. The horse is a herbivore. This means it eats plants and its teeth are suited to cutting and grinding tough grass.*

🔺 *Hyenas are aggressive pack hunters, but they will also scavenge, or steal, dead animals that have been killed by other predators.*

▶ *Each claw on this lion's paw is curved and very sharp – a perfect tool for digging into its prey. Even a pet cat has claws like this.*

○ Some mammals eat only one or two kinds of food. The giant panda feeds mainly on the shoots and roots of the bamboo plant. It may spend all day eating up to 12 kg of bamboo. Some mammals, such as bears and humans, will eat a varied diet, including both plant matter and meat. They are called omnivores.

○ The numbat lives in southwest Australia. It rips open termite nests with the sharp claws of its front paws then licks up termites and, occasionally, ants. It has 52 teeth – more than most other land mammals – and a sticky tongue.

▶ *The giant panda will occasionally vary its normal diet of bamboo, and eat small creatures, such as fish, mice and eggs.*

Baby whales

Like land mammals, whales nurse their babies with their own milk. Whale milk is so rich that babies grow incredibly fast. A baby blue whale, for example, drinks 500 l of milk a day. Its mother's milk is so packed with nutrients that the baby will grow extremely quickly, and put on an extra 100 kg in weight every day for about seven months.

○ Meerkats enthusiastically attack and eat venomous scorpions, first rendering them harmless by biting off their tail stings. By eating these dangerous creatures, meerkats are able to enjoy a supply of food that would be avoided by most predators.

○ Some mammals, such as hyenas, wild dogs and wolves, hunt in packs for their food. By working together, mammals can chase bigger prey and are more likely to be successful in their hunts.

World of Mammals

Mammals are able to live almost everywhere in the world. They can survive in every major habitat because, like birds, they are able to adapt to different climates by keeping their body temperatures constant. This means that they can be found all over the world.

Arctic foxes are well-camouflaged in their cold northern habitat. They sport white coats in winter, but grow brown fur in the summer.

American black bears prefer to inhabit forests, where they can find fruit, berries and nuts. They also scavenge food from rubbish bins.

The world's oceans and rivers have become home to many mammal species that returned to water and have adapted to an aquatic lifestyle, such as dolphins.

Southern elephant seals and other mammals are able to survive the plummeting temperatures of the Antarctic thanks to their thick layers of fat, or blubber.

Thick-furred alpacas live high in the South American Andes. Their dense wool keeps them warm at heights of up to 4800 m.

At the time of the dinosaurs tropical rainforests were common. The few that remain still provide a habitat for a huge array of animal life, such as this squirrel monkey.

Woodlands and forests offer plenty of opportunities for long-eared bats to hunt for insects.

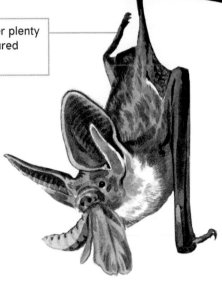

The mysterious clouded leopard lurks in the forests of Southeast Asia. As the trees are being cut down, so the numbers of this endangered species fall.

The endangered European mink lives in wetlands where it can prowl, searching for fish, frogs, waterbirds and crayfish.

The land of Australia broke away from the rest of the continents millions of years ago and a different range of mammals evolved, such as wallabies.

Keeping cool is as essential to survival as keeping warm. Mammals of hot and dry regions rest in the shade and pant to lower their temperatures. Lions live on the African grasslands. They rest during the hottest part of the day.

Massive herds of African wildebeest migrate for hundreds of kilometres in search of fresh grass, which only grows after seasonal rainfalls.

Find out more
Strange mammals pp. 386–387

Senses – Keeping in Touch

T he mammals are an enormously successful group of animals, and one of the reasons for this is their brain power. Animals with big brains are able to use information that comes from their five senses – sight, hearing, smell, taste and touch – to stay safe, and to find food, water and mates.

▶ The strongest, or dominant, leopard bares its fangs and stands over the other animal, which lies down on its back to show that it does not want or intend to fight.

▲ By displaying his strength, a male mandrill, which can weigh up to 35 kg, may avoid having to fight a competitor or intruder.

❍ Mammals communicate with one another. They may use special scents to send messages to one another and, more obviously, they use sounds, facial expressions and body postures.

❍ Scents, or strong-smelling secretions, are produced by a mammal's glands. These special regions may be found on faces, feet and bottoms. Mammals use their scents to mark their territory, mates, food and even youngsters.

❍ Male mandrills have bright red and blue markings on their faces, and bluey-purple bottoms, which they use to attract females. They scare away other males by yawning to show off their enormous fangs, which can reach nearly 7 cm in length.

❍ Like many mammals, horses rely on a strong sense of smell. They recognize each other by scent. A mother can pick out her foal from a herd purely by smell and a male horse can tell if a female is in a nearby field by sniffing the air.

❍ Whales migrate, or travel, great distances across the world's oceans. They find their way by sensing the Earth's magnetic field, using particles of the mineral magnetite in their bodies.

Amazing

Baby wood mice make ultrasonic distress calls to summon their mother.

○ Carnivorous mammals, such as tigers, usually have eyes at the front of their heads. This helps them focus on prey before attacking. Herbivores, such as rabbits, usually have eyes on either side of their heads, so they can spot a predator in almost any direction.

○ At dawn and dusk, when it is hard to see, mammals often rely on whiskers and their sense of touch to give them information about their surroundings. Moles live underground, so they do not need good hearing or sight. Instead they rely on smell and touch. Long sensory hairs, or whiskers, cover their sensitive snouts.

▲ *Touch is one of the most developed senses in horses. They can sense a fly landing on any part of their body and use their tail to flick it off. Horses respond to touch all over the body – especially on their ears and eyes.*

○ Some dogs have such good senses of smell that they can match a person to their shoes, just by sniffing.

○ Whales can see well up to 1 m underwater, but they have no sense of smell. Their sense of hearing, however, is excellent and allows them to communicate with one another. Many whales communicate by clicks, which can even be heard by humans.

Polar bears

Polar bears can smell seals up to 60 km across the ice. Their white coats camouflage them against the Arctic snow when hunting seals, although their black nose sometimes gives them away. They catch seals when the seals poke their heads up through breathing holes in the Arctic ice. Polar bears often swim underwater and come up under an ice floe to tip seals off. They may also throw huge chunks of ice at seals to stun them.

▼ *Sperm whales have the biggest brains of any living mammal. Fat deposits in their skulls help to focus the sounds made by echolocation.*

Noisy mammals

The noisiest land animals are the red and black howler monkeys of South America. They live in groups and howl, whoop and call to define their territory and scare away intruders. The sound is made louder by echo chambers beneath their chins and can be heard several kilometres away.

Find out more

Seals and sea lions pp. 418–419

Family Life

Most mammals give birth to live young. Inside the female's body, the developing young are nourished by a special organ, called the placenta. Most mammal babies are fairly well developed when born, although they still need parental care to begin with.

○ Before mammals can reproduce, or breed, they need to find a suitable partner. Courtship is the time when animals get together to breed. Usually the male has to show a female that he is fit, strong and healthy before she will mate with him.

○ The time when a baby is growing inside its mother is called pregnancy, or gestation. Mammals, such as deer, that are in danger of being attacked by predators give birth to well-developed offspring that are able to run just a few hours after they are born.

▼ *In its first weeks of life, a foal stays close to its mother at all times. As it gradually becomes more confident, it moves away from her to explore.*

▶ *Meerkats live underground in large family groups of 30 members or more. Standing on rocks or bushes, 'sentries' cluck and cheep to warn of predators nearby.*

Mammal groups

Mammals are divided into three groups, according to how they reproduce, or have young. Monotremes, such as the platypus, lay eggs. Marsupials, such as kangaroos, give birth to tiny babies that are poorly developed and are nourished with their mother's milk. Placentals, such as humans, grow inside their mother's womb. They get nutrients through a placenta until they are developed enough to be born.

▶ *A male zebra mates with all of the females in his group, or harem. In return, he protects the group, and their territory, against would-be intruders and predators.*

○ One of the most dangerous times in an animal's life is the time immediately after it has been born, or has hatched. Some species, such as frogs and insects, lay hundreds of eggs so that some of the young may have a chance of survival. Mammals, however, normally have just a few offspring, which the parents protect.

○ The only egg-laying mammals are the duckbilled platypus and the five species of spiny anteaters, or echidnas. These curious animals live in Australia and lay their eggs in burrows. Once the youngsters are hatched, they feed on their mother's milk, just like other types of mammal.

Longest gestation

It takes a long time for a mammal baby to develop: 280 days (just over nine months) for a human, but even longer for other large mammals.

Elephant	660 days
Whale	500 days
Rhinoceros	450 days
Walrus	480 days
Giraffe	430 days

▲ *Only one female in a colony of naked mole rats can breed. She may have more than 20 babies, or pups, at a time.*

Amazing

Tiger cubs depend entirely on their mothers to bring them food until they are about 18 months old, when they begin to make their own first kills.

Father's milk

In some bat species males are known to produce milk, but it is not known if they ever suckle (feed) their young.

❍ Young meerkats care for their younger brothers and sisters while their mother forages for food to maintain her milk supply. Other members of the colony, known as sentries, stand guard on high mounds and scan the horizon for predators.

❍ When animals live in social groups they often perform different roles, or jobs. Naked mole rats, for example, live underground in a colony of up to 80 animals led by just one female – the queen. Other colony members dig burrows to find food, as well as looking after the queen.

▲ *Rutting between two mammals, such as wild goats, determines who gets to mate. The loser will have to wait for the chance to compete with another male.*

❍ Many mammals live in groups or societies. This way of life offers them protection and safety in numbers. Burchell's zebras, for example, form close family groups consisting of several females and their offspring. They are led by one male – the stallion – which mates with all of the females.

▲ *The platypus lives in rivers in Western Australia. It has webbed feet and a paddle-tail for swimming.*

❍ For many wild animals the most dangerous time is infancy. Wild gorillas can live into their forties, but nearly two out of every five baby gorillas die before they are one year old. Some die of disease, others are killed by adult male gorillas, or poachers or leopards.

❍ While smaller mammals may have quite short life spans – of only a few years – larger mammals tend to live for longer. Elephants may reach 70 years of age, and when one dies other members of the herd may circle the body and appear to mourn and cry.

How Mammals Move

Mammals live in many different places, from the oceans to the treetops. These extraordinary and adaptable animals have developed different ways of moving through those habitats – from swimming to crawling, and even flying. Animals need to move to find food, shelter and mates, and being able to move quickly may help them escape from predators.

Moving through water

Water is dense and this means it takes extra energy to move through it. Only three groups of mammals are adapted to life in water: whales and dolphins, seals and sea lions, and dugongs and manatees.

Some species of seal and sea lion can dive as deep as 1500 m and stay underwater for an hour before returning to the surface to breathe.

Mammals that live underwater usually have flippers and fins instead of legs. A dolphin's tail, called its flukes, looks similar to a fish's tail, but a dolphin swims by arching its body up and down, not bending from side to side like a fish.

Otters can live in oceans, seas, rivers and lakes. They have webbed feet and waterproof coats. Otters live at the water's edge and swim to find prey, such as frogs and fish.

Manatees often live in rivers or near the seashore, and can stay underwater for up to 20 minutes.

A polar bear's fur traps air, helping to keep this huge animal afloat. Polar bears dive into freezing water to hunt for seals and sea birds.

Humpback whales have been seen to leap out of the water as many as 100 times in quick succession. They may weigh up to 30 tonnes, yet they are able to 'breach' into the open air using their powerful tail.

Life in the trees

Flying is another high-energy form of movement. Bats are the only mammals that can fly, although others, such as the flying squirrel, can glide. Most mammals that live in trees move around by climbing or swinging.

A squirrel's bushy tail works as a balance and rudder when it scampers along branches or leaps between trees.

Gibbons are the most agile of all the apes. They have long arms with which they hurtle through the forest, flying up to 15 m between hand-holds.

Fruit bats fly from tree to tree in search of food, but they sometimes get blown off course by tropical storms. They can even get carried off to neighbouring islands.

The dwarf cuscus is a tree-living marsupial. Its prehensile (grasping) tail curls around branches and has furless skin for a good grip.

The three-toed sloth is the world's slowest mammal. It moves at around a mere 11–16 m/h.

Life on land

Most land-living mammals walk on four legs, although some, such as kangaroos and humans, walk on two. Flexible spines help cats achieve great bursts of speed, while antelope and deer can run for long distances without tiring.

The cheetah is the fastest land mammal in the world, reaching speeds of 105 km/h. Within just two seconds, a cheetah can reach speeds of 75 km/h, but will run out of energy after a mere 30 seconds of sprinting.

One of the world's bounciest mammals is the serval. This slender cat can leap 1 m high and travel a distance of 4 m as it jumps upon its prey.

Despite weighing 2 tonnes or more, a rhinoceros can run at 50 km/h.

The red kangaroo is a champion bouncer. It can leap along at 40 km/h or more, leaping 9 or 10 m in a single bound. Its tail is used as a balance when hopping, and to hold the kangaroo up when walking.

Strange Mammals

The strangest mammals are monotremes and marsupials. Monotremes are egg-laying mammals, of which there are only two types: the duck-billed platypus and the echidna. Marsupials are born in a tiny, undeveloped form. There are nearly 300 species of marsupial, including kangaroos and opossums.

Amazing

The newly born mouse opossum is no larger than a grain of rice – the smallest newborn mammal in the world.

Tasmanian devil

Tasmania, a small island off the southern coast of Australia, is home to the largest marsupial carnivore: the Tasmanian devil. This nocturnal creature hunts at night and eats almost any meat, dead or alive, including insects, opossums and wallabies. It stuffs its food into its mouth using its front feet then grinds and chews it with sharp teeth and powerful jaws.

○ Marsupials probably originated in America some 100 million years ago, at a time when America and Australia were still joined. Most marsupials now live on the continent of Australasia, but some species still inhabit the Americas.

○ Most marsupials develop inside their mother's pouch, where they remain attached to a teat, sucking milk. Small marsupials, including some opossums, do not have pouches.

○ A koala baby spends six months inside its mother's pouch, and another six months riding on her back. Adult koalas spend up to 18 hours a day sleeping. When they are not sleeping, they are likely to be eating leaves from eucalyptus trees.

○ Other Australian marsupials include wombats, several kinds of wallaby, bandicoots (which look like rats), marsupial moles and possums.

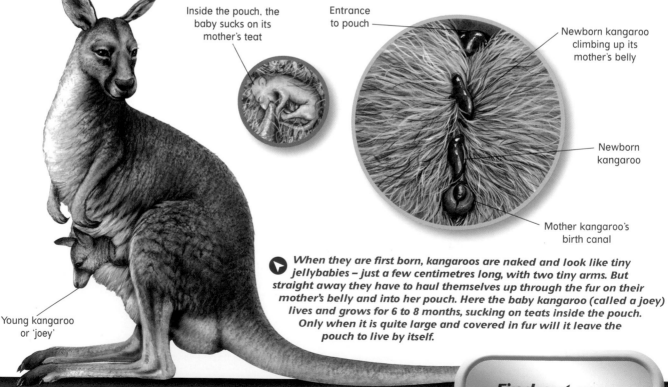

Inside the pouch, the baby sucks on its mother's teat

Entrance to pouch

Newborn kangaroo climbing up its mother's belly

Newborn kangaroo

Mother kangaroo's birth canal

Young kangaroo or 'joey'

▶ *When they are first born, kangaroos are naked and look like tiny jellybabies – just a few centimetres long, with two tiny arms. But straight away they have to haul themselves up through the fur on their mother's belly and into her pouch. Here the baby kangaroo (called a joey) lives and grows for 6 to 8 months, sucking on teats inside the pouch. Only when it is quite large and covered in fur will it leave the pouch to live by itself.*

Find out more
Family life pp. 382–383

○ **The American or Virginia opossum is nocturnal and a good climber and swimmer. The young stay attached to the mother's teats for around 50 days after birth.**

○ The name koala comes from an aboriginal term meaning 'no drink', because koalas get nearly all of their water from their food.

○ Echidnas are also known as spiny anteaters because they are covered in spines and eat ants, termites, worms and grubs. They live in a wide range of habitats including woods, desert, mountains, and grasslands in Australia and New Guinea.

○ **There are more than 60 species of opossum and they all live in the Americas. Most opossums are the size of a domestic cat, or smaller. They can eat many types of food, including fruit, insects and eggs.**

○ The wombat's pouch faces backwards, so the young are protected from flying earth when the mother is digging. Wombats are heavily built with muscular bodies that suit their burrowing way of life. They can dig tunnels that measure up to 200 m.

○ Opossums have lived in the Americas for around 55 million years. They have spread as far northwards as Canada, but are vulnerable to frostbitten ears and toes. When attacked, opossums go into a death-like trance, called 'playing possum'.

○ Once a baby opossum has attached itself to a teat, it cannot let go until it is fully developed. Opossums entwine their tails around those of their young when they carry them.

○ New Guinea bandicoots are the size of rabbits. These marsupials are related to cuscuses and opossums and eat all kinds of small animals, as well as seeds and fruits that they dig for on the forest floor.

○ **Although koalas mainly eat eucalyptus or gum tree leaves, they will munch the leaves of other trees and also swallow some soil to obtain extra minerals and nutrients.**

○ **The stocky wombat is related to the koala, but cannot climb trees and digs large burrows for protection.**

Platypus

Duck-billed platypuses have webbed feet and spend much of their time in water. The females lay eggs in a burrow by a river bank, and when the young hatch they lick the milk that oozes out over the fur of their mother's belly. The platypus's burrow can extend 30 m from the water's edge to the nest. It blocks the entrance to deter snakes. Before the discovery of fossil platypus teeth in Argentina, the animal was believed to have existed only in Australia and New Guinea.

○ **In the breeding season the female echidna develops a temporary pouch on her stomach. After she lays her egg, she transfers it into the pouch for incubation, where it remains for 8 or 9 days.**

Insect-eating Mammals

Shrews, hedgehogs, moles and similar animals are known as insectivores. This name means 'insect-eaters', but many of these small, busy, active, darting mammals feed on a variety of tiny prey, including worms, snails, slugs and spiders. There are about 345 species of insectivores around the world.

Amazing

Moonrats look like mice. They mark their territories with scent that smells like rotting onions.

○ Most insectivores have long, pointed, whiskery noses, little eyes and ears and very sharp teeth. They are mainly active at night and they use their keen senses of smell and touch, rather than sight, to catch prey.

○ Pygmy shrews are the smallest of all land mammals, weighing only 2 g and measuring hardly 6 cm long – including the tail. They rely on their quick reactions to hunt and catch creatures larger than themselves, including beetles and grasshoppers.

▶ *Desmans are suited to life in water and they can swim very fast as they chase fish, tadpoles and water insects.*

○ A mole is seldom seen above ground unless floods drive it to the surface. It spends most of its life in its large burrow network, feeding on worms and grubs and other creatures found in the soil. Moles are virtually blind.

○ Desmans are amongst the rarest of mammalian insect-eaters. There are only two types in the world – one that lives in the Pyrenees Mountains of Europe and one that lives in Asia. They are related to moles, but look more like water shrews, with their webbed feet and dense, waterproof fur.

◀ *The Hispaniolan solenodon is an endangered species. It has black or reddish-brown fur and measures 28–32 cm in body length, and has a tail of up to 26 cm long.*

Hibernation

Hedgehogs, like many other mammals, save energy during the cold winter months by hibernating. A hedgehog's body temperature drops to around 6°C in the middle of the winter, and it survives on stores of body fat. During a spell of mild weather, a hibernating hedgehog may rouse itself to feed. The mottled brown colour of a hedgehog's spines helps to camouflage it as it sleeps, burrowed beneath hedges, or nestled amongst piles of fallen leaves.

Find out more
What mammals eat pp. 376–377

The large eyes of an elephant shrew give it keen vision, even in the dark undergrowth of its African habitat.

Making a molehill

The mole's front feet are almost like shovels and are used to push aside earth. Molehills are loose soil that the mole thrusts up from its tunnels – which can stretch for up to 150 m.

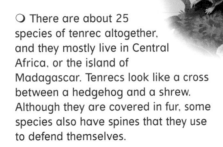

Pygmy shrews are so small and active, and use up so much energy, that they must feed every 4–6 hours, or face starvation.

○ There are about 25 species of tenrec altogether, and they mostly live in Central Africa, or the island of Madagascar. Tenrecs look like a cross between a hedgehog and a shrew. Although they are covered in fur, some species also have spines that they use to defend themselves.

○ The water shrew is huge amongst shrews. It has 9-cm head–body length with a 5-cm tail. It swims in water to catch fish, frogs and worms. It is an extremely active creature and needs to eat its own weight daily. It may hunt along river banks for extra food, such as grubs, slugs and spiders.

○ Hedgehogs are familiar garden predators that feed mainly on worms, slugs and caterpillars. They are usually helpful to a gardener, but they may be poisoned by eating slugs that have fed on slug pellets. Rolling into a tight prickly ball protects the hedgehog from predators such as foxes and stoats.

○ It is believed that some species of shrew hunt using echolocation. This means that they send out high-pitched squeals, which bounce off nearby objects, such as small animals. When the sound returns to the shrew's ear it can tell how far away the object is.

○ Solenodons look like rat-sized shrews. There are only two kinds – both found in the Caribbean and both very rare. They use their flexible snouts to sniff out insects from cracks and crevices. They can also pounce on larger prey, such as lizards and mice, using their long, sharp claws.

○ The elephant shrew owes its name to its long, flexible snout (a proboscis). Although similar in appearance to other shrews, elephant shrews are so unusual that they have been put in their own group of mammals. To escape predators they run swiftly along special pathways that they keep clear by removing twigs and leaves.

○ The common tenrec rears more young than any other mammal on the planet, with litters containing up to 24 babies.

Tree shrews are not true shrews, but they do look and act similarly. They live in the tropical forests of Southeast Asia.

It is believed that water shrews have toxin, or poison, in their saliva, which helps them to catch and kill their prey. A bite from a water shrew can produce a burning pain that lasts several days.

The Anteater Family

Anteaters, sloths and armadillos may not look very similar, but they all belong in the same group of mammals – the xenarthrans. These creatures are all characterized by small brains, and few or no teeth. Despite their size, anteaters, pangolins and armadillos survive on a diet of ants.

⬆ *Like other sloths, the three-toed sloth moves extremely slowly through its forest habitat. Although sloths spend most of their time in the trees, they can crawl on the ground and even swim well.*

⬆ *The leathery skin and the bony armour of the nine-banded armadillo account for more than one-sixth of its weight.*

⬅ *Two-toed sloths, like this one, do not have tails. They have long, coarse fur, small brains, tiny eyes and ears, and few teeth.*

○ Ants and termites fight and bite when caught, but they are so tiny that big ant-eating mammals have little to fear. These mammals lick and pick up their miniature victims dozens at a time, with their long, sticky tongues.

○ Unlike most other xenarthrans, sloths do not eat ants – they survive on a diet of leaves and fruit. A sloth's large stomach is divided into many compartments. The food inside can account for up to one-third of the animal's entire body weight.

○ A sloth's fur grows in the opposite direction to that of most mammals, so when the sloth is upside down its fur points towards the ground – this means that rain can run off the body.

⬆ *Tree pangolins hunt at night for nests of ants and termites high in the branches. They sleep in their own nests by day.*

Sunbathers

Unlike other mammals, the body temperature of a sloth varies. Every morning they bask in the sun in the forest treetops to get warm.

Amazing

A sloth's thick fur is home to a large number of algae (small plant-like organisms). The algae turn the sloth's coat green, helping it to remain hidden (camouflaged) as it hangs from leaf-covered branches.

Find out more
How mammals move p. 385

▲ The tamandua lives mostly in trees. It can walk on the ground, but it is slow, clumsy and at greater risk from predators when it does so.

○ Sloths live in the forests of South America. They spend almost all of their time hanging upside down in trees, making the effort to come down to the ground only once a week or so to empty their bowels.

○ Armadillos have a tough covering that is similar to armour. It is made up of small bone plates covered in heavy skin. The giant armadillo has 100 teeth. Pangolins, however, have a covering made from overlapping plates of horn, and no teeth.

▶ The mother sloth carries her infant for up to nine months on her belly, where it feeds on the leaves it can reach.

○ The small-scaled tree pangolin is one of four African pangolins. The long, curving prehensile (grasping) tail helps it to climb in the branches of trees, using its sharp-edged scales to get an even better grip on the bark.

○ The giant anteater is an odd-looking mammal with its brush-like tail, shaggy fur and long, curved nose. It grows to 2 m long, including the tail, and shuffles through wood or scrub in Central and South America.

○ The appearance of the silky anteater is deceptive. Despite its soft golden or silvery fur, this mammal is far from cuddly – it can slash out with its fearsome sharp and curved claws. Rather than destroy a nest, it makes a small hole in the side and just takes a small number of inhabitants at a time.

▲ Like other armadillos, the fairy armadillo has special bones in its spine, which give its body extra strength and support when burrowing.

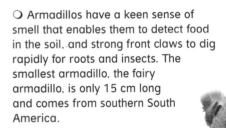

○ Armadillos have a keen sense of smell that enables them to detect food in the soil, and strong front claws to dig rapidly for roots and insects. The smallest armadillo, the fairy armadillo, is only 15 cm long and comes from southern South America.

○ Tamanduas are smaller, tree-living versions of the giant anteater. They can use their strong, flexible, furless tail to wrap around branches like a fifth foot. They live in the forests of Central and South America.

▶ The silky anteater of South and Central America hunts at night, searching for the nests of tree ants.

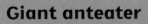

Giant anteater

The mouth of a giant anteater is so small that you could not insert even a finger into it. Giant anteaters have no teeth, and rely on their extremely long, sticky tongues to gather up termites after breaking into their concrete-hard mounds. The tongue of one of these extraordinary creatures can reach for more than 60 cm.

Bats

Few people see bats because they usually fly at night, often in dense forest or woodland habitats. Yet of all the species of mammal, about one in five is a bat. They are found in all but the coldest places on Earth. Most bats are small and feed on other flying creatures, such as moths.

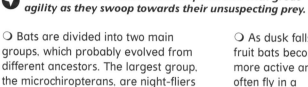

● *Bats can move at considerable speed and with great agility as they swoop towards their unsuspecting prey.*

● *Bats' wings are formed from special layers of skin that make up a membrane, called a patagium, which extends beyond their limbs.*

Fruit bat

There are more than 130 types of fruit bat across Africa, Asia and Australia. The body of the Wallace's fruit bat is about 20 cm long and it has a wingspan of 40–45 cm.

○ Bats are divided into two main groups, which probably evolved from different ancestors. The largest group, the microchiropterans, are night-fliers and use echolocation to find their prey. The megachiropterans are bigger bats. These bats have fox-like faces and do not echolocate.

○ Most bats sleep during the day in sheltered places, such as tree holes or caves. A few sleep out in the open, on tree branches or on cliff faces. They rely on keeping still or camouflage, for safety from predators.

○ Fruit bats, which belong to the megachiropteran group of bats, have long snouts and their faces resemble dogs or foxes – giving them the common name of flying fox. Most types roost in trees by day and flap their wings to keep cool.

● *Microchiropterans often rely on their senses of hearing and smell to locate mates, predators or prey.*

○ As dusk falls, fruit bats become more active and often fly in a group hunting for food. They usually live in tropical areas, where there is a good supply of soft, ripe fruits throughout the year.

○ Bats have hook-like leg claws with which they grip branches or rock ledges when they roost. They usually roost in groups for warmth and safety. Each bat wraps its wings around its body for extra protection and to preserve its body heat.

○ The lesser long-nosed bat is unusual in that it feeds on nectar – the sweet syrup produced by many flowering plants. As nectar is full of sugar, it is an energy-packed fuel.

Amazing

Mexican free-tailed bats form the largest colonies of any bat (and of almost any animal). As many as 10 million may cluster together in a single cave.

Factfile

Longest living	
Little brown bat	33 years
Largest wingspan	
Malayan flying fox	1.8 m
Smallest skull	
Bumblebee bat	11 mm
Fastest flyer	
Big brown bat	64 km/h
Longest hibernation	
Little brown bat	7 months a year

Find out more

World mammals pp. 378–379

The lesser long-nosed bat lives in desert regions of North America. It feeds on plants such as organ-pipe and barrel cacti.

○ Australia's ghost bat is the continent's only meat-eating bat. It hunts and devours frogs, birds, lizards, small mammals, and even other bats.

○ The famous vampire bat feeds on blood, and it is the only bat with this bizarre diet. At night it seeks a victim, such as a cow or horse, and crawls up its leg onto its body. The bat uses its sharp teeth to shave away a small area of flesh and uses its tongue to lap up the blood that oozes from the wound.

○ Many tropical nectar- and pollen-eating bats are important pollinators of plants, including some trees. They transfer the pollen from one plant to another as they feed inside the trees.

Microchiropteran bats have large ears and small eyes. They often have a strangely shaped nose, called a nose leaf, which plays a vital role in the use of echolocation.

Echolocation

Night-flying bats rely on a special sense to help them find their way. It is called echolocation, and is similar to the method many whales use to find objects in the ocean depths. The bats send out high-pitched squeaks, which are directed by their strangely shaped noses. When the sounds hit something, such as a moth, the sounds' echoes are reflected, or bounced, back to the bat. With their extra-large ears, the bats are able to 'catch' the sounds and work out where the object is positioned.

Vampire bats are very agile and can run along the ground at some speed. Their saliva, or spit, contains special chemicals that stop blood from clotting and they often spend about 30 minutes at a time feeding. Apart from the obvious harm they cause to their victim, vampire bats also spread the deadly disease rabies.

Bats up-close

Fruit bat
Fruit bats do not tend to echolocate, but instead use their sight to hunt.

Horseshoe bat
The strangely shaped flesh on this bat's nose helps it to echolocate.

Pipistrelle bat
The pipistrelle's face is blackish and prominent with dark, long ears.

Vampire bat
This bat's incisor teeth slice into flesh without alerting the victim.

Rodents

There are more than 1700 types, or species, of rodent and they make up the largest group of mammals. Rodents are usually small, four-legged creatures with long tails and sharp senses. They have four long incisor teeth, which keep growing throughout the animal's life. Rodents are often intelligent, agile and adaptable, and can be found living all over the world, in almost every habitat.

The cavy is the original 'guinea pig' from which many kinds of pet guinea pigs are bred. It lives in grassy and rocky scrub in southern South America.

The woodchuck, or groundhog, spends the winter in hibernation. The males fight one another during the spring mating season and defend their burrows by flicking their tails and clicking their teeth.

Voles are mouse-like rodents. They normally eat plant matter and often live in meadows and on farmland.

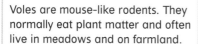

Rodents have long and strong teeth, and powerful jaws that are suited to gnawing. Like this chipmunk, most rodents eat plant matter, such as seeds, nuts and fruits.

Porcupines move with a slow, shuffling waddle. They do not need to run from their enemies as they are equipped with long, sharp spines.

The capybara is the largest-living rodent and measures about 1.3 m long. It lives around ponds, lakes and rivers in South America.

Amazing

Forty per cent of all mammal species are rodents. Some are considered pests, as they eat human food and spread disease.

There are more than 270 different types of squirrel. They help spread woodland trees by burying nuts to eat later – and then forgetting where they left them.

Find out more

How mammals move p. 385

Black rats have spread around the world by travelling on ships. They carry fleas, which harbour the plague – a terrible disease that has caused the deaths of millions of people over the centuries.

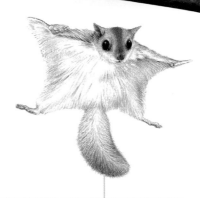

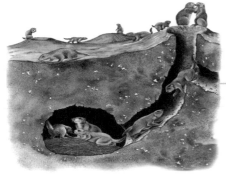

Prairie dogs are some of the best burrowers of the mammal world. (Despite their name they are ground squirrels.) Families live together in groups called coteries and their underground warrens can extend for hundreds of kilometres.

Flying squirrels are gliders rather than true flyers. They have a hairy membrane that reaches between their limbs and which acts like a parachute. They use their tails like a rudder, to direct them in the air.

Beavers are well-suited to their watery lifestyle. They have nostrils and ears that shut when underwater and a glossy, waterproof coat. Families often work together to build dams across streams.

Lemmings, like many rodents, prefer to live in groups. They build their nests under the snow in winter and dig tunnels through the snow to find grass, berries and lichen to eat.

North American gerbils avoid overheating in their dry desert home by feeding only at night. They are so well-suited to their habitat that they get all their water from food and never need to drink.

Rats and mice are often regarded as pests as many of them live with or near humans. They eat stores of grain and will invade cupboards and kitchens, given the opportunity.

The harvest mouse makes its nest from grass stems that are carefully woven together. They feed on shoots, seeds and insects.

Rabbits, Hares and Pikas

Rabbits and hares live in open, grassy country. With their huge ears, large eyes and twitching noses, they are always alert to danger and ready to escape into their burrows, hide in the undergrowth, or race off at great speed. Pikas are small vole-like cousins of rabbits and live mainly in Asia.

Amazing

With feet up to 15 cm long, hares can reach speeds of 60 km/h when running flat out.

○ The common rabbit originally came from Spain and North Africa, but it has travelled to many other countries where it has pushed native animals out of their habitats and eaten local plants in huge quantities.

○ Rabbits, hares and pikas belong to a group of mammals called lagomorphs. They are similar to rodents, and like them have large incisor teeth that grow continuously. They have superb senses of hearing and sight, and strong, muscular legs that help them to move at great speed.

○ Pikas are small creatures that resemble voles or guinea pigs, with rounded ears and almost no tail. Like rabbits, they feed mainly on grasses and other plants.

○ Baby rabbits are called kittens, adult males are called bucks and adult females are called does. Baby hares are called leverets.

○ The hairy feet of the snowshoe hare allow it to run over snow without sinking. It lives in the northern forests of North America and is a favourite prey of the lynx.

○ The Arctic hare is known by other names, such as tundra hare and mountain hare, depending on where it lives. In the summer this animal has a brown coat, but in the winter it grows a white coat, which camouflages it against the fallen snow.

○ Rabbits dig burrows, but hares do not. The burrows may connect to make a huge underground labyrinth, or warren. Each burrow is wide enough for one rabbit to pass at a time, and may end in chambers where females give birth.

○ The huge ears of the desert hare, the antelope jackrabbit, can hear the tiny sounds of an approaching predator, and can lose body heat, helping the animal to keep cool. Its long legs help it reach enormous speeds.

Fast breeders

Rabbits are well known for their highly successful breeding habits. The females of some species are able to mate and get pregnant when only three months old. The gestation period (pregnancy) may last for only four to six weeks. By the time the babies, or kittens, are born, the mother rabbit may already be growing the next litter inside her. A mother rabbit may have up to 12 kittens each time, and can have six litters every year.

At birth

Hares are born with fur and their eyes open; rabbits are born naked and with their eyes closed.

▶ *During periods of drought (dry weather), the antelope jackrabbit braves the thorns of cacti and yuccas to nibble their fleshy parts for precious moisture.*

○ Brown hares can leap a distance of 3 m when scared, but they prefer to crouch still and wait until danger passes. When rabbits are threatened they thump the ground to warn other members of their colony.

○ Pikas tend to live in mountainous regions of the world. Large-eared pikas live higher than almost any other mammal, 6000 m up in the mountains of the Himalaya.

▼ *On the approach of spring, the snowshoe hare's brain detects the extra hours of daylight, and begins to moult its thick, white fur.*

Find out more

What mammals eat pp. 376–377

Northern pika

Snowshoe hare

Mountain hare

Black-tailed
jackrabbit

Rabbit

Brown hare

Steppe pika

Red pika

Northern pika
Pikas are small creatures resembling voles or guinea pigs, with rounded ears and almost no tail. Like rabbits they feed mainly on grasses and other plants.

Snowshoe hare
The hairy feet of this hare allow it to run over snow without sinking. It lives in the northern forests of North America and is a favourite prey of lynx.

Mountain hare
This dappled hare lives mainly in the Arctic and mountain habitats. The more snow that falls in the region where it lives, the whiter its coat turns in winter.

Black-tailed jackrabbit
This North American hare's huge ears detect very faint noises. They also give off heat and help the jackrabbit stay cool in the hot summer sun.

Rabbit
The common rabbit is all too common in many places. It came originally from Spain and North Africa, but it has invaded many other countries, eating local plants so that other animals starve, as well as destroying crops and digging its home burrows, called warrens.

Brown hare
Found in many parts of Europe and Asia, the brown hare can cover 3 m in one leap. However, it runs only as a last resort, preferring to crouch still until danger has passed.

Red pika
Most pikas prefer rocky upland slopes. The red pika lives in the Tien Shan mountain range in Central Asia, making its home at heights of up to 4000 m.

Steppe pika
The steppe pika digs an elaborate network of burrows in the steppes or grasslands of Asia. It retreats underground to escape its many predators.

Mustelids

Otters, stoats, weasels and badgers all belong to the mammal group of mustelids. They are long-bodied, short-legged, sharp-toothed hunters. They are active, flexible, fast-moving and often race into holes or burrows after their prey. Many species are extremely fierce and willing to attack animals bigger than themselves.

○ The mustelid group of mammals contains a wide variety of animals living in different habitats. Martens, for example, live in trees, badgers burrow, and minks live on the water's edge. Most mustelids have short ears and five toes on each foot. They usually have long tails and slender bodies.

○ Badgers are very strong, powerful animals that come out at night. They live in family groups in huge networks of underground chambers and tunnels, called setts. Badgers eat a variety of foods, including worms, insects, frogs, lizards, birds and fruit.

Weasels

Tribesmen in Burma are reported to have used trained weasels to kill wild geese and the young of wild goats.

▷ Polecats are closely related to the domestic ferret. When threatened, this marbled polecat releases a foul smell from glands beneath its tail.

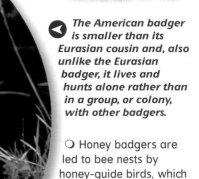

○ Sea otters rarely come onto land, and rarely go into water that is more than 15 m deep. They live along the coasts of the North and West Pacific and eat shellfish, worms, starfish and sea urchins.

○ The biggest otter is the giant or Brazilian otter of South American rivers and swamps. It grows to 2 m in total length and 30 kg in weight.

▷ The American least weasel is the world's smallest mammalian carnivore. It measures 15 cm in length and weighs just 30 g.

◁ The American badger is smaller than its Eurasian cousin and, also unlike the Eurasian badger, it lives and hunts alone rather than in a group, or colony, with other badgers.

○ Honey badgers are led to bee nests by honey-guide birds, which attract it with special calls. Once a honey badger has opened the nest with its long front claws, the bird can eat its fill of beeswax, bees and grubs, while the honey badger eats the honey and grubs. The honey badger is protected from bee stings by its extremely tough skin.

○ A female Eurasian badger sometimes has female helpers that babysit her cubs while she forages for food. Badgers are very clean animals and regularly change their bedding and dig latrines some distance from the sett.

Find out more

How mammals move p. 385

▶ *The sea otter is the world's smallest marine mammal. It has thick fur that keeps it warm and dry and a strong tail that it uses to steer itself in the water, like a rudder.*

Clever otter

The sea otter is an intelligent mammal that has developed some interesting behaviour. It can crack open shells by using a rock. It collects the rock from the sea floor then lies on its back, rests the rock on its belly and smashes the shell against it. A few hard whacks later, and the shell is broken. To stop itself from being pulled out to sea by the tide, a tired sea otter may wrap itself in kelp (seaweed) to anchor itself before it sleeps.

◀ *A honey badger's skin is so loose that the animal can twist right round and bite its attacker.*

○ Skunks typically have small heads, fluffy tails and a black and white colouring. These bold stripes of colour act as a warning to any attackers; they warn of the foul liquid a skunk can spray from its rump. Before spraying, a skunk stamps its feet and raises its tail.

○ Weasels are amongst the smallest animals in the mustelid group, although the males are often twice the size of females and eat different prey. They hunt on mice, which they can pursue down burrows thanks to their narrow skulls and thin bodies.

Amazing

The sea otter has the densest fur of any mammal in the world. Approximately 150,000 hairs occupy just 1 sq cm of the sea otter's skin!

▶ *A skunk's spray can travel up to 6 m and consists of seven different foul-smelling chemicals that can cause temporary blindness.*

▲ *Otters are well-adapted to life in water, where they prey on fish, frogs, shellfish and even other aquatic mammals, such as water voles.*

○ Stoats have long been farmed for their fur. Although these common mustelids have reddish-brown fur in the summer, their winter coat is white. White stoat fur is known as ermine.

○ The marbled polecat has unusual markings on its fur. It has black fur that is speckled, striped or spotted in yellow or white. This polecat lives across central Asia and hunts mice, voles and lemmings at dusk.

Rhinoceroses and Tapirs

Rhinoceroses might look like hippopotamuses or elephants, but they are actually more closely related to tapirs and horses. Rhinos are massive, hoofed creatures with extremely thick skin, bulky, strong bodies and at least one horn on the nose. Tapirs resemble pigs, and have changed very little in the last 25 million years.

▲ Young tapirs, like this one from Brazil, often have reddish-brown coats that are striped and flecked in white. This pattern provides them with camouflage in dappled forest shade.

○ The Javan rhino is the rarest, and one of the world's most threatened animals. It is now found only in wildlife reserves in the west of the island of Java, where its population numbers tens rather than hundreds. It lives mainly in forests, but these are disappearing as their trees are being felled for timber and to make way for farmland.

○ The largest of all rhinos, the white rhino, reaches a length of 4.2 m, with a shoulder height of 1.9 m and a weight of 3.5 tonnes. The 'white' of its name does not refer to the beast's colour, which is grey, but means 'wide' from the rhino's broad snout.

▲ The white rhino has two horns. The front one is the largest and may reach 1.3 m in length.

○ The Sumatran rhino of Southeast Asia has two horns, like the two African types. It is the smallest rhino, up to 3 m in body length and 750 kg in weight.

○ The Indian rhino prefers open scrub and grassland to forests. Its heavy skin, almost 2 cm thick, is divided into distinct plates, which give it the appearance of a suit of armour.

○ Black rhinos, which are actually grey-brown, range widely across Africa, but they have suffered badly from the traps and guns of poachers and have been wiped out in some areas. The black rhino's long, flexible upper lip can grasp leaves and shoots as it browses.

○ One of the main problems facing all rhinos is that they breed very slowly. The female usually has one young every two to four years. This means that rhino numbers take a long time to build up or replenish.

Rhino horns

Rhinos are in grave danger of extinction and there are believed to be no more than 12,000 alive in the wild today. This is largely owing to the great value of a rhino's horn. Rhino horns are powdered and used in Chinese medicine, or carved to make ornate handles for daggers. To save the rhinos from poachers, their horns are often cut off by trained staff. The procedure is painless.

Hoofed animals

Hoofed animals are called ungulates. The type of hoof they have is used to further separate them into different groups.

Equidae	Horses and zebras
Rhinocerotidae	Rhinos
Tapiridae	Tapirs
Suidea	Pigs
Hippopotamidae	Hippos
Camilidae	Camels
Cervidae	Deer
Giraffidae	Giraffe and okapi
Bovidae	Cattle

▲ *The Malayan tapir has unusual black-and-white markings, which possibly help camouflage it in the dimly lit forest undergrowth. These mammals eat twigs and leaves.*

○ Rhinos have poor eyesight and cannot locate a motionless object further than 30 m away. They rely on their senses of hearing and smell to detect possible predators and intruders. They defend their territories and will charge at other animals, or humans, if they feel threatened.

Amazing

Rhino horns are not made of real horn, but very tightly packed hairs. The largest belonged to a white rhino and was more than 1.5 m long.

○ Rhinos may look like fearsome hunters, but they are timid herbivores that exist on a diet of branches, leaves, stems and grass.

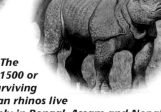

○ Fossil remains of bones and teeth show that tapirs were roaming forests more than 25 million years ago. They eat plants and live in woods and forests in Southeast Asia and Central America.

○ There are only four species of tapir: South American tapir, Mountain tapir, Baird's tapir and Malayan tapir. They have slender pig-like bodies and long snouts. Their sense of smell is excellent and they also have good hearing.

○ Tapirs spend much of the day underwater to escape predators and keep cool in their hot forest homes. They use their long snouts as snorkels.

◀ *Javan rhinos have no hair, except on the tips of their tails and on their ears. They are nocturnal and live alone.*

◀ *The 1500 or so surviving Indian rhinos live mainly in Bengal, Assam and Nepal.*

Rare rhino

The Sumatran rhino is partly covered in long hair. It is a rare rainforest animal with a total number of only 100 to 200 in the world.

▼ *Black rhinos are often active at night. They tend to live alone and spend the day resting or wallowing in mud.*

Find out more

Family life pp. 382–383

Pigs and Hippopotamuses

Pigs are an adaptable group of animals that includes boars and hogs. They have rounded stocky bodies, large heads and slender legs. Hippopotamuses spend most of their time under, or near, water and it is now believed that they are more closely related to whales than any other of the world's hoofed mammals.

▶ *When they graze during the daytime, hippos can get uncomfortably hot. A brief wallow in a nearby pool helps them to cool down and soothes their sensitive skin.*

▲ *Hippo calves may stay with their mothers until they are four or five years old. The family group forms a close bond.*

○ Female pigs are called sows, males are called boars and the youngsters are called piglets. They usually live in family groups, called sounders, of one sow and her young.

○ The warthog is a wild pig that grazes on grasslands in Africa. Warthogs have manes of dark hair that run down their spines and large curved tusks that are used for fighting.

▶ *Even when eating waterlettuce a hippo must stay alert, keeping its eyes, ears and nostrils above water.*

○ Peccaries are closely related to pigs. They live in South America and have complex stomachs that can digest tough plant fibres. They live in large herds, or sounders, with the adult males and may, as a group, attack other animals that are larger than themselves.

○ The wild boar is believed to be the ancestor of all domestic pigs. Boars have thick, coarse fur that is striped in piglets. The sows often form groups for safety and they are very protective of their young.

○ Domestic pigs do not deserve their reputation as dirty animals – they lie in mud only to cool down because they are unable to sweat. They are also highly intelligent creatures and can be trained just as easily as some breeds of dog.

Fierce protectors

Hippos are widely regarded as one of Africa's most dangerous mammals, despite the fact that they are not predators or hunters. Hippos will, however, attack to protect their territory or young. They have been known to swim below a boat and capsize it when it has come too close to a young hippo lurking underwater. A hippo can kill humans by crushing them with their mighty jaw.

○ Hippos lie in water with just their nostrils, eyes and ears visible at the surface. Each hippo herd occupies a stretch, or territory, of river. Male hippos sometimes fight each for territory or for females at breeding time. They can inflict fatal wounds on one another, using their enormous canine teeth.

○ Hippos come out of water at night and graze on the shore of the river. Their diet is mostly grass, although they have been known to eat small animals or nibble at other plants.

○ Hippos travel on land up to 30 km a night in search of food, but if they are frightened they will run back to water to hide. They will spend up to five hours a night feeding.

Agile and powerful warthogs roam across the savannah, often living in family groups and seeking shelter in burrows.

○ Baby hippos are called calves. They stay with their mothers well after they have weaned (moved from milk onto solid food). Hippos suckle their young underwater and often sleep submerged, surfacing regularly to breathe while still unconscious.

○ The pygmy hippo is only about 90 cm tall, but it can still weigh as much as 250 kg. It lives in the swampy forests of West Africa but is rare – and at some risk of extinction in the wild – with just a few thousand remaining.

The collared peccary, or javelina, has a pale stripe around its neck. It mostly eats plant matter and small animals, such as lizards.

Hippo 'hitchers'

The plump, steady back of a wallowing hippo provides a safe and convenient resting place for birds. Some African birds, such as bee-eaters and egrets, make a habit of settling on hippos where they can find a good supply of insects to eat. The hippos tolerate these 'hitchhikers' because they are glad to be rid of the biting insects, which irritate and damage their skin.

Pigs are kept on farms to supply the meat trade, but they are becoming increasingly popular as pets.

Amazing

A male hippo can grow to 4 m in length and can weigh well over 3 tonnes.

Giraffes, Camels and Deer

With their extremely long necks and ungainly stick-like legs, giraffes are easy to spot in their favoured habitat, the open bush of Africa. Here they use their height to reach tasty twigs and shoots almost 6 m above the ground.

❍ Camels, deer and giraffes all belong to a large group of hoofed mammals called artiodactyls. They are placed in this group because they have an even number of toes in their hooves. (The toes may not be visible, but the bones are still there.)

❍ There is only one species of giraffe, but this includes several varieties each with a different coat pattern. Reticulated giraffes of East Africa have triangular patches, while South African Cape giraffes have blotchy markings. The fur of a giraffe is patched-in brown on cream, and each giraffe has its own unique pattern.

▶ *With their thick fur, Bactrian camels can survive the harsh, cold lands of China and Mongolia.*

❍ A giraffe's neck may be more than 2 m long, but it has only seven bones in it. That is the same number as is found in a human neck. Its long tongue is so tough that it can wrap around the thorns of an acacia tree without becoming damaged.

❍ When giraffes walk they move the two legs on one side of their body then the two on the other side. Their long legs mean that when it comes to running they can gallop along at speeds of 50 km/h.

Alpacas and llamas

Alpacas and llamas are close relatives of camels. They live at great heights in the South American Andes and are prized for their fine wool.

Amazing

Giraffes are the world's tallest animals, but one giraffe is five times lighter than an elephant.

❍ Female giraffes with calves have been seen to severely beat, and drive off, attacking lions. They use their hoofs, necks and heads as weapons. Newly born and young giraffes are at particular risk from lions and other African predators.

❍ Camels are specialized for harsh habitats and can withstand drought (a long dry spell) well. They have long eyelashes that protect their eyes when desert winds whip up sand, slit-like nostrils, and broad feet that keep them steady on the unstable ground.

◀ *Giraffes tend to form social groups, or herds, often containing 15 to 20 individuals. Generally giraffes are not aggressive animals.*

Find out more

Animal sizes p. 372

When a whitetail deer senses danger it raises its tail, flashing white fur to warn other deer nearby.

Most camels today are domesticated and are used by people as beasts of burden to transport belongings many kilometres through the desert. They are also used to provide milk, meat, wool and skins. When carrying its load, a camel travels at around 3 to 8 km/h and can walk at this speed for up to 18 hours without rest.

Reindeer are known as caribou in North America. Some herds migrate, or travel, hundreds of miles a year as they search for food.

A close-up of a giraffe's coat. The criss-crossed lines produce a clever camouflaging effect in the shimmering light of the African savannah.

Bactrian camels have two humps and shaggy fur, which helps to keep out the bitter cold wind of the Mongolian high grasslands where they live. A camel's hump does not contain water, but fat. This fat is converted into energy when fresh-food supplies are short.

Dromedaries endure the heat and drought of the deserts in North Africa, the Middle East and Australia. While most dromedaries are used to carrying loads, one variety is bred for racing. Like the Bactrian, dromedaries mostly eat plant material, although they will also nibble at bones and dried meat.

A newborn giraffe may be 2 m tall, but it is defenceless against even smaller predators, such as lions.

Deer are characterized by their antlers. These growths emerge directly from the animal's skull and are covered in thin skin, called velvet. The velvet has disappeared by the mating, or rutting, season, when the antlers are used by males to fight one another. Antlers fall off when the mating season is over.

The male fallow deer, or buck, has broad-spreading antlers, but the doe (female) lacks antlers. Fallow deer are common in woodland habitats where they forage for plants, shrubs and grass to eat. They live in large groups called herds. A young deer is called a fawn.

Most deer species live in woods and grasslands in cold regions, such as northern Europe and North America. Reindeer cope with harsh winters by finding lichen to eat under the snow, perhaps by smell.

A fallow deer's antlers are a good indicator of a male's general health. Large antlers, in good condition, tell a female that a male will make a good mate and produce healthy strong offspring.

Okapi

The rare okapi of West African forests is a close cousin of the giraffe. It is a shy forest-dweller that is seldom seen, living on a diet of leaves, fruits, twigs and shoots, which are abundant in the okapi's forest home. It gathers leaves using its curly, dark-blue tongue, which is almost 50 cm long. Okapis are coated in fine brown fur and have zebra-like white stripes on their legs. They live so deep in thick tropical forests that they were not discovered by Europeans until the 1900s.

405

The Horse Family

Horses, ponies, zebras and asses all belong to the same mammalian family – the equids. Equids have manes of long hair on their heads and necks, and thick, tufted tails. Their long legs, deep chests and powerful muscles allow them to run a long way, at great speed, without becoming tired.

○ **Wild Connemara ponies have lived on the moors of western Ireland since the 16th century. They are now bred throughout Europe, and are both sturdy and intelligent.**

○ Ponies are usually smaller than horses, with wider bodies and shorter legs. They are hardy creatures that can tolerate difficult habitats, including steep and rocky hillsides. Some breeds of wild pony still live in the moors and grasslands of the world.

○ An ass is a wild equid that is sure-footed and able to survive in very harsh conditions. They are shorter than most other members of the horse family and are famous for their ability to live in places where there is little food or water.

○ Przewalski's horses are the only truly wild horses left in the world. Until recently they existed only in zoos and parks, but a small herd has been put back into the wild.

△ **Arab horses are purebred hotbloods. They are thought to be the oldest breed of domestic horse and are used for racing.**

○ Since earliest times horses have been used by people to help them pull loads, plough fields and fight wars. Without the help of horses, the story of human history would be very different. Even today many people throughout the world rely on horses, ponies, donkeys and mules for transport.

○ Tame, or domestic, horses are of three main types: hotbloods, coldbloods and warmbloods. Hotbloods are used for riding and racing. Coldbloods are heavy horses used for pulling loads, and warmbloods are a mixture of the two, and the most common.

Early horses

Propalaeotherium was one of the earliest ancestors of the horse. It lived in thick forests between 49 and 43 million years ago, in the Early Tertiary Period. It had four small hooves on its front feet and three hooves on its back feet. It walked on the pads of its feet, like a dog or a cat.

△ **Shetland ponies have thick fur and manes to protect them from the cold weather. They first arrived in Scotland around 10,000 years ago, from Scandinavia.**

Horse terms

Stallion	Male over 4 years old
Mare	Female over 4 years old
Colt	Male under 4 years old
Filly	Female under 4 years old
Foal	Male or female under 1 year old

○ Horses were once hunted by predators, and they developed excellent senses of sight, hearing and smell to help them detect prowlers nearby. Horses also rely on their senses of smell to recognize one another – this is why they are often seen nuzzling each other.

○ Wild equids can see well at night, so often continue to graze when the sun has gone down. They need little sleep and can nap for a few minutes at a time while still on their feet.

○ Zebras have startling patterns of black-and-white striped fur. They live in Africa, where they inhabit the savannah. There are three types of zebra: Grevy's, Burchell's and the Mountain zebra.

○ A horse's teeth continue to grow throughout its life and the age of a horse can be determined from its teeth. Equids have sharp incisor teeth at the front of its mouth and grinding molars at the back. In old age a horse begins to lose its molars.

① *No one knows why zebras have stripes, but they may confuse predators, such as lions, or simply help zebras identify one another.*

○ Equids are highly social animals and prefer to live in family groups, called herds. The herd is usually led by a mare and contains only one adult male. If startled, horses can run away quickly. The mares stay close to their youngsters to protect them.

○ Horses can communicate with other members of the herd using both their voices and their body language. By pointing their ears backwards, horses show that they feel scared or anxious.

② *Przewalski's horse is heavily built. It has a large head, thick neck and short legs.*

Zebra skin

There are three types, or species, of zebra – Grevy's, Burchell's and mountain. A Grevy's zebra lives further north than the other two species. It is the tallest of the three types and has very thin stripes, particularly on its face. The mountian zebra has a dark muzzle and thick black stripes on its rump. It is in danger of becoming extinct. The most common the of the three types is Burchell's zebra. Zebra types can be identified by the pattern of stripes on their fur.

Grevy's   Burchell's   Mountain

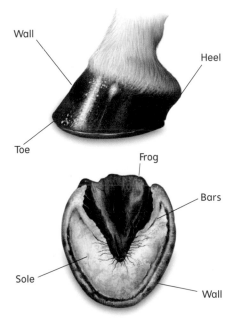

Wall

Heel

Toe

Frog

Bars

Sole

Wall

③ *A horse's hoof is made of the same substance as human nails and hair and takes nine months to grow.*

Amazing

The very first horse-like animal is thought to have lived about 50 million years ago. It is called *hyracotherium* or *eophippus*.

The Cattle Family

Cattle and their relatives belong to a mammalian family called the bovids. They have horns that, unlike deer horns, are almost never lost, and their hooves are divided into two. Bovids are a large group of mammals – there are about 140 species. Although they are found throughout the world, Africa has the biggest range of bovids. The family includes cows, bison, goats, sheep and antelope.

Amazing

The last truly wild European bison was killed in 1919, but new herds – bred from zoo animals – have been established in reserves, in particular in the Bialowieza Forest in Poland.

Waterbuck live in Africa in all kinds of habitat, but they are never far from water, especially marshes. When threatened by their natural predators – lions and leopards – they hide in water.

Domestic cows are reared for milk, which is used to make cheese, butter and yogurt. Male domestic cattle are mainly reared for their meat, which is called beef.

Mountain goats have woolly coats to keep them warm in their snowy home in western Canada and the USA. Their hooves have sharp edges that dig into cracks in the rock, and hollow soles that act like suction pads.

Dali sheep are well-equipped for mountain life, with woolly coats and nimble feet. They are always alert to predators.

The only antelope in America, the pronghorn, inhabits open prairie (grassland). It is one of the fastest runners in the world and, unusually for antelope, it sheds its horns every year.

Thomson's gazelle is one of the smallest, daintiest and fastest of the gazelles. It grows to only 100 cm head–body length and is a main food item of many savannah predators, such as lions and cheetahs.

Find out more

The cat family pp. 414–415

Also known as bison, the buffalo is a huge, powerful and aggressive mammal. Buffalo rest by day and graze at night and may form herds of 2000 or more.

Sheep were first domesticated more than 10,000 years ago. There are now more than 700 million sheep in the world.

With its long and shaggy outer coat, the musk ox is well-protected from bitingly cold winds of the tundra. Adults are about 2 m long from head to rump. Both males and females have broad, curling horns.

Bighorn sheep live wild in the mountains of North and Central America. The males sport huge, curved horns, which they use for fighting one another (rutting) during the mating season.

The pronghorn can see the white warning patches on the rump of another pronghorn from several kilometres away.

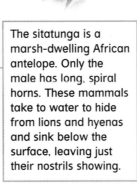

The sitatunga is a marsh-dwelling African antelope. Only the male has long, spiral horns. These mammals take to water to hide from lions and hyenas and sink below the surface, leaving just their nostrils showing.

The graceful gerenuk balances on its back legs and stretches its long neck upwards to eat the foliage of trees and tall bushes. Only the male gerenuk has horns. This species inhabits grasslands in East Africa.

Bears and Raccoons

There are eight species, or types, of bear. They tend to be very large, strong and aggressive mammals. While bears have an excellent sense of hearing, their eyesight and sense of smell are poor. Most bears have thick brown, black or white coats and immensely strong paws that are equipped with dagger-like claws.

Amazing

Bamboo is so poor in nutrients that a giant panda may have to spend up to 16 hours a day eating it.

❍ Bears generally live in woodlands and forests. They inhabit areas of Europe, Asia and North America, and are found in smaller numbers in South America and parts of Africa. Those bears that live in cool climates, sleep, or become dormant, for much of the winter to conserve their energy.

◄ The Asian bear eats mainly fruit, nuts, shoots, grubs and insects.

❍ The Asian black bear has a jet-black coat of soft, silky fur with white markings on its chest. It is an agile climber and often clambers into branches to rest.

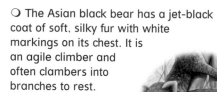

❍ Brown bears are known as grizzlies in North America, where they are widespread in areas of forest wilderness. They are the largest land-living carnivores in the world, and can stand up to 3.5 m tall. Brown bears eat mostly plant matter, but they will eat meat and fish if the opportunity arises.

❍ The yellow-white fur of the polar bear blends with the snow and ice of its Arctic home, allowing it to creep up on its prey of seals. Polar bears also hunt fish and swim well; they are the only species of bear that exists almost entirely on a diet of meat.

❍ The sun bear of Southeast Asia is the smallest bear, at around 100 cm in length. It lives in tropical forests and feeds on shoots, leaves, birds, mice and other small animals, including termites.

◄ Also known as the lesser panda, the red panda is fox-like in appearance. It is an agile tree-climber and likes to sunbathe in the treetops.

❍ North American bears that inhabit national parks have learned to scavenge food left behind by people. Many have lost their natural fear of humans and come very close to homes, cars and trailers. As a precaution these bears may be tranquillized and moved further away.

Bears in winter

Bears do not hibernate, but they do sleep for long periods in the winter in a specially prepared den. They survive on stores of body fat, but their body temperatures do not drop. Cubs are often born at this time.

▼ Female polar bears may go without eating for up to eight months, surviving only on their body fat, while over-wintering and feeding their newborn young.

Polar bears p. 381

◀ *Grizzlies catch salmon as the fish swim upstream. One bite, or a cuff from the bear's large paws, is usually enough to stun or kill a fish.*

◀ *In many suburban areas of the USA, raccoons have moved into sheds and roof spaces, emerging at night to raid rubbish bins.*

○ South America's only bear is the spectacled bear, which builds feeding and sleeping platforms in the branches of fruit trees.

○ Raccoons are small or medium-sized carnivores that walk on flat feet, like bears. They have similar lifestyles to bears, but they mostly live in trees. They come from the Americas and have long bodies, long tails and are active at night.

○ Raccoons eat a huge variety of foods, from small animals, like mice, birds, frogs and fish, to shoots, fruits and berries. Most have brown or grey fur and they often have mask-like face markings and ringed tails. Animals, like raccoons, that will eat almost any type of food they can find are called 'opportunists'.

▲ *Kinkajous live in a range of habitats in Central and South America. They have very strong tails.*

○ The red panda is actually more closely related to raccoons than it is to panda bears. It lives in China and nearby countries, preferring dense mountain forests. Its diet consists of bamboo, leaves, grass, fruit, nuts and small creatures.

▲ *A sun bear's tongue can reach 25 cm into cracks and crevices to scoop up bees, grubs, termites or honey. Its claws are unusually long for a tree-climbing mammal.*

▲ *Spectacled bears feed on fruit, but they occasionally wander onto farmland and raid the crops.*

Protecting the giant panda

There are around 1600 giant pandas left in the wild, almost all of them in Western China. About 100 pandas are kept in captivity. These endangered animals have become an international symbol of animal conservation. The Chinese government has established around 50 nature reserves, where about 980 of the remaining pandas are protected from poaching and the loss of their habitat. The population of pandas is so small, and they reproduce so slowly, that it is still doubtful that they will avoid extinction in the long term.

Elephants

The three kinds of elephant are the largest land animals in the world. They also come from a truly ancient group of mammals. Various kinds of elephant and mammoth have lived on Earth for more than 30 million years.

Elephant relatives

Rock hyraxes may look like rabbits or chinchillas, but they are believed to be the closest living relatives of the elephant. They eat grass and other plants and live in Africa, especially on inland cliffs and among the rocky outcrops. There are actually two species of hyrax: the rock hyrax and the tree hyrax. The rock hyrax is smaller than the tree hyrax – and a great deal smaller than its other relative, the elephant!

○ A large African elephant male stands more than 3 m tall, has a head and body nearly 7 m long and weighs over 5 tonnes. The huge ears of the African elephant help to keep it cool by losing heat over their large surface area. An elephant may also flap its ears to fan its body.

◭ *All elephants are sociable animals, but African elephants form the largest groups, or herds. These herds may number several hundred individuals particularly when there is plenty of food available.*

○ Asian elephants are slightly smaller in size than their African cousins. They also have smaller ears and shorter tusks. Female Asian elephants may lack tusks altogether. The molar (chewing and grinding) teeth of Asian elephants are so similar to fossilized teeth of extinct mammals that it is believed the two species are closely related.

○ Like the African and Asian elephants, the third species of elephant – the African forest elephant – is an endangered species. It lives in the forests of west and central Africa.

◭ *The African elephant (on the left) is the largest of the three elephant species. The Asian elephant (on the right) has smaller ears than its close relative, and the tusks are either short, or (in females) absent altogether.*

Find out more

Mammoths p. 375

Amazing

An elephant eats about 150 kg of food a day – that's the weight of two adult people.

○ The elephant's trunk, which is really its very long nose and upper lip, is like a multipurpose fifth limb. It can grasp and pull leaves and similar food into its mouth for chewing. It sucks up water and squirts it into the mouth when the elephant drinks. The trunk is also able to sniff the air for scents.

○ Elephants live in small herds, usually of females and their young. The eldest female is known as a matriarch, and she leads the group. Male elephants are called bulls and they join a herd only at mating time.

○ Elephants are very intelligent mammals, with the largest brains of all land animals. They also have very good memories – Asian elephants have been domesticated and have learnt to follow simple instructions and perform tasks.

○ Elephant tusks are actually very large upper incisor teeth. They are made of a hard white substance called ivory. The elephant uses them to dig for food and water, and to defend itself against predators, such as lions (in Africa or Asia) or tigers (in Asia).

◁ *When the leader of the herd senses danger, she lifts her trunk and sniffs the air – then warns the others by using her trunk to give a loud blast called a trumpet. If an intruder comes too close, she will roll down her trunk, throw back her ears, lower her head and charge at up to 50 km/h.*

▷ *Elephants have long incisor teeth, called tusks, and huge molars, which can grow to more than 30 cm long.*

○ Elephants communicate over long distances using low frequency sounds (too low for humans to hear). They are good swimmers, and some Asian elephants have been seen to swim 10 km.

○ Elephants sometimes enter caves in order to lick rocks that contain essential minerals, such as salt, which they need to include in their diet.

▽ *Young elephants (called calves) are closely protected by their mothers and the other female members of the herd.*

Elephants in danger

Although around 30,000 Asian elephants are believed to live in the forests of Southeast Asia, they are a species in danger of extinction. They are poached for meat and ivory, but the major threat comes from loss of habitat. As the human population grows, demand for land for farming and housing increases. In 1990 the sale of ivory was banned worldwide in the hope that this would stop the killing of thousands of African elephants. Despite the ban elephants are still killed and their ivory finds its way on to the market. There are around half a million African elephants, but as poaching and loss of habitat continue the numbers are expected to decline.

The Cat Family

Big cats are the most fearsome hunters in the animal world. They stalk in stealthy silence, charge like lightening, pounce, and slaughter their victims using razor-sharp teeth and claws. Like the smaller cats, they are carnivores with keen senses, quick reactions and great agility. Cats belong to a group of mammals called felidae.

Amazing

An adult male lion can eat up to 30 kg of meat in one go, and will not need to eat again for several days.

○ The tiger is not only the biggest of the cats, it is also one of the largest carnivores living on land. Siberian tigers are the largest of the five surviving varieties of tiger, and may weigh as much as 350 kg and measure up to 3 m in length.

○ All cats have rough tongues – a scratchy surface is ideal for scraping meat off bones. Cats can turn their tongues into a scoop shape, which enables them to lap up large quantities of water at a time.

○ Most cats are loners and inhabit a territory, which they defend against intruders. Youngsters normally stay with their mothers until they are between one and three years old. Lions normally live in groups called prides.

○ Cheetahs are the world's fastest land animals. They live in the grasslands and deserts of Africa, the Middle East and western Asia. Although a female may have between four and six cubs in each litter, only one in 20 cubs survives to adulthood – the others are usually killed by lions and hyenas.

○ Male lions help to look after the young when the lionesses are hunting. Males eat before the females, but often let the youngsters eat first. All lions have tufts of fur on their tails. These tufts have no known purpose – except as playthings for cubs.

Lions usually live in prides of four to six adults and their cubs. Adult males stay with a pride only for a few years at a time, having to leave when younger, healthier males fight them for superiority.

○ Pumas inhabit a wide range of habitats, from the southern tip of South America all the way northward to Alaska. They are often regarded as the most graceful species of big cat and they can spring up, silently and smoothly, 2 m into a tree.

Only 6000 or so tigers remain living in the wild. They live in South and East Asia where their habitat is under threat. Tigers are also poached for their skins and bones, which are used, illegally, in traditional Chinese medicines.

Like all cats, the cheetah has a rounded head, short muzzle and forward-facing eyes. It has excellent vision and can even see well in the dim light.

> *Jaguars are immensely powerful beasts, and can attack and kill cattle and horses. They can even feed on turtles, which they crack open with their huge jaws.*

Silent steps

The bottom of a cat's paw has tufts of soft fur that help muffle the sound of this fearsome predator as it silently stalks its prey.

○ Of all the big cats, jaguars are the most water-loving. They live in swampy areas in Central America and in the Amazon basin. They have been ruthlessly hunted for their beautiful fur, but now the greatest danger to their survival comes from the destruction of forest habitats.

○ Leopards are probably the most common of all big cats. They hunt at night and will hunt and eat almost anything that comes along, including dung beetles. They inhabit the forests of Africa and Asia.

○ There are around 37 species of cat in the world, and 300 breeds of domestic, or pet, cat. Most of the big cats are in danger of extinction, but one of the world's rarest cats is the small Iberian lynx.

< *The Canadian lynx inhabits forests where it can hunt its favourite prey – the snowshoe hare. Lynxes usually hunt at night and will wait in ambush for several hours before pouncing on their victim.*

> *Ocelots have been hunted for their fine fur. This practice is now illegal.*

▲ *Pumas, also known as cougars, panthers and mountain lions, usually hunt small animals, such as rabbits, squirrels and beavers.*

Rough tongue

When they lick themselves with their rough tongues, cats spread their own scent around their bodies, while cleaning and smoothing their fur. The tiny growths on a cat's tongue, which make it rough, are called papillae.

○ The body of an ocelot measures around 100 cm long. It is extremely agile and can leap from the ground on a dark night and grab a low-flying bat in its paws.

○ A tiger's stripes help to camouflage it as it hides in tall grass and thick vegetation. As the sunlight and shadows flicker on the tiger's coat, it blends into the background. Tigers spend most of the day resting, coming out to hunt only when the sun is setting and their camouflage is at its best.

Find out more

Past and present pp. 374–375

The Dog Family

All dogs, whether they are domestic or wild, are members of the mammalian family of canids. There are 36 species of canids, including wolves, foxes, coyotes and jackals. They are all intelligent animals with long, lean bodies, slender legs and bushy tails.

Third eyelid

Dogs have a membrane called the 'third eyelid' that protects their eyeballs. It sweeps across the eye to clear away dirt.

○ Wild dogs inhabit almost all regions of the world, except the African island of Madagascar, and New Zealand. Many species of wild dog are in danger of extinction because they are hunted, or their habitats are being destroyed. Domestic dogs, however, are thriving and are found almost everywhere that humans live.

▶ *Known for their cunning, coyotes often live near to humans and have been known to attack family pets.*

○ The largest wild dog is the grey wolf, which can measure up to 1.5 m in length and can weigh up to 60 kg. Wolves live in family groups called packs that number between eight and twelve individuals. They hunt as a group, and can kill animals, such as caribou, that are much larger than themselves.

○ Red wolves are smaller and rarer than their grey relatives. They live in only North Carolina, USA, and there may be as few as 100 of them alive in the wild.

Amazing

Domestic dogs are one million times better at smelling sweat than humans.

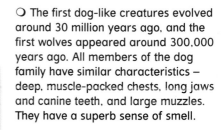

○ The first dog-like creatures evolved around 30 million years ago, and the first wolves appeared around 300,000 years ago. All members of the dog family have similar characteristics – deep, muscle-packed chests, long jaws and canine teeth, and large muzzles. They have a superb sense of smell.

○ It is believed that dogs were first tamed by humans around 12,000 years ago, during the last ice age. They were probably bred from wild wolves and dogs and may have been used for hunting, or to scare away predators.

▶ *Unlike cats, dogs cannot retract, or pull in, their claws. A dog's back paws have four claws each, but their front paws have five.*

◀ *The grey wolf is the ancestor of all domestic dogs. The similarities between the two are obvious.*

Fennec fox

The smallest wild dog in the world is the fennec fox. It is no bigger than a pet cat and lives in the desert lands of North Africa, where it hunts lizards and bugs. The fennec fox has very large ears in relation to its body size and can detect very quiet sounds, even over long distances.

Unusual dogs

Bloodhound
Droopy-eared and with a fantastic sense of smell

Chinese-crested Dog
Almost hairless and needs to wear sunscreen.

Chow Chow
Fluffy dog and one of the world's oldest breeds.

Shar Pei
The wrinkliest dog, once bred to hunt in China.

> *Like other members of the dog family, jackals are good hunters. Adult jackals bring food back to their waiting cubs.*

○ Coyotes are very fast runners and can reach speeds of 65 km/h when chasing rabbits. These wolf-like wild dogs live in North and Central America, and at night their howling can be heard across mountains and plains.

○ African wild dogs live in large packs with more than 30 members. They used to roam across the African plains hunting zebra, wildebeest and antelope, but their numbers are much reduced now.

○ A well-known member of the dog family, the red fox is found all over Europe, Asia, America and Australia. Like other foxes, red foxes dig burrows below ground where they can protect their cubs.

○ Jackals are fearless defenders of their family groups and a single jackal will attack a hyena five times its weight. Jackals live mostly on the continent of Africa and normally live in pairs. They often live close to humans and scavenge food from them.

> *Red foxes are not fussy eaters and will hunt rabbits and hares, forage for beetles and grubs, or even eat food discarded by humans.*

> *African wild dogs live in huge packs that have more than 30 members. They have lost their habitat to people and other animals and are now in danger of extinction.*

Find out more
World of mammals p. 378

Seals and Sea Lions

Seals and sea lions are superbly equipped for life in the water. Most live in oceans, but a few dwell in large lakes and rivers. They are excellent divers and some seals may stay underwater for more than an hour at a time, although, as mammals, they must surface to breathe.

❍ Seals, sea lions and walruses all belong to a mammalian family called pinnipeds. Their bodies are shaped like bullets and perfectly suited to movement in water. They are covered in fine, waterproof hair, and have thick layers of blubber, or fat. Blubber keeps them warm and acts as an energy store for times when food is scarce.

❍ Pinnipeds are descended from land-living mammals. Their limbs have evolved, over millions of years, to become flippers, which are perfectly adapted for swimming.

❍ The common seal is one of the most familiar of all seals. It lives in northern oceans and often stays close to land, scavenging food at harbours and ports. Common seals usually feed on fish, squid and shellfish and can live for 30 years or more.

❍ The walrus is the largest member of the pinniped family. It lives along Arctic coasts and swims with its flipper-like limbs. The tusks of the walrus are very long canines and can reach up to 1 m in length. They are used for fighting during the mating season. Walruses are sociable animals and live in groups, or herds, of about 100 individuals.

Amazing

The world's largest mammal herd consists of up to 1.5 million northern fur seals, which breed on two islands in the Pacific sub-Arctic region.

In Australia

Australian sea lions feed mainly on octopus, lobster and fish. They are themselves hunted by great white sharks.

⌄ Antarctic fur seals were hunted close to extinction in the 19th century. Now they are threatened by a shortage of their main food, krill.

⌄ A walrus has about 300 stiff whiskers on either side of its muzzle, which it uses to help it find food in murky waters.

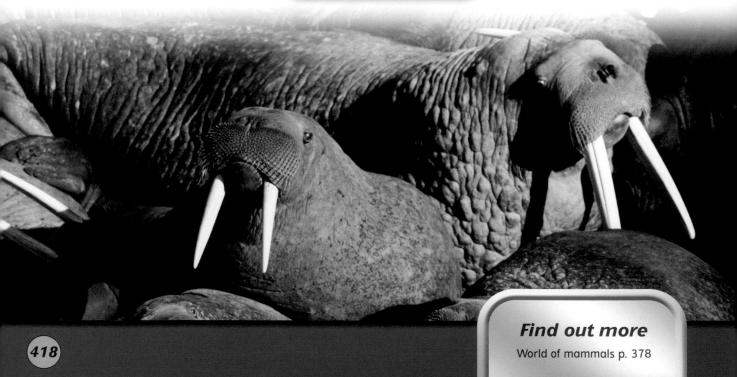

Find out more

World of mammals p. 378

❍ Although pinnipeds spend much of their lives in water, they stay on land during mating and breeding times. Males establish and defend their territories on land – and females mate with males who have the best territories. The females return to the sea, and come back to land when it is time for them to give birth, between eight and 15 months later.

🔺 *A harp seal pup has white fur that camouflages it against the snow and ice of its northern home.*

❍ One-third of a walrus's total weight is made up from blubber. This layer of insulating fat also protects the walrus during fights. In the summer months basking walruses turn pink as their blood vessels expand to lose heat, and cool the body.

❍ Harp seals rarely come to land. They spend most of their lives swimming in the sea or resting on icebergs. Their pups are even born on floating pack ice. The young pups have soft, silky white fur, which develops darker markings in the following months.

▶ *Common, or harbour, seals are the most widespread and numerous of all seals.*

▶ *Newborn harp seals have fluffy, yellowish fur. This first turns white, and then short and grey in adulthood.*

❍ Australian sea lions are one of the rarest pinnipeds, with only between 3000 and 5000 individuals alive today. Males can reach up to 2.5 m in length and weigh up to 300 kg. These are very sociable mammals and live in large groups, coming to land to mate and breed. Gestation (pregnancy) lasts 18 months. However, many cubs are killed, mainly by adult sea lions.

❍ When a seal dives deep, its heartbeat slows from 55 to 120 beats a minute to just four to 15 beats a minute. By breathing more slowly, the seal needs less oxygen, and can stay longer underwater.

◀ *Manatees are graceful swimmers. moving in water as if in slow motion. They can swim steadily at 8 km/h, steering with their flippers and moving their tails up and down. In shallow water manatees use their flippers to walk slowly on the seabed.*

Dugongs and manatees

Dugongs and manatees are similar in body-shape to seals, but they belong to a different mammalian family – the Sirenians. Sirenians are similar in appearance, but manatees have rounded tails, while dugongs have crescent tails. They are the only plant-eating sea mammals in the world. Long ago, manatees were mistaken for mermaids. Sirenians are very slow breeders, and more of them die every year than are born, threatening these unusual creatures with extinction. Sirenians live in the sea, estuaries and rivers. Their diet of plants produces large amounts of gas in their guts – which helps them to remain buoyant (float) in water.

Manatee

Whales and Dolphins

Oceans and seas cover *two-thirds of our planet. They teem with life and potential food, so it is no wonder that, long ago, mammals returned to water. Seals, sea lions and walruses are superb swimmers, but only the whales and dolphins have truly mastered life at sea.*

Whale song

It is known that whales are intelligent animals, and that they are able to communicate with one another in complex ways – although their methods are not entirely understood. Some whales communicate with a range of sounds that humans cannot hear, and male humpbacks sing elaborate 'songs' lasting 20 minutes or so, perhaps to woo females.

▼ *The sperm whale is one of the greatest diving whales and may perform this sequence each time it dives to the cold, dark depths of the ocean.*

Amazing

A sperm whale can stay underwater, holding its breath, for up to two hours at a time.

❍ It is believed that the very first mammals evolved from land animals that moved to the sea to escape predators. This probably happened around 50 million years ago, but whales did not live fully in the water until around five to ten million years ago – a very short time in evolution.

❍ Whales, dolphins and porpoises all belong to the family of mammals called cetacea, and they are known as cetaceans. They may look very different from mammals that live on land, but they all have mammalian features, such as breathing air, giving birth, and feeding their young with milk.

◗ *When frightened, Fraser's dolphins swim close together with lots of low leaps and splashing*

Indus River dolphin

The Indus River dolphin has tiny eyes and is almost blind. It travels through muddy water by using echolocation, or by feeling its way – it drags its flipper through the riverbed.

❍ As, like all mammals, whales and dolphins have lungs, they tend to come to the surface to breathe every ten minutes or so, although they can stay underwater for up to 40 minutes.

❍ The blue whale is thought to be the largest creature that ever lived on Earth. Despite its great size, it feeds solely on tiny sea creatures, called krill. Instead of teeth, a blue whale has large, horny plates, called baleens, that trap the creatures like a sieve. Blue whales devour up to 4 tonnes of krill daily in summer – that is 4 million krill a day.

1. The sperm whale surfaces and breathes in and out powerfully several times

2. It then straightens out its body and may disappear beneath the surface

3. The whale then reappears and begins to arch its back

Find out more

What is a mammal? pp. 372–373

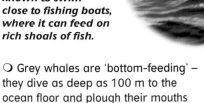

▶ *The Atlantic humpback dolphin mainly inhabits shallower waters, but it is known to swim close to fishing boats, where it can feed on rich shoals of fish.*

○ Grey whales are 'bottom-feeding' – they dive as deep as 100 m to the ocean floor and plough their mouths through the mud to scoop up shellfish, worms and other seabed animals.

○ For centuries, whales have been hunted by humans. The value of their blubber, bones and meat made the dangerous task of tracking and killing these mammals worthwhile. In the last century, with the aid of safer and more efficient ships, humans have brought some whale populations to the brink of extinction.

○ Most dolphins live in the oceans or seas but some are adapted to life in freshwater. These river dolphins are shy and little is known about them, except that, thanks to competition for food and the effects of pollution, they are in danger of extinction.

○ Groups of common dolphins, travelling and feeding together, may number up to 2000 individuals. They have been known to follow boats and aid humans in the water by keeping them afloat and driving away sharks. A group of dolphins is called a pod.

◀ *Humpback whales feed by rising up through shoals of fish with their mouths open and throat skin bulging. They scoop up water, push it out through the baleen and eat the food left inside their mouths.*

▲ *Dusky dolphins prefer warm, shallow water and live in groups of up to 1000 individuals.*

○ Some whales and dolphins can find and catch their prey using echolocation. They send out sounds, and use the echoes to work out where the prey is positioned. Although they have no sense of smell – which would be useless underwater – whales do have excellent hearing.

◀ *Killer whales, or orcas, are big deep-sea predators. They are actually a type of dolphin, rather than whale, and can reach 9 m in length.*

4. By arching its back and tipping its head downwards, the whale prepares to dive

5. Its tail is lifted out of the water as it begins to dive

6. The sperm whale dives deep into the darkness of the ocean

Lemurs and Lorises

Lemurs, lorises, tarsiers and aye-ayes belong in the mammalian family of primates, along with monkeys, apes and humans. Like all primates, they have large brains and well-developed hands with gripping thumbs. They possess forward-facing, large eyes that enable them to see and hunt at night.

○ *Pottos move slowly and can remain completely still for hours if they are threatened or scared.*

○ The golden potto is a slow-moving prosimian that is active at night. It lives in the rainforests of Central Africa where it feeds mainly on maggots, caterpillars and similar grubs. Like other prosimians, pottos have huge eyes that can reflect light, improving their vision during the night.

○ The aye-aye, a close relative of the lemur, uses its extra-long middle finger to tap on tree trunks and branches, where it listens for bugs inside. It has huge ears and can hear grubs chewing wood beneath bark. The aye-aye gnaws at the wood to make a hole and picks out the grubs with its middle finger.

○ Lemurs groom one another using a special claw on one finger, and their front teeth, which resemble a comb.

▶ *Aye-ayes were believed to be extinct, but they are now bred in captivity and then returned to the wild in Madagascar.*

○ Lemurs, lorises and aye-ayes are more primitive than monkeys and apes and are placed in their own group, the prosimians. These mammals have snouts and a highly developed sense of smell.

○ Most prosimians live in trees, and can leap from branch to branch with great accuracy and agility. Lemurs are able to move quickly, while lorises tend to creep more slowly along branches and tree trunks.

Island life

All lemurs live on the island of Madagascar where they evolved in isolation, separated from the African mainland by the 300-km wide Mozambique Channel. Lemurs were able to evolve into their many species on Madagascar mainly because they had no competition from monkeys or other primates.

▲ *Lemurs spend most of their time in trees. Ruffed lemurs leap and climb with ease, grace and speed, grabbing at branches as they balance themselves with their long tails.*

Lemurs...

Have grasping hands and feet
Are intelligent and adaptable
Have forward-facing eyes
Have flat nails rather than claws
Live in groups

○ In the mating season ring-tailed lemurs have stink fights for females. They rub their wrists and tails in stink glands under their arms and rear, then wave them at rivals to drive them off.

○ Tarsiers are found only in Southeast Asia, including parts of the Philippines. They have huge eyes and very flexible necks, which allow them to swivel their heads almost all the way round, like an owl's head.

○ The thick-tailed bushbaby is the largest of all bushbabies, with a nose to tail length of 75 cm. It lives in the forest and bush of east and southern Africa and eats many foods, including lizards and birds. Bushbabies are also known as galagos.

○ Fat-tailed dwarf lemurs sleep through the dry season in July and August, living on the fat stored in the thick bases of their tails.

◊ *Ring-tailed lemurs are graceful inhabitants of Madagascan forests. They live in groups of up to 25 and, like most lemurs, eat fruit, leaves, insects and flowers.*

Flying lemur

Despite its name, the flying lemur is neither a lemur, nor does it fly. Flying lemurs (there are only two species) live in woodlands and mountains in Southeast Asia, where they are common. They glide through the air by means of membranes that extend from the neck to the tips of the fingers, toes and tail. When these sheets of skin are spread out they work like a kite and enable the animal to leap and glide safely from tree to tree, up to distances of 130 m.

◊ *Bushbabies, such as this lesser bushbaby, get their name from the child-like crying sound they make, and their large, appealing eyes.*

○ The slow loris creeps silently and stealthily upon its prey and suddenly lunges forward to grasp it. This mammal inhabits forests of Southeast Asia and has superb night vision thanks to its huge eyes.

Amazing

The sifika lemur has one alarm call to warn of birds of prey, and another to warn of snakes.

◊ *The tarsier sits still on a branch and, when a lizard, mouse or insect ambles past, it quickly pounces.*

◊ *Lorises are normally smaller than lemurs and have larger eyes. They also tend to move more slowly than lemurs.*

Find out more

Monkeys pp. 424–425

Monkeys

Monkeys are busy, active, inquisitive creatures who live in groups, leap about in trees and make various whooping and screeching noises. Most kinds of monkey live in social groups, often led by one dominant and powerful male. Monkeys, like all primates, are intelligent, quick learners with good memories.

○ Monkeys belong to the primate group of mammals, but they are further divided into two groups: Old World and New World. Old World monkeys (from Africa and Asia) are more closely related to apes and usually have flatter faces. New World monkeys (from the Americas) have long, grasping tails and longer muzzles.

○ The mandrill is a type of baboon that lives in West African forests and is one of the biggest kinds of monkey. A male mandrill can weigh up to 90 kg, but the females are much smaller and their markings are less bright.

○ The eastern black-and-white colobus monkeys are familiar animals across the middle of Africa, although they rarely come out of the trees. In the morning and evening they search for food in the treetops and they live on a diet of plants, mainly leaves.

○ Some female red colobus monkeys in Gambia gang up to attack, and even kill, strange males. They may also travel in the company of Diana monkeys, as the Diana monkeys are better at spotting the chimps that prey on colobus monkeys.

◀ *Tree-dwelling colobus monkeys relax during the midday heat and groom one another. They live in groups of four or five monkeys, led by one male.*

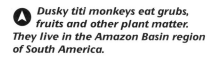

▲ *Dusky titi monkeys eat grubs, fruits and other plant matter. They live in the Amazon Basin region of South America.*

Amazing

Spider monkeys use their gripping tails to hang from low branches to drink.

▲ *Vervet monkeys are excellent communicators and make different sounds to warn of a variety of approaching predators.*

Clever primates

Monkeys, such as this Japanese snow monkey, have large skulls to accommodate their big brains. They live in complex social groups. Members of the group look out for one another to find food and shelter and they all keep a look-out for predators. They will even team up to look after younger members of the group. Primates are superb communicators. They can express moods – such as fear, anger or pleasure – using facial expressions, body language, and sounds.

Woolly monkeys have stout, compact bodies and powerful muscles. Their strength is essential for leaping and swinging through trees.

○ All monkeys can move through trees with great ease, often using a long, grasping tail as a fifth limb. Baboons' feet, however, are more suited to walking than grabbing branches.

○ Monkeys normally move using four limbs, but they can sit on their rumps, or even walk on two feet. This frees their front limbs for picking food, grooming and holding their young.

○ While many New World monkeys live in large groups, dusky titi monkeys form close pair bonds. This means that one male and one female stay together to defend their territory and look after the young. The pair will even link their tails and sing together at dawn to keep intruders away.

○ Spider monkeys are found in the jungles of central and South America. They are notable for their prehensile (grasping) tails, which are bald on the undersides and so can grip branches, as well as take the monkey's weight. They live in large groups, or troops.

○ Slim and long-legged, an African patas monkey can climb much better than a human and can also run faster – reaching 50 km/h. An old, experienced male leads his troop of about ten females and their young. They feed on the ground by day and sleep at night.

Healthy colour

It is thought that strong colours indicate good health in an animal. Female macaque monkeys prefer to mate with males who have rosy faces, and are more likely to ignore males with pale complexions.

○ Marmosets and tamarins are small New World monkeys. They often live in social groups in dense forest habitats. Females normally give birth to twins that are mainly carried by the father.

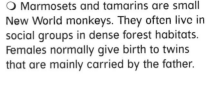

Olive baboons are olive-green in colour and live in closely knit social groups of up to 140 individuals.

When female spider monkeys reach maturity, they must leave their troop and join another.

The elegant and slender patas monkey is one of the swiftest primates and can move quickly on land and in the trees.

Find out more
World of mammals p. 378

Apes

Apes are close cousins of monkeys and our closest living relatives. They have large heads and brains, relative to body size, forward-facing eyes, front limbs that are longer than the hind limbs and no tail. Apes are primates and they are further divided into two groups: great apes (gorillas, chimps and orang-utans) and lesser apes (gibbons).

▶ *Like other ape babies, the young orang-utan depends upon its mother for milk and care. It will stay with her until it is about eight years old. Despite laws to protect them, young orang-utans are sometimes stolen and sold as pets.*

○ There are two main types of gorilla: western and eastern (which includes the shaggy-haired mountain gorilla). Both types are endangered as a result of poaching and the destruction of their forest homes.

Ape groups

Most apes live in social groups or in pairs, but orang-utans live alone.

○ Huge, muscular gorillas are peaceful animals that spend much of their time on the ground, eating plant matter in the dense African forests. At nighttime they make nests in the trees by bending branches together.

○ A mature male gorilla is known as a silverback, owing to the greying of his fur. Silverbacks play with their youngsters and will protect their family groups, even to the death. In order to capture youngsters (for zoos or illegal pets), poachers sometimes have to kill the entire family to get to them.

◀ *At 80 kg, the male orang-utan is twice as big as the female.*

▶ *A young ape depends upon its mother during its early years, and may soon die if separated from her.*

○ Chimpanzees are becoming scarce in their natural habitat – the savannahs, bush and forests of Central Africa. They face destruction of their home areas and illegal trapping for the pet trade.

○ Like other apes, chimps eat a largely vegetarian diet, but they also eat termites, ants and caterpillars. Groups of males sometimes band together to hunt for other animals, such as small deer or birds. They have even been known to attack and kill other chimps.

○ If a chimpanzee finds a tree laden with fruit, it drums on a tree trunk and makes loud panting cries to summon other chimps to come and share the feast. It is estimated that chimps can make more than 30 calls with different meanings.

Grooming is an essential part of a chimp's daily routine. It helps to create strong bonds between individuals, and to establish the group's pecking order.

Skilled apes

Apes are highly intelligent, social animals with great skills of communication and learning. In tests they have been able to solve complex problems and can even learn sign language. Chimps, orang-utans and gorillas have been seen to use tools – once thought of as only a human characteristic. Orang-utans. like chimps, use sticks as tools to poke into crevices and remove tasty bugs, or to scratch their backs. Gorillas have been observed testing a river's depth with a stick, and then using the stick to help it balance as it crossed the river.

❍ Orang-utans live only in the thick forests of Sumatra and Borneo. They are rare, shy and seldom seen. Their bright reddish-brown coats grow long and shaggy with age. They spend many hours eating soft fruits, such as figs and mangoes, but they also eat leaves, shoots, nuts and, occasionally, small animals.

❍ Orang-utans spend much more time in trees than the other great apes, and are the largest tree-dwelling mammals in the world. They are hunted by tigers and clouded leopards, but the biggest threat to their survival is the cutting down of trees in their forests.

❍ Gibbons have the longest arms relative to body size, of all primates and can hang by just one arm. They are more closely related to orang-utans than to chimps and gorillas. Some gibbons live in pairs of one male and one female and they 'sing' to one another to reinforce and strengthen their relationship.

Despite their huge size and enormous canine teeth, gorillas are not normally aggressive animals, unless attacked.

Amazing

The population of mountain gorillas is slowly growing thanks to conservation work. The latest reports suggest that there are now about 700 of these mammals left.

Monkeys and most apes move swiftly through the trees by hanging from their long arms and swinging forward from branch to branch. This method of movement is called brachiation.

Find out more
How mammals move p. 385

Glossary

Ancestor An animal that lived long ago, from which one of today's animals is descended.

Antlers The horns of a member of the deer family.

Apes Primates with either no tail, or only a very short tail.

Aquatic In water, or to do with water.

Artiodactyls Hoofed mammals with an even number of toes on each hoof.

Babook Monkeys with dog-like muzzles.

Baleen Horny material in the upper jaws of some whales.

Beasts of burden Animals that are used to carry loads.

Blubber Thick layer of fat to keep marine mammals warm.

Brachiation The way that monkeys swing through the trees using their arms to go from branch to branch.

Bovids Members of the cattle family.

Camouflage Pattern or colour that blends in with the surroundings.

Canid Member of the dog family.

Canine Fang-like tooth, used for stabbing and tearing food.

Carnivore Animal that mostly or totally eats meat.

Cetacean Member of the whale family.

Colony A group of animals that live together.

Conservation Careful protection of animals, plants and their habitats.

Continent Large area of land surrounded by water, such as Africa.

Courtship Behaviour that occurs before mating.

Domesticated Animals that are tamed and used to being around humans, such as pets and farm animals.

Drought Long period of dry weather, often leading to a shortage of water.

Echolocation A method used by some animals to find prey, or their own position.

Endangered An animal or plant species that is in danger of becoming extinct.

Endothermic Warm-blooded – an animal that can keep its body temperature constant.

Equid Member of the horse family.

Estuary The habitat where the fresh water of a river meets the salty water of a sea or ocean.

Evolution Process by which animals and plants change and develop over long periods of time.

Exothermic Cold-blooded – animals that cannot control their body temperature.

Extinction When an animal species completely dies out.

Felidae The cat family.

Flipper the limbs of marine mammals adapted for movement in the water.

Foliage Leaves and twigs of a tree.

Forage Look for food.

Fossil Remains of a long-dead animal or plant that have been preserved as stone.

Genes Instructions or information, in the form of the chemical DNA, for how the body develops, grows and functions.

Gestation The time it takes for a baby, or offspring, to grow inside its mother (or inside an egg).

Gibbon Tree-living ape with long limbs and no tail.

Gland Part of the body that makes hormones or other substances needed by the body.

Graze Feed on grassland or meadow.

Habitat The place an animal or plant lives.

Herbivore Animal that mostly or totally eats plants.

Herd Group of mammals, such as horses or elephants.

Hibernation A period of rest and deep sleep that occurs over winter.

Hormone A chemical that carries messages around the body.

Ice Age A long period of time when the Earth is cool and glaciers (rivers of ice) cover large parts of its surface.

Incisor Cutting tooth.

Incubation Keeping a young animal warm while it develops.

Insectivore Animal that mostly or totally eats insects.

Invertebrate Animals without backbones.

Ivory Tough white substance that makes up the tusks of elephants and walruses.

Krill Small shrimp-like creatures that live in the oceans.

Lagomorph A member of the rabbit and hare family.

Lichen A type of plant that grows as crusty patches, or small bushes, on rocks or trees.

Mammoth An extinct relative of the elephant.

Marsh Wet land, usually between dry land and a river or lake.

Mating The way a male animal and a female animal come together to reproduce (have young).

Matriarch The leading female in a group of animals.

Migration Movement by animals to find better conditions, such as food or weather.

Molar Grinding tooth.

Monotreme Mammal that lays eggs and may have a pouch.

Mustelids Members of the otter family.

Muzzle The jaws and nose of some animals, such as dogs.

Native Belongs to, or comes from, a certain area.

Nectar Sweet liquid produced by flowers.

Nocturnal Active at night rather than during the day.

Nutrients Contained in food and essential for a healthy life.

Omnivore Animal that eats a varied diet.

Opportunists Animals that eat almost whatever they find, such as rats.

Oxygen The gas that animals need to breathe.

Pinniped Member of the seal family.

Placenta Special organ that supplies nourishment to the unborn young in a pregnant animal.

Pod Group of whales or dolphins.

Predator An animal that hunts, or preys, on other animals.

Prehensile Grasping.

Prey An animal that is hunted upon by another.

Pride Group of lions.

Primate Member of the monkey family.

Rainforest A large habitat with trees that has lots of rain throughout the year.

Reproduction Method by which animals or plants make more of their own kind.

Respiration Another word for breathing, or releasing energy from food and gases.

Rodent Small, gnawing animal, such as a rat or mouse.

Roost Settle down to rest or sleep – a place where bats sleep.

Savannah Grasslands in Africa.

Scavenge Search for and eat discarded or leftover food.

Sett A badger burrow.

Sounder Group of pigs or peccaries.

Species A type of animal or plant that reproduces solely with only others like itself.

Swamp A habitat that is flooded for much or all of the year.

Territory An area or place where an animal lives and feeds, and which it defends by chasing away others of its kind.

Therapsid Probable ancestor of mammals.

Troop Group or colony of monkeys.

Tundra Huge area of treeless land close to the Arctic.

Ungulate Hoofed animal.

Vertebrate An animal with a backbone.

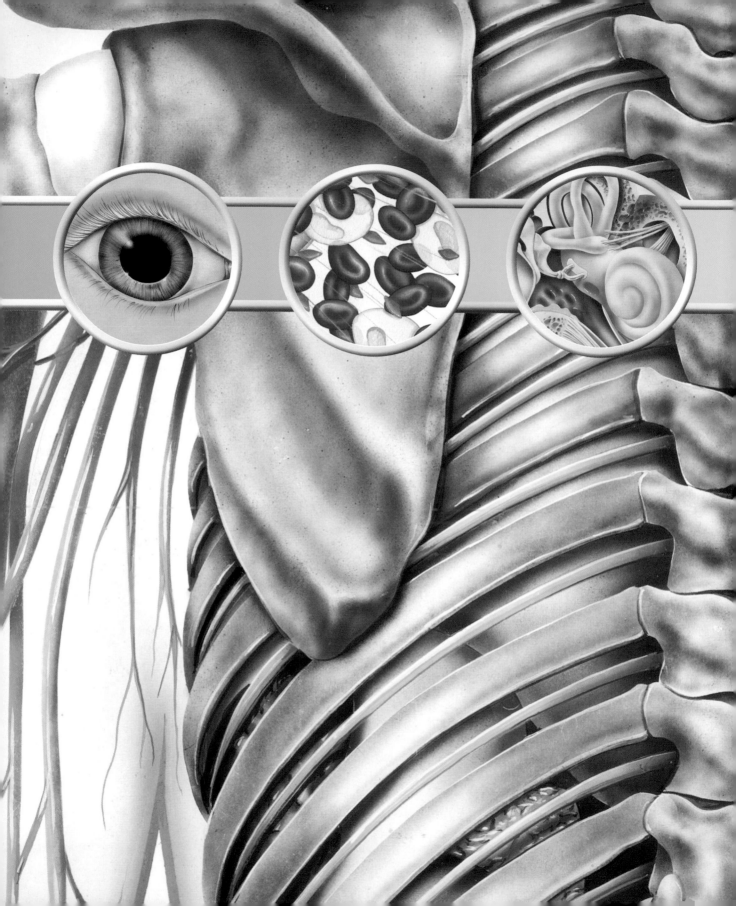

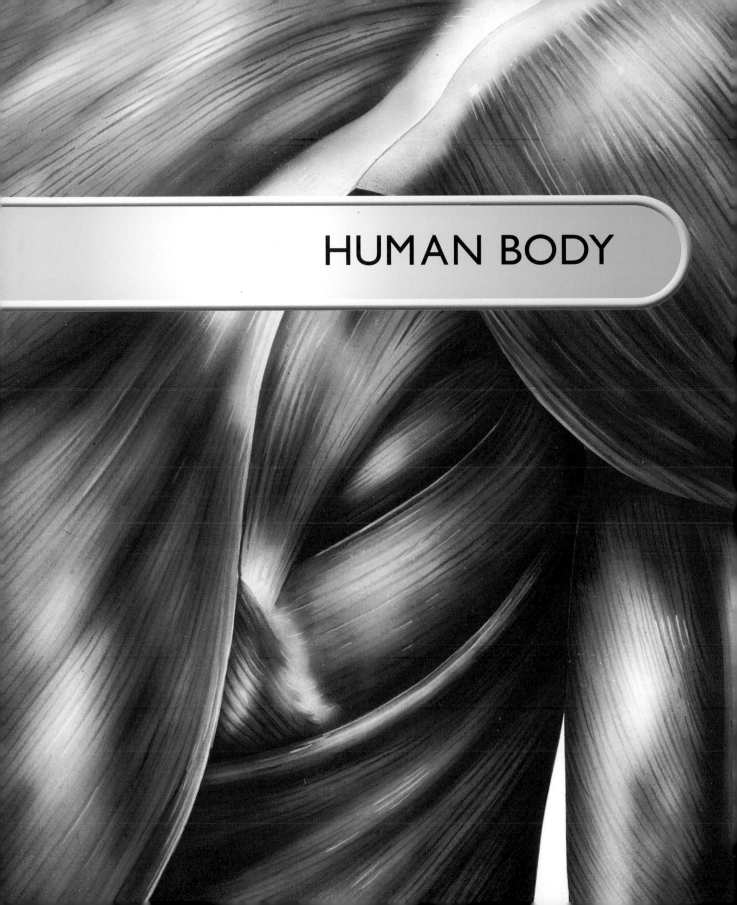

HUMAN BODY

Amazing Bodies

Even though human beings all look different, inside, these bodies are almost identical. They all have the same inner parts, or organs, the same muscles and bones, and they all work in the same way.

❍ Human beings are the most common large, living creatures on Earth.

❍ There are more than 6000 million humans in the world – far more than any kind of similar-sized animals such as lions, dolphins or even sheep.

❍ A few exceptional people break through the 'average' barrier in their size or age and grow to be incredibly tall, remain very short, become enormously heavy or reach an extremely old age.

❍ The body is made of hundreds of different parts, including organs, muscles and bones.

❍ Organs are packed closely together – and they work with each other, too.

❍ Organs include lungs, liver, kidneys, stomach, eyes, ears, heart, bladder, intestines and brain.

❍ All these organs are wrapped up in the largest organ, the skin.

❍ Each of these organs, in turn, is made from millions of cells.

❍ Our body is made of 50 million million cells. Each cell contains the genetic code that makes us all unique individuals.

❍ The genetic code is found in a chemical called DNA. Each DNA molecule is shaped like a coiled ladder.

Human bodies are different sizes and form various shapes – women and men, girls and boys, old and young, wide and slim, dark and light, tall and short – with different clothes and hairstyles.

Find out more

Body systems pp. 434–435

○ The full set of instructions in all the DNA for the whole human body is called the human genome. If all the DNA in all the cells in the body was joined end to end it would stretch from the Earth to the Sun and back more than 100 times.

○ Your bladder can comfortably stretch enough to accommodate half a litre of liquid. When you need to urinate a message is sent from the nerves in the bladder wall to your brain.

○ The skin is made up of two layers – the upper layer is made of dead skin and is continually flaking off your body. It is possible to shed up to ten billion flakes a day.

○ The brain has two halves both called hemispheres. The left half or hemisphere of the brain receives sense information from and controls the right side of the body, and vice versa.

○ If you knock your leg just below your kneecap it stretches your thigh muscles, which causes your leg to jerk upwards. This is called an involuntary reflex reaction and does not involve your brain.

○ Skin covers your entire body accounting for about 16 per cent of your body weight.

▶ *Front (anterior) view of the human body.*

○ Skin varies in thickness from approximately 0.5 mm to 4 mm in thickness.

○ Your heart is about the size of a grapefruit. During one day it pumps blood around your body about 1000 times.

○ During pregnancy the uterus swells from about the size of an apple to the size of a basketball.

Amazing

The body begins as a tiny speck, the fertilized egg, which increases in size more than five billion times to become a fully grown adult.

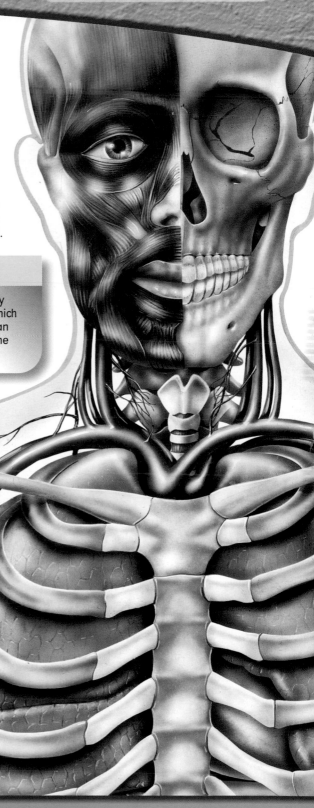

Average weight

Skin	11,000 g
Liver	1600 g
Brain	1400 g (male)
Lungs	1100 g
Heart	300 g

Body Systems

A body system is a group of parts that work together to carry out one job or particular task to help keep the body alive and working well. The human body has about a dozen main systems.

Anatomy

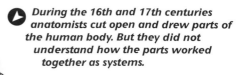

The study of the structure of the human body is called anatomy. The first great book of anatomy *On the Fabric of the Human Body* was written in 1543 by the Flemish scientist Andreas Vesalius (1514–1564).

○ The heart, blood vessels (tubes) and blood make up the circulatory system. This pumps or circulates blood all around the body.

○ The skeleton supports the body, protects the major organs, and provides an anchor for the muscles.

○ The nervous system is the brain and the nerves – the body's control and communications network.

Fig. 1

○ The digestive system breaks down food into chemicals that the body can use to its advantage.

○ The respiratory system takes air into the lungs to supply oxygen, and lets out waste carbon dioxide.

○ The urinary system controls the body's water balance, removing extra water as urine and getting rid of impurities in the blood by filtering it through the kidneys.

◀ *When the body is very active, several main systems work hard together, including the muscles, the bones and joints, the respiratory system to take in oxygen, and the circulatory system to pump blood.*

▶ *During the 16th and 17th centuries anatomists cut open and drew parts of the human body. But they did not understand how the parts worked together as systems.*

○ The immune system is the body's defence against germs. It includes white blood cells, antibodies and the lymphatic system.

○ The other body systems are the hormonal system (controls growth and internal co-ordination by chemical hormones), integumentary system (skin, hair and nails), and the sensory system (eyes, ears, nose, tongue, skin, balance).

○ The reproductive system is the sexual organs that enable people to have children. It is the only system that is different in men and women.

Artificial parts

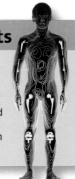

Some body parts, such as bones and joints, can be replaced by artificial versions made of tough plastics, stainless steel and titanium. Artificial or prosthetic joints are shown here coloured in white.

Amazing

The world 'muscle' comes from an old Latin word *mus* meaning 'mouse'. The reason for this is that people thought that when muscles rippled it looked like a mouse running along under the skin.

Find out more

Studying the body pp. 438–439

Major systems

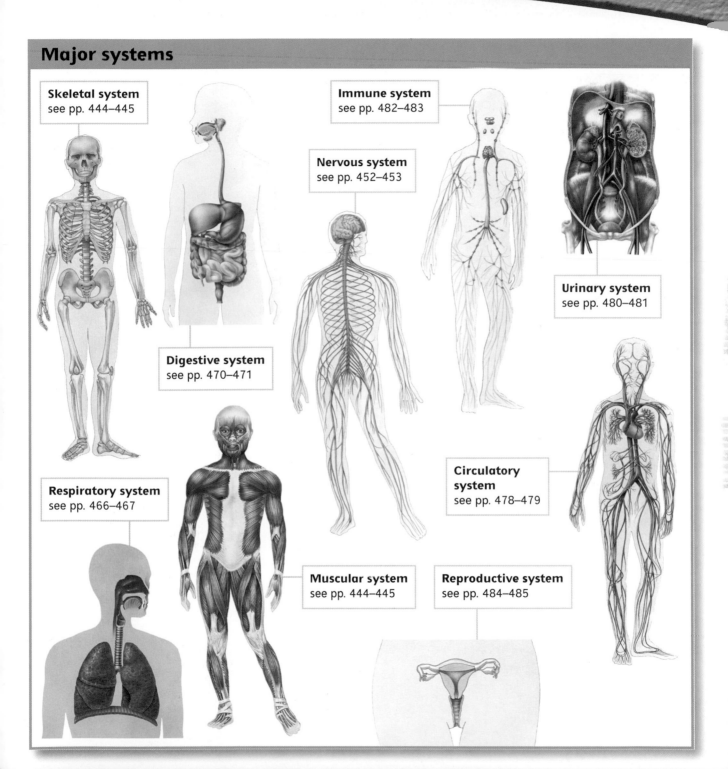

Skeletal system
see pp. 444–445

Immune system
see pp. 482–483

Nervous system
see pp. 452–453

Urinary system
see pp. 480–481

Digestive system
see pp. 470–471

Circulatory system
see pp. 478–479

Respiratory system
see pp. 466–467

Muscular system
see pp. 444–445

Reproductive system
see pp. 484–485

Body Cells and Tissues

The human body is made of more than 50 million million microscopic cells. A typical cell is 0.02 mm across – about 1000 would fit on this full stop. There are at least 200 kinds of cells in the body, with different sizes and shapes, and different functions.

○ The cell's outside layer is the cell or plasma membrane. Inside the cell, many tiny organelles (cells with specialized functions) float in the jelly-like cytoplasm.

Amazing

Every second, more than two million new red cells for the blood are made by the bone marrow.

○ Most cells do not live for long. They wear out and die naturally at the rate of 5 million every second. However, specialized types of cells, called stem cells, are always dividing, to produce new cells that replace the old ones.

○ Tissues are groups or collections of microscopic cells that are all the same type and do the same job. Examples include muscle tissue, which can shorten or contract to cause movement, and nerve tissue, which carries nerve signals.

Brain scans

A head scan reveals the inside of the brain's tissues as if 'sliced' into layers. Carrying out many scans at different levels builds up a 3-D structure of the brain and head.

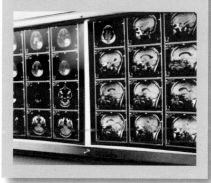

▶ The cell membrane is the outer layer, controlling what comes into and goes out of the cell. Mitochondria break down glucose sugar to release its stored chemical energy, which powers the cell's processes. Ribosomes are like tiny factories making new substances, especially proteins, which are the cell's main structural parts or 'building bricks'. Lysosomes are the cell's dustbins, breaking up any unwanted material. Golgi bodies are the cell's dispatch centre, where chemicals are bagged up inside tiny membranes to send where they are needed. The nucleus is the cell's control centre, sending out instructions via a chemical called messenger RNA whenever a new chemical is needed.

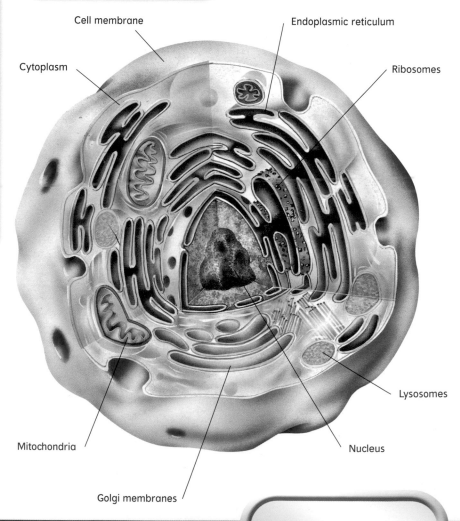

Cell membrane

Cytoplasm

Endoplasmic reticulum

Ribosomes

Lysosomes

Nucleus

Golgi membranes

Mitochondria

Find out more

Blood and vessels pp. 478–479

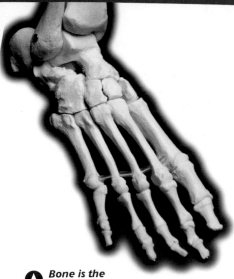

Bone is the second-strongest tissue in the body. It lasts longest and resists decay most. The hardest of all tissues is the enamel that covers the surface of the teeth.

○ Connective tissue holds all the other kinds of tissue together in various ways. Adipose tissue makes fat, and tendons and cartilage are also connective tissue.

○ Epithelial tissue is lining or covering material, making skin and other parts of the body. It may combine three kinds of cell to make a thin waterproof layer – squamous (flat), cuboid (box-like) and columnar (pillar-like) cells.

○ Organs include the heart, brain, stomach and kidneys and are the body's main parts or structures. The biggest organ in the body is the liver, while the largest organ of the whole body is the skin. Usually, several organs work together as a body system.

Under the microscope

Bacteria, the commonest kinds of microbes, are tiny blobs compared to body cells.

Blood is viewed as a tissue – a collection of similar cells all doing much the same task, like these red blood cells.

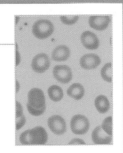

The immune system includes white blood cells that can change shape and flow along.

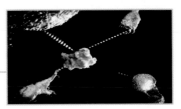

Lungs are largely made from special lung tissues, but the mucous membrane that lines the airways is epithelial tissue.

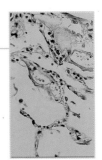

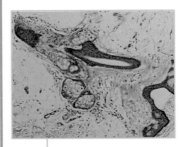

Epithelial tissues of many kinds form the outer coverings and inner linings of many body parts. Skin is one complex form of epithelial tissue.

This microscope picture shows the gum tissue around a tooth.

Cell life

Epithelial cell (inside of cheek)	10 hours
Epidermal cell (skin surface)	4 weeks
Red blood cell	3 months
Liver cell	18 months
Bone cell	10 years
Nerve cell in brain	50-plus years

Size of cells

Among the smallest cells in the human body are red blood cells, which are only 0.007 mm across. Among the largest cells in the human body are giant muscle cells or fibres, 0.1 mm wide and up to 50 mm long.

Studying the Body

We know more about the human body than anything else in the Universe. Yet every day we find more about how the body moves, digests food, gets rid of wastes, controls its internal conditions, fights germs and disease, and stays fit and healthy. To do this, scientists and medical researchers use a huge variety of modern machines, gadgets and technologies. They include scanners, chemical tests, microscopes and electrical monitors.

❍ Chemical tests on the blood and other parts show the substances they contain. Microscopes reveal the smallest cells and even genes.

❍ Electrical devices, such as heart (ECG) and brain (EEG) monitors, show readings as wavy lines on a paper sheet or screen for doctors to examine.

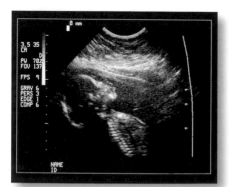

▲ One or two ultrasound scans are routine during pregnancy to check the development of the baby in the uterus.

❍ Ordinary X-rays show the hardest, heaviest or densest body parts, such as bone, cartilage and teeth, as white or pale against a black background.

❍ CT or CAT (computerized axial tomography) scans use very weak X-rays to show bones and also softer parts such as blood vessels and nerves, in three dimensions.

❍ MR or NMR (nuclear magnetic resonance) scans use powerful magnetic fields and pulses of radio signals to show similar images to CT scans in even more detail.

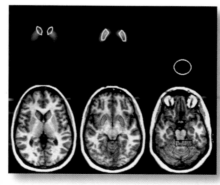

▲ MR scans are taken at different levels in the head and show soft tissues like the brain's folded outer surface, the cortex.

▶ Transmission electron microscopes (TEMs) are the most powerful kind of microscope and can show even the tiniest germs, like these influenza (flu) viruses.

❍ Ultrasound scans use the reflections or echoes of very high-pitched sound waves beamed into the body to build up an image such as an unborn baby in the womb.

❍ All of these images can be given added colours by computers to make the details even clearer.

CT scanning

A common type of CT scanner looks like a very large washing machine. Like MR and X-rays, CT scans are painless. The scanner rotates an X-ray beam around the patient while moving him or her slowly forward. This gives a set of picures showing different slices of the patient's body.

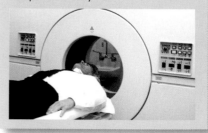

Key dates

160	Galen of ancient Rome carries out some of the first studies of the human body, seeing its insides through the terrible wounds suffered by gladiators
1543	Andreas Vesalius produces the first detailed book of body anatomy – *On the Fabric of the Human Body*
1610	The newly invented microscope reveals cells and other tiny body parts
1628	William Harvey discovers that blood is pumped around the body by the heart, rather than continually being made and used up
1895	Wilhelm Röntgen discovers X-rays and how they pass through flesh but not bone
1900	Karl Landsteiner works out the system of blood groups, making blood transfusions safer
1970s	Early CT and MR scanners show detailed pictures of inside the body
2000	The order of chemicals is worked out in the entire set of the body's genetic material, DNA, known as sequencing the human genome

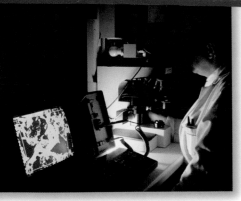

Computers are used to store, display and play back scanned images and also highlight any unusual growths in colour.

SEMs

Scanning electron microscopes (SEMs) fire beams of tiny charged particles called electrons. They magnify much more than light microscopes, showing details of individual cells like these fat cells.

Thermal imagers detect tiny differences in the temperature of various body parts, such as the knee.

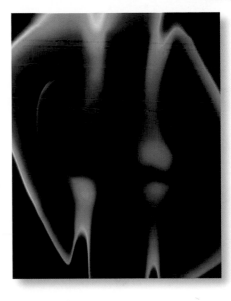

○ Optical microscopes use lenses and light to magnify things (make them look bigger). By combining two or more lenses, they can magnify specimens up to 2000 times and reveal individual blood cells.

○ To magnify things more, scientists use electron microscopes – microscopes that fire beams of tiny charged particles called electrons. Scanning electron microscopes (SEMs) are able to magnify things up to 100,000 times. SEMs show such things as the structures inside body cells.

○ Transmission electron microscopes (TEMs) magnify even more than SEMs – up to five million times. TEMs can reveal the individual molecules in a cell.

Amazing

Using a type of ultrasound scanner called an echocardiograph, a person's heart can be seen beating 'live' on screen.

The surgical team is headed by the surgeon. There is also an anaethetist to make sure the patient stays asleep, as well as surgical assistants and nurses.

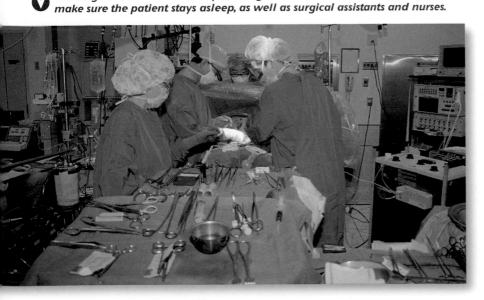

In this X-ray of the hands of a young child, the wrist bones have not yet fully hardened and so do not show up clearly.

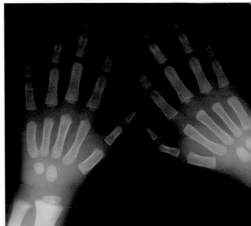

Find out more
Body systems pp. 434–435

Skin

Skin is often said to 'glow with health'. In fact, its surface is dead. The surface of the skin is made of hard, toughened, flattened, dead cells. They rub away and flake off in their thousands every minute as we move about, wear clothes, wash and dry with towels.

○ The upper layer of skin is called the epidermis. At its base are fast-multiplying cells that replace the old, keratin-hardened cells that rub off the surface.

○ Under the epidermis is the thicker dermis. It contains strong, stretchy fibres of another body protein – collagen. The dermis also contains microscopic blood vessels, the growing bases or roots of hairs, sweat glands and nerves ending in micro-sensors to detect touch.

○ Human skin is very tough. It can repair many minor cuts and replace itself in grazes. But certain types of damage are more serious. In particular, too much strong sunshine is bad for skin.

▲ *Sunbathing not only causes the skin to become brittle and wrinkled, it also increases the risk of developing skin cancer.*

Dead skin

Skin may feel smooth, but its surface is made of millions of tiny flakes, too small to see. These are flat, dead cells that rub away. Each year the body loses about 4 kg of rubbed-off skin flakes. During a lifetime the body sheds about as much skin as is equal to its adult weight – around 20 bucketfuls.

○ The sun's invisible rays, called UV-B (ultraviolet B), can harm the fast-dividing epidermal cells just under the skin's surface. This may cause a serious form of cancer called malignant melanoma.

◄ *Skin colour varies from person to person because of melanin, a pigment that protects skin from the sun's harmful rays. The more melanin you have in your skin, the darker it is.*

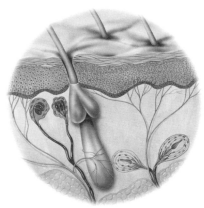

▲ *Around the base of each hair is a sebaceous gland. It makes a natural oily substance, sebum, which keeps skin supple and fairly waterproof.*

Amazing

Spread out flat, the skin of an adult would cover about 2 sq m, which is about the same area as the surface of a standard single bed.

Find out more

Touch pp. 464–465

If the body is too hot, for example when exercising, tiny sweat glands in skin release watery sweat, which oozes onto the surface of the skin. As sweat dries, it draws heat from the body to cool it.

Thick and thin

The thinnest skin, on the eyelids, is only 0.5 mm thick. The sole of the foot has the thickest skin, up to 5 mm thick.

○ Skin protects the softer, inner parts of the body from knocks and harm. It keeps in moist body fluids and keeps out dirt, germs and harmful substances such as strong chemicals.

○ Skin grows thicker to adapt and protect the body where it is pressed or rubbed often, such as on the soles of the feet.

○ As the body gets older, the skin wrinkles as the rubbery elastin and collagen fibres that support it sag.

The outer or surface layer of skin, the epidermis, is mostly dead. The lower layer or dermis is alive and packed with microscopic parts.

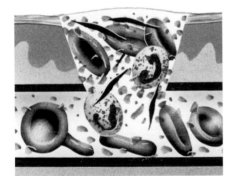

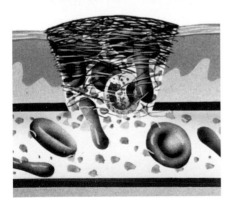

Blood clots to seal a cut. The blood chemical fibrin forms a web of micro-fibres. Platelets help to form the clot, which traps red blood cells.

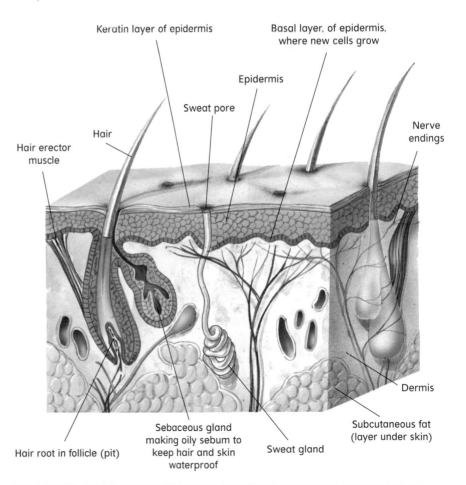

Keratin layer of epidermis

Basal layer, of epidermis, where new cells grow

Epidermis

Sweat pore

Hair

Nerve endings

Hair erector muscle

Hair root in follicle (pit)

Sebaceous gland making oily sebum to keep hair and skin waterproof

Sweat gland

Dermis

Subcutaneous fat (layer under skin)

Hair and Nails

There are up to 120,000 hairs on the head, called scalp hairs. There are also eyebrow hairs and eyelash hairs. Grown-ups have hairs in the armpits and between the legs, and men have hairs on the face. And everyone, even a baby, has tiny hairs all over the body – up to 20 million of them.

Nail growth

Nails grow about half a millimetre each week. The fingernails on the favoured hand grow slightly faster. So if you are left-handed, the nails on that hand grow faster than those on your right hand.

○ Hairs, like skin, are dead. The only living part of a hair is at its base, where it grows in a tiny pit called a follicle. The upper part, or shaft, is made of old, dead, stuck-together hair cells filled with the tough substance keratin.

○ Hair helps to protect the body, especially where it is thicker and longer on the head. It also helps to keep the body warm in cold conditions.

❤ *Each eyelash lasts only one to two months before it falls out, then a new one grows from the same follicle in the eyelid. Eyebrows do the same but grow for several months before falling out.*

◀ *A nail has its root under the skin and grows along the nail bed, which is the skin underneath it. The paler, crescent-like area is the lunula or 'little moon'. Nails make the fingertips stronger and more rigid when applying pressure.*

○ No hairs live for ever. Each one grows for a time, then it falls out, and its follicle has a 'rest' before a new hair sprouts. This is happening all the time, so the body always has some hairs on each part.

○ A typical head hair grows up to 3.5 mm each week.

○ Hair colour, like skin colour, depends on the genes inherited from parents. It is due to natural pigments, mainly the very dark brown substance melanin, contained in cells known as melanocytes.

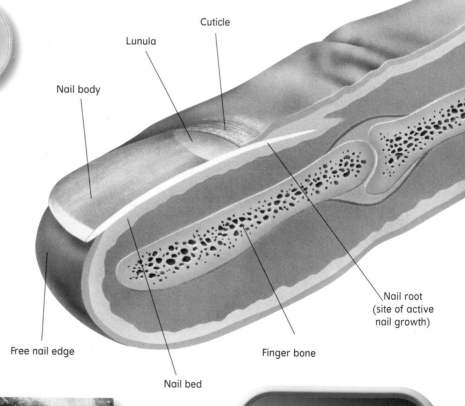

Cuticle

Lunula

Nail body

Nail root (site of active nail growth)

Free nail edge

Nail bed

Finger bone

Number of hairs

The average number of head or scalp hairs depends partly on their colour.

Light, fair or blond	120,000
Reddish or ginger	110,000
Brown	100,000
Black	90,000

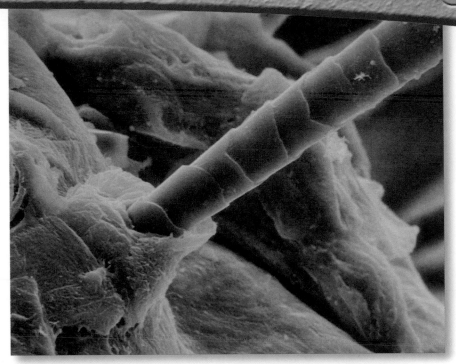

A nail is hard, tough and dead, and made mainly of keratin. The only living part is its root, buried in the skin, which makes new nail tissue as the whole nail grows towards the fingertip or toetip.

A hair is alive and growing only at its root, down in the base of the follicle. The shaft that sticks out of the skin is dead, and is made of flattened cells stuck firmly together.

Hair colour

Hair contains pigments (coloured substances) – mainly melanin (dark brown) and some carotene (yellowish). Different amounts of pigments, and the way their tiny particles are spread out, cause different hair colours.

Black curly hair
The result of black melanin from a flat hair follicle

Hair growth

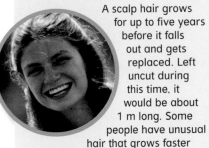

A scalp hair grows for up to five years before it falls out and gets replaced. Left uncut during this time, it would be about 1 m long. Some people have unusual hair that grows faster and for longer. Each hair can reach more than 4 m in length before dropping out.

Toenails grow about two to three times slower than fingernails.

Thumbnails and the nail on the big toe grow faster than the nails on the rest of the fingers and toes.

Like hairs, nails grow faster in summer than in winter, and faster at night than by day.

It takes about six months for a fingernail to grow from base to top, although it varies depending on the time of year.

At the base of the nail is a half moon that is called the lunula. This is covered by the cuticle, which is a flap of skin.

Blonde wavy hair
The result of carotene from an oval hair follicle

Straight black hair
The result of black melanin from a round follicle

Straight red hair
The result of red melanin from a round hair follicle

Nails form a stiff backing for the flexible fingertips and toetips, so we can feel, touch, sense pressure and grip objects.

Find out more

Skin pp. 440–441

Skeleton and Muscles

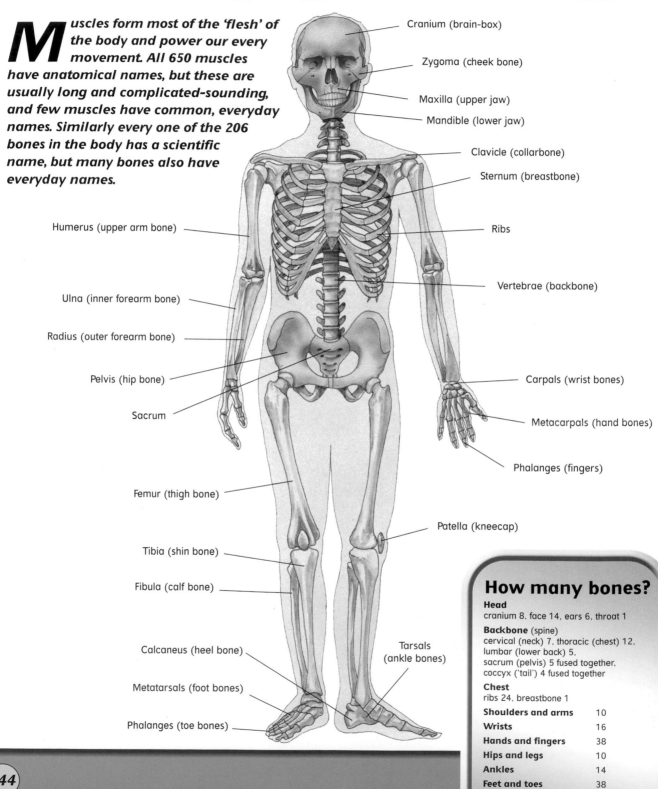

Muscles form most of the 'flesh' of the body and power our every movement. All 650 muscles have anatomical names, but these are usually long and complicated-sounding, and few muscles have common, everyday names. Similarly every one of the 206 bones in the body has a scientific name, but many bones also have everyday names.

Cranium (brain-box)

Zygoma (cheek bone)

Maxilla (upper jaw)

Mandible (lower jaw)

Clavicle (collarbone)

Sternum (breastbone)

Humerus (upper arm bone)

Ribs

Ulna (inner forearm bone)

Vertebrae (backbone)

Radius (outer forearm bone)

Pelvis (hip bone)

Sacrum

Carpals (wrist bones)

Metacarpals (hand bones)

Phalanges (fingers)

Femur (thigh bone)

Patella (kneecap)

Tibia (shin bone)

Fibula (calf bone)

Calcaneus (heel bone)

Tarsals (ankle bones)

Metatarsals (foot bones)

Phalanges (toe bones)

How many bones?

Head
cranium 8, face 14, ears 6, throat 1

Backbone (spine)
cervical (neck) 7, thoracic (chest) 12, lumbar (lower back) 5, sacrum (pelvis) 5 fused together, coccyx ('tail') 4 fused together

Chest
ribs 24, breastbone 1

Shoulders and arms	10
Wrists	16
Hands and fingers	38
Hips and legs	10
Ankles	14
Feet and toes	38

Find out more

Joints pp. 448–449

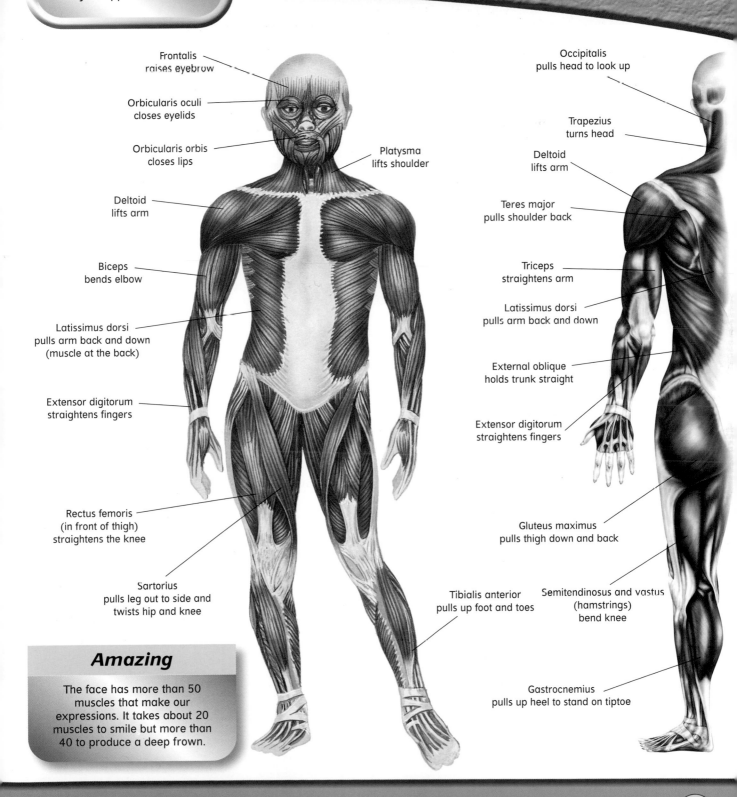

Frontalis
raises eyebrow

Orbicularis oculi
closes eyelids

Orbicularis orbis
closes lips

Deltoid
lifts arm

Biceps
bends elbow

Latissimus dorsi
pulls arm back and down
(muscle at the back)

Extensor digitorum
straightens fingers

Rectus femoris
(in front of thigh)
straightens the knee

Sartorius
pulls leg out to side and
twists hip and knee

Platysma
lifts shoulder

Occipitalis
pulls head to look up

Trapezius
turns head

Deltoid
lifts arm

Teres major
pulls shoulder back

Triceps
straightens arm

Latissimus dorsi
pulls arm back and down

External oblique
holds trunk straight

Extensor digitorum
straightens fingers

Gluteus maximus
pulls thigh down and back

Tibialis anterior
pulls up foot and toes

Semitendinosus and vastus
(hamstrings)
bend knee

Gastrocnemius
pulls up heel to stand on tiptoe

Amazing

The face has more than 50
muscles that make our
expressions. It takes about 20
muscles to smile but more than
40 to produce a deep frown.

Bones

More than 200 bones form the body's internal supporting framework, called the skeleton. Bones are strong and stiff, giving the body its shape, protecting internal organs and holding together the soft parts such as blood vessels, nerves and guts.

Amazing

An adult's skeleton has 206 bones – but a baby's skeleton has over 340. This is because as the body grows, some separate bones join together to form one bone.

○ Bones are very strong, yet they are also very lightweight. They are made of active living tissue, so if they break because of too much pressure on them, they can usually repair themselves.

○ Some bones protect very delicate body parts. For example, the skull bone protects the brain and main sense organs. Two deep bowl-like sockets called orbits, in the face, protect much of the eyeballs.

○ The 12 pairs of ribs are the thin, flattish bones that curve around your chest. Together, the rib bones make up the rib cage. Along with the backbone and breastbone, the ribs protect your vital organs – heart, lungs, liver, kidneys, stomach and spleen.

Periosteum (covering)

Hard bone layer

Spongy layer

Marrow

○ Most bones are not solid bone throughout. They have three layers. Outside is a 'shell' of hard or compact bone, which is very strong and stiff. Inside this is a layer of spongy or cancellous bone, with tiny holes for lightness. In the middle of most bones is marrow, a soft and jelly-like substance that makes new red and white cells for the blood. The whole bone is covered by a tough skin-like layer, the periosteum.

○ Marrow is not found in all bones, and not all marrow is the same. In babies, nearly all bones contain red marrow (which makes new blood cells), but as the body grows some changes to yellow marrow (which stores fat).

► *A tendon is where the end of a muscle tapers into a tough, slimmer, rope-like part that is anchored very strongly into a bone or cartilage.*

► *A typical bone has a hard outer layer, a spongy, honeycomb-like middle layer, and marrow at the centre, as well as tiny blood vessels and nerves.*

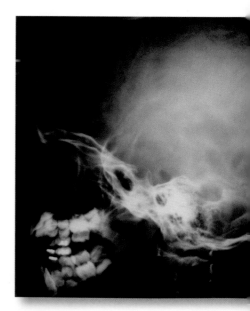

▲ *A child's skull, shown here in this X-ray photo, is quite large in relation to the rest of the child's body. As our bodies grow, our skull starts to look smaller in proportion.*

Find out more

Skeleton and muscles pp. 444–445

🔻 *Inside the tough casing of most bones is a soft, jelly-like core called the marrow, which can be either red or yellow. Red marrow contains cells called haemopoetic stem cells that are continually dividing to produce many kinds of blood cells.*

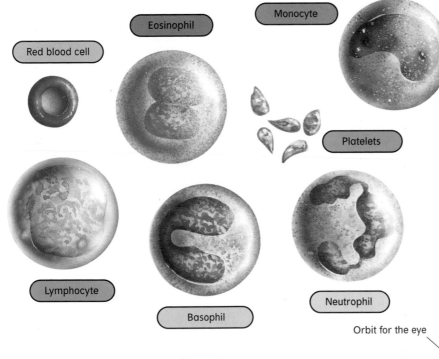

Red blood cell

Eosinophil

Monocyte

Platelets

Lymphocyte

Basophil

Neutrophil

Micro-bone

A microscopic view of the inside of a bone shows just why the skeleton is so light and strong. Bone is actually full of holes, like a honeycomb. Its structure is provided by criss-crossing struts called trabeculae, each angled perfectly to cope with stresses and strains.

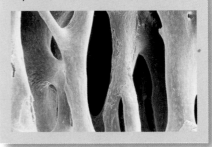

Large and small

The longest bone in the body is the thighbone or femur, about one-quarter of the body's height. The smallest bone is the stirrup bone in the ear, shown here – it is only slightly bigger than this U.

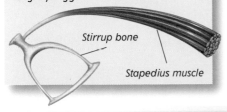

Stirrup bone

Stapedius muscle

○ Long bones in the arms and legs work as rigid levers, so when muscles pull on them, they can push, lift or make other movements.

○ Most of the body parts are about two-thirds water, but bones are only one-fifth water.

○ Skulls vary in size and shape, and this greatly affects the appearance of someone's face – long and thin, or broad.

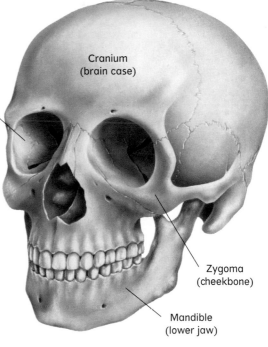

Cranium (brain case)

Orbit for the eye

Zygoma (cheekbone)

Mandible (lower jaw)

🔺 *The skull is not one bone, but 22 separate bones bound tightly together with fibres so that they cannot move. These fibrous joints, which can hardly be seen, are called sutures.*

The spine (backbone)

The spine or spinal column is the body's central support.

It is made of 26 block-like bones called vertebrae, one on top of the other, which hold up the skull and head while allowing the main body to flex and bend.

The spinal column also protects the body's main nerve, the spinal cord, which links the brain to all body parts.

The spinal cord is inside a tunnel formed by the lined-up gaps or holes within the vertebrae.

Joints

A single bone is rigid and tough, and can hardly bend. But the whole skeleton can move because its bones are linked at flexible joints, designed to reduce rubbing and wear.

Artificial joints

In some people, joints become stiff and painful due to disease, injury or stressful use over a long period of time. These natural joints can be replaced with artificial ones – joint prostheses. These are usually made of supertough plastics and strong metals. An artificial hip or knee (as shown) allows people to walk again without pain.

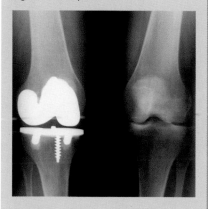

○ Where bones meet in a joint, they are covered with a shiny, slightly softer substance known as cartilage, which is moistened by a slippery fluid (synovial fluid) that allows the joints to move smoothly.

○ Ligaments are strips of strong tissue that hold bones together at the joints.

○ Hinge joints, such as the elbow, let the bones swing to and fro in two directions like door hinges do.

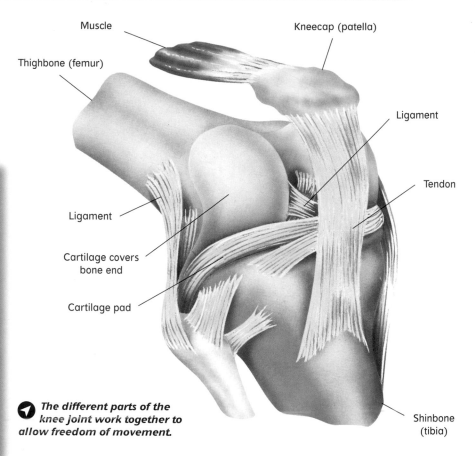

Muscle

Kneecap (patella)

Thighbone (femur)

Ligament

Tendon

Ligament

Cartilage covers bone end

Cartilage pad

Shinbone (tibia)

The different parts of the knee joint work together to allow freedom of movement.

○ In ball-and-socket joints, such as the shoulder and hip, the rounded end of one bone sits in the cup-shaped socket of the other, and can move in almost any direction.

○ Swivel joints turn like a wheel on an axle. Your head can swivel to the left or to the right on your spine.

The hip joint is a ball-and-socket joint which takes a great deal of wear and tear. When the cushioning layer of cartilage breaks down, it can be replaced with an artificial joint made of special plastics.

○ Saddle joints such as those in the thumb have the bones interlocking like two saddles. These joints allow great mobility with considerable strength.

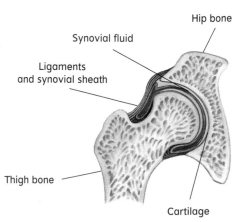

Hip bone

Synovial fluid

Ligaments and synovial sheath

Thigh bone

Cartilage

Find out more
Studying the body pp. 438–439

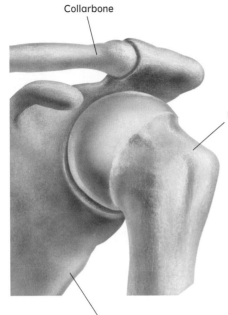

Collarbone

Upper arm bone

Shoulder blade

◀ *In the shoulder the ball-shaped end of the upper arm bone fits into a cup-like socket formed by the shoulder blade and collarbone.*

◯ Costal cartilage forms the innermost part of each rib where the bone joins to the breastbone.

◯ Hyaline cartilage forms many structural parts. The laryngeal cartilages making up the framework of the larynx or voicebox are hyaline cartilage. So are the cartilages forming the nose and the strengthening C-shaped rings in the windpipe (trachea).

◀ *No joint in the body is put under more stress than the knee. Besides ligaments and tendons to support it, it has thick cushions of cartilage.*

Amazing

The body has more than 200 joints. The largest are in the hips and knees. The smallest are between the tiny bones inside each ear, which help you hear.

◯ Elastic cartilage forms the bendy framework inside the outer ear flap (pinna).

◯ Cartilage grows more quickly than bone, and the skeletons of babies that are in the womb are mostly cartilage, which gradually ossifies (hardens to bone).

◯ The relatively inflexible joints between the bones (vertebrae) of the spine are cushioned by pads of cartilage.

◯ In some joints, there are not only cartilage coverings over the bone ends but also pads of cartilage between the cartilage. These extra pads are called articular discs. There are two of these extra cartilages, known as menisci, in each knee joint. They help the knee to 'lock' straight so that we can stand up without too much effort.

◯ Joints are also called articulations. The cartilage that covers the bone ends in the joint is technically known as articular cartilage.

◯ There are also other types of cartilage that, in general, are strong and light but slightly bendy and flexible.

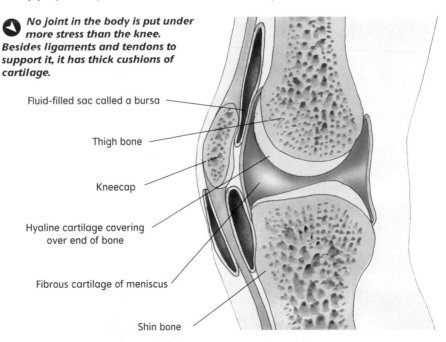

Fluid-filled sac called a bursa

Thigh bone

Kneecap

Hyaline cartilage covering over end of bone

Fibrous cartilage of meniscus

Shin bone

How Muscles Work

*T*he body's 650 muscles make up almost half of its total weight. As muscles contract, they pull on the bones they are attached to, and so move the body. The contraction of the muscles is controlled by nerve signals sent out from parts of the brain called the motor centres and cerebellum.

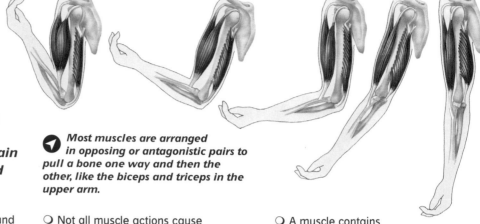

○ A typical muscle is striped, long and slim, bulging in the middle, and joined to a bone at each end. However, some muscles are shaped like triangles or sheets and may be joined to several bones, to each other, or not attached to bone, such as the layer of muscle in arteries.

○ Just under the skin are dozens of muscles called the outer or superficial layer. Under these is usually another, intermediate layer, and there is also a third or deep muscle layer.

● *Most muscles are arranged in opposing or antagonistic pairs to pull a bone one way and then the other, like the biceps and triceps in the upper arm.*

○ Not all muscle actions cause movement. Several muscles may tense to hold a part steady and still. For example, when the body is standing, the neck and back muscles tense to keep it upright and balanced.

○ Muscle pairs work together with other pairs as large muscle teams to move bones in many directions. When playing sport, our muscles are working in groups of pairs to respond to the moves we require.

▶ *A reflex is an automatic body movement, without conscious control by the brain. Nerve signals go from the finger to the spinal cord and back to the arm muscles, to jerk the finger away from pain.*

○ A muscle contains bundles of long, thin muscle fibres (myofibres), about the width of human hairs. Each fibre is made of even thinner parts called muscle fibrils (myofibrils). And each fibril contains even narrower parts, myofilaments.

○ There are two kinds of filaments, made of different types of protein: actin, which is thin, and myosin, which is thick. These slide past each other to shorten the fibrils, causing the whole muscle to contract.

○ 'Fast-twitch' muscles in the fingers, face and eyes can contract in less than one-twentieth of a second. They are speedy but soon tire. 'Slow-twitch' muscles, such as those in the back, take longer but can keep contracting for a greater period of time.

Brain

Nerve signals into spinal cord

Nerve signals out to muscle

Finger detects pain

Sensory nerve signals

Reflex cascade

Many reflexes to avoid injury or damage happen one after the other in a 'cascade'. For example, if an object comes fast towards the face:

Eyelids close to guard the delicate surfaces of the eyes.

Face 'screws up' as facial muscles tense and harden.

Neck muscles twist the face away.

Shoulder and upper body muscles jerk the head away.

Shoulder and arm muscles throw up the arms and hands to block the object.

Tapering end or head of muscle

Body or belly of muscle

Fasciae enclose large groups of muscle fibres

▶ *A large muscle contains thousands of myofibres, grouped in bundles called fascicles. These are separated from each other by layers of tough connective tissue known as fascia. The smallest muscles have just a few dozen myofibres.*

Tendon

Epimysium (outer covering)

Facial muscles

There are seven muscles on each side of the mouth, which can pull it wider, up or down. More than 50 muscles are needed to make the facial expressions that show other people our thoughts and feelings.

Actin (thin myofilament)

Muscle fibres (myofibres)

Nerve branches

Myosin (thick myofilament)

Muscle fibril (myofibrils)

▼ *Exercise does not make 'more muscles', but it does make each muscle bigger, stronger and better able to cope with strain and fatigue, with a larger blood supply.*

Brain muscle

Heart muscle is a unique combination of skeletal and smooth muscle. It has its own built-in contraction rhythm of 70 beats a minute, and special muscle cells that work like nerve cells for transmitting the signals for waves of muscle contraction to sweep through the heart.

Amazing

The biggest muscle is the gluteus maximus, in the buttocks. The smallest muscle is the stapedius, attached to the stirrup bone in the ear, which is the size of this dash —.

Find out more

Skeleton and muscles pp. 444–445

The Nervous System

T*he body consists of many different organs and tissues. These must work together in an organized way for the whole body to stay healthy and active. The main system that controls and co-ordinates all these parts is the nervous system.*

▼ *The spinal cord is encased in a tunnel in the backbone at the back of each vertebra. Nerves branch off to the body in pairs either side.*

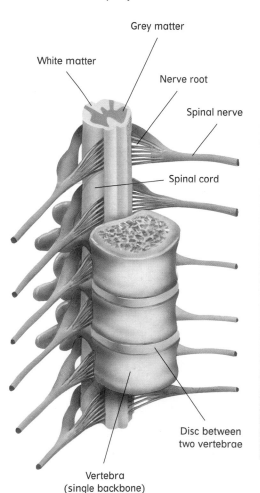

Grey matter

White matter

Nerve root

Spinal nerve

Spinal cord

Disc between two vertebrae

Vertebra (single backbone)

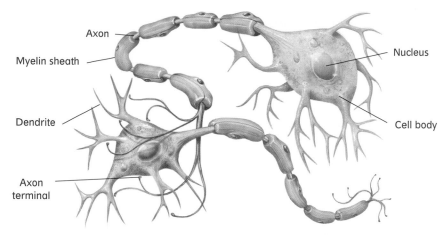

Axon

Myelin sheath

Dendrite

Axon terminal

Nucleus

Cell body

○ Like a computer network, the nerve system sends tiny electrical signals to and fro, carrying information from one part of the body to another. The electrical signals are called nerve messages.

Nerve signal speed

Different types of nerve fibres carry signals at different speeds. The fastest signals travel at more than 120 m per second. The slowest signals travel at 1–2 m per second. These runners on the starting block should take a minimum of 0.1 seconds to hear the start gun and react to it by leaping from the blocks. If they set off in less than 0.1 seconds, it is a false start.

▲ *Nerve cells, or neurons, are the 'wires' of the body's nervous sytem. They carry messages within, to and from the central nervous system.*

○ The nervous system has three main parts: brain, spinal cord and peripheral nerves.

○ The brain consists of billions of nerve cells and other tissues in the top half of the head. Its lower end merges into the spinal cord, the body's main nerve.

○ The spinal cord is inside a tunnel formed by the row of holes inside the vertebrae of the backbone or spine.

○ Peripheral nerves branch out from the spinal cord and brain to reach every body part.

Number of nerves

12 pairs of cranial nerves branch directly from the brain.

31 pairs of main peripheral nerves branch from the spinal cord – 8 cervical nerve pairs, 12 thoracic pairs, 5 lumbar pairs, 5 sacral pairs and one coccyx pair.

The spinal cord is about 45 cm long.

Some nerve cells are more than 30 cm in length, making them the longest cells in the body.

Nerve signals travel so fast that we can sense a situation and react to it in less than 0.2 seconds.

Find out more

The brain pp. 454–455

○ A nerve has a tough, shiny, greyish covering, called the epineurium. Inside are bundles, or fascicles, of nerve fibres that carry the tiny electrical pulses of nerve signals.

○ A thick nerve has hundreds of thousands of fibres, while the thinnest nerves, as fine as a human hair, have just a few.

○ A motor nerve carries nerve signals from the brain, out to the muscles and glands.

○ Sensory nerves carry signals the other way, from the eyes, ears and other sense organs, to the brain.

▼ *Nerve signals are transmitted across a synapse as chemical messengers called neurotransmitters. These lock on to receptors on the receiving nerve.*

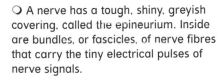

Amazing

If all the nerves in the body were taken out and joined end to end they would stretch more than 80,000 km – twice around the world.

▶ *The nervous system is an incredibly intricate network of nerves linking your brain to every part of the body. The nerves of the peripheral nervous system branch out to every limb and body part from the central nervous system (the brain and spinal cord).*

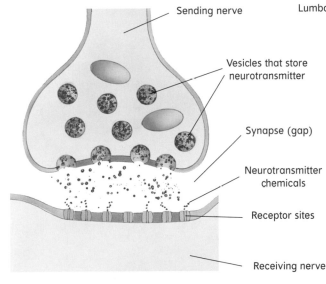

Sending nerve

Vesicles that store neurotransmitter

Synapse (gap)

Neurotransmitter chemicals

Receptor sites

Receiving nerve

Brain

Cranial nerves

Lateral pectoral nerve

Brachial 'plexus' (nerve junction)

Spinal cord

Ulnar nerve

Lumbar nerves

Sacral nerves

Sciatic nerve

Femoral nerve

Peroneal nerve

Radial nerve

Lateral plantar nerve

Nerve cells

A spider has a nervous system with about 100,000 nerve cells, while a human being has around 60 billion.

The Brain

The brain is the site of the human mind. It is where we think, imagine, receive information from our senses, work out what it means, make decisions, store memories, experience emotions, such as fear and happiness, and control body movements.

Amazing

The brain is the first part to develop in the womb – at one stage it is bigger than all of the rest of the body.

❍ Most of these processes happen in the cerebral cortex – the thin, layer that covers the domed, wrinkled surface of the brain.

❍ Some processes, such as creating a picture in the mind of what the eyes see, happen mainly in one part of the cortex. Other processes, such as storing and recalling memories, involve several areas of the cortex and also other parts of the brain.

❍ The brain's cortex is only 5 mm thick, but flattened out it would cover an area almost as big as a pillow case – and it contains at least 50 billion nerve cells.

❍ The two halves (hemispheres) of the brain look the same, but they work in different ways.

❍ In most people, the left hemisphere is important in using numbers and words, working out problems in a logical way, planning, reasoning and comprehension.

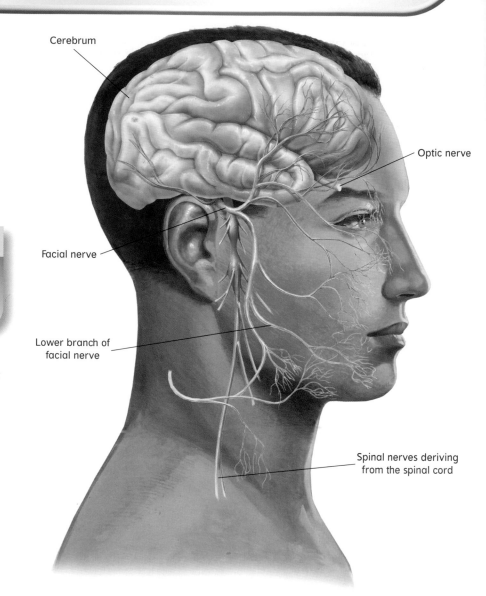

Cerebrum

Optic nerve

Facial nerve

Lower branch of facial nerve

Spinal nerves deriving from the spinal cord

▲ *The cranial nerves cover the cerebrum and branch out to the face. They carry signals from the head and neck to the brain. Instructions from the brain travel in the opposite direction.*

Brain and body

The human brain is about 1/50th of the weight of the whole body. In one of the most intelligent animals, the dolphin, this proportion is about 1/150th.

Find out more

Brain scans p. 436

▼ Different parts of the cortex deal with nerve signals that are either coming from the senses or being sent to muscles.

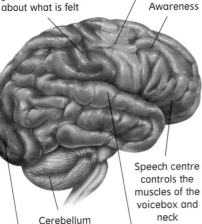

Movement or motor centre controls muscles and movements

Touch centre receives signals from the skin about what is felt

Awareness

Speech centre controls the muscles of the voicebox and neck

Cerebellum (movement co-ordination)

Hearing centre receives messages from the ear along the auditory nerve

Visual centre receives nerve signals from the eyes and works out what is seen

Brain evolution

Brain size is linked to intelligence, but size isn't everything. What makes humans and our ancestors intelligent is our brain's complex structure. *Homo habilis'* brain was 50 per cent bigger than its *Australopithecine* predecessors. It had a brain capacity of 750 ml. *Homo sapiens*, the species to which human beings belong, has a brain capacity of 1400 ml.

Australopithecus afarensis

Homo sapien

Homo habilis

▼ About nine-tenths of the brain is the large dome of the two cerebral hemispheres. The outer cerebral cortex is where many conscious thoughts happen. Inside are blob-like parts called ganglia.

▲ Billions of nerve signals flash around the brain every second, bringing information from the senses, sending out instructions to the muscles, and carrying thoughts and memories. Some of these signals 'leak' through the skull bone where they can be picked up by sensor pads on the skin on an EEG machine.

❍ The right hemisphere deals with recognizing patterns in shapes, colours and sounds, imagination and having ideas and inspiration.

❍ The two hemispheres are linked by a 'bridge', the corpus callosum, which contains 100 million nerve fibres.

❍ Under the cortex is 'white matter', which is mainly nerve fibres to lower parts of the brain.

Parts of the brain

The visual centre or area of the brain is at the lower rear of the cortex and receives nerve signals from the eyes and works out what is seen.
The movement or motor centre controls the body movements by making muscles contract and relax.
The touch centre just behind the motor centre receives signals from the skin about what is felt on different parts of the body surface.
At the lower rear is a smaller wrinkled part, the cerebellum. It makes muscle-powered movements smooth, skilful and co-ordinated.
The central parts of the brain, such as the thalamus, are involved in awareness, memories and emotions.
The hippocampus is linked to mood, willpower, learning and memory.
The lowest part is the brain stem, which is responsible for automatic body processes such as digestion and heartbeat.
The hypothalamus controls body heat, water and hunger, and wakes you up.

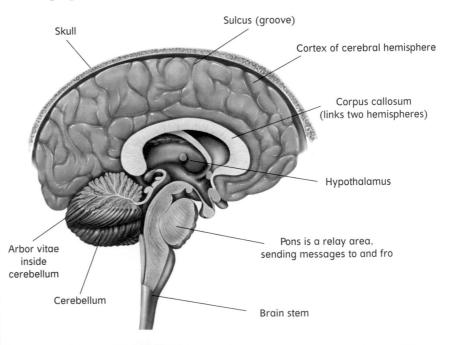

Skull

Sulcus (groove)

Cortex of cerebral hemisphere

Corpus callosum (links two hemispheres)

Hypothalamus

Arbor vitae inside cerebellum

Pons is a relay area, sending messages to and fro

Cerebellum

Brain stem

Eyes and Sight

More information about the outside world enters the body through the eyes – from pictures, words on paper, real scenes and screens – than through all the other senses combined. The eye detects light as rays of different colours and brightness, and produces patterns of tiny nerve signals that are sent to the brain.

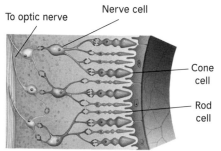

To optic nerve

Nerve cell

Cone cell

Rod cell

● The eye's retina has two kinds of light-sensitive cells. Rods are tall and slim, and number about 125 million. They detect shades of light and work well in dim light but cannot see colours. The 7 million cones are shorter and wider and clustered at the rear where the central part of the image falls. They see colours and fine details in bright light.

❍ Your eyes are tough balls that are filled with a jelly-like substance called vitreous humour.

❍ The eyeball, about 2.5 cm across, has a tough outer cover, the sclera. Inside this is a blood-rich layer, the choroid, which nourishes parts of the eye.

❍ At the front is a transparent window, the dome-shaped cornea, which lets in light rays.

● Tear fluid is made in the lachrymal glands and drains from the inner eyelids through the lachrymal ducts into the nose. Inside the eye is the light-sensitive lining, the retina.

Optic chiasma where signals from each eye partly cross over

Muscles that turn the eye

Outer sheath of eyeball (sclera)

Tear fluid gland

Iris

Pupil

Tear duct in to nose

❍ The light rays pass through a hole, the pupil, in a ring of coloured muscle, the iris. The iris makes the pupil smaller in bright conditions, preventing too much light from entering the eye and damaging the inside.

❍ These rays then pass through the lens that bends (refracts) them to shine a clear image of the world on to the retina lining the eyeball.

Defective sight

The eye's own lens, just behind the dark hole or pupil, can become thicker or thinner to focus on near or far objects. When the lens is not working properly, some people need extra lenses, so glasses or contact lenses help them see clearly.

Find out more
Braille p. 464

Optic nerve which carries the signals to the brain

Choroid layer

Retina – the lining of light-sensitive rods and cones

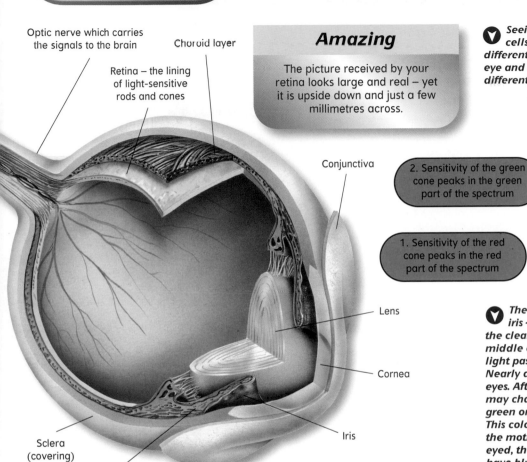

Sclera (covering)

Ligaments supporting the lens

Amazing

The picture received by your retina looks large and real – yet it is upside down and just a few millimetres across.

Conjunctiva

Lens

Cornea

Iris

○ On the retina, more than 130 million light-sensitive cells change the patterns of light into nerve signals.

○ Each of your two eyes gives you a slightly different view of the world. The brain combines these views to give an impression of depth and 3-D solidity.

○ The brain uses information such as the inward-looking angle of each eye, and the amount the lens is thinned or thickened, to assess the distance of objects.

○ All the thousands of different colours, shades and hues we can see are worked out by the brain from combinations of signals from the three types of cones, known as red, green and blue cones due to the colour of light they detect.

Laser eye surgery

A narrow beam of high-power laser light can be shone accurately into the eye, to carry out treatment for various eye disorders. The heat from the beam can seal a leaky blood vessel, or sculpt and reshape the lens and cornea to make vision clearer.

Seeing in colour depends on eye cells called cones. There are three different types of cone in the human eye and each are sensitive to a different part of the spectrum.

3. Sensitivity of the blue cone peaks in the blue part of the spectrum

2. Sensitivity of the green cone peaks in the green part of the spectrum

1. Sensitivity of the red cone peaks in the red part of the spectrum

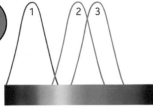

White light spectrum

The coloured part of the eye is the iris – a ring of muscle seen through the clear cornea. The dark hole in the middle of the iris is the pupil, where light passes to the inside of the eye. Nearly all babies are born with blue eyes. After a few months the colour may change to a shade of brown, green or grey, then it stays the same. This colour is inherited from parents. If the mother and father are both blue-eyed, their child will almost certainly have blue eyes. However, if one or both parents are brown-eyed, then their child may have brown or blue eyes.

Parents' eye colour

Genes for eye colour

Possible colours for children

Ears, Hearing and Balance

The ear detects vibrations of sound that reach it as invisible waves of changing pressure in air, known as sound waves. The level of a sound, whether high or low, is called its pitch and is measured in Hz (Hertz or vibrations per second). The volume or loudness of a sound is a measure of the energy intensity in the sound waves. Our ears can only respond to a limited range of frequencies and intensities.

Amazing

Sound waves travel through air at about 340 m/sec. A sound from the left reaches the left ear first, and the right ear less than one-thousandth of a second later.

Outer ear flap

Cartilage in ear flap

Ear canal

Skull bone

○ Pinnae (singular, pinna) are the ear flaps you can see on the side of your head, and they are simply collecting funnels for sounds.

○ Sound waves pass into a slightly S-shaped tube, the outer ear canal, and hit the small, flexible eardrum at the end.

○ The vibrations pass along three tiny bones – the hammer, anvil and stirrup. These three ear bones are known as the ossicles and are the smallest bones in the body. Surrounding muscles tense to hold them firmly so that they vibrate less when very loud sound waves hit them.

○ The vibrations then pass into the fluid inside the snail-shaped cochlea. The vibrations cause ripples that are sensed by microscopic hairs on auditory cells, and then changed into nerve signals.

○ Each ear's cochlea has 25,000 auditory cells, with a total of more than 2 million micro-hairs to detect sound vibrations.

○ We know the direction of sounds because we have two ears. This is known as stereophonic or binaural hearing.

○ The ear facing the sound's direction hears sounds earlier and more loudly than the other ear because sounds fade as they travel.

▶ The loudness or intensity of sounds is measured in decibels, dB. Sound volumes of more than about 90 dB can damage the ears, especially if they are high-pitched and continue for a long time.

Whispering 20–30 dB

Motorcycle 70–90 dB

Vacuum cleaner 60–80 dB

Jet take-off 120–140 dB

Talking 40–60 dB

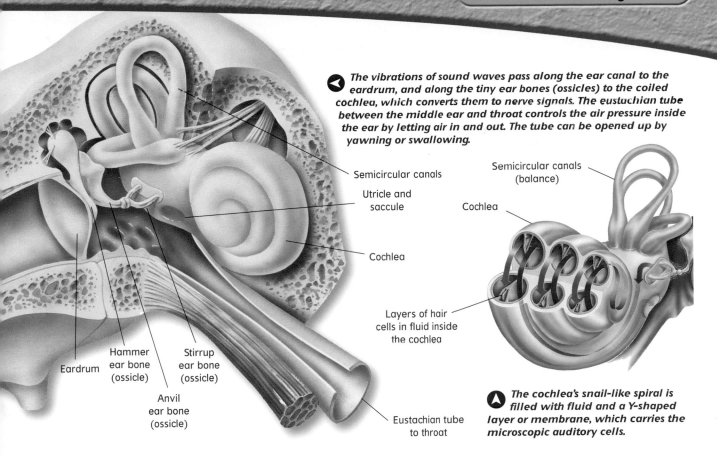

The vibrations of sound waves pass along the ear canal to the eardrum, and along the tiny ear bones (ossicles) to the coiled cochlea, which converts them to nerve signals. The eustachian tube between the middle ear and throat controls the air pressure inside the ear by letting air in and out. The tube can be opened up by yawning or swallowing.

Semicircular canals

Utricle and saccule

Cochlea

Semicircular canals (balance)

Cochlea

Layers of hair cells in fluid inside the cochlea

Eardrum

Hammer ear bone (ossicle)

Anvil ear bone (ossicle)

Stirrup ear bone (ossicle)

Eustachian tube to throat

The cochlea's snail-like spiral is filled with fluid and a Y-shaped layer or membrane, which carries the microscopic auditory cells.

○ The brain works out these time and volume differences to tell the sound's direction.

○ To stay upright, your body must send a continual stream of data about its position to your brain – and your brain must continually tell your body how to move to keep its balance.

○ Balance is controlled in many parts of the brain, including the brain's cerebellum.

○ Your brain finds out about your body position from many sources, including your eyes, proprioceptors around the body, and the semicircular canals and other chambers in the inner ear.

○ The semicircular canals are three, tiny, fluid-filled loops in your inner ear. Two chambers (holes) called the utricle and saccule are linked to the semicircular canals.

○ When you move your head, the fluid in the canals and cavities lags a little, pulling on hair detectors, which tell your brain what is going on. The canals tell you whether you are nodding or shaking your head, and which way you are moving.

Staying balanced

To stop you losing your balance, it helps to fix your eyes on a single focal point, so that your brain does not become confused or distracted.

Spinning

A rollercoaster ride can make you feel dizzy because the liquid inside your inner ear keeps spinning after you have stopped.

Find out more

The brain pp. 454–455

Nose and Smell

Smells are tiny scent particles or molecules that are taken into your nose by breathed-in air. A particular smell may be noticeable even when just a few scent molecules are mixed in with millions of air molecules.

Blocked nose

When we have a cold, the nose produces lots of extra slimy mucus. This covers the smell patches, olfactory epithelia, so we cannot smell so well. It also blocks out the smell of foods as we chew, making them seem to have less 'taste'.

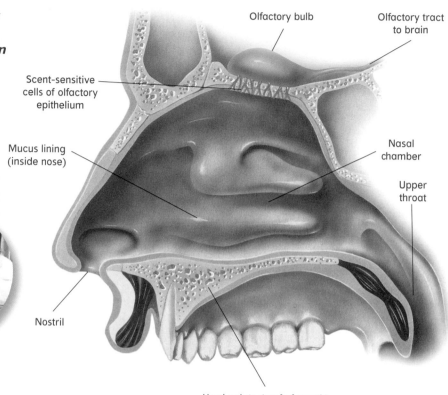

Olfactory bulb

Olfactory tract to brain

Scent-sensitive cells of olfactory epithelium

Mucus lining (inside nose)

Nasal chamber

Upper throat

Nostril

Hard palate (roof of mouth)

○ Olfactory means 'to do with the sense of smell'.

○ The sensory parts for smell are two patches called olfactory (smell) epithelia. They are in the roof of the nasal chamber, inside the skull bone behind the nose.

○ Each patch contains olfactory cells, which have bunches of micro-hairs, cilia. These detect certain odorant particles from the air that float into the nose and land on them.

Amazing

The human nose can tell the difference between more than 10,000 different chemicals. Dogs can pick up smells that are 10,000 times fainter than the ones humans can detect.

⬥ The hairy-looking patches called olfactory epithelia, which detect smells, are in the top of the air space known as the nasal chamber, inside the nose and above the mouth.

○ The olfactory epithelium contains over 25 million receptor cells. Each of the receptor cells in the olfactory epithelium has up to 20 or so scent-detecting hairs called cilia.

○ When they are triggered by scent molecules, the cilia send signals to a cluster of nerves called the olfactory bulb, which then sends messages to the part of the brain that recognizes smell.

○ The part of the brain that deals with smell is closely linked to the parts that deal with memories and emotions.

◀ Olfactory (smell) cells have micro-hairs facing down into the nasal chamber. If the particles fit into landing sites called receptors on the micro hairs, like a key into a lock, then nerve signals flash along the olfactory nerve to the brain.

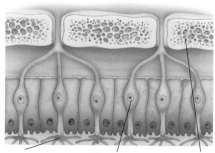

Micro-hair   Olfactory cell   Bone

Cartilage is a rubbery substance used in various places around the body. A single blow to the nose can easily damage nasal cartilage, as often happens to boxers.

○ The two closely linked parts of the brain may be why smells can often evoke vivid memories and trigger powerful emotions.

○ By the age of 20, you will have lost 20 per cent of your sense of smell. By 60, you will have lost 60 per cent.

○ Rarely a person has no sense of smell. This is called anosmia.

○ Loss of smell is usually caused by a problem in the development of the olfactory bulb or olfactory tract (nerve) leading from the nose to the brain.

Professionals

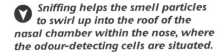

Several professions rely on an expert sense of smell, including winemakers and manufacturers of scents, perfumes and air fresheners.

Tiny bits of dust, germs and floating particles in air can block the nose and also damage the airways and lungs. People who work in dusty places, or with powders, vapours and fumes, wear masks to protect themselves. Surgeons wear masks so they cannot breathe germs onto their patients.

Sniffing helps the smell particles to swirl up into the roof of the nasal chamber within the nose, where the odour-detecting cells are situated.

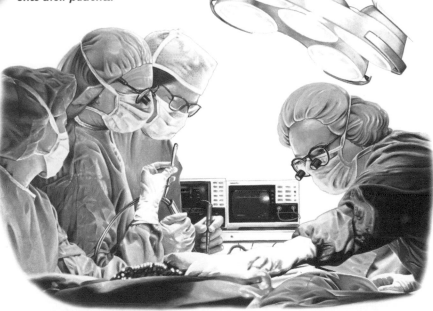

Tongue and Taste

The sense of taste gives us less information about the world than the other senses. Taste is triggered by certain chemicals in food, which dissolve in the saliva in the mouth, and then send information to a particular part of the brain via sensory nerve cells on the tongue.

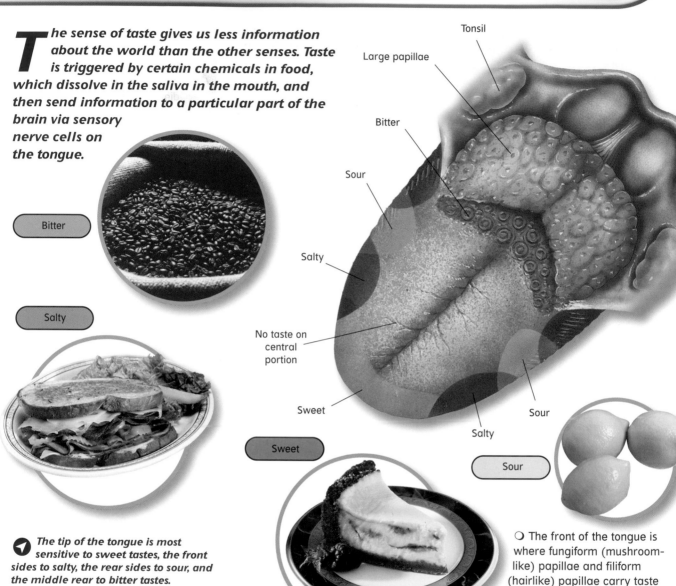

Tonsil

Large papillae

Bitter

Sour

Salty

No taste on central portion

Sweet

Salty

Sour

Bitter

Salty

Sweet

Sour

➤ **The tip of the tongue is most sensitive to sweet tastes, the front sides to salty, the rear sides to sour, and the middle rear to bitter tastes.**

❍ The tongue is almost all muscle and can stretch itself long and thin or short and wide.

❍ The front, sides and rear of the tongue have 10,000 taste buds set into the surface. These taste buds are scattered between the larger 'lumps' called papillae.

❍ Taste buds are sensitive to four basic flavours: sweet, sour, bitter and salty.

❍ The back of the tongue contains big round papillae shaped like an upside-down V. This is where bitter flavours are sensed.

❍ The front of the tongue is where fungiform (mushroom-like) papillae and filiform (hairlike) papillae carry taste buds that detect sweet, sour and salty flavours.

❍ Each taste bud is one-tenth of a millimetre across. It contains about 25 gustatory (taste) cells, which have tufts of micro-hairs called cilia. These detect chemical flavouring particles in food.

Find out more

The digestive system pp. 470–471

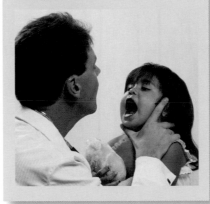

As well as tasting the flavour of ice cream, the tongue can also tell that it is cold and smooth.

Detecting illness

The tongue's colour and texture can give clues about illness. When we are ill it sometimes looks 'furry'. It may also have raw spots or patches called ulcers, which can be a sign of being run down and stressed.

○ In your mouth you also have other sense receptors. These include sensors for pressure, moisture, cold, heat and touch.

○ Taste bud cells only last for about a week before the body starts to renew them.

○ When you have a cold you often lose your sense of taste. This is because your nose is blocked and you lose your sense of smell. Your taste buds continue to work.

The large pimple–like lumps at the back of the tongue, called papillae, have tiny taste buds in their deep clefts.

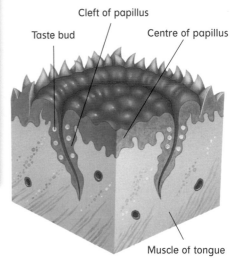

Cleft of papillus

Taste bud

Centre of papillus

Muscle of tongue

○ It is not clear how the micro-hairs, or cilia, on taste and smell cells respond to chemical particles. It is possible that the surfaces of the cilia have tiny pits in them of different shapes. A certain odorant or flavorant particle fits into one shape of pit, but not the others – like a key into its lock.

○ Only when the particle fits properly, is a nerve signal sent to the brain.

○ As well as taste, the tongue can also feel the texture, consistency and temperature of food.

○ A baby has a very developed sense of taste, with taste buds all over the inside of its mouth.

○ In the mouth there are three main pairs of salivary glands. These are the parotid, the submandibular and the sublingual.

○ The parotid glands are found in front of the ears – they are the largest. Ducts open into the mouth from the cheek.

○ The submandibular glands are situated at the back of the lower jaw, under the mouth. The ducts enter the mouth under the middle of the tongue.

○ The sublingual glands are found under the tongue.

The tongue

The tongue's other jobs, besides taste, including moving the food around the mouth for thorough chewing, licking the lips clean, and helping to shape the sounds of speech from the vocal cords.

Touch, Pressure and Pain

Touch, or physical contact, is a complicated set of sensations that are detected all over the surface of your body, by your skin. These sensations include feeling heat, cold, pressure, movement or vibration, and pain.

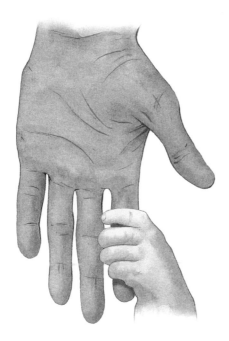

Babies have soft skin and explore touch sensations as they learn. The fingertips are where your sense of touch is most sensitive.

❍ There are sense receptors or sensors everywhere in your skin, but places like your face have more than your back.

❍ There are at least seven different kinds of microsensors in skin. In sensitive areas such as the lips and fingertips, hundreds of different microsensors are packed into an area the size of this 'o'.

❍ The sensors work together to detect the various features of touch, from light contact to the pain that warns us that skin may be damaged.

❍ Free nerve-endings are rather like the bare end of a wire. They respond to most kinds of skin sensation and are almost everywhere in your skin.

❍ There are specialized sensors in certain places, each named after their discoverer.

❍ Pacini's corpuscles and Meissner's endings react instantly to sudden pressure. Krause's bulbs, Merkel's discs and Ruffini's endings respond to steady pressure. Krause's bulbs are also sensitive to cold. Ruffini's endings react to changes in temperature.

Braille

The sense of touch is vital to a person who is blind. Braille is a system of raised dots and patterns, which each symbolize different letters or words. Through the use of braille, a blind person can feel, and so read, the words on a page.

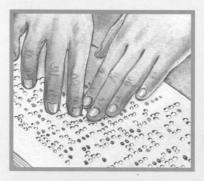

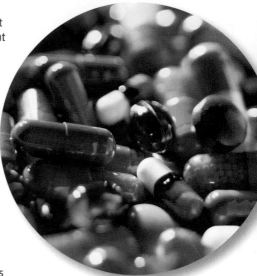

Thousands of different drugs are used today, such as antibiotics that are used to treat bacterial infections and analgesics that help to relieve pain.

❍ The parietal (side) lobe of the brain is where you register touch, heat and cold, and pain.

❍ Analgesic drugs such as aspirin relieve pain, working mainly by stopping the body making prostaglandin, the chemical that sends pain signals to the brain.

❍ The brain is thought to work out the sensation of touch from the patterns of millions of nerve signals coming in from all kinds of touch sensors, so that it knows if an object is hard or soft, cold or warm, rough or smooth, and wet or dry.

Your skin

All over your skin you have about:

3500 various detectors on a fingertip
200,000 hot and cold sensors
500,000 touch and pressure sensors
3,000,000 pain sensors

Find out more

Skin pp. 440–441

○ Hairs are dead and so cannot feel touch. But around the root of each hair, in the follicle, are wrapped sensors such as free nerve endings. These detect if the hair is pulled or tilted. If the hair is wrenched out the sensors register pain.

○ These hair root sensors can even feel the hair being tilted by the wind, when there is no physical contact at all. This happens when we feel 'the wind on our face', as the wind bends the tiny hairs on the cheeks.

○ Strong tastes, such as spicy food, rely less on the sense of smell than on pain-sensitive nerve endings in the tongue.

▼ *Fingertips are patterns of wavy ridges on the tips of the fingers. The ridges help the skin to grip well, especially when it is slightly dampened by sweat. No two people have the same fingerprints – even identical twins.*

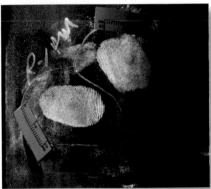

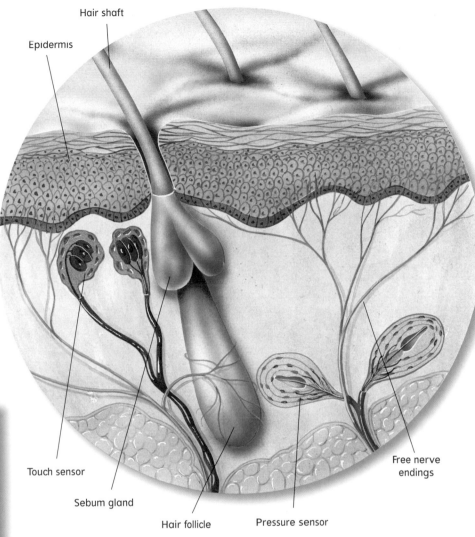

Hair shaft

Epidermis

Touch sensor

Sebum gland

Hair follicle

Pressure sensor

Free nerve endings

▲ *Three types of touch sensor are shown in this close-up through skin. They are free nerve endings (green branches), light touch endings (red blobs next to the hair) and heavy pressure detectors (blue 'onions').*

Rough skin

When undertaking hard physical work, the rubbing on the skin of the hands may cause calluses or rough patches of skin. However, this reduces the sense of touch, because the outer layer of skin, epidermis, is thicker and shields the touch sensors below in the dermis.

Amazing

The disease called leprosy destroys nerves carrying touch signals, so people suffer injuries without realizing it.

The Respiratory System

The air around us contains the gas oxygen. It is needed for chemical changes inside the body, which break apart the high-energy substance glucose (blood sugar) obtained from food. The parts specialized to take in air and pass oxygen from it into the blood are known as the respiratory system.

○ The respiratory system consists of the nose, throat, larynx (voice box), trachea (windpipe), bronchi (main airways in the chest) and the lungs.

○ Breathing in, or inspiring, draws fresh air into the lungs, where oxygen is taken in or absorbed into the blood.

○ The main breathing muscle is the diaphragm, which is dome-shaped and sits under the lungs. When it tenses or contracts, it becomes flatter, expanding the lungs to suck in air.

Breathing

As you rest or sleep, you breathe once every three or four seconds, moving half a litre of air each time. After much exercise, you may breathe as fast as once each second, moving up to 3 l of air each time.

○ Intercostal muscles between the ribs also contract when breathing in, to lift the front of the chest and help expand the lungs.

○ Breathing out, or expiring, causes the low-oxygen 'used air' to be pushed up along the airways and out of the body.

○ As the diaphragm relaxes, the stretched lungs shrink back to their smaller size, pushing out air.

▶ *This side view diagram shows a cross-section of the upper respiratory tract – the mouth, nose, throat and windpipe or trachea, with the vocal cords at the top of the trachea.*

▼ *Breathing in is powered by contraction of the diaphragm and rib muscles. To breathe out these muscles relax.*

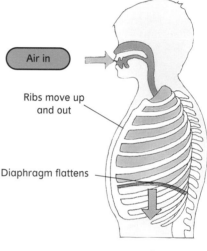

Air in

Ribs move up and out

Diaphragm flattens

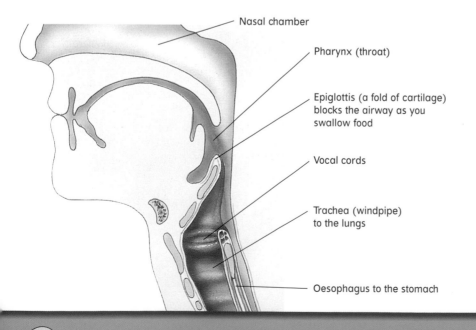

Nasal chamber

Pharynx (throat)

Epiglottis (a fold of cartilage) blocks the airway as you swallow food

Vocal cords

Trachea (windpipe) to the lungs

Oesophagus to the stomach

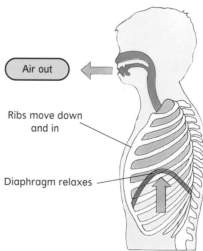

Air out

Ribs move down and in

Diaphragm relaxes

Find out more

Nose and smell pp. 460–461

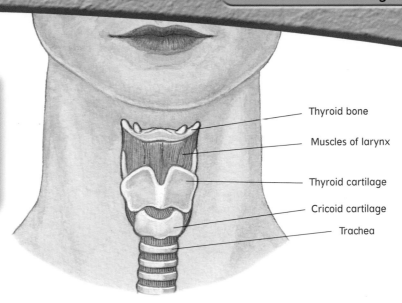

- Thyroid bone
- Muscles of larynx
- Thyroid cartilage
- Cricoid cartilage
- Trachea

Amazing

The basic sound of the voice comes from the vocal cords. But the shape and position of the air chambers in the throat, mouth, nose and sinuses (air-filled spaces in the skull bone) all affect the voice quality.

○ Inside the larynx (voice box), in the front of the neck, two stiff ridges called vocal cords stick out from the sides. During normal breathing there is a triangle-shaped gap for air.

○ To speak, muscles pull the ridges almost together. Air passing through the narrow gap makes them vibrate (shake to and fro rapidly), which produces sound.

▲ This front view shows the muscles and cartilages of the larynx or voice box. The main thyroid cartilage forms the 'Adam's apple' bulge in the front of the neck.

○ To make a vocal sound louder, the chest and abdomen muscles force air through the gap at greater speed.

○ To make higher-pitched sounds, the larynx muscles pull the vocal cords tighter.

○ Men's vocal cords are about 30 mm long and women's are about 20 mm.

▶ The vocal cords are soft flaps in the larynx, situated at the base of the throat. Our voices make sounds by vibrating these cords, as shown in the diagram. The gap between the cords is called the glottis and opens sudddenly when we say a hard 'g' sound, as in 'good'.

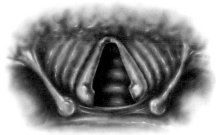

When the cords are apart no sound is made, as air can move freely past them

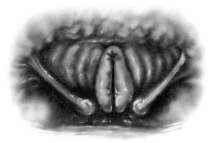

When the cords are pulled together by tiny muscles, air is forced through a small gap and the cords vibrate to create a sound

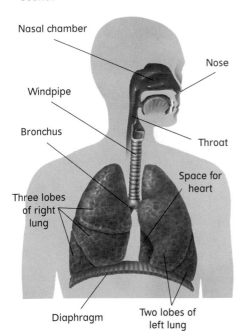

- Nasal chamber
- Nose
- Windpipe
- Bronchus
- Throat
- Space for heart
- Three lobes of right lung
- Diaphragm
- Two lobes of left lung

▲ The right lung is larger than the left lung, which has a scooped-out space for the heart.

In space

There is no air in space, so astronauts must take their own in a special kind of backpack. This holds a main air tank and a reserve air tank for emergencies. The main tank is connected to the astronaut's helmet.

Deep in the Lungs

You breathe because every single cell in your body needs a continuous supply of oxygen to burn glucose, the high-energy substance from digested food that cells get from blood. Scientists call breathing 'respiration'. Cellular respiration is the way that cells use oxygen to burn glucose.

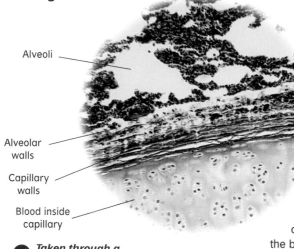

Alveoli

Alveolar walls

Capillary walls

Blood inside capillary

Taken through a powerful microscope, this photo of a slice of lung tissue shows a blood vessel and the very thin walls of an alveolus next to it.

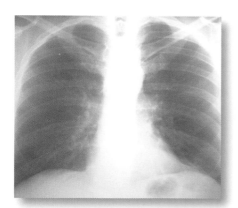

An X-ray gives a clear picture of the inside of the chest, showing the ribs, the spine, and the branching airways in the lung. Any lung problems and blockages show up as white shadows.

Controlling breathing

Wind musicians, such as this trumpeter, use their diaphragm and chest to control the air flowing in and out of their lungs. This allows them to produce a better quality sound.

○ After air is taken in through the nose or mouth, it travels down the throat, down the windpipe held open by cartilage rings, and into the lungs.

○ The lungs' airways branch many times, becoming too thin to see. At the end of each branch is a group of microscopic air bubbles, called alveoli, surrounded by a network of equally tiny blood vessels, called capillaries.

○ Oxygen seeps or diffuses from the air inside the alveoli, into blood in the capillaries, and is carried away around the body.

○ Fresh air when breathed into the body contains about 21 per cent oxygen and almost no carbon dioxide. After air has been in the lungs and breathed out, the proportion of carbon dioxide rises to 4 per cent. The proportion of oxygen falls to 16 per cent.

○ Waste carbon dioxide is collected by the blood, passes into the air in the alveoli and is breathed out.

○ The surface of the airways is protected by a slimy film of mucus, which gets thicker to protect the lungs when you have a chest infection.

Colour of blood

Red blood cells can actually be brown in colour, but they turn bright scarlet when their haemoglobin is carrying oxygen. After the haemoglobin passes its oxygen to a cell, it fades to dull purple. So oxygen-rich blood from the lungs is red, while oxygen-poor blood that is returning to the lungs is a purplish-blue colour.

How much air?

Restful breathing
Less than 10 l of air in and out of the lungs each minute

Restful breathing rate
12–15 breaths per minute

Strenuous breathing
150 l each minute

Strenuous breathing rate
60-plus breaths per minute

Maximum amount of air in lungs
On breathing in hard up to 6 l

Minimum amount of air in lungs
On breathing out hard 0.5 l

Newborn babies
Faster than adults, about 40 times a minute

If you live to the age of 80,
You will have taken well over 600 million breaths

Find out more

The respiratory system pp. 466–467

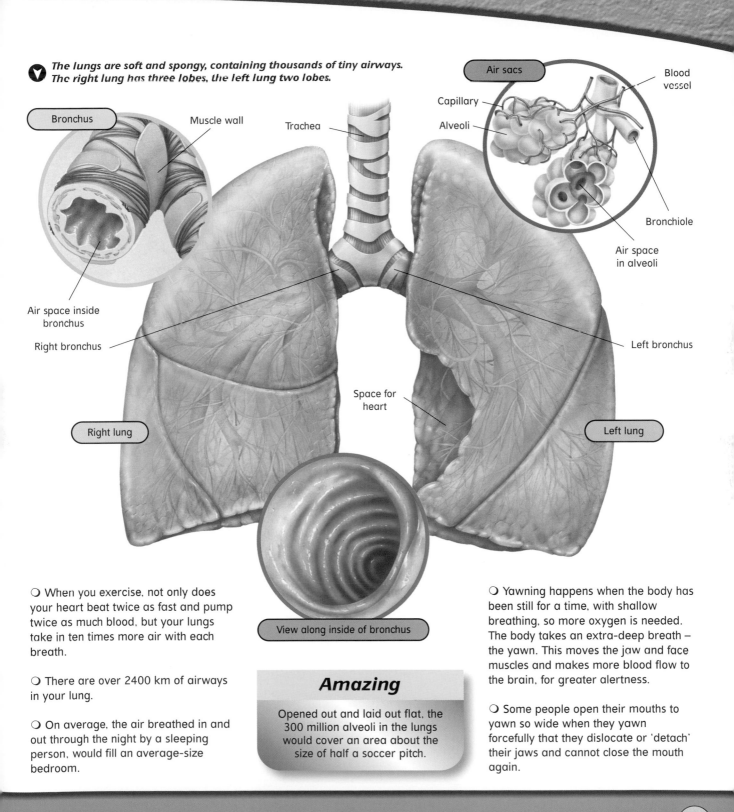

The lungs are soft and spongy, containing thousands of tiny airways. The right lung has three lobes, the left lung two lobes.

Bronchus

Muscle wall

Trachea

Air sacs

Capillary

Alveoli

Blood vessel

Bronchiole

Air space in alveoli

Air space inside bronchus

Right bronchus

Left bronchus

Space for heart

Right lung

Left lung

View along inside of bronchus

○ When you exercise, not only does your heart beat twice as fast and pump twice as much blood, but your lungs take in ten times more air with each breath.

○ There are over 2400 km of airways in your lung.

○ On average, the air breathed in and out through the night by a sleeping person, would fill an average-size bedroom.

Amazing

Opened out and laid out flat, the 300 million alveoli in the lungs would cover an area about the size of half a soccer pitch.

○ Yawning happens when the body has been still for a time, with shallow breathing, so more oxygen is needed. The body takes an extra-deep breath – the yawn. This moves the jaw and face muscles and makes more blood flow to the brain, for greater alertness.

○ Some people open their mouths to yawn so wide when they yawn forcefully that they dislocate or 'detach' their jaws and cannot close the mouth again.

The Digestive System

The body takes in a huge range of foods including meat and fish, bread, rice and pasta, and fresh fruits and vegetables. But the journey for all these foods is the same. They pass into the digestive tract, which is a passageway looped and coiled within the body.

Amazing

In one year a person eats about ten times their whole body weight in food.

○ As foods pass along the tract they are broken down or digested into smaller, simpler substances, called nutrients, which can be absorbed into the blood stream. The whole journey for food, from one end of the tract to the other, lasts about 24 hours.

○ In the mouth, foods are chewed and moistened by saliva (spit). They are swallowed down the oesophagus (gullet) into the stomach.

Endoscope tube

Image from endoscope

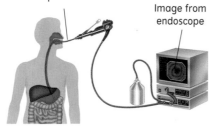

▲ *The endoscope is a flexible telescope made of fibre-optic strands. It is inserted into the body to give a view of what is going on inside, for example, in the stomach.*

Vitamins and minerals are needed for many body processes, such as calcium for strong bones and iron for blood.

Carbohydrates (sugars and starches) are used mainly for energy.

Oils and fats provide some energy and building materials for body parts. Healthiest are plant-based oils.

Proteins are vital for growth, to maintain and repair body parts, and for strong muscles and bones.

Fibre is not absorbed into the body, but keeps the digestive system working well.

▲ *Different food groups contain different types of nutrients, all of which play a vital role in keeping the body healthy.*

Digestion time

0 hour
Food is chewed and swallowed

1 hour
Food is churned with acids and juices in the stomach

2 hours
Partially-digested food begins to flow into the small intestine for further digestion and absorption

4 hours
Most food has left the stomach and passed to the small intestine

6 hours
Leftover and undigested foods pass into the large intestine, which takes the water and returns it to the body

10 hours
Leftovers begin to collect in the last part of the system, the rectum, as faeces

16–24 hours
Faeces pass through the last part of the system, the anus, and out of the body

Fats

Fats are an important source of energy. Together with carbohydrates and proteins they make up three main components of foods. Fats are either saturated or unsaturated. Saturated fats are linked to high levels of the substance cholesterol in the blood and may increase certain health risks, such as heart attacks.

Find out more
Tongue and taste pp. 462–463

○ When food is swallowed, muscle action closes the top of the windpipe so the food passes only into the gullet or oesophagus, down to the stomach.

○ In the stomach foods are churned around with gastric juices that contain chemicals called acids and enzymes. These enzymes turn food into a thick soup-like substance, called chyme, which oozes into the small intestine.

○ In the small intestine nutrients are absorbed into the blood. Waste products are stored in the rectum and leave the body through the anus.

○ The liver is not part of the digestive tract, but it is part of the digestive system. It receives nutrient-rich blood from the small intestine. The liver makes a green liquid called bile, which breaks down fatty foods. Bile is stored in the gall bladder.

○ To the left of the liver and behind the stomach is another digestive organ, the pancreas. It produces powerful enzymes to aid food breakdown in the small intestine.

▶ *The digestive system includes the mouth, teeth, tongue, throat, gullet, stomach, the small and large intestines, which together form a long tube, the digestive tract, and also the liver and pancreas.*

Three pairs of salivary glands make saliva

Swallowed food goes down the oesophagus (gullet)

Liver (plays an important role in processing digested food)

Stomach

Pancreas (secretes pancreatic juices)

Large intestine

Small intestine

Appendix

Rectum

Anus

▼ *Swallowing involves a series of complicated muscle actions as the tongue pushes the lump of food (shown in yellow) into the throat, past the entrance to the windpipe and down the gullet.*

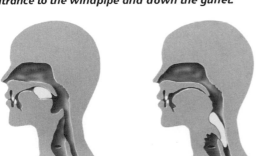

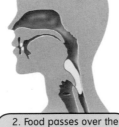

1. Tongue presses food to back of mouth

2. Food passes over the top of the windpipe

3. Food is pushed down the gullet

Barium X-ray

To help doctors investigate problems within the digestive system, patients drink barium meal, a special substance that shows up as white on an X-ray. This helps doctors to diagnose exactly what and where the problem might be.

Mouth and Teeth

Digestion starts as soon as food gets into the mouth. The teeth bite off lumps of food, chew them and mix them with watery saliva (spit) to make the food soft and easy to swallow in small lumps.

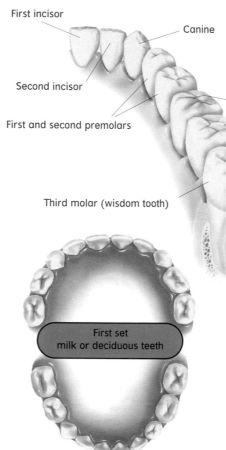

First incisor

Canine

Second incisor

First and second premolars

First and second molars

Third molar (wisdom tooth)

▶ *In each side of the jaw, the adult set of teeth includes two incisors at the front for biting, one taller canine for tearing, and two broad premolars, plus three wider molars for crushing and chewing.*

○ Each tooth is covered by whitish, very hard enamel. Under the enamel is slightly softer dentine. The centre of the tooth has a living pulp of blood vessels and nerves.

○ Incisors are the four pairs of teeth at the front of an adult's mouth. They have sharp edges for cutting food.

○ Canines are the two pairs of big, pointed teeth behind the incisors. Their shape is good for tearing food.

Second set
adult or permanent set

First set
milk or deciduous teeth

○ A person has 52 teeth, but not at the same time. The first (baby) set appear soon after birth and number 20.

○ These deciduous teeth begin to fall out when children are about six years old, and are replaced by the second (adult) or permanent set of 32 teeth.

○ The adult set of teeth is usually fully developed by about 18-20 years of age.

▶ *There are 20 small teeth in the first set. The earliest ones usually appear above the gum by about six months of age, the last ones at three years old. As the mouth grows, the baby teeth fall out from about seven years old. They are replaced by 32 large teeth in the second (adult) set.*

Amazing

From the moment you take your first bite of food, enzymes in your saliva begin to break carbohydrates down into glucose, preparing the food for digestion.

Dental X-rays

Sometimes cracks and tiny pieces of decay hardly show at the surface of a tooth. But they can widen out and become more serious beneath. Dental X-rays reveal holes or cavities inside a tooth caused by decay or injury. They can also show an abscess (pus-filled area of infection) lower down, inside the jaw bone.

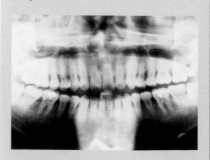

Find out more
The digestive system pp. 470–471

Teeth

Teeth are strong and tough, but need regular cleaning. Bacteria live on old bits of food in the mouth. They make waste products, which are acid and eat into the enamel and dentine causing holes, called cavities. Regular trips to the dentist to check that the teeth are cleaned properly is important. Dentists will also look for any small problems like tiny cracks that can be treated before they worsen.

○ Premolars are four pairs of teeth in front of the molars.

○ Molars are the (usually) six pairs of big, strong teeth at the back of the mouth. Their flattish tops are a good shape for grinding food.

○ In some people the rearmost molars, which are situated at the very back of the upper and lower jaws, may never grow above the gum. They are called the wisdom teeth.

Dentine

Enamel

Pulp in pulp cavity

Gum

Cementum

Jaw bone

Root canal

Blood vessels and nerves

Sets of teeth

Average ages when teeth appear

First set

First incisors	6–12 months
Second incisors	9–15 months
Canines	16–24 months
First premolars	14–18 months
Second premolars	24–30 months

Second set

First incisors	5–8 years
Second incisors	7–9 years
Canines	9–12 years
First premolars	10–12 years
Second premolars	10–12 years
First molars	6–8 years
Second molars	10–13 years
Third molars	15–20 years
(wisdom teeth)	

○ The canines are sometimes called 'eye teeth'. The molars are known as 'cheek teeth', with the rearmost ones being called 'wisdom teeth'.

○ Tooth colour varies from person to person. Some people have slightly yellowish teeth but these can be just as strong and healthy as white teeth, or even more so.

○ Fluoride is often added to the drinking water at source to help protect teeth from decay.

▲ *This cutaway of a molar shows its two roots firmly fixed into the jaw bone with 'living glue', cementum. Incisors and canines have only one root each. The part of the tooth that shows above the gum is called the crown.*

○ As a person ages the gums, called gingivae, shrink slightly and pull away from the roots of the tooth. This is why there is a saying that older people are 'long in the tooth' – even though their teeth have not actually become longer.

473

Stomach, Liver and Intestines

When you swallow, food travels down your oesophagus (gullet) into your stomach. The stomach is a muscular-walled bag which mashes the food into a pulp, helped by chemicals that are called gastric juices.

○ During a large meal the stomach stretches to hold about 1.5 l of chewed food. Its lining makes a powerful acid – hydrochloric acid – to attack and digest food. This acid also helps to kill germs (harmful microbes) in the food.

○ The stomach does not digest its own lining because it is coated with a layer of slimy mucus, which resists the acid attack.

Amazing

The length of the whole digestive system is up to 9 m – that's about six or seven times the height of the body it is in.

The pancreas

This is a microscopic view of the pancreas, with the islets of Langerhans (shown in purple) embedded in the exocrine tissue. The islets of Langerhans secrete two important hormones, which are insulin and glucagon. Insulin and glucagon regulate blood sugar levels.

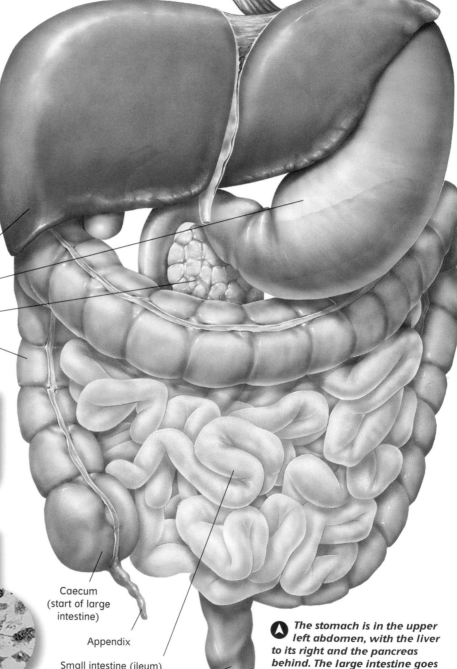

Liver

Stomach

Pancreas

Large intestine

Caecum (start of large intestine)

Appendix

Small intestine (ileum)

Rectum

▶ The stomach is in the upper left abdomen, with the liver to its right and the pancreas behind. The large intestine goes around the outside of the lower abdomen, with the small intestine coiled inside it.

Hiccups

If the stomach gets too full, it presses on the diaphragm breathing muscle and its nerve, just above. This can make the diaphragm contract suddenly, out of control, producing hiccups (hiccoughs).

○ Most nutrients are absorbed through the small intestine lining into the blood flowing through its walls.

○ The liver is the body's chemical processing centre, and the body's biggest internal organ. The word hepatic means 'to do with the liver'.

○ The liver's prime task is handling all the nutrients and substances digested from food and sending them out to the body cells when needed.

○ The liver turns carbohydrates into glucose, the main energy-giving chemical for body cells. It keeps the levels of glucose in the blood steady. It does this by releasing more when levels drop, and by storing it as glycogen, a type of starch, when levels rise.

○ The pancreas is made from a substance called exocrine tissue, embedded with about one million nests of hormone glands called the islets of Langerhans.

Surface area

The small intestine's lining is folded into ridges called plicae.

The surfaces of the plicae are also folded, into tiny finger-like structures about 1 mm tall, called villi.

Each villus is covered with thousands of microvilli.

The plicae, villi and microvilli give a huge surface area in the small intestine for absorbing nutrients – more than 20 times the body's whole skin area.

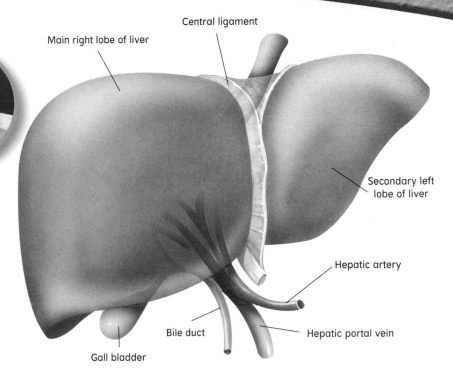

Main right lobe of liver · Central ligament · Secondary left lobe of liver · Hepatic artery · Bile duct · Hepatic portal vein · Gall bladder

The liver has two parts or lobes linked by the central falciform ligament. It is a very blood-rich organ, soft and easily damaged.

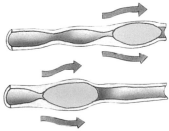

Food is pushed through the long, winding digestive tract by waves of contraction (tightening) that pass along its muscular walls. These waves are called peristalsis.

○ The exocrine tissue secretes pancreatic enzymes such as amylase into the intestine to help digest food. Amylase breaks down carbohydrates into simple sugars such as maltose, lactose and sucrose.

○ The pancreatic enzymes run into the intestine via a pipe called the pancreatic duct, which joins on to the bile duct. This duct also carries bile from the liver.

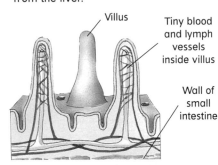

Villus · Tiny blood and lymph vessels inside villus · Wall of small intestine

The small intestine is lined with tiny, finger-like folds called villi. On the surface of each villus are even tinier, finger-like folds called microvilli. These folds give a huge area for absorbing food.

Find out more
Barium X-ray p. 471

The Heart

Blood flows round and round the body in a system of tubes called blood vessels. It is pumped by the heart, which has hollow chambers with strong muscular walls that contract to push the blood through the vessels.

Pulse (heart) rate

The pulse is felt by pressing two fingertips on the inside of the wrist, just below the mound of the thumb, where the radial artery nears the surface. Other pulse points include the carotid artery in the neck and the brachial artery inside the elbow.

Pulmonary artery takes blood to the lungs to pick up oxygen

Two big veins called the venae cavae bring blood low in oxygen back from the body to the right side of the heart

Amazing

During an average lifetime, the heart pumps 200 million litres of blood – enough to fill New York's Central Park to a depth of 15 m.

A large artery called the aorta sends blood rich in oxygen out to the whole body

Pulmonary veins bring blood back from the lungs

Tricuspid valve between the atrium and ventricle of the right side of the heart

Right ventricle pumps blood to the lungs

Blood loaded with oxygen from the lungs enters the left atrium

Blood rich in oxygen returns from the lungs

Pulmonary valve at entrance to pulmonary arteries

Septum

Mitral valve between the atrium and ventricle of the left side of the heart

The heart is a remarkable double pump, with two pumping chambers, the left and the right ventricles. It contracts automatically to squeeze jets of blood out of the ventricles and through the arteries.

Aortic valve at entrance to aorta

Left ventricle pumps blood out to the whole body via the aorta

Heartbeat rate

New baby
120–130 per minute, even when asleep

Seven years
80–90 per minute

Adult at rest
70 per minute

Adult during great activity
150-plus per minute

ECG

An exercise ECG (electro-cardiograph) machine can show how healthy someone's heart is, by monitoring how much the heart rate goes up and down during activity. As the heart's muscles make it pump they produce tiny pulses of electricity. Pads on the skin pick up these pulses, whch are displayed as a wavy line on a screen.

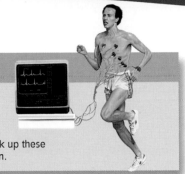

○ There are two valves in each side of the heart to make sure that blood flows only one way – a large one between the atrium and the ventricle, and a small one at the exit from the ventricle into the artery.

○ The heartbeat rate is measured in the wrist as the pulse rate.

○ The heart is not a single pump, but two, because the body has two circulations.

○ The right side of the heart sends blood through the pulmonary circulation to the lungs, to pick up supplies of oxygen.

○ This blood returns to the left side of the heart, which pumps it all around the body in the systemic circulation, to deliver the oxygen. The blood comes back to the heart again to continue its endless journey.

○ Each side of the heart has two chambers. There is an atrium (plural atria) at the top where blood accumulates (builds up) from the veins, and a ventricle below which contracts to pump blood out into the arteries.

Workings of the heart

The heart's coordinated beat is produced by waves of nerve-like signals passing through its muscles.

These signals start in a small patch of the upper right atrium, where it joins to the main vein, called the sino-strial or SA node.

The SA node is the heart's own natural pacemaker.

The signals are relayed to the ventricles by the atrio-ventricular or AV node between the right atrium and right ventricle.

If the beat is irregular an artificial device, a cardiac pacemaker, can be put into the chest and linked to the heart by wires.

Some pacemakers respond to the body's need and make the heart speed up or slow down.

The cardiac cycle

The heart's beating action can be divided into stages, but in reality these merge into one continuous sequence of movements, the cardiac cycle.

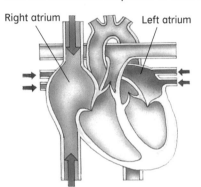

Right atrium — Left atrium

The heartbeat or cardiac cycle is the regular squeezing of the heart muscle to pump blood. First blood flows into the atria of the relaxed heart.

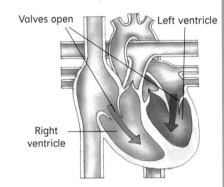

Valves open — Left ventricle

Right ventricle

Systole, the contracting phase, begins when a wave of muscle contraction sweeps across the heart and squeezes blood from the atria into the ventricles

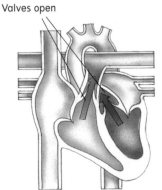

Valves open

When the muscular contraction reaches the thicker-walled ventricles, they squeeze blood out into the main arteries.

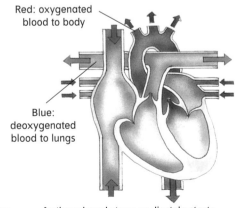

Red: oxygenated blood to body

Blue: deoxygenated blood to lungs

As the relaxed stage or diastole starts again, the heart muscle relaxes and the atria fill with blood from the main veins.

Blood and Vessels

Blood carries many substances that are vital for life. These include oxygen and glucose (blood sugar) for energy, nutrients and raw materials for growth and repair, and natural body chemicals, called hormones that control internal processes. At the same time, blood also takes away wastes and unwanted materials, including carbon dioxide, which is breathed out in the lungs.

○ The heart sends blood out into strong-walled vessels, called arteries.

○ Arteries have thick, stretchy walls to cope with pressure as blood surges out of the heart at high speed. Each heartbeat makes the arteries bulge all through the body. The bulge or pulsation is felt as the pulse.

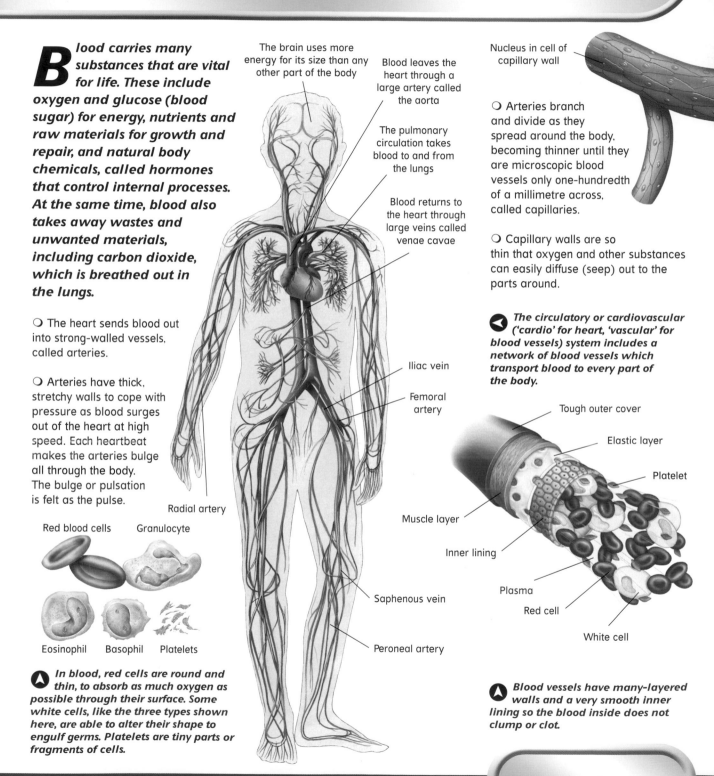

The brain uses more energy for its size than any other part of the body

Blood leaves the heart through a large artery called the aorta

The pulmonary circulation takes blood to and from the lungs

Blood returns to the heart through large veins called venae cavae

Iliac vein

Femoral artery

Saphenous vein

Peroneal artery

Radial artery

Red blood cells

Granulocyte

Eosinophil   Basophil   Platelets

▲ In blood, red cells are round and thin, to absorb as much oxygen as possible through their surface. Some white cells, like the three types shown here, are able to alter their shape to engulf germs. Platelets are tiny parts or fragments of cells.

Nucleus in cell of capillary wall

○ Arteries branch and divide as they spread around the body, becoming thinner until they are microscopic blood vessels only one-hundredth of a millimetre across, called capillaries.

○ Capillary walls are so thin that oxygen and other substances can easily diffuse (seep) out to the parts around.

◄ The circulatory or cardiovascular ('cardio' for heart, 'vascular' for blood vessels) system includes a network of blood vessels which transport blood to every part of the body.

Tough outer cover

Elastic layer

Platelet

Muscle layer

Inner lining

Plasma

Red cell

White cell

▲ Blood vessels have many-layered walls and a very smooth inner lining so the blood inside does not clump or clot.

Find out more

Size of cells p. 437

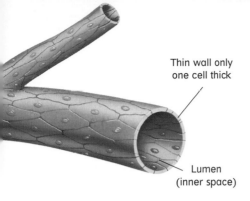

Thin wall only one cell thick

Lumen (inner space)

⊙ Capillaries join to make wider vessels, veins, that take blood back to the heart.

⊙ On average, a drop of blood takes one minute to travel from the heart, through these vessels and back again.

⊙ About 55 per cent of blood is a pale liquid, plasma, containing dissolved oxygen, nutrients and hundreds of other substances.

⊙ The rest of blood contains three main kinds of cells – red cells to carry oxygen, white cells to fight disease and platelets to help blood clot.

⊙ At any moment about 70 per cent of all the body's blood is in the veins, 25 per cent in the arteries and 5 per cent in the capillaries.

Ⓐ *Capillaries, shown here in this diagram, are tiny tubes, barely wider than the blood cells they carry. They form an extensive network that twists and turns through the body's tissues.*

Ⓥ *In this greatly enlarged cutaway of a small vein, the valve prevents the blood from flowing backwards, away from the heart.*

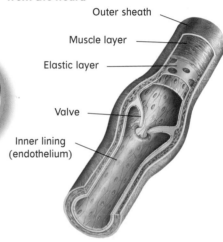

Outer sheath

Muscle layer

Elastic layer

Valve

Inner lining (endothelium)

Amazing

One cubic mm of blood (the size of a pinhead) contains 5 million red cells, 8000 white cells and 350,000 platelets.

Blood banks

Blood given by a donor is usually separated into various constituents or ingredients, and then stored in a blood bank like this until it is needed for a transfusion.

Ⓐ *Arteries have thick walls. Capillaries are microscopic and supply almost every body part, except for a few regions such as the lens of the eye. Veins are thin-walled and carry slow-moving blood.*

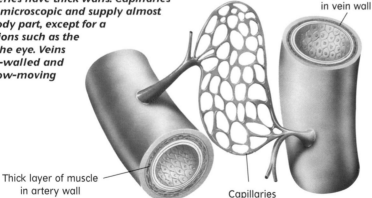

Thin layer of muscle in vein wall

Thick layer of muscle in artery wall

Capillaries

Blood volume

An average adult man has a blood volume of 5 to 6 l. An average adult woman has a blood volume of 4 to 5 l. Compared to an adult, a baby has slightly less blood for its body size.

Blood groups

Donated blood is tested to determine its blood group. The blood must belong to a suitable group, otherwise patients undergoing a blood transfusion could become very ill.

Most people's blood belongs to one of four different groups or types – A, O, B and AB.

Blood type O is the most common, followed by blood group A.

Blood is also either Rhesus positive (Rh+) or Rhesus negative (Rh-).

Around 85 per cent of people are Rh+, the remaining 15 per cent are Rh-.

The Rhesus factors got their name because they were first identified in Rhesus monkeys.

If your blood is Rh+ and your group is A, your blood group is said to be A positive.

If your blood is Rh- and your group is O, you are O negative, and so on.

Waste Disposal

The body's thousands of internal chemical processes, which work together, are known as its metabolism. This produces wastes of many kinds. Two main systems get rid of such body wastes.

○ The digestive system removes not only bits of leftover and undigested food, but also some wastes of metabolism.

○ The solid wastes are removed from the end of the digestive tract through the anus. They contain mainly rubbed-off bits of intestine lining and undigested parts of food.

○ The other waste disposal system is the urinary system whose main organs are the kidneys. They filter waste products, unwanted salts and water from the blood, and dispose of them in a watery fluid called urine. The amount of urine that is produced is controlled by hormones.

○ The kidney has two layers, the cortex and medulla. The space where urine collects is called the renal pelvis.

Dialysis

In some cases the kidneys do not work properly and wastes build up in the blood. Many such people can be treated by renal dialysis using an 'artificial kidney'. The blood is led along a tube to the dialysis machine, which filters out the waste products and returns it to the body. This usually takes a few hours, several times each week.

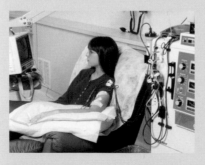

The urinary system controls the balance of water in the body.

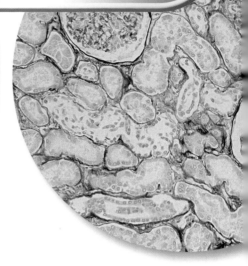

A microscopic view of cells in the kidney.

○ The kidneys receive more blood for their size than almost any other body organ – about 1.2 l every minute.

○ Inside each kidney are about one million tiny filters called nephrons. These take waste substances from the blood, along with excess water, to form urine.

○ The urine flows down a tube, the ureter, to the bladder in the lower body.

○ The urine collects in the bladder until there is about 300 ml, when you feel the need to empty the bladder. This happens by urination along a tube to the outside, the urethra.

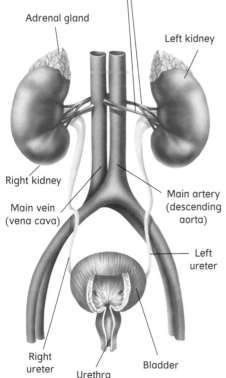

Renal artery and vein

Adrenal gland

Left kidney

Right kidney

Main vein (vena cava)

Main artery (descending aorta)

Left ureter

Right ureter

Urethra

Bladder

Water balance

Water in		
Foods		750 ml
Drinks		1650 ml
Water made in the body by chemical processes (water of metabolism)		300 ml
Total		**2700 ml**

Water out		
Sweat from skin, vapour from lungs		850 ml
Urine		1750 ml
Faeces (bowel motions)		100 ml
Total		**2700 ml**

Find out more

The digestive system pp. 470–471

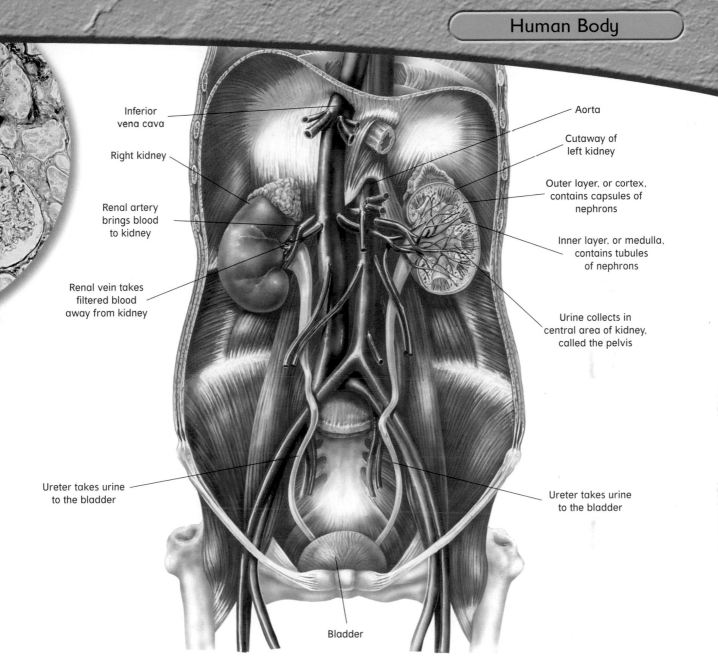

Inferior
vena cava

Right kidney

Renal artery
brings blood
to kidney

Renal vein takes
filtered blood
away from kidney

Ureter takes urine
to the bladder

Aorta

Cutaway of
left kidney

Outer layer, or cortex,
contains capsules of
nephrons

Inner layer, or medulla,
contains tubules
of nephrons

Urine collects in
central area of kidney,
called the pelvis

Ureter takes urine
to the bladder

Bladder

❑ Urine is mostly water, but there are substances dissolved in it. These include urea, various salts, creatinine, ammonia and blood wastes.

❑ In an average day (24 hours) the body produces about 1.5–2 l of urine. But this amount varies hugely with activity and weather conditions. If hot and active, the body loses more water in sweat, and so makes less urine.

The urinary system controls the body's water balance, removing extra water as urine and getting rid of impurities in the blood. The kidneys manage to recycle or save every reusable substance from the blood. They take 85 l of water and other blood substances from every 1000 l of blood, but only let out 0.6 l as urine.

Urine testing

Doctors can get clues to illnesses by testing what substances there are in urine. Diabetes, for instance, is shown up by the presence of glucose in the urine.

Hormones and Defences

*T*he hormonal or endocrine system consists of glands that make substances called hormones. These travel around the whole body in the blood, but each hormone affects only certain parts, known as its target organs.

○ The pea-sized pituitary gland, under the brain, is in overall control of the hormonal system.

○ The thyroid gland in the neck makes thyroxine, which controls how fast cells use energy.

○ The amount of urine made by the kidneys is controlled by the hormone ADH (antidiuretic hormone). As water is lost in urine or through sweat during strenuous activity, it must be replaced by water in drinks.

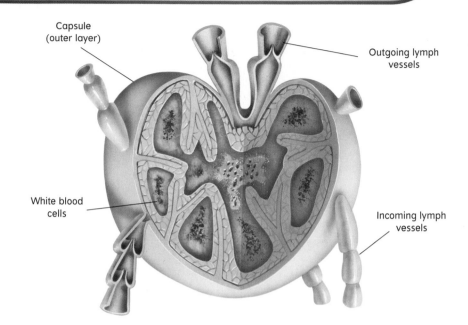

Capsule (outer layer)

Outgoing lymph vessels

White blood cells

Incoming lymph vessels

▼ **Main hormonal glands within the female body.**

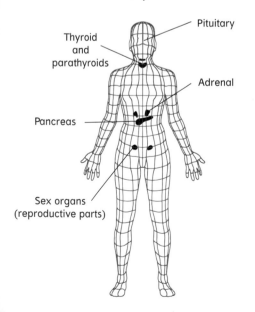

Pituitary

Thyroid and parathyroids

Adrenal

Pancreas

Sex organs (reproductive parts)

○ The adrenal glands above the kidneys make hormones that regulate how the body uses water and its reactions to stress, such as adrenaline.

○ The main stress hormone is adrenaline from the adrenal glands. In a frightening or energetic situation, it makes the heart beat faster and the liver release glucose for extra energy. More blood flows to the muscles so that the body can take fast action.

○ The pancreas makes two hormones, insulin and glucagon, which control the amount of energy-giving glucose (sugar) in the blood.

Amazing

Body defences include various types of fluids, such as tear fluid. This protects your vulnerable eyes by washing away germs. Tears also contain an enzyme called lysozome, which kills bacteria.

▲ **Nerve cells, or neurons, are the 'wires' of the body's nervous system. They carry message within, to, and from the central nervous system along fine branches called dendrites and long tails called axons.**

AIDS

The disease AIDS (Acquired Immune Deficiency Syndrome) is caused by a virus called HIV (Human Immunodeficiency Virus). This virus gets inside vital cells of the body's immune system and weakens its ability to fight against other infections.

○ The body's self-defences, which attack invading germs and prevent illness, are called its immune system.

○ The immune system includes many lymph nodes and vessels, which contain the pale fluid lymph.

Find out more
The pancreas p. 474

The thyroid

The thyroid is a small gland about the size of two joined cherries. It is situated at the front of the neck, just below the larynx. It secretes three important hormones: tri-iodothyronine (T3), thyroxine (T4) and calcitonin. The thyroid hormones affect how energetic you are by controlling your metabolic rate – the rate at which your body cells use glucose.

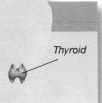

Thyroid

Adenoids

Tonsils

Armpit lymph nodes

Thymus gland

Spleen

Abdominal lymph nodes

Groin lymph nodes

▶ *The immune system includes many lymph nodes, found particularly in the neck, chest, armpits, lower body and groin. There are also lymph tissues in the adenoids, tonsils and the spleen, which sits behind the stomach.*

○ During infection, lymph nodes enlarge with extra fluid and white cells as 'swollen glands'.

○ Lymph fluid collects in the tiny spaces between and around cells and tissues. It oozes into lymph ducts that carry it to lymph nodes, and into the blood.

○ Lymph collects wastes of metabolism and the lymph nodes contain white blood cells that destroy harmful or unwanted substances, especially germs.

○ The body contains about 1–2 l of lymph fluid.

Bacteria and viruses

The herpes virus may not cause any symptoms until activated by an event such as an illness.

0.00015 mm

The adenovirus virus is found in the respiratory system and can cause infections, such as colds and sore throats.

0.00008 mm

E. coli are very common bacteria. Some are found in the human intestine where they are helpful rather than harmful.

0.002 mm

The influenza virus likes the slimy mucus that lines the passages of the nose, throat, windpipe and lungs.

0.0001 mm

The phage virus attacks and invades bacteria. There are types of phage for each kind or strain of bacteria.

0.00025 mm

Staphylococcus bacteria live on the skin causing few problems. More harmful types can cause problems.

0.001 mm

Genes and Reproduction

Every second, another three human beings enter the world. They are new babies, born after nine months of growing and developing inside their mothers. The parts of the body that produce new human beings are known as the reproductive system.

○ The reproductive parts are the only body system that is not fully formed and working at birth. The reproductive system completes its development around the ages of 11 to 13 in girls, and 14 to 16 in boys, which is the time known as puberty.

○ The process of reproduction begins with the joining of two single cells – the egg from the mother, and the sperm from the father.

Cap
Head
Nucleus
Sperm tail
Neck

◀ *A single sperm cell has a rounded head containing genetic material (DNA).*

○ The main female sex organs, the ovaries, contain many thousands of egg cells. Every month one egg becomes ripe and is released into the oviduct or egg tube (fallopian tube) in a process called ovulation.

○ The egg cell is relatively large, 0.1 mm across. It passes along the tube, where it may meet a sperm cell and be fertilized.

Single chromosome

DNA unravelling

DNA coiled into the chromosome

DNA's double helix shape, like a twisted rope ladder

▲ *The genetic material, DNA, (de-oxyribonucleic acid) is shaped like a long, twisted ladder. The DNA for this full set, called the genome, is copied every time a cell divides to form two cells. Each cell is copied by splitting into two, and each half of DNA builds a new other half.*

○ The main male sex organs, the testes, make millions of sperm each day and they live for about one month.

○ Compared to the egg cell, the sperm cell is tiny, just 0.05 mm long. If the sperm cells do not pass along the vas deferens or sperm tube, and then out of the body through the penis, they gradually die and break apart as new ones form.

▼ *Two sets of chromosomes, one each from the mother and the father, combine at fertilization.*

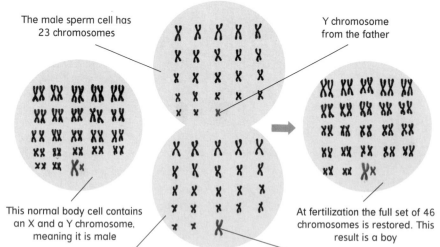

The male sperm cell has 23 chromosomes

Y chromosome from the father

This normal body cell contains an X and a Y chromosome, meaning it is male

The female egg cell has 23 chromosomes

X chromosome from the mother

At fertilization the full set of 46 chromosomes is restored. This result is a boy

Amazing

Long ago people thought there was a tiny yet complete human being curled up in the head of a sperm cell. Now we know it is DNA.

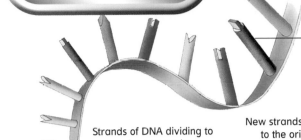

Strands are linked by chemical subunits called bases

Strands of DNA dividing to make new copies

New strands are identical to the original ones

Each of these bases pairs up with only one other base

New strands are built upon the original ones

IVF babies

In IVF, in vitro fertilization, egg cells are removed from the woman's ovaries, added to sperm cells in a shallow dish, and observed under the microscope. If an egg and sperm join and the fertilized egg begins to grow, it is put into the woman's womb to continue development.

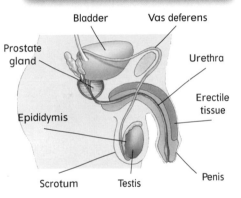

Bladder

Vas deferens

Prostate gland

Urethra

Erectile tissue

Epididymis

Scrotum

Testis

Penis

In a man's reproductive organs, sperm are made in the two testes. During sex they pass along the vas deferens tubes, which join and continue as the urethra, to the outside.

Twins

Identical twins come from the same fertilized egg and so have exactly the same genes. Non-identical twins occur when a woman releases two eggs together, and both get fertilized.

○ The egg cell is only able to join with a sperm for a few days when a woman is ovulating (when an egg has been released from the ovary). Thousands of sperm cells swim near to the egg in the oviduct, but only one can join with or fertilize it.

○ Both the egg and sperm contain sets of the body's genetic material, made of DNA. At fertilization the sets combine to form a unique set of genes for the new baby.

Inside the oviduct of the woman, many sperm cells lash their tails to swim towards the egg cell. However, only one sperm cell can merge with the egg cell, adding its genetic material (DNA) to the egg's.

Egg cell's outer coat

Sperm

Egg cell cytoplasm

Egg cell nucleus

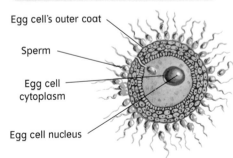

Oviduct

Ovary

Womb (uterus)

Vagina

Cervix

The parts of the body specialized to produce a baby are known as the reproductive organs. In the woman, egg cells are contained in the two ovaries. Each month the menstrual cycle causes one egg to ripen and pass along the oviduct into the womb, where a sperm cell may join with it.

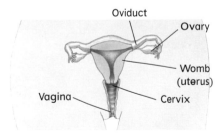

DNA and chromosomes

The full set of human genetic material, known as the human genome, contains about 30,000 genes.

Inside a human cell, this genetic material as DNA is in 46 separate lengths called chromosomes.

These 46 chromosomes are in 23 pairs, inside the nucleus of each cell.

When eggs and sperm form they have only one chromosome from each pair.

When egg and sperm join their chromosomes pair up to total 46 again.

If all the DNA from all the 46 chromosomes in a single cell were joined together, it would stretch almost 2 m.

New Life

About four weeks after a new baby is born, we say it is 'one month old'. But really it has been ten months since its body began to form. After fertilization, the unborn baby spent nine months developing and growing inside its mother.

Ultrasound scan

An ultrasound scan uses a pen-like probe moved over the skin to show an image of the unborn baby on a screen, which helps doctors to determine that the baby is healthy and developing well.

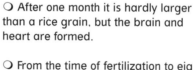

○ Inside the uterus the single fertilized egg divides into two cells, then four, eight and so on.

○ After a week it is a ball of a few hundred cells that buries itself in the blood-rich lining of the uterus and takes in nourishment for continued growth.

○ After one month it is hardly larger than a rice grain, but the brain and heart are formed.

○ From the time of fertilization to eight weeks later, the developing baby is known as an embryo. The lungs, intestines and other parts take shape towards the end of this time.

○ After two months the baby is still smaller than a thumb, yet all its main parts and organs have formed.

○ From eight weeks after fertilization until birth, the unborn baby is known as a foetus. It spends most of this time growing in size and developing smaller body parts such as eyelids, fingernails and toenails.

○ In the womb it is dark, with nothing to see, yet the eyes are working, even though the lids are closed. Oxygen and food comes from the mother into the baby's blood through the part called the placenta.

○ The opening or neck of the womb is called the cervix. The cervix was tightly closed during pregnancy but as birth starts it widens, or dilates, to let the baby through.

○ The contractions of the womb push the baby along the birth canal, or vagina, until it emerges and is born.

○ The baby takes its first gasps of air, often crying as it does so. This is a good sign, since it opens up the baby's airways and lungs. These were not used in the womb, but now the baby must breathe to get oxygen for itself.

○ The baby also needs food and soon takes a first meal of its mother's milk. The milk provides all the nourishment it needs for the first months of its life.

8 weeks, small as a thumb tip, all main organs formed

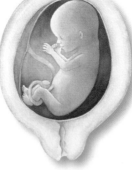

12 weeks, heart beats, kicking movements begin

16 weeks, mother's abdomen bulges

20 weeks, first hair grows, placenta fully formed

24 weeks, thumb-sucking may begin

Find out more
IVF babies p. 485

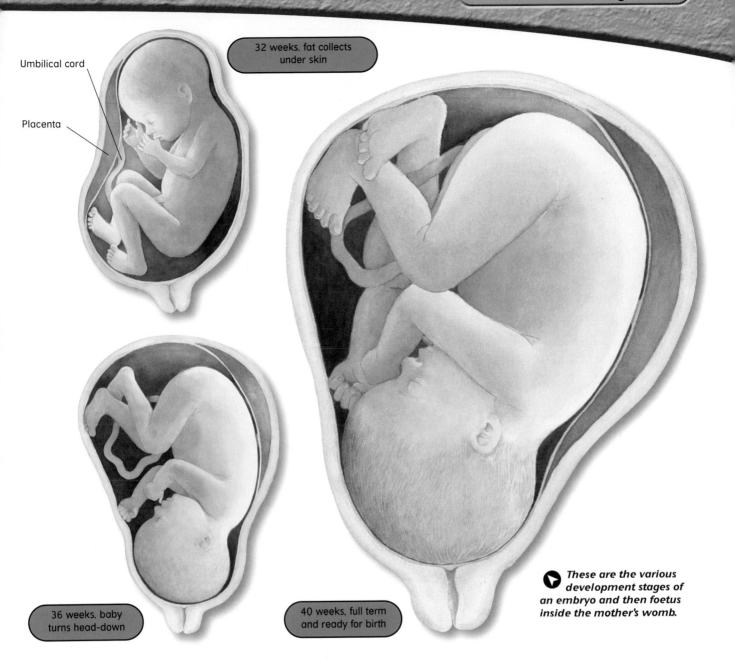

32 weeks, fat collects under skin

Umbilical cord

Placenta

36 weeks, baby turns head-down

40 weeks, full term and ready for birth

▶ *These are the various development stages of an embryo and then foetus inside the mother's womb.*

Amazing

The average time from fertilization of the egg by the sperm, to the time of birth, is 266 days.

Breech birth

Most babies are born head-first, cephalic presentation. In some cases the baby may be bottom-first, breech presentation. One option is to make an incision (cut) in the mother's abdomen and womb wall, remove the baby, and stitch or fasten the incision. This is a Caesarean birth.

Glossary

Actin A long, thin substance (protein) found in partnership with myosin inside muscles, which causes the muscle to contract.

Artery A main blood vessel that carries blood away from the heart to the tissues and organs.

Auditory To do with the ear and hearing.

Bronchus One of the main airways inside the lungs, branching from the windpipe (trachea).

Capillary A microscopic blood vessel, with walls so thin that substances such as oxygen and glucose can pass from the blood, to the cells and tissues around.

Carbon dioxide A waste product formed when glucose (blood sugar) is broken down to provide energy, and which is breathed out from the lungs.

Cartilage A light, strong, slightly bendy substance that forms parts of the skeleton and covers the ends of bones inside a joint.

Cell A microscopic living unit or 'building block' of the body (and of all living things).

Cell membrane The outer layer or 'skin' of a cell, also called the plasma membrane.

Cerebral To do with the large, domed, wrinkled upper part of the brain, the cerebrum, and also to do with thinking and mental processes.

Cochlea The small, snail-shaped part deep in the ear, which changes patterns of sound vibrations into nerve signals.

Cones Conical or tapering cells in the retina of the eye, which detect details and colours.

Conjunctiva The very thin sensitive covering over the clear, domed front of the eye (the cornea).

Cortex The outer layer of a part, such as the cerebral cortex of the brain, or the renal cortex of the kidney.

Cranial To do with the head and brain (the cranium is the domed part of the skull covering the brain).

Dental To do with the teeth and their role in biting and chewing food.

DNA De-oxyribonucleic acid, the chemical that carries genetic information in the form of a code, as the order of its subunits known as bases.

ECG Electrocardiogram, a wavy line or trace showing electrical pulses given off by the beating heart, produced by an electrocardiograph machine.

EEG Electro-encephalogram, a wavy line or trace showing the electrical pulses given off by the brain. It is produced by a machine called an electro-encephalograph.

Endocrine To do with hormones and the hormonal system. Endocrine glands make hormones releasing them directly into the blood flowing through the gland, rather than along a tube or duct.

Enzyme A substance that speeds up the breakdown (or build-up) of chemicals, for example when digesting food into nutrients.

Epithelium A covering or lining layer of cells, around or inside a body part.

Excretion Getting rid of waste products from the body, chiefly by filtering the blood through the kidneys (excretory system).

Exocrine A tissue or gland that makes a product, such as an enzyme, and releases this along a tube or duct.

Follicle In the skin, a tiny pocket-like pit from which a hair grows. In the ovary, a fluid-filled container for a ripe egg cell.

Gastric To do with the stomach and its role in digestion.

Genes Instructions in the form of the chemical DNA, which act as a 'blueprint' for how the body grows, develops and maintains itself.

Gland A body part that makes and releases a product, usually in liquid form, such as the salivary glands that make saliva (spit).

Glucose A type of sugar, also known as blood sugar, obtained from the breakdown of carbohydrates in food. It is broken apart inside cells to provide energy.

Grey matter Type of tissue forming the outer layer of the brain (cortex), and the inner part of the spinal cord, which consists mainly of nerve cells.

Hepatic To do with the liver and its role in digestion.

Lumen The tunnel-like space in a tube or duct, such as inside a blood vessel or part of the intestine.

Lymph Pale milky fluid gathered from around and between cells and tissues that flows through the lymph vessels and nodes, and finally into the blood.

Lymph node A rounded grouping of lymph tissue containing lymph fluid and white blood cells, which enlarges during illness and is sometimes called a 'swollen gland'.

Medulla The inner layer of a part, such as the renal medulla of the kidney.

Metabolism A general name for all of the body's chemical processes and reactions inside its cells.

Mitochondria Tiny sausage-like parts (organelles) inside a cell, which make energy available to power the cell's life processes.

Motor To do with muscles and movements – motor nerves carry signals from the brain to the muscles.

Mucus A sticky, slimy substance produced by many body parts as protection and to lubricate movements.

Muscle A body part specialized to get shorter or contract.

Myo- To do with the muscles, such as myofibres, the hair-like strands that make up a muscle.

Myosin A long, thick substance (protein) found in partnership with actin inside muscles, which causes the muscle to contract.

Nucleus The 'control centre' of a cell, which contains the genetic material, DNA.

Oesophagus The gullet or food pipe, carrying swallowed food from the throat down to the stomach.

Olfactory To do with the sense of smell and the nose.

Optic To do with the eye and seeing.

Organ A main part of the body, such as the heart, lung, stomach, pancreas, or liver.

Oxygen A colourless, odourless gas that makes up about one-fifth of air, which the body needs to break down glucose (blood sugar) to obtain energy.

Papilla Small projection or 'pimple', such as the papillae on the tongue.

Pulmonary To do with the lungs and breathing.

Pulmonary circulation The part of the blood circulation carrying blood to the lungs (rather than to the rest of the body).

Pupil The hole in the iris (coloured ring of muscle) at the front of the eye, through which light passes into the eyeball.

Reflex A fast, automatic body reaction or movement, usually for defence or to avoid injury, which happens without involving our conscious thought.

Renal To do with the kidneys.

Respiration The movements of breathing to get oxygen into the body (bodily respiration). Also the chemical processes inside cells, which break apart glucose (blood sugar) to obtain energy (cellular respiration).

Retina The light-sensitive layer inside the eyeball, which changes patterns of light rays into nerve signals.

Ribosomes Tiny ball-like parts inside cells, which make substances such as proteins.

Rods Cylindrical or pencil-shaped cells in the retina of the eye, which work in dim light but cannot detect colours.

Suture A type of joint where the bones are linked firmly and tightly together, allowing no movement.

Synapse Junction between two nerve cells, where their outer membranes are very close but do not touch, and where a nerve signal is passed on in the form of chemicals known as neurotransmitters.

Synovial fluid The slippery, oil-like fluid inside some joints (synovial joints).

System Body parts that work together to carry out one main task or function, such as the respiratory system, which takes oxygen into the body.

Systemic circulation The part of the blood circulation that carries blood around the body (rather than to the lungs).

Tendon Tapering, rope-like part that joins a muscle to a bone.

Tissue A grouping or collection of body cells that are all very similar or the same, such as muscle tissue or nerve tissue.

Vein A main blood vessel that carries blood from the tissues and organs, back to the heart.

Vertebra One of the individual bones that makes up the backbone or spine (spinal or vertebral column).

White matter Type of tissue inside the brain, and forming the outer part of the spinal cord, which consists mainly of nerve fibres.

Index